PETER HALSTEAD

UNLOCKING
HUMAN RIGHTS

SERIES EDITORS:
JACQUELINE MARTIN & CHRIS TURNER

HODDER
EDUCATION
AN HACHETTE UK COMPANY

Orders: please contact Bookpoint Ltd, 130 Milton Park, Abingdon, Oxon OX14 4SB. Telephone: (44) 01235 827720. Fax: (44) 01235 400454. Lines are open from 9.00–5.00, Monday to Saturday, with a 24-hour message answering service. You can also order through our website www.hoddereducation.co.uk

If you have any comments to make about this, or any of our other titles, please send them to educationenquiries@hodder.co.uk

British Library Cataloguing in Publication Data
A catalogue record for this title is available from the British Library

ISBN: 978 0 340 972915

First Edition Published 2009
Impression number   10 9 8 7 6 5 4 3 2 1
Year   2012 2011 2010 2009 2008

Hachette UK's policy is to use papers that are natural, renewable and recyclable products and made from wood grown in sustainable forests. The logging and manufacturing processes are expected to conform to the environmental regulations of the country of origin.

Cover photo © Image Source/Punchstock
Index compiled by Dr. Laurence Errington, 15 Kirkhill Terrace, Edinburgh EH16 5DQ
Typeset by Phoenix Photosetting, Chatham, Kent.
Printed in Malta for Hodder Education, An Hachette UK Company, 338 Euston Road, London NW1 3BH

CONTENTS ■

Acknowledgements	xiv
Preface	xv
Human rights study skills	xvii
Table of cases	xxiv
Table of statutes	xxxv
Table of international legislation	xxxviii
List of figures	xliii

1	**Introduction to human rights**	**1**
	1.1 Overview	**1**
	1.1.1 Hard and soft law	2
	1.2 Rights and freedoms	**3**
	1.2.1 Rule of law	3
	1.2.2 Separation of powers	3
	1.2.3 Democracy	4
	1.3 Where did 'rights' start?	**4**
	1.3.1 Slavery	4
	1.3.2 Civil and human rights in Europe	6
	1.3.3 League of Nations	9
	1.3.4 Aftermath of the Second World War	10
	1.3.5 End of colonialism	10
	1.3.6 Diplomats and heads of state	11
	1.3.7 Non-combatants, refugees and migrants	12
	1.4 EU Charter of Fundamental Rights	**12**
	1.4.1 Legal scope of EU Charter	13
	1.5 Jurisprudential nature of human rights	**14**
	1.5.1 *Universal v cultural relativism*	14
	1.5.2 Implications of universalism	15
	1.5.3 Basic human goods	16
	1.5.4 Generational rights	17

	1.5.5	The Dembour analysis	19
1.6	UK rights today		21
1.7	Acronyms and glossary		22
1.8	Summary		24

2	European Convention on Human Rights		26
2.1	Introduction		26
	2.1.1	Early twentieth century	26
	2.1.2	The UN	27
	2.1.3	The Council of Europe	27
2.2	The European rights regime		28
2.3	European Union		29
2.4	Council of Europe institutions and personnel		30
	2.4.1	The Commission	30
	2.4.2	The Court	31
	2.4.3	The Committee of Ministers	31
	2.4.4	The Parliamentary Assembly	32
	2.4.5	The Commissioner for Human Rights	33
	2.4.6	The Judiciary	33
2.5	The Convention Principles		35
	2.5.1	International treaty	35
	2.5.2	Prohibition on discrimination	36
	2.5.3	Protocols	38
	2.5.4	Reservations	39
	2.5.5	Derogations	40
	2.5.6	Hierarchy of rights?	42
	2.5.7	Lawfulness	42
2.6	Inter-state applications		44
2.7	Individual applications		46
2.8	Operating principles of the ECHR		47
	2.8.1	Proportionality and purposive interpretation	47
	2.8.2	The margin of appreciation	48
	2.8.3	Advisory opinions	49
2.9	Conclusions		51

3	Human Rights Act 1998		54
3.1	A proud English tradition		54
	3.1.1	Reluctant Europeans	55

	3.1.2	Need for change	56
3.2	**Genesis of the Act**		**57**
	3.2.1	Bringing rights home	59
	3.2.2	Constitutional significance	60
3.3	**The Human Rights Act 1998**		**62**
	3.3.1	Structure of the Act	62
	3.3.2	Summary explanation	63
3.4	**Introduction to the Act**		**64**
	3.4.1	The Convention rights s 1	64
	3.4.2	Interpretation of Convention rights s 2	65
	3.4.3	Preamble	66
3.5	**Legislation**		**66**
	3.5.1	Interpretation of legislation s 3	66
	3.5.2	Purposive interpretation	67
	3.5.3	Declarations of incompatibility s 4	68
	3.5.4	Incompatibility case law	69
	3.5.5	Right of Crown to intervene s 5	71
3.6	**Public authorities**		**71**
	3.6.1	Acts of public authorities s 6	71
	3.6.2	Proceedings under s 7	72
	3.6.3	Judicial remedies s 8	73
3.7	**Remedial action s 10**		**73**
3.8	**Other rights and proceedings**		**74**
	3.8.1	Freedom of expression s 12	74
	3.8.2	Freedom of thought, conscience and religion s 13	74
3.9	**Derogations and reservations**		**74**
	3.9.1	Derogation	75
	3.9.2	Reservations	77
3.10	**Judges of the European Court of Human Rights**		**78**
3.11	**Parliamentary procedure**		**78**
3.12	**Implementation**		**79**
3.13	**Human rights in the UK**		**79**
4	**Right to life**		**83**
4.1	**Introduction**		**83**
	4.1.1	Global conventions	83
	4.1.2	The European Convention	84
	4.1.3	Abolition of the death penalty	85

	4.1.4	Preliminary considerations	85
4.2	Investigation of mistakes		91
4.3	Wartime deaths		96
	4.3.1	Positive state obligation	99
4.4	Deaths in custody		100
4.5	Right to die?		105
	4.5.1	Competency	105
	4.5.2	Insoluble dilemma	107
	4.5.3	The doctrine of double effect	108
	4.5.4	Absence of competency	109
4.6	Right to live		111
	4.6.1	Competency	111
	4.6.2	Absence of competency	111
4.7	Self defence		112
4.8	Right to life in Europe		115
	4.8.1	Turkey	115
	4.8.2	Germany	116
	4.8.3	Italy	117
4.9	Conclusions		117
	4.9.1	Common law	117
	4.9.2	Rights law	118
5	**Prohibition against torture, inhuman and degrading treatment**		**121**
5.1	Background		121
	5.1.2	What is torture?	122
5.2	The Milgram experiment		123
5.3	Absolute unacceptability		124
5.4	Meaning and sources		125
5.5	UN Special Rapporteur		126
5.6	Changing perceptions		127
5.7	Chastisement of children		129
	5.7.1	Earlier cases	129
	5.7.2	Current law	130
5.8	UK legislation		131
	5.8.1	School Standards and Framework Act 1998 c 31	131
	5.8.2	The Children Act 2004	132
5.9	Children with disability		133
5.10	Punishment of young criminals		134

5.11		Interrogation of terrorists	135
	5.11.1	The Parker Report	136
5.12		Deportation	137
5.13		Europe	140
5.14		Torture elsewhere	141
	5.14.1	USA	141
	5.14.2	China	142
	5.14.3	Chile	143
5.15		Conclusions	145
6		**Prohibition against slavery**	**147**
6.1		Slavery, servitude, forced or compulsory labour	147
	6.1.1	Background	147
	6.1.2	Common law	148
	6.1.3	Statutory reform	149
	6.1.4	A global problem	150
6.2		Definitions	150
	6.2.1	ECHR Article 4	152
6.3		Slavery and servitude	152
6.4		Servitude and forced labour	154
6.5		Military Service	156
6.6		Forced labour and Article 4(3) civil exceptions	157
	6.6.1	Jury service	157
	6.6.2	Legal service	158
	6.6.3	Fire service	158
	6.6.4	Sport	159
6.7		Council of Europe Convention against Trafficking in Humans	160
	6.7.1	Examples of trafficking	161
	6.7.2	Operation Pentameter	162
6.8		Conclusions	162
7		**Right to liberty and security**	**165**
7.1		English civil liberties	165
7.2		Human rights	165
	7.2.1	Universal rights	166
	7.2.2	The European Convention	166
	7.2.3	Circumstances permitting deprivation of liberty	167
7.3		Case law	170

	7.3.1	Breach of the peace	170
	7.3.2	Detention without warrant and 'honest belief'	171
	7.3.3	Courts martial	171
	7.3.4	Crime	172
	7.3.5	Natural justice	172
7.4		**Balancing liberty and security: detention without charge**	**173**
7.5		**Anti-libertarian policies**	**176**
7.6		**Non-criminal detention under Article 5**	**178**
	7.6.1	Art 5(1)(a) Detention after conviction	179
	7.6.2	Art 5(1)(b) Non-compliance with lawful court order	179
	7.6.3	Art 5(1)(c) Prevention of commission of an offence	181
	7.6.4	Art 5(1)(d) Detention of minors	182
	7.6.5	Art 5(1)(e) Detention on medical or social grounds	183
	7.6.6	Art 5(1)(f) Unauthorised entrants	184
7.7		**Detention involving foreign states**	**185**
	7.7.1	Guantanamo	186
	7.7.2	Iraq	187
7.8		**European Union**	**188**
8		**Right to a fair trial**	**193**
8.1		**Trials and hearings**	**193**
8.2		**Background**	**193**
	8.2.1	Magna Carta (1215)	194
	8.2.2	English Bill of Rights 1689	195
8.3		**Fair process**	**196**
	8.3.1	Kevin at the police station	196
8.4		**Judicial independence**	**198**
	8.4.1	Protection of judicial office	198
	8.4.2	Judicial bias in hearings	198
	8.4.3	Jury bias	203
8.5		**ECHR Article 6 Right to a fair trial**	**205**
	8.5.1	Types of hearing	206
	8.5.2	Fair hearings despite flaws	209
8.6		**Article 6(1)**	**210**
	8.6.1	Access to the Court	210
	8.6.2	Fair and public hearing and judgment	214
	8.6.3	Within a reasonable time	216
	8.6.4	Independent court and absence of bias	217

8.7	Article 6(2) presumption of innocence		217
	8.7.1	The reversed burden of proof	218
8.8	Article 6(3) minimum rights		220
	8.8.1	Article 6(3)(a) prompt information	220
	8.8.2	Article 6(3)(b) adequate time and facilities	221
	8.8.3	Article 6(3)(c) defending oneself and legal assistance	221
	8.8.4	Article 6(3)(d) witnesses	222
	8.8.5	Article 6(3)(e) interpreters	224
	8.8.6	Misuse of Article 6(3)	225
9	**No punishment without law**		**229**
9.1	Introduction		229
9.2	Due process (of law)		229
9.3	Legislative power of Parliament		230
9.4	Development of the *nullum crimen* principle		232
9.5	Modern international provisions		233
	9.5.1	UDHR Art 11	233
	9.5.2	The ICCPR Article 15	233
	9.5.3	ECHR Art 7	234
9.6	The 'Kevin test'		234
	9.6.1	Example of Principle 1	236
	9.6.2	Examples of Principle 2	236
9.7	Retrospective crime and punishment		239
	9.7.1	Retrospective law	239
	9.7.2	Retrospective punishment	240
9.8	Scope of Art 7 cases		243
	9.8.1	What kinds of case?	243
	9.8.2	Strictly criminal in scope	244
	9.8.3	Presumption of innocence	244
9.9	Conclusions		245
10	**Privacy and respect for private and family life**		**247**
10.1	Introduction		247
10.2	Privacy under the common law		248
10.3	Rights brought home		251
	10.3.1	Convention provisions	252
	10.3.2	Development of 'right to privacy'	252
	10.3.3	Framing the claim under Art 8	254

10.3.4   Difficulty of categorisation   257
10.4   Exclusion of evidence   274
10.5   Importance of Art 8   276
10.6   Marriage and founding a family   277

11   Freedom of thought, conscience and religion   280
11.1   Introduction   280
11.2   Freedoms interconnectivity   282
11.3   Analogous provisions   283
11.4   Manifestation of religion   284
11.5   Human Rights Act s 13   288
11.6   Variety of religious beliefs   289
11.7   UK state recognition of religion   290
11.8   Secular beliefs   292
11.9   EU policy   297
11.10   European examples   297
11.11   Scope of Art 9   300

12   Freedom of expression   302
12.1   The foundation freedom   302
12.2   Importance of freedom of expression   302
12.3   Treaty provisions   304
12.4   Analysis of ECHR Article 10(1)   306
12.5   Analysis of Article 10(2)   307
12.6   Limitations on freedom of expression   307
12.6.1   Prescribed by law   307
12.6.2   Necessary in a democratic society   308
12.6.3   Legitimate aims   309
12.7   Art 10(2) duties and responsibilities   310
12.8   Human Rights Act 1998   316
12.9   Anti-terrorism laws   317
12.10   United Nations periodic review report   318

13   Freedom of assembly and association   321
13.1   Strength in numbers   321
13.2   Employment   322
13.3   Domestic law   322
13.4   International instruments   325

13.5	Assembly and association	326
	13.5.1 UDHR Art 20	326
	13.5.2 EU Charter freedoms	327
	13.5.3 ECHR Article 11	327
13.6	Analysis of 'association'	327
	13.6.1 Case law on association	328
13.7	Meaning of 'assembly'	332
	13.7.1 Case law on assembly	333

14	**Right to marry**	**338**
14.1	Global recognition	338
	14.1.1 UDHR 1948 Article 16	339
	14.1.2 ICCPR 1966 Article 23	339
14.2	European recognition	340
	14.2.1 ECHR 1950 Article 12	340
	14.2.2 EU Charter of Fundamental Rights 2000 Article 9	340
14.3	Overview of ECHR case law	340
14.4	Understanding the meaning of marriage	341
14.5	Relationship between Arts 8 and 12	342
14.6	Right of prisoners to marry and found a family	345
	14.6.1 Marriage	345
	14.6.2 Founding a family	345
14.7	Consanguinity	347
14.8	Immigrants, illegal entrants, asylum seekers	348
14.9	Divorce/legal separation	350
14.10	Transsexuals	352
14.11	Tax	355
14.12	Protocol 7 Art 5	356

15	**Rights and remedies**	**358**
15.1	Establishing the principle	358
15.2	Rights must be enforceable	358
	15.2.1 *Ubi jus, ibi remedium*	358
	15.2.2 *Magna Carta* Arts 39 and 40	360
	15.2.3 Equitable maxims	361
	15.2.4 Rule of law	362
	15.2.5 Equality before the law	363
	15.2.6 Petitions of right	364

		15.2.7	UDHR Article 8	366
		15.2.8	ECHR Article 13	366
		15.2.9	HRA 1998 s 1(1)	366
	15.3	Rights and remedies		367
		15.3.1	Enforceability of remedies	367
		15.3.2	Legal systems enforcing law	367
		15.3.3	UN global enforcement	368
	15.4	Enforcement of ECHR remedies under HRA		371
		15.4.1	Rights protected by the HRA	371
		15.4.2	Summary of HRA remedies	371
		15.4.3	Limitations on enforcement ability	372
	15.5	Case law		373
		15.5.1	Asylum seekers	373
		15.5.2	Medical negligence and *stare decisis*	374
		15.5.3	Higher education	375
		15.5.4	Deprivation of place of abode	376
		15.5.5	Failures to provide remedy	377
16	Prohibition of discrimination			381
	16.1	Background		381
		16.1.1	Domestic legislation	381
		16.1.2	Consolidation of domestic provisions	382
		16.1.3	International declarations and treaties	383
	16.2	ECHR Article 14		384
	16.3	Discrimination and equality		384
	16.4	Getting a case heard		385
	16.5	What is discrimination?		387
		16.5.1	Rational justifiability	387
		16.5.2	The *Michalak* Catechism	388
	16.6	Other kinds of discrimination		389
		16.6.1	Property status	390
		16.6.2	Probationary tenancy	391
		16.6.3	Bankrupt's possessions	392
		16.6.4	Right to marry	393
		16.6.5	Sex discrimination	393
		16.6.6	Asylum	395
		16.6.7	Terrorism	396

17	**Regional rights regimes**	**400**
	17.1 The Americas	**400**
	17.1.1 American Declaration of the Rights and Duties of Man 1948	400
	17.1.2 Organisation of American States (OAS)	400
	17.1.3 American Convention on Human Rights 1969	401
	17.1.4 Forced disappearances	401
	17.2 Africa	**402**
	17.2.1 Organisation of African Unity	402
	17.2.2 African Union	403
	17.3 Minsk Convention	**404**
	17.4 Arab Declaration and Charter	**405**
	17.4.1 Cairo Declaration	405
	17.4.2 Arab Charter on Human Rights	405
	17.5 Asia	**406**
	17.6 Conclusions	**408**
Index		**410**

ACKNOWLEDGEMENTS

The author would like to express his sincere gratitude to his students past and present without whose help and curiosity this book would not have been written, and to the readers who generously offered practical advice which improved the book considerably. Any errors of course remain the responsibility of the author.

This book is dedicated to Jack and Florence Halstead.

PREFACE ▮

The *Unlocking the Law* series is an entirely new style of undergraduate law textbook. Many student texts are very prose dense and have little in the way of interactive materials to help a student feel his or her way through the course of study on a given module.

The purpose of this series, then, is to try to make learning each subject area more accessible by focusing on actual learning needs, and by providing a range of different supporting materials and features.

All topic areas are broken down into 'bite-size' sections, with a logical progression and extensive use of headings and numerous sub-headings. Each book in the series will also contain a variety of charts, diagrams and key facts summaries to reinforce the information in the body of the text. Diagrams and flow charts are particularly useful because they can provide a quick and easy understanding of the key points, especially when revising for examinations. Key Facts charts not only provide a quick visual guide through the subject but are useful for revision purposes also.

The books have a number of common features in the style of text layout. Important cases are separated out for easy access and have full citation in the text as well as in the table of cases, for ease of reference. The emphasis of the series is on depth of understanding much more than breadth. For this reason, each text also includes key extracts from judgments, where appropriate. Extracts from academic comment from journal articles and leading texts are also included to give some insight into the academic debate on complex or controversial areas. In both cases these are indented to make them clear from the body of the text.

Finally, the books also include much formative 'self-testing', with a variety of activities ranging through subject-specific comprehension, application of the law, and a range of other activities to help the student gain a good idea of his or her progress in the course.

Symbols used in this series:

 This is a small extract from a judgment in a case. It may follow a case example or the case may be identified immediately above.

 This is a section from an Act.

 This is an Article of the EC Treaty or of the European Convention on Human Rights.

 This is a clause from a draft Bill or Code.

> Where a paragraph is indented, this is an extract from an academic source such as an article or a leading textbook.

Note also that for all incidental references to 'he', 'him', 'his', we invoke the Interpretation Act 1978 and its provisions that 'he' includes 'she' etc. are invoked.

The twentieth century generally and, more particularly, the World Wars and subsequent conflicts taught us that unless we develop a global culture of respect, billions of people will continue to suffer unnecessarily from political oppression, poverty, ill-health, lack of education and insecurity of existence. Addressing political, economic, social and cultural rights issues after the Second World War provided a start. However, more recently there has been a realisation that other factors require us radically to expand what we understand by human rights, especially global warming which seems to threaten us all, and contradictions arising from scientific and technological developments. There is widespread debate about what human rights mean, or should mean, and perhaps the one word that comes nearest to telling us is the need to recognise and respect human 'dignity'.

This book is designed to cover all the main areas of undergraduate and professional syllabuses and starts with a wide-ranging introductory chapter followed by a detailed examination of the European Convention on Human Rights and the Human Rights Act. The substantive Convention Articles are dealt with by close reference to UK and European case law and the book concludes with a survey of the global and regional rights regimes.

The law is stated as I believe it to be on 1st January 2009.

Peter Halstead

HUMAN RIGHTS STUDY SKILLS

Essay writing

No amount of reading, study and knowledge will do the student much good unless he can produce a high standard of assessed work. This section is designed to help you to plan and write good essays, dissertations and indeed any extended piece of writing on human rights and the following section deals with tackling problems or scenarios.

Consider the following essay titles:

ACTIVITY

Practice essay titles

Essay 1: 'Human rights can mean different things depending on where you are and when.' Discuss.

Essay 2: Analyse the scope of Article 2 of the European Convention on Human Rights (right to life) and evaluate in detail two leading cases.

Many assessments are framed like Essay 1 with a real or imagined 'quotation' and a separate instruction as to what to do with it. In such cases the quotation comprises the 'content words' and the instruction 'discuss' provides the 'process word'. The process words are important and there are many of them (see Figure 1.8 following).

For Essay 2 the process words are contained and conjoined in the title and require two separate parts to the answer – analysis of Art 2 and evaluation of two unspecified original law reports. You should not use a secondary account to answer this question but must refer to the primary law report source. Neither of the titles is particularly easy but you can write an excellent answer for each essay, given sufficient time, research and care in execution. That means dealing with the coursework when you receive it, not the night before the hand-in deadline.

Consider the process word(s) first because they will affect the approach to be taken. Some of them may also reflect the level of work expected, in that by the end of undergraduate studies, students are often required to 'critically analyse' or 'evaluate' which implies a greater degree of thought and depth than a simple 'discuss' or 'explain'. The adverb 'critically' may be added to

Process words	What is needed
Advise	Identify and explain the legal points involved before coming to a conclusion on the likely outcome either for a particular individual or in answer to a specified question.
Analyse	Study in depth, identifying and describing the main characteristics in detail before reaching a conclusion.
Assess	Weigh up two or more options or arguments, considering their advantages and disadvantages before reaching a conclusion.
Comment	Express an opinion or reaction to given material in speech or writing.
Compare	Look for qualities or characteristics that resemble each other: emphasise similarities but do not ignore differences.
Consider	Think carefully about something before making a decision or reaching (a) conclusion(s).
Contrast	Stress the dissimilarities between the items but do not ignore points of similarity.
Critically	Incorporate a detailed and scholarly analysis or commentary alongside whatever other process word is indicated.
Define	Give concise, clear and authoritative meanings: start with treaty or statutory reference(s) if relevant, then expand by reference to cases.
Discuss	Examine and analyse carefully, considering both or all sides of the problem and reach a balanced conclusion.
Draft	Draw up a document.
Evaluate	Examine closely with a view to weighing up both sides of a situation in a balanced way before reaching a conclusion.
Examine	Look in detail at the arguments, theories, points at issue and evidence and come to a conclusion.
Explain	Make clear and illustrate the point(s): clarify, interpret and spell out the material you present.
Justify	Prove, make out a case for something: give reasons for decisions or conclusions, taking pains to be convincing.
List	Identify and set out clearly in an appropriate and rational order.
Outline	Provide a brief explanation of the main points.
Present	Introduce or announce the various items of a prepared piece of work, either individually or as part of a team, sometimes assisted by visual aids (and if so check in advance what equipment is available).
Refute	Rebut or repel and prove the falsity or error of a statement, opinion or argument by your own argument.
Suggest	Put forward ideas, with a rationale.

■ Essay instructions

emphasise the requirement of a scholarly approach to whatever the other process word(s) are. Consider the following table and always think carefully about exactly what is required before starting to research the topic and frame the answer.

Important qualification

The above table of essay instructions is designed to give you food for thought with regard to the process words, but the definitions may not invariably be authoritative or exactly what is needed in particular contexts, so care must always be given to match the process word(s) with the content words and any other instructions given for the required work.

Planning the essay

Although quite different things are required from the questions themselves, for both of these essays you would need to do several things in common:

- Identify the point(s) requiring discussion, ie prepare a draft answer plan.
- Research the required data keeping track of your sources, ie an accurate list of where you find your information, with the exact references – it is infuriating if you are unable to retrace a source because you failed to note sufficient details.
- Sort out the presentation order.
- Engage in the discussion, analysis and evaluation respectively, supporting the points you make with authority.
- When you have written your essay, insert a brief relevant introduction at the beginning and draw appropriate conclusions at the end.
- Do not forget to use appropriate referencing (Oxford, Harvard or other designated system) with bibliography, case and statute list, as stipulated.
- Throughout the process, aim to complete the coursework ahead of the actual deadline.

Choosing the material tends to be the easier part, whilst executing the exact requirement of the essay is often less successfully achieved.

Essay 1 requires you to identify what you think is important. Key words are:

- discuss
- human rights
- different things
- where
- when.

How many 'rights' and 'things' will depend to some extent on how long your essay must be but obviously involves some elements of comparison and contrast although not explicitly saying so. Here, a balance of numbers and depth is implied; you would not be advised simply to make a list, and you will want some depth and substance to your answer. Thus, you might choose to frame your discussion in terms of comparing and contrasting freedom of speech in the UK and Myanmar (Burma), or the right to private and family life under the European Convention and in the Sudan.

If that seems to require too much research into unfamiliar areas, there are many aspects of the ECHR which have changed over the last 50 years, and where attitudes vary considerably from one country to another. Examples might be changing attitudes to corporal punishment or the death penalty, or comparisons of freedom of religion in (say) Greece and France. The essay leaves it up to you and if you choose well, there is much you can say. Consider what resources are available as well as what interests you. The instruction to 'discuss' allows you considerable scope but remember that discussion can be carried on at any level; a rambling discussion is tedious and will not gain high marks.

Essay 2 defines your subject matter which pins you down so far as your analysis of the right to life provisions is concerned, but leaves you free to choose the subject matter of your case law evaluation in the second part of the question. In the absence of any indication you are entitled to conclude that roughly equal weight should be given to each part, although common sense is needed depending on the exact wording of this type of question. If a question falls, or is split, into more than one part, the examiner will usually indicate clearly if one part is worth more or less than the other(s).

Key words and targets here are:

* analyse and evaluate
* scope of the right to life article
* two leading cases.

After your introduction you may wish to quote Art 2 (or the relevant part(s) of it) which says:

1. Everyone's right to life shall be protected by law. No one shall be deprived of his life intentionally save in the execution of a sentence of a court following his conviction of a crime for which this penalty is provided by law.

2. Deprivation of life shall not be regarded as inflicted in contravention of this Article when it results from the use of force which is no more than absolutely necessary:

(a) in defence of any person from unlawful violence
(b) in order to effect lawful arrest or to prevent the escape of a person lawfully detained
(c) in action lawfully taken for the purpose of quelling a riot or insurrection.

Doing this will bring home to you that the actual key word is 'scope' and simply describing the article would be insufficient. It is complex, starting with the bald statement:

(1) everyone's right to life 'shall be' protected by law, then going on to

(2) provide justification for judicial killing, and

(3) in Art 2(2) indicating no less than six circumstances where protection is removed:

- self-defence
- defence of another
- lawful arrest
- prevention of escape from lawful custody
- killing whilst quelling a riot
- killing whilst trying to prevent insurrection.

Most people would assume that if there is one right above all others that cannot be qualified or compromised, it would be the right to life. Your analysis will demonstrate that the ECHR is much more complex than that simplistic and erroneous conclusion would suggest. One aspect of analysis is to show the essence and component parts of something, and here you could do this by providing case law examples of the three constituents identified above, for example:

(1) successfully argued in *McCann and others v United Kingdom* (1995) 21 EHRR 97 but not in *LCB v United Kingdom* (1998) 27 EHRR 212

(2) that would require explanation of the gradual acceptance *via* protocols of complete abolition of the death penalty

(3) examples of cases that might be used here could include *Re Jordan's Applications for Judicial Review* [2004] NICA 29; *Jordan and others v United Kingdom* (2001) *The Times*, 18th May; *McShane v United Kingdom* [2002] ECHR 43290/98; and *Finucane v United Kingdom* [2003] ECHR 29178/95.

It is important to refer back to the title occasionally to ensure that you choose two appropriate leading cases and that you do not just recount, describe or summarise them, but evaluate their content and significance, ie put a value on their importance.

Hence, it is important that you think carefully about what is required, address the questions in a methodical manner, and answer in an organised and disciplined way. Refer throughout to exactly what is asked for, ensure that you fully reference the work in respect of case, statutory and treaty citation, journal articles and other preferably primary sources, and undertake the work in a timely manner so that it does not have to be printed and submitted in a hurry at the last minute.

Problem solving

Some legal topics lend themselves more easily than others to scenarios or problem-solving, as students of land law and equity often find, and in such cases they may be required to advise one or more of the characters depicted. It may be more appropriate to use the essay format for human rights, but similar criteria apply if there is a scenario to address. What is needed is fourfold:

- identifying relevant facts on which the answer will depend
- identifying and locating relevant law

- applying that law to the facts
- drawing appropriate conclusions and, if required, advising the scenario characters in the manner required by the assessment.

In most scenarios there is a choice to be made regarding the structure that can often be reduced to deciding whether to:

- deal with the facts chronologically, or
- deal in turn with each of the characters involved.

Although you must identify which circumstances apply to whom and when, it is important to avoid repeating the facts *verbatim* as this is simply padding and will not qualify for any marks.

ACTIVITY

Practice scenario question

Ben arrived in the UK in June 2001 from Barbados by using a false passport in the name of Robert. He was refused entry, detained for a short period, and removed. He returned in September 2001 using his real name Ben and obtained leave first to enter as a visitor and later to stay as a student. In 2002 he married a UK national Janet and was then granted indefinite leave to remain on account of the marriage.

In 2003 he was arrested on drugs and firearms offences but was acquitted. Following his trial he was detained under immigration powers and notice was served for his removal under the Immigration and Asylum Act 1999 s 10 on the ground that he had obtained leave to remain based on deception. Throughout he denied that he had ever attempted to enter the UK as Robert, although eventually it was established by facial recognition technology that Ben and Robert were one and the same person.

His claim to remain has now been certified as unfounded under the Nationality, Immigration and Asylum Act 2002 s 94(2).

Advise Ben.

Approach to the scenario task

Here the definition of 'advise' given above is entirely appropriate: 'identify and explain the legal points involved then come to a conclusion on the likely outcome for a particular individual'. Identifying the law involved should be fairly straightforward: you have been given the relevant statutory provisions governing the way his case has been dealt with so far, so you would locate and study these to provide yourself with the necessary detailed understanding of the law needed to address the scenario. Ben would probably use Art 8 of the ECHR and would wish to challenge the decision by means of judicial review.

He might wish to argue other articles, for example that he had not had fair hearings under Art 6, although you would point out that there is no indication that this was the case from the facts given in the scenario, so it is not a line to be pursued. The basis of his argument would be that the Secretary of State had failed to establish as a precedent fact to the exercise of the removal power that he had obtained leave to remain by deception because his true name and identity is in fact Ben.

It is imperative that you reach a conclusion and provide Ben with the required advice, even though you may not be sure as to how the court would deal with his case. Arts 6 and 8 are not absolute and unqualified, so you would apply them to his circumstances, and in light of his continued deception the court is likely to refuse his application for judicial review and he will probably be deported.

TABLE OF CASES ■

A v B (a company) [2002] EWCA Civ 337; [2002] 3 WLR 542 253
A v Essex CC; J v Worcestershire CC; S v Hertfordshire CC; B v Suffolk CC [2008] EWCA
   Civ 364 133
A v Netherlands (App No 9322/81); (1983) 5 EHRR CD 598 159
A v Secretary of State for the Home Department; X v Secretary of State for the Home
   Department [2004] UKHL 56, [2005] 2 AC 68, HL; *reversing* [2002] EWCA Civ
   1502, [2004] QB 335, [2003] 1 All ER 816, CA 174, 390, 397
A v United Kingdom (1999) 27 EHRR 611...130, 131
A (and others) v Secretary of State for the Home Department (No 2) [2005]
   UKHL 71, [2006] 2 AC 221, HL; *reversing* [2004] EWCA Civ 1123, CA.......122, 128, 138, 145, 191
A (Children) (Conjoined Twins: Surgical Separation), *Re* [2001] 2 WLR 480.....................112, 115, 120
A (FC) and others (FC) (Appellants) v Secretary of State for the Home Department
   (Respondent); X (FC) and another (FC) (Appellants) v Secretary of State for the Home
   Department (Respondent) [2004] UKHL 56; [2005] 2 AC 68; [2002] EWCA Civ 1502 76
AL (Serbia) v Secretary of State for the Home Department; R. (on the application of Rudi) v
   Secretary of State for the Home Department [2008] 1 WLR 1434 37
Ahmed v United Kingdom (2000) 29 EHRR 1 328
Airedale NHS Trust Respondents v Bland Appellant [1993] 2 WLR 316; [1993] AC 789 ....109, 120
Airey v Ireland (1979–80) 2 EHRR 305...341, 350, 351
Aksoy v Turkey (1996) 23 EHRR 553...141
Aldwyck Housing Association v Cunningham [2000] CLY 52 200
Anderson and Others v The Scottish Ministers and Another (2001) *The Times,* 29 October;
   [2001] All ER (D) 240 (Oct)...192
Angelini v Sweden, App 10491/83, Decision of 3 December 1986 (1986) 51 DR 41, ECmHR.............290
Arrowsmith v United Kingdom, App 7050/75, decision of 12 October 1978 (1978) 19 DR 5,
   ECmHR; (1980) 19 DR 5; (1981) 3 EHRR 218 ....292, 310
Antoun v Queen (2006) (unreported)...203
Aston Cantlow and Wilmcote with Billesley Parochial Church Council v Wallbank [2004] 1 AC 546..378
Attorney-General v Guardian Newspapers Ltd [1987] 1 WLR 1284 56
Attorney-General v Jonathan Cape Ltd; Attorney General v Times Newspapers Ltd [1976] QB 752;
   [1975] 3 WLR 606...315
Attorney-General's Reference No 1 of 2004 [2004] EWCA Crim 1025; [2004] 3 WLR 976...................50
Austin v Commissioner of Police of the Metropolis [2009] UKHL 5, HL; *affirming* [2007]
   EWCA Civ 989 CA; *affirming* [2005] EWHC 480 (QB) 182, 192
Autio v Finland (1991) 72 DR 245, ECtHR...292
Aydin (Sukran) v Turkey (1997) 25 EHRR 251, 3 BHRC 300.....................................141
Aydin v Turkey App 25660/94, Decision of 25 May 2005 (2006) 42 EHRR 44 140

B and L v United Kingdom [2006] 42 EHRR 11 ....341, 348, 354
B and P v United Kingdom (Apps 36337/97 and 35974/97), Judgment of 24 April 2001;
   (2002) 34 EHRR 19...215

Barbera, Messegue and Jabardo v Spain (1988) 11 EHRR 360 218
Barrow v United Kingdom (App no 42735/02) 386
Beet v United Kingdom (47676/99) (2005) 41 EHRR 23 180
Belilos v Switzerland (1988) 10 EHRR 466 40
Bellinger v Bellinger [2003] UKHL 21; [2003] 2 AC 467................................341, 354, 355
Benham v United Kingdom (App 19380/92), Judgment of 10 June 1996; (1996) 22
    EHRR 293 180
Bernstein v Skyviews Ltd [1978] QB 479..249, 251, 256
Birmingham City Council v Bradney, Birmingham City Council v McCann [2003] EWCA
    Civ 1783; [2003] All ER (D) 163 (Dec), CA...267
Birmingham City Council v H (a Minor) [1993] 1 FLR 883 112
Bliss v Hall 132 ER 758; (1838) 4 Bing NC 183 Common Pleas...264
Brannigan and McBride v United Kingdom, Judgment of 26 May 1993, Series A, No 258-B;
    (1993) 17 EHRR 539...41, 75, 77
Brogan and others v United Kingdom, Judgment of 29 November 1988, Series A, No 258-B;
    (1988) 11 EHRR 117 ....41, 63, 75, 171
Brüggemann & Scheuten v Germany (1977) 3 EHRR 244 ....255, 256
Buckley v United Kingdom (1996) 23 EHRR 101..255, 256
Bull v Bull [1955] 1 QB 234 CA..362
Burden v United Kingdom (2007) 44 EHRR 51 ....341, 356
Burmah Oil Company v Lord Advocate [1965] AC 75..231, 232
Burton v UK (1996) 22 EHHR 135 270
Bushell's Case (1670) Vaughan's Reports, 135; (1670) 124 ER 1006 ....303, 309, 319

CG v United Kingdom (43373/98) Judgment of 19 December 2001; (2002) 34 EHRR 31 214
Caballero v United Kingdom (App 32819/96), Judgment of 8 February 2000; (2000) 30
    EHRR 643...172, 191
Campbell v Hall (1774) 1 Cowp 204; 98 ER 1045, KB 377
Campbell v MGN Ltd [2004] UKHL 22; [2004] 2 AC 457 253
Campbell and Cosans v United Kingdom (Application 7511/76) (1982) 4 EHRR 293....................39, 130
Chahal v United Kingdom (1996) 23 EHRR 413; 1 BHRC 405 65
Chapman v UK (2001) 33 EHRR 399..255, 256, 272
Chappell v United Kingdom (1989) 12 EHRR 1; App12587/86, Decision of 14 July 1987
    (1987) 53 DR 241...290
Chassagnou and others v France (2000) 29 EHRR 615..328
Church of Scientology Moscow v Russia (Application No 18147/02), Decision 5 April 2007;
    (2008) 46 EHRR 16...290
Connolly v DPP [2007] 2 All ER 1012 (DC); [2007] EWHC Amin.....................................293
Connors v United Kingdom (2005) 40 EHRR 9...271
Corcoran and others v United Kingdom (App No 60525/00)..386
Cossey v United Kingdom (1991) 13 EHRR 622..269, 341, 353
Costello-Roberts v United Kingdom (Application 13134/87) [1993] 19 EHRR 112; [1994]
    1 FCR 65..130
Council of Civil Service Unions v Minister for the Civil Service [1985] AC 374 ....330, 377
Council of Civil Service Unions and Others v United Kingdom App No 11603/85 (1988)
    10 EHRR CD269 ....330, 331
Countryside Alliance v Attorney-General [2007] UKHL 52; [2007] 3 WLR 922 ....71, 254, 257, 278
Craxi v Italy (2004) 38 EHRR 47 263

Croke (A Minor) v Wiseman [1982] 1 WLR 71 CA (Civ Div) 374
Cuscani v United Kingdom (32771/96) (2003) 36 EHRR 2..225
Cyprus v Turkey (App 25781/94 ECHR), Judgment of 10 May 2001 [2001] 11 BHRC 45,
    (2002) 35 EHRR 731 ....44, 45, 152

D v France App 10180/82, Decision of 6 December 1983 (1983) 35 DR 199...................................290
Dabas v High Court of Justice, Madrid (Dabas v Spain) [2007] 2 AC 31 HL...............................189
Derbyshire County Council v Times Newspapers Ltd [1993] AC 534; [1992] QB 770...................56, 254
Dickson v United Kingdom (44362/04) (2008) 46 EHRR 41 ....341, 345, 346
Dimes v Grand Junction Canal 10 ER 301; (1852) 3 HL Cas 759 ....199, 201, 202
Douglas v Hello! Ltd [2001] 2 WLR 992 CA..253
Draper v UK (1981) 24 DR 72...56
Dyson v Watson; HM Advocate v JK, [2002] UKPC D1, [2004] 1 AC 379...................................216

E (Alleged Patient), Re, see Sheffield City Council v E—
ELH v United Kingdom (32094/96) (1998) 25 EHRR CD 158 Eur Com HR 347
Eastham v Newcastle United Football Club [1963] 1 Ch 413..159
Eccleston v United Kingdom (App no 42841/02) 386
Edwards v United Kingdom (App 46477/99), Judgment of 14 March 2002; (2002)
    35 EHRR 19; (2002) 35 EHRR 487 ....101–103, 120
Eisenstecken v Austria (2002) 34 EHRR 35...40
Evans v Amicus Healthcare Ltd [2003] 4 All ER 903 Fam D..248
Evans v United Kingdom (Application 6339/05) (2008) 46 EHRR 34; [2007] 1 FLR 1990
    (Grand Chamber)..341, 343, 347
Ezelin v France, Judgment of 26 April 1991, Series A, No 202; (1992) 14 EHRR 362 333

F (Mongolia) v Secretary of State for the Home Department [2007] All ER (D) 384 (Jul);
    [2007] EWCA Civ 769..390, 395
FK (Kenya) v Secretary of State for the Home Department [2008] EWCA Civ 119.............341, 349, 355
Findlater v United Kingdom (App no 38881/97)...386
Findlay v United Kingdom (App 22107/93) (1997) 24 EHRR 221...171
Finucane v United Kingdom (App 29178/95), Judgment of 1 July 2003; (2003) 37 EHTT 656......92, 95
Fitzpatrick v Sterling Housing Association [2001] 1 AC 27..394
Fox, Campbell and Hartley v United Kingdom, Judgment of 30 August 1990, Series A, No 182;
    (1991) 13 EHRR 157...171
Friend v Lord Advocate [2007] UKHL 53 328

G & E v Norway (1983) 35 DR 30 ....255, 256
Galstyan v Armenia [2007] ECHR 26986/03...328
Gammell v Wilson [1982] AC 27 HL..375
Ghaidan v Godin-Mendoza [2002] EWCA Civ 1533 ....390, 394, 395
Giacomelli v Italy (2006) 45 EHRR 871...255
Glass v United Kingdom (61827/00) [2004] 39 EHRR 15...260
Golder v United Kingdom, Judgment of 21 February 1975, Series A, No 18; (1979–80)
    1 EHRR 524..212
Goodwin v United Kingdom (2002) 35 EHRR 447...341, 354, 355
Gouriet v Union of Post Office Workers (1978) AC 435..359
Grande Oriente D'Italia Di Palazzo Giustiniani v Italy [2001] ECHR 500; (2002) 34 EHRR 22 328

Greek Case, The (1969) 12 Yearbook 1, European Commission of Human Rights 125
Guisto v Governor of Brixton Prison [2003] 2 WLR 1089 HL 191
Guzzardi v Italy Series A, No 39 (1981) 3 EHRR 333...169, 170, 183

H v United Kingdom (1993) 16 EHRR CD 44, ECmHR 294
H v United Kingdom aka L v UK (45508/99), Judgment of 5 October 2004 (2004) 40 EHRR 761 ...184
H v United Kingdom, Judgment of 8 July 1987, Series A, No 120; (1988) 10 EHRR 95.....................216
Halsey v Esso Petroleum Co Ltd [1961] 1 WLR 683 QBD..264
Hamer v UK Application No 7114/75 (1982) 4 EHRR 139; (1979) 24 DR 5.....................56, 341, 345
Handyside v United Kingdom, 7 December 1976, App No 5493/72; (1979–80) 1 EHRR 737 ....308, 309
Harrow London Borough Council v Qazi [2003] UKHL 43; [2004] 1 AC 983.............256, 266, 267, 276
Hashman and Harrup v United Kingdom (2000) 30 EHRR 241 ....262, 335
Hatton v United Kingdom (2003) 37 EHHR 28 265
Hepple and others v United Kingdom (App no 65731/01) 386
Heydon's Case (1584) Co Rep 7a..67
Hill and 12 others v United Kingdom (App no 28006/02); (consolidated with many other cases).........386
Hood v United Kingdom (App 27267/95), Judgment of 18 February 1999; (2000) 29 EHRR 365......171
Howell v Lees Millais [2007] EWCA Civ 720...200, 203
Hunt v London Borough of Hackney etc. [2002] 3 WLR 247; [2002] 4 All ER 156 361

ISKONA and others v United Kingdom, App 20490/02, Decision of 8 March 1994 (1994)
    76-A DR 41; ECmHR 290
International Transport Roth GmbH v Secretary of State for the Home Department [2002]
    EWCA Civ 158; [2002] 3 WLR 344...73, 208
Iqbal v Whipps Cross University Hospital NHS Trust [2007] EWCA Civ 1190....................374, 379
Ireland v United Kingdom (Application 5310/71), Judgment of 18 January 1978, Series A,
    No 25; (1978) 2 EHRR 25 ....44, 77, 126
Iversen v Norway (App 1468/62), Decision of 17 December 1963 (1963) 6 Yearbook 278;
    EComHR...155, 157

JE v DE (aka Re DE) [2006] EWHC 3459..183
Johansen v Norway (1987) 9 EHRR CD 103 ....156, 157
Johnston v Ireland (1987) 9 EHRR 203...341, 350, 351
Jones v Ministry of the Interior of the Kingdom of Saudi Arabia (Secretary of State for
    Constitutional Affairs intervening); Mitchell v Al-Dali [2006] UKHL 26, [2007]
    1 AC 270; reversing in part [2004] EWCA Civ 1394...144
Jordan and others v United Kingdom; McKerr v UK; Kelly and Others v UK; Shanaghan v UK
    (Application No 24746/94) (Application No 28883/95) (Application No 30054/96)
    (Application No 37715/97), Judgment of 4 May 2001, (2003) 37 EHRR 52; (2001)
    The Times, 18 May 92–95, 102, 103
Jordan's Application for Judicial Review, Re [2004] NI 198; [2004] NICA 29 ....93, 94

K (A Child) (Secure Accommodation Order: Right to Liberty), Re [2001] 2 WLR 1141;
    [2000] All ER (D) 1834 (CA) 178, 183
K v Federal Republic of Germany (1961) 4 Yearbook 240; 6 Coll. 17.................................341, 345
K v United Kingdom (38000/05) (2008) The Times, 13 October 375
Khan v United Kingdom Application No 35394/97; (2002) EHRR 45...275
Kalac v Turkey (App 20704/92) Judgment of 1 July 1997; (1999) 27 EHRR 552...............................287

Karaduman v Turkey (App 16278/90) Decision of 3 May 1993 (1993) 74 DR 199 290
Karlheinz Schmidt v Germany (1994) 18 EHRR 513 159
Kay v Lambeth London Borough Council [2006] UKHL 10; [2006] 2 AC 465; [2004] EWCA
    Civgf 926 256
Kaye v Robertson [1991] FSR 62 ....250, 251, 256
Kelly v United Kingdom (2001), *see* Jordan and others v United Kingdom; McKerr v UK;
    Kelly and Others v UK; Shanaghan v UK—
Kelly v United Kingdom (Application 17579/90) (1993) 16 EHRR CD 20 ....89–91, 119
Kimber and others v United Kingdom (App 65900/01) 386
Klass and others v Federal Republic of Germany (1979–80) 2 EHRR 214 261
Knudsen v Norway (1986) 8 EHRR 45, Cm; (1985) 42 DR 247, ECmHR 292
Kokkinakis v Greece (1993) 17 EHRR 397, ECtHR 287, 300
Koniarska v United Kingdom (App 33670/96), admissibility decision of 12 October 2000 183
Kyprianou v Cyprus (App No 73979/01, 15 December 2005 (2007) 44 EHRR 27 220

L v Lithuania (2008) 46 EHRR 22 ....341, 354
LCB v United Kingdom (App 23413/94), Judgment of 9 June 1998; (1998) 27 EHRR 212 ...86, 88, 115
Lancashire County Council v Taylor (Secretary of State for the Environment, Food and Rural
    Affairs intervening) [2005] EWCA Civ 284; [2005] 1 WLR 2668 390
Larissis and others v Greece (1999) 27 EHRR 329 287
Le Compte and others v Belgium (1981) 4 EHRR 1 328
Le Cour Grandmaison and Fritz v France (1989) 11 EHRR 46 292
Leakey v National Trust [1980] QB 485 CA 264
Leyla Sahin v Turkey (App 44774/98), initial Judgment of 29 June 2004 confirmed by Grand
    Chamber Judgment of 10 November 2005 298
Litwa v Poland (App no 26629/95) (2000) 63 BMLR 199; [2000] ECHR 26629/95 178
Liversidge v Anderson [1941] 3 All ER 338 HL 191
Lloyd v United Kingdom (29798/96) [2006] RA 329 180
Locobail (UK) Ltd v Bayfield Properties Ltd [2000] QB 451 ....200, 201
Loizidou v Turkey (1996) 20 ECHRR 1995 40
Lord Advocate, The, Petitioner, 2007 SLT 849 207

M v Secretary of State for Work and Pensions [2006] UKHL 11; [2006] 2 AC 91 ....390, 394
M and H (Minors), *Re* [1990] 1 AC 686 56
McBride v United Kingdom App No 1396/06 (2006) 43 EHRR SE 10 ....113–115, 119
McCann v United Kingdom (Application 19009/04) [2008] All ER (D) 146 (May), ECtHR 266, 267
McCann and others v United Kingdom, (Application 18984/91), Judgment of
    27 September 1995, Series A, No 324; (1995) 21 EHRR 97; [1995] ECHR
    18984/91 ....87, 88, 91, 104, 119, 276
McFeeley and others v United Kingdom (App 8317/78) (1981) 3 EHRR 161 293
McGinley and Egan v United Kingdom (1999) 27 EHRR 1 87
McKerr v United Kingdom, *see* Jordan and others v United Kingdom; McKerr v UK; Kelly and
    Others v UK; Shanaghan v UK—
McR's Application for judicial review, *Re* [2002] NIQB 58; [2003] NI 1 73
McShane v United Kingdom (App 43290/98), Judgment of 28 May 2002; (2002)
    35 EHRR 523 ....92, 94, 119
Malcolm, *Re* [2004] EWCA Civ 1748; [2005] 1 WLR 1238 ....390, 392, 395
Malone v UK (Application 8691/79) (1984) 7 EHRR 14; (1985) 7 EHRR 14 ....56, 262, 276

Manoussakis and others v Greece (1996) 23 EHRR 387, ECt HR................290, 297
Mansur v Turkey (A/321) (1995) 20 EHRR 535 ECHR 217
Marckx v Belgium (1979) 2 EHRR 330 ....341, 343
Markovic v Italy (App No1398/03) (2007) 44 EHRR 52 209
Mastromatteo v Italy (App No 37703/97)......................................117
Matthews v United Kingdom (App no 40302/98) 386
Max Mosley v News Group Newspapers Limited [2008] EWHC 1777 (QB); 2008
  WL 2872466..274, 308, 309
Menesheva v Russia App 59261/00, Decision of 9 March 2006 (2007) 44 EHRR 56............141
Metropolitan Church of Bessarabia v Moldova (2002) 35 EHRR 13................298
Ministry of Justice v Prison Officers Association [2008] EWHC 239 (QB)............332
Moreno Gomez v Spain (2005) 41 EHRR 40......................................266

N v United Kingdom (26565/05) *The Times*, 6 June 2007........................139
Nadarajah v Secretary of State for the Home Department and conjoined cases [2003] EWCA
  Civ 1768, CA 185
'Negotiate Now' v United Kingdom (1995) 19 EHRR 93 328
Neill and others v United Kingdom (App no 56721/00)..........................386
Nerva v UK (App No 42295/98) 385, 386
Niemietz v Germany (1992) 16 EHRR 97 ....255, 256
Notham v London Borough of Barnet [1978] 1All ER 1243 47

Ogur v Turkey (App No 21594/93) (2001) 31 EHRR 40 116
Osman v United Kingdom (App 23452/94), Judgment of 28 October 1998; (1998) 29 EHRR 24599,
  103
Othman (Jordan) v Secretary of State for the Home Department [2008] EWCA Civ 290 139

P (A Child) (Adoption: Unmarried Couples), *Re* [2008] UKHL 38................352
PG & JH v UK Reports of Judgments and Decisions 2001-IX, p 195; (App 44787/98),
  Judgment of 25 September 2001 ....255, 256
Pearson v United Kingdom (App 8374/03), Decision of 27 April 2004 154
Peck v UK (Application 44647/98) [2003] IP & T 320; [2003] All ER (D) 255 (Jan);
  (2003) 36 EHRR 41 ....255, 256, 273, 276
Pendragon v UK (1999) 27 EHRR Co 179; [1999] EHRLR 223 (Commission)................289
Pepper (Inspector of Taxes) v Hart [1993] AC 593 47
Perks and others v UK (1999) 30 EHRR 33, ECtHR................172, 178, 179
Perry v United Kingdom (2004) 39 EHRR 3........................248, 263
Pickett v British Rail Engineering Ltd [1980] AC 136 HL 374, 375
Pickstone v Freemans plc [1988] 2 All ER 803....................................67
Pinochet Ugarte (Habeas Corpus) (2000) 97(1) LSG 24 144
Platform Arzte fur das Leben v Austria (1991) 13 EHRR 204 328
Poplar Housing and Regeneration Community Association Ltd v Donoghue [2001] EWCA
  Civ 595; 3 WLR 183 71
Powell and Raynor v United Kingdom (1990) 12 EHRR 355 265
Pretty v United Kingdom (App 2346/02), Judgment of 29 April 2002;
  (2002) 35 EHRR 1 ....105, 108, 115, 134, 255, 256, 296, 377, 379

R v Abdroikov, R v Green and R v Williamson [2007] UKHL 37; [2007] 1 WLR 2679......204

R v Arthur Alan Murray [2004] EWCA Crim 2211; 2004 WL 1808966 312
R v Bhajan Singh [1976] QB 198...341, 348
R v Big M Drug Mart Ltd [1985] 1 SCR 295; [1986] LRC (Const) 322, Can SC.....................300
R v Bow Street Metropolitan Stipendiary Magistrate ex parte. Pinochet Ugarte (No 1)
    [2001] 1 AC 61...143
R v Bow Street Metropolitan Stipendiary Magistrate ex parte. Pinochet Ugarte (No 2)
    [2001] 1 AC 119, HL...144, 199, 201–203, 205
R v Bow Street Stipendiary Magistrate ex parte Pinochet Ugarte (No 3) [1999]
    2 WLR 827; [2000] 1 AC 147...11, 144
R v Cole and R v Keet [2007] EWCA Crim 1924; [2007] 1 WLR 2716 210
R v Conroy and R v Glover [1997] 2 Cr App R 285..204
R v Davis (Iain) and others [2008] 3 WLR 125; [2006] 1 WLR 125 ....223, 224
R v Deyemi (Danny) [2007] EWCA Crim 2060 244
R v DPP, ex parte Kebilene and others [2000] 2 AC 326; [1999] 3 WLR 175 219
R v Dundon [2004] EWCA Crim 621...209
R v Goldstein; R v Rimmington [2006] 2 All ER 257 HL 241–243, 245
R v Gough (Robert) [1993] AC 646 HL 201, 203, 204, 227
R v H (Assault of Child: Reasonable Chastisement) [2001] EWCA Crim 1024 131
R v Home Secretary ex p Brind [1991] 1 AC 696..56
R v Kearley (1992) 2 AC 228...194
R v Khan (Sultan) [1997] AC 558 HL..275
R v Knowles, ex parte Somersett, or Somerset v Steuart (1772) 20 State Tr 1;
    (1772) Lofft 1; (1772) 98 ER 499 ....4, 6, 148, 149, 157, 163
R v Lambert (Steven) (and others) [2001] 2 WLR 211 218
R v Lewis [2005] EWCA Crim 859 209
R v McGuigan (William Joseph) [2005] EWCA Crim 2861; CA (Crim Div)....................237
R v Malik [1968] 1 WLR 353..312
R v MHRT North and East London Region, ex parte H (2001) 3 WLR 512 69
R v Misra and another [2004] All ER (D) 107 243
R v Sang (Leonard Anthony) [1980] AC 402 HL...275
R v Secretary of State for the Home Department ex parte Khawaja [1984] AC 74 HL...........186
R v Secretary of State for the Home Department ex parte Pinochet Ugarte [1999] CLY 2291 QBD 144
R v Secretary of State for the Home Department ex parte Simms (and O'Brien)
    [2000] 2 AC 115...303, 304, 309, 316
R v Secretary of State for Transport, ex p Richmond-upon-Thames London Borough
    Council [1994] 1 All ER 577, [1994] 1 WLR 74, QBD..265
R v Secretary of State for Transport, ex p Richmond upon Thames London Borough Council
    (No 4) [1996] 1 WLR 1460, CA; affirming [1996] 4 All ER 93, QBD 265
R v Spencer [1987] AC 128, HL 203, 227
R v Taylor (Paul Simon) [2001] EWCA Crim 2263; [2002] 1 Cr App Rep 519 ....289, 290
R v Ulcay (Erdogan) and another [2007] EWCA Crim 2379 ....225, 226
R v Umran Javed and Others [2007] EWCA Crim 2692 ....328, 334
R (on the application of Abbasi) v Secretary of State for Foreign and Commonwealth Affairs
    [2002] EWCA Civ 1598; [2003] 3 LRC 297 ....186, 189
R (on the application of Al-Jedda) v Secretary of State for Defence [2006] 3 WLR 954 CA 187, 189
R (on the application of Al-Skeini and others) v Secretary of State for Defence (The Redress
    Trust and others intervening) [2007] UKHL 26; [2008] 1 AC 153................................99, 100

R (on the application of Amin Imtiaz) v Secretary of State for the Home Department [2004]
1 AC 653; [2003] UKHL 51, HL, *reversing* [2002] EWCA Civ 390, CA.................................101, 120

R (on the application of Amirthanathan) v Secretary of State for the Home Department [2003]
EWCA Civ 1768, CA; *affirming* [2003] EWHC 1107 (Admin)..185

R (on the application of Anufrijeva) v Southwark LBC [2003] EWCA Civ 1406 (consolidated
case) 373, 379

R (on the application of Baiai) v Secretary of State for the Home Department; R (on the
application of Bigoku) v same; R (on the application of Tilki) v same [2008] UKHL
53, HL; on appeal from [2007] EWCA Civ 478, CA; *affirming* [2006] EWHC 823,
Admin Ct 341, 349, 390, 393, 395

R (on the application of Bancoult) v Secretary of State for Foreign and Commonwealth
Affairs [2008] UKHL 61 377

R (on the application of Begum) v Denbigh High School Governors [2006] UKHL 15;
[2005] EWCA Civ 199...285, 289, 298

R (on the application of Bennett) v HM Coroner for Inner South London [2006] EWHC
196 (Admin)..113, 119

R (on the application of Black) v Secretary of State for the Home Department [2008] EWCA
Civ 359 70

R (on the application of Burke) v General Medical Council [2005] EWCA Civ 1003; [2004]
EWHC 1879 ....111, 120

R (on the application of Carson) v Secretary of State for Work and Pensions and Conjoined
cases [2005] UKHL 37 ....387, 390, 398

R (on the application of Countryside Alliance and others (Appellants) and others) v Her
Majesty's Attorney General and another (Respondents) (Conjoined Appeals), *see*
Countryside Alliance v Attorney-General—

R (on the application of Countryside Alliance and others) v Attorney General and another; R
(on the application of Derwin and others) v Same, *see* Countryside Alliance v Attorney-General—

R (on the application of Daskaloulis) v University of West England, Queen's Bench Division
(Administrative Court), 22 October 2008 ....375, 379

R (on the application of E) v Secretary of State for the Home Department [2007] EWHC 1731
(Admin); [2007] ACD 83...221

R (on the application of Gentle) v Prime Minister [2008] UKHL 20.................96, 97, 99, 104, 115, 119

R (on the application of H) v London North and East Region Mental Health
Review Tribunal (Secretary of State for Health intervening) [2001] EWCA
Civ 415; [2002] QB 1, CA; *reversing* [2000] All ER (D) 1837, Admin Ct..........................73

R (on the application of H) v Secretary of State for Health [2005] UKHL 60; *reversing* [2005]
3 All ER 468..69

R (on the application of Heather) v Leonard Cheshire Foundation [2002] EWCA Civ 366; [2002]
2 All ER 936..71

R (on the application of Laporte) v Chief Constable of Gloucestershire [2006] UKHL 55.....................181

R (on the application of McLellan v Bracknell Forest BC) [2001] EWCA Civ 1510 ....390, 391, 395

R (on the application of Mellor) v Secretary of State for the Home Department [2001]
3 WLR 533 ....341, 345

R (on the application of Morris) v Westminster City Council and another; Regina (Badu) v
Lambeth London Borough Council [2005] EWCA Civ 1184; [2006] 1 WLR 505 CA 70

R (on the application of Playfoot (A Child)) v Millais School Governing Body [2007]
EWHC 1698 (Admin)..285, 286, 289, 298

R (on the application of Pretty) v Director of Public Prosecutions (Secretary of State for the Home Department intervening) [2001] UKHL 61; [2002] 1 AC 800, HL; *affirming* [2001] EWHC Admin 788, DC 105, 108, 115, 120, 134, 255, 295, 377

R (on the application of Q) v Home Secretary [2003] 3 WLR 365...134

R (on the application of Saddi and others) v Secretary of State for the Home Department [2002] 1 WLR 3131 ....184, 185

R (on the application of Stewart) v HM Advocate; Gough (Stephen Peter) v HM Advocate, *see* Robertson, Petitioner; Gough v McFadyen—

R (on the application of Swami Suryananda) v Welsh Ministers [2007] EWCA Civ 893 ....48, 289, 294

R (on the application of Ullah) v Special Adjudicator; Do v Secretary of State for the Home Department [2004] 3 All ER 785; [2004] UKHL 26...137, 243

R (on the application of Uttley) v Secretary of State for the Home Department [2004] 4 All ER 1; [2004] UKHL 38; [2004] 1 WLR 2278; [2003] EWCA Civ 1130 ....237, 240

R (on the application of Watkins-Singh) v Aberdare Girls' High School Governors [2008] EWHC 1865 (Admin) 286, 298

R (on the application of Williamson and others) v Secretary of State for Education and Employment and others [2005] UKHL 15...132

R (on the application of X) v Headteachers and Governors of Y School [2007] EWHC 298 (Admin)...286

RSPCA v Attorney-General [2002] 1 WLR 448 328

Rassemblement Jurassien Unitö Jurassienne v Switzerland (1979) 17 DLR 93.................................333

Reay and Hope v British Nuclear Fuels Plc [1994] Env LR 320..87

Rees v UK (1987) 9 EHRR 56; (1985) 7 EHRR 429..268, 269, 341, 353

Republic of Ireland v The United Kingdom (1979–80) 2 EHRR 25..135, 145

Robertson (Stewart) v HM Advocate; Gough (Stephen Peter) v HM Advocate; aka: Robertson, Petitioner; Gough v McFadyen [2007] SLT 1153 309

Rogers v Secretary of State for the Home Department [1973] AC 388 HL...315

Rylands v Fletcher (1868) LR 3 HL 330...264

SW and CR v UK [1996] 21 EHRR 363; [1991] 4 All ER 481 238–240

Schmidt and Dahlstrom v Sweden [1976] 1 EHRR 632 331

Secretary of State for Justice v Walker and others [2008] EWCA Civ 30 179

Secretary of State for the Home Department v JJ and others [2008] 1 AC 385; [2007] 3 WLR 642; [2007] UKHL 45 ....76, 174, 190

Secretary of State for the Home Department v MB [2007] UKHL 46, [2008] 1 AC 440, HL; *affirming* [2006] EWCA Civ 1140; [2007] QB 415 CA; *reversing* [2006] EWHC 1000 (Admin) 68, 72

Serif v Greece (App 38178/97, Judgment of 4 December 1999 (2001) 31 EHRR. 20 297

Shanaghan v United Kingdom (2001), *see* Jordan and others v United Kingdom; McKerr v UK; Kelly and Others v UK; Shanaghan v UK—

Sheffield and Horsham v UK (1999) 27 EHRR 163..269, 270

Sheffield City Council v E (also known as Re E (Alleged Patient)) [2005] 2 WLR 953.................341, 342

Sheffield City Council v Smart [2002] EWCA Civ 4; [2002] LGR 467, CA 256

Sheldrake v DPP; Attorney-General's Reference No 4 of 2002, [2004] UKHL 43; [2005] 1 AC 264; [2004] 3 WLR 976, HL; *reversing in part* [2003] EWCA Crim 762; [2003] 3 WLR 1153, CA; *reversing* [2003] EWHC 273; [2004] QB 487, DC 219

Shobiye v UK (1976) ECmHR..178

Sidabras and Dziautas v Lithuania (Apps 55480/00 and 59330/00), Judgment of 27 July 2004; (2004) 42 EHRR 104...255

Sigsworth, *Re* [1935] Ch 89...67

Sigurjonsson (Sigurdur A) v Iceland Judgment of 30 June 1993, Series A No 264; (1993) 16 EHRR 462...328

Sijakova and others v FYRM (App 67914/01), Decision of 27 April 2004.........................152

Siliadin v France (App 73316/01), Judgment of 26 July 2005; (2006) EHRR 16.........152–154, 157

Silver and others v UK (1983) 5 EHRR 347 ....43, 56, 57

Smith v Scott 2007 SC 345...69

Soering v United Kingdom (A/161) (1989) 11 EHRR 439 ....85, 137, 145

St Helens Smelting Co v Tipping (1865) 11 HL Cas 642 264

Staff Side of the Police Negotiating Board, The, John Francis v The Secretary of State for the Home Department [2008] EWHC 1173 (Admin) 330

Stec v United Kingdom (2006) 43 EHRR 1017 37

Steel and Morris v United Kingdom (App 68416/01), Judgment of 15 February 2005; (2005) 41 EHRR 22...213

Steel and others v United Kingdom (App 24838/94), Judgment of 23 September 1998; (1998) 28 EHRR 603; [1998] Crim LR 893; 5 BHRC 339 ....170, 191, 243, 325

Stewart v United Kingdom (1984) 39 DR 162, ECmHR 119

Stichting Collectieve Antennevoorziening Gouda and others Case C-288/89 (Judgment of 25 July 1991 [1991] ECR I-4007)...305

Streletz v Germany (App No 34044/96); Kessler v Germany (App No 35532/97); Krenz v Germany (App No 44801/98) (2001) 33 EHRR 31...116, 120

Sturges v Bridgman (1878) 11 Ch D 852 CA...264

Sumukan Ltd v Commonwealth Secretariat [2007] EWCA Civ 243 [2007] 1 CLC 282.........207

Sunday Times v United Kingdom, 26 April 1979 (App No 6538/74); (1979) 2 EHRR 245 307

T v United Kingdom (App 24724/94); and V v United Kingdom (App 24888/94) Judgments of 16 December 1999; (2000) 30 EHRR 121...134, 145

TP v UK [2001] ECHR 28945/95...212

Tammer v Estonia (2001) 37 EHRR 857 308

Tatishvili v Russia (App No 1509/02); (2007) 45 EHRR 52 209

Thoburn v Sunderland City Council [2003] QB 151 361

Thompson and Venables v News Group Newspapers [2001] 2 WLR 1038 ....253, 257

Tolstoy Miloslavsky v UK (A/323) (1995) 20 EHRR 442...314

Tomasi v France (1992) 15 EHRR 1 146

Tremblay v France (Application No 37194/02)...164

Tyrell v United Kingdom (App 28188/95), Decision of 4 September 1996; Tyrer v UK Judgment of 25 April 1978, Series A, No 26; (1979–80) 2 EHRR 1 129

Van der Leer v Netherlands (1990) 12 EHRR 567...172

Van der Mussele v Belgium, Series A, No 70 (App No 8919/80); (1984) 6 EHRR 163; [1983] ECHR 8919/80...158, 222

Van Droogenbroeck v Belgium (1982) 4 EHRR 443 ....155, 157

Van Oosterwijck v Belgium (1981) 3 EHRR 557...268

Vo v France (2005) 40 EHRR 12 ....120, 344

W, X, Y and Z v United Kingdom (App 3435–38/67); (1968) 11 YB 562 ....156, 157

Waddington v Miah alias Ullah [1974] 1 WLR 683..232
Wainwright v Home Secretary [2003] UKHL 53; [2003] 3 WLR 1137.........................253, 254, 257, 258
Wainwright v United Kingdom (2007) 44 EHRR 40..258
Wandsworth London Borough Council v Michalak [2003] 1 WLR 617 CA.................388, 389, 390, 395
Watson v Durham University [2008] EWCA Civ 1266, CA 376, 379
Welch v UK [1995] 20 EHRR 247..236
Whaley v Lord Advocate [2007] UKHL 53; 2008 SC (HL) 107 332
Whitely v Chappell (1868) 4 LR QB 147..67
Wilson & the NUJ and Others v United Kingdom (2002) *The Times*, 5 July 2002 328
Wilson v First County Trust Ltd (No 2) [2004] 1 AC 816; *reversing* [2001] EWCA Civ 633,
   [2002] QB 74 69
Worm v Austria (App No 22714/93) (1998) 25 EHRR 454..316

X v Austria (1979) 18 DR 154, ECmHR 173
X v Belgium (1969) 12 Yearbook 174, ECmHR..119
X v France (App 5442/72), Decision of 20 December 1974 (1974) 1 DR 41................................289
X v United Kingdom (App 8121/78), Decision of 6 March 1982 (1982) 28 DR 5................................289
X, Y and Z v United Kingdom (1997) 24 EHRR 143..341, 353
Xenides-Arestis v Turkey [2006] ECHR 46347/99 376

Y v United Kingdom [1994] 17 EHRR 238..130
Young v Bristol Aeroplane Co Ltd [1944] KB 718 CA 375
Young v United Kingdom (App No 60682/00); (2007) 45 EHRR 29..207
Young, James and Webster v United Kingdom, Judgment of 13 August 1981, Series A, No 44;
   (1982) 4 EHRR 38..329

Z and others v United Kingdom (App 29392/95) (ECHR), Judgment of 10 May 2001; (2001)
   10 BHRC 384; (2001) *The Times*, 31 May..212
Zarb Adami v Malta (App No 17209/02); (2007) 44 EHRR 3 ...., 157
Zentrum Omkarananda and the Divine Light Zentrum v Switzerland (App 8118/77), Decision of
   19 March 1981 (1981) 25 DR 105 289

TABLE OF STATUTES ■

Abortion Act 1967 109
Act of Union of Parliaments 1706.............................60
Act of Union of Parliaments 1707.............................60
Acts of Union 1800 60
Agricultural Holdings Act 1986......................390, 391
Aliens Act 1905..57
Aliens Act 1914..57
Animal Health Act 1981—
   s 32...294
Anti-terrorism, Crime and Security Act
   2001 ....42, 75, 173, 189,
                    324, 396
   Pt 4 ....75, 175
   s 21.......................................138, 396, 397
   s 23.......................................138, 174, 175, 191,
                    396, 397
   s 25..138
Asylum and Immigration (Treatment of
   Claimants, etc.) Act 2004—
   s 19 ....349, 350
   s 19(3)(b)...350

Bill of Rights 1688–89...............8, 55, 60, 85, 195, 226,
                  228, 230, 296, 365
   Art 9...302, 319

Child Support Act...393
Children Act 1989 215
   s 25..183
Children Act 2004—
   s 58..132
Children and Young Persons Act 1933.....................132
Civil Aviation Act 1982—
   s 78..265
Civil Contingency Act 2004 176
Civil Partnership Act 2004.........363, 379, 382, 394
Colonial Laws Validity Act 1865 377
Commonwealth Immigrants Act 1962........................57
Commonwealth Immigrants Act 1968........................57
Constitutional Reform Act 2005 ....3, 61
Consumer Credit Act 1974.................................70
   s 127(3) 70
Conventicle Act 1664......................................303
Criminal Evidence (Witness Anonymity) Act
   2008 ....224, 227
Criminal Justice (Terrorism and Conspiracy)
   Act 1998..173
Criminal Justice Act 1988—
   s 134...144

s 160..312
Criminal Justice Act 1991...............................237
   s 35...70
   s 35(1)..70
Criminal Justice Act 2003..................151, 173, 194, 204
   s 114...194
Criminal Justice and Public Order Act 1994..............324
   s 25..172
Crown Proceedings Act 1600 ....364, 379
Crown Proceedings Act 1947 ....366, 373
   s 1..359

Data Protection Act 1998 303
Disability Discrimination Act 1995.................382, 395
Drug Trafficking Offences Act 1986 236

Education (No 2) Act 1986 ....39, 77, 130
Education Act 1996...............................39, 77
   s 548...131
   s 548(1)..132
Equal Pay Act 1970 ....363, 379, 381, 395
Equality Act 2006...................286, 363, 379, 382,
                   387, 395,
                   398
European Communities Act 1972 ....55, 60, 66, 231
   s 2..361
Extradition Act 2003....................................189
   s 64(2)...189

Forced Marriage (Civil Protection) Act 2007 339
Freedom of Information Act 2000 ....178, 303

Gender Recognition Act 2004 270
   Sch 1 270
Genocide Act 1969 ....231, 232

Habeas Corpus Act 1679 60
Homicide Act 1957—
   s 2..218
   s 2(2)...218
   s 4(2)..50
House of Lords Act 1999 ....55, 61
Housing Act 1985.......................................266
   s 113...388
Housing Act 1996—
   s 185(4) 70
Human Fertilisation and Embryology Act
   1990 ....343, 344
   Sch 3, para 6(3) 248

Human Rights Act 1998 ....1, 8, 15, 21, 24–26,
28, 29, 36, 50, 54, 58, 59,
61–67, 69, 71, 72, 74, 75,
78–81, 92, 93, 100, 104, 111,
118, 178, 186, 188, 246, 247,
250–253, 259, 266, 274, 296,
316, 350, 354, 365–367,
371–373, 379, 380,
388, 394, 396
ss 1–17 62
ss 1–10 63
s 1 ....63, 64
s 1(1) 360, 366, 371, 389
s 1(4) 65
s 2 63–65
s 2(1) 65
s 3 ....63, 66–69
s 3(1) 66
s 4...63, 66, 68, 70, 71, 73,
80–82, 354, 372
s 5 ....63, 66, 71
s 6...63, 69, 71, 72, 92, 372
s 6(1) 71, 100, 188
s 6(3) 71
s 7...63, 69, 72, 182
s 7(1) 188, 372
s 7(3) 372
s 7(4) 372
s 8 ....63, 73
s 8(1)–(3) 73
s 8(1) 372, 373
s 8(3) 372
s 8(4) 372
s 10..63, 64, 68, 71,
73, 372
s 10(2) 73
s 10(7) 63
ss 11–22 64
s 11...74, 316, 372
s 12...74, 316, 372
s 13...74, 280, 288, 316,
320, 372
s 13(1), (2) 288
ss 14–17 74
s 14 ....75, 77
s 14(1) 75
s 15..77
s 15(1) 75
s 16..42
ss 18–22 63
s 18..78
s 19..78
s 19(1)(a), (b) 78
s 19(2) 78
s 20..79
s 21 ....67, 79
s 22..79

Sch 1 ....64, 371
Sch 1, Pt I 50, 63, 70, 102, 183, 396
Sch 1, Pt II 63, 70
Sch 1, Pt III 63
Sch 2 ....63, 64, 71
Sch 3 ....63, 64
Sch 3, Pt I 63, 75
Sch 3, Pt II 63, 77
Sch 4 ....63, 64
Hunting Act 2004 ....72, 254–256

Immigration Act 1971...................................232
Immigration and Asylum Act 1999—
Pt II...73, 208
s 35(8) 208
s 65...185
Incitement to Disaffection Act 1934 ....310, 311
s 1 ....292, 310
s 2..292
Insolvency Act 1986......................................392
s 283(1) 392
s 352...50
s 436..392
Interception of Communications Act 1985............56, 262
s 2..262
International Criminal Court Act 2001 231

Magna Carta 1215 ....8, 9, 55, 60, 61, 194,
226, 228, 360, 361, 363
Cl 28 194
Cl 29 ....195, 229
Cl 36 62
Cl 38 62
Cl 39 ....62, 360
Cl 40 ....62, 359, 360
Magna Carta (1297 Version) 360, 361
Cl 1 62
Cl 9 62
Cl 29 62
Malicious Communications Act 1988.........................293
Matrimonial Causes Act 1973................................354
s 11(c) 354
Mental Health Act 1983......................................184, 258
s 72..73
s 73..73
Misuse of Drugs Act 1971 289
s 5(4) 218
s 28..218
Murder (Abolition of the Death Penalty) Act
1965 ....8, 109

Nationality, Immigration and Asylum Act 2002—
s 125..73
Sch 8 73
Northern Ireland (Emergency Provisions) Act
1978—
s 1 171

Offences against the Person Act 1861............................132
  s 62 73

Parliament Act 1911 ....55, 60
Parliament Act 1949 ....55, 60
Petition of Right 1628 8
Police Act 1996 331
  s 64 330
  s 91 330
Police and Criminal Evidence Act 1984.................32, 193
  s 78 ....274, 275
Prevention of Terrorism (Temporary Provisions)
  Act 1989—
  s 16A 219
Prevention of Terrorism Act 2005 ....42, 76, 174,
                                        175, 189
  s 1 76
  s 2 192
  s 3 192
Protection from Eviction Act 1977................................50
Public Order Act 1936 ....323, 324
  s 1 323
Public Order Act 1986 ....289, 324
  s 12 324
  s 17 311
  s 18 311
  s 18(1) 334

Race Relations Act 1965 ....311, 363, 379, 382
  s 6(1) 312
Race Relations Act 1968 382
Race Relations Act 1976.......................................286, 382
Race Relations (Amendment) Act 2000 382
Registration of Business Names Act 1916 57
Regulation of Investigatory Powers Act 2000 262
Rent Act 1977...394
  Sch, paras 2, 3..394
Road Traffic Act 1988 219
  s 5(1) 219
  s 5(2) 219

School Standards and Framework Act 1998.......130, 131,
                                           145
  s 131 131
Scotland Act 1998...54
Sex Discrimination Act 1975 ....363, 379, 381

Sexual Offences (Amendment) Act 1976—
  s 1 238
Sexual Offences Act 2003 73
Slave Trade Act 1807 ....6, 149, 163
Slavery Abolition Act 1833.............................149, 163
Special Immigration Appeals Commission Act
  1998 66
Statute Law Revision Act 1863.......................................61
Suicide Act 1961................................105, 108, 296, 378
  s 1 295
  s 1(1) 295
  s 2 ....295, 296
  s 2(1) 105, 106, 295
  s 2(2) 295
  s 2(4) 106, 295

Terrorism Act 2000 ....173, 324
  s 1 317
  s 11(2) 219
Terrorism Act 2006 ....319, 324
Theatres Act 1968 303

Valerie Mary Hill and Alan Monk (Marriage
  Enabling) Act 1985 348

War Crimes Act 1991.......................................231, 231
War Damage Act 1965......................................231, 232
Weights and Measures Act 1985....................................361

Table of Statutory Instruments

Adoption (Northern Ireland) Order 1987
  (SI 1987 No 2203) 352

Gender Recognition Act 2004 (Commencement)
  Order 2005 (SI 2005 No 0054) 270

Human Rights Act 1998 (Amendment) Order 2005
  (SI 2005 No 1071) 76

Human Rights Act (Designated Derogation)
  Order 2001 (SI 2001 No 3644) 75, 174, 189,
                                           396, 398

Mental Health Act 1983 (Remedial) Order 2001
  (SI 2001 No 3712) 73

TABLE OF INTERNATIONAL LEGISLATION ■

Abolition of Forced Labour Convention
(ILO No 105) (1948)...............................149, 157, 325
African Charter on Human and Peoples'
Rights (1981) (the Banjul Charter) 188, 402
Art 8...284
Art 9...306
Art 20..339, 357
Art 68...404
African Charter on the Rights and Welfare of
the Child (1990)—
Art 48...404
African Unity Charter 402
Art II...402
Art III...403
American Bill of Rights..85
American Convention on Human Rights (1969)
(Pact of San Jose, Costa Rica) 15, 188,
401, 402
Art 3...401
Art 12...284
Art 13...306
Art 17..339, 357
Art 18...401
Art 19...401
Art 20...401
Art 21...401
Art 22...401
Art 23...401
Art 24...401
Art 25...401
American Declaration of the Rights and Duties
of Man (1948)...400–402
Arab Charter on Human Rights (1994) 405–407
Art 7(1) 406
Art 7(2) 406
Art 30...284
Arab Charter on Human Rights (2004) 408

Bavarian Code (1815) 233
Beijing Rules (UN Standard Minimum Rules for
the Administration of Juvenile Justice) 217
r 13.1...217
r 20.1...217

Cairo Declaration (1990).................................405, 407

Commonwealth of Independent States
Convention on Human Rights and
Fundamental Freedoms of the (1995)
(Minsk Convention)..........................51, 188, 404, 407
Art 11...306
Congress of Vienna 1815...6
Council Directive 89/552/EC 305
17th Recital...305
Council Framework Decision 2002/584/JHA
(of 13 June 2002) on the European Arrest
warrant and the surrender proceedures between
Member States (originally Agreed at the Laeken
Summit in December 2001.....................................188
Council of Europe Convention on Action
against Trafficking in Human Beings
(2005) (CETS No 197) 149, 150, 160, 163
Covenant of the League of Nations—
Art 21 9

Declaration of Arbroath (1320) 55
Declaration of Independance (America) (1776).......8, 191
Declaration of the Rights of Man (France)
(1789) 8, 233
Declaration of Tokyo (1975)...............................125, 140
Declaration on the Elimination of All Forms
of Intolerance and Discrimination Based on
Religion or Belief (1981) 284, 384
Declaration on the Elimination of All Forms
Racial Discrimination (1963) 383
Art 1 383
Declaration on the Rights of Persons Belonging
to National or Ethnic, Religious and Linguistic
Minorities (1992) 384

European Community Treaty, Protocol on the
system of public broadcasting in the Member
States...305
European Convention against Torture and other
Cruel, Inhuman or Degrading Treatment or
Punishment (1984)...128
European Convention Concerning Forced
Labour (1957) (ILO No 29).................151, 157, 325
European Convention on the Protection of
Human Rights and Fundamental Freedoms
(1950) 1, 2, 6, 7, 10,

12, 13, 15, 21–33, 35, 36, 38, 39, 41–43, 45–47, 49–59, 61–75, 77–81, 84, 86–90, 97, 98, 100, 101, 105, 106, 115, 117, 118, 120, 127, 128, 130, 138–140, 150, 152, 161, 163, 166, 168, 170, 172, 173, 177, 178, 183–184, 186–188, 193, 197, 204, 206, 210, 217, 218, 222, 224, 228, 229, 236, 238, 240, 241, 243, 245, 246, 249, 252, 254, 257–259, 261, 266, 268, 279–282, 284–290, 293, 296, 297, 300–302, 304, 305, 307, 308, 316, 317, 320, 323, 325, 326, 335–340, 342, 343, 346, 347, 350, 351, 353–355, 366, 367, 371, 372, 374, 380, 384, 385, 389, 391, 394, 398, 399, 401, 404, 407, 408

Art 1 ....36, 63, 70, 93, 98, 100, 137, 153, 215, 297, 371
Arts 2–14..36
Arts 2–12 ....358, 360, 366, 371, 379
Art 2 ....36, 40, 43, 45, 63–65, 75, 83, 84, 86–107, 112–117, 120, 137, 175, 296, 305, 343, 344, 396
Art 2(1) 84, 85, 98, 104, 117–119
Art 2(2) 84, 86, 89–91, 117
Art 2(2)(a) 89–91, 112, 119
Art 2(2)(b) 89–91, 118, 119
Art 2(2)(c) 89–91, 118, 119
Art 3 ....36, 39, 40, 44–46, 63–65, 75, 85, 86, 88, 105, 106, 122, 125, 127–130, 132–135, 137–139, 141, 169, 212, 259, 271, 343
Art 4 ....36, 40, 43, 63–65, 147, 149, 150, 152–155, 158–160, 163
Art 4(1) 40, 75, 150, 155, 156
Art 4(2) 151, 155, 156, 158, 222
Art 4(3) 151, 157, 158
Art 4(3)(a) 155
Art 4(3)(b) 156
Art 4(3)(d) 158, 159
Art 5 ....36, 42–44, 63–65, 76, 77, 152, 155, 165, 166, 169, 174–177, 180–185, 187, 190–192, 262, 397
Art 5(1) 41, 45, 73, 75, 155, 166, 169–171, 177, 180, 182, 183
Art 5(1)(a)..............................76, 168, 169, 179, 189
Art 5(1)(b) 76, 168–170, 178, 179, 189

Art 5(1)(c) 76, 168–170, 181, 182, 185, 189
Art 5(1)(d) 76, 168, 169, 178, 182, 189
Art 5(1)(e) 76, 168, 169, 178, 182–184, 189
Art 5(1)(f)........................76, 168–170, 178, 184, 185, 189, 349, 396
Art 5(2) 41, 45, 167, 169, 171
Art 5(3) 41, 45, 167, 169, 171, 172, 217
Art 5(4) 45, 70, 73, 134, 167, 169, 171, 179, 184
Art 5(4)(a) 179
Art 5(5) 41, 167, 169–172
Art 6 ....36, 43, 50, 63–65, 70, 73, 87, 137, 139, 168, 169, 171, 180, 193, 197, 204–213, 215, 216, 221, 226–228, 240, 244, 245, 259, 261, 265, 272, 275, 351, 391
Art 6(1) 57, 70, 134, 192, 206, 210, 212, 213, 216, 217, 221, 225, 227, 236, 244
Art 6(2) 50, 206, 215, 217–219, 227, 244
Art 6(3) 193, 206, 211, 220, 225, 227
Art 6(3)(a) 220, 221
Art 6(3)(b) 220, 221
Art 6(3)(c) 215, 220–222
Art 6(3)(d) 215, 220, 222, 223
Art 6(3)(e) 220, 224, 225
Art 7 ....36, 40, 43, 63–65, 75, 168, 193, 197, 229, 233–235, 237–246, 259, 275
Art 7(1)......................................116, 235–237, 245
Art 7(2) 235, 245
Art 8...............................36, 37, 42, 43, 45, 46, 49, 56, 57, 63–65, 72, 73, 87, 105, 106, 169, 212, 247, 248, 252, 254–263, 265–269, 271–278, 308, 340, 342–344, 346, 347, 351–354, 366, 373–376, 393, 394
Art 8(1) 48, 257, 266, 278, 391
Art 8(2) 48, 257, 258, 261, 267, 271, 278, 344, 391
Art 9 ....36, 42, 43, 46, 63–65, 74, 90, 105, 106, 138, 169, 280, 282–293, 297, 300, 326, 340, 351
Art 9(1) 284, 294, 297, 310
Art 9(2)....................................284, 292–294, 297
Art 10 ....36, 43, 57, 63–65, 181, 213, 282, 285, 293, 302, 306, 308–310, 314, 316, 319, 326, 333, 334
Art 10(1)..................................306, 307, 309, 310, 319

Art 10(2)......................292, 307–311, 316, 317, 319
Art 11 ....36, 63–65, 72, 168, 181,
282, 285, 322, 323,
326–333, 336
Art 11(1) 328, 330
Art 11(2) 330, 332
Art 12 ....36, 43, 56, 63–65, 247,
248, 268, 269, 277, 278,
340, 342–356, 395
Art 13 ....36, , 41, 43, 44, 46, 57, 64,
65, 87, 137, 212, 259,
261, 262, 265, 266, 271,
272, 288, 330, 351, 359,
360, 365–367, 371, 373,
375, 379
Art 14 ....36–38, 43–45, 63–65, 70, 72,
105, 106, 114, 115, 158,
175, 191, 271, 272, 285,
343, 344, 351–353, 360,
366, 373, 381, 384, 385,
387–398
Art 15...........................40, 41, 45, 77, 151, 174, 397
Art 15(1) 135, 397
Art 15(2) 40
Art 15(3) 40
Arts 16–18 ....63–65, 360, 366
Arts 19–51 33
Art 19 77
Art 21 51
Art 22 51
Art 25 ....87, 385
Art 25(1) 261
Art 27(1) 386
Art 27(2) 90
Art 28 ....45, 136
Art 33 44
Art 34 46
Art 35 46
Art 38 141
Art 41 373
Art 46...87, 376
Art 47..50, 51
Art 50 88
Art 57 77
Art 64 39
European Convention on the Protection
of Human Rights and Fundamental
Freedoms (1950), Protocol 1 ....39, 43, 63, 77,
80, 169, 366, 371
Art 1 ....45, 46, 63–65, 72, 272,
309, 343, 360, 376, 392
Art 2 ....39, 43, 63–65, 75, 77,
134, 169, 360
Art 3 ....39, 43, 63, 64, 360
European Convention on the Protection
of Human Rights and Fundamental
Freedoms (1950), Protocol 2.......................29, 31, 51

European Convention on the Protection of
Human Rights and Fundamental Freedoms
(1950), Protocol 3...29
European Convention on the Protection of
Human Rights and Fundamental Freedoms
(1950), Protocol 4...172
Art 4..172
European Convention on the Protection of
Human Rights and Fundamental Freedoms
(1950), Protocol 5...29
European Convention on the Protection
of Human Rights and Fundamental
Freedoms (1950), Protocol 6 ....38, 39, 43, 63,
75, 85, 366
Art 1...63, 360
Art 2...63
Art 6..360
European Convention on the Protection of
Human Rights and Fundamental Freedoms
(1950), Protocol 7...29, 43
Art 5..248, 277, 278, 356
Art 7..277
European Convention on the Protection of
Human Rights and Fundamental Freedoms
(1950), Protocol 8...29
European Convention on the Protection of
Human Rights and Fundamental Freedoms
(1950), Protocol 9...29
European Convention on the Protection of
Human Rights and Fundamental Freedoms
(1950), Protocol 10...29
European Convention on the Protection
of Human Rights and Fundamental
Freedoms (1950), Protocol 11...............29–31, 33, 38,
46, 385
Art 5(2) 385
European Convention on the Protection
of Human Rights and Fundamental
Freedoms (1950), Protocol 13.....................29, 43, 57,
65, 80, 85, 371
Art 13 64
European Convention on the Protection of
Human Rights and Fundamental Freedoms
(1950), Protocol 14...29
European Convention Relating to the Status
of Refugees (1951)...12, 13, 325
Art 15 325
Art 26 168
European Union Charter of Fundamental
Rights (2000)................................12, 13, 21, 304, 305,
327, 336, 338
Art 9...340, 357
Art 10 297
Art 11 305
Art 12 327
Art 51 13
Art 52(3) 297, 305

Art 52(5) 14

Forced Labour Convention (1932)
(ILO No 29) 149, 151, 157, 325
Art 2(1) 154
Freedom of Association and Protection of the
Rights to Organise Convention (1948)....................321
French Constitution 1791 233
Art 1 298

General Assembly Resolution on respect for
human rights and freedoms without distinction
as to race, sex, language or religion (47/135 of
18 December 1992) 384
Geneva Conventions 12, 142
Geneva Convention, No 4—
Art 78 188
Art 103 188
German Penal Code (1871) 233

Hague Convention 12

Inter-American Convention on the Forced
Disappearance of Persons (1994)....................401, 402
International Covenant on Economic, Social
and Cultural Rights 17, 23, 384
International Covenant on Civil and Political
Rights (1966) 17, 22, 23, 116,
234, 245, 325,
338, 384
Part III..83
Part IV..166
Art 6 ....83, 104, 116
Arts 9–13 ....166, 177
Arts 9–12 190
Art 12..168
Art 15..233, 235
Art 18..284
Art 19..306
Art 21..325
Art 22..325
Art 23..339, 356
International Covenant on Civil and Political
Rights (1966), Optional Protocol One 166
International Covenant on Economic, Social
and Cultural Rights (1966) 17, 22, 325
Art 8 325
International Convention on the Elimination
of all forms of Discrimination against Women
(1973) (CEDAW) 22, 384
International Convention on the Elimination of
all forms of Discrimination against Women
(CEDAW) Optional Protocol 1999........................384
Art 21 384
International Convention on the Elimination of
all forms of Racial Discrimination (1966)
(CERD) 383

International Convention on the Suppression and
Punishment of the Crime of *Apartheid* (1973) 383
Irish Constitution—
Art 41.3.2..350, 355
Irish Constitution Act (1995), Fifteenth
Amendment..351

Norwegian Act on Exemption from Military
Service—
s 19..156
s 20..157

Organisation of American States (1951) 400

Organisation of African Unity Convention
Governing Specific Aspects of Refugee Problems
in Africa (1969)—
Art15 404

Paris Principles 406
Protocol on the Establishment of an African Court
on Human and Peoples' Rights (1998)—
Art 35..404
Protocol to the UN Convention against
Transnational Organised Crime (UNTOC) 2000,
known as the Protocol to Prevent, Suppress and
Punish Trafficking in Persons, especially Women
and Children 161

Rome Statute of the International Criminal Court
(1998) 245
Art 22..233
Art 23..233

Schengen agreement..30, 34
Single European Act 1987..29
Slavery, Servitude, Forced Labour and Similar
Institutions and Practices Convention (1926)
(as amended by the 1953 Protocol)....6, 149, 150, 154
Statute of the Council of Europe................................27
Art 1(a)..27
Supplementary Convention on the Abolition of
Slavery, the Slave Trade, and Institutions and
Practices Similar to Slavery........................154

Treaty of Amsterdam (1997)..30
Treaty of London (1949)..27, 59
Treaty of Rome (EEC Treaty) (1957)..................29, 254
Treaty of Versailles (1919)..7, 26
Treaty of Westphalia (1648)........................11, 370
Treaty on the European Union (1992) (Maastricht
Treaty)..30

United Nations Charter................................97, 403, 405
Art 1 369
Art 2 368
Art 5 371

Art 19..371
Arts 39–51...369
Art 41..369, 371
Art 42.......................................187, 369
Art 51..369
United Nations Convention against Torture and
other Cruel, Inhuman or Degrading Treatment
or Punishment (1984) 127, 128, 142,
144, 146, 402
Art 1..126
United Nations Convention on Consent to
Marriage, Minimum Age for Marriage, and
Registration of Marriages (1964) 338, 357
United Nations Convention on the Prevention
and Punishment of the Crime of Genocide
(1948)..............................54, 101, 231, 402
United Nations Convention on the
Rights of the Child (1989) 133, 217, 325, 367
Art 1..217
Art 6(1) 84
Art 15..325
Art 37(d) 217
Art 40(2)(iii)..217
United Nations Declaration on the Right to
Development 18
United Nations International Bill of Human
Rights..384, 405
United Nations International Covenant on Civil
and Political Rights 402
Art 26..397
United Nations resolution 40/33 29 November
1985 217
United Nations resolution 1386 (XIV) 20 November
1959 83
United Nations resolution 1985/33 126
United Nations resolution 3452 (XXX) 9 December
1975 125

United Nations Security Council resolution
1244/1999 370
United Nations Stockholm Declaration (1972) 1, 2, 13
United Nations Supplementary Convention on
the Abolition of Slavery, the Slave Trade, and
Institutions and Practices Similar to Slavery
(1956) 6, 149
Art 1..151
Art 7(b) 151
United States Constitution (1791)................................246
Art 1, s 9(3) 233
Eighth Amendment 85
Universal Declaration of Human Rights
(GA resolution 217 A (III)
(10th December 1948))...............8, 15, 18, 22, 23, 27,
34, 59, 101, 127, 128,
168, 234, 245, 302, 325,
326, 336, 339, 384, 402,
403, 408
Arts 3–21...17
Art 3.......................................83, 166, 190
Art 4.......................................149, 150
Art 5.......................................125, 128, 177
Art 8..................359, 365, 366, 373, 379
Art 11.......................................233, 235
Art 13..168
Art 16.......................................339, 356
Art 18..284
Art 19.......................................304–306, 319
Art 20.......................................325, 326
Arts 22–27...17
Art 23..325

Vienna Convention on Consular Relations (1963)........11
Vienna Convention on Diplomatic Relations (1961) 11

LIST OF FIGURES

	Essay instructions	xviii
1.1	Key terms	5
1.2	Timeline	8
1.3	The Council of Europe	10
1.4	*Universality v cultural relativity*	14
1.5	Connectivity of universal rights	16
1.6	Generational rights table	17
1.7	Dembour categories	20
1.8	Table of acronyms	22
1.9	Glossary of words and phrases	23
2.1	Timeline	29
2.2	Procedural Protocols	31
2.3	Categories of ECHR protection	36
2.4	Summary of Art 14 characteristics	38
2.5	Qualification of rights	43
2.6	Admissibility questions	46
3.1	Table of key dates	59
3.2	Basis for a written constitution	61
3.3	Contents of Human Rights Act 1998	63
3.4	Rules of statutory interpretation	67
3.5	Remedying incompatibility	73
4.1	Lawful deprivation of life	91
4.2	Lacunae	115
5.1	Justification of torture?	125
5.2	Definitions	126

5.3	Dr Manfred Nowak	126
5.4	UN links	127
5.5	Types of mistreatment	135
5.6	The five techniques	136
6.1	Triangular slave trade	148
6.2	Slavery and related crimes	149
6.3	Exploitation of children	150
7.1	Prescribed criteria applicable to Art 5	169
7.2	Reasons for detention	178
8.1	Judicial independence	199
8.2	Types of bias	203
8.3	Summary of Art 6 principles	206
8.4	Summary minimum rights	220
9.1	Dicey's theory of parliamentary sovereignty	231
9.2	Development of the 'nullum crimen' maxim	233
9.3	The 'Kevin test'	235
10.1	Breach of confidence — privacy	253
10.2	The Flitcroft guidelines	253
10.3	Aspects of private and family life	256
10.4	Environmental torts	264
11.1	Rights language table	281
11.2	Art 9	283
11.3	Equivalent Articles	284
11.4	Variety of beliefs	289
12.1	Freedom of speech and expression	306
13.1	Association and assembly	321

13.2   Examples of domestic provision   324

13.3   Public Order Act 1986 as amended   324

13.4   International provisions   325

13.5   Associations   328

14.1   Contexts   341

14.2   Interconnections   344

15.1   Crown Proceedings Act 1600   364

15.2   Mind map   368

16.1   Anti-discrimination overview   381

16.2   International provisions   383

16.3   Applications alleging discrimination   386

16.4   Michalak catechism   389

16.5   Types of discrimination   390

16.6   Art 14 steps for asylum seekers   396

17.1   African rights documents   404

chapter 1 INTRODUCTION TO HUMAN RIGHTS ■

AIMS AND OBJECTIVES □ □ □

- This book deals primarily with the European Convention on Human Rights (ECHR) and the Human Rights Act (HRA) but, as human rights are of universal concern, in chapter 17 there is wider discussion

- Chapter 1 provides an introduction whose objectives are indicated below, and Chapter 17 explains the global rights regime and regions other than Europe

- To provide an overview of the meaning of human rights and an introduction to the ideas discussed in this book

- To consider the nature of the rights, freedoms, prohibitions and other concepts

- To consider some important historical rights developments

- To provide a table of key terms, acronyms and glossary

1.1 Overview

Principle 1 of the United Nations Stockholm Declaration 1972 states that

> 'Man has the fundamental right to freedom, equality and adequate conditions of life in an environment of a quality that permits a life of dignity and well-being and he bears a solemn responsibility to protect and improve the environment for present and future generations.'

This declared principle encapsulates the essence of human rights. The word 'freedom' as used here represents the 'first generation' of individual civil and political rights arising from western philosophy and political theory.

'Equality' suggests a post Second World War socialist or 'second world' view as it would have been described during the Cold War (1945–89) meaning that the collective rights of peoples should be accorded prominence rather than private and individual rights. An underlying

implication may be that claims to individual rights are a luxury that many people in the world cannot afford.

Individual civil and political rights are taken to mean the enjoyment of such things as personal freedom of thought, conscience and religion, to associate with others, to fair judicial hearings and the ability to follow whatever way of life one chooses, and similar privileges. On the other hand, economic, social and cultural rights (rather than freedoms) tend to refer to the collective need for everyone to have access to adequate provision for health, education, housing, job security and pensions.

In order to achieve the types of objective in either category, however, it is argued that a third generation of more amorphous collective minority and developmental rights should also be recognised. Perhaps the most important of these must be a healthy and supportive environment in which mankind can live and thrive, the 'adequate conditions of life' referred to in the Stockholm Declaration.

Underlying and underpinning all aspects of the concept of **universal human rights** is the absolute requirement that everyone, however rich or poor, whoever they may be and wherever they may live, is entitled to respect from others and should be allowed and enabled to live an adequately resourced and supported life in dignity. The earth should be used, protected and improved by its inhabitants and enhanced for their children and grandchildren, the present and future generations of which the declaration speaks, emphasising that mankind possesses a life interest in, rather than full ownership of, the world – tenants of the planet, not freeholders.

It should be noted that not everyone accepts the universality of rights, and the philosophical approach representing this alternative view is referred to as **cultural relativism**. There is thus a fundamental divide in human rights between universalism and cultural relativism.

1.1.1 Hard and soft law

The fact that this is a Declaration also indicates another important thing about human rights: namely, that many of them exist as aspirational 'soft law'. Globally, only a small proportion of human rights are enshrined in and protected by 'hard' or enforceable law, and where this is the case they are restricted to particular defined rights in limited parts of the world, for example the ECHR. The recognition and growth of human rights, like other human regimes, is always work in progress and is difficult to measure on any meaningful scale because there is no entirely satisfactory objective rights system that is humanly achievable. Circumstances constantly vary, and mankind is now caught up in global warming and climate change momentum that is intimately connected to rights claims.

It is a truism that states place more importance on economic self-interest than on working towards a fair system of global governance that respects and protects everyone. Promotion and promulgation of human rights should be protected like the economic and trade interests governed by the World Trade Organisation (WTO). This first chapter selects a few of the rights issues that are vital for the world today, and examines them briefly.

1.2 Rights and freedoms

The idea of natural rights arises from belief in natural law, that there were in nature gods or in later times one God who created the universe, from whom everything springs and who makes everything possible. From early primitive chthonic notions mankind developed a variety of more sophisticated religious sentiments and beliefs, a common characteristic of which is that they usually prescribe ways in which people should behave towards others, but without the flexibility of positive law (human imposed law) that can be changed as circumstances require; so both primitive natural law and religious beliefs and more sophisticated positive laws throughout the ages have fed and continue to feed into the development of human rights.

1.2.1 Rule of law

Fundamentally modern rights and freedoms need to be based on the rule of law if they are to be effective and enforceable, although this is a problematical and ambiguous concept that requires explanation. Most modern states lay claim to running their affairs in accordance with their interpretation of the rule of law, but if the European Union, China and the United States all sincerely believe that they adhere to the rule of law, it quickly becomes obvious that their respective visions differ considerably, one from another.

1.2.2 Separation of powers

One component theory supportive of the rule of law is that power should be divided and thus limited in order to prevent too great a concentration in the hands of one individual or clique – the doctrine of separation of powers.

> 'Unlimited power is apt to corrupt the minds of those who possess it.'
>
> William Pitt the Elder, 1770

> 'Power tends to corrupt, and absolute power corrupts absolutely. Great men are almost always bad men.'
>
> Lord Acton, 1887

The doctrine that the principal state functions should be kept separate goes back to classical times of the Greeks and Romans but was reformulated for the French Enlightenment by Baron de Montesquieu. He identified the executive or government that proposes and carries out policy, the legislature as makers of law, and the judiciary who interpret law. Keep them separate, goes the theory, and oppression should be avoided.

The model currently works but imperfectly in the UK, with the executive effectively controlling the legislature by the whipping system and the Prime Minister's ability to make and break other ministerial careers, although the position of the judiciary has been strengthened by establishing the Judicial Appointments Commission and Supreme Court under the Constitutional Reform

3

Act 2005, thus removing the senior judiciary from the legislature. In the United States the separation between the three is much clearer.

1.2.3 Democracy

The ability to choose how one lives and is governed is at the root of democracy. This is another key ingredient in the human rights mix and it too gives rise to a widely differing range of interpretation in different parts of the world. To live in a truly democratic state means that the way in which the justice system operates requires a broad and sympathetic approach to the application of law by means of principles or rules of natural justice, not the same thing as the rule of law. Some sense of what these fundamental ideas mean can be seen from the following table of key terms. For any system or regime of human rights to operate, a reasonable and workable version of these principles should be present.

1.3 Where did 'rights' start?

There is no simple or obvious answer to this question, but a few indicative examples are considered here by way of introduction.

1.3.1 Slavery

One of the oldest institutions or practices accepted as normal by mankind until recent times is slavery, which brings a variety of human rights questions into focus. In the past, 'civilisations' became so reliant on slavery that eventually they could not function without it. Examples include the ancient Egyptians, Greeks and Romans, and European settlers in the West Indies and United States. In other places native peoples were subjugated and ill-treated by mostly European colonialists in ways analogous to slavery, as in the case of Australian Aborigines, New Zealand Maoris, throughout the African continent and in parts of Asia.

It is interesting that societies not only depended on slaves but mostly thought it quite natural that some humans should be accorded a subservient civic status precluding virtually all rights and dignity for the benefit of others. In this they were supported by different religions, including Christianity. Enslavement of one human being by another is fundamentally and entirely antipathetic to every modern idea of what is meant by human rights, representing as it does negation and removal of virtually all *indicia* of humanity, but recognition of this is relatively recent in the history of mankind.

English law

English law prides itself on being a protector of slaves' rights, despite the contradictions inherent in the enthusiasm with which English slave traders (or 'merchant adventurers' as they saw themselves) used to operate throughout the world. In the eighteenth century Lord Mansfield pronounced in *R v Knowles, ex parte Somersett*, or *Somerset v Steuart* (1772) Lofft 1, 98 ER 499 that slavery was odious and quite unsupportable in any circumstances:

4

KEY TERMS	
Concept	**Meaning**
Natural law	The theory that law originates in nature so possessing general validity transcending place and time, providing legitimacy that all peoples should recognise, supporting the idea that human rights are universal
Positive law	In a sense the opposite of natural law: the theory that law is imposed (posited) by (a) human being(s) on others rather than by God or nature. It is law made by the legitimate authority within a given state enacting rules of conduct and stipulating sanctions ensuring obedience
Religious law	The belief that law comes neither from vague 'natural' sources nor ultimately from humans, but is knowledge revealed by God governing all human affairs and behaviour. Wider in scope than positive law, it also incorporates aspects of moral and ethical behaviour and although administered by humans, it is believed to be holy and unalterable, revealed through prophets and applied by clerics
Rule of law	An expression of Dicey's theory about the British Constitution that individuals' rights are determined by clear and fair legal rules and not the arbitrary actions of any authority over them. It includes the right to have legal disputes or prosecutions heard by independent courts only when the law has been broken, with everyone treated equally. More generally it is taken to mean a set of rules of fairness applicable everywhere to safeguard justice and protect human rights
Separation of powers	A theory originating with the Greeks and developed by the Romans having influence in modern times as expressed by Montesquieu. Power should be divided between three branches of state: the government (executive), legislature (parliament) and courts (judiciary). The executive proposes and implements policy; laws are made and changed by the legislature; and breaches of law are adjudicated upon by the judges. Power is divided and dictatorship of one person or group (and thus tyranny) is avoided
Democracy	A political theory taken to mean representative government chosen by a wide electorate who can change the government regularly. It tends to accept that the majority is right (or should have its way) and implicitly incorporates ideas of freedom of thought, opinion and choice, individual rights and the general presence of civil liberties
Rules of natural justice	A general political philosophy in a similar way to democracy or the doctrine of separation of powers, but with more specific meaning as it can be split into particular 'rules' that should apply in all societies. An example is procedural fairness in court or other judicial proceedings – the right to be represented, call witnesses, have an unbiased judge, and not to be forced to incriminate oneself

Figure 1.1 Key terms

J ' . . . The state of slavery is of such a nature, that it is incapable of being introduced on any reasons, moral or political; but only positive law, which preserves its force long after the reasons, occasion, and time itself from whence it was created, is erased from memory: it is so odious, that nothing can be suffered to support it, but positive law. Whatever inconveniences, therefore, may follow from a decision, I cannot say this case is allowed or approved by the law of England; and therefore the black must be discharged.'

What Lord Mansfield meant was that slavery is totally contrary to natural law but that were it to be legalised by human positive law it would be the law of the land, albeit repugnant and morally unacceptable. His decision in any event only related to ownership of slaves within the realm.

The case arose because the slave James Somersett, who was owned by an American, had been brought to England where he escaped. It became a *cause célèbre* as people vied to take sides in the litigation instituted to decide on his freedom and to determine whether in such a case he became free simply by breathing English air. It was at that time by no means obvious which side had the moral high ground, and indeed it is salutary to remember that when slavery was eventually abolished by the Westminster Parliament in 1833, the Bishop of Exeter, who had retained ownership of his 655 slaves right up to the bitter end, was compensated by the British taxpayer in the sum of £12,700 for his loss. The slave trade had been outlawed by Parliament by the Abolition of the Slave Trade Act 26 years previously in 1807, but the message had not sunk home even in some high clerical palaces.

It was William Wilberforce MP and other colleagues known as the 'Clapham Sect' who eventually forced the legislation. As the pre-eminent nineteenth-century naval power, Britain then entered into various bilateral agreements with other European states which gave crews of navy ships the right to board and search vessels in international waters to ensure that slave traders were apprehended and slaves freed.

International abolition

The Congress of Vienna 1815 said that the slave trade was morally repugnant and inhumane and although progress was made throughout the nineteenth century to remove the scourge of slavery, in some places it lasted until recent times. Saudi Arabia and the Yemen did not abolish slavery until 1962 and in the preceding decade it was estimated that there were perhaps half a million slaves still held in captivity there and in the Middle East. In parts of Africa slavery still persists today.

It is perhaps not surprising, therefore, that despite all the nineteenth-century activity, the League of Nations, which had been established in 1919 in response to the First World War, found it necessary to promote a Slavery Commission in 1924 with a Slavery Convention of 1926 codifying international law. Needed still later was the 1956 Supplementary Convention on the Abolition of Slavery, the Slave Trade and Institutions and Practices. It is estimated that there are still up to 27 million slaves in the modern world.

Chapter 6 deals in detail with the prohibition of slavery and forced labour under the ECHR, but the seeds were sown some two centuries ago by English common law and UK legislation.

1.3.2 Civil and human rights in Europe

Political factors

Towards the end of the nineteenth century the incipient decline of the British Empire and the growing strength of a Germany lacking a maritime and colonial history with the glory, wealth

and power that that would have provided seem to have destined the early part of the twentieth century to early disintegration into the conflict of the First World War (1914–18). By the 1940s human rights had become a serious global issue because of atrocities committed in Europe and Asia prior to and during the Second World War (1939–45) that prompted the establishment of the United Nations Organisation in 1945.

Some of the causes of the Second World War lay in the nature and execution of the peace arrangements established after the Great War. The Peace Conference was punitive to the defeated states, and when the League of Nations was inaugurated in 1919 under the Treaty of Versailles, it was given no human rights role to play, nor was it supported by the United States (see section 1.3.3). Population transfers after 1918 opened the door to resurgence of an embittered and humiliated Germany with a messianic leader mandated to redress the balance yet lacking any coherent policy or idea of how Germany could rule the world if their ambitions had been fulfilled.

These were all factors relevant to the need to establish a new rights era after 1945. Those aspects of human nature that allowed slavery to be tolerated up to modern times and elected a government under which apparently civilised people could commit mass murder in factory conditions were and still are part of the human psyche. Yet whilst all these things were happening in the real world, philosophers and others were thinking deeply about what it is that motivates people to act as they do, and planning for what they hoped would be a very different world.

Philosophical influences

In the eighteenth century in western countries there had been recognition of civil rights that were sparked by the American and French revolutions, and before that less violently and more gradually in the 1689 'Glorious Revolution' in England when the Crown was forced to start following an early parliamentary road to representative democracy, although Ireland and Scotland escaped neither violence nor glory. Before these events, earlier roots can be identified which go right back into the mists of pre-history, to codes of early civilisations and to the Greeks.

In Europe at the end of the Dark Ages philosophical discourse can be said to have started as far back as 1088 when the University of Bologna was established. By 1400 there were some 30 or so institutions that we would now call universities throughout Europe. They prospectively and perhaps indirectly played their part in the advancement of thought that eventually led to the Enlightenment. Although those were very different times to the present day, the seeds were being sown, and there were many other influences that fed into the process.

Who can say, then, where human rights started? Mankind has always railed against oppression, and different ages and societies have suffered under and fought it. From earlier civilisations and their philosophers grew ideas that eventually became modern theory and practice of human rights.

One way of tracing this developmental process of ideas and events that helped to develop modern human rights is to construct a timeline, although this can only provide a brief summary of highly selected information. What is important depends on what you want to identify – ideas, events, people, states, civilisations, dates and so on. The following timeline highlights a few of these highly selective and subjective yet seminal events that have led to current understanding of what is meant by human rights in the UK. Another person's list could look very different but be equally valid.

Date	Event/document	Reasons
1215	*Magna Carta*	
1628	Petition of Right	
1688	(English) Bill of Rights	
1776	American Declaration of Independence	
1790	French Declaration of the Rights of Man	
1833	Abolition of slavery in UK	
1948	Universal Declaration of Human Rights	
1950	European Convention on Human Rights	
1965	Abolition of death penalty in UK	
1998	Human Rights Act	
2002	Establishment of International Criminal Court	

■ Figure 1.2 Timeline

ACTIVITY

Timeline

Construct your own timeline based on the five events, documents, persons or otherwise that you consider the most significant in the development of human rights using a third column to set out your reasons: you can use the examples given or choose different ones.

The subject-matter discussed in the preceding introductory pages provides insight into what people consider to be some of the constituent elements of human rights. The following self-assessment questions give an opportunity to reflect on this.

General philosophical considerations and specific examples of inhumanity such as slavery only begin to scratch the surface of the nature of rights. The following sections elaborate and consider other contributions to the rights agenda.

1.3.3 League of Nations

The League of Nations was established in 1919 but from the beginning it had a number of defects that restricted its usefulness as an international body and that eventually led to its decline and demise. It was largely unsupported by the USA, without whose backing as the emerging pre-eminent world power it was doomed to fail. Its specific objectives did not include the protection of human rights, although some of its wider aims were analogous, for example Art 21 of the Covenant of the League of Nations imposed an obligation on its Members to:

'... secure and maintain fair and humane conditions of labour for men, women and children' [and to] 'secure just treatment of the native inhabitants of territories under their control.'

The reference to securing just treatment for native inhabitants relates to colonial states' mandates for territories under their jurisdiction and resonates with contemporary ideas of minorities and self-determination. The only surviving body of that era operating today with continuing significance is the International Labour Organisation (ILO), also dating from 1919.

The motivation for establishing the ILO was certainly humanitarian and in contemporary terms would have been tied to and supported by the human rights agenda, as working conditions in the nineteenth century had been grim and did not look set to change much after the first two disastrous decades of the twentieth century.

ACTIVITY

Self-assessment questions

1 What do the events and documents listed in the Figure 1.2 timeline demonstrate:

  (a) Modern societies could not have developed without the institution of slavery.

  (b) Rights other than civil and political ones are unimportant.

  (c) Only in the twenty-first century did criminal matters become the subject matter of international human rights.

  (d) Britain is the most important country in the development of human rights.

  (e) All human rights can be traced back to *Magna Carta*.

  (f) The failure of the League of Nations was due to lack of support by the United States and lack of interest in human rights at the time.

  (g) Religious leaders ought to have spoken out sooner against unfairness and iniquity rather than taking advantage of western colonialism to enslave others?

2 You may not agree with any of the suggestions, in which case formulate your own conclusions. You may decide that truth is multi-faceted. When you have decided, consider what this tells you about the type and nature of human rights discussed so far.

Another progressive aspect of the ILO is that although half the executive body of the Organisation was represented by governments, the other half comprised equal representation by workers and employers. Its ongoing success can be judged by the fact that on its fiftieth anniversary in 1969 the organisation was awarded the Nobel Peace Prize.

1.3.4 Aftermath of the Second World War

As if to emphasise the need for changes the word 'genocide' emerged from the chaos and ruin of the Second World War. People have killed each other since the dawn of time, often in great numbers, so the idea of one group or tribe or nation attempting to exterminate another was nothing new: Genghis Khan did it in the early thirteenth century and an assortment of cavalier Europeans through the length and breadth of the world ever since, or so it sometimes seems. However, the word 'genocide' itself was coined by the Polish scholar Raphael Lemkin during the Second World War by combining 'geno' (people) and 'cide' (kill).

The persecution and wholesale massacre of a number of minorities and resultant chaos in 1945 acted as urgent stimulants for the Allies to reinvent post-war solutions and avoid making the same mistakes as with the failed League of Nations. Planning for the UN was undertaken during the Second World War and in 1945 the Potsdam Conference, or Conference of Berlin, took place in which the so-called tripartite states of the UK, USA and USSR (Soviet Union) participated.

The destruction that had been caused, ongoing physical chaos on the ground and the incalculable human cost in death, injury, displacement and deprivation are now almost unimaginable, but were all factors that helped to lead to the establishment of the UN in New York whilst the Council of Europe was also set up with various rights objectives. Out of the latter grew the European Convention, Commission and Court of Human Rights.

The Council of Europe is an intergovernmental organisation with 47 Member States whose objectives are to:
• protect human rights, pluralist democracy and the rule of law
• promote awareness and encourage the development of Europe's cultural identity and diversity
• seek solutions to problems facing European society including discrimination against minorities, xenophobia, intolerance, environmental protection, human cloning, Aids, drugs, organised crime, etc
• help consolidate democratic stability in Europe by backing political, legislative and constitutional reform

■ Figure 1.3 The Council of Europe

1.3.5 End of colonialism

The demise of the last European colonial period occurred quickly after the Second World War, in some instances assisted by armed resistance as in Malaya, Kenya and Cyprus. The remnants of the Portuguese, Spanish, Dutch, French and British empires disappeared, sometimes with indecent haste considering the unpreparedness left behind. Confusion and worse were caused by poorly drawn boundaries, weak political, economic and social systems, warring tribes and factions, and inadequate ongoing support.

Other difficulties arose because of claims to minority rights. People who had not wanted to be governed by colonial powers were sometimes equally unhappy to be governed by the emergent ruling factions in the newly independent states, and religious and tribal differences that had been ignored or subjugated under colonial regimes now came to the fore. Political or religious minority claims of this kind helped to highlight the need to recognise other minority rights – women, children, indigenous populations. Therefore, both in Europe as a direct result of the Second World War and in much of the rest of the world because of the decline in European colonialism, claims of minorities pointed to the need for development of human rights responses.

1.3.6 Diplomats and heads of state

The Treaty of Westphalia 1648 marked the beginnings of nation states which in turn began to form modern ideas of citizenship. The 'new order' it started to establish in Europe based on national sovereignty came to replace the Holy Roman Empire that had previously held sway; but long before the seventeenth century the need for different peoples to communicate freely was recognised, even if such discourse was sometimes more honoured in the breach than the observance. Official envoys representing states travelled the world for millennia bearing messages in times when, and to places where, that was the only way of communicating. Customary international law developed to afford protection to those messengers, eventually leading to present-day laws of diplomacy.

Special recognition has always been afforded to monarchs and heads of state and diplomatic law functioned as an adjunct to this. Modern law is the result of work by the International Law Commission and is contained in the Vienna Convention on Diplomatic Relations 1961 and the Vienna Convention on Consular Relations 1963. The special rights accorded to heads of state and diplomats are now based around the idea that communication is essential to the conduct of international relations and even where there are serious differences between states it is better to retain contact than to stop talking to each other. Only in extreme cases do states 'break off diplomatic relations' and even then they are obliged to maintain dialogue through a neutral party such as Switzerland.

For many years there was a general theory that rights afforded to heads and former heads of state were inviolate, but the case of the late Chilean Head of State General Pinochet may alter this perceived immunity from process in future (*R v Bow Street Stipendiary Magistrate ex parte Pinochet Ugarte* (No 3) [1999] 2 WLR 827). The general benefited from the then Home Secretary Jack Straw's decision to use the dictator's health as a reason not to accede to a Spanish judge's request that Senator Pinochet be extradited to Spain to answer murder charges relating to the 'disappeared' victims of his regime in Chile in the 1970s and 80s. The House of Lords had held

that (former) heads of state are not entitled to unlimited immunity for crimes committed whilst enjoying that status, but the circumstances precluded the legal issues being carried to conclusion.

1.3.7 Non-combatants, refugees and migrants

Rules also grew up to deal with warfare and the treatment of non-combatants. These are now represented by the Geneva and Hague Conventions respectively, the former dealing with the rules of war and the latter, humanitarian law. Other aspects of human rights grew out of earlier international custom and later law.

The disruption of the Second World War created the need for large-scale resettlement of refugees and realignment of peoples into new political entities, such as the creation of the former Yugoslavia and transfer of land from Germany to Poland. The Convention Relating to the Status of Refugees 1951 was designed to address European issues arising from the war, but its continued application today has led to enormous problems as it was clearly not designed to deal with and could not anticipate current world problems of political and economic mass migration. Modern transport, cheap and widely available, and a flourishing market in people traffickers hinders governments trying to apply the Convention to inappropriate categories of person.

Treatment of migrants under international law has other human rights implications. There are two broad approaches to what states' responsibilities ought to be towards aliens, ie the **international minimum standard of treatment** approach, or the **national or equality treatment** standard. Simply expressed, the former means that a state should apply minimum internationally based human rights standards to aliens within their jurisdiction, regardless of how the state's own citizens are treated, which is a form of universalism. The latter only requires the state to give the same rights to foreigners as it does to its own citizens, however low those standards might be, which is a species of relativism.

1.4 EU Charter of Fundamental Rights

The ECHR is the main treaty of the Council of Europe and is discussed in detail in Chapter 2. The European Union (EU) also has its own Charter of Fundamental Rights which can be accessed, together with explanatory notes, via the Department of Constitutional Affairs' website listed under useful resources at the end of this chapter. The Charter brings together in one text existing civil, political, economic and social rights of the EU's Member States, divided into six chapters under the headings of:

- dignity
- freedoms
- equality
- solidarity

ACTIVITY

Self-assessment questions

1	The underlying principle of the Stockholm Declaration is that people should be enabled to live dignified lives and enjoy freedoms and equality in a decent environment.	True	False
2	The rule of law and the rules of natural justice are two different ways of saying the same thing.	True	False
3	Heads and previous heads of state are entitled to absolute protection from prosecution whatever they may have done or been responsible for whilst acting as such.	True	False
4	The Convention Relating to the Status of Refugees 1951 still applies to the UK but is out of date and no longer suited to dealing with today's refugee problems.	True	False
5	One problem faced by former colonised states is that their peoples and boundaries do not fall within natural social and geographical areas but were artificially imposed by the former colonial rulers for their own purposes.	True	False

- citizens' rights
- justice.

The Charter has no legal force but is intended to operate as a political declaration. The reason the EU agreed this separate document is that the ECHR does not apply to the EU as an entity nor to its constituent institutions, although it does apply separately to all the individual Member States. The Charter declares rights not included in the ECHR such as the right to vote in European parliamentary elections, to establish businesses and work throughout the EU and to exercise other rights to information and complain to the EU ombudsman.

1.4.1 Legal scope of EU Charter

The Charter does not create new powers nor extend any EU powers established in other treaties and only applies to Member States when they are applying Union law. Specifically Art 51 states that:

'This Charter does not extend the scope of application of Union law beyond the powers of the Union or establish any new power or task for the Union, or modify powers and tasks defined in the other Parts of the Constitution.'

Under Art 52(5) of the Charter rules of interpretation establish that most of the solidarity provisions are to be construed as guiding principles rather than legal or human rights.

1.5 Jurisprudential nature of human rights

There are many different theoretical approaches to what is meant by human rights, and the implications and practicalities of interpreting and applying them. Some broad ideas or theories have been explained earlier in this chapter and this section provides a brief synopsis of selected views on rights theory.

1.5.1 *Universal v cultural relativism*

Perhaps *the* defining characteristic of modern human rights is their claim to be universal. There are many humane and civilised people who would not hurt a fly, yet who would deny categorically that there are any such things as 'universal human rights'. They argue that it is self-evident that the earth is populated by several billion people who are unable to exercise rights and freedoms in any meaningful way. More easily understood is the proposition that by virtue of being human everyone *ought to be* entitled to universal rights. Such claim may be founded on the notion of innate dignity or respect that should be accorded to all and arising from the essence of humanity.

Universalism is in origin a western concept and many people argue that, literally understood, the idea is nonsense because varying standards and criteria apply in different parts of the world. Different beliefs suggest cultural relativism but one of that creed's obvious and main weaknesses is that it is often trumpeted by ruling cliques and elites in states where the majority of the population is patently down-trodden and enjoys few rights. Cultural relativism is therefore sometimes portrayed by its opponents as self-serving. Another way of viewing this is to argue that universal rights are objective whilst culturally relative rights are subjective. The two opposing views are summarised in the following table:

Universal rights	The idea that so-called 'primitive' or 'undeveloped' cultures will eventually become 'advanced' and adopt the same laws and human rights as western societies. Universality stems from the belief that some rights are intrinsic by virtue of one's humanity and should have no bearing or dependence on cultural criteria, for example the right not to be enslaved or tortured cannot depend on relativity (where you are and in which society you are located), but are absolute and available to all.
Cultural relativism	The assertion that rights are not universal but differ from one society to another according to their individual cultures, allowing human rights to be interpreted differently throughout the world. If the right not to be enslaved or tortured is universal and absolute, what about the right to education? There is little likelihood of universal agreement that every child has a human right to be educated to an agreed age.

■ Figure 1.4 *Universality v cultural relativity*

1.5.2 Implications of universalism

Largely because of the Allies' victory in the Second World War, the current version of rights which predominates globally is universalism. A number of claims are made as to what this means and how it should operate whether in worldwide UDHR terms, regional contexts such as the ECHR or the American Convention on Human Rights 1969, or domestic legislation such the HRA.

It is claimed that rights are inalienable, interconnected, interdependent, interrelated, indivisible and obligatory rather than aspiratory, which can be represented diagrammatically as in Figure 1.5.

Inalienable means that an individual is not able to give away or sell his rights, nor those of others. Thus, a parent has no right to exploit his child, let alone sell the child into servitude or slavery, or to misuse other members of his family.

Interconnectivity of rights brings together individual rights such as that of personal security with the collective need of everyone to live in a healthy and safe environment. Security is not limited to personal safety but to the general welfare of mankind, present and future.

Interdependence and **interrelatedness** exist because of the very nature of rights, the idea being that they all contribute to enhancement and realisation of human dignity and development, whether a person's needs are physical, psychological, cultural or spiritual. An educated person is generally more likely to be healthy and for education he needs information, the ability, skills and means of achieving knowledge, and an environment that allows him to flourish; all are essential and intertwined. Once the person achieves healthy and educated maturity, he needs to be able to work to support himself and his family, with all the other rights that allow him to survive and prosper.

Indivisibility of rights comes from the idea that whether the right in question is civil or political, economic, social or cultural, or for that matter a less clearly defined right to (say) development or a clean environment, they all relate to the inherent dignity of man and cannot be placed in any order of hierarchy or priority. In this view, it does not mean anything and indeed it would be wrong to argue that individual political rights are more or less important than collective social, economic or cultural rights: all should be treated with equal respect and given equal priority. This causes problems, however, because it tends to assume without specifically saying so that everyone starts from the same place, which is obviously not the case.

Using the word **'obligation'** introduces a different element, one which is often overlooked or not understood by people claiming 'rights', and there are two points to make here. The first is that rights do not and cannot exist in isolation from everything else, universal or not, so the existence of a right implies the likelihood of some corresponding obligation. The second point is that very few rights granted in legal regimes are unconditional, as will be seen when we examine the ECHR.

Non-discriminatory: apart from the absolute nature of the requirement that there should be no discrimination, and that torture and slavery can never be tolerated, other rights and freedoms are qualified to lesser or greater degrees; yet even the definition of torture is linked to inhuman

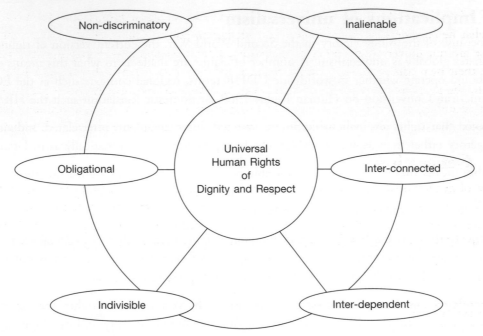

■ Figure 1.5 Connectivity of universal rights

treatment, and slavery to certain types of compulsory labour, both of which provide 'wriggle room' for those who wish to question the limits. Such an approach is not only damaging but dangerous; picking and choosing which aspects of human rights or international law to observe leaves the field free for every rogue regime to do the same.

1.5.3 Basic human goods

Another way of considering rights is to examine what is required to sustain life in a way that enables freedoms to be enjoyed. In Chapter IV of *Natural Law and Natural Rights* the Australian legal philosopher John Finnis identifies what he describes as the basic forms of human goods which comprise:

- life and its capacity for development
- acquisition of knowledge, as an end in itself
- capacity for recreation
- aesthetic expression
- sociability and friendship
- practical reasonableness
- capacity for intelligent and reasonable thought processes
- religion, or the capacity for spiritual experience.

Cultural relativists would attack this view of rights on the basis that Finnis provides a subjective list of what he considers to be the basic forms of human goods. This is alright as far as it goes but these are not universal and other people with different backgrounds and purposes could produce their own lists with, they would claim, equal authority. Even if this is not a valid objection, the forms of what are in practice acceptable as basic forms of human goods will be different according to which part of the world one examines. These objections are removed if one accepts that this is what ought to be the case, even if it is not and is not likely to be.

1.5.4 Generational rights

The idea of generational rights provides a less well-known and very different overview of post Second World War human rights. Karel Vasak's 1979 theory metaphorically likens human rights to the French revolutionary slogan, *liberté, égalité et fraternité*, translated as first, second and third generations of human rights development. They are set out in the following table:

Liberté: first generation
Characteristic *freedoms* • civil and political in nature • designed to protect citizens from excesses perpetrated by the state • basically negative in nature, for example Arts 3–21 UDHR and ICCPR • often expressed as freedoms, for example of speech, religion, assembly.
Égalité: second generation
Characteristic *equality* • based on social, economic and cultural factors • mostly positive requiring the state to make provision • include employment and family rights, for example Arts 22–27 UDHR and ICESC • needs institution of programmes to implement them, for example educational, health.
Fraternité: third generation
Characteristic *solidarity* • group and collective rights, for example peace, a healthy environment, ownership of universal commons such as the seabed • issues of self-determination • not represented in earlier and traditional rights agendas and programmes.

■ Figure 1.6 Generational rights table

1 **First-generation rights** may be described as clear and sharply defined although not unrestricted: freedom of speech constrained by the right to protection from defamation, or freedom of assembly whilst not unduly impinging on other people's comfort and privacy.

2 **Second-generation rights** become less concrete and more generalised, such as the collective right of a given society to be provided with medical care and educational facilities for which the people as a whole provide the necessary resources, the more able and capable subsidising the less well-off. This type of right would exist in a successful welfare or socialist state.

3 **Third-generation rights** are more global and less easily achieved and some people would deny that they should be characterised as 'rights' at all. The trend is expansionary from individual to society to the wider world. With civil and political individual rights states normally provide hard law to enforce them. For social and economic rights, states sometimes provide policies that may or may not be enforceable by or on behalf of individuals.

In the fraternity phase, issues affecting large groups or the whole of mankind emerge, and if law is involved at all it will usually be soft in character. The essential characteristics of third-generation rights are the embracing of joint and collective obligations by all states. Those requirements are wider than are expected from individual states and extend to international actors such as INGOs and transnational corporations.

Concretisation

There is a 'concretisation' process taking place in the development of rights moving from theoretical idealism, whose origins can be identified in the American and French revolutions and earlier, to the practical implementation of rights regimes after the Second World War. The UDHR was an attempt to identify a combination of types of right but is only a Declaration and as such not hard international treaty law, although it has (perhaps) acquired the status of international custom, as evidence of general practice accepted as law. Therefore, concretisation is only slow and partial.

An example of practical application of third-generation rights is the 1986 UN Declaration on the Right to Development together with various documents, charters and treaties providing support for the emergence of fraternal rights to peace and a healthy environment. It should be understood that the use of the generational metaphor is not meant to imply that the first and second generations die and are replaced by the 'grandchildren' but more a loose family growth and development.

There is other debate about whether *fraternite* or solidarity implies either a quantitative or qualitative shift in the nature of human rights, birth of a generation of entirely new rights, or extensions of the old. In other words, are the joint responsibilities of developmental rights of a different nature and dimension to previously recognised traditional and individual rights? The question does not lend itself to easy conclusions.

Objections

Opposition to Vasek's theory has been based on differing suppositions:

1 Human rights have to be individual so that they can be enforceable as such by law.

2 Solidarity rights are collective so they either cannot be so enforceable or at best would be more difficult to enforce because of the practical problems of demonstrating that the right applies to the claimant (whether this is correct is questionable, as legal systems can and do countenance class actions or claims by groups of individuals).

3   Attempting to add these to the currently accepted International Bill of Human Rights would dilute the efficacy of those fundamental rights and freedoms and damage the progress made so far.

Despite doubts and opposition, Vasek's theory provides an elegant metaphorical, theoretical approach and aid to understanding the origins, development, implementation and possible future trends of international human rights, and is not intended to be a literal application of the French revolutionary slogan. The metaphor provides a simple way to grasp the existing and potential scope of post Second World War human rights, whilst acknowledging that not everyone would agree with extending rights in this way.

A different way of trying to get to grips with the nature rather than the content of human rights is provided by Marie-Benedict Dembour's book *Who Believes in Human Rights?* Details are given at the end of this chapter. The main proposition is briefly described here as the Dembour analysis.

1.5.5 The Dembour analysis

Marie-Benedict Dembour does not believe that human rights exist outside of social recognition, by which she means that they only exist to the extent that they are talked about. This sceptical attitude is understandable on the basis that to assert that rights *are* universal is one thing, but it is more realistic to argue that rights *ought to be* universal although in the real world they are not. This *is/ought* discussion is also well known outside rights discourse. From an empirical sceptical viewpoint and using as her subject matter European Convention cases, she identifies four main concepts of human rights which, in summary, she classifies as given, agreed, fought for or talked about.

1 Given rights

This represents the approach of natural law scholars who believe that human rights comprise 'minimal entitlements originating from an immanent source'. The philosopher Emmanuel Kant can be associated with this group and the origins of their beliefs lie from early times in Nature, later gods or God, and more recently in Reason and Humanity. Although that is taken to be where rights originate they can be provided by positive law, ie man-made law imposed by rulers on societies and if they are to be effective, enforced by sanctions. Therefore, since the Second World War, rights developments have been 'progress'.

2 Agreed rights

'Deliberative scholars' take this view of rights. The idea is that there must be agreement as to how the rules of the political game are to be formulated and implemented, ie how they operate as procedural principles reflecting a consensus within a given society, as in the writings of Habermas.

3 Fought for rights

Scholars taking this approach are fewer in number and may be characterised as 'protesters'. The need for rights persuades them that people must fight for what they believe in so as to establish rights. They cannot simply hope that right reason will prevail and a world of dignity and respect by and towards human beings will emerge. They take a Levinasian view (after the Lithuanian Jewish–French philosopher Emanuelis Levinas) which means responding to unacceptable conditions when they occur.

4 Talked about

This refers to a small number of 'discourse scholars' and is Dembour's own stance. The belief here is that human rights 'have no essential immanence but exist only because they are talked about'. They are neither good nor bad but have to be judged by what they are stated to be at particular times and in particular places, assessed against whatever outcomes are achieved. The influence here is post-modernism.

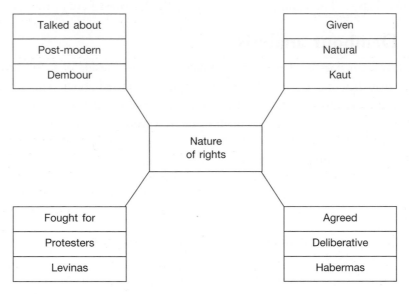

Figure 1.7 Dembour categories

These sections of Chapter 1 can only provide a précis of some approaches to rights theory, and there are other methods of classification. However, the theories discussed will repay some thought and help in achieving individual insight and reaching conclusions as to what is meant by 'human rights'.

ACTIVITY

Self-assessment questions

1 Why does the EU have its own Charter of Fundamental Rights rather than simply adopting the ECHR?

2 Explain the differences between universalism and cultural relativism in the context of human rights.

3 What is meant by 'connectivity' of human rights?

4 Identify what Finnis means when he writes about basic forms of human goods: are they definitive?

5 Explain Vasek's three generations of human rights with examples of each.

6 What are the categories of Dembour's analysis and what theoretical approach to human rights underlies each?

1.6 UK rights today

Renewed interest in human rights was established in the UK when the opposition Labour Party undertook during the 1997 election campaign to 'bring rights home', by which they meant allowing UK subjects to claim rights under the ECHR through UK domestic law. Previously, although the UK was a signatory to the European Convention from the start, the benefits had not generally been accessible to individuals, perhaps because successive governments believed that long-established protections such as jury trial, *habeas corpus* and judicial review were adequate. Nevertheless, after a campaign lasting several decades, those who believed that such protection needed strengthening prevailed, and after the 1997 election the Human Rights Bill 1998 was brought forward and enacted; it is dealt with in detail in Chapter 3.

This chapter has shown that human rights find their origins in history, their development through various theories, processes and events, and their concrete existence now at local, national, continental regional and global levels. They have grown from notions of individual freedoms such as thought, speech, assembly and religion through claims to collective social and economic rights of health, education, employment and so on to, some would say, universal rights (or claims) to a safe and healthy environment, free from war, poverty and cruelty.

This book goes on to deal with the body of hard law comprising conventional rights and freedoms arising from the European Convention and Human Rights Act, and also a number of other important aspects of human rights that are essential to understanding rights in the modern world.

1.7 Acronyms and glossary

Rights books tend to make frequent reference to acronyms and some of the more common ones are set out in the following alphabetical table.

CEDAW	Convention on the Elimination of all forms of Discrimination against Women
ECHR	European Convention of Human Rights
ECOSOC	(UN) Economic and Social Council
EIDHR	(EU) European Initiative for Human Rights and Democracy
ICC	International Criminal Court
ICCPR	International Covenant on Civil and Political Rights
ICESCR	International Covenant on Economic, Social and Cultural Rights
ICJ	International Court of Justice
ICRC	International Committee of the Red Cross
ILO	International Labour Organisation
INGO	International Non-Governmental Organisation
NGO	Non-Governmental Organisation
UDHR	Universal Declaration of Human Rights
UN	United Nations
UNHCHR	United Nations High Commissioner for Human Rights
UNHCR	United Nations High Commissioner for Refugees

■ Figure 1.8 Table of acronyms

References are also made to various words, phrases, or descriptions the meaning of which may not be obvious at first sight, so a glossary of some of these is set out below.

Civil and political rights	First-generation citizens' individual rights to liberty, civil rights and freedoms
Collective rights	The claim of native aboriginal groups to have their rights as a whole preserved, as opposed to individual rights such as to be given a fair hearing.
Convention	A legally binding agreement between states, entered into voluntarily and enforceable only to the extent acknowledged by signatories, and used more or less interchangeably with the words 'covenant' and 'treaty' (Note that it has an entirely different meaning to a 'constitutional convention', which is an unwritten rule followed within UK government in the absence of a clear written constitution).
Covenant	See Convention
Customary international law	This is one of the sources of international law.
Declaration	A set of non-legally binding standards to be observed by states. It can also mean an interpretive statement by a state entering into a treaty obligation setting out its understanding of what a particular provision means.
Denunciation	Some but not all treaties allow a state to denounce individual petition rights.
Derogation	Withdrawal by a state from particular rights obligations in times of armed conflict or public emergency, threatening the life of the nation
Economic, social and cultural rights	Second-generation rights giving people rights to the material necessities of life rather than to individual freedoms
Environmental and development rights	Third-generation rights of mankind to enjoy a safe and healthy environment, and for peoples generally to live in harmony
Hard law	Commitments between states that are regarded as valid under international law and so are binding on those who enter into them
INGO (see NGO)	International NGO
International Bill of Rights	The combined totality of the UDHR, ICESCR, ICCPR and its optional protocol
Margin of appreciation	The amount of discretion given to individual states to take account of their own social and cultural conditions when applying international human rights, especially with reference to the ECHR
NGO (see INGO)	An institution created outside of any intergovernmental agreement, bringing together private or public legal bodies or natural or legal persons of different nationalities, on a volunteer basis, and not operating for profit
Non-derogable rights	Rights from which states are not allowed to derogate, usually taken to include the right to life, prohibition of torture and slavery, freedom of thought, conscience and religion, and prohibition of retroactive penal legislation
Protocol	An addendum to a treaty which modifies it, often used to incorporate optional provisions not acceptable to all states parties
Ratification	Confirmation by a state's legislative machinery of intended adherence to a convention or treaty
Reservations	Legally binding statements of limitation made by states entering into treaty obligations so that specified provisions of the treaty do not have to apply to that state
Soft law	These are commitments made between states that they do not regard as binding and which are unenforceable under international law, and so they can be ignored with impunity.
State	A territorial area occupied by a society that possesses the same government and under the same laws: states are mostly synonymous with countries although not exactly the same
Treaty	See Convention

■ Figure 1.9 Glossary of words and phrases

1.8 Summary

This first chapter has introduced a wide range of subject matter about the origins and nature of human rights, the language used and the techniques necessary for successful study. There are various activities which will repay some attention before moving on to the close study of the European Convention and Human Rights Act.

In particular, the advice given about how to tackle different types of assessment is important because too many students disregard the actual requirements and convert the question to 'Write everything you know about X'. It should be needless to say, but this does not ensure success.

KEY FACTS

Fact	Explanation
Universalism	Post Second World War human rights almost entirely pre-suppose that human rights are universal, without too closely defining what that means, and denying that they are culturally relative.
Rights and law	The ECHR and HRA are hard law, enforceable through the courts, but there are many other claims to rights which are soft law and not easily or directly enforceable through any legal system.
Democratic institutions	Respect for human rights mostly presupposes the existence of democratic systems which respect the rule of law, rules of natural justice, and rights of people to elect and remove their rulers.
Variety of rights	Claims vary but include rights, freedoms and prohibitions, and in nearly all instances are qualified in some way and need to be balanced against other people's needs.
Council of Europe	The Council of Europe is the most successful existing human rights organisation in terms of establishing enforceable rights machinery, responsible for the ECHR and European Court of Human Rights.
United Nations	The UN is widely regarded as not having been really successful in promulgating human rights in a world which regards *realpolitik* as more important but nevertheless the UN plays an important role.

CONTINUED ▸

KEY FACTS

ECHR	The European Convention is the main focus of the rest of this book and requires detailed study of the Court and its case law.
Human Rights Act 1998	Knowledge of the Act and domestic case law is essential for modern implementation of human rights in the UK.

Useful resources

Department of Constitutional Affairs: http://www.dca.gov.uk/peoples-rights/human-rights/faqs.htm.

Morales, Dr M C P, 'UNESCO's Philosophy of "intellectual and moral solidarity" in attaining peace': http://www.onlineunesco.org/UNESCO's%20Philosophy.html.

Think Quest Project: http://library.thinkquest.org/C0126065/index.html.

The National Archive: http://www.nationalarchives.gov.uk/humanrights/.

Council of Europe: http://www.coe.int/.

Stanford Encyclopaedia of Philosophy: http://plato.stanford.edu/entries/rights/#2.2.

Further reading

Dembour, M-B, *Who Believes in Human Rights? Reflections on the European Convention* (Cambridge University Press, Law in Context Series, 2006).

Finnis, J, *Natural Law and Natural Rights* (Oxford University Press, Clarendon Law Series, 1980).

Halstead, P, *Human Rights Key Facts* (2nd edn, Hodder Arnold, London, 2008).

Smith, R K M, *Textbook on International Human Rights* (3rd edn, Oxford University Press, 2007).

Toggenburg, G N, 'The Role of the New EU Fundamental Rights Agency: Debating the "Sex of Angels" or Improving Europe's Human Rights Performance?' EL Rev 2008, 33(3), 385–398.

Wellman, C, 'Solidarity, the Individual and Human Rights', *Human Rights Quarterly*, August 2000, 22(3), 639–657.

chapter
2 EUROPEAN CONVENTION
ON HUMAN RIGHTS ■

AIMS AND OBJECTIVES

At the end of this chapter, you should be able to:

■ understand the institutions and objectives of the Council of Europe

■ distinguish it from the Common Market or EU

■ consider the main operating principles of the Convention.

2.1 Introduction

This chapter needs to be read in conjunction with Chapter 3 on the Human Rights Act 1998, because some of the ideas introduced in Chapter 2 require further explanation and elaboration in the context of the Act. The Convention is set out in a Schedule to the Act but, as will be seen, it is not actually incorporated lock, stock and barrel into English law.

This chapter introduces the basic ideas and principles, and will amplify and explain how they work in English law in more detail; subsequent chapters of the book then analyse the particular rights, freedoms and prohibitions established by the Convention and given flesh in European and domestic case law.

2.1.1 Early twentieth century

At the beginning of the twentieth century two strong power blocs faced each other in Europe in an atmosphere of growing hostility and mistrust. Industrialisation in the nineteenth century had encouraged the growth of mass production techniques, and during the First World War, 1914–18, these mass production processes were applied to the war effort, with devastating consequences to military and civilian populations and with destruction of property.

There had been attempts in the nineteenth century to achieve understanding and co-operation between the great European powers, with the 'Concert of Europe' or 'Congress System' in the first part of the century after the Napoleonic Wars and towards the end of that century through the 'Inter-Parliamentary Union', which was formed with the eventually unsuccessful objective of preventing war.

After the First World War the League of Nations was formed in 1919 as part of the arrangements under the Treaty of Versailles. The Covenant of the League of Nations established the League of Nations itself whose objective was to avoid future wars by providing an organisation and machinery to forestall and prevent misunderstandings. For a number of reasons the League of Nations failed in its primary purpose, two of the main ones being that it did not ensure the rehabilitation of Germany and it lacked adequate support and involvement on the part of the USA.

2.1.2 The UN

After the Second World War, the United Nations Organisation (UNO) was established with renewed determination that a global body with sufficient support and authority should do what the League of Nations had failed to do. At the time it was known as UNO (nowadays as the UN) and in 1948 it set about establishing a code of human rights which was to be known as the Universal Declaration of Human Rights (GA resolution 217 A (III) of 10th December 1948). Although it is a 'declaration' and falls short of being an international treaty enforceable under international law, it has acquired a respected status over the years. The furtherance of human rights is only one of the UN's roles but nevertheless an important one which provided inspiration and a precedent for European states to emulate when they came to consider the ECHR.

2.1.3 The Council of Europe

Both World Wars had started in Europe, so it was important that the European powers should take some responsibility to reinforce the global UN process by taking steps to avoid making the same mistakes again. Taking note of the League of Nations' defects it was decided that more emphasis should be placed on encouraging democracy and the rule of law, and establishing effective machinery to protect human rights.

The primary objective of the Statute of the Council of Europe is clearly stated in its first Article:

'1(a) The aim of the Council of Europe is to achieve a greater unity between its members for the purpose of safeguarding and realising the ideals and principles which are their common heritage and facilitating their economic and social progress.'

Other objectives of the Council included developing respect for and observance of democracy and human rights, and harmonising policies designed to further common educational, cultural, social welfare, health, local government and justice policies.

The original Treaty of London was signed on 5th May 1949 by 10 founding states: Belgium, Denmark, France, Ireland, Italy, Luxembourg, the Netherlands, Norway, Sweden and the United Kingdom. The Council's headquarters are at the Palais de l'Europe in Strasbourg, France, and it now has 47 Member States including Iceland, Georgia and Ukraine, although they are not actually geographically located in Europe.

2.2 The European rights regime

One of the first tasks of the Council's Assembly was to prepare a report recommending the drafting and adoption of a human rights treaty. This was done and the Convention opened for signature on 4th November 1950 in Rome. Commonly called the European Convention on Human Rights (ECHR), its full title is the Convention for the Protection of Human Rights and Fundamental Freedoms, and usually in this book it will be referred to as the 'ECHR' or 'the Convention'. The UK Westminster Parliament ratified the Convention in 1951 and it came into force generally in Europe on 3rd September 1953.

The European Commission of Human Rights was established in 1954 to consider complaints by individuals, groups of individuals or NGOs who or which claimed to have suffered because of breach of the Convention, and it started to deal with complaints in the following year. The part-time European Court of Human Rights was established in 1959 to deal with cases deemed to be admissible, because by then the necessary quorum of nine states had accepted the authority of a European Court to interpret the Convention. Prior to 1966, UK subjects were not allowed to take individual cases either to the Commission or the Court and even after 1966 the 'right to individual petition' could only be exercised with the government's permission. This limited right of redress to UK citizens lasted until 2000 when the Human Rights Act came into force.

The system started very slowly: it was 1961 before the first case was dealt with by the Court, and even by 1977 only 17 cases had been heard. However, from the 1980s onwards the position changed, increasingly rapidly, and once a certain momentum was reached it did not take long for the system to become overloaded as the number of Member States increased. Consequently, changes were needed both to structures and procedures.

Before 1998 a complaint had to be lodged with the Commission for it to make a decision on admissibility. The facts would be established and an attempt made to secure a 'friendly settlement', ie one agreed between the complainant and the alleged offending state. Failing that, the Commission would prepare a report summarising the facts and providing an opinion as to whether the case should go forward either to the Council of Ministers or to the Court. If referred to the Council of Ministers, they had three months to deal with it or to pass it on to the Court anyway.

It was also in 1998, after almost half a century of the Convention's existence, that UK subjects became entitled under domestic law *via* the Human Rights Act 1998 to have recourse to the European Court if dissatisfied after all domestic UK remedies had been exhausted. As an international treaty, ie an agreement between states, under the UK's unwritten constitution the Convention did not provide individuals with rights; it was only the enactment of a statute specifically awarding such rights that enabled individuals to take action.

This is because treaties made under international law (which is what the ECHR is) only bind the UK as a state, and do not automatically become part of domestic law. A Statute of the Westminster Parliament was required to do this and it had clearly to establish the extent of rights of action granted to individuals.

Year	Event
1950	ECHR opened for signature
1951	Westminster Parliament ratified the Convention
1953	Convention came into force
1954	European Commission of Human Rights was established
1959	Part-time European Court of Human Rights was established
1966	UK subjects granted right to individual petition with government's permission
1977	By this year only 17 cases had been heard by the Court
1998	Human Rights Act passed by Westminster Parliament
1998	Full-time European Court of Human Rights was established
1999	European Commission of Human Rights ceased to operate
2000	Human Rights Act came into force in the UK

■ Figure 2.1 Timeline

Because of the huge increase in business the full-time European Court was also established in 1998 and after an interim period of one year the Commission ceased to operate. This was brought about by Protocol 11 which entered into force on 1st November 1998 and which became an integral part of the Convention replacing substantial parts of the original Convention. Protocols 2, 3, 5, 8, 9 and 10 were superseded by Protocol 11, which established a fundamental change in the Convention's machinery. With the abolition of the Commission, individuals could apply directly to the Court and the Committee of Ministers lost its judicial functions. Protocol 11 has not been entirely successful so Protocol 14 has been adopted, although it has not yet entered into force.

2.3 European Union

The EU also sets itself high human rights standards but it is important not to confuse it with the Council of Europe. The origins of the EU also lie in the objective of ending wars in Europe but in this case by forming initially in 1950 the European Coal and Steel Community with six founder members – France, Germany, Italy and the Benelux countries (Belgium, the Netherlands and Luxembourg). The Treaty of Rome in 1957 created the European Economic Community (EEC) or 'Common Market' and the way it was intended to prevent further European wars was primarily by combining the former warring states' industrial and economic interests.

In 1973, Denmark, Ireland and the UK joined, followed by Greece in 1981 and Spain and Portugal in 1985. The Single European Act 1987 (an EU treaty, not a UK statute) provided the basis for creating the 'single market'. When communism collapsed between 1989 and 1991

(opening the door to Eastern European states being able to join later on), and the single market was completed, it provided four freedoms of movement, goods, services and people. This was followed by the Treaty on European Union in 1993 and the Treaty of Amsterdam 1998, with Austria, Finland and Sweden joining in 1995.

The Schengen agreement, named after a small village in Luxembourg, allowed inter-state travel without passports for those countries that adopted it (which the UK declined to do). In 2001 the new European currency – the euro – was introduced by some EU Member States and, as many of the political divisions in Europe healed following the end of the Cold War, 10 more states joined in 2004, making a total of 27 members.

The EU's court is the European Court of Justice, usually referred to as the ECJ, which sits at Luxembourg and is not to be confused with the European Court of Human Rights, which sits at Strasbourg. References in this book to the 'European Court' will mean the latter unless otherwise indicated.

This is a brief synopsis but it is important not to confuse the two organisations and to understand that although all Member States of the EU must accede to the ECHR and the human rights standards established by the Council of Europe, the primary purpose of the EU is economic whilst the fundamental objective of the Council of Europe is democracy and human rights standard setting. The Council of Europe is not a political and economic organisation, unlike the EU.

2.4 Council of Europe institutions and personnel

The four main institutions of the Council of Europe were the:

- European Commission on Human Rights established in 1954
- European Court of Human Rights established part-time in 1959 and reconstituted full-time in 1998
- Committee of Ministers of the Council of Europe whose membership comprises the foreign ministers of the 47 Member States
- Parliamentary Assembly of the Council of Europe.

2.4.1 The Commission

The European Convention as originally adopted made provision for complaints to be brought by Contracting States against other Contracting States. It was also possible for individual applicants (which meant not only individuals but groups of individuals and NGOs) to bring complaints, but recognition of them was optional. It was only by virtue of Protocol 11 to the Convention that it became compulsory for States to be subject to individual complaints.

The role of the Commission was to subject complaints to scrutiny in order to determine their admissibility. If it was decided that a complaint was admissible, the Commission then carried on its business with the purpose of brokering a friendly settlement. If it was unsuccessful in reaching a settlement, it produced a report setting out its factual findings and indicating its conclusions on the merits of the case. This was then forwarded to the Council of Ministers.

The system came under increasing strain as membership of the Council of Europe expanded. In 1981 the number of applications registered with the Commission was 401 but by 1997 that had increased to 4,750. The Commission's role ceased altogether from 31st October 1999 when the reconstituted full-time Court replaced it for all ongoing complaints.

2.4.2 The Court

A total of 13 protocols have been adopted since the ECHR came into force, some adding further rights and liberties to those guaranteed by the Convention and others reforming and updating the procedures. The following protocols were of particular relevance in this procedural context:

Protocol No 2	gave the Court power to provide advisory opinions
Protocol No 9	allowed individuals to bring cases before the Court subject to ratification by the respondent State and acceptance by a screening panel
Protocol No 11 from 1st November 1998	provided for restructuring of the enforcement machinery by replacing the Commission and existing part-time Court with a single full-time Court.

Figure 2.2 Procedural protocols

Much of the rationale for these reforms was the huge increase in Convention complaints business arising from the accession of new Member States, particularly from 1990 onwards as the Cold War ended. The Court's business grew rapidly along with that of the Commission, from seven in 1981 to 119 in 1997. From then onwards the growth rate accelerated with a 130 per cent increase in applications following the entry into force of Protocol 11 from 5,979 applications in 1998 to 13,858 in 2001. By 2007 the total number of applications to the Court had reached 54,000 according to the *Survey of Activities 2007* available *via* HUDOC.

2.4.3 The Committee of Ministers

The Committee of Ministers is the Council of Europe's decision-making body, comprising all the Member States' Foreign Affairs ministers or their permanent diplomatic representatives in Strasbourg. It operates as a governmental body where national approaches to problems facing European society can be discussed on an equal basis. It also works as a collective forum to formulate Europe-wide responses to challenges. It collaborates with the Parliamentary Assembly and together they comprise the guardian of the fundamental values of the Council of Europe, monitoring Member States' compliance with their undertakings.

From May 1951 onwards, deputies were appointed to work at Strasbourg to allow Member States to stay in constant touch with the organisation. They are in effect civil servants and

operate as the permanent representatives. The Committee meets annually at ministerial level in May or November and usually takes the form of political dialogue or discussion on matters of mutual interest other than defence.

The role of the ministers is threefold:

1. as the emanation of the governments which enables them to express on equal terms their national approaches to the problems confronting Europe's societies

2. as the collective forum where European responses to these challenges are worked out

3. as the guardian, alongside the Parliamentary Assembly, of the values for which the Council of Europe exists.

2.4.4 The Parliamentary Assembly

The Parliamentary Assembly of the Council of Europe is sometimes referred to as 'PACE' (not to be confused with the UK's Police and Criminal Evidence Act 1984). The parliamentarians who represent the Member States describe themselves as 'Greater Europe's democratic conscience' and the Assembly 'sees itself as the driving force in extending European co-operation to all democratic states throughout Europe', according to its website. The members can choose the subject matter they wish to discuss and request that European governments take various initiatives and report back to the Assembly.

They were primarily responsible for the ECHR and must be consulted about all international treaties drawn up by the Council. The larger powers, ie the UK, Germany, France, Italy and the Russian Federation, each have 18 representatives. The official languages used are English and French, but PACE also uses German, Italian and Russian as working languages.

The Assembly has 315 members comprising five political groupings, although members are able to choose not to belong to any of these groups:

- Socialists Group (SOC)
- Group of the European People's Party (EPP/CD)
- Liberal, Democratic and Reformers' Group (LDR)
- European Democratic Group (EDG)
- Group of the Unified European Left (UEL).

It meets quarterly for a week in public plenary session and also holds a spring meeting in one of the Member States. The President is elected from amongst the members, and there are 19 Vice-Presidents together with Chairs of the five political groupings and Chairs of the 10 parliamentary committees. It has further important roles in that it also elects the Secretary-General and Deputy Secretary-General of the Council of Europe, the judges of the European Court and the Council of Europe's Commissioner for Human Rights.

2.4.5 The Commissioner for Human Rights

The Commission for Human Rights operates as an independent institution within the Council of Europe, mandated to promote awareness of and respect for human rights in the Member States. The role of Commissioner was established in 1999, the first Commissioner being Alvaro Gil-Robles (1999–2006) and the current one being Thomas Hammarberg.

The Commissioner is mandated to:

- foster the effective observance of human rights, and assist Member States in the implementation of Council of Europe human rights standards
- promote education in and awareness of human rights in Council of Europe Member States
- identify possible shortcomings in the law and practice concerning human rights
- facilitate the activities of national ombudsmen institutions and other human rights structures
- provide advice and information regarding the protection of human rights across the region.

The office of Commissioner is non-judicial, so he is not able to entertain complaints but he does play an important role by co-operating with a wide range of national and international institutions, the UN, EU and OSCE, as well as liaising with leading human rights NGOs, think tanks and universities.

2.4.6 The Judiciary

The present structure of the Court as a permanent body with full-time judges was established on 1st November 1998 by Protocol 11, replacing the original part-time Court established in 1950 and the European Commission of Human Rights set up in 1954. It made the process entirely judicial as the Court took on the Commission's screening role and the former adjudicatory function of the Council of Ministers was abolished.

Protocol 11 amended the Convention S II Arts 19–51 and the new judges were elected by the Parliamentary Assembly for renewable six-year terms. The Court has the same number of judges as there are signatory parties to the ECHR but there is no requirement that they should strictly correspond to or represent the 47 nationalities, as they are expected to apply the Convention impartially and not in accordance with their respective national legal systems; Liechtenstein, for example, elected a Swiss judge. The retirement age is 70 but judges can finish dealing with their existing cases on reaching that age.

The ECHR gives the Plenary Court a number of functions, including electing the President, two Vice-Presidents and three more Section Presidents, as the Court has five Sections. The UK judge, Sir Nicolas Bratza, is one of the Vice-Presidents. The composition of the five Sections is geographically and gender-balanced, also taking into consideration the different legal systems of the Contracting States, and is varied every three years.

Most cases are dealt with by Chambers comprising seven judges and Committees of three judges whose function is to dispose of applications that are clearly inadmissible. The Court's Grand Chamber comprises 17 judges including, as *ex-officio* members, the President, Vice-Presidents and Section Presidents. The Grand Chamber deals with cases that raise a serious question of interpretation or application of the Convention or a serious issue of general importance, and a Chamber can relinquish responsibility for a case at any time if it becomes clear that it would be more appropriate for the Grand Chamber to take over.

ACTIVITY

	Self-assessment questions	True	False
1	The Council of Europe has 27 Member States.		
2	The full-time European Court of Human Rights was established in 1998.		
3	The Universal Declaration of Human Rights is a treaty.		
4	The European Union has 47 Member States.		
5	The European Commission on Human Rights was abolished in 1999.		
6	The right to individual petition has been available to UK individuals since 1966.		
7	The Schengen agreement is an EU instrument that allows freedom of movement without a passport between Signatory States.		
8	The role of the Council of Europe's Commission for Human Rights is principally judicial.		
9	A Grand Chamber of the European Court of Human Rights comprises 17 judges.		
10	The Committee of Ministers regard themselves as being co-guardians with the Parliamentary Assembly of the Council of Europe's values.		
11	The European Court of Human Rights sits at Strasbourg and the ECJ of the EU sits at Luxembourg.		
12	Before 1998 a complaint had to be lodged with the Commission for it to make a decision on admissibility.		

ACTIVITY

Self-test question

Compare and contrast the respective roles of the Commissioner for Human Rights and the Judges of the European Court of Human Rights.

KEY LINKS

League of Nations	http://www.indiana.edu/~league/ http://www.library.northwestern.edu/govinfo/collections/league/
United Nations	http://www.un.org/
Council of Europe	www.coe.int
Statute of the Council of Europe	http://conventions.coe.int/Treaty/EN/Treaties/Html/001.htm
ECHR	www.conventions.coe.int
European Court of Human Rights	http://www.echr.coe.int/echr/
HUDOC	http://www.echr.coe.int/ECHR/EN/hudoc

2.5 The Convention Principles

2.5.1 International treaty

The ECHR is an international treaty whose emphasis is on individual and political rights rather than collective economic, social and cultural rights, reflecting particularly English, French and North American philosophy and values. 'Convention' here means the same thing as 'treaty'. International law observed by accession to treaties is different from domestic law in that states choose whether or not to 'join up', and if they do so they can often restrict the extent of their compliance by making reservations or by derogating (explained in sections 2.5.4 and 2.5.5).

The post-war division of Europe by the 'iron curtain' described by Churchill, and the subsequent Cold War brought out these differing civil and economic/social emphases more clearly in the decades from 1945 to 1990. A further human rights dimension developed in those post-war years brought about by the virtual ending of European colonialism and the emergence of self-

governing third-world states. This is not to say that the values are entirely polarised because they are not, and in some ways attempting to classify them can be an artificial exercise. Nevertheless, there are some benefits in taking a bird's-eye view. There is further discussion of the nature of these various rights in Chapter 1 at section 1.5.4.

Art 1 of the ECHR imposes an obligation on the High Contracting Parties to secure to everyone within their jurisdiction the rights and freedoms in Section 1 of the Convention, which makes the internal distinction between rights and freedoms. Arts 2–14 enumerate 13 rights, freedoms and a third category of prohibitions.

Of those 13 provisions, 11 are self-standing and two are pervasive. Art 13 sets out the right to an effective remedy and Art 14 prohibits discrimination. These articles cannot in themselves form the subject matter of a complaint, but they apply to all the other articles without exception and there is no provision allowing derogation from them. A useful overview is therefore to place the substantive articles within the description of right, freedom, prohibition and pervasiveness:

Rights	Freedoms	Prohibitions	Pervasiveness
Art 2 right to life	Art 9 freedom of thought, conscience and religion	Art 3 prohibition of torture	Art 13 right to effective remedy
Art 5 right to liberty and security	Art 10 freedom of expression	Art 4 prohibition of slavery and forced labour	Art 14 prohibition against discrimination
Art 6 right to a fair trial	Art 11 freedom of assembly and association	Art 7 prohibition on punishment without law	
Art 8 right to respect for family and private life			
Art 12 right to marry			

Figure 2.3 Categories of ECHR protection

With regard to the right to an effective remedy under Art 13 somewhat different considerations apply and this is dealt with in Chapter 3 on the Human Rights Act. Rights and remedies are more fully considered in Chapter 15 and there is a more detailed analysis of the prohibition of discrimination in Chapter 16.

2.5.2 Prohibition on discrimination

The characteristic that makes Art 14 more than a self-standing substantive prohibition is that it always applies without exception to the other 11 subject-specific provisions. It is useful to keep this in mind when considering the individual Convention articles and reading the case law, as it helps in understanding the multiple issues that often apply to complaints.

The following case example indicates how the prohibition on discrimination provisions work.

CASE EXAMPLE

AL (Serbia) v Secretary of State for the Home Department; R (on the application of Rudi) v Secretary of State for the Home Department [2008] 1 WLR 1434

AL and R appealed to the House of Lords against Court of Appeal decisions that they could not benefit from the Home Secretary's Family Indefinite Leave to Remain exercise because they had come to the UK as unaccompanied children from Kosovo, having lost their parents. Indefinite leave to remain until reaching 18 years of age was granted but, thereafter, steps were taken to secure their removal.

The Family Indefinite Leave to Remain exercise assisted children who were seeking asylum if they were included in a family. However, unaccompanied children who fled to the UK were excluded and on reaching the age of 18 were liable to be returned to their country of origin.

The applicants considered that they were being discriminated against because they did not have a family. They argued that the decision to remove them was irrational on ordinary judicial review principles and contrary to the common law principle that like cases had to be treated alike.

Their appeal was dismissed by the House of Lords, who held that the Home Secretary's exercise fell within the scope of the Convention's Art 8 rights whilst their circumstances fell within the residuary category of 'other status' for the purpose of Art 14.

Article 14

Baroness Hale discussed the way in which Art 14 operates in her speech. She said it has no independent existence and there is no room for its application except in conjunction with one of the self-standing articles, in this case the Art 8 right to respect for family and private life. Nor does it forbid every difference in treatment such as occurred here.

She located the core explanation of this in a passage from *Stec v United Kingdom* (2006) 43 EHRR 1017 which said that treating people differently is discriminatory if there is no reasonable justification for it and it has no objective. The point is that it should pursue a legitimate aim and should be proportionate, allowing the contracting state to enjoy a margin of appreciation in assessing the distinctions.

Had the difference in treatment been founded on their race, colour, ethnic origin or sexual orientation, much stricter interpretation would have been applied. Whilst it might

CONTINUED ▸

appear that unaccompanied children should be entitled to more rather than less consideration than those who arrived with their families, when they reached adulthood as single persons the policy seemed to be based on the premise that then they had less reason to stay in the UK. This is perhaps revealed by the statement that had the policy discriminated between the children while they were children, it would have been particularly hard to justify.

Sections 2.8.1 and 2.8.2 later in this chapter explain proportionality and the margin of appreciation.

1	prohibits discrimination on grounds *such as* sex, race, colour, language, religion, political or other opinion, national or social origin, association with a national minority, property, birth or *other status*
2	the grounds specifically identified are not exclusive, 'such as' and 'other status' being subject to *sui generis* interpretation
3	it complements the Convention and protocol substantive provisions
4	it has no independent existence as it has effect solely in relation to 'the enjoyment of the rights and freedoms' safeguarded by the substantive provisions
5	this means it cannot apply unless one or more of the substantive provisions is engaged
6	it is not an open-ended guarantee of equal protection of the laws
7	it does not forbid every difference in treatment in the exercise of the rights and freedoms recognised
8	difference of treatment is discriminatory if it has no objective and reasonable justification
9	it must pursue a legitimate aim and apply proportionality between the objective and the means
10	it is less to do with comparability and more to do with justification
11	the difference in treatments must be on a prohibited ground

Figure 2.4 Summary of Art 14 characteristics

2.5.3 Protocols

Protocols as used in the ECHR are additional and later forms of agreement dealing with specific aspects of human rights. The reason that some of them were not included in the original Convention is that not all states were able or prepared to accept what was suggested at the time of signing and ratification. In other cases the protocols were agreed at a later date to take account of changes and procedural developments that had occurred.

For example, the Sixth Protocol (1983) dealing with the abolition of the death penalty contained provisions that were unacceptable to most of the States' Signatories in 1950, whilst the Eleventh

Protocol agreed in 1994 dealt with restructuring the control machinery established by the ECHR due to the enlargement of membership and increase in work, the extent of which had not been envisaged back in 1950.

It should be noted that not all the protocols still exist as originally agreed over the years, as some of them have been consolidated.

2.5.4 Reservations

High Contracting Parties can enter 'reservations' when they accede to treaties, which means that although they agree to be bound by the substantive provisions of the treaty, there are one or more aspects with which they are not willing to comply. This can only be done to the extent that the treaty itself allows: it would be unacceptable under the ECHR, for example, to countenance High Contracting Parties reserving the right to ignore the provisions of Art 3 so that they could use torture and inhuman and degrading treatment on opponents.

Reservations are not permissible in respect of Protocols 6 (1983 abolition of the death penalty) and 13 (2002, which again dealt with abolition of the death penalty but also made various other provisions covering derogations, reservations and territorial application).

The UK entered a reservation in respect of educational rights contained in Protocol 1 Art 2, the effect of which was that the government would only observe the principle so far as was compatible with provision of efficient instruction and training and avoidance of unreasonable public expenditure.

In *Campbell and Cosans v United Kingdom* (1982) 4 EHRR 293 the European Court found that this did not prevent the UK from being in violation of Protocol 1 Art 2 of the ECHR. The reason is that under ECHR Art 64 a 'reservation in respect of any provision is permitted only to the extent that any law in force in a State's territory at the time when the reservation is made is not in conformity with the provision'.

Protocol 1 Art 2 of the ECHR states as follows:

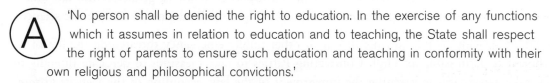

(A) 'No person shall be denied the right to education. In the exercise of any functions which it assumes in relation to education and to teaching, the State shall respect the right of parents to ensure such education and teaching in conformity with their own religious and philosophical convictions.'

The terms of the UK's reservation made on 20th March 1952 are as follows:

(C) 'At the time of signing the present (first) Protocol I declare that, in view of certain provisions of the Education Acts in the United Kingdom, the principle affirmed in the second sentence of Article 2 is accepted by the United Kingdom only so far as it is compatible with the provision of efficient instruction and training, and the avoidance of unreasonable public expenditure.'

The European Court of Human Rights has on a number of occasions addressed the effect of reservations by different states and considered the validity of those reservations including:

- *Belilos v Switzerland* (1988) 10 EHRR 466
- *Loizidou v Turkey* (1996) 20 ECHRR 1995
- *Eisenstecken v Austria* (2002) 34 EHRR 35.

2.5.5 Derogations

Derogations occur under Art 15 of the ECHR when a state withdraws from specific obligations because of war or other public emergency, but only so far as the exigencies of the situation warrant. It is not allowed in respect of the following:

- right to life
- prohibition of torture
- prohibition of slavery and servitude
- prohibition of punishment without law.

These exclusions need to be treated with caution as the following examples indicate:

- The right to life is clearly connected to abolition of the death penalty but there remain residual rights to impose the death penalty in wartime for those states which have not fully accepted all the protocol provisions.
- Torture is always proscribed but what is inhuman or degrading treatment, and how or when it merges into torture, are problematic areas as has been demonstrated in recent years by some western states' policies dealing with the 'war on terror'.
- Slavery is absolutely banned, but compulsory labour is allowed in some circumstances under Art 4.
- That there should be no punishment without law under Art 7 seems to be axiomatic, yet issues were raised with the introduction of the retrospective crime of genocide into law and removal of double jeopardy protective provisions in light of developments in forensic science.

What Art 15 provides is that in time of war or other public emergency threatening the life of the nation it is permissible for High Contracting Parties to take measures to derogate (literally to 'detract, take away part', ie lessening the impairment of the law, according to the *Concise Oxford Dictionary*). This is subject to the proviso that such measures are not inconsistent with the State's other obligations under international law. Article 15(2) prevents derogation from Art 2 except in respect of deaths resulting from lawful acts of war, or from Arts 3, 4(1) and 7.

When states do derogate there is a further obligation under Art 15(3) to keep the Secretary-General of the Council of Europe fully informed of:

- the measures taken

- why they were taken

- when they ceased to operate.

Derogating under anti-terrorism legislation

The UK has made a number of derogations from the ECHR in connection with anti-terrorism policies during the Northern Ireland troubles and more recently in response to Al-Qaeda and home-grown terrorist threats.

CASE EXAMPLES

Brogan and others v United Kingdom (1989) 11 EHRR 117

The four applicants had been arrested on suspicion of being involved in terrorist activities in Northern Ireland and were detained for periods varying between four days and 11 hours to six days and 16.5 hours. Although they were questioned about specific alleged terrorist offences none of them was charged or brought before any judicial officer or tribunal prior to release.

The European Court held that there had been violations of Arts 5(1), 5(2), 5(3), 5(5) and Art 13 in that none of the applicants had either been brought 'promptly' before a judicial authority, nor released 'promptly' following his arrest. The fact that the arrests and detention were motivated by the legitimate objective of protecting the public against terrorism did not in itself ensure compliance with the strict terms of Art 5(3) which provides that everyone arrested is, in addition to the promptness requirements, entitled to trial within a reasonable time or release pending trial, if appropriate conditioned by guarantees to appear for trial.

Judgment was given on 29th November 1988 and on 23rd December 1988 the Government derogated under Art 15.

Brannigan and McBride v United Kingdom (1994) 17 EHRR 539

The legality of the government's derogation was tested some five years later when the suspects had been detained for six and four days respectively. It was held that the UK's exercise of the right to derogate was justified even though the extension to their detention was not judicially supervised.

There was a public emergency in Northern Ireland but there were safeguards in place to provide protection against arbitrary decisions, including *habeas corpus* and the right to consult a lawyer on arrest or if the period of detention was extended after 48 hours. These were susceptible to judicial review and regular independent review of the legislation, so the right to an effective remedy under Art 13 had not been violated.

41

Early in this century the rise in international terrorism led to further derogation under the Anti-Terrorism, Crime and Security Act 2001 and the Prevention of Terrorism Act 2005 which is discussed in Chapter 3. The purpose of the 2005 Act is to provide for the making of 'control orders' which impose obligations on individuals who are suspected of being involved in terrorist-related activities. They are set out in preventative orders designed to prevent or restrict involvement by individuals in terrorist plots.

Two kinds of control order were created, either involving or not involving derogation from the ECHR. The non-derogating category could be made by the Secretary of State, but in more serious cases which came within the derogating category supervision had to be by the court, apart from emergency situations where the Secretary of State had to seek the immediate confirmation of his actions by the Court.

Under the Human Rights Act s 16 designated derogations cease to have effect under UK law after five years unless they are renewed, but this provision does not apply to reservations.

2.5.6 Hierarchy of rights?

Figure 2.5 sets out the ECHR rights, freedoms and prohibitions and considers whether they have comparative importance. To what extent is it legitimate to suggest that some may be more important than others? If there are differences in importance, what criteria should be used to determine a hierarchy?

In fact there is no *formal* hierarchy of precedence and cases frequently involve the need to take several provisions into account in order to establish whether or not rights breaches have occurred. Bear in mind that one of the ideas discussed in Chapter 1 was that human rights are interdependent, interrelated and indivisible (section 1.5.2). There is, however, another way to classify the various articles, ie into qualified and unqualified rights, some of the latter being non-derogable. Qualified rights only exist subject to the State being able to restrict or interfere with the right to secure particular interests, which vary according to the right in question.

2.5.7 Lawfulness

If there are any restrictions imposed on Convention rights, they must be 'lawful' but this requirement is referred to in different ways. For example in Art 5 the word 'lawful' is used but in Art 8 the preferred phrase is 'in accordance with the law' and in Art 9 'prescribed by law'.

Whatever the wording, any restriction on Convention rights is only going to be lawful if it conforms to the following criteria:

• Legislation, either primary or secondary, must exist as the legal basis under domestic law to establish legality.

• The provision must be 'accessible', which means that it must be available to those who are affected by it.

Qualified	Unqualified	Derogable
Art 8 respect for private and family life	Art 2 right to life (subject to exceptions)	Art 2 No
Art 9 freedom of thought, conscience and religion	Art 3 prohibition of torture, inhuman or degrading treatment or punishment	Art 3 No
Art 10 freedom of assembly and association	Art 4 prohibition of slavery and forced labour	Art 4 No
Protocol 1 right to protection of property	Art 5 right to liberty and security	
	Art 6 right to a fair trial	
	Art 7 prohibition on punishment without law	Art 7 No
	Art 12 right to marry	
	Art 13 right to an effective remedy	
	Art 14 prohibition of discrimination	
	Prot 1 Arts 2 and 3 right to education and free elections	
	Prot 6 prohibition of death penalty (except in time of war or imminent threat thereof)	Prot 6 No
	Prot 7 (expulsion of aliens, criminal appeals and compensation, double jeopardy)	Prot 7 No
	Prot 13 abolition of death penalty.	Prot 13 No

Figure 2.5 Qualification of rights

- The law in question must be 'foreseeable', which means that it must be worded in such a way as to enable those affected by it to understand what it means and to moderate their behaviour accordingly.

In *Silver and others v UK* (1983) 5 EHRR 347 discussed in Chapter 3, prisoners were successful in claiming that secretive prison rules failed to conform to these criteria even though the legislation in the form of statute and rules made thereunder were valid and in conformity with the Convention. Similarly, Home Office guidelines may also fail to comply. The extent of foreseeability in this context varies so that in some cases there will be flexible interpretation whilst in others the construction will be narrow.

ACTIVITY

Quick quiz

1 What are the main responsibilities of the Committee of Ministers?

2 What are the political groupings in the Parliamentary Assembly?

3 What are the main responsibilities of the Human Rights Commissioner?

4 In what circumstances would a case be heard by a Grand Chamber?

5 Which six articles protect rights and what are those rights?

6 Which three articles protect freedoms and what are those freedoms?

7 Which four articles deal with prohibitions and what are they?

8 How do Arts 13 and 14 differ from the others?

9 What are protocols, derogations and reservations?

10 Is there a hierarchy of rights and if not, how might they be classified?

2.6 Inter-state applications

Inter-state applications are covered by Art 33:

 'Any High Contracting Party may refer to the Court any alleged breach of the provisions of the Convention and the protocols thereto by another High Contracting Party.'

Such referrals are uncommon but two cases where there was a need to settle interstate disagreements involved Turkey and Cyprus and the UK and Ireland respectively:

* *Ireland v United Kingdom*, Judgment of 18th January 1978, Series A, No 25; (1978) 2 EHRR 25

* *Cyprus v Turkey* (App. 25781/94) Judgment of 10th May 2001; (2001) 35 WHRR 731

CASE EXAMPLE

Ireland v United Kingdom (A/25) (1979–80) 2 EHRR 25

Ireland brought this case against the UK, alleging that the detention of IRA suspects contravened the torture provisions of Art 3 of the ECHR. Suspects were subjected to wall-standing in stress positions, hooding, deprivation of sleep and sustenance. It was also alleged that rights to liberty and security under Art 5 were breached, that the

CONTINUED ▶

treatment was discriminatory under Art 14 because it singled out the IRA as one group of people, and that nothing done was excused as an emergency by virtue of Art 15.

The Commission of Human Rights were of the opinion that there had been breaches of the Convention and the Court regretted that the British Government were in specific breach of Art 28 because they had failed to assist the Commission.

Detention without trial infringed Arts 5(1)–5(4) but it was permitted in the circumstances of public emergency. No discrimination was found by the Court under Art 14.

The interrogation techniques used by the British did constitute a form of inhuman or degrading treatment so there had been a breach of Art 3.

CASE EXAMPLE

Cyprus v Turkey (25781/94) (2002) 35 EHRR 30

Turkey invaded Cyprus in 1974 and established the Turkish Republic of Northern Cyprus in 1983. The UN Security Council decided that this was invalid and the international community refused to recognise it. Greek Cypriots living in the north were displaced to the south and the Turkish Republic regarded their properties as having been abandoned. Cyprus claimed breach of various human rights including Art 2 because many Greek Cypriots were missing. Some had been killed or detained, and no satisfactory investigation had been carried out by Turkey.

Other alleged breaches included Art 3 inhuman treatment arising from the absence of information as to what had happened to people, Art 8 in lack of respect for private and family life, and Art 1 Prot 1 by refusal to allow displaced Greek Cypriots to return and take possession of their former properties in Northern Cyprus.

It was held that Cyprus did have a 'legitimate legal interest' to enable it to bring the action. Although there was not enough evidence to prove that the missing people had been killed or were being held by the Turks, many of them had last been seen in the hands of the Turkish military and this added up to disappearance in life-threatening circumstances.

There was an ongoing breach of Art 2 because Turkey had failed to carry out any investigation. A breach of Art 5(2) occurred because of the failure to keep records of detainees and condemning relatives of missing persons to live in a prolonged state of

CONTINUED ▸

anxiety was a violation of Art 3. Further violations extended to Arts 8, 9, 13 and Art 1 Prot 1.

Although this comprehensive condemnation occurred in 2002, the partition of Cyprus still continues and agreement is yet to be reached between the various parties to allow the many injustices to be rectified and the whole of Cyprus to take up membership of the EU.

2.7 Individual applications

Individual applications are covered by Art 34:

(A) 'The Court may receive applications from any person, non-governmental organization or group of individuals claiming to be the victim of a violation by one of the High Contracting Parties of the rights set forth in the Convention or the protocols thereto. The High Contracting Parties undertake not to hinder in any way the effective exercise of this right.'

As indicated in section 2.4.2 previously, there were some 54,000 applications received by the Court in 2007. There is a filtering process to remove those which it would be inappropriate or a waste of time placing before the Court, following which those that get through are registered. Initial consideration is by a three-judge Committee tasked with ensuring that the complaints meet the Court's admissibility criteria. Unanimity is needed if the application is to be ruled inadmissible. The basis of this part of the process is Arts 34 and 35 as amended by Protocol 11 and involves consideration by the three judges of the nine questions indicated in Figure 2.6.

1	Can the applicant claim to be a victim of a violation of a Convention right?
2	Is the defendant State a party to the Convention?
3	Have domestic remedies been exhausted?
4	Is the application filed within the six-month time limit?
5	Is the application signed?
6	Has the application been brought before?
7	Is the application compatible with the Convention?
8	Is the application manifestly ill-founded?
9	Is there an abuse of the right of petition?

■ Figure 2.6 Admissibility questions

The process continues with a seven-judge Chamber that includes the judge for the defendant state considering the parties' written arguments. If necessary, material facts are investigated, a decision is reached as to whether the complaint is admissible, and the possibility of a friendly settlement explored. The parties must undertake to abide by the final judgment and the case is then considered on its merits; if it is one of particular difficulty it can be referred to a Grand Chamber of 17 judges.

2.8 Operating principles of the ECHR

The replacement of the Commission and part-time Court was effected by Protocol 13 which provided for a permanent court from 1st November 1998, combining the administrative procedure for dealing with applicability and the judicial trial of issues.

The European Court of Human Rights is not able to operate legislatively nor to overrule treaty provisions, but it takes a purposive or teleological approach to treaty interpretation: ie the Court strives to achieve the desired objectives of the various articles. This mode of applying the Convention may be seen as somewhat broader than the literal rule of English law statutory interpretation and a development of the mischief and golden rules (see sections 3.5.1 and 3.5.2 in Chapter 3).

In *Notham v London Borough of Barnet* [1978] 1 All ER 1243 Lord Denning said that purposive interpretation would 'promote the general legislative purpose underlying the provisions' and Lord Browne-Wilkinson said in *Pepper (Inspector of Taxes) v Hart* [1993] AC 593 that the idea was 'to give effect to the true intentions of the legislature' with Lord Griffiths providing a more comprehensive explanation:

> 'The days have long passed when the courts adopted a strict constructionist view
> of interpretation which required them to adopt the literal meaning of the
> language. The courts now adopt a purposive approach which seeks to give effect
> to the true purpose of legislation and are prepared to look at much extraneous
> material that bears upon the background against which the legislation was
> enacted.'

The purposive approach to statutory and treaty interpretation shows the influence of continental civil law methodology and has proved a flexible tool that enabled the European Court to adapt to the profound changes which have occurred over the past 50 years, not merely because of modernity but by virtue of the rich variety of cultures and social and legal systems now operating within the province of the ECHR.

2.8.1 Proportionality and purposive interpretation

This richness and diversity has many positive aspects but can also sometimes give rise to interpretative problems. For this reason the Court utilises the principle of 'proportionality' in

reaching decisions, maintaining a balance between individuals' rights and legitimate interests of states. Proportionality means that the way in which rights are exercised has to be applied so as to keep society's requirements in proportion to those of the individual, not interfering with his rights unless there is a pressing societal need to do so.

Proportionality and how it relates to a similar process of balancing is explained in a report, 'Public Protection, Proportionality, and the Search for Balance', published in 2007 for the Ministry of Justice by a group of University of Oxford researchers:

'At its most rigorously applied, proportionality requires a multi-stage analysis:

- First, the court must ask whether the purpose of any rights restriction is legitimate
- Second, the court must then ask whether the measure in question is suitable to attaining the identified purpose
- Third, the court must ask whether the measure is necessary for the attainment of the purpose
- Finally, the court must establish whether the measure is proportionate in the strict sense, namely whether it strikes a proper balance between the purpose and the individuals' rights in question.

Proportionality as a legal concept must be distinguished from the concept of balancing. Balancing, as identified in this report, involves a broad brush, and sometimes opaque, analysis aimed at a resolution of the interests and rights involved. When balancing, courts are effectively applying a utilitarian analysis of the rights and public interest goals in question, giving no significantly greater weight to rights than to security measures.'

The practical implications of proportionality can be seen in widely differing contexts. At one end of the spectrum there is the need to balance the requirements of protecting society against terrorist outrages weighed against the right of individuals to go about their daily lives and business without state interference, whilst on a more mundane level there is the question of how far it is necessary to apply animal welfare and public health rules in circumstances where this was never intended (*R (Suryananda) v Welsh Ministers* [2007] EWCA Civ 893).

2.8.2 The margin of appreciation

This can best be understood by examining those Articles that are expressed to be subject to qualification(s). For example, Art 8(1) clearly provides that everyone is entitled to be accorded respect for his private and family life, his home and his correspondence, but Art 8(2) then goes on to qualify the right by saying that although there must be no interference by public authorities with the exercise of these four rights, some interference will be justified if it is necessary in a democratic society in the interests of:

- national security

- public safety

- the economic well-being of the country

- to prevent disorder or crime

- to protect public health or morals

- to protect the rights and freedoms of others.

Because Art 8 is qualified in so many ways, it allows different domestic courts and tribunals to exercise considerable discretion in the way that, in their particular societies, they choose to protect their citizens' private and family lives, their homes and correspondence, and this is understood and applied by the European Court of Human Rights.

ACTIVITY

Quick quiz

1 What are the basic objectives of the European Union and the Council of Europe?

2 What are the main Council of Europe institutions?

3 What is the generic role of the protocols, ie why were the provisions in the various protocols not simply included in the ECHR itself?

4 Explain in your own words the meaning of the following:

- proportionality

- purposive interpretation

- margin of appreciation.

5 What admissibility questions are asked to establish whether a case should be heard by the European Court of Human Rights?

6 What is an inter-state application and how does it differ from an individual application?

2.8.3 Advisory opinions

The operation of the English legal system is fundamentally pragmatic, learned and understood by studying real cases involving real people with very real problems to be resolved. The courts hear cases either because the Crown is prosecuting individuals for minor offences or major crimes, or because there is some actual legal issue to be settled between parties – a claim to be made, a right exerted, an interest to be protected and so on. English courts are not theoretical debating chambers where interesting jurisprudential conundrums can be picked over and discussed. English courts are mostly not in the business of providing advisory opinions, although there are

some circumstances where cases can be referred to the Court from time to time where guidance is needed by a public official.

CASE EXAMPLE

Attorney-General's Reference No 1 of 2004 [2004] EWCA Crim 1025; [2004] 3 WLR 976

The issue to be determined here was whether reverse burdens of proof imposed by different statutes (ie the defendant being required to prove his innocence rather than the Crown having to prove his guilt) was compatible with the presumption of innocence under Art 6 of the ECHR and the Human Rights Act 1998.

Five defendants E, D, J, H and C appealed against their respective convictions and the Attorney-General referred two points of law to the Criminal Division of the Court of Appeal. The defendants had to prove statutory defences. Two had relied on s 352 of the Insolvency Act 1986, and two others had used the statutory defence under the Protection from Eviction Act 1977. The fifth appellant claimed to be the survivor of a suicide pact and relied on the defence under s 4(2) of the Homicide Act 1957.

The issues to which answers were required were: first, whether a reverse burden contravened Sched.1 Part I Art 6(2) of the Human Rights Act 1998 Act (everyone charged with a criminal offence shall be presumed innocent until proved guilty according to law); and second, when it was appropriate to hold a preparatory hearing.

The Court allowed the reference and one of the appeals, but dismissed the other four appeals. Determining whether a reverse burden contravened the Convention's Art 6(2) presumption of innocence and, if so, whether it could be interpreted in such a way as to make it compatible, involved deciding what kind of burden was placed on the defendant by the relevant statute: legal or evidential. If it was legal, could it be justified? If it could not be justified, could it be 'read down' to be construed in the alternative as an evidential burden?

The appeal court went on to hold that reverse burdens of proof are valid under the common law and the Human Rights Act and 'probably justified' if there were significant and fair reasons to shift the Crown's overall burden to the defendant. It was assumed that Parliament had considered such cases to be proportionate.

Similarly, under Art 47 of the ECHR the European Court has jurisdiction to give advisory opinions when requested to do so by the Council of Ministers, in which case consideration must be given by the Court sitting as a Grand Chamber. The Court interprets this role narrowly and so, for example, was not prepared to provide an advisory opinion on the extent to which the

ECHR could co-exist with the CIS Convention (ie the Convention on Human Rights and Fundamental Freedoms of the Commonwealth of Independent States entered into by Belarus, the Kyrgyz Republic, the Russian Federation and Tajikistan). The question arose because the Council of Europe's Parliamentary Assembly and Council of Ministers were uneasy about the efficacy and enforceability of the CIS machinery and the possibility of conflict and contradictions arising between the two human rights conventions.

In contrast on 17th July 2006 the Committee of Ministers asked the Court to provide an Art 47 Advisory Opinion on two questions of a much narrower nature:

1. Can a list of candidates for the post of judge at the Court which satisfies the criteria listed in Art 21 be refused solely on the basis of gender-related issues?

2. Are Resolutions 1366 (2004) and 1426 (2005) in breach of the Parliamentary Assembly's responsibilities under Art 22 to consider a list of candidates, or a name on such a list, on the basis of the criteria listed in Art 21?

The Court held that it did have jurisdiction to answer the first question and it was not necessary to answer the second one. In reaching this conclusion the Court considered the *travaux préparatoires* to Protocol No 2, an example of purposive interpretation previously discussed, the preparatory documents providing insight into the intention of the protocol. The issue here was election of judges to the Court: candidates must be of high moral character and possess the qualifications required for appointment to high judicial office or must be *jurisconsults* of recognised competence.

The actual basis of the question was whether it was valid for the Parliamentary Assembly in its Resolutions 1366 (2004) and 1426 (2005) to resolve that it would not consider lists of candidates which did not contain at least one candidate of each sex except when the candidates belong to the sex which is under-represented in the Court. The conclusion reached was that the question posed by the Committee of Ministers did not lend itself to a straightforward 'yes' or 'no' answer. This was only the second time that the Court had been asked to provide an Advisory Opinion.

2.9 Conclusions

This chapter, and the next one dealing with the Human Rights Act, are important because they establish the context for understanding the individual rights contained in the various Convention Articles. Both the Council of Europe and what is now the EU came into existence directly as a result of the Second World War and although they have very different agendas, they are at one in the fundamental belief that an enforceable rights regime must lie at the root of the European project. The background to this has been explained, and the structure of the Council of Europe.

The guiding principles of the ECHR and the machinery have been considered: the Convention and its protocols, derogations and reservations, the non-absolute nature of most rights, individual

and state applications. Proportionality and purposive interpretation and the margin of appreciation help to explain how countries as diverse as the UK and Greece, or Romania and The Netherlands, manage in broad terms to live in the same human rights tent. The next chapter focuses on how after nearly half a century the Convention rights have been 'brought home' to the UK.

KEY FACTS

The European Union (EU) is an organisation of 27 Member States which, whilst adhering to high human rights standards, has primarily economic objectives of freedom of trade, movement, goods, services and people in a single market with a single currency

The Council of Europe is an organisation of 47 Member States (which includes all 27 EU Member States) whose primary objective is to establish and enforce high human rights standards throughout Europe but with some non- or partially European members, for example Iceland, Moldova, Turkey and the Ukraine

The main current institutions of the Council of Europe are the Committee of Ministers, the Parliamentary Assembly and the European Court of Human Rights

The Council of Europe's chief instrument to achieve its human rights objectives is the Convention for the Protection of Human Rights and Fundamental Freedoms (1950) commonly called the European Convention on Human Rights or ECHR

The substantive articles of the ECHR and its protocols provide a range of human rights, freedoms and prohibitions which can be enforced by individuals against states once all domestic remedies have been exhausted

The European Commission on Human Rights operated as a filtering body for applications between 1954 and 1999 but is now defunct

The European Court of Human Rights was established as a part-time body in 1954 and was reconstituted as a full-time court in 1998

The European Court has developed a range of procedures that differ from those of the UK and other Signatory States which include the principle of proportionality, purposive interpretation and the margin of appreciation

The office of Commissioner for Human Rights was established in 1999 and its role is to foster and encourage development of human rights, promote education and awareness, and provide advice and information

Useful resources

European Court of Human Rights Home Page: www.echr.coe.int/.

Goold, B, Lazarus, L and Swiney, G, 'Public Protection, Proportionality, and the Search for Balance', Ministry of Justice, 2007 accessible at: http://www.justice.gov.uk/docs/270907.pdf.

HUDOC survey: cmiskp.echr.coe.int/tkp197/search.asp.

Justice, 'Review of the UK's Reservations to International Human Rights Treaty Obligations', accessible at: http://www.liberty-human-rights.org.uk/pdfs/policy02/interventions-dec-2002.pdf.

Further reading

Amos, M, *Human Rights Law* (Hart Publishing, Oxford and Portland, Oregon, 2006) Part II.

Ghandi, P R, *Blackstone's International Human Rights Documents* (latest edn, Oxford University Press).

Helfer, L R, 'Redesigning the European Court of Human Rights: Embeddedness as a Deep Structural Principle of the European Human Rights Regime', EJIL 2008, 19(1), 125–159.

O'Boyle, M, 'On Reforming the Operation of the European Court of Human Rights', EHRLR 2008, 1, 1–11.

Ovey, C and White, R, *Jacobs and White, The European Convention on Human Rights* (4th edn, Oxford University Press, 2006), 1–54; 432–525.

chapter 3

HUMAN RIGHTS ACT 1998

AIMS AND OBJECTIVES

This is one of the most important pieces of legislation enacted by Parliament in recent years and the key to understanding why that is, and how it operates, lies in the Council of Europe and the establishment and operation of the European Convention on Human Rights (ECHR) discussed in Chapter 2.

The first part of this chapter examines the background and considers various reasons why the Convention was not made part of UK domestic law in 1953 when it was ratified by the UK. Growing pressure over the years eventually led to the Convention rights being 'brought home' by the 1998 Act, which came into operation in October 2000; although by virtue of the Scotland Act 1998, they were already operative in Scotland. The chapter goes on to provide a detailed analysis of the Act and how it operates, discussing the substantive sections and schedules together with examples of relevant case law.

3.1 A proud English tradition

It took almost half a century for the Convention rights to become directly accessible to UK individuals as of right once all domestic routes had been exhausted, and there are various suggestions as to why this was the case, some more convincing than others. As explained in Chapter 2 the ECHR was conceived following the Allies' eventual victory in the Second World War and there was a belief that the Axis powers and especially Germany needed to have spelled out in clear terms what human rights meant and what standards of civilised behaviour should in future be observed by European states.

The Nuremberg trials were held between 1945 and 1949 and some of these heard accounts of the mass murders perpetrated in the name of the German people. The crime of genocide was defined for the first time under international law in the United Nations Convention on the Prevention and Punishment of the Crime of Genocide 1948. Given the emerging facts it was no doubt understandable that Europeans were keen to establish their own human rights regime, and the British were at the forefront of this movement. Germany was not one of the original signatories as it was under Allied occupation at the time.

In earlier history England and later the UK took pride in their record of protecting rights and particularly individual rights, although of course over the centuries the record on this score was somewhat patchy, to say the least. However, there were seminal events and documents that supported the civil liberties record such as *Magna Carta* 1215, which established rights to jury trial and fair process, and the Bill of Rights 1689, which shifted the balance of power from Crown to Parliament. The Scots had their own ideas of freedom and resistance to oppression which they expressed in the Declaration of Arbroath 1320.

These and other constitutional documents were reinforced by the development of rights philosophy through writers such as John Locke (*Treatise on Government* 1690) and later by Tom Paine (*Common Sense* 1776) and J S Mill (*On Liberty* 1859). Other positive progress on the general rights agenda included the abolition of slavery, introduction of universal suffrage and curtailment of hereditary powers in government by the Parliament Acts of 1911 and 1949 and the House of Lords Act 1999. From the UK perspective in 1945, as victors after a gargantuan struggle and enriched by their liberal tradition, they were ideally placed to sow the seeds to establish a new human rights order in Europe. This view was evidently supported by the other original signatories, including the defeated Italy.

There were other laudable aspects to the UK's freedom tradition including trial by one's peers, whether by jury or lay magistrate, *habeas corpus*, judicial review and protection against 'double jeopardy', that is the right not to be threatened with further trial once an accused had been acquitted. Civil liberties appeared to be comprehensive and effective and 'human rights' perhaps not quite so relevant or necessary for the UK. Great Britain, with its parliamentary democracy, common law legal system and belief that it had brought enlightenment *via* the British Empire to all those parts of the globe then still coloured red on the world map, was the home of civil rights and birthplace of freedoms that were the envy of the world.

So it seemed, and so perhaps it might have been; yet much was to change in the following decades. Thus, although the UK was highly instrumental in framing the ECHR and ratifying it promptly, there was no intention to make it part of domestic law to give direct domestic rights to individual British subjects.

3.1.1 Reluctant Europeans

As an off-shore island and traditional nautical nation, Great Britain was and to a considerable extent still is less enthusiastic than (say) France and Germany, or the East European states, to commit fully to Europe, whether by embracing the new human rights jurisprudence or the European Economic Community in the 1950s. It was only in 1972 that the UK joined the EEC (by virtue of the European Communities Act 1972 c 68) but in the following years it could not really be said that UK courts enthusiastically adopted broader European attitudes to enrich English notions of civil liberties.

Nevertheless, the courts did begin to be influenced both by EC and ECHR jurisprudence so that the Convention was recognised and used indirectly by domestic courts prior to 1998 in several ways, although there was some reluctance to acknowledge the 'pervasive' importance of the Convention and its centrality to all law as it applies in relationships between state and subjects.

Examples of pre-1998 limited recognition of the Convention include the following:

- The right of individual petition with government permission was granted to individuals in the UK in 1966.

- Exercise of judicial discretion (as opposed to the exercise of administrative discretion) was to some extent informed by the Convention (*A-G v Guardian Newspapers Ltd* [1987] 1 WLR 1284).

- The courts accepted there was a presumption that legislation would not intentionally breach the ECHR (*Re M and H (Minors)* [1990] 1 AC 686).

- It could help to establish the scope of the common law (*Derbyshire CC v Times Newspapers Ltd* [1992] QB 770 pp 812 and 830).

It was also recognised that Convention jurisprudence was available as a general aid to construction where there was ambiguity in legislation (*R v Home Secretary ex p Brind* [1991] 1 AC 696 at p 760) and according to Lord Ackner it was by then well-settled law that the Convention could be deployed in order to resolve ambiguity in English primary or subordinate legislation.

3.1.2 Need for change

However, as the 1970s and 1980s progressed there were signs that all was not well. The government allowed individuals to bring some cases against the UK but lost several significant ones which demonstrated a number of serious flaws. These included defective procedures, failure to treat individuals with respect and treatment of individuals that purported to further state policies that had little or no merit.

The following provide a few examples:

- In *Hamer v UK* (1979) 24 DR 5; (1982) 4 EHRR 139 and *Draper v UK* (1981) 24 DR 72 the Commission ruled that there had been interference with Art 12 rights and that no legitimate state objectives or interests were served in preventing prisoners from marrying.

- *Silver and others v UK* (1983) 5 EHRR 347 demonstrated that the totality of procedures and remedies had failed a Sikh prisoner – prison board of visitors, ombudsman, Home Secretary and judicial review – when his correspondence had been unlawfully interfered with contrary to Art 8.

- The common law had failed to protect British citizens against police telephone tapping (*Malone v UK* (1984) 7 EHRR 14), which resulted in the enactment of the Interception of Communications Act 1985.

CASE EXAMPLE

Silver and others v UK (1983) 5 EHRR 347

A number of convicted prisoners complained that the control of their mail by the prison authorities constituted a breach of their rights to respect for correspondence and freedom of expression contrary to Arts 8 and 10 of the ECHR. They alleged that they were being denied the right to an effective remedy under Art 13 and one applicant also claimed that he had been refused permission to seek legal advice under Art 6(1).

The European Court held that there had been a violation of Arts 6(1), 8 and 13 and that it was not necessary to deal with Art 10 as it was covered by the other findings.

The measures complained about conformed to English law and although the primary and secondary legislation were accessible, the unpublished orders and instructions to officials were not, so the prisoners did not have the necessary information to protect their interests and foresee the consequences of their actions. More particularly, the interference in question did not have a legitimate aim under Art 8 and some of the restrictions imposed on their correspondence by the prison authorities were not necessary in a democratic society.

The Court also said that the Home Secretary was insufficiently independent to enable the Court to treat complaints to him as an effective remedy where the validity of an instruction was being questioned by the complainants; nor was judicial review adequate in these circumstances because although they contravened the Convention, the High Court would not have been able to find the relevant measures arbitrary, taken in bad faith for improper motives or *ultra vires*.

3.2 Genesis of the Act

Interest began to grow in bringing the ECHR with enforceable rights and remedies within the ambit of UK domestic law. Joining the European Economic Community in 1973 meant that European law and practices were being applied in the UK and rights cases such as those cited above in section 3.1.2 indicated that despite some hesitation and reluctance European jurisprudence was beginning to influence the domestic common law courts.

Furthermore, even allowing for English law's respect for individual freedom, civil liberties only represented one aspect of English law. There was a considerable volume of other laws that were quite illiberal, whether or not justified by circumstances at the times they were enacted. Examples of these include the Aliens Acts of 1905 and 1914 and the Registration of Business Names Act 1916, or the Commonwealth Immigrants Acts of 1962 and 1968. In the 1990s there was a spate of restrictive immigration legislation, and a trend had developed for the executive, ie the government to bludgeon Parliament into doing the government's will, at the cost of sacrificing some of the protection offered by an independent legislature under the doctrine of separation of powers (see section 1.2.2).

Considering the overall position at the end of the twentieth century, the introduction of the Human Rights Act 1998 provided some direct rights of action to individuals but the cumulative effect of various twentieth-century problems and the impact of terrorist activities, formerly IRA and latterly international, had done little to reverse the trend for the executive to sideline Parliament and occasionally the courts by enacting authoritarian legislation. One of the objectives of the Human Rights Act would be to redress the balance to some extent in favour of the individual.

Entrenched written constitutions in other western democracies guarantee basic rights, but English constitutional historians and lawyers refer with pride to the unwritten constitution which, although not actually 'unwritten', is vague, indeterminate and has a tendency to mean what one wants it to mean, which does not always support or underpin human rights. There is little agreement about which documents and practices categorically define and encompass the UK's constitution, which is why it is widely characterised as being 'unwritten' (see section 3.2.2 on constitutional significance below). Therefore, when it came to the 'fundamental rights' enunciated in the Convention, English law was sometimes found wanting. Parliamentary sovereignty and other constitutional provisions were not proving sufficiently robust to guarantee human rights and freedoms.

Some of these weaknesses had been presaged in earlier decades by proponents of constitutional reform. During the 1970s and 80s there were a number of attempts to advance the cause of incorporating the Convention into domestic UK law. Anthony Lester (now Lord Lester of Herne Hill QC) published a Fabian pamphlet in 1968 entitled *Democracy and Individual Rights*, and subsequently there were debates instigated by politicians of all the major parties in both Houses of Parliament. Sir Leslie Scarman (the late Lord Scarman) delivered the Hamlyn lecture in 1974 entitled *English Law – The New Dimension* which argued for an entrenched instrument in the form of a new Bill of Rights that would protect basic liberties against the whims of Parliament.

Ideas for reform were developed and carried forward in subsequent years by conservative politicians such as Sir Keith Joseph, Sir Geoffrey Howe and others of differing political hues. Charter 88 (now known as *Unlock Democracy*) was established in 1988 as a pressure group advocating constitutional and electoral reform in response to what was seen by some people as authoritarian 'Thatcherism', its objectives being to bring about:

- fair, open and honest elections
- rights, freedoms and a written constitution
- stronger parliament and accountable government
- bringing power closer to the people

- a culture of informed political interest and responsibility.

Therefore, for some people the progress made regarding the ECHR was only limited in light of what they saw as the need for wider constitutional change, in particular a clearly drafted constitution and electoral and parliamentary reform.

3.2.1 Bringing rights home

Eventually in the mid-1990s the Labour Party pledged to reform the law. After a Consultation Paper *Bringing Rights Home* was published in 1996 the ideas expressed therein were developed in the White Paper *Rights Brought Home: The Human Rights Bill* (CM 3782) which made the case for change, explained the government's proposals for enforcing Convention rights, indicated how this would improve compliance, and set out the derogations and reservations that the government considered to be necessary.

When the Human Rights Act was passed in 1998, to come into effect in October 2000 in order to allow time for training and adjustment, it provided that existing UK domestic law would be interpreted and future laws enacted and interpreted by government and courts in accordance with the Convention, and at last empowered individuals and organisations to enforce Convention rights directly in domestic courts. However, it did not directly incorporate the Convention into domestic law.

Event	Date
Universal Declaration of Human Rights	1948
Treaty of London established the Council of Europe	1949
Convention for Protection of Human Rights and Fundamental Freedoms	1950
UK's Westminster Parliament ratified the Convention	1951
European Convention came into force	1953
European Commission was established	1954
Original European Court (part-time) was established	1959
Individual right of petition (with permission) granted to UK individuals	1966
Fabian pamphlet *Democracy and Individual Rights*, Anthony Lester	1968
Hamlyn lecture *English Law – The New Dimension*, Sir Leslie Scarman	1974
Consultation paper *Bringing Rights Home* published	1996
White Paper *Rights Brought Home: The Human Rights Bill* (CM 3782)	1997
Human Rights Act passed	1998
Reconstituted European Court established	1998
Human Rights Act came into effect	2000

Figure 3.1 Table of key dates

3.2.2 Constitutional significance

It has been noted that the UK has neither an entrenched nor a written constitution and is one of the very few states where this is the case, the others being Israel and New Zealand. 'Entrenchment' means protection by stipulating additional requirements in order to bring about change, such as requiring a two-thirds or three-quarters legislative majority vote in favour. A 'constitution' is the body of fundamental principles according to which a State is governed, which indicates that those principles are more important than the day-to-day laws that continually change, such as road traffic, taxation, housing or health legislation. In states where there is a written constitution, there tends to be more awareness of what comprise the fundamental values that apply, as, for example, with the US Constitution.

What the UK Constitution does comprise is a collection of Acts of Parliament, Orders in Council, treaties, court decisions, and (actually unwritten) constitutional conventions or modes/codes of behaviour that are ill-defined and easily changed by those who are supposed to be bound by them. This provides flexibility and the ability to institute change that does not exist under a written constitution, where extraordinary procedures usually requiring a high level of agreement are needed to bring about change. As previously indicated, there is no agreement about what exact rules, procedures, practices and statutes constitute the UK's 'unwritten constitution' but perhaps most people would agree that the following would have a strong claim to be included:

Date	Document/event	Reason
1215	*Magna Carta*	Granted important individual rights such as jury trial and *habeas corpus*
1688	Bill of Rights	Crown acknowledged supremacy of Parliament and established beginnings of the constitutional monarchy
1603	Coronation	Union of the Crowns: James VI of Scotland became James I of England on death of Queen Elizabeth I
1679	Habeas Corpus Act	Still on the statute book, albeit amended, this was one of a number before and after that stemmed from *Magna Carta* and guaranteed due process
1706 1707	Acts of Union of Parliaments	Brought into effect the treaty that formed Great Britain out of the Kingdoms of England and Scotland
1800	Acts of Union	Merged the Kingdom of Ireland with the unified Kingdom of Great Britain
1911 1949	Parliament Acts	Increased Commons' authority over the hereditary Lords by removing latters' powers to amend money Bills and reducing the length of time they could delay a Bill
1920s	Various statutes	Dealt with the establishment of the independent Irish Republic
1972	European Communities Act	Enlarged the European Communities then comprising only the original six states to include the UK, Ireland and Denmark

CONTINUED ▸

Date	Document/event	Reason
1998	Various statutes	Dealt with the establishment of the Scottish Parliament and Assemblies for Wales and Northern Ireland
1998	Human Rights Act	'Brought home' Convention rights to UK subjects by providing protection and remedies for human rights
1999	House of Lords Act	Removed the right of the majority of hereditary peers to take part in government by virtue of automatic right
2005	Constitutional Reform Act	Provides for the law lords to be replaced by a Supreme Court and removes Speaker functions in the House of Lords and control of the judiciary from the Lord Chancellor

Figure 3.2 Basis for a written constitution

People will quite rightly have different views as to what should be incorporated in or omitted from such a list, but they cover a range of matters, some of which are concerned with individual rights and the remainder with the structure of the realm and the relationship between the Crown and Parliament. In any worthwhile constitution, however, all these aspects need to be clearly established. *Magna Carta Libertatum* as it is sometimes called was reissued after 1215 on a number of occasions throughout the thirteenth century, although the bulk of it was repealed by the Statute Law Revision Act 1863 and much of the rest since then.

ACTIVITY

Self-assessment questions

1 Why did the UK Government not grant the right to individuals to access the European Commission and Court directly from 1953 when the ECHR came into force?

2 Name as many of English law's 'civil rights' (as opposed to ECHR 'human rights') as you can remember.

3 List ways in which English case law recognised the influence of the ECHR prior to 1998.

4 Can you name any European cases that suggested English civil liberties law was not fit for purpose?

5 What other influences played a part in bringing about recognition of the desirability of bringing the ECHR within the ambit of UK domestic law?

6 Do you think a written constitution is desirable now that the Human Rights Act has been enacted? What are the reasons supporting your conclusion?

However, three clauses of the 1297 version of *Magna Carta* are still law in England and Wales:

- Clause 1 guarantees freedom of the English Church (now the established Church of England).
- Clause 9 guarantees the ancient liberties of the City of London.
- Clause 29 guarantees due process.

The right of *habeas corpus*, although no longer stemming directly from *Magna Carta*, originally arose from the provisions of clauses 36, 38, 39 and 40 of the 1215 version.

3.3 The Human Rights Act 1998

3.3.1 Structure of the Act

The following table sets out the structure of the Act. It is followed by some explanatory notes which should be studied carefully as this is an unusual piece of legislation, bringing into domestic UK law the right for individuals to take advantage of an international treaty, and one that is truly fundamental to their status and basic rights.

The Sections

Introduction
s1   The Convention Rights
s2   Interpretation of Convention rights

Legislation
s3   Interpretation of legislation
s4   Declaration of incompatibility
s5   Right of Crown to intervene

Public authorities
s6   Acts of public authorities
s7   Proceedings
s8   Judicial remedies
s9   Judicial acts

Remedial action
s10   Power to take remedial action

Other rights and proceedings
s11   Safeguard for existing human rights
s12   Freedom of expression
s13   Freedom of thought, conscience and religion

Derogations and reservations
s14   Derogation
s15   Reservation
s16   Period for which designated derogations have effect
s17   Periodic review of designated reservations

CONTINUED ▶

Judges of the European Court of Human Rights
s18   Appointment to European Court of Human Rights

Parliamentary procedure
s19   Statements of compatibility

Supplemental
s20   Orders, etc under this Act
s21   Interpretation
s22   Short title, commencement, application and content

The Schedules

Schedule 1 The articles

Part I The Convention rights and freedoms
Sets out the rights and freedoms contained in Convention Arts 2–12, 14, and 16–18, from the right to life to limitations on the use of restrictions on rights (see the previous chapter on the Convention for more detail of the actual articles)

Part II The First Protocol
Arts 1–3 deal with protection of property, the right to education and free elections; Pt II of the HRA sets out the reservation made in 1952 to the right to education, Art 2 being accepted by the UK only so far as it is compatible with the provision of efficient instruction and training, and the avoidance of unreasonable public expenditure

Part III The Sixth Protocol
Art 1 abolishes the death penalty and Art 2 allows states to make provision for the death penalty in times of war or imminent threat of war

Schedule 2 Remedial orders
Section 10 of the Act gives power to take remedial action where legislation has been declared under s 4 to be incompatible with a Convention right, and this schedule makes further provision on procedure, urgent cases and definitions for such action under s 10(7)

Schedule 3 Derogation and reservation
This Schedule explains why the UK has derogated (Pt I) or made reservations (Pt II) from the Convention, the derogation relating to terrorism measures introduced by the government in 1974 arising from the Northern Ireland disturbances and the adverse European Court's decision of *Brogan and others* in 1988

Schedule 4 Judicial pensions
This obliges the appropriate Minister to ensure that there are pension provisions for any holder of a judicial office who serves as a European Court Judge, with statutory instruments providing rules in connection with the HRA

Figure 3.3 Contents of Human Rights Act 1998

3.3.2 Summary explanation

(a) First part of the Act (ss 1–10)

- **Introduction** ss 1 and 2 define and interpret the ECHR rights and terms.

- **Legislation** is explained in ss 3–5, comprising interpretation of the Act (as opposed to the Convention), the introduction into English law of the power of higher courts to make declarations of incompatibility, and the right of the Crown to intervene.

- **Public authorities**, ie what they are, how they deal with their proceedings, and what judicial remedies are available are covered by ss 6, 7 and 8.

- **Remedial action** under s 10 deals with the power of government ministers to do what is necessary after a declaration of incompatibility by the court.

(b) Second part of the Act (ss 11–22)

- **Other rights and proceedings** refer to safeguards for existing human rights in s 11 and ss 12 and 13 dealing with freedom of expression and freedom of thought, conscience and religion.

- **Derogations and reservations** are defined and the length of time for which they exist validated under ss 14–18.

- **Appointment of judges** to the European Court is covered in s 18.

- **Statements of compatibility** must be made by ministers to certify all new legislation as ECHR compatible or to provide justification if not, contained in s 19.

- **Supplemental** provisions as to orders under the Act, interpretation and the usual short title and commencement provisions are in ss 20–22.

(c) Third part of the Act (Schedules)

- There are four **Schedules** to the Act, those numbered 2–4 clearly referring to specific aspects requiring implementation: remedial orders, derogations and reservations, and judicial pensions.

- The **First Schedule** defines the relevant rights and freedoms for the purposes of the Act, and deals with rights of property, education and free elections, and abolition of the death penalty.

The Human Rights Act 1998 c 42 is 'An Act to give further effect to rights and freedoms guaranteed under the European Convention on Human Rights; to make provision with respect to holders of certain judicial offices who become judges of the European Court of Human Rights; and for connected purposes [9th November 1998]'.

3.4 Introduction to the Act

3.4.1 The Convention rights s 1

Sections 1 and 2 are introductory, s 1 defining the Convention rights and Protocols to the extent they are meant to apply in domestic law, indicating how they are to take effect subject to any designated derogations or reservations, and how the Secretary of State can amend the statute by order to reflect the effect of protocols.

The 'Convention rights' as defined by s 1 comprise Arts 2–12 and 14 of the ECHR, Arts 1–3 of the First Protocol, and Art 1 of the Thirteenth Protocol (as read with Arts 16–18 of the Convention). It is important to be clear as to exactly what this includes and excludes:

- It *omits* the crucial Convention Art 13 which gives the right to an effective remedy (discussed further below).

- In addition to the other substantive rights established by Arts 2–12 and Art 14 it also *includes* four other rights that were established by Protocol after the original ECHR was agreed and ratified:
  - protection of **property** under Prot 1 Art 1
  - right to **education** under Prot 1 Art 2 (although the UK made a reservation as it was not prepared to accept this as an unqualified obligation regardless of possible expense)
  - right to **free elections**
  - right to **protection from capital punishment** (Prot 13 eventually provided for abolition of the death penalty without the right to derogate or make reservations – Arts 16–18 of the Convention referred to restrictions on political activities of aliens, prohibition of abuse of rights, and limitations on use of restrictions on rights).

The 'Secretary of State' has power under s 1(4) by order to make amendments to the Act in order to reflect the effect of protocols. This power can currently be exercised by the Secretary of State for Constitutional Affairs. The way the Act defines 'the Convention rights' is not simply to incorporate them into domestic law and it specifically omits Art 13 of the ECHR which provides:

(A) 'Right to an effective remedy

Everyone whose rights and freedoms as set forth in this Convention are violated shall have an effective remedy before a national authority notwithstanding that the violation has been committed by persons acting in an official capacity.'

This seems at first sight rather odd as it is the motor which drives the individual's right to the effective remedies provided by the Convention. The answer is that the Act itself does the job of complying with Art 13, and part of the reason for omitting the Article was fear that it would give too much interpretative power to the judiciary. The government's view was that to have done so would have caused confusion and prompted the courts to devise novel remedies not contemplated by the Act, so Art 13 remains outside the direct scope of the Act.

3.4.2 Interpretation of Convention rights s 2

Section 2 requires courts and tribunals determining Convention questions to 'take into account' a wide range of matters that would have brought aspects of Art 13 into consideration (see below) and in this way the Article is indirectly applied. By s 2(1) these include judgments, decisions, declarations and advisory opinions of the European Court, opinions and decisions of the Commission, and decisions of the Committee of Ministers.

Therefore, the omission from the statute does not preclude UK courts having to consider Art 13 when it comprises an essential part of a claim as in *Chahal v United Kingdom* (1996) 23 EHRR 413. In that case (although it arose prior to the Act) the government claimed that details of the case against an alleged Sikh terrorist could not be disclosed in order to protect national security,

which left the claimant without an effective remedy and necessitated the enactment of the Special Immigration Appeals Commission Act 1998 that created through SIAC a specific right of appeal in such cases.

3.4.3 Preamble

The general idea of the Act as indicated in the preamble was to give 'further effect' to the Convention in a number of ways. The relevance of the words 'further effect' is that the Act avoids actually incorporating the Convention lock, stock and barrel into domestic law, which is what would be needed at common law to ensure that all the rights incontrovertibly have to be applied. The Act also tries to preserve the supremacy of Parliament given that, as a state, international obligations have been entered into which seem to restrict that supremacy.

The position here is analogous to that of UK membership of the EU. It is sometimes argued that Parliament has the absolute ability to legislate without any fetters or restrictions, reflecting Dicey's exposition of the doctrine of parliamentary supremacy. The explanation of this dichotomy lies in the differences between what is theoretically legally possible under the doctrine of supremacy of parliament and the rather more restricted realistic version of what may be politically practicable. The theory that the omnipotent Westminster Parliament can enact any legislation whatsoever would be tested were it to try, for example, to:

- re-establish the British Empire
- repatriate all immigrants since (say) 1945
- repeal the European Communities Act 1972
- repeal the Human Rights Act 1998
- abolish the Scottish Parliament or the Welsh Assembly.

3.5 Legislation

Sections 3, 4 and 5 deal with interpretation of legislation, declarations of incompatibility, and the right of the Crown to intervene respectively.

3.5.1 Interpretation of legislation s 3

With regard to interpretation of domestic legislation s 3(1) provides that Acts of Parliament and subordinate legislation (statutory instruments and by-laws) must be read so far as possible compatibly with Convention rights, with the qualification that this does not affect the validity, operation or enforcement of pre-existing legislation. What the section is doing, therefore, is specifying a rule of how the courts are to read and interpret ECHR jurisprudence. In the past, judges usually took as their starting point a 'literal' reading of Acts of Parliament but they were also free to interpret statutes in different ways, depending on the context and their personal inclinations and Parliament does not usually restrict or attempt to influence this judicial discretion.

Under the interpretation section of the Human Rights Act (s 21) 'primary legislation' includes public general Acts, local, personal and private Acts, Orders in Council and various Church of England measures but it does not deal with interpretation of treaties such as the Convention itself or other international agreements.

Section 3 is stated to operate 'so far as it is possible to do so', which sounds tentative and perhaps this is because such approach to statutory interpretation is different from the traditional English one. The basic rationale means primarily trying to ascertain the true meaning of a statute by reading it literally, and other methods were categorised as the golden and mischief rules of statutory interpretation. These are not consciously applied in the usual course of events but may be used in a judgment to explain how the *ratio* of the decision was reached. Here, 'statutory' also means the way in which other instruments such as treaties are interpreted.

Rule	Operation	Rationale	Case
Literal	The court gives the words their plain, ordinary or literal meaning even if that leads to some absurdity in the meaning	It is not up to a judge to 'second guess' Parliament and anyway most statutes are fairly clear as to their meaning	*Whitely v Chappell* (1868) 4 LR QB 147
Golden	The court avoids absurdity by modifying the literal rule to make sense of the words	The judge's job involves equitable common sense in cases where a statute's meaning was not clear	*Re Sigsworth* [1935] Ch 89
Mischief	The court looks at the law prior to its being changed by legislation and applies what appears to be the 'cure' supplied by the Act	This provides the judge with more discretion, and to some extent is similar to the purposive approach	*Heydon's Case* (1584) Co Rep 7a
Purposive	National courts are required to interpret their national law in light of the purpose of the relevant statute or treaty	This is necessary when the relevant law is only expressed in general terms: the continental approach to EU and human rights law	*Pickstone v Freemans plc* [1988] 2 All ER 803

Figure 3.4 Rules of statutory interpretation

3.5.2 Purposive interpretation

Continental jurisprudence, based on civil law jurisdictions, allows the judge to adopt a broad and 'purposive' approach, which means seeking out the substance and reality of what the law is and avoiding a narrow or technical interpretation. That is because much civil (originally Roman) law is expressed in widely drawn codes rather than in detailed statutes. In some ways it may perhaps be seen as a more liberal version of the mischief rule. The original logic of *Heydon's Case* is compelling in that it was said that in attempting to interpret the law the court should consider four things:

1. What was the Common Law before the making of the Act?

2. What was the mischief and defect for which the Common Law did not provide?

3. What remedy the Parliament hath resolved and appointed to cure the disease of the commonwealth?

4. The true reason of the remedy; and then the office of all Judges is always to make such construction as shall suppress the mischief, and advance the remedy

The Human Rights Act 1998 s 3 says that legislation 'must be read and given effect in a way which is compatible with the Convention rights' not quite directly applying the mischief rule, but certainly telling judges to keep a sharp eye open to address the mischief of denial of human rights and freedoms.

In *Secretary of State for the Home Department v MB* [2006] EWCA Civ 1140; [2007] QB 415 CA a non-derogating order was sought by the Home Secretary in the case of an alleged Islamic terrorist who was refused even a summary of the charges against him. The trial judge made a declaration of incompatibility which was reversed by the Court of Appeal. The court said that a purposive approach to the matter, and the Home Secretary's obligation to keep the matters under review, were sufficient to keep the terrorist legislation within the boundaries. In balancing the interests of society against protection of individual rights, the purposive element is not always that easy to discern.

3.5.3 Declarations of incompatibility s 4

Section 4 empowers the higher courts to make 'declarations of incompatibility' where in any proceedings dealing with primary legislation the court is satisfied that some provision is incompatible with Convention rights. There are six courts that have this power:

- House of Lords
- Judicial Committee of the Privy Council (until replaced by the Supreme Court)
- Court of Appeal
- High Court
- Courts Martial Appeal Court
- Scottish High Court of Judiciary sitting otherwise than as a trial court or the Court of Session.

Where any of these courts is considering making a declaration of incompatibility, notice should be given to the Crown so that the relevant minister or nominee can be joined as a party to the proceedings. The likely result is that the law would probably then be amended and failure on the part of the government to ensure that this is done would lead to inevitable bad publicity and probable action in the European Court. The higher courts are not themselves, however, able to set aside legislation.

The lower courts (including county and magistrates' courts and other tribunals) cannot make declarations of incompatibility and must apply the legislation; nor can they trigger the s 10 remedial order provisions providing a fast-track procedure for ministers to amend defective legislation. This does not prevent the Convention being argued before the lower courts by virtue of the effects of ss 3, 6 and 7 but lower courts are constrained to abide by legislation even if they think it might contravene the ECHR.

The natural inclination of judges is to find rational and sensible answers within the law to the problems with which they are confronted. Usually the law will be found to be compatible with the Act and, whilst most of the cases seem to bear this out, there have been a number of declarations of incompatibility.

3.5.4 Incompatibility case law

According to the Department of Constitutional Affairs, up until August 2006 some 20 declarations of incompatibility had been made. These concerned a variety of matters including mental health, offences against the person, immigration, criminal sentencing, human fertilisation and embryology, matrimonial causes, social security and housing. Fourteen declarations made in respect of primary legislation had not at that date been overturned but six of the cases had been overturned on appeal.

One of the first examples of a declaration of incompatibility was *R v MHRT North and East London Region, ex parte H* (2001) 3 WLR 512 which concerned the burden of proof on patients seeking relief in applications to Mental Health Review Tribunals. Following the case the government was obliged to take a number of steps including making a remedial order in November 2001 to which retrospective approval was given by Parliament in April 2002. The result of this was that patients subjected to similar injustice could claim compensation. Under s 6 an obligation is imposed on public authorities to act compatibly with Convention rights, public authorities being courts, tribunals and any person certain of whose functions are of a public nature but excluding Parliament and its activities. Prior to the Act public bodies were not subject to a requirement to act in accordance with the Convention.

In *R (on the application of H) v Secretary of State for Health* [2005] 3 All ER 468 the Court of Appeal made a declaration of incompatibility in the case of another mental patient whom the court said should have been allowed to return to a tribunal in order to obtain a judicial decision as to her continued detention. That case was later reversed by the House of Lords (*Regina (H) v Secretary of State for Health* [2005] UKHL 60), who held that there had been several courses of action available to the applicant including judicial review, so there had been no incompatibility.

In a recent Scots law case *Smith v Scott* 2007 SC 345 the court declined to make a declaration as, in the circumstances, it would amount to the court acting as legislator. The issue here concerned the complaint of a convicted prisoner that he was not allowed to vote in the Scottish parliamentary elections because his name was not on the electoral register.

In *Wilson v First County Trust Ltd (No 2)* [2004] 1 AC 816 the Home Secretary appealed against a decision ([2001] EWCA Civ 633, [2002] QB 74) that the restriction on the enforcement of improperly executed credit agreements enacted in s 127(3) of the Consumer Credit Act 1974 was incompatible with the Human Rights Act 1998 Sched 1 Pt I Art 6(1) and Sched 1 Pt II Art 1. The Court of Appeal had held that a pawn-broking loan agreement breached regulations made under the Consumer Credit Act 1974 because the correct amount of credit had not been stated. Under the 1974 Act this absolutely barred the court from enforcing the agreement, which the CA said arguably infringed the Art 6 right to a fair trial and failed to protect property under Art 1 of the First Protocol. The House of Lords allowed the appeal and held that the Court of Appeal had been wrong to make a declaration of incompatibility.

Incompatibility may arise in any context and in *Regina (Morris) v Westminster City Council and another* and *Regina (Badu) v Lambeth London Borough Council* [2005] EWCA Civ 1184; [2006] 1 WLR 505 CA the High Court Judge had declared that s 185(4) of the Housing Act 1996 was incompatible with the claimant's rights under Art 14 of the Convention and, although the judge's order was modified, the Secretary of State in this case lost his appeal against that decision.

CASE EXAMPLE

R (on the application of Black) v Secretary of State for the Home Department [2008] EWCA Civ 359

Black appealed against the dismissal of his application for judicial review of the Home Secretary's decision to reject the recommendations of the Parole Board for his early release after serving 11 years' imprisonment. He had been sentenced to a total of 20 years for offences of kidnap and robbery, plus an additional consecutive four years for escaping from custody and assault. Both sets of offences occurred prior to April 2005 which meant that any early release was governed by s 35(1) of the Criminal Justice Act 1991. The Home Secretary decided that he still posed a risk to the public.

The case hinged on ECHR jurisprudence which made a clear distinction between cases where a person was deprived of his liberty by virtue of administrative decisions (those made by the Home Secretary) and judicial ones made by a court. Here, responsibility was shared between them and although the Parole Board's procedures met the criteria for a sufficiently independent body to be Art 5(4) compliant, leaving the final decision to the Home Secretary did not.

Section 35 of the 1991 Act left the decision as to release in the hands of the executive and so could be applied arbitrarily, which was the mischief at which Art 5(4) was directed. Although Black's appeal had to be dismissed, because the procedure complied with domestic law, the court granted a declaration of incompatibility under the Human Rights Act 1998 s 4.

3.5.5 Right of Crown to intervene s 5

The Human Rights Act s 5 gives the Crown the power to intervene in accordance with rules of court where the court is considering whether to make a declaration of incompatibility. A minister or nominee is joined as a party to the proceedings. Appeal can be made against this to the House of Lords with leave in criminal cases except in Scotland. If there has been a declaration of incompatibility under s 4 and intervention on behalf of the Crown under s 5, the remedial action required to be taken is covered in s 10 and Sched 2 of the Act.

3.6 Public authorities

3.6.1 Acts of public authorities s 6

'6(1)   It is unlawful for a public authority to act in a way which is incompatible with a Convention right...

6(3)   In this section 'public authority' includes

(a) a court or tribunal, and

(b) any person certain of whose functions are functions of a public nature, but does not include either House of Parliament or a person exercising functions in connection with proceedings in Parliament

(c) In subs (3) 'Parliament' does not include the House of Lords in its judicial capacity.'

Public authorities in this context include those legislatively designated, meaning courts and tribunals under s 6 and others whose functions are obviously public such as the police and prison services, government departments and local authorities. In addition there are:

- 'hybrids' such as housing associations (*Poplar Housing and Regeneration Community Association Ltd v Donoghue* [2001] EWCA Civ 595; 3 WLR 183)

- 'non-hybrid' bodies, for example charities (*R (on the application of Heather) v Leonard Cheshire Foundation* [2002] EWCA Civ 366; [2002] 2 All ER 936).

It does not, however, include either House of Parliament, except the House of Lords when it is operating as a court.

The effect of s 6 is to make it unlawful for a public authority to act in a way that is incompatible with one of the above Convention rights, unless it has to do so because of some primary legislation that cannot be interpreted compatibly with the Convention.

Baroness Hale of Richmond clearly explained the duty of public authorities to act compatibly with the Convention in *Regina (Countryside Alliance and others) v Attorney General and another; Regina (Derwin and others) v Same* [2007] UKHL 52; [2007] 3 WLR 922 at paras 113 and 114. She said that the Act for the first time outside EC law gave people rights against the State, and

public bodies and officials have to act compatibly with Convention rights. Therefore, if Parliament did in fact make incompatible laws, the courts had to read and apply the legislation compatibly as far as possible. Lower courts had to comply with the law as found, but higher courts had to make a declaration of incompatibility.

She went on to say that such declarations have proved themselves to be powerful incentives to the executive and legislature to put things right. The purpose of such human rights instruments is to place limits on the powers of a democratically elected Parliament in order to protect fundamental rights and freedoms, and minorities, against the will of those who are taken to represent the majority.

> 'Democracy is the will of the people, but the people may not will to invade those rights and freedoms which are fundamental to democracy itself. To qualify as such a fundamental right, a freedom must be something more than the freedom to do as we please, whether alone or in company with others.'

The case was a challenge by the Countryside Alliance and others to the Hunting Act 2004 seeking judicial review by way of a declaration that the 2004 Act infringed and was incompatible with their rights under Arts 8, 11 and 14 of the ECHR and Art 1 of the First Protocol. The claim was comprehensively dismissed by the Divisional Court, Court of Appeal and House of Lords although their lordships had a variety of opinions as to why in each case.

Baroness Hale again had views on how to deal with the question of compatibility in another recent case *Secretary of State for the Home Department v MB; Same v AF* [2007] UKHL 46; [2007] 3 WLR 681 involving non-derogating control orders made by the Secretary of State, the result of which was that both cases were remitted to the High Court for further consideration. She said that in interpreting the Act compatibly, the Court was doing its best to make it work and this gave the maximum incentive to all the parties, the judge and the Home Secretary to obtain procedural justice.

3.6.2 Proceedings under s 7

Section 7 allows the victim of an act by a public authority which has infringed Convention rights as provided for by s 6 to bring appropriate court or tribunal proceedings and to rely on Convention rights with a limitation period basically of one year. This can be longer if the court or tribunal think it fair and subject to a stricter time limit if any particular procedure requires such limitation. Nothing in the Act is to be taken as having created any criminal offence. Rules governing incidental jurisdictional matters have been made by the Lord Chancellor.

The effect of these provisions is that the Act does three substantive things to help victims in that it:

- creates the right to take action for breach of statutory duty
- provides a specific head of illegality to use in judicial review proceedings
- provides a defence for an individual in an action brought by a public authority.

3.6.3 Judicial remedies s 8

Where a public authority has been found to have acted unlawfully by the court, s 8(1) authorises it to make such relief, remedy or order as it considers just and appropriate. There is power to award damages, although this can only be done by a court which already has the power to do this or to order payment of compensation in civil proceedings by virtue of s 8(2).

Awarding damages is not particularly encouraged as the section goes on to say that it should only be done if it is necessary to afford 'just satisfaction', taking into account any other relief or remedy granted and the consequences of any decisions that have been made (s 8(3)). References to 'court' are also to apply to tribunals.

3.7 Remedial action s 10

Section 4 enabled higher courts to make declarations of incompatibility with the Convention if they decided that domestic law did not comply with ECHR criteria. Ministers must then consider what, if anything, they are going to do about it, as soon as rights of appeal have been exhausted or abandoned.

'10(2) If a Minister of the Crown considers that there are compelling reasons for proceeding under this section, he may by order make such amendments to the legislation as he considers necessary to remove the incompatibility.'

The following table, adapted from Department of Constitutional Affairs' online information (details are given at the end of the chapter) provides an indication of how s 10 operates.

Case	Incompatibility	Section 10 remedy
R (on the application of H) v Mental Health Review Tribunal etc [2001] EWCA Civ 415	Mental Health Act 1983 ss 72 and 73 were incompatible with Arts 5(1) and (4) as they did not require a Tribunal to discharge a patient if it was not shown that he suffered from mental disorder requiring detention	Legislation amended by Mental Health Act 1983 (Remedial) Order 2001 (SI 2001 No 3712)
McR's Application for judicial review (Kerr J) [2003] NI 1	Offences Against the Person Act 1861 s 62 (attempted buggery then still applicable in Northern Ireland) was incompatible with Art 8 as it interfered with consensual sexual behaviour between individuals	Sexual Offences Act 2003 repealed s 62 as it applied in Northern Ireland
International Transport Roth GmbH v Home Secretary [2002] EWCA Civ 158	Immigration and Asylum Act 1999 Pt II penalty scheme incompatible with Art 6 as fixed nature of penalties removed the right to have decision made by independent tribunal and also offended property rights	Nationality, Immigration and Asylum Act 2002 s 125 and Sched 8 amended the 1999 statute

Figure 3.5 Remedying incompatibility

3.8 Other rights and proceedings

The Human Rights Act next contains three sections whose purpose is to safeguard existing human rights. Section 12 refers to freedom of expression and s 13 to freedom of thought, conscience and religion.

'11 A person's reliance on a Convention right does not restrict –
(a) any other right or freedom conferred on him by or under any law having effect in any part of the United Kingdom; or
(b) his right to make any claim or bring any proceedings which he could make or bring apart from ss 7 to 9.'

Section 11 refers to 'any law', so the intention is to safeguard all rights and freedoms whatever their origin and to make it clear that they are not restricted, constrained or reduced by the Act. Any right or freedom previously possessed and any pre-existing right to make a claim or bring proceedings are protected.

3.8.1 Freedom of expression s 12

When a court is considering whether or not to grant any relief which might affect the exercise of the Convention right of freedom of expression, the person affected should be present or represented in court. If he is not, no relief is to be granted unless all practicable steps have been taken to notify him or there are compelling reasons why he should not be notified.

If the question at issue concerns restraint of publication prior to trial, no such restraint is to be allowed unless the court concludes that the applicant is likely to establish that this will be the outcome. It operates as a presumption against gagging in such circumstances. The court is also required to pay particular regard and attention to the Convention's protective measures for freedom of expression where the materials in question appear to be journalistic, literary or artistic. The availability of the material to the public, and any relevant privacy code, must also be considered.

3.8.2 Freedom of thought, conscience and religion s 13

This section adds emphasis to the importance of Art 9. If a court or tribunal's determination of any question arising under the Act might affect the exercise by a religious organisation or its members of the Convention Art 9 freedom, it must have 'particular regard to the importance of that right'.

3.9 Derogations and reservations

Derogations and reservations are dealt with in ss 14–17 of the Act. The statutory definitions of each of these are as follows:

'14. – (1) In this Act 'designated derogation' means any derogation by the UK from an Article of the Convention, or of any protocol to the Convention, which is designated for the purposes of this Act in an order made by the Secretary of State.

15. – (1) In this Act 'designated reservation' means –

(a) the United Kingdom's reservation to Article 2 of the First Protocol to the Convention; and

(b) any other reservation by the United Kingdom to an Article of the Convention, or of any protocol to the Convention, which is designated for the purposes of this Act in an order made by the secretary of State.'

3.9.1 Derogation

Derogation allows a State not to comply with the Convention in a strictly limited way in the event of a public emergency that threatens the country, or war, although not at the expense of its other international obligations. If the government considers derogation to be necessary, it must lodge a declaration with the Secretary of the Council of Europe and keep him informed until the derogation can be removed.

However, some of the Convention's provisions are so fundamental that, whatever the circumstances, states are not allowed to derogate despite s 14. The first of these is the Art 2 right to life, except where the deaths occur because of lawful acts of war. Derogation from the prohibitions against torture (Art 3) or slavery (Art 4(1)) are not permissible, nor is it acceptable to impose retrospective criminal penalties (Art 7). No derogation or reservation can be made with regard to the death penalty (Sixth Protocol) apart from the limited exception in time of war.

When the Human Rights Act was implemented in October 2000 the UK's derogations were contained in Sched 3 Pt 1 of the Act and referred to notifications of 23rd December 1988 and 23rd March 1989, both relating to terrorism matters arising from the Irish troubles and specifically as a result of the ECHR's decision in *Brogan v United Kingdom* (1988) 11 EHRR 117. The derogation was subsequently unsuccessfully challenged in *Brannigan and McBride v United Kingdom* (1993) 17 EHRR 539. The provision was replaced by the Terrorism Act 2000 so the derogation was withdrawn.

Derogation by statutory instrument

Following the 9/11 terrorist attacks on the New York World Trade Center twin towers, the government gave notice of derogation from Art 5(1) as they believed the American outrage gave rise to a state of emergency in the UK, and in response they enacted the Anti-terrorism, Crime and Security Act 2001. Implementing Pt 4 of the Act they detained a number of terrorist suspects in Belmarsh Prison without charge or trial. The derogation was implemented by The Human Rights Act 1998 (Designated Derogation) Order 2001 No 3644.

The nine-member Appellate Committee of the House of Lords ruled by a majority of 8:1 that this was illegal on 16th December 2004 in *A (FC) and others (FC) (Appellants) v Secretary of*

State for the Home Department (Respondent); X (FC) and another (FC) (Appellants) v Secretary of State for the Home Department (Respondent) [2004] UKHL 56 on appeal from: [2002] EWCA Civ 1502. The Court of Appeal had upheld the Home Office's position. Despite having lost the case, the government kept the suspects in custody until April 2005, when they introduced further legislation providing for control orders.

Lord Hoffmann summarised the importance of the issues at stake:

> 'The real threat to the life of the nation, in the sense of a people living in accordance with its traditional laws and political values, comes not from terrorism but from laws such as these. That is the true measure of what terrorism may achieve. It is for Parliament to decide whether to give the terrorists such a victory.'

In 2005 the government withdrew its derogation by the Human Rights Act 1998 (Amendment) Order 2005 (SI 2005 No 1071).

The issue of derogation has more recently been brought to the fore by the provisions of the Prevention of Terrorism Act 2005 s 1 which authorises control orders to be made in respect of persons believed by the Home Secretary to pose a terrorist risk to the public. Two types of order are envisaged:

- non-derogating orders, effective for 12 months, made by the Home Secretary
- more draconian orders amounting to deprivation of liberty that would contravene Art 5 of the ECHR, which are derogating orders.

Secretary of State for the Home Department v JJ and others [2008] 1 AC 385; [2007] 3 WLR 642

The Home Secretary appealed to the House of Lords against the dismissal of his appeal by the Court of Appeal against the High Court decision that the obligations imposed on six suspected terrorists by non-derogating control orders under the Prevention of Terrorism Act 2005 violated the right to liberty and security provisions of Art 5 of the ECHR. None of the cases fell within the Arts 5(1)(a)–(f) exemptions.

The defendants were all confined to one-bedroom flats for 18 hours a day with further restrictions on their visitors and movements when outside. They were electronically tagged and subject to spot searches. At first instance and in the Court of Appeal it was found that the intrusive totality of the restrictions in effect amounted to detention in an open prison.

The House of Lords dismissed the Home Secretary's appeal, Lords Hoffman and Carswell dissenting. The Home Secretary had no power to make an order that was incompatible with Art 5.

Thus, if the orders were intended to be derogating orders they would have to be made by a judge and prior derogation would be needed under the Human Rights Act 1998 s 14 and in accordance with the provisions of Art 15 of the ECHR. What the Home Secretary had attempted to do was to make non-derogating orders but he had couched them in such wide and restrictive terms that he had contravened Art 5 of the Convention.

The Art 15 test was satisfied in the earlier case of *Ireland v United Kingdom* (1978) 2 EHRR 25 in light of the long-term IRA threat to UK security but the role of the Court when Art 15 was challenged was considered. Contracting States have responsibility for the life of their respective nations and must determine how far it is necessary to go to overcome emergencies. The national authorities are in principle in a better position than the international judge (and presumably also than domestic judges) to decide on the:

(a) existence of the emergency, and

(b) nature and scope of derogations needed to avert it.

Even so, State power is limited and it is the Court that bears responsibility under Art 19 to ensure the observance of the States' engagements. In short, the 'domestic margin of appreciation is . . . accompanied by a European supervision'. As noted the discussion was revisited in *Brannigan and McBride v United Kingdom* (1993) 17 EHRR 539 and at para 43 the Court said that 'in exercising its supervision the Court must give appropriate weight to such relevant factors as the nature of the rights affected by the derogation, the circumstances leading to, and the duration of, the emergency situation.'

3.9.2 Reservations

Art 57 of the ECHR allows any State to make a reservation on signature or ratification of the Convention in respect of any particular of its domestic law that did not conform to Convention requirements, although they have to be specific and reservations of a general nature are not permitted. In the Human Rights Act s 15 defines designated reservations, and the actual terms of the First Protocol reservation made in 1952 are set out in Sched 3 Pt II:

'At the time of signing the present (First) Protocol, I declare that, in view of certain provisions of the Education Acts in the United Kingdom, the principle affirmed in the second sentence of Article 2 is accepted by the United Kingdom only so far as it is compatible with the provision of efficient instruction and training, and the avoidance of unreasonable expenditure. Dated 20 March 1952. Made by the United Kingdom Permanent Representative to the Council of Europe.'

The purpose of this reservation was to ensure that in fulfilling its obligations to provide education the UK would not be placed in a position where the expenditure required to do so became more than the government wished or was able to commit.

3.10 Judges of the European Court of Human Rights

Section 18 defines the meaning of 'judicial office' for the purposes of the Act and provides that the holder of a judicial office may become a judge of the European Court of Human Rights without being required to relinquish his domestic judicial office. For England and Wales those entitled are Lords Justices of Appeal, Justices of the High Court and Circuit Judges. For Scotland they comprise judges of the Court of Session and sheriffs, and for Northern Ireland Lords Justices of Appeal, High Court and County Court Judges. The section does not authorise Lords of Appeal in Ordinary to be appointed to the European Court of Human Rights. Any judge appointed is not required to perform the duties of his domestic judicial office while serving in Europe.

The first and current UK judge appointed to the European Court is Sir Nicholas Bratza, who was appointed both as a High Court Judge and the UK's judge in the European Court of Human Rights in 1998. He was re-elected again in 2001 and 2004 as one of the five section presidents and since January 2007 has been the European Court's vice-president.

3.11 Parliamentary procedure

Section 19 contains the important provision that Ministers of the Crown in charge of Bills in either House of Parliament must, prior to the Second Reading of the Bill, make a statement to the relevant House. This will usually be 'a statement of compatibility' under s 19(1)(a) to the effect that in the minister's view the provisions of the Bill are compatible with Convention rights. If he is not able to do this he is required to make a statement under s 19(1)(b) to the effect that although he is unable to make a statement of compatibility the government nevertheless wishes the House to proceed with the Bill. No doubt any such statement would be heavily fortified with good reasons why not. Section 19(2) says that the statement must be in writing and be published in such manner as the minister making it considers appropriate.

Lord Woolf believed that this provided strong encouragement for government to ensure that future legislation would conform to the Convention rights. In a speech to the British Academy on 15th October 2002 entitled 'Human Rights: Have the Public Benefited?' he made the point that:

> 'It is important also to bear in mind the effect of the HRA on the legislative process and the actions of the executive and other public bodies. When legislation is introduced to Parliament, the Minister is required to make a statement of compatibility. This assurance to Parliament is not given lightly. In the determination of policy and in the drafting of the bill, considerable care will be exercised to identify and resolve any possible human rights issues. In the

parliamentary process the bill will be scrutinised by the Human Rights Committee of both Houses of Parliament. In addition, in every government department there has been intense focus on the need to provide ongoing training in human rights for civil servants. A human rights culture is managing to survive even in the most dust-ridden corridors of Whitehall.'

3.12 Implementation

The supplemental provisions under s 20 authorise ministers including the Lord Chancellor to make orders under the Act by statutory instrument which has to be laid before Parliament for approval. Section 21 is the interpretation section and the short title, commencement, application and extent provisions are in s 22 and confirm that the Act binds the Crown.

3.13 Human rights in the UK

The Human Rights Act has not provided the UK with a written constitution, nor has it much altered the constitutional position. Either of those propositions would be likely to involve a variety of significant other matters such as parliamentary and electoral reform, entrenchment of fundamental principles, crystallisation of constitutional conventions and much else. What it has done, however, is provide a much clearer set of identifiable rights and freedoms which are developing the civil liberties agenda and upon which a fertile body of human rights case law is being constructed.

It has not proved to be the panacea that some people wanted, nor the disaster that others expected. It does bring into the sphere of English law a wide range of continental wisdom that enriches domestic law. A mark of its success is that when most people think of human rights nowadays, they have in mind the rights and freedoms provided by the Convention and an idea that if needs be they can now make these rights stick in the local court.

What they may often overlook is that with rights and freedoms come duties and obligations. Almost nothing in the Convention apart from the prohibitions on torture and slavery is unqualified, and the ongoing development of European and domestic case law continually demonstrates changing attitudes within jurisdictions and considerable variations in the interpretation of the Convention between states. This can be seen, for example, in matters involving banning corporal punishment, marriage, civil partnerships, gender transfer and freedom of thought in a religious context.

ACTIVITY

Self-test questions

1. Which substantive Convention right is omitted from the Human Rights Act and why?

2. What four important rights are dealt with in Protocols 1 and 13?

3. What statutory interpretative method is applied by the judiciary to the ECHR and how does it operate?

4. Which six UK courts have the authority to deal with declarations of incompatibility under s 4?

5. Explain with examples what is meant by a 'public authority'?

6. What are the *practical* rights, remedies and procedures to which the Act gives rise for individuals?

7. What remedial action needs to be taken if the court makes a declaration of incompatibility?

8. What has the Act to say about freedom of expression and why is this different from other rights and freedoms?

9. Why is freedom of thought, conscience and religion specifically addressed by the Act?

10. Explain the differences between reservations and derogations, with examples of each.

ACTIVITY

Essay practice

Using the Human Rights Study Skills at the beginning of this book prepare an answer plan for the following title:

Discuss the arguments for and against 'bringing rights home' into UK domestic law and analyse how successful the process has been in light of twenty-first century case law.

KEY FACTS

1	The European Convention on Human Rights came into force in 1953
2	From 1966 onwards UK individuals could petition the European Commission for relief but only with the consent of the government
3	Traditional civil liberties are allied to other constitutional rights but over several decades were sometimes found to be wanting in human rights terms
4	Increased lobbying gradually persuaded government to resolve to 'bring rights home', ie to make them enforceable under domestic law within the UK when all other remedies had been exhausted
5	The Human Rights Act 1998 gave UK subjects access to the European Court of Human Rights from October 2000
6	The Act comprises 22 sections and four schedules and should be interpreted in a purposive manner
7	Ministers introducing all new legislation must certify it conforms to Convention requirements or provide an explanation as to why it does not do so
8	Senior judges have the power to make declarations of incompatibility regarding non-conforming law which effectively forces government to amend the law
9	Public authorities are required and can be obliged to act in conformity with the Convention
10	The Act has proved to be neither the disaster that opponents forecast nor the panacea for which supporters hoped

Useful resources

Office of Public Sector Information text of the HRA 1998:
    http://www.opsi.gov.uk/ACTS/acts1998/ukpga_19980042_en_1.
Department of Constitutional Affairs Study Guide to the HRA, 3rd edn 2006:
    http://www.dca.gov.uk/peoples-rights/human-rights/pdf/act-studyguide.pdf.
Ministry of Justice human rights links: http://www.justice.gov.uk/whatwedo/humanrights.htm.
Department of Constitutional Affairs: Table of s 4 incompatibility cases:
http://www.dca.gov.uk/peoples-rights/human-rights/pdf/decl-incompat-tabl.pdf.

Further reading

Amos, M, *Human Rights Law* (Hart Publishing, Oxford and Portland, Oregon, 2006), Pt I, Chapters 1–6.

Feldman, D, 'Deprivation of liberty in anti-terrorism law', CLJ 2008, 67(1), 4–8.

Fenwick, H, *Civil Liberties and Human Rights* (Routledge-Cavendish, Abingdon, 4th edn, 2007) Part I, Chapters 1–4.

Foster, S, *Human Rights and Civil Liberties* (Pearson Longman, London, 2nd edn, 2008) Part I, Chapters 1–3.

Hoffman, D and Rowe, J, QC, *Human Rights in the UK: An Introduction to the Human Rights Act 1998* (Pearson Longman, London, 2nd edn, 2006) Chapters 1–7.

chapter

4 RIGHT TO LIFE ■

AIMS AND OBJECTIVES

This chapter examines the different contexts in which the right to life has to be considered and aims to do the following:

- Identify the main Convention provisions that apply

- Examine Art 2 of the ECHR and the defences

- Consider UK domestic and European case law

- Examine the requirements for investigation of mistakes

- Explore deaths that occur as a result of war

- Examine the implications that arise when deaths occur whilst the deceased is in custody

- Consider the parameters of the right to life and whether there is a right to die

- Examine self-defence and its impact on Art 2.

4.1 Introduction

4.1.1 Global conventions

Art 3 of the Universal Declaration of Human Rights (1948) (UDHR) declares that everyone has the right to life, liberty and the security of person. Liberty and security of person are dealt with in Chapter 7. Pt III Art 6 of the International Covenant on Civil and Political Rights (1966) (ICCPR) amplifies the UDHR statement by saying that every human being has the inherent right to life which shall be protected by law so that no one shall be arbitrarily deprived of his life. Art 6 goes on to refer to the death penalty, the illegality of imposing it on anyone under 18 years of age, and the crime of genocide.

The Proclamation by the UN General Assembly in resolution 1386 (XIV) of 20th November 1959 in the third and fifth recitals identifies the kinds of duty owed to children:

 ' . . . the child, by reason of his physical and mental immaturity, needs special safeguards and care, including appropriate legal protection, before as well as after birth . . . mankind owes to the child the best it has to give.'

Thirty years later in Art 6(1) the Convention on the Rights of the Child stated that all children should be recognised by States as having the inherent right to life. It is the most widely adopted of all international conventions although the USA takes the view that the text protecting children goes 'too far when it asserts entitlements based on economic, social and cultural rights'. The other state that has not adopted this Convention is Somalia.

None of these instruments define what 'life' means or whether and, if so, to what extent it implies some quality applicable to life; nor does the ECHR. There is much to consider about quality of life in relation to other provisions – prohibitions on torture and inhuman treatment, slavery and discrimination, rights to and freedom of thought, conscience, religion, association, assembly and so on; but even disregarding any qualitative element, scientific, religious and legal views vary as to when life begins and ends.

The case law, domestic and European, demonstrates the wide scope of this subject, from abortion and separation of conjoined twins to euthanasia and removal of life support from persons in a persistent vegetative state (PVS). Other aspects involve self-defence, deprivation of life in custody, war and circumstances where states may or may not have failed in their positive duty to create and permit conditions where life can flourish. As suggested above, sometimes philosophical and ethical issues arise such as what is the precise moment at which life begins or ends, which is an important consideration in modern medical research and practice.

4.1.2 The European Convention

The right to life is contained in Art 2 of the ECHR as follows:

'2(1) Everyone's right to life shall be protected by law. No-one shall be deprived of his life intentionally save in the execution of a sentence of a court following his conviction of a crime for which this penalty is provided by law.

2(2) Deprivation of life shall not be regarded as inflicted in contravention of this Article when it results from the use of force which is no more than absolutely necessary in:

(a) defence of any person from unlawful violence;
(b) order to effect a lawful arrest or to prevent the escape of a person lawfully detained;
(c) action lawfully taken for the purpose of quelling a riot or insurrection.'

The right to life is fundamental to all human rights. Capital punishment, often compounded by torture, has been considered acceptable and normal by most societies throughout human history, yet recognition that it should be abolished is central to modern human rights. There are a number of reasons for this, from the practical if counter-intuitive one that it is largely ineffective as a deterrent, to the moral one that it is wrong to take human life even if that life is flawed or dangerous. There is also the vital point that mistakes are made, and the rights position is that it is unacceptable for just one innocent person to be wrongly executed even if that might mean that guilty people go free.

Stated positively, acknowledgement of transgression and rehabilitation should underpin human rights, even where punishment is essential. This is not to be taken as an assertion that the right to life is actually respected by many individuals, societies or governments, and it may well be the case that a majority of people would in fact prefer to retain the death penalty.

However, the implications of this right are that states have a positive duty to protect human life, which also requires providing the means and fostering the conditions which allow life to flourish. Adequate procedures should be put in place by states to enable this to happen. One of the complaints in the English Bill of Rights (1688) was that 'illegal and cruel punishments' had been inflicted by the Crown and this was taken up in America by the Eighth Amendment to the United States Constitution in 1791, part of the American Bill of Rights, which prohibits the Federal Government from imposing excessive bail and fines, and cruel and unusual punishments.

4.1.3 Abolition of the death penalty

Although capital punishment is still carried out in the USA, Saudi Arabia, China and other parts of the world, abolition by many other states increasingly means that the death penalty may come to be regarded as 'cruel and unusual'. Thus, in Europe the exception dealt with in the second sentence of Art 2(1) has been overtaken by events. Protocol 6 abolishes the death penalty in peacetime and has been signed by all 47 Member States of the Council of Europe and ratified by all except Russia, where a moratorium on its use is in place. Protocol 13 abolishes the death penalty completely and this has been ratified by 33 states. If European rights *mores* gradually prevail, so recognition of the supreme value of human life should spread to other parts of the world where life is currently held in cheap regard.

Use of this punishment by the state and public attitudes towards capital punishment provide good examples of why human life should be valued, but the right to life extends far beyond those issues, as indicated in the introductory paragraph of this chapter. Later discussion will explore this further together with related aspects such as claims of fear of death that may also come within Art 3. States have positive obligations to protect life and by the very nature of the right to life many claims are in fact brought by relatives of people who have died or been killed.

4.1.4 Preliminary considerations

(a) Prerequisite to membership

The Council of Europe has a policy of requiring all new members to undertake to abolish capital punishment as a condition of acceptance into membership, and Member States are not allowed to extradite anyone to another state where that person might be subject to the death penalty, for example to China, the USA or Saudi Arabia, unless a prior undertaking is obtained from the relevant government that the death penalty will not be imposed.

In *Soering v United Kingdom* (1989) 11 EHRR 439 where a West German national alleged that the Home Secretary's decision to extradite him to Virginia on a capital murder charge would

breach his ECHR rights, the case was not argued on Art 2 but on Art 3 (torture or inhuman treatment) because if sentenced to death he would be exposed to the so-called 'death row phenomenon', although in the event the only breach found in this case was of the Art 13 right to an effective remedy.

(b) Scope of Article 2

Article 2(2) stipulates a number of instances where contravention will not occur if no more force causing death is used than absolutely necessary. The use of the adverb 'absolutely' indicates in effect that there should be no alternative available. Self-defence and defence of others by anyone is the first exception, and effecting lawful arrest or preventing unlawful escape is the second. The third is lawful action to deal with public unrest. Often it is the actions of the police, military, prison officers and similar state officials that are called into question, although other types of life preservation or termination questions have also arisen for adjudication under Art 2 such as abortion and whether there is a concomitant right to die.

(c) Case law

CASE EXAMPLE

LCB v United Kingdom (1998) 27 EHRR 212

The unusual case of *LCB v United Kingdom* was too problematical for the applicant to prove violation of Art 2. Her father was in the RAF and present on Christmas Island during the 1957–8 nuclear tests, and had helped to clear the site afterwards. She was born in 1966 but in 1970 developed leukaemia and claimed that if warning had been given to her about her father's exposure to radiation, more timely pre- and post-natal monitoring might have led to earlier diagnosis and treatment.

However, it was held unanimously that:

(1) The Court had no jurisdiction to consider the applicant's complaint under Art 2 of ECHR concerning the State's failure to monitor the extent of her father's exposure to radiation on Christmas Island

(2) There had been no breach of Art 2 of ECHR in relation to the State's failure to advise the applicant's parents and monitor her health prior to her diagnosis with leukaemia

It was also found that there had been no breach of Art 3 (prohibition of torture, inhuman or degrading treatment) and the Court had no jurisdiction to consider the applicant's complaints concerning the State's failure to create individual dose records of

CONTINUED ▸

her father's exposure to radiation and the withholding of contemporaneous records of levels of radiation on Christmas Island.

The Court's reasoning

The Court's ability to consider the applicant's contentions in this case was limited by the fact that she had not raised the question of the State's failure to monitor the extent of her father's exposure to radiation before the Commission, and she was not able to raise new issues before the Court. A further problem was that her father's exposure had occurred in 1958 prior to the UK's Arts 25 and 46 Declarations of 14th January 1966. The ECHR itself had been ratified by the UK on 8th March 1951, whilst the Declaration under Art 25 recognised the competence of the European Commission of Human Rights to receive individual petitions, and under Art 46 the compulsory jurisdiction of the European Court of Human Rights.

As there was no question here that the State had intentionally done anything to deprive the applicant of her right to life, her case hinged on whether sufficient and appropriate steps had been taken to protect those (including her father) within its jurisdiction. There was a shortfall of evidence about radiation dosage levels at the time of the nuclear tests, insufficient to satisfy the Court that there was a causal link between her father's exposure to radiation and his subsequently conceived daughter's leukaemia. Indeed, in 1993 French J had found in *Reay and Hope v British Nuclear Fuels Plc* [1994] Env LR 320 after considering expert evidence that 'the scales tilted decisively' in favour of a finding that there was no such causal link.

The European Court also found that it was uncertain whether monitoring the claimant's health *in utero* and after her birth would have resulted in earlier diagnosis and treatment. Given all the information available to the State at the appropriate time and to the Court at the hearing, there had been no violation of Art 2 as it had not been established that the State could have been expected of its own volition to notify the applicant's parents or to take any other special action in relation to her.

It is worth mentioning that another case in the following year, also based on exposure to nuclear testing but making complaint under Arts 6, 8 and 13, also failed (*McGinley and Egan v United Kingdom* (1999) 27 EHRR 1).

Many of the cases involving the UK Government arise out of the Northern Ireland troubles, one of the most important being *McCann and others v United Kingdom*.

under Art 2 so the application was manifestly ill-founded within the meaning of Art 27(2) of the Convention. The exception of death being caused whilst attempting to effect lawful arrest was successfully pleaded and the force used was not disproportionate.

The test of necessity

The Commission said that this includes an assessment of whether the interference was proportionate to the legitimate aim pursued. Qualification of the word 'necessary' by the adverb 'absolutely' indicated that a stricter and more compelling test of necessity was required than for other ECHR provisions (where limitations are measured as being 'prescribed by law and necessary in a democratic society in the public interest by reference to such factors as public order, health or morals, or the protection of the rights and freedoms of others', as, for example, in the Art 9 provisions relating to freedom of thought, conscience and religion).

In particular the Commission considered that ' . . . Article 2(2) permits the use of force for the purposes enumerated in sub-paragraphs (a), (b) and (c) subject to the requirement that the force used is strictly proportionate to the achievement of the permitted purpose. In assessing whether the use of force is strictly proportionate, regard must be had to the nature of the aim pursued, the dangers to life and limb inherent in the situation and the degree of the risk that the force employed might result in loss of life. The Commission's examination must have due regard to all the relevant circumstances surrounding the deprivation of life'.

The UK judge had concluded that the soldiers' intention in firing at the car had twofold objectives of preventing crime and attempting to effect lawful arrest. That conclusion had been supported by the judge having heard all the evidence, including that of the other occupants of the car as well as the soldiers, and had addressed the issue of whether sufficient consideration had been given by the soldiers to the likelihood that persons other than terrorists might be attempting to breach the roadblock. The way the car had been driven put the soldiers at risk, and the Commission was able to conclude that the balance here fell in favour of the UK authorities and against the joyriders so as to allow a finding of non-violation of Art 2.

Perhaps this case should have been discussed under the following heading of investigation of mistakes, but the evidence available in *Kelly v United Kingdom* did not really merit it being classified as a 'mistake'. Rather, the conclusion was that it was an unfortunate death caused, according to the evidence adduced, more by the recklessness of the victims than errors on the part of the security forces.

ACTIVITY

Self-test questions

1 What is the significance of the words 'absolutely necessary' in Art 2(2) as compared with the more commonly used words in a number of other articles 'prescribed by law and necessary in a democratic society'?

2 Given that the death penalty no longer operates in the UK or Europe, make brief notes as to how the defences contained in Art 2(2) applied or did not apply to the cases discussed so far in this chapter.

3 If the criteria applicable to Art 2 were those explained under the test of necessity in the case example just mentioned of *Kelly v UK*, how might the decisions have been different?

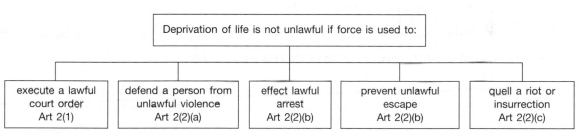

Figure 4.1 Lawful deprivation of life

4.2 Investigation of mistakes

Sometimes, however, the conduct of the authorities gives rise to rather more concern. Cases such as *McCann* which the army called 'Operation Flavius' and the more recent case of Jean Charles de Menezes mistakenly shot by the metropolitan police give rise to questions about effective training of state operatives, their rules of engagement, supervision of the actual operations and how investigations are conducted when something goes wrong.

In the de Menezes case, issues arose as to who was responsible or who should have taken responsibility for the way the operation was conducted and serious flaws were revealed. The investigation into the *McCann* case was found to be satisfactory in that there were comprehensive public inquest proceedings although public interest certificates had been issued at the inquest to allow the government to prevent aspects of SAS training from becoming generally known. It was not the actual killing of known terrorists by the SAS but the way the operation was handled that led to the adverse finding against the UK. The terrorists should have been arrested at an earlier stage rather than being allowed to continue to a point when the soldiers believed they were about to detonate a bomb. It would seem that, had the metropolitan police operation been better managed, the same point would have applied to de Menezes.

The following case examples are particularly pertinent to consideration of how the UK authorities deal with the aftermath of deaths caused by state operatives:

- *McKerr* illustrates the criteria applied to investigations by the European Court of Human Rights and found that there were shortfalls in UK practice.

- In *Jordan* the applicant won in the European Court but still failed to obtain the justice he wanted from the domestic legal system.

- In *McShane* the applicant also succeeded in the European Court, as did the victim's widow in *Finucane*.

Taken together, and bearing in mind that they are all recent decisions, there is some cause for concern that UK investigatory procedures are not entirely satisfactory and may sometimes be seriously defective.

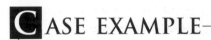

CASE EXAMPLE

McKerr v United Kingdom [2001] ECHR 28883/95

The European Court held unanimously that there had been a breach of Art 2 where the applicant's unarmed father had been shot and killed by RUC officers in Northern Ireland in 1982 but there had been no effective investigation into or redress for his death.

Three police officers had stood criminal trial for Gervaise McKerr's death with two other men killed in the same car, but evidence had been concealed during the trial and the officers had been acquitted, the inquest closing without reaching any conclusion. The deceased's son Jonathan McKerr was awarded £10,000 as just satisfaction in respect of the frustration, distress and anxiety suffered.

That was not the end of the matter, however. The government decided not to hold a further investigation, so Jonathan McKerr commenced judicial review proceedings seeking:

   (a) declarations that the continuing failure to provide an Art 2 compliant investigation was unlawful and in breach of s 6 of the Human Rights Act 1998
   (b) an order compelling the Secretary of State for Northern Ireland to conduct such an investigation; and
   (c) damages.

The application was dismissed at first instance but an appeal was allowed by the Northern Ireland Court of Appeal. The Secretary of State appealed to the House of Lords where he was upheld, as the Human Rights Act is not retrospective and the

CONTINUED ▸

previously unincorporated treaty created no rights or obligations in domestic law. Nor was there any overriding common law right to an effective investigation corresponding to the procedural right implicit in Art 2.

The relevant part of the European Court's judgment on the investigatory element of death at the hands of state actors said that the implication of Arts 1 and 2 of the ECHR was that there had to be a satisfactory 'effective official investigation'. The purpose of this was to secure that domestic laws ensuring the right to life were properly implemented along with accountability of the state officials at whose hands the victim had died.

The form of such investigation might vary but what was necessary was that the State took the initiative and did not leave it to relatives to have to try to find out what had happened. The investigation had to be independent and be able to reach a conclusion whether or not the force used was justified. There was a long list of deficiencies applicable in *McKerr* that led the European Court to conclude that the investigatory procedures were deficient and Art 2 violated.

CASE EXAMPLE

Re Jordan's Applications for Judicial Review [2004] **NICA 29**

Jordan and others v United Kingdom (2001) *The Times*, 18th May

This was an appeal to the Northern Ireland Court of Appeal by Jordan's father against refusal to grant judicial review of the Director of Public Prosecution's decision not to prosecute a police officer who had shot and killed Jordan's son in 1992. An inquest commenced in 1995 but was repeatedly adjourned. The Coroner's Court was in any event prevented under Northern Ireland's laws from allowing a jury to reach a verdict of unlawful killing. The applicant objected to this but was overruled by the coroner at a hearing that eventually took place in 2002.

Subsequent judicial review proceedings also failed but before Jordan's father could take his case to the Court of Appeal the House of Lords decided in a Northern Ireland case that Art 2 of the ECHR did not apply to cases occurring prior to implementation of the Human Rights Act 1998 (2nd October 2000).

At this hearing the Northern Ireland Appeal Court held *inter alia* that the jury was entitled to make findings and reach conclusions of fact on the central issue of whether the force used was unjustified, so a verdict of 'unlawful killing' was unnecessary.

CONTINUED ▸

Jordan's case, together with three similar ones including the previous case example *McKerr*, was considered by the European Court of Human Rights and judgments given on 4th May 2001 *sub nom Jordan v United Kingdom; McKerr v United Kingdom; Kelly and Others v United Kingdom; Shanaghan v United Kingdom*. In each case there was a finding that the Art 2 right to life had been violated. More pertinently from the point of view of investigatory procedures, the European Court made the following findings regarding procedural obligations under Art 2:

'In all four cases, the Court found it was not for it to specify in any detail which procedures the authorities should have adopted in providing for the proper examination of the circumstances of a killing by state agents . . . it could not be said that there should be one unified procedure providing for all requirements ... however, in all four cases, the available procedures had not struck the right balance.'

The Court went on to say that in all four cases it had 'identified shortcomings in transparency and effectiveness which ran counter to the purpose identified by the domestic courts of allaying suspicions and rumours . . . proper procedures for ensuring the accountability of agents of the state were indispensable in maintaining public confidence and meeting the legitimate concerns that could arise from the use of lethal force (and) lack of such procedures would only add fuel to fears of sinister motivations, as was illustrated, among other things, by submissions made concerning an alleged shoot-to-kill policy'.

The Court accordingly found, unanimously, that, in each of the four cases, 'there had been a failure to comply with the procedural obligation imposed by Article 2 and that there had been, in that respect, a violation of Article 2'.

It is interesting to note that despite winning the cases in the European Court, the eventual outcome was still deeply unsatisfactory to the complainants and demonstrated delays and procedural faults in UK practice dealing with deaths caused by state actors.

The other two case examples are also taken from Northern Ireland, and both showed that there were deficiencies in addressing circumstances of death.

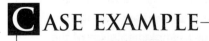 CASE EXAMPLE

McShane v United Kingdom [2002] ECHR 43290/98

The applicant was a US citizen whose husband had been killed when an Armoured Personnel Carrier ran over him during a major disturbance in Londonderry, but after an investigation it was decided that there was insufficient evidence to prosecute the driver.

CONTINUED ▶

As in *Jordan's* case the DPP refused to act because statements concerning the events were produced under conditions of anonymity.

After two-and-a-half years the case was sent to the coroner whose proceedings were adjourned. The applicant complained that her husband had been killed by the security forces and that she had no effective remedy in respect of his death.

The European Court of Human Rights held that although there was insufficient evidence concerning the circumstances surrounding the death to enable the Court to make a determination on the State's alleged responsibility, the fact that he was killed as a result of use of force to quell public disorder gave rise to an obligation on the part of the State to investigate the death.

There had, however, been a number of shortcomings in both the police investigation and inquest, including a lack of independence with the Royal Ulster Constabulary investigating a death in which one of their own officers had been involved, together with some dilatoriness. The failure to comply with Art 2 procedural requirements was therefore upheld.

ASE EXAMPLE

Finucane v United Kingdom [2003] ECHR 29178/95

Another recent high-profile Northern Ireland case was *Finucane v United Kingdom.* The facts and circumstances were complicated, if not Byzantine, but essentially Patrick Finucane was a lawyer who had represented individuals from both sides of the religious divide and in so doing had made a number of enemies. Mrs Finucane believed that her husband had received threats from RUC officers but in any event in 1989 he was shot and killed by two masked men who broke into their house and, although various members of the protestant Ulster Freedom Fighters (UFF) were interviewed, no one was charged.

Accusations abounded about the involvement of undercover agents and there was an inquiry by a British police officer who published a secret report whose findings were not made public. Eventually an earlier suspect called William Stobie was put on trial, acquitted and then murdered apparently by loyalist paramilitaries.

The investigatory requirement into deaths in such circumstances meant that independence should be not only hierarchical or institutional but also practical and effective, by leading to a clear conclusion whether the force used had been justified

CONTINUED ▸

(which clearly it was not in these circumstances) but also leading to the identification and punishment of those responsible. Here there had been a lack of independence in the initial RUC investigation and the inquest had failed to address serious and legitimate concerns of both the family and general public. The secret Stevens report, although carried out by an independent police officer from the Cambridgeshire Constabulary, had also lacked the necessary elements of public scrutiny and accessibility for the applicant. This was compounded by the DPP failing to provide any reasons why timely prosecutions had not been initiated.

Given all these factors there had been no effective investigation into her husband's death, which had occurred in circumstances giving rise to suspicions of collusion by the security forces with his killers, and it was held unanimously that there had been a breach of Art 2.

ACTIVITY

Self-assessment questions

1 What do you understand by the investigatory procedural requirements into the circumstances of death caused by state actors?

2 Which of the preceding case examples in your opinion best illustrates these requirements, and why?

3 What would be the attitude of the English court or the European Court of Human Rights to an extradition request from a US court in respect of someone charged with a capital offence?

4.3 Wartime deaths

The previous section examined deaths arising out of the Northern Ireland troubles which at their most serious amounted to what might be described as a low-level civil war despite the initial welcoming of British troops by the Catholic community. The emphasis was on procedural investigatory aspects because where the state itself has been actively involved in conflict, it is particularly important that fair and objective procedures be established and followed when complaints of irregularity or illegality are made.

This section considers death occurring in actual wartime conditions and examines the important case *R (on the application of Gentle) v Prime Minister* [2008] UKHL 20, which has some similarities in that executive decisions and the ways in which Parliament were persuaded to support them were being challenged. How does Art 2 operate in conventional wartime conditions, even if not formally declared, compared with times of serious internal disturbance?

Aspects of this question were tested in an application for judicial review by Rose Gentle and Beverley Clarke, the mothers of two soldiers killed in Iraq. They appealed against refusal of an application for judicial review of the Government's denial of an independent inquiry into the circumstances that led to the invasion of Iraq, but lost in the Court of Appeal and again in the House of Lords where their case was heard by nine Lords of Appeal in Ordinary (the usual number is five). The applicants considered there was a serious question to be answered as to whether the invasion was illegal under international law and contended that it was in the public interest that there should be full consideration by an independent inquiry.

Inquests were held, but although these investigated the circumstances surrounding the individual deaths, they did not provide and were not intended to provide a forum to examine wider questions about the war itself. Because the status of human rights is so important in context of war, a detailed analysis is given of the law lords' reasoning in this case.

CASE EXAMPLE

R (on the application of Gentle) v Prime Minister [2008] UKHL 20

At the Court of Appeal hearing, the claimants' case was that Art 2 of the ECHR imposed a substantive obligation on the Government to ensure that when servicemen were committed to military activities the legality under international law of those activities should first be established. They contended that this had not been done in the case of the Iraq war. If there was such a duty it would impose on the Government a procedural obligation under Art 2 to establish an effective and public investigation into the deaths, the purpose of which would be to address the question of whether the Government had taken reasonable steps to act within international law. The Court of Appeal dismissed the claim, as did the House of Lords.

The Court's reasoning

The implied procedural duty was 'parasitic' on the clearly stated substantive duty, and could not exist independently. The claimants therefore had to show that the facts supported an arguable case. Dealing with interpretation of Art 2 it was held that 'Article 2 was not a generalised provision protective of life, irrespective of any specific death or threat, or an absolute guarantee that nobody would be exposed by the state to situations where his life was in danger, whatever the circumstances'. Art 2 was not engaged merely by troops being put at risk, and the ECHR did not deal with this situation as it 'did not provide a suitable framework for resolving questions about the resort to war'. The UN Charter provided the relevant code and enforcement means, so it was nothing to do with Art 2 of the ECHR.

CONTINUED ▸

Other elements of the ratio were that the soldiers had been outside UK jurisdiction so Art 1 of the ECHR was not engaged, and the complaints were 'too remote from the true purview of Article 2'. They could not, therefore, establish a substantive arguable case under Art 2. Even had they been able to do so, 'they would have still been unable to establish a right, pursuant to Article 2, to a wide ranging inquiry such as they sought since the signatories to the Convention could not have contemplated binding themselves legally to establish an independent public inquiry into the process by which a decision had been made to commit a state's armed forces to war'.

Lord Bingham of Cornhill pointed out that Art 2 had never been applied to the process of deciding the legality of resorting to arms, for three very good reasons:

1   Lawfulness or otherwise has no bearing on the risk of fatalities
2   The draftsmen of the ECHR could never have intended Art 2 to apply to situations of war
3   The obligation to apply the Convention refers to everyone within the jurisdiction, which in the context of the ECHR means the individual territories of Member States.

Lord Hope of Craighead said at para 24:

'The question whether the invasion was lawful was, without doubt, of cardinal importance to the decision whether it was proper to commit British troops to the invasion. But it was no more relevant to the Article 2(1) Convention right of each individual than the question whether it had the approval of the Cabinet or of Parliament.'

The real reason behind the mothers' claims is indicated by Lord Roger of Earlsferry at para 35:

[The criticism of a Government legal adviser who had resigned] 'was that, despite having the requisite information and having initially considered that an invasion would be unlawful, for no good reason [the Attorney-General] had subsequently changed his mind – once, in giving his written opinion on 7 March, and, again, in his written statement on 17 March. In her view – because of points of which he was fully aware – the Attorney General's advice was quite simply wrong. The claimants also think that it was wrong. Therefore the inquiry which they really want is one that would investigate why – as they see it – the Attorney General changed his mind and gave the wrong advice, and how the Government came to go to war on the basis of that wrong advice.'

In his next para 36 Lord Roger also explains the legal position under international law that led to the war itself and to these challenges:

'Understandably, the claimants themselves do not distinguish between Trooper Clarke and Fusilier Gentle. But, in terms of international law, the cases are different. Trooper

CONTINUED ▸

> Clarke was killed shortly after the invasion in March 2003 when the Government relied on Security Council resolutions 678, 687 and 1441 as authority for using force against Iraq. By the time Fusilier Gentle was killed, the Security Council had adopted resolution 1511, authorising the creation of the multinational force, and resolution 1546, governing the position when sovereignty passed to the Iraqi Interim Government. There can be no doubt whatever that those resolutions gave authority for the operations of the multinational force, of which Fusilier Gentle was a member, on 28 June 2004. So it is Trooper Clarke's case which raises the issue about the legal situation at the time of the invasion.'

The effect of this case is that the Government cannot successfully be challenged in the courts on the legitimacy of the Iraq War. The decision whether or not to hold an inquiry, and if so when and on what terms, remains within the executive's prerogative. In this kind of matter the ultimate judgement will be a political one by the executive and not a legal one by the judiciary which leaves in question the role that Parliament did play in supporting the Government, and the probity of the information on which decisions were made.

4.3.1 Positive state obligation

The speeches in *Gentle* give an indication of how difficult it can be to impose a positive obligation on governments to protect life, although what was effectively a political challenge through the courts was not likely to succeed and the law lords were almost unanimously (with some dissent from Baroness Hale) of a mind about the outcome.

Nor is it easy in other circumstances to prove that states have positive obligations to take preventative measures to protect individuals whose lives may be at risk. This was examined by the European Court in *Osman v United Kingdom* (1998) 29 EHRR 245 which involved a teenage boy who had been stalked and threatened by a former teacher who eventually broke into the boy's house injuring him and killing his father. There had been previous warning signs with damage having been caused apparently by the killer, and Osman and his mother unsuccessfully brought negligence proceedings against the police.

The European Court held that there had been no breach of Art 2 because none of the incidents prior to the killing had been life-threatening and there was no evidence that the killer was mentally ill or prone to violence. Furthermore, there was no clear evidence that it was the eventual killer who had been responsible for the earlier incidents; so, although there is a general duty on the part of the state to take appropriate steps to protect its citizens, taking into consideration the operational choices that have to be made regarding resources and priorities, the obligation has to be interpreted so as not to impose disproportionate or impossible burdens on the authorities.

Sitting between the previous section on wartime deaths and the next section addressing deaths in custody is the case of *Regina (Al-Skeini and others) v Secretary of State for Defence (The Redress*

Trust and others intervening) [2007] UKHL 26; [2008] 1 AC 153. It was a case brought by relatives of five Iraqi civilians who had been killed by British troops before the Iraqi Interim Government had been formed, and a sixth case where the deceased Iraqi civilian had died after allegedly having been tortured whilst in custody at a British military base. In all the cases judicial review was sought of the Secretary of State's failure to conduct independent inquiries into the deaths or accept liability for what had happened.

The preliminary issue was whether the Human Rights Act 1998 applied outside the UK. With the exception of Lord Bingham of Cornhill's dissenting speech the House of Lords held that although legislation did not generally apply outside the UK, interpretation should nevertheless be consistent with comity of nations and international law as long as other states' sovereignty was not infringed. Section 6(1) contained no geographical limitation and applied only to UK public authorities but it would not be offensive to allow its remedies to be available to other states. The rights were therefore to be understood as applying wherever the UK had jurisdiction in respect of Art 1. In broad terms, therefore, on the preliminary issue the Act could apply.

Bearing in mind the constraints of construing ECHR jurisprudence in its European regional context it could only be applied outside that jurisdiction if 'a contracting state had such effective control over an area as to enable it to provide the full package of rights and freedoms guaranteed by s 1 of the Convention to everyone within that area'. That was the case within the British military base but not elsewhere, so jurisdiction in *Al-Skeini* extended to the sixth victim but not to the other five killed in the wider armed conflict.

The five cases would be dismissed but the sixth remitted to the Divisional Court for determination, Lord Bingham again dissenting.

4.4 Deaths in custody

Deaths occurring in custody perhaps better demonstrate the government's positive Art 2 duties but can give rise to particular difficulties as evidence may be difficult to obtain. In some parts of Europe problems have also occurred because of 'disappearances' of the kind that occurred under the Pinochet regime in Chile in the 1970s, and Turkey in particular has lost a number of such cases.

The House of Commons and House of Lords Joint Committee on Human Rights in their Third Report considered the question of deaths in custody and the obligations of the relevant public authorities in these circumstances in the following terms:

'16. Every unnatural death in custody presents a human rights issue. In this report, we examine the problem of deaths in custody in light of the human rights obligations of the institutions which compulsorily detain people and those which investigate deaths of people who are so detained. These institutions are subject to a number of obligations. Under the Human Rights Act 1998, the police and prison service are "public authorities" with obligations to comply with rights under the European Convention on Human Rights, including the right to life.

Private contractors operating prisons, immigration removal centres and mental health detention facilities are also considered to be public authorities when exercising powers of detention delegated to them by the state, and are therefore also required to comply with Convention rights. In international law, the state, in protecting people in its custody and in investigating deaths, has obligations to comply with international standards, including those under the European Convention on Human Rights, and United Nations human rights treaties.'

The report went on to say that the number of people who die in custody is extremely shocking (something over 100 a year for the UK in the early years of the present century), many of them are suicides, and it is within this context that the positive obligations of Art 2 are vital.

Fault on the part of the prison authorities sometimes leads to the murder of a prisoner, as in the case of Zahid Mubarek, killed by his racially motivated cell mate Robert Stewart at Feltham Young Offenders Institution in 2002. On 29th April 2004 the Home Secretary announced the establishment of a non-statutory inquiry into Zahid Mubarek's murder with interesting terms of reference:

'In the light of the House of Lords judg(e)ment in the case of *Regina v Secretary of State for the Home Department ex parte Amin*, to investigate and report to the Home Secretary on the death of Zahid Mubarek, and the events leading up to the attack on him, and make recommendations about the prevention of such attacks in the future, taking into account the investigations that have already taken place – in particular, those by the Prison Service and the Commission for Racial Equality.'

An extract from the Preface to the Inquiry seems to provide a fair summary of the circumstances:

'Shortly after the attack on Zahid, the police discovered that Stewart had strong racist views. They also learned that he had had a violent past while previously in custody, and that his mental health had been questioned. Much of that had been known to some of the prison officers at Feltham at the time. Not surprisingly, questions began to be asked about how he and Zahid had ended up in the same cell. How had Stewart come to share a cell with someone from an ethnic minority? What exactly had been known about Stewart? Had any information about him been passed to the wing? And had any assessment been carried out of the risk Stewart might have posed to any prisoner who shared a cell with him?

To its credit, the Prison Service never sought to deny that it had failed to fulfil its responsibility to look after Zahid while he had been in its care.'

Mubarek is not the only case where this happened. In *Edwards v United Kingdom* (2002) 35 EHRR 19 the applicants' son died after being attacked by a fellow prisoner. His family complained that the authorities had failed to protect their son's life and were responsible for his death. They contended that the investigation into his death was not adequate or effective, and the European Court upheld these claims and found that there had been a breach of Art 2. The assessment procedure of his mental state following arrest was defective and the prison screening procedures were ineffective. Edwards should have been in hospital rather than placed in a cell with a paranoid schizophrenic with a known history of mental illness and violence to others.

The killer in that case, Linford, pleaded guilty to manslaughter and as a result there was no witness evidence given at a criminal trial nor was there an inquest. There was an Inquiry at which the applicants were not represented and were thus unable to put questions to witnesses. That occurred in 1994 so the authorities seem to have done little, if anything, to improve their procedures when they came to deal with *Mubarek* in 2002 when it ought to have been clear to them that the killer Stewart was the one who needed to be isolated.

What this demonstrates is that when there is an investigation into a death in custody there should be an appropriate level of involvement on the part of the deceased's relatives, even where the state admits liability and the assailant has been convicted of murder. The question is to what extent lessons have been learned.

CASE EXAMPLE

R (on the application of Amin (Imtiaz)) v Secretary of State for the Home Department [2003] UKHL 51

The uncle of a young Asian offender, who had been murdered by his cell mate whilst in prison, appealed against the first instance decision (EWCA Civ 390) that the state had complied with this statutory duty under the Human Rights Act 1998 Sched I Pt I Art 2.

A police investigation had taken place to determine whether anyone should be prosecuted and an internal inquiry held by the prison service, as well as a coroner's inquest although that had been adjourned and not reopened. The Commission for Racial Equality had also conducted an investigation that made specific reference to the case; but what the uncle wanted was an independent public investigation in order to satisfy the state's obligations under Art 2.

The House of Lords allowed his appeal. Although the European Court had not prescribed a specific single investigatory process to be applied in all cases, there were clear minimum standards laid down that had to be met, whatever kind of investigation was thought to be appropriate, as per the cases *Edwards v United Kingdom* (2002) and *Jordan v United Kingdom* (2001) discussed earlier in this chapter, and here those requirements were not met.

CONTINUED ▶

The House of Lords held that the state's duty to secure the right to life guaranteed by Art 2 particularly required it to take steps to protect the lives of those involuntarily in its custody from the criminal acts of others. Where death occurred, the state's procedural obligation to carry out an effective investigation of the circumstances required, whatever mode of inquiry was adopted as a minimum standard of review, sufficient public scrutiny to secure accountability and an appropriate level of participation by the next-of-kin to safeguard their legitimate interests. None of the investigations undertaken satisfied the minimum threshold and there had been no inquest.

The Court of Appeal was reversed and Hooper J's order restored. The deficiencies were clearly documented:

> 'There had been no inquest to discharge the state's investigative duty. The police investigation raised many unanswered questions and could not discharge the state's duty. The Commission for Racial Equality's investigation was necessarily confined to race related issues and the murder trial had involved little exploration, as could sometimes occur, of wider issues concerning M's death. The prison service's internal inquiry had been conducted by an official who had not enjoyed institutional or hierarchical independence. That inquiry had been conducted in private and the consequent report had not been published ... In order to satisfy Art 2, a full public investigation was required with legal representation, provision of relevant material and opportunity to cross examine witnesses.'

Lord Bingham of Cornhill adopted the views of the European Court of Human Rights in *Osman v United Kingdom* (1998) 29 EHRR 245 to interpret the primary and secondary purposes of Art 2. There are certain well-defined circumstances where a positive obligation is placed on the authorities to take preventative operational measures to protect an individual whose life is at risk from the criminal acts of another individual.

There is added importance to ensuring effectiveness in the context of the right to life, and the procedural aspect includes the minimum requirement of a mechanism to enable public and independent scrutiny where a life has been taken.

How that is done will vary from one case to another. The particular vulnerability of persons in custody is one of the important factors, and it is also vital that the authorities act of their own volition and do not have to be chased and coerced by the victim's family.

Edwards v UK was a crucial precedent in this case because of its similarity to *Amin's* circumstances whereas other cases involved killing by agents of the state. The trial judge had been correct; the Court of Appeal were reversed; and *Edwards v UK* and *Jordan v UK* were applied.

ACTIVITY

	Statement	True	False
1	Art 6 of the ICCPR is largely consistent with the provisions of Art 2 of the ECHR		
2	Defence, self-defence, effecting lawful arrest, preventing unlawful escape and action to quell riots or insurrections are all valid reasons for causing death under Art 2 ECHR		
3	Carrying out the death penalty is authorised and permissible under Art 2(1) of the ECHR		
4	'Absolutely necessary' is a less demanding requirement under Art 2 ECHR than limitations 'prescribed by law and necessary in a democratic society in the public interest' required by other Arts		
5	Neither the 1966 right of individual petition nor the Human Rights Act 1998 are retrospective in effect		
6	The SAS squad who killed the team of IRA suspects in *McCann* were exonerated from blame for the deaths by the European Court		
7	*Gentle* demonstrated that judicial review and human rights challenges *via* the courts are ineffective ways of trying to hold the government to account for executive decisions on matters involving the national interest		
8	The case law shows that the system of investigating deaths in custody is robust and working well		
9	The Human Rights Act 1998 contains legal provisions governing domestic law and so can never operate outside the UK		
10	By the very nature of things, cases brought under the right to life provisions of Art 2 of the ECHR always have to be instituted by surviving relatives of the deceased		

4.5 Right to die?

4.5.1 Competency

The question of whether there exists a 'right to die' is considered here, which may at first sight seem odd but which is in fact closely connected with what is called 'autonomy' or control of one's own fate. By this is meant whether there is a right to die by means and at a time of one's own choosing. It will be seen that although there is no direct Convention right as such, in practical terms most individuals are able to choose to die by their own hand and to commit suicide is no longer a criminal act under English law, although helping a person to do so is. The question of competency arises where an individual with full mental faculties lacks the physical capacity to act. This is different from the position where the person in question is in a coma or PVS, as will become clear by comparing the cases of *Pretty* and *Bland*.

CASE EXAMPLE

Regina (Pretty) v Director of Public Prosecutions (Secretary of State for the Home Department intervening) [2001] UKHL 61 [2002] 1 AC 800

Pretty v United Kingdom (2002) 35 EHRR 1

The question of whether individuals have the right to die had to be faced by Diane Pretty. As a motor neurone sufferer she had passed beyond the stage where she could physically take her own life and although her mental faculties were unimpaired, she was terminally ill and knew that she would die in distress. She wished to be able to choose to die before reaching such dire straights, but would need assistance to do so. Killing herself would not have been a criminal action, but if her husband assisted her his actions would have been criminal under the Suicide Act 1961.

She therefore asked the Director of Public Prosecutions (DPP) to give an undertaking not to prosecute her husband for the offence of aiding and abetting the suicide of another contrary to s 2(1) of the Suicide Act 1961 should he help her. The DPP refused and she applied for judicial review of that decision, seeking amongst other things a declaration that s 2(1) was incompatible with her Convention rights. The Divisional Court refused the application and she appealed with leave of an Appellate Committee of the House of Lords (Lord Bingham of Cornhill, Lord Steyn and Lord Hope of Craighead) granted on 30th October 2001 directly to the House of Lords, arguing that the section was incompatible with Arts 2, 3, 8, 9 and/or 14 of the ECHR.

CONTINUED ▶

The Divisional Court itself had refused leave to appeal but certified that the following points of law of general public importance were involved in the decision:

'(1) Does the Director of Public Prosecutions have power under s 2(4) of the Suicide Act 1961 or otherwise not to consent to prosecute in advance of the relevant events occurring?

(2) If so, was he required in this case to undertake not to prosecute the claimant's husband if he were to assist her to commit suicide having regard to her rights under articles 2, 3, 8, 9 and 14 of the European Convention for the Protection of Human Rights and Fundamental Freedoms and his obligation to act compatibly with the Convention?

(3) If not, is s 2(1) of the Suicide Act 1961 incompatible with articles 2, 3, 8, 9 and/or 14 of the Convention?'

The Home Secretary intervened in both the Divisional Court and the House of Lords as an interested party.

It was argued for the claimant that Art 2 does not protect life but the right to life and its purpose was to protect individuals from third parties such as public authorities and the state. What the ECHR does not do is require that withholding of life-prolonging treatment should be criminalised or that citizens' lives have to be protected at all costs. Individuals can choose whether to live and can refuse life-saving or prolonging medical treatment. They can lawfully choose to commit suicide and Art 2 protects the right of self-determination in relation to life and death. The right to die is not the antithesis of the right to life but is its corollary, which means that positive obligations are imposed on the state and the DPP has a positive duty to provide the undertaking requested so that the claimant could control how and when she was to die.

The Secretary of State's counter arguments were adopted by the DPP. There was an absence of support in the case law and the negative obligation not to take a person's life intentionally was not overruled by any of the positive implied obligations. The *raison d'etre* of Art 2 is to guarantee a person's right to life, which means entitlement not to have one's life ended unnaturally by intentional human intervention. If there were a right to die it would extinguish the benefit on which it is supposedly based.

Whilst their lordships expressed great sympathy for Diane Pretty's dilemma, the appeal was dismissed and it was held that regarding Art 2 the starting point was the:

CONTINUED ▸

'language of the article itself, the thrust of which was to reflect the sanctity which, particularly in western eyes, attached to life. The article protected the right to life and prevented the deliberate taking of life except in very narrowly defined circumstances. It could not be interpreted as conferring a right to die or to enlist the aid of another in bringing about one's own death. Whatever the benefits which, in the view of many, attached to voluntary euthanasia, suicide, physician-assisted suicide and suicide assisted without the intervention of a physician, they were not benefits which derive protection from an Article framed to protect the sanctity of life.'

She subsequently took her case to the European Court of Human Rights, repeating her argument that the refusal of the DPP to grant her husband the desired immunity from prosecution if he assisted her in committing suicide, and the prohibition in domestic law on assisting suicide, infringed her rights under (*inter alia*) Art 2 of the ECHR but it was unanimously held that the application was inadmissible and that there had been no violation of Art 2.

Diane Pretty's medical condition deteriorated sharply three days after she was denied her application to the European Court. She died on Sunday 12th May 2002 in a hospice following 10 days of the severe breathing difficulties she had striven to avoid, her husband pointing out that this was exactly what she had foreseen and of which she had been afraid.

4.5.2 Insoluble dilemma

Despite the emotive ethical issues raised by this case the law remains unchanged but as the problem persists for a small minority of sufferers there is inevitably ongoing litigation. In October 2008 Debbie Purdy lost her High Court case in which she requested protection for her husband should he accompany her to a Swiss clinic for euthanasia. Aiding or abetting suicide is still punishable with up to 14 years' imprisonment. It emerged that over 100 UK citizens have attended the Swiss Dignitas Clinic, although no relative who has provided assistance has been prosecuted, indicating that the Government's policy is one of turning a blind eye to apparent breaches of the law. It was reported that the decision would be appealed but success is unlikely because, as Lord Justice Scott Baker pointed out, it is only Parliament that can change the law in such circumstances.

The absence of prosecutions for assisted suicide does not resolve the question because the uncertainty engendered leads to other threats of official action, such as local authority intervention and police investigations. The parents of a young rugby player who was paralysed during a training session in 2007 and who also died in the Swiss clinic were the subject of a

police investigation in 2008 which was to report to the DPP for a decision to be made as to whether they should be prosecuted. Eventually a decision was notified that no prosecution would be instituted. In November 2008 Herefordshire Primary Care Trust eventually dropped High Court proceedings after accepting that a 13-year-old girl had sufficient autonomy to refuse a heart transplant operation because she did not wish to suffer further effects from the medical treatment she had received throughout her life.

In light of the widespread and real concerns caused by high-profile cases such as the Baby P prosecution in 2008 where a mother and two men were convicted of causing the death following horrific injuries of an 18-month-old child, the difficulties of social services, the police, relatives and medical staff are obvious and the human rights issues unresolved.

4.5.3 The doctrine of double effect

Pretty demonstrates the problem of a person who has good reason to make a decision at some point in time to end her life in order to avoid intolerable suffering. Domestic law has been ameliorated by the terms of the Suicide Act which removed the criminal stigma from committing suicide whilst retaining criminal liability for those who assist another person's suicide. Diane Pretty's circumstances, and those of Debbie Purdy, were different from those of most people in that they had reached such a stage of physical degeneration that the option of suicide was no longer available to them. What they both needed was help to bring their suffering to an end at the time of their choosing, and the law was unable to assist them.

UK legislators have not addressed this and analogous problems, despite attempts to enact Private Members' Bills. If patients wish to fight death to the last, help is available, but if the fight is hopeless, painful and frightening, only the doctrine of 'double effect' is available whereby an increasing dosage of medication to relieve pain is administered which eventually is itself the proximate cause of death. However, that leaves *lacunae* in the law which puts doctors and nurses at risk of prosecution.

> 'The doctrine (or principle) of double effect is often invoked to explain the permissibility of an action that causes a serious harm, such as the death of a human being, as a side effect of promoting some good end. It is claimed that sometimes it is permissible to cause such a harm as a side effect (or "double effect") of bringing about a good result even though it would not be permissible to cause such a harm as a means to bringing about the same good end. This reasoning is summarized with the claim that sometimes it is permissible to bring about as a merely foreseen side effect a harmful event that it would be impermissible to bring about intentionally.'
>
> *Stanford Encylopaedia of Philosophy*

What this means in practice is that doctors, nurses, relatives and carers are faced with difficult decisions in respect of which legal uncertainty persists, at least with regard to consequences if not in relation to the law itself. The 'slippery slope' argument is used to oppose change although in the Netherlands, Switzerland and the US State of Oregon regimes have been implemented that are acceptable to the citizens of those states and which seem to work in practice.

UK governments sometimes seem to have a problem with providing a lead on certain moral and ethical questions and in the past have been rescued by private members' Bills and by allowing MPs a free vote according to conscience. Examples include the Murder (Abolition of the Death Penalty) Act 1965 and the Abortion Act 1967. Perhaps eventually the current problem will also be addressed in this way. In the meantime doctors are occasionally still prosecuted for causing death and despite the activities of the late Dr Shipman the overwhelming majority of doctors are driven by the highest motives and deserve to have *their* human rights protected as well as those of their patients.

4.5.4 Absence of competency

A different problem involves cases of PVS victims, where brain damage is so severe that the patient is unconscious and unable to communicate. One difficulty here is that in some rare instances the victim may suddenly recover, after many years *incommunicado*, and regain his faculties. Another factor is that consciousness may exist even though it is not apparent to bystanders and the patient may be unable to communicate although aware of what is going on. This is indeed a difficult dilemma for relatives and medical staff when the time comes to decide whether that patient should continue to live, or be released from his persistent condition.

'Release' is the operative word because as euthanasia is illegal the method used is to withdraw the patient's support. 'Support' is typically hydration, feeding and sometimes medication. The patient who was being kept alive by a combination of these medical procedures is denied them and starts to die. Withdrawal of support takes some time and is arguably a less humane way of dealing with a patient than assisted suicide, as the former results in a slower death typically caused by starvation and dehydration.

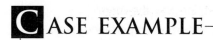

CASE EXAMPLE

Airedale NHS Trust Respondents v Bland Appellant [1993] 2 WLR 316 [1993] AC 789

A leading case is the House of Lords decision in *Bland* where their lordships struggled with a morally insoluble conundrum. Tony Bland, then aged 17, was grievously injured in the Hillsborough football ground disaster in 1989. His lungs were crushed and punctured and the supply of oxygen to his brain was interrupted. He sustained catastrophic and irreversible damage to the higher centres of the brain which left him in a PVS. The unanimous medical diagnosis was that this was irrecoverable.

CONTINUED ▶

Tony Bland had never indicated what he would have wished to happen to him in such circumstances but his father felt that 'he would not want to be left like that'. Those involved in his welfare were obliged to seek court approval, ie declarations to:

(i) lawfully discontinue all life-sustaining treatment and medical support measures designed to keep the patient alive in his existing PVS including the termination of ventilation, nutrition and hydration by artificial means; and

(ii) lawfully discontinue and thereafter not furnish medical treatment to the patient except for the sole purpose of enabling the patient to end his life and die peacefully with the greatest dignity and the least of pain, suffering and distress.

The President of the Family Division Sir Stephen Brown had granted the declarations sought and, on appeal by the Official Solicitor, the Court of Appeal upheld the President's order. The House of Lords considered the whole dilemma very carefully and, dismissing the further appeal, said that 'the object of medical treatment and care was to benefit the patient, but since a large body of informed and responsible medical opinion was of the view that existence in the PVS was not a benefit to the patient, the principle of the sanctity of life, which was not absolute, was not violated by ceasing to give medical treatment and care involving invasive manipulation of the patient's body, to which he had not consented and which conferred no benefit upon him, to a PVS patient who had been in that state for over three years; that the doctors responsible for the patient's treatment were neither under a duty'.

Lord Browne-Wilkinson said that 'nor (were they) entitled, to continue such medical care; that since the time had come when the patient had no further interest in being kept alive, the necessity to do so, created by his inability to make a choice, and the justification for the invasive care and treatment had gone; and that, accordingly, the omission to perform what had previously been a duty would no longer be unlawful'.

This was an extremely difficult case for their lordships to determine and the moral dilemmas were significant, so the following opinions are of considerable importance here:

'The interests of the protection of patients and their doctors, the reassurance of the patients' families and that of the public, render it desirable that, until a body of experience and practice has been built up, application should be made to the Family Division in any case where it is considered by the medical practitioners in charge of a PVS patient that continued treatment and care no longer confer any benefit upon him'
(Lord Keith of Kinkel, Lord Goff of Chieveley, Lord Lowry and Lord Browne Wilkinson).

'It is imperative that the moral, social and legal issues of the present case should be considered by Parliament'
(Lord Browne-Wilkinson and Lord Mustill)

However, Parliament has so far not legislated on this matter either.

4.6 Right to live

4.6.1 Competency

In an almost diametrically opposed situation to that of Diane Pretty and Debby Purdy, another litigant, Leslie Burke, wanted assurances that when he reached the stage of not being able to make his own decisions, the doctors then providing him with medical treatment would not terminate it but would continue making all efforts to keep him alive. He had won such assurance at first instance and the General Medical Council (GMC) appealed against that decision in *R (on the application of Burke) v General Medical Council* [2005] EWCA Civ 1003.

The GMC had published a guidance paper entitled 'Withholding and Withdrawing Life prolonging Treatments: Good Practice in Decision making' addressing issues involved in withdrawing artificial nutrition and hydration (ANH). Burke wished such treatment to continue until he died of natural causes. The trial judge had held ([2004] EWHC 1879) that both at common law and under the Human Rights Act 1998 a competent patient who had made an advance directive could so direct and it would be determinative of the issue. He had made three directions referring to Burke and three more declaring paragraphs in the guidance to be unlawful.

The Court of Appeal held that there was no reason for Burke to fear that ANH would be withdrawn prior to the last stages of his disease and the guidance did not suggest anything to the contrary. It appeared that he had been persuaded to seek judicial review by third parties who were trying to raise other issues (Diane Pretty had also had considerable third-party support). The Court of Appeal specifically warned against future courts selectively using the trial judge's declarations. The guidance was extremely important and necessary. Leave to appeal to the House of Lords was refused and Burke's subsequent attempt to have the matter referred to the European Court of Human Rights was found to be inadmissible.

4.6.2 Absence of competency

Another important case on the right to live is that of the conjoined twins Jodie and Mary, a different kind of insoluble moral dilemma. In this Court of Appeal case, J (Jodie) and M (Mary) were conjoined (Siamese) twins in the care of a hospital administered by an NHS Trust who were the respondent.

CASE EXAMPLE

**Re A (Children) (Conjoined Twins: Surgical Separation) (2000) CA
[2001] 2 WLR 480**

Jodie was medically assessed as being capable of independent existence but an operation to separate them would have resulted in Mary's certain death. Mary was only alive because a common artery enabled Jodie to circulate oxygenated blood for both. Without an operation both children would die within three to six months because Jodie's heart would eventually fail. As devout Roman Catholics the parents refused to consent to the operation even to save one twin, although the doctors believed that they could carry out the operation so as to give Jodie a worthwhile life. Consequently a declaration was sought that the proposed operation would be lawful. The judge decided the operation was in the best interests of both twins and lawful, so granted the parents' declaration. Appeal was made to the Court of Appeal.

It was held that Art 2 of the Convention was to be construed as an autonomous text without regard to any special rules of English law, and the word 'intentionally' in Art 2 had to be given its natural and ordinary meaning. It thus applied only to cases where the purpose of the prohibited action was to cause death and did not import any prohibition of the proposed operation other than those which were to be found in English common law. The trial judge had been right to conclude that the operation would be in J's best interests. However it was not in M's best interests as death for M was the certain consequence of the operation and there was no contravening advantage for her.

Following *Birmingham City Council v H (a Minor)* [1993] 1 FLR 883 the court had to balance the interests of one against the other. The respect the law had to have for the right to life of each had to balance the right to life of each twin alongside other considerations. Choosing the lesser of two evils, the court found the operation to be justified in all the circumstances as the lesser evil and no unlawful act would be committed. The proposed operation would not in any event offend the sanctity of life principle. The availability of a plea of *quasi* self defence, modified to meet the exceptional circumstances nature had inflicted on the twins, made intervention by the doctors lawful.

4.7 Self-defence

It will be recalled that ECHR Art 2(2)(a) provides that deprivation of life is not to be regarded as being inflicted in contravention of the protection of everyone's right to life when it results from the use of force which is no more than absolutely necessary to defend any person from unlawful violence. The cases discussed previously do not come within either of the other two exceptions, which were use of force no more than absolutely necessary to effect lawful arrest or to prevent unlawful escape, and action to quell a riot or insurrection. Indirectly, therefore, they raised issues of protecting people from unlawful violence. However, in many cases the exception of self-defence will be more apparent.

It can be justified in situations even where the person exercising the right is mistaken as to the circumstances. In *R (on the application of Bennett) v HM Coroner for Inner South London* [2006] EWHC 196 (Admin) the claimant applied for judicial review of a coroner's verdict where the jury had not been allowed to consider a verdict of unlawful killing but only the alternatives of lawful killing or an open verdict. The circumstances in *Bennett* were that his son had been brandishing what a police officer thought was a gun and had been shot by the officer, but it transpired it had been a cigarette lighter disguised as a gun. The officer was not prosecuted and a verdict of lawful killing was reached.

The application was refused and Collins J pointed out that the European Court of Human Rights had considered what English law requires for self defence and had not suggested that there was any incompatibility with Art 2. Here a verdict of unlawful killing could properly be regarded as one that would have been unsafe; there was no real difference between the reasonableness test in English law and the test under Art 2.

In the inquest in December 2008 into the death of Jean Charles de Menezes, the victim of a mistaken identity killing in 2005 by the Metropolitan Police, the coroner (former High Court Judge Sir Michael Wright) also refused to allow the jury to consider a verdict of unlawful killing, instructing them that they had to decide it was lawful, or return an open verdict.

CASE EXAMPLE

McBride v United Kingdom **Application No 1396/06 (2006) 43 EHRR SE 10**

Being a soldier is no protection against an accusation of and sometimes conviction of murder. The obvious response to any such charge would be that they killed in self-defence, but that contention may be rejected by the court depending on the circumstances. Wright and Fisher were two guardsmen who had been so convicted and sentenced to life imprisonment, having shot Peter McBride in September 1992 for little more than having been 'a cheeky young man' who 'after an impudent and improper confrontation' had run away.

The self-defence argument that they feared he was a bomber was not borne out by the evidence, nor did the soldiers impress the trial judge with what they had to say, and he

CONTINUED ▸

found them guilty beyond reasonable doubt of murder. In their appeal to the Northern Ireland Court of Appeal there was no doubt of the conclusion reached, the court saying that they considered that 'the evidence clearly established that when they fired the appellants were acting in concert and shared a common intention to stop the deceased by shooting him'. They were refused leave to appeal to the House of Lords.

The guardsmen served terms of six years' imprisonment and on release were retained by the Army without loss of status or career progression on the basis that they had shown contrition. This occasioned judicial review proceedings by Peter McBride's mother. The trial judge indicated that the decision to allow them to remain in the Army should be considered again. Consequently the matter was considered afresh by a differently constituted Army board with representations being made by Amnesty International and other interested bodies. However, the soldiers were still not discharged from the Army after taking into consideration a variety of mitigating factors such as their age and lack of experience at the time of the offence and their utter loyalty to the Army.

Mrs McBride again challenged the decision by judicial review, and losing this she appealed to the Northern Ireland Court of Appeal which rejected the grounds used to justify the Army's latest decision by saying that 'taken together, the reasons expressed by the Army Board for the retention in Army service of Guardsmen Fisher and Wright in its determination of 21 November 2001 do not amount to exceptional reasons'.

The Army board refused to reconsider the matter but in her last effort to obtain the soldiers' dismissal from the Army she made another attempt to have the circumstances judicially reviewed. This was also rejected by the High Court partly on the basis that the Court of Appeal had previously refused to grant such coercive relief, although the purpose of judicial review is in fact to cause the decision to be revisited rather than overruled by the court.

In the final stage of the proceedings Mrs McBride made application to the European Court of Human Rights under Arts 2 and 14 of the Convention, but Art 14 is not a freestanding right as another article has to be engaged before it can be used. It prohibits discrimination in the application of other articles, not discrimination *per se*. Therefore, at the end of a long period of litigation that involved every possible step available to her, Mrs McBride was left having to face the fact that the two soldiers who had been convicted of murdering her son were both able to continue with their military careers.

Article 14 which prohibits discrimination states that:

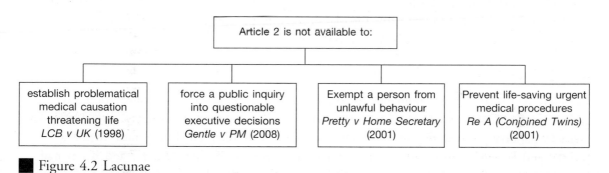

(A)   'The enjoyment of the rights and freedoms set forth in this Convention shall be secured without discrimination on any ground such as sex, race, colour, language, religion, political or other opinion, national or social origin, association with a national minority, property, birth or other status.'

McBride is interesting because it illustrates the length and complexity of some litigation that may arise where relatives seek justice following the death of a loved one. The repeated judicial review proceedings and appeals that found in favour of the family were insufficient to achieve the result of preventing the soldiers from continuing with their military careers, despite their convictions for murder. The case demonstrates the peculiar difficulties of balancing the distress caused by the family's tragic loss against the instantaneous actions of two inexperienced and possibly inadequately trained soldiers, whose lives had also been damaged by what occurred. The perception of self-defence in such circumstances is often instinctive, the reaction of a split second, which perhaps makes the outcome understandable even though not providing closure for the McBride family.

Article 2 is not available to:			
establish problematical medical causation threatening life *LCB v UK* (1998)	force a public inquiry into questionable executive decisions *Gentle v PM* (2008)	Exempt a person from unlawful behaviour *Pretty v Home Secretary* (2001)	Prevent life-saving urgent medical procedures *Re A (Conjoined Twins)* (2001)

■ Figure 4.2 Lacunae

4.8 Right to life in Europe

Compliance with Art 2 of the European Convention has obviously been tested in the UK during the latter part of the twentieth century by the Irish troubles and more recently by international terrorism, and in the context of a variety of medical cases. Other European states have been subjected to pressures and problems of their own and a brief idea of what some of these are is given in this section in order to provide wider insight into the right to life under the ECHR.

4.8.1 Turkey

Turkey is a candidate to join the EU amidst some controversy. A secular NATO Muslim state, most of whose territory is situated in Asia, Turkey finds itself confronting opposition from some of the existing members of the EU although its geographical location at the crossroads of Eastern

Europe, the Middle East and Asia gives it great strategic importance. It has a large population estimated to be around 71 million in mid-2007 and joining the EU would be an important factor in helping to settle the direction in which Europe moves in the twenty-first century. Turkey has devoted much effort into adapting and conforming to the criteria and standards set by the Council of Europe but is beset with the problem of the Kurds, those stateless people who occupy parts of Turkey, Iran and Iraq and who want a homeland of their own. Not surprisingly, therefore, Turkey has encountered problems with Art 2.

In *Ogur v Turkey* (21594/93) (2001) 31 EHRR 40 the claimant was a Turkish national living in part of Turkey where a state of emergency had been declared during which his son was killed by security forces. The case was reported to the public prosecutor but the investigation undertaken failed to identify the individual responsible for the killing. The absence of prosecution, it was argued by Ogur, was a violation of Art 2.

A majority of the European Commission on Human Rights upheld his complaint first on the basis that the use of force had been disproportionate and unnecessary, and second because the investigation had not been conducted by an independent authority and was deficient in a number of ways. There had been no proper post-mortem examination or thorough forensic examination of the scene, so the investigation could not have uncovered sufficient evidence to identify and punish those responsible for Ogur's son's death, which was found to be a violation of Art 2 requiring an award of compensation

4.8.2 Germany

Germany had very different problems to confront in the 1990s following reunification after the end of the Cold War and demolition of the Berlin wall. A number of cases were brought by East German nationals who were previously senior officials in the German Democratic Republic (GDR) and Socialist Unity Party in the former East Germany. Streletz, Kessler and Krenz had been convicted of homicide in respect of the responsibility they shared for the deaths of people killed whilst trying to escape to the West from East Germany. Relying on Art 7(1) of the Convention (no punishment without law, dealt with in Chapter 9) they contended that at the time the acts were committed they did not constitute offences under either German domestic or international law.

The complaints were dismissed. The convictions had been made by the reunified courts and were based on the 'appearance of legality' created by the former GDR but in fact they had ordered the killing of people trying to escape to the West. It was therefore not possible to invoke the protection of Art 7(1) and to find otherwise would be contrary to the whole purpose of the article. The acts in question were offences under GDR law and in any event not justifiable in terms of national security. The GDR had also ratified the International Covenant on Civil and Political Rights 1966 and the acts in question were contrary to Art 6 of the Covenant (*Streletz v Germany*; *Kessler v Germany* (35532/97); *Krenz v Germany* (44801/98) (2001) 33 EHRR 31).

4.8.3 Italy

Although Italy has perhaps suffered more than her fair share of terrorist activities, she is better known for the activities of the Mafia. The question in *Mastromatteo v Italy* (Application No 37703/97) was whether there had been a violation of Art 2 where the applicant's son had been murdered in 1989 by three criminals who were attempting to escape after a bank robbery. Why might this involve any question of state responsibility to its citizens?

It subsequently came to light that two of the robbers had been serving prison sentences for repeated violent offences and the one who had fired the shot had been released on prison leave whilst the other was subject to a semi-custodial regime. The judges responsible for their release had relied on reports from the prison authorities, based on their conduct in prison, that they did not constitute a danger to society. All three were subsequently sentenced to long terms of imprisonment.

The applicant was applying for compensation under a law that made provision for aid to be given to victims of organised crime and terrorism, but was refused relief by the Minister of the Interior and then by the President of Italy. The Grand Chamber decided unanimously that there had been no violation of Art 2 and, by 16 votes to 1, that there had been no violation of the Convention's procedural guarantees either.

4.9 Conclusions

Other European states have been the subject of Art 2 findings and many other cases could have been cited here. However, the purpose of mentioning these examples is simply to emphasise the European-wide scope of the provisions and the fact that a variety of influences and circumstances differing from those in the UK may be applicable

4.9.1 Common law

The common law did not concern itself with the 'right to life' in the sense in which the phrase is used today in human rights instruments. It did recognise that there are degrees of killing such as manslaughter and murder, and in earlier times suicide, but these have now been turned into statutory offences, and suicide decriminalised. In some common law jurisdictions the degrees of killing are made more explicit and classified as first- or second-degree murder, with differing consequences. To the extent that they may be comparable, these were the equivalents to Art 2(1) of the ECHR.

The defences to deprivation of the right to life now extant in Art 2(2) are similar to those that were available under the common law. Self-defence and death arising from reasonable actions taken to prevent harm to others was, and is, justifiable although there has been debate in recent times as to how acceptable the use of violence is when one person is attacked by another. Probably the law was and is fairly clear, although lack of judgement on the part of some people

purporting to defend themselves and their property on the one hand, and occasional over-zealous prosecuting authorities on the other may be the reason there has been concern.

Actions taken by the police and military, when prescribed by whatever the contemporary laws were at the relevant times and undertaken in as reasonable a manner as can be achieved given the inevitable circumstances of dealing with dangerous people, or people acting in a dangerous manner, are within the parameters of what the law allows. This obviously covers arrest and escape of persons who were or should have been lawfully detained, now Art 2(2)(b), or controlling dangerous mobs as under Art 2(2)(c)

4.9.2 Rights law

Given the pervasive existence and nature of human rights and other anti-discriminatory and pro-equality provisions today, when a person has been deprived of what is now recognised as a primary human right to life it is always going to be possible for a complainant to try to engage the European machinery once all domestic remedies have been exhausted.

The ECHR reflects global provisions dealing with the right to life and there is a wealth of European case law on the various aspects of the right itself, and defences where lives have been lost. The Key Facts chart at the end of this chapter provides a brief summary demonstrating some of the more important points. The three exceptions are clear as to their purpose and extent, although it should be noted that the first one (defence of any person from unlawful violence) is considerably wider than self-defence or defending others from overt violence, extending as it does to situations where other vulnerable or helpless people may need protection as in the medical cases.

It is also important to note that the abolition of capital punishment throughout Europe in peacetime needs to be considered in the context of the qualification to Art 2(1) (save in the execution of a sentence of a court following his conviction of a crime for which this penalty is provided by law).

The cases discussed in this chapter show that the ECHR and HRA machinery do not always achieve what the applicant and perhaps the wider public in some cases would regard as a fair outcome, but they do serve as a reminder that even on something as fundamentally important as the human right to stay alive as long as possible, nothing that pertains to human existence is absolute. Exceptions exist, and the circumstances of every case need to be examined with care so that the conflicting interests of individuals and society are kept in kilter.

ACTIVITY

Self-assessment questions

1 Explain in your own words the doctrine of 'double effect' and how it relates to the right to life.

2 Work out the sequence of court cases and their respective identities and functions as described in *McBride v United Kingdom* App No 1396/06 (2006) 43 EHRR SE 10 and make a short summary of your view as to whether human rights were well served by the eventual outcome.

3 What was the nature of the violation found against the UK in *McCann v UK* Judgment of 27th September 1995, Series A, No 324; (1995) 21 EHRR 97 and from other later cases and do you think the lessons have been learned?

KEY FACTS

Principle	Authority
Everyone's right to life shall be protected by law	European Convention on Human Rights Art 2(1)
There is no contravention if death occurs in defence of any person from unlawful violence	ECHR Art 2(2)(a); *R (on the application of Bennett) v HM Coroner for Inner South London* (2006)
There is no contravention if death occurs in order to effect a lawful arrest or to prevent the escape of a person lawfully detained	ECHR Art 2(2)(b); *Kelly v United Kingdom* (1993)
There is no contravention if action lawfully taken for the purpose of quelling a riot or insurrection	ECHR Art 2(2)(c); *Stewart v UK* (1984) pp 172–3; *X v Belgium* (1969)
Failure to investigate death properly	*McShane v United Kingdom* (2002)
Court unable to challenge legitimacy of decisions and actions of the executive	*R (on the application of Gentle) v Prime Minister* (2008)

CONTINUED ▸

KEY FACTS

Failure of prison authorities to protect incarcerated prisoner	*Edwards v United Kingdom* (2002); *R Amin (Imtiaz) v Home Sec* (2004)
No right to die	*R (on the application of Pretty) v DPP* (2001)
Considerations where patient is in a PVS	*Airedale NHS Trust Respondents v Bland Appellant* (1993)
Positive right to preservation of life	*R (on the application of Burke) v General Medical Council* (2005)
The 'lesser of two evils' principle	*Re A (Children) (Conjoined Twins: Surgical Separation)* (2000) CA
'Appearance of legality' will not prevent finding of violation of Article 2	*Streletz v Germany; Kessler v Germany; Krenz v Germany* (2001)

Useful resources

Kelly, M, 'The Right to Life' (Practical Guide 2005):
   www.nihrc.org/dms/data/NIHRC/attachments/dd/files/12/TheRighttoLife.pdf accessed 9th July 2008.
International Planned Parenthood Federation site, accessed 9th September 2008:
   http://www.ippf.org/en/Resources/Statements/The+Right+to+Life.htm.

Further reading

Amos, M, *Human Rights Law* (Hart Publishing, Oxford and Portland, Oregon, 2006) 175–201.
Kretzmer, D, 'Targeted Killing of Suspected Terrorists: Extra-judicial Executions or Legitimate Means of Defence?' (2005) EJIL 171.
Leverick, F, 'Is English Self-defence law incompatible with Article 2 of the ECHR?' (2002) Crim LR 347.
Ovey, C and White, R C A, *Jacobs & White The European Convention on Human Rights* (4th edn, Oxford University Press, Oxford, 2006) 56–73.
Papadopoulou, D, 'Environmental Calamities and the Right to Life: State Omissions and Negligence Under Scrutiny', Env L Rev 2006, 8(1), 59–65.
Plomer, A, 'A Foetal Right to Life? The Case of Vo v France', HRL Rev 2005, 5(2), 311–338.

chapter 5 PROHIBITION AGAINST TORTURE, INHUMAN AND DEGRADING TREATMENT

AIMS AND OBJECTIVES

The chapter discusses the meaning of torture and the historical willingness of people to resort to its use. A variety of examples are discussed to demonstrate that this is no longer the case and that the use of torture is now completely unacceptable to civilised people. The prohibition against torture is global, not merely regional or domestic, although there are variations in how it is actually defined. Torture is not addressed as if it stood alone but in conjunction with other kinds of inhuman treatment. There have been considerable changes in attitudes over time in particular with reference to use of physical punishment and the way children should be treated.

Torture is perhaps analogous to slavery in that it is now recognised as being absolutely repugnant to everything that human beings should strive to achieve. Other rights and freedoms are important but are enjoyed in different ways, depending on the society under discussion. The universal view of human rights brooks no exceptions or qualifications to the prohibition against torture.

5.1 Background

Torture has been used throughout the world and for as far back as history and even archaeology can trace. What would today be regarded as 'cruel and unusual' interrogation methods or punishments were routinely used to extract confessions during the Inquisition. The word 'torture' itself comes from the Latin word *tortus* which means twisted and there was often a link between the occasions on which torture was used and the alleged behaviour of the torture victim. The more heinous the crime, the more severe the perceived risk to the authorities, and the more savage the torture inflicted.

In ancient Greece freemen were not tortured but slaves were, whilst the Romans allowed it for accused persons but not witnesses unless treason was suspected, in which case the status of the traitor ceased to be relevant. In England torture was used in the Middle Ages although perhaps not as widely as is sometimes portrayed. Heresy and treason were regarded as particularly serious, however, and the methods and implements used can be seen in museums.

121

Although the common law precluded evidence obtained by torture it was nevertheless used as Lord Bingham of Cornhill pointed out in his speech in *A (and others) v Secretary of State for the Home Department* [2005] UKHL 71:

> 'Despite this common law prohibition, it is clear from the historical record that torture was practised in England in the sixteenth and early seventeenth centuries. But this took place pursuant to warrants issued by the Council or the Crown, largely (but not exclusively) in relation to alleged offences against the state, in exercise of the Royal prerogative: see Jardine; and Lowell, pp 290–300.'

Lord Bingham's speech in this case provides a fascinating account of the early use of torture in English law. One of the best-known examples is that of the Gunpowder Plot where a group of English Catholics planned to blow up the Houses of Parliament during the State opening on 5th November 1605. They hoped to abduct King James' children and foment rebellion in the English Midlands. The plan was discovered because one of the conspirators warned his brother-in-law not to attend Parliament on that day. The notorious 'Hanging Judge Jeffries' acquired his reputation by sentencing and torturing suspects in the West Country in the following year. Torture was used for a variety of reasons, not only to exact revenge on the King's enemies but to act as an example and deterrent to others.

In the twentieth century it was only after the Second World War that concerted international steps were taken to ban torture. Even so, the practice is still used in parts of Europe and is widespread throughout much of the rest of the world, albeit often now implemented in subtler ways, such as brain-washing or the use of drugs, that may leave no physical traces. It remains a weapon of coercion used by states against their enemies. This chapter goes on to discuss some of the human rights and legal aspects of torture and severe mistreatment.

5.1.2 What is torture?

Although the title of this chapter is prohibition against torture, relatively little torture as such is discussed, particularly with reference to the UK. Human rights law usually deals with torture together with inhuman or degrading treatment or punishment and much of the emphasis is on Art 3 of the ECHR, but because torture is relatively rare in Europe compared with other parts of the world, there is in this chapter more emphasis on other relevant treaties and legal provisions. Torture is prevalent in some parts of the world but not unknown in Europe.

Torture is the manipulation of the body and/or mind in order to elicit information, or sometimes it is inflicted because of less obvious or easily understood psychological motivations. In addition to extraction of information the motivation may be revenge, deterrence or sadism. What perhaps originated in earlier times as physical mistreatment inflicted to obtain information has expanded to include psychological or mental cruelty carrying connotations of punishment, brain-washing and re-education.

Thus, torture may comprise a direct assault on the victim causing immediate and ongoing pain but it might be indirect where the victim is shown implements of torture that cause terror, or involve threats to loved ones or administration of drugs that the body is unable to resist. There seem to be few if any limits to the willingness of people who think it is justified in using such techniques to inflict torture and inhuman treatment in order to obtain some end or advantage.

Political expediency and belief that the means justifies the end are probably the usual primary causes. This does give rise to an important question, however: is torture the preserve of exceptional people, whom we might regard as single-minded zealots or deviant psychopaths, or is there a deeper problem that might affect the majority of mankind?

5.2 The Milgram experiment

In the early 1960s Dr Stanley Milgram, a social psychologist at Yale University, conducted an experiment in which subjects were told that the purpose of the exercise was to study the effects of punishment on the learning process. A 'learner' in an adjacent room (in reality an actor, although the subject of the experiment did not know this) was supposed to be memorising information but if he made a mistake the subject was instructed to inflict punishment by way of electric shocks of increasing severity *via* a set of 30 levers. The subject was told that these shocks varied from 15 volts to 450 volts. When the 'learner' made a mistake the subject heard prerecorded sounds of distress that eventually culminated in screams and the actor banging on the wall, but the subject was not aware of the deception.

The purpose of the experiment was to study the extent of 'submissive compliance', ie how far ordinary people would go in following instructions (which in other contexts would be described as 'obeying superior orders') without bringing into play their individual consciences. Students and colleagues of Professor Milgram were asked beforehand to estimate what they thought would be the likely incidence of unquestioning obedience when the subjects genuinely believed that they were causing real pain and punishment. The general opinion was that it would probably be about 1 or 2 per cent whereas in fact it transpired that over 60 per cent of participants were prepared to inflict extreme pain because they had been instructed (or ordered) to do so.

> 'The extreme willingness of adults to go to almost any lengths on the command of an authority constitutes the chief finding of the study and the fact most urgently demanding explanation. Ordinary people, simply doing their jobs, and without any particular hostility on their part, can become agents in a terrible destructive process. Moreover, even when the destructive effects of their work become patently clear, and they are asked to carry out actions incompatible with fundamental standards of morality, relatively few people have the resources needed to resist authority.'
>
> Stanley Milgram, 'Behavioral Study of Obedience', *Journal of Abnormal and Social Psychology* 67, 371–378

This apparently deep-seated aspect of human behaviour may help to explain why even today civilised states are prepared to ignore the Geneva Conventions and use or condone techniques such as 'water boarding', 'extraordinary rendition' and concentration camps, denying fundamental elements of the rule of law and human rights, in order to extract information from suspects.

ACTIVITY

Self-assessment questions

1 Explain what torture means in your own words.

2 Consider whether, and if so to what extent, Professor Milgram's experiments if repeated today would be likely to demonstrate a similar level of submissive compliance.

3 If you think not, what would be the probable reasons for the changes in attitude?

5.3 Absolute unacceptability

Despite what states still do or tolerate, torture is totally unacceptable according to global, European and other regional human rights provisions and under UK domestic law. A wide range of treaties, statutes and case law prohibit certain practices and activities either absolutely or by restricting the ways in which they can be used. However, 'torture' is usually dealt with in the same definition as 'inhuman' or 'degrading' 'treatment' or 'punishment' and as these are disjunctive it is not always easy to differentiate treatment and punishment, and more difficult again to distinguish the boundaries between what is degrading, inhuman or torture.

International human rights law is clear that the prohibition of torture is without qualification, restriction or exception and derogation from it is never acceptable whatever the prevailing circumstances of public emergency, civil unrest, insurrection, terrorist activities or outright war. Thus, there should be no room for excuse, equivocation or argument on this: torture is negation and denial of humanity, even if it is inherent in human nature.

There is a problem here: many people, perhaps a majority, do believe that *in extremis* the end justifies the means. This being the case, torturing a suspect on the premise that by extracting information other lives might be saved is hard to resist in a populist context. Take the following examples:

Authoritarian proposition

Many people accept it is legitimate to torture a suspected terrorist if it is believed that a bomb has been planted and by immediately obtaining the details of its location, type and so on many innocent lives might be saved

Rights objection

The flaw in this line of thought is that it is a fundamental tenet of the rule of law that a person is innocent until proven guilty before a legitimate tribunal or court

Second authoritarian proposition

What if the suspect is caught red-handed committing a terrorist act and the suspected bomb and bomber have not been located?

Rights objection

Will argue the first proposition again, and that the end does not justify the means – but these are founded on theory when human lives may be at stake

■ Figure 5.1 Justification of torture?

What people actually think about the use of torture is discussed in section 5.6 later in the chapter.

5.4 Meaning and sources

Source/authority	Definition
Universal Declaration of Human Rights 1948 Art 5	'No one shall be subjected to torture or to *cruel*, inhuman or degrading treatment or punishment.'
European Convention on Human Rights 1950 Art 3	'No one shall be subjected to torture or to inhuman or degrading treatment or punishment.'
The Greek Case (1969) 12 Yearbook 1, European Commission of Human Rights	Suffering must be inflicted intentionally and torture is an aggravated form of inhuman treatment ' . . . which has a purpose, such as the obtaining of information or confession, or the infliction of punishment'.
Declaration of Tokyo 1975 Guidelines for Medical Doctors concerning Torture and Other Cruel, Inhuman or Degrading Treatment or Punishment in relation to Detention and Imprisonment Adopted by the 29th World Medical Assembly, Tokyo, Japan, October 1975	' . . . torture is defined as the deliberate, systematic or wanton infliction of physical or mental suffering by one or more persons acting alone or on the orders of any authority, to force another person to yield information, to make a confession, or for any other reason'.
Declaration on the Protection of All Persons from Being Subjected to Torture and Other Cruel, Inhuman or Degrading Treatment or Punishment Adopted by General Assembly resolution 3452 of 9th December 1975	' . . . torture means any act by which severe pain or suffering, whether physical or mental, is intentionally inflicted by or at the instigation of a public official on a person for such purposes as obtaining from him or a third person information or confession, punishing him for an act he has committed or is suspected of having committed, or intimidating him or other persons. It does not include pain or suffering arising only from, inherent in or incidental to, lawful sanctions to the extent consistent with the Standard Minimum Rules for the Treatment of Prisoners . . . (it) constitutes an aggravated and deliberate form of cruel, inhuman or degrading treatment or punishment'.

CONTINUED ▸

Source/authority	Definition
Ireland v United Kingdom (1978) 2 EHRR 25	' . . . deliberate inhuman treatment causing very serious and cruel suffering'.
United Nations Convention against Torture and other Cruel, Inhuman or Degrading Treatment or Punishment 1984 Art 1	'For the purposes of this Convention, the term "torture" means any act by which severe pain or suffering, whether physical or mental, is intentionally inflicted on a person for such purposes as obtaining from him or a third person information or a confession, punishing him for an act he or a third person has committed or is suspected of having committed, or intimidating or coercing him or a third person, or for any reason based on discrimination of any kind, when such pain or suffering is inflicted by or at the instigation of or with the consent or acquiescence of a public official or other person acting in an official capacity. It does not include pain or suffering arising only from, inherent in or incidental to lawful sanctions'.

■ Figure 5.2 Definitions

It will be seen that although the basic elements are common to these various definitions, there are different emphases in the meaning and the language sometimes also differs.

5.5 UN Special Rapporteur

By resolution 1985/33 the UN Commission on Human Rights decided to appoint a special *rapporteur* to examine questions relating to torture, covering all countries, whether or not they had ratified the Convention against Torture and other Cruel, Inhuman or Degrading Treatment or Punishment. Currently, the *rapporteur* is an Austrian, Manfred Nowak whose mandate covers three main activities:

- transmitting urgent appeals to States regarding individuals reported to be at risk of torture and dealing with communications on past alleged cases
- undertaking fact-finding country visits
- submitting annual reports on activities, mandate and methods of work to the Human Rights Council and the General Assembly.

■ Figure 5.3 Dr Manfred Nowak

The *rapporteur* has an advantage over the complaints mechanisms of human rights treaty monitoring bodies because he is not prevented from undertaking investigation by the requirement that all domestic remedies must first be exhausted. This is obviously useful, as waiting for that to be done may leave it too late for the alleged victim. He can also act in conjunction with other mandates established by the UN Commission on Human Rights, which from June 2006 has been replaced by the UN Human Rights Council, based in Geneva. Access to UN information about various aspects of torture is given in the following table.

UN body	www address
Committee Against Torture	http://www2.ohchr.org/english/bodies/cat/
Special rapporteur on torture and other cruel, inhuman or degrading treatment or punishment	http://www2.ohchr.org/english/issues/torture/rapporteur/
Voluntary Fund for Victims of Torture	http://www.ohchr.org/EN/Issues/Pages/TortureFundMain.aspx

■ Figure 5.4 UN links

5.6 Changing perceptions

In addressing alleged breaches of Art 3 of the ECHR, it is necessary to take into account the extent of legitimate behaviour or punishment. If the treatment in question goes beyond acceptable limits it may be regarded as inhuman or degrading under ECHR provisions although the UDHR refers additionally to 'cruel' treatment or punishment and the 1984 UN Torture Convention elaborates in more detail and refers to additional elements such as intimidation, coercion and discrimination.

Since and because of the Second World War there has been interest and concern about the role of doctors in interrogation. There can be a fine borderline between ensuring that suspects are not mistreated and providing a cloak of legitimacy to actions or procedures used by interrogators. The terms of Art 3 of the ECHR are as follows:

 'No one shall be subjected to torture or inhuman or degrading treatment or punishment.'

To establish contravention of treaty provisions it is necessary to set a threshold of behaviour beyond which interrogators must not go. At the same time, however, it must be made clear that this does not condone less serious types of treatment. Additionally, as is the case for other Convention issues, what is acceptable in one time or place may not be so at a later date. A good example of this is infliction of corporal punishment where the case law provides examples both of lesser kinds of breach of Art 3 and changing social attitudes within the UK.

An Opinion Poll of some 27,000 people in 25 different countries conducted for the BBC World Service by Globescan in conjunction with the University of Maryland's Program on International Policy Attitudes in October 2006 suggested that 59 per cent of the world's population were unwilling to condone the use of torture but that 29 per cent think that governments should in some circumstances be able to use torture to combat terrorism.

Israelis had the highest percentage (43 per cent) of people in favour of some use of torture and Italy the highest number of people opposed (81 per cent). Other countries with over 70 per cent of the population against the use of torture were Australia, France, Canada, the UK (72 per cent) and Germany. Only in India did more people approve of the use of torture than who disapprove of it. The poll also found that education and average incomes did not seem to affect people's views (to access the data, see resources at the end of this chapter).

KEY FACTS

Rule/principle/meaning	Source/authority
Torture was not supposed to be used under the common law, but for serious crimes such as heresy and treason confessions were extracted from accused persons	Lord Bingham's speech in *A (and others) v Secretary of State for the Home Department* (2005)
Derivation of 'torture': Middle English, from Old French, from Late Latin *tort_ra*, from Latin *tortus*, past participle of *torqu_re*, to twist	Answers.com
'No one shall be subjected to torture or to *cruel*, inhuman or degrading treatment or punishment.'	UDHR Art 5 and ECHR Art 3 provide identical definitions except that the UDHR includes the word 'cruel'
People appear to have an alarming propensity to 'obey orders' even when the consequences may lead to 'inhuman behaviour'	Dr Stanley Milgram of Yale University's experiments on seemingly slow learners subjected to apparent electric shocks by 'ordinary people'
Torture is totally unacceptable in global, European and other regional human rights terms and under UK domestic law	UN Declaration, UN Torture Convention, European Convention for the Prevention of Torture and Inhuman or Degrading Treatment or Punishment, ECHR, English common law

The rest of this chapter deals with torture with three main headings of treatment of children, treatment of adults and extra-territorial torture.

A   TREATMENT OF CHILDREN

Examination of the law relating to treatment of children in the UK reveals a number of circumstances in which questions of inhuman or degrading suffering have or may have been caused. This includes corporal punishment in schools or by parents, dealing with children who have disabilities, and treatment of young criminals. One of the significant pertinent factors here is that of changing societal attitudes: what was widely acceptable for a decade or two after the Second World War can today appear anachronistic and in some cases cruel. It is also clear that whereas formerly physically disciplining children was common, this is no longer the case.

5.7 Chastisement of children

5.7.1 Earlier cases

Although torture allegations are rare in the UK, there have been cases under Art 3 of the ECHR which are examined in this chapter and some, although not all, of these relate to corporal punishment of children. In the 1950s, for example, corporal punishment was commonly administered in Scottish schools not only for serious but also for relatively minor offences, such as talking in class, but attitudes changed during the 1960s and 70s.

In *Tyrer v UK* (1978) 2 EHRR 1, the European Court of Human Rights considered the case of a 15-year-old boy sentenced to three strokes of the birch by order of the Isle of Man Juvenile Court, having been convicted of assault. Corporal punishment inflicted directly or condoned by the state is today no longer acceptable and had come to be considered problematical by the 1970s. When examining changing social conditions and the margin of appreciation:

> 'the Court must ... recall that the Convention is a living instrument which, as the Commission rightly stressed, must be interpreted in the light of present-day conditions. In (this) case the Court cannot but be influenced by the developments and commonly accepted standards in the penal policy of the member States of the Council of Europe in this field.'

> para 31

The punishment inflicted on Tyrer was found to attain the level of humiliation inherent in the notion of degrading punishment within the meaning of Art 3, aggravated by the 'indignity of having the punishment administered over the bare posterior'. It did not, however, amount to torture.

Four years later in 1982 another case was heard in the European Court where the respective applicants each had children of compulsory school age attending Scottish State schools in which

corporal punishment was still routinely administered as a disciplinary measure (*Campbell and Cosans v United Kingdom* (1982) 4 EHRR 293). In these instances Mrs Campbell's son was never subjected to this and Mrs Cosan's son refused to submit to it and was suspended. He was refused readmission when his parents continued to deny the right of the education authorities to administer corporal punishment.

The European Commission referred the case to the Court which unanimously held that there had been no violation of Art 3 as no physical or psychological damage actually occurred, but by a majority of 6:1 the Court decided that the right to education and respect for the religious and philosophical convictions of the parents had been breached.

In 1992 a private school headmaster caned a 15-year-old boy across his clothed buttocks leaving the boy with four weals. There was no prosecution and a county court civil claim was dismissed. The European Commission considered that it was a severe caning causing physical injury and humiliation and therefore amounted to degrading treatment, and a financial settlement of £8,000 was awarded. In light of this settlement the case did not proceed in the European Court, despite regret expressed by the Commission's Delegate, who argued that it was a strong case to be answered (*Y v United Kingdom* (1994) 17 EHRR 238).

In the following year a seven-year-old schoolboy was smacked by his private school headmaster with a slipper on his clothed bottom without any injury resulting and this instance was not sufficiently harsh, according to the Commission, to amount to a violation of Art 3 (*Costello-Roberts v United Kingdom* (1993) 19 EHRR 112). Thus, similar cases could produce contradictory results depending on the exact circumstances.

5.7.2 Current law

The use of the birch in UK schools had been abolished in 1948 before the ECHR came into existence and in State schools corporal punishment was discontinued in 1986 by the Education (No 2) Act 1986 (c 61). Some independent schools continued with the practice up to 1998 after which they were prevented by the School Standards and Framework Act 1998 (c 31).

The criteria to be taken into consideration for ill-treatment to amount to the requisite level of severity in order to fall within the Art 3 proscription were examined more recently in *A v United Kingdom* (1999) 27 EHRR 611 where a nine-year-old child who had been beaten by his stepfather was referred to a paediatrician whose examination revealed bruising indicating that the child had been beaten with a garden cane. A charge of assault occasioning actual bodily harm (ABH) was brought against the stepfather who used the defence of reasonable chastisement which resulted in his acquittal by a majority jury verdict.

The case was then referred to the European Court where it was held unanimously that the assessment of the level of severity depended on 'the particular circumstances of the case including the nature and context of the ill treatment, its duration, its physical and mental effects and, in some cases, the victim's age, sex and state of health'.

That level was found to have been reached in A's case but a further question arose which was whether the UK Government should be held responsible for that treatment, bearing in mind its responsibility for ensuring protection of those within the jurisdiction, in particular with respect to children and other vulnerable persons. On this score, English law on reasonable chastisement failed to provide such protection because the stepfather had been acquitted when, by implication, he should have been convicted. This decision appears to some extent to discount the important role played by the jury in English law and the importance of the prosecution being obliged to prove their case beyond reasonable doubt.

Earlier cases were considered and reviewed by the Court of Criminal Appeal in *R v H (Assault of Child: Reasonable Chastisement)* [2001] EWCA Crim 1024, where a father had been charged with assault occasioning ABH on his son after punishing him with a leather belt for disobedience. The criteria to be applied now are that the judge should 'direct the jury having regard to those factors which were identified in *A v United Kingdom* namely the nature, context and duration of H's behaviour, the physical and mental consequences to his son, his son's age and H's reasons for administering the chastisement'.

5.8 UK legislation

As can be seen from these cases, beating children as a legitimate form of educational discipline was still permissible in the UK almost to the end of the twentieth century. In England and Wales it is still a permissible punishment when inflicted by parents, although some 23 states throughout the world had by 2007 completely abolished corporal punishment of children by everyone, including parents.

5.8.1 School Standards and Framework Act 1998 c 31

'131 Abolition of corporal punishment in schools etc

(1) For s 548 of the Education Act 1996 c. 56 there shall be substituted—

"548 No right to give corporal punishment

(1) Corporal punishment given by, or on the authority of, a member of staff to a child—

   (a) for whom education is provided at any school, or

   (b) for whom education is provided, otherwise than at school, under any arrangements made by a local education authority, or

   (c) for whom specified nursery education is provided otherwise than at school, cannot be justified in any proceedings on the ground that it was given in pursuance of a right exercisable by the member of staff by virtue of his position as such.

(3) Battery of a child causing actual bodily harm to the child cannot be justified in any civil proceedings on the ground that it constituted reasonable punishment.'

5.8.2 The Children Act 2004

Section 58 deals with reasonable punishment of children, but does not ban it outright:

 '(1) In relation to any offence specified in subs (2), battery of a child cannot be justified on the ground that it constituted reasonable punishment . . . '

What this means is that the offences of assault occasioning ABH, wounding and causing grievous bodily harm under the Offences against the Person Act 1861 (c 100) and cruelty to persons under the age of 16 under the Children and Young Persons Act 1933 (c 12) cannot be committed whilst having the defence of reasonable punishment available to avoid conviction. It may be that the Government's reluctance to abolish all corporal punishment for children is because there is considerable public support for its retention in the UK.

CASE EXAMPLE

R (on the application of Williamson and others) v Secretary of State for Education and Employment and others [2005] UKHL 15

Despite abolition of educational corporal punishment the House of Lords considered it again in the context of Christian independent schools in 2005. The applicants were a combination of teachers working at, and parents whose children attended, independent schools. The common factor between them was belief that it is an essential element of Christian education that teachers should be able physically to punish children guilty of indiscipline by virtue of the duty of acting *in loco parentis*, presumably under the adage of 'spare the rod and spoil the child'. The applicants sought judicial review of the Education Act 1996 s 548(1).

They objected to the ban on corporal punishment in state schools being extended to independent schools, thus effectively precluding physically administered discipline from all UK education. Obviously there was no wish to infringe Art 3, rather a contention that their right to freedom of thought, conscience and religion and to manifest their religious beliefs in an educational context were being thwarted by this legislative restriction.

Their claim was unsuccessful in the High Court and before the Court of Appeal. They argued that as parents still had some residual common law rights physically to discipline their children, this responsibility could be delegated by them to teachers so that they would not in that capacity be teachers 'as such'.

It was held that the statutory distinction differentiated the situation where a teacher acted as a teacher compared with that where he might also be a parent. The ban on corporal punishment was clearly imposed by primary legislation and fulfilled the

CONTINUED ▸

legitimate aim of protecting vulnerable children and promoting their well-being. The means chosen were appropriate and proportionate. The conclusion was that banning all educational corporal punishment as illegitimate is valid, and the challenge failed.

Baroness Hale at several points in her speech kept bringing the matter back to its true and proper focus:

'My Lords, this is, and has always been, a case about children, their rights and the rights of their parents and teachers. Yet there has been no one here or in the courts below to speak on behalf of the children. No litigation friend has been appointed to consider the rights of the pupils involved separately from those of the adults. No NGO ... has intervened to argue a case on behalf of children as a whole. The battle has been fought on ground selected by the adults ... The practice of corporal punishment involves what would otherwise be an assault upon another person . . . Instead the argument was about "the nature of religious belief itself". That is, of course, a most important question, but it is not the question in this case . . . A child has the same right as anyone else not to be assaulted; the defence of lawful chastisement is an exception to that right.'

She went on to consider the relevance and importance of the UN Convention on the Rights of the Child (1989) and other evidence and concluded that given the existence of a large body of authority and professional support:

'If a child has a right to be brought up without institutional violence, as he does, that right should be respected whether or not his parents and teachers believe otherwise.'

5.9 Children with disability

Punishment of children within the judicial or educational systems raises a number of issues, but there are other circumstances where children may be subjected to or not receive treatment that gives rise to questions of whether Art 3 becomes engaged. Children with disabilities who are not in any way at fault need careful protection, as do healthy children guilty of misbehaviour.

CASE EXAMPLE

A v Essex CC; J v Worcestershire CC; S v Hertfordshire CC; B v Suffolk CC [2008] EWCA Civ 364

These cases involved a number of children and different local education authorities, although on cost grounds the appeal was made only on behalf of the anonymised child A, confusingly described in the case analysis as X.

CONTINUED ▸

As Sedley LJ said, essentially his case was that 'for want of even minimally suitable provision for his education, he was shut out of the state (education) system for 18 or 19 months. The consequences are said to have amounted to inhuman or degrading treatment and an unjustified disruption of his private and family life, as well as to discrimination in the enjoyment of the A2P1 (Article 2 Protocol 1) right.'

The child had been removed from school because of teachers' problems in knowing how to deal with him, the reason being his state of health which meant that he was a danger to himself and others. He was severely autistic, had considerable learning difficulties, was doubly incontinent; he self-harmed and despite medication suffered between 10 and 15 epileptic fits a day. The main basis of the claim was alleged failure by the authority to satisfy his right to education and to show respect for his private and family life, but it was also argued on his behalf that the inhuman and degrading aspect was that whilst he was out of school his life and that of his family was extremely stressful because he was understimulated and his parents had an exasperating and emotionally draining time trying to cope with him.

Hard as these consequences were, neither the trial judge Field J nor the Court of Appeal thought it came anywhere near the level of degradation needed to engage Art 3. This conclusion was reached taking into consideration *Pretty v United Kingdom* (2002) 35 EHRR 1 that exacerbation of a naturally occurring physical or mental condition could in some circumstances be sufficient to violate Art 3 and *R (Q) v Home Secretary* [2003] 3 WLR 365 where the Court of Appeal had set the level of entry into the protection of Art 3 below simple destitution.

5.10 Punishment of young criminals

The European Court of Human Rights considered the nature and level of ill-treatment needed to engage and contravene Art 3 in the virtually identical cases brought by Thomson and Venables, who had been convicted of killing the toddler Jamie Bulger when they were 11 years of age (*T and V v United Kingdom* (2000) 30 EHRR 121). They complained that Art 3 had been breached in respect of their trial and sentence. Both complaints were dismissed, the former by 12 votes to 5 and the latter by 10 votes to 7, although the Court did find against the UK Government under Art 6(1) (fair hearing) and 5(4) (speedy release from unlawful detention).

What T and V were asserting essentially was that in view of their young age, compounded by their immaturity and state of emotional disturbance, their public trial in an adult Crown Court amounted to inhuman and degrading treatment. They claimed that it had been unfair because of their inability fully and properly to participate in the proceedings. In the European Court's analysis of Art 3 it was emphasised that it enshrines one of the most fundamental values of democratic society. The prohibition on torture or inhuman and degrading treatment or punishment is absolute and in no way can be made to relate to the victim's conduct. This means that the horrific nature of their crime was totally immaterial to their rights under Art 3.

The following table provides a summary of some of the essential elements of Art 3.

Minimum severity of treatment	Inhuman	Degrading	Humiliation
It is relative and depends on such circumstances as the nature and context of treatment or punishment, manner and method of its execution, duration, its physical or mental effects and, in some cases, the sex, age and health of the victim	Behaviour that is premeditated, applied for a long period of time, causing actual bodily injury or intense physical and mental suffering	Treatment such as to arouse in its victims feelings of fear, anguish and inferiority capable of humiliating and debasing them	The suffering or humiliation involved must go beyond that inevitable element of suffering or humiliation connected with a given form of legitimate treatment or punishment

Figure 5.5 Types of mistreatment

B   TREATMENT OF ADULTS

Examining attitudes to disciplining children reveals some interesting changes and developments into what is perceived as their human rights. This next section provides a similar investigation into how adults are treated and focuses on terrorists and deportation. Reasons for resisting deportation differ; often they are because of fear of what the receiving state might do to them on their return, but sometimes it is the wish to retain the benefits of remaining in the UK, for example to enjoy NHS medical facilities.

5.11 Interrogation of terrorists

CASE EXAMPLE

The Republic of Ireland v The United Kingdom (1979–80) 2 EHRR 25

The allegations here arose out of terrorist activities of the IRA and Loyalist groups in Northern Ireland. Because of the 'troubles' the British Government had given notice of derogation under Art 15(1) of the Convention on grounds of the 'public emergency threatening the life of the nation'. The Irish Government challenged the use of extra judicial detention alleging infringement of Art 3 and, more particularly, they objected to a

CONTINUED ▸

number of interrogation methods known as the 'five techniques' that included wall-standing, hooding, infliction of loud noise and deprivation of sleep and food, all taking place over a considerable period of time. The UK Government did not deny the allegations but said that they had been discontinued.

The European Commission of Human Rights was of the opinion that the practices amounted to torture but on reference to the plenary Court, torture was not upheld. Instead, the European Court found that there had been inhuman treatment and:

> '(l) Since the five techniques were such as to arouse in the victims feelings of fear, anguish and inferiority capable of humiliating and debasing them and possibly breaking their physical or moral resistance, they were also degrading.
>
> (m) The distinction between torture and inhuman or degrading treatment derived principally from a difference in the intensity of the suffering inflicted.'

The European Court regretted that the British Government failed to accord the Commission full assistance as required by Art 28.

Wall standing	The victim is made to stand on his toes with legs and feet apart
Hooding	A bag is put over the detainee's head
Noise	Subjection to continuous hissing and loud noises
Sleep	Deprivation of sleep
Food and drink	Starving and dehydrating the subject

Figure 5.6 The five techniques

5.11.1 The Parker Report

This report produced by Lord Parker of Waddington (technically the 'Report of the Committee of Privy Counsellors appointed to consider authorised procedures for the interrogation of persons suspected of terrorism' (Cmd 4901 SBN 10 149010 0)) had made it clear that under domestic law such behaviour was illegal:

> '10. Domestic Law . . . (c) We have received both written and oral representations from many legal bodies and individual lawyers from both England and Northern Ireland. There has been no dissent from the view that the procedures are illegal alike by the law of England and the law of Northern Ireland . . . (d) This being so, no Army Directive and no Minister could lawfully or validly have authorized the use of the procedures. Only Parliament can alter the law. The procedures were and are illegal.'

5.12 Deportation

Attempts by the Government to deport persons from the UK provide a number of examples of how Art 3 comes to be engaged. The fear of what may happen to the subject when he arrives in the foreign jurisdiction is usually real and immediate. The risk may be that he is likely to be subjected to actual torture, or to be held in conditions that are inhuman and degrading.

CASE EXAMPLE

Soering v United Kingdom (A/161) (1989) 11 EHRR 439

Soering was a German national who had lived in the USA since the age of 11 and the US and German authorities wanted him extradited from the UK to the USA to be tried for murders allegedly committed in the USA. He sought and failed to obtain the writ of *habeas corpus* in his attempt to resist extradition and so made application to the European Court on the basis that trial in the USA would probably lead to him being held for perhaps six to eight years on death row. This would mean not only that his trial would not be fair in terms of Art 6, and that he would not have any remedy for violation of his rights under Art 13, but that his treatment would also be inhuman and degrading in contravention of Art 3.

The House of Lords agreed that Soering's complaints regarding breaches of Arts 1 and 13 were ill-founded but that Art 3 would be contravened were he to be extradited to the USA, even though under some circumstances the death penalty itself was still allowed under Art 2. The delay between sentence and execution and resultant severe stress would comprise the causation here. He could, however, be extradited to Germany because there was no death penalty there and the legitimate purpose of extradition would be fulfilled.

CASE EXAMPLE

R (on the application of Ullah) v Special Adjudicator; Do v Secretary of State for the Home Department [2004] UKHL 26

In *Ullah* the Court of Appeal had held ([2002] EWCA Civ 1856) that where the ECHR was invoked on the sole ground of the treatment to which an alien was likely to be subjected by the receiving state, and that treatment was not sufficiently severe to engage Art 3, the English courts were not required to recognise that any other article of the Convention was or could be engaged.

CONTINUED ▸

In a conjoined appeal against that decision a Pakistani national, Ullah, and a Vietnamese national, Do, claimed that they each had a well-founded fear of persecution if returned to their states of origin because of their religious practices or beliefs that would be a contravention of the freedom of thought, conscience and religion provisions of Art 9.

The House of Lords dismissed their appeals on two grounds. The first was that 'an Article of the Convention other than Art 3 could be engaged in relation to a removal of an individual from the UK where the anticipated treatment in the receiving state would be in breach of the requirements of the Convention, but such treatment did not meet the minimum requirements of Art 3'.

Their Lordships went on to say that it was unlikely that someone could successfully resist expulsion relying on Art 9 without then being entitled to asylum based on Art 9 or Art 3. The second reason was that a very strong case was needed for successful reliance on articles other than Art 3 and neither appellant here met that standard.

CASE EXAMPLE

A (and others) v Secretary of State for the Home Department [2005] UKHL 71

Here the House of Lords considered the relationship between English common law and the ECHR where three appeals were allowed. Their Lordships said that from its earliest days English common law had been against the use of torture to obtain confessions and had insisted on an exclusionary rule. The law refused to accept that inducement or oppression should 'go to the weight rather than the admissibility of the confession'. Indeed, they went on to say, it was perhaps the most fundamental rule of English criminal law that a confession not proved to be voluntary was inadmissible. Even standing alone unaided by the ECHR, common law principles insisted on third-party torture evidence being excluded as unfair, unreliable, incompatible with the principles applied by tribunals and offensive to ordinary standards of decency and humanity.

The case examines, emphasises and reinforces these principles and Lord Bingham of Cornhill explains how in the opening sentence of his speech:

> 'My Lords, may the Special Immigration Appeals Commission ("SIAC"), a superior
> court of record established by statute, when hearing an appeal under s 25 of the Anti-
> terrorism, Crime and Security Act 2001 by a person certified and detained under ss 21
> and 23 of that Act, receive evidence which has or may have been procured by torture
> inflicted, in order to obtain evidence, by officials of a foreign state without the

CONTINUED ▸

complicity of the British authorities? That is the central question which the House must answer in these appeals.'

The Secretary of State seems to have been prepared to accept that torture evidence could be admitted before SIAC as long as there had been no complicity on the part of the UK. This did not accord with English law and the appeals were allowed with the cases being remitted to SIAC for reconsideration.

In the absence of very exceptional circumstances, the deportation of an asylum seeker who was suffering from AIDS to Uganda, where access to medical treatment and facilities was problematic, would not breach ECHR 1950 Art 3 (*N v United Kingdom* (26565/05) *The Times*, 6th June 2007).

When a UK court is contemplating deportation of someone it should consider Convention issues separately. Extradition or expulsion can be resisted where the person to be removed risks suffering a flagrant denial of a fair trial in the receiving state. In *Othman (Jordan) v Secretary of State for the Home Department* [2008] EWCA Civ 290, SIAC had 'understated or misunderstood' the fundamental character of how the ECHR prohibited admission of evidence obtained by torture. It was not simply that it would make the trial unfair, but that in no circumstances should a person be subjected to inhuman or degrading treatment. This prohibitive principle is 'fundamental, unconditional and non-derogable'.

The Home Secretary was attempting to deport a Jordanian national (who had been granted asylum in the UK) on the ground that it was now thought that he was an Islamic extremist with terrorist links and as such was believed to be a danger to UK national security. He had been convicted in his absence by the Jordanian court but evidence was given to the English court that witnesses at Othman's Jordanian trial had been tortured.

Although it was accepted by SIAC that Art 6 would probably not be fully complied with if he was returned to Jordan, it concluded that it would not amount to a complete denial of justice. This somewhat illogical conclusion, and an apparent ignoring of the provision of evidence obtained by torture, was the wrong approach and Othman was entitled not to be deported.

English courts find themselves dealing on many occasions with allegations of torture and the lesser manifestations addressed by Art 3, but fortunately for the English legal system these are only rarely complaints against the UK or its agents. From some of the decisions it might occasionally be concluded that this could make it difficult for English courts fully to appreciate the circumstances facing potential deportees, whether on a humanitarian basis as in *N v UK* (2007) or because of fear of state-inspired action being taken against them on their return home or to their country of origin.

Balancing the broad interests of the UK as a whole against the widely differing individual

circumstances of litigants or defendants in light of the Convention and other domestic civil liberty requirements is especially fraught with difficulty and it is not made any easier by the frequently changed complexities of UK immigration and asylum law.

ACTIVITY

Self-assessment questions

1   Can you write from memory a clear short definition of (a) torture and (b) inhuman or degrading treatment?

2   What are the 'five techniques?

3   Who, if anyone, is allowed to inflict corporal punishment on children under English law?

4   Who is the UN special *rapporteur* on torture and what are his remits?

5   What results were revealed by Professor Stanley Milgram's research into ordinary people's behaviour in the early 1960s?

6   How is the question of the minimum severity of treatment assessed?

7   What are the essential differences between humiliation, degrading treatment and inhuman treatment?

8   What is the current law on corporal punishment of school children?

9   Which state has the highest proportion of its population (a) against and (b) in favour of the use of torture to extract information from suspects?

10   Which body of professionals was the subject of advice under the Declaration of Tokyo 1975 and what was that advice?

C   EXTRA-TERRITORIAL TORTURE

5.13 Europe

This chapter has considered a number of instances of inhuman and degrading treatment in differing contexts, and some European cases involving the UK where torture has been alleged. It has also looked at cases heard in English courts where torture would have been possible, and perhaps likely, had the parties before the court been deported. In this section some instances of actual torture are considered.

Torture can take many forms. One of a number of Turkish examples is *Aydin v Turkey* (2006) 42 EHRR 44, where the applicant was the wife of a Turkish citizen of Kurdish origin whose husband had been held in isolation, beaten and shot through the head. The applicant herself alleged that she had been mistreated and she was subsequently granted asylum in Switzerland. The nature of her mistreatment was that she had been grabbed by the hair, slapped in the face, ordered to strip naked and detained in a police cell for four days.

The European Court's determination was that her husband's treatment had amounted to torture but the claim that her own treatment had been inhuman and degrading was not upheld. It should be said that the state strongly contested the allegations but also failed to fulfil its obligation under Art 38 to furnish all necessary facilities to the Commission and the Court to assist their job of investigating the allegations and reaching conclusions.

In *Aksoy v Turkey* (1996) 23 EHRR 553 it was found that torture had been inflicted where the victim was stripped naked and suspended with his arms tied behind his back. In another case a Turkish woman of Kurdish origin claimed that when she was arrested in June 1993 by Turkish security forces she had been detained for three days during which she was beaten, tortured and raped. Other components of her torture were being kept blindfolded, paraded naked in humiliating circumstances and 'on one occasion she was pummelled with high pressure water while being spun around in a tyre' (*Aydin (Sukran) v Turkey* (1998) 25 EHRR 251).

It has been alleged that during the Greek military dictatorship between 1967 and 1974 torture was used for two purposes, namely the gathering of information to use against its opponents, and to intimidate and discourage dissidents (Mika Haritos-Fatouros, *The Psychological Origins of Institutionalised Torture*, Routledge Research International Series in Social Psychology).

In *Menesheva v Russia* (2007) 44 EHRR 56, the applicant was a 19-year-old woman whose flat was invaded by police without warrants on a number of occasions and when she took exception to this she was beaten, kicked, thrown against a wall, carried upside down and dragged down stairs, administratively detained and refused medical treatment. Forensic medical examination revealed multiple bruises and cuts to her body, and a traumatic swelling of the soft tissue of her head, but she was denied all domestic law remedies. The ill-treatment was found to amount to torture within the meaning of Art 3 having regard to her age, gender and the purpose, severity and duration of her ill-treatment.

5.14 Torture elsewhere

It is apparent that torture can and does occur in many countries and has not been abolished despite human rights progress in recent years. We can now look briefly at a few snapshots of what is still happening across the world. They are not the only examples but are important because they point to states who claim to adhere to rights standards or hold themselves out as exemplars to others.

5.14.1 USA

Human Rights Watch, an American INGO, summarise their understanding of the stance of the US George W Bush Government on the use of interrogative techniques as follows:

'Each day brings more information about the appalling abuses inflicted upon men and women held by the United States in Iraq, Afghanistan, and elsewhere around the world. US forces have used interrogation techniques including hooding, stripping detainees naked, subjecting them to extremes of heat, cold, noise and light, and depriving them of sleep – in violation of the Geneva Conventions and the Convention against Torture and Other Cruel, Inhuman or Degrading Treatment or Punishment. This apparently routine infliction of pain, discomfort, and humiliation has expanded in all too many cases into vicious beatings, sexual degradation, sodomy, near drowning, and near asphyxiation. Detainees have died under questionable circumstances while incarcerated.

This must end. Torture or other cruel, inhuman, or degrading practices should be as unthinkable as slavery. US Department of Defense officials have announced that certain stress interrogation techniques will no longer be used in Iraq. But President Bush should ban all forms of abuse during interrogation in Iraq and everywhere else that the United States holds people in custody. It is wrong in itself and leads to further atrocities.'

http://www.hrw.org/campaigns/torture.htm

An editorial in the *New York Times* published the following opening paragraph on 26th October 2005:

'Amid all the natural and political disasters it faces, the White House is certainly tireless in its effort to legalize torture. This week, Vice President Dick Cheney proposed a novel solution for the moral and legal problems raised by the use of American soldiers to abuse prisoners and the practice of turning captives over to governments willing to act as proxies in doing the torturing. Mr. Cheney wants to make it legal for the Central Intelligence Agency to do this wet work.'

These are serious allegations but it should be noted that they are made by a highly reputable and respected US INGO and newspaper respectively.

5.14.2 China

The UN's special *rapporteur* on torture, Manfred Nowak, was reported by the BBC to have had his fact-finding efforts in China 'obstructed'. He said that although Beijing outlawed torture in 1996 and it had declined in cities, it still occurred and was used to extract confessions. However, he was allowed to visit detention centres in Beijing, Tibet and Xinjiang. He was concerned about psychological torture in labour camps but considered that on the whole it was 'on the decline, but still widespread'.

Methods used included 'use of electric shock batons, cigarette burns, and submersion in pits of water or sewage'. Continuous monitoring meant that intimidation also continued and this produced 'a palpable level of fear and self-censorship ... until major legal reforms allowed for an independent judiciary, the problem of torture could not be brought under effective control in China'.

5.14.3 Chile

The case of the late Senator Pinochet Ugarte, former President of Chile, provides an interesting study of the legal processes that may be involved in attempts to bring to justice persons accused of torture. On 11th September 1973 General Pinochet, Commander-in-Chief of the Chilean Military, instituted a *coup d'etat* against the democratically elected socialist president and government of Chile and established a military dictatorship. Assisted by the American CIA, he then oversaw the harsh detention of tens of thousands of the regime's opponents and the killing or 'disappearing' of an estimated several thousand others.

During the currency of his regime victims were incarcerated without trial and many were tortured. He was later appointed president, which was confirmed by a questionable plebiscite in 1980, and stayed in power until 1988 although remaining head of the Chilean Military until 10th March 1998 when he became a Life Senator. In 1998 he was in the UK seeking medical treatment when international legal action was taken in an attempt to hold him to account for human rights abuses including torture of victims. As can be seen from the following Case Example, the legal history of this case is somewhat complex.

CASE EXAMPLE

R v Bow Street Metropolitan Stipendiary Magistrate, ex p Pinochet Ugarte (No 1) [2001] 1 AC 61

A Spanish judge Baltasar Garzon attempted to have Senator Pinochet extradited to Spain for the alleged torture and murder of a Spanish citizen in Chile and provisional warrants were granted by an English Stipendiary Magistrate. Application was made on the Senator's behalf for judicial review which was resisted by the Spanish Government. The issue was essentially a conflict between the alleged commission of crimes of torture and murder, and the claim of Senator Pinochet to immunity regardless of what might have occurred based on his being a former head of state. In November 1998 the House of Lords by a 3:2 majority in *R v Bow Street Metropolitan Stipendiary Magistrate, ex p Pinochet Ugarte (No 1)* [2001] 1 AC 61 upheld the Spanish Government and found that the Senator did not have immunity.

However, his legal representatives discovered that Lord Hoffmann, one of the judges in that decision, had been an unpaid director and chairman of Amnesty International Charity Ltd which was wholly controlled by Amnesty International, who had been

CONTINUED ▸

allowed to intervene and give evidence in the previous decision. On the principle that justice must not only be done but must be seen to be done, the House of Lords ruled in January 1999 that there had to be a re-hearing of the case by a differently constituted Committee of the House of Lords (R v Bow Street Metropolitan Stipendiary Magistrate, ex p Pinochet Ugarte (No 2) [2001] 1 AC 119.

The Criminal Justice Act 1988 s 134 in force on 29th September 1988 made torture a crime under UK law and triable in the UK, regardless of where it was committed. The statute gave effect to the UN Convention against Torture and other Cruel, Inhuman or Degrading Treatment or Punishment 1984. The Convention had been ratified by both the UK and Chile. The effect of this was that the reconstituted Committee of the House of Lords decided in March 1999 that Senator Pinochet had no immunity in respect of authorising or organising torture after 8th December 1988 (R v Bow Street Metropolitan Stipendiary Magistrate, ex p Pinochet Ugarte (No 3) [2000] 1 AC 147). What this did was to reduce dramatically the charges against Pinochet from 32 charges of conspiracy to torture and murder, hostage-taking and actual torture, to two charges of conspiracy to torture and one of torture.

In May 1999 his application for judicial review of that latest decision was refused by Ognall J on the ground that such further proceeding would not assist the smooth and efficient conduct of the process and that Senator Pinochet could challenge the decision in the actual extradition proceedings that were now to go ahead (R v Secretary of State for the Home Department, ex p Pinochet Ugarte (1999) CLY 2291 QBD). A further attempt by a number of human rights organisations to be served with papers and to intervene in the case was refused by the Divisional Court in December 1999 (Re Pinochet Ugarte (Habeas Corpus) (2000) 97(1) LSG 24).

In January 2000 the Home Secretary Jack Straw, on the basis of medical evidence and without further legal proceedings, allowed Senator Pinochet to return to Chile, although by then the governments of Spain, Belgium, France and Switzerland had become involved in attempts to bring him to justice for alleged torture or murder of their respective citizens. Following his return to Chile continuing attempts were made there to bring him to trial without success until his death on 10th December 2006.

The effect of these cases, although ultimately unsuccessful in terms of actually dealing with the alleged crimes of Senator Pinochet, was to challenge previously held assumptions that heads of state could act with impunity and be protected from the consequences by the law. However, in *Jones v Ministry of Interior Al-Mamlaka Al-Arabiya AS Saudiya (the Kingdom of Saudi Arabia) and others* [2006] UKHL 26, attempts by two UK subjects to bring civil claims against Saudi officials for alleged torture in Saudi Arabia were not upheld by the House of Lords who unanimously agreed that there is no removal of State immunity from either the State or its officials for the purposes of international civil claims for torture.

5.15 Conclusions

With regard to treatment of persons within the UK, allegations of torture are almost unthinkable and most unlikely. This is not say that UK courts are unfamiliar with it, usually in the context of considering cases where potential deportees are resisting deportation or extradition. Cases involving inhuman or degrading treatment have been successfully brought against the UK Government in cases including children and adults, educational and judicial procedures, and in connection with treatment of handicapped persons. In Europe torture does not seem to be common but is not unknown and study of the case law shows that much of it tends to arise out of ethnic or cultural circumstances. In the wider world it appears that torture is a commonly used weapon, with rape and physical attacks resorted to in order to spread terror and subdue enemies.

KEY FACTS

Rule/principle/meaning	Authority
Corporal punishment is absolutely prohibited in all UK educational establishments	Schools Standards and Framework Act 1998
Parental physical punishment is still permissible in England and Wales	Common law defence of 'reasonable chastisement' is still available
The European Commission has found the UK Government guilty of torture but this was not upheld by the European Court	*The Republic of Ireland v The United Kingdom* (1979–80)
Extradition is not allowed to a State where inhuman or degrading treatment may be inflicted	*Soering v United Kingdom* (1989) *A (and others) v Secretary of State for the Home Department* (2005)
Behaviour is relative and assessed according to circumstances such as nature and context of treatment or punishment, manner and method of its execution, duration, its physical or mental effects and, in some cases, the sex, age and health of the victim	*T and V v United Kingdom* (2000)

CONTINUED ▸

KEY FACTS

Rule/principle/meaning	Authority
Where an individual is in custody the threshold for infliction of inhuman treatment is lowered	*Tomasi v France* (1992) 15 EHRR 1 para 113

Useful resources

Globescan and University of Maryland research on support for torture: www.globescan.com or
    www.pipa.org.
Human Rights Watch: US Torture and Abuse of Detainees: http://www.hrw.org/campaigns/torture.htm.
International Rehabilitation Council for Torture Victims: online Torture Journal:
    http://www.irct.org/Default.aspx?ID=61.
Stanford Encyclopedia of Philosophy: Torture: http://plato.stanford.edu/entries/torture/.
UN Convention against Torture and Other Cruel, Inhuman or Degrading Treatment or Punishment:
    http://www.unhchr.ch/html/menu3/b/h_cat39.htm.
World Organisation Against Torture: http://www.omct.org/.

Further reading

Bates, E, 'State Immunity for Torture (Case Comment)', HRL Rev 2007, 7(4), 651–680.
Burchard, C, 'Torture in the Jurisprudence of the Ad Hoc Tribunals: A Critical Assessment', JICJ 2008,
    6(2), 159–182.
Duffy, A, 'Expulsion to Face Torture? Non-refoulement in International Law', IJRL 2008, 20(3),
    373–390.
Gaeta, P, 'When is the Involvement of State Officials a Requirement for the Crime of Torture?', JICJ
    2008, 6(2), 183–193.
Orakhelashvili, A, 'State Immunity and Hierarchy of Norms: Why the House of Lords got it Wrong
    (Case Comment)' EJIL 2007, 18(5), 955–970.
Ovey, C and White, R C A, *Jacobs and White The European Convention on Human Rights* (4th edn,
    Oxford University Press, 2006), 74–109.
Sweeney, J A, 'The Human Rights of Failed Asylum Seekers in the United Kingdom', PL 2008, Sum,
    277–301.

6 PROHIBITION AGAINST SLAVERY ■

AIMS AND OBJECTIVES   □ □ □

The aims of this chapter are to:

- Obtain an overview of the historical and common law background, and statutory abolition of slavery and the slave trade

- Consider slavery and associated evils as a global phenomenon

- Identify the principal treaties, conventions and protocols

- Analyse the terms of Article 4 of the ECHR and case law

- Examine aspects of human trafficking and governmental policy to tackle it.

6.1 Slavery, servitude, forced or compulsory labour

6.1.1 Background

No one knows for certain where or when slavery began but it was certainly thousands of years ago. What we do know is that ancient civilizations regarded the institution as both normal and essential to supporting their ways of life. Humans have had domesticated animals for at least the last 10,000 years for agricultural purposes and as domestic pets, although obviously this is not regarded as slavery; but it is interesting to note that humans are not unique in this regard: kinds of servitude also seem to exist in the insect kingdom. Ants use aphids as slaves, and worker bees are destined to serve the greater interest of the hive. This chapter will, of course, concentrate on how human beings treat other human beings.

Most historically recorded civilizations seem to have believed that slavery was not morally wrong. There is controversy about whether, and if so the extent to which, the ancient Egyptians needed slaves to build pyramids, but the practice was certainly regarded as normal by the Greeks and Romans. More recently, European nations, particularly those adjacent to the western seaboard, regarded it as natural and highly profitable to trade with Africans, who themselves were prepared to sell their own compatriots in order to survive, dominate, punish or grow rich. The campaign to abolish the triangular trade between Europe, West Africa and the West Indies was waged for decades in the late eighteenth and early nineteenth centuries but, despite abolition both of the institution itself and slave trading, slavery is still practised today with painful consequences in Europe and the wider world.

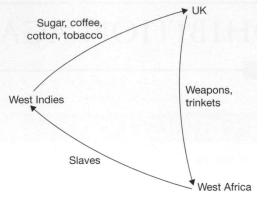

Figure 6.1 Triangular slave trade

Like piracy, slavery is regarded as a heinous crime that offends all humanity because it flies in the face of every tenet of moral and ethical human behaviour and potentially threatens everyone. There are a number of conventions devoted to it and related mistreatment, together with articles in other more general treaties, as can be seen in Figure 6.2.

6.1.2 Common law

After the Romans had finally left England from about the year 400 AD, slavery in the classical sense no longer existed, although the majority of the population lived in conditions of what might now be called servitude both before and after the Norman invasion. The common law that developed following the Norman Conquest had little to say about slavery for several centuries even though, later on, British traders became involved along with the Portuguese, Spanish, French and Dutch in the triangular slave trade between Europe, West Africa and the West Indies. Slavery was not introduced into England, however, although British traders did make fortunes out of it. There is a moral ambiguity here in that the practice was accepted so far as the lucrative overseas trade was concerned, but it seemed to give rise to controversy when brought home to England.

Towards the end of the eighteenth century the case of *R v Knowles, ex parte Somersett* (1772) 20 State Tr 1; (1772) Lofft 1 brought the slavery question before the English court because an African American slave, who had been purchased in Virginia by a man called Charles Stuart, was brought to England and managed to escape. A reward was offered; he was recaptured; and Stuart intended to return him to Jamaica where he was to be sold. Before that could be done, a writ of *habeas corpus* was issued and the case was heard by the Chief Justice of King's Bench, Lord Mansfield.

There has been much written about the case and background to it, but part of Lord Mansfield's judgment delivered on the 22nd June 1772 stated that:

Translated into modern terms Lord Mansfield was saying that slavery is so odious to the common law that only positive law, meaning a deliberate statutory enactment, could impose it in England or today in the UK. It provides an interesting anticipation of Benthamite and Austinian

> **J** 'The state of slavery is of such a nature, that it is incapable of being introduced on any reasons, moral or political; but only positive law, which preserves its force long after the reasons, occasion, and time itself from whence it was created, is erased from memory: it is so odious, that nothing can be suffered to support it, but positive law. Whatever inconveniences, therefore, may follow from a decision, I cannot say this case is allowed or approved by the law of England; and therefore the black must be discharged.'

theories of positive law, and completely refuses to accept that there is any natural law justification for the institution.

English law can be rightly proud of Lord Mansfield's stance in *Somersett*, which is why it was highlighted in Chapter 1.3.1, as was the UK's role in international abolition. Between them, prohibition of torture and slavery form the bedrock upon which all other human rights can be constructed.

6.1.3 Statutory reform

Shortly after that decision and from about 1785 onwards, anti-slave trade activists known as the Clapham Sect campaigned to have a new positive law enacted for the opposite purpose which eventually led to the Slave Trade Act 1807 and Slavery Abolition Act 1833. The former abolished the slave trade in the British Empire and the latter the institution of slavery itself, but only in the British Empire.

For much of the remainder of the nineteenth century the Royal Navy attempted to stamp out both evils across the oceans of the world. British trading in slaves had begun during the reign of Elizabeth I in 1562, and those who had profited and were still at the time of abolition profiting

Convention/Declaration	Year
Slavery, Servitude, Forced Labour and Similar Institutions and Practices Convention of 1926 (Slavery Convention of 1926) (as amended by the 1953 Protocol)	1926 1953
Convention Concerning Forced Labour (ILO No 29)	1932
Universal Declaration of Human Rights Art 4	1948
European Convention on Human Rights Art 4	1950
Supplementary Convention on the Abolition of Slavery, the Slave Trade, and Institutions and Practices Similar to Slavery	1956
Abolition of Forced Labour Convention (ILO No 105)	1959
Council of Europe Convention on Action against Trafficking in Human Beings	2005

Figure 6.2 Slavery and related crimes

from the trade were compensated by the taxpayer in the sum of £20 million, although the ex-slaves themselves were not compensated.

6.1.4 A global problem

Abolition of slavery is even today still a work in progress and one that by the nature of things will never be completely eradicated. In the twentieth century slavery still persists, as can be seen from the following table setting out a number of League of Nations, ILO, UN, EU and Council of Europe conventions and declarations.

'Related crimes' or violations here refer to the fact that slavery, servitude and forced or compulsory labour are dealt with in Art 4 of the Universal and European Conventions, whilst people-trafficking is addressed separately in the 2005 Council of Europe Convention. Nevertheless the offences are closely connected, as a considerable amount of people-trafficking of one kind or another goes on both within and into Europe. The victims of this end up and survive, rather than live, in conditions that amount at least to servitude or forced labour and sometimes what might be described as *quasi,* if not technically, full-blown slavery.

The conventions that address these issues are global and regional, some stemming from the days of the League of Nations in the 1920s, some under the auspices of the only remaining League of Nations body, the International Labour Organisation (ILO), and others from the UN or Council of Europe. It is worth noting that the Council of Europe has been responsible for over 200 treaties and its interest and activities are not solely restricted to the ECHR (see links at the end of this chapter).

Children are amongst the most badly affected victims of slavery and servitude-connected activities in the modern world, as indicated in the next table:

Problem	Estimated numbers	Source
Forced and bonded child labour	246 million	ILO
Trafficked children	1.2 million	UNICEF
Sexually exploited children	1 million	UNICEF
Child soldiers	300,000	UNICEF

Figure 6.3 Exploitation of children

6.2 Definitions

Article 4(1) of the ECHR states categorically that 'No one shall be held in slavery or servitude', so providing an absolute prohibition on both evils. The Article is set out in full at the end of this section at 6.2.1. According to Art 1 of the 1926 Slavery Convention, 'slavery is the status or condition of a person over whom any or all of the powers attaching to the rights of ownership are exercised'. No derogation with regard either to slavery or servitude is possible under Art 15 of the ECHR.

Aspects of servitude are addressed indirectly in the UN 1956 Supplementary Convention Art 7(b) by reference to 'a person of servile status' characteristics of whom are established in Art 1 as debt bondage, serfdom, or more generally institutions or practices that allow people to be exploited by others. The difficulty with this 'combined' approach is analogous to the way that torture and its lesser gradations are dealt together. Slavery is less common yet relatively easy to identify, whilst servitude can imply many shades of deprivation of freedom and servility ranging from virtual or quasi slavery to benign treatment of someone who otherwise could be much worse off.

Article 4(2) of the ECHR is also couched in categorical terms stating that 'No one shall be required to perform forced or compulsory labour', but rather than defining what is meant by 'forced or compulsory labour' Art 4(3) identifies a number of things which are excluded, these being work done:

- whilst in legitimate detention
- of a military character, or substituted work done as a conscientious objector
- perforce in case of emergency or calamity that threatens life or the well-being of the community
- by way of 'normal civic obligations'.

The origin of the expression 'forced or compulsory labour' lies in the 1932 ILO Convention supplemented by that of 1957, and as the ILO still exists as a functioning organisation specialising in this field the European Commission on Human Rights has been, and the European Court of Human Rights still is, influenced by ILO interpretation of the phrase. As it describes itself, 'the International Labour Organization (ILO) is the tripartite UN agency that brings together governments, employers and workers of its member states in common action to promote decent work throughout the world'. The essential underlying element of slavery is the practice of a master or mistress extracting work out of the slave whilst providing no remuneration or reward, thus denying and negating the slave's very humanity.

What emerges, therefore, is that slavery and servitude are considered to be conditions of ongoing status, with servitude being a lesser degree of slavery. Slavery would last for life and servitude for a long period, if not for life. Forced labour is different, understood as something that may become necessary from time to time and be imposed legitimately by society on people who otherwise enjoy the usual freedoms of that society, but subject to valid exceptions by way of punishment imposed by the state, or to other contributory obligations arising in times of stress, natural disaster or war.

Examples of the practical effects of this in an acceptable context if properly used are that, in peacetime, law-abiding subjects (now under the Criminal Justice Act 2003 including lawyers and judges) are required to undertake jury service, whilst criminals may be forced to undertake

community service or be subjected to the terms of Anti-Social Behaviour Orders (ASBOs). In wartime, conscription may be introduced and civilians directed to contribute agricultural work towards the war effort on the land or by manufacturing munitions, although perhaps the nature of modern warfare makes such impositions less likely for the future. These and similar duties are, or would be, acceptable as 'normal civic obligations' if fairly applied and are discussed in more detail in s 6.

6.2.1 ECHR Article 4

Art 4 of the ECHR provides as follows:

> **(A)** 'Prohibition of slavery and forced labour
>
> 1 No one shall be held in slavery or servitude
>
> 2 No one shall be required to perform forced or compulsory labour
>
> 3 For the purpose of this article the term 'forced or compulsory labour' shall not include:
>
> a any work required to be done in the ordinary course of detention imposed according to the provisions of Article 5 of this Convention or during conditional release from such detention;
>
> b any service of a military character or, in case of conscientious objectors in countries where they are recognised, service exacted instead of compulsory military service;
>
> c any service exacted in case of an emergency or calamity threatening the life or well-being of the community;
>
> d any work or service which forms part of normal civic duties.'

6.3 Slavery and servitude

In Europe claims that certain groups of people, subject to protection by the ECHR, are slaves have not been upheld by the Commission or the Court. For example the argument in *Sijakova and others v FYRM* (App 67914/01), Decision of 27th April 2004 that children who had joined the monastic order of the Macedonian Orthodox Church were being held in conditions of slavery was dismissed.

It was argued in *Cyprus v Turkey* (2002) 35 EHRR 731 that missing Greek Cypriots would effectively be held in servitude if it turned out that they were detained in Turkish custody, but as a hypothetical proposition this was also dismissed by the Commission and Court.

The European Court of Human Rights has recently given detailed consideration to the provisions of Art 4 of the ECHR as discussed in the French case of *Siliadin*.

CASE EXAMPLE

Siliadin v France Application No 73316/01 (2006) 43 EHRR 16

This case heard by the European Court of Human Rights in July 2005 provides a useful recent consideration of a modern instance of servitude. The applicant here was not a slave nor subjected to compulsory labour and was not in the strict sense of the word trafficked. Nevertheless, she and her family were tricked and she was subjected to forced labour induced by fear and ignorance.

The applicant was from Togo, aged 15 years and seven months, and Mrs D the woman who took her to France was a French national but herself also of Togolese origins. The agreement was that the applicant would work at Mrs D's home to earn sufficient money to pay for her air fare and in the meantime her immigration status would be regularised and she would be educated.

Reality turned out to be rather different. Her passport and tourist visa were confiscated by Mrs D and after working a few months for her she was 'lent' to Mr and Mrs B where she was obliged to work 15 hours a day without pay, education, identity documents or resolution of her immigration status. She escaped after a time but returned following pressure from her uncle, although her living conditions did not improve.

At some point her lot was reported to the French authorities by the Committee Against Modern Slavery, which resulted in criminal proceedings and conviction of Mr and Mrs B of the offence of obtaining performance of unpaid or inadequately remunerated services, but the conviction was overturned on appeal. Further appeals eventually upheld the applicant's contentions although the final domestic court decision still failed to establish the offence of subjecting the applicant to working or living conditions incompatible with human dignity.

The court did find, however, that the treatment had caused her extensive psychological trauma. She was awarded damages and subsequently arrears of salary and compensation in lieu of notice. Domestic remedies at that stage having been exhausted, the applicant claimed that her right to be free from slavery, forced labour and servitude had been violated due to the lack of protection provided by French law.

The European Court held unanimously that there had been a violation of Art 4. The government's argument that she had lost her status as a victim was dismissed and the fact that the state had itself refrained from infringing her rights did not suffice to conclude that France had complied with its obligations deriving from Art 1. In other words, there was a positive obligation on the state to ensure that Art 4 was not breached, and in ensuring that her right to respect for her private life was not infringed.

CONTINUED ▶

That obligation could therefore extend to the state adopting measures governing inter-personal relationships to prevent ill-treatment administered by private individuals against children and other vulnerable individuals. Had this conclusion about the state's positive obligations not been reached, the protection of the relevant international instruments would have been rendered ineffective. Art 4, which enshrines one of the fundamental values of democratic societies, made no provision for exceptions or derogation even in the event of war or other public emergency threatening the life of the nation.

The facts here were not under any substantial dispute, and the circumstances contravened other treaty obligations, for example the ILO Forced Labour Convention 1930 Art 2(1). Although not directly menaced by any 'penalty', she had been intimidated by her absence of legitimate immigration status and was fearful of being arrested by the police. The bottom line was that she had not performed the required work of her own free will.

The Court went on to consider other treaty obligations under the 1927 Slavery Convention, finding that these circumstances did not constitute slavery as defined by that Convention, although the concept of 'servitude' was linked and this brought in the Supplementary Convention on the Abolition of Slavery, the Slave Trade, and Institutions and Practices Similar to Slavery. France had not observed its obligations to take all practicable and necessary steps to bring about the complete abolition or abandonment of unacceptable practices such as freedom of movement or free time, quite apart from the individual's broken promises.

The state's case was not assisted by the fact that a French Parliamentary Committee had drawn attention to deficiencies in French criminal law in this regard. The domestic judicial system had only been partially effective and significantly had failed to uphold a criminal conviction of exploiting the applicant's labour and subjecting her to conditions incompatible with human dignity, so in effect the offences were not being taken sufficiently seriously by the state.

6.4 Servitude and forced labour

Compared with slavery and servitude the issue of forced labour has given rise to many more cases, with mixed results. In *Pearson v United Kingdom* (App 8374/03), Decision of 27th April 2004 the claim that the discrepancy between women's and men's retirement ages of 60 and 65 respectively meant that men had to suffer five years' forced labour was rejected.

The difference between 'servitude' and 'forced labour' was considered in *Siliadin v France* at para 104 where, from the case law of the Commission and the Court, it was concluded that servitude appeared to characterise situations in which denial of the individual's freedom was not limited to the compulsory provision of labour, but also extended to his or her living conditions, and that there was no potential for improvement, an element which was absent from the concept of 'forced or compulsory labour'.

Complaints concerning forced labour go back to 1962 when the Commission heard the case of *Iversen v Norway* (App 1468/62), Decision of 17th December 1963 (1963) 6 Yearbook 278 in which a dentist who had been forced to work for the Norwegian Public Dental Service had been convicted and sentenced for refusing to complete the required stint in the service. The application was considered to be inadmissible, although there were differences of opinion in the Commission as to whether this was because it was not forced labour or alternatively that it was acceptable public service.

CASE EXAMPLE

Van Droogenbroeck v Belgium (1982) 4 EHRR 443

Belgian law provides that habitual criminals with a long history of offences and convictions may be labelled as 'recidivists', which means that they can be detained and forced to undertake work. The applicant here had such a history and was so designated but complained that he had been held in servitude and forced to work, contrary to Arts 4(1) and (2) of the ECHR, as well as being deprived of his liberty contrary to Art 5(1). He claimed that he was refused judicial review and the Commission upheld his complaint under Art 5 but by majority rejected the other complaints. The Court agreed that Art 5 had been violated because of his inability at reasonably regular intervals to test the lawfulness of his detention by judicial review, but they too rejected the Art 4 forced labour complaints.

With regard to prison work the Court said that:

(a) The detention of habitual offenders at the discretion of the Government did not involve a sufficiently serious form of denial of freedom to amount to servitude.

(b) The work which the applicant was asked to do in prison was imposed in the ordinary course of detention and was justified under Art 4 (3) (*a*) of the Convention.

To have been regarded as 'servitude' it would have needed to involve a 'particularly serious denial of freedom' which was not present here. The work was designed to help him reintegrate himself into society. The legal basis for doing this had equivalence in provisions imposed by other Member States of the Council of Europe and so was in line with what was acceptable.

6.5 Military Service

There is little case law on whether, and if so to what extent, military service might be construed as forced or compulsory service. In the UK conscription ended in 1960, so for almost 50 years there has been little need for it to be raised in the context of domestic law, although the question was considered in the late 1960s in *W, X, Y and Z v United Kingdom* (App 3435–38/67); (1968) 11 YB 562. Four 15- and 16-year-olds had joined the British Army and Navy and signed on for a period of nine years to commence on their eighteenth birthdays. They later changed their minds about serving in the armed forces but were refused permission to be discharged. Amongst other things they claimed that their right not to be held in servitude under Art 4(1) had been violated and that they should not be required to perform forced or compulsory labour under Art 4(2).

Those contentions were not upheld because the provisions of Art 4(3)(b) state that forced or compulsory labour shall not include any service of a military character or conscientious objector alternatives. The applicants' claims must have been founded on the hope that having signed up when under age the Commission would hold that this could be interpreted as compulsion when extended into majority for such a long period, but the words of the Convention are clear enough on this score and parental consent had been given in each case.

In English law civil cases there are some circumstances where minors can repudiate contracts entered into during minority and on reaching majority but this was not applied by analogy. The four applications were held to be inadmissible although revised regulations were introduced subsequently under which boy entrants could decide to leave after three years' service upon reaching 18 years of age.

CASE EXAMPLE

Johansen v Norway (1987) 9 EHRR CD 103

In 1987 the Norwegian Ministry of Justice recognised a conscientious objector as being exempt from military service and required him to undertake 16 months' civilian service as an alternative. The objector refused on the ground that this was also unacceptable and offended his conscience, and he argued that it was an attempt by the State to uphold respect for the military service.

In such circumstances Norwegian law provided two kinds of procedure:

* prosecution under s19 of the Act on Exemption from Military Service and sentencing to a fine or imprisonment of not more than three months, or

CONTINUED ▶

- placement of the conscientious objector in a special camp supervised by the Prison Administration Service under s 20 of the same Act to spend the period of service there

The applicant was at the time waiting to be summoned to such a special camp but argued that the conditions for s 20 to be applied had not been met in his case. His contention that his obligation was simply that he had to submit to some sixteen months of imprisonment, was rejected by the commission who took the view that his obligation was not to submit to detention, but to perform civilian service The Commission found that the complaint was manifestly ill-founded.

ACTIVITY

Self-assessment questions

1 Explain the differences between:
- slavery
- servitude
- forced or compulsory labour.

2 Summarise the main issues raised and conclusions to be reached from the following cases:
  (a) *R v Knowles, ex parte Somersett* (1772)
  (b) *W, X, Y and Z v United Kingdom* (1968)
  (c) *Van Droogenbroeck v Belgium* (1982)
  (d) *Johansen v Norway* (1987)
  (e) *Siliadin v France* (2006).

3 What is the ILO and which ILO Conventions are still applicable?

4 What analogous crime is endemic in Europe in addition to slavery, servitude and forced or compulsory labour?

5 What is the ILO's estimated number of children who are victims of forced and bonded labour in the world today?

6.6 Forced labour and Article 4(3) civil exceptions

Sometimes there is only a fine distinction between characterising types of work either as forced labour or as some other form of compulsory, but perhaps acceptable, service to the community as appeared in the case of the dentist in *Iversen v Norway.*

6.6.1 Jury service

A different type of service to the community was addressed in *Zarb Adami v Malta* Application No 17209/02; (2007) 44 EHRR 3, where a Maltese pharmacist's name was placed on the jurors'

list from 1971 to 2005. Between 1971 and 1997 he was called upon to serve either as a juror or foreman of the jury on three separate occasions in connection with criminal proceedings.

When he was required to attend on a fourth occasion he failed to turn up and refused to pay the fine that was imposed which led to a court summons the purpose of which was to convert his fine into a term of imprisonment. The applicant alleged violations of Art 4(3)(d) read in conjunction with Art 14. The European Court found that there had been violations and that it was three times more likely that as a man he would be required to undertake jury service as part of his civic obligations than it would have been had he been a woman.

6.6.2 Legal service

The Court had on a previous occasion (*Van der Mussele v Belgium* (1983) 6 EHRR 163) provided an interpretation of how Art 4 should be applied in such cases. The Belgian case dealt with a pupil advocate who was obliged to represent a defendant without remuneration and in that case no violations had been found. By way of explanation it was stated that:

> J 'paragraph 3 [of Art 4] is not intended to "limit" the exercise of the right guaranteed by paragraph 2, but to "delimit" the very content of this right, for it forms a whole with paragraph 2 and indicates what "the term 'forced or compulsory labour' shall not include" . . . this being so, paragraph 3 serves as an aid to the interpretation of paragraph 2.'

The Court went on to hold that:

> J 'the four sub-paragraphs of paragraph 3, notwithstanding their diversity, are grounded on the governing ideas of the general interest, social solidarity and what is in the normal or ordinary course of affairs. The final sub-paragraph, namely sub-paragraph (d) which excludes "any work which forms part of normal civil obligations" from the scope of forced or compulsory labour, is of especial significance in the context of the present case.'

Art 4 is somewhat complex in structure because in two sub-clauses it proscribes two kinds of behaviour, whilst the other sub-clauses set out exceptions, so this guidance is useful as an aid to interpretation.

6.6.3 Fire service

There was a requirement of German law that men, but not women, should either serve as firemen or alternatively pay a financial levy. Karlheinz Schmidt claimed that this was discriminatory and that it contravened Art 4(3)(d) but his action and appeal were dismissed by the Commission. When he took his complaint to the European Court it was held that compulsory fire service was indeed part of the normal civic obligations compatible with Art 4 but that there had been discrimination in his case (*Karlheinz Schmidt v Germany* (1994) 18 EHRR 513).

6.6.4 Sport

The favourable bases on which many professional sportspersons are employed nowadays may seem generous, but lucrative contracts were not always available and in particular the profession of footballer used to be much more of a working man's trade than a celebrity sport, at least in the way it was remunerated and with regard to the terms of employment.

In 1963 Wilberforce J, as he then was, held in the case of *Eastham v Newcastle United Football Club* [1963] 1 Ch 413 that a declaration should be made in favour of a footballer against the Football Association and the Football League to the effect that the 'retention and transfer' system then operated was an unlawful restraint of trade. The system prevented players from taking up new employment even after their contracts had ended. It would have been interesting to see the outcome had it gone to the European Commission as Eastham was not being forced to undertake work but was being prevented from so doing.

In *A v Netherlands* (App No 9322/81); (1983) 5 EHRR CD598 a professional football player had also concluded his club contract. Although he was offered a further contract he declined to sign it and it was alleged that his club were insisting on 'prohibitive' compensation to let him go. The applicant argued that this was in effect forced or compulsory labour and was discriminatory. He blamed not only his club but the Dutch Football Association and State for authorising and tolerating such a system.

The Commission's *jurisprudence constante* was interpreted so that the concept of forced or compulsory labour contained in Art 4 of the Convention comprised two main elements which it is reasonable to take into account when interpreting this provision. These were that the:

- labour or service must be either unjust or oppressive, or
- the service itself must constitute an avoidable hardship.

Jurisprudence constante is the civil law doctrine according to which a long series of previous decisions applying a particular rule of law carries considerable weight and may be determinative in subsequent cases. This is comparable with the common law doctrine of *stare decisis* or 'let the decision stand', otherwise known as the doctrine of judicial precedent. In *A v Netherlands* only the Dutch State was subject to the Commission's jurisdiction and because, as an individual, A's own possessions would not be diminished it rendered his case inadmissible as he could not be forced to carry on playing for his original club.

ACTIVITY

Quick Quiz

1 What was the status of slavery under the common law?

2 What was the name given to the late eighteenth-/early nineteenth-century reformers who brought about the abolition of slavery and the slave trade in the British Empire?

3 What were the two Acts of Parliament that dealt with the ending of slavery and the slave trade?

4 Name three treaties/conventions dealing with twentieth-century slavery.

5 What are the four things prohibited by ECHR Art 4?

6 What are the four things that are allowed as exceptions to two of the prohibitions under Art 4?

7 Name and briefly outline the significance of one case relating to each of the following:
- military service
- jury service
- legal service
- fire service
- sport.

8 Explain *jurisprudence constante*.

6.7 Council of Europe Convention against Trafficking in Humans

Closely connected to traditional understanding of slavery, servitude, and forced or compulsory labour is trafficking in human beings. In explaining concern about trafficking, the Council of Europe have said in justification of a new treaty that 'this phenomenon has hit unprecedented levels, to the extent that it can be considered as a new form of slavery'.

For that reason the Council of Europe prepared a comprehensive treaty which focused primarily on protection of victims of trafficking and safeguarding their rights. Its objectives include protection of victims as well as prosecution of perpetrators. The Council of Europe Convention on Action against Trafficking in Human Beings (CETS No 197) was adopted by the Committee of Ministers on 3rd May 2005 and opened for signature in Warsaw on 16th May 2005.

Provision is made in the Convention for establishing an independent monitoring mechanism which guarantees parties' compliance with its provisions. It applies to national or transnational forms of trafficking, whether or not it involves organised crime. It draws no distinction between types of victim – men, women or children – and applies whatever sexual, labour or other forms of exploitation may have occurred.

The definition of trafficking under the Convention is as follows:

'Trafficking in human beings' shall mean the recruitment, transportation, transfer, harbouring or receipt of persons, by means of the threat or use of force or other forms of coercion, of abduction, of fraud, of deception, of the abuse of power or of a position of vulnerability or of the giving or receiving of payments or benefits to achieve the consent of a person having control over another person, for the purpose of exploitation.

Exploitation shall include, at a minimum, the exploitation of the prostitution of others or other forms of sexual exploitation, forced labour or services, slavery or practices similar to slavery, servitude or the removal of organs.'

In summary, therefore, what the treaty does is threefold in that it:

1 prevents trafficking

2 protects the human rights of trafficking victims

3 provides for prosecution of the traffickers.

In its campaign to prevent and deal with human trafficking the UK Government uses the definition from the Protocol to the UN Convention against Transnational Organised Crime (UNTOC) 2000, known as the Protocol to Prevent, Suppress and Punish Trafficking in Persons, especially Women and Children, which is in identical form. It is important to distinguish trafficking with the smuggling of migrants voluntarily into the UK, the Protocol definition of this activity being 'the procurement, in order to obtain, directly or indirectly, a financial or other material benefit, of the illegal entry of a person into a State Party of which the person is not a national or a permanent resident'.

6.7.1 Examples of trafficking

In June 2000, 60 illegal Chinese immigrants were trapped in a sealed lorry container and, as the air ran out, 58 of them including four women died of asphyxiation. The Dutch lorry driver was sentenced to 14 years' imprisonment and his co-accused, Ying Guo, to six years for conspiring to smuggle illegal immigrants into Britain. In June 2002 a Dutch appeal court increased the sentences of seven men convicted of belonging to a people-smuggling network responsible for the deaths of the Chinese immigrants.

In February 2004, 21 cockle pickers were drowned in Morecambe Bay. They were all Chinese, 20 from Fujian and one from Liaoning province. It was believed that two more people may also have died. Many of the bodies were identified from fishing permits, some of which contained

false names. In March 2006 a gang master Lin Liang Ren was convicted on 21 counts of manslaughter and of facilitating breaches of immigration law.

6.7.2 Operation Pentameter

One particular type of employment is especially unpleasant. In 2006 a multi-agency task force under the title of Operation Pentameter funded by the Home Office was launched. It brought together Britain's 55 police forces, the Immigration Service and the Serious and Organised Crime Agency. During that year, according to the UK Human Trafficking Centre (UKHTC) 84 victims of trafficking were identified following visits to an estimated 10 per cent of the country's sex establishments. It was found that the majority of the women came from Eastern Europe, the Baltic States and the Balkans, or from the Far East, particularly Malaysia, Thailand and China.

In January 2006 the Home Office in conjunction with the Scottish Executive launched a national consultation exercise on proposals for a UK Action Plan on human trafficking and this was followed up by a report published in March 2007. The plan had a number of objectives which effectively seemed to amount to joining up the relevant government departments with other interested agencies and making their work more transparent.

The scope of the Action Plan was described as taking the human rights approach, ie placing greater emphasis on combating human trafficking from a rights perspective rather than 'through the prism of organised immigration crime'. Whilst it is difficult enough to pin down the traffickers, it is often also hard to differentiate the women who are victims from those, perhaps a minority, who have chosen to come to the UK for purposes of prostitution. The report goes on to address forced labour and child trafficking and identifies key areas as:

- prevention
- investigation, law enforcement and prosecution
- providing protection and assistance to adult victims
- proposing specific measures to deal with child trafficking.

There are 62 objectives with their respective plans of action, timetables, parties responsible for implementation and means of assessment and it remains to be seen how successful this policy is in deterring and dealing with this human rights scourge.

6.8 Conclusions

Despite the high profile of anti-slavery, servitude, forced/compulsory labour and trafficking provisions in the twenty-first century, they all persist. They constitute a global problem and in some parts of the world outside Europe are endemic. This chapter has considered the origins of slavery, refusal of English common law to recognise it as legitimate within the realm, and the campaign to have it abolished in the rest of the world, and has addressed a range of activities analogous to slavery which are amongst the more serious of human rights breaches.

The number of treaties, conventions and protocols dealing with these topics serve as a reminder that these unfortunate victims, like the poor, are always going to exist and so particular vigilance and effort are required to combat these evils. With regard to Europe, the problems arise from trafficking humans into the continent for a variety of reasons, and the conditions in which some people live under duress in the UK and on the continent. Slavery in the historical sense is rare in Europe, but servitude, forced and compulsory labour brought about as a result of people-trafficking is not uncommon, as indicated in the previous examples.

According to the charity ECPAT UK (End Child Prostitution, Child Pornography and the Trafficking of Children for Sexual Purposes), quoting ILO sources in 2005, 2.45 million people are victims of trafficking annually, of which 50 per cent are children. UNICEF reported in 2003 that there were 250 child-trafficking cases in the UK between 1998 and 2003.

Many more examples could be quoted. Although to most people in the UK and in Europe, slavery may seem to be something that occurred in history and has been abolished, in its modern manifestations it still constitutes large-scale abuse of human rights throughout the world.

KEY FACTS

Whilst the common law prohibited slavery in England (*Somersett's Case* (1772)) and later the UK, British traders made fortunes out of slaves and the slave trade in the rest of the world

English activists – the Clapham Sect – were instrumental in having the slave trade (Slave Trade Act 1807) and slavery itself (Slavery Abolition Act 1833) abolished in the British Empire

The rest of the nineteenth century saw the gradual reduction of slavery and trade in slaves throughout the world, but not entirely successfully

In the twentieth century, international treaties continued the abolition work *via* the ILO, UN, Council of Europe and others

In the twenty-first century, slavery still exists together with modern forms of abuse including people-trafficking, bond-servitude, child labour, people-smuggling and a range of other child abuses

The ECHR anti-slavery provision is Art 4 which prohibits slavery, servitude, forced or compulsory labour whilst providing exceptions to forced or compulsory labour

The Council of Europe has strengthened international law in this area with the Convention on Action against Trafficking in Human Beings 2005

163

Useful resources

Anti-Slavery International: www.antislavery.org/.

Anti-Trafficking Alliance: http://www.atalliance.org.uk/.

Council of Europe treaties with links:

http://conventions.coe.int/Treaty/Commun/ListeTraites.asp?CM=8&CL=ENG.

Home Office UK Action Plan on Tackling Human Trafficking:

http://www.homeoffice.gov.uk/documents/human-traffick-action-plan.

International Labour Organisation Home Page:

http://www.ilo.org/global/lang-en/index.htm.

Joseph Rowntree Foundation, *Modern Slavery in the United Kingdom*, February 2007, Ref 2035:

http://www.jrf.org.uk/knowledge/findings/socialpolicy/2035.asp.

United Kingdom Human Trafficking Centre: http://www.ukhtc.org/uk.htm.

Further reading

Case comment on *Tremblay v France* (Application No 37194/02), 'Prostitution: Prostitute Required to Make Social Security Contributions – Forced Prostitution – Art 3 and 4(2)', EHRLR 2008, 1, 135–137.

Drew, S, 'Human Trafficking: A Modern Form of Slavery?' EHRLR 2002, 4, 481–492.

Egan, S, 'Protecting the Victims of Trafficking: Problems and Prospects', EHRLR, 2008, 1, 106–119.

Mantouvalou, V, 'Servitude and Forced Labour in the 21st Century: The Human Rights of Domestic Workers', ILJ 2006, 35(4), 395–414.

McArdle, D, 'One Hundred Years of Servitude: Contractual Conflict in English Professional Football before Bosman', Web JCLI 2000, 2, Internet.

Piotrowicz, R, 'The UNHCR's Guidelines on Human Trafficking', IJRL, 2008, 20(2), 242–252.

Ramage, S, 'Human Trafficking in 2008 – Blowing Away some Myths', Crim Law 2008, 184, 8–11.

chapter 7

RIGHT TO LIBERTY AND SECURITY ■

AIMS AND OBJECTIVES

This chapter examines a number of aspects of the right to liberty and security and aims to do the following:

■ Introduce civil liberties and human rights

■ Outline the scope of universal and European human rights

■ Consider Art 5 of the European Convention on Human (ECHR) and its case law.

7.1 English civil liberties

Traditional English law textbooks dealing with civil liberties address a wide range of issues under headings such as freedom of expression, protection of privacy and personal liberty. Within those broad categories are found more detailed discussion of freedom of speech, the law of contempt, protection from offensive speech, official secrecy and freedom of protest and assembly. Liberty here also refers to freedom from arbitrary arrest, protection whilst undergoing police questioning, and in respect of one's property. To make it clear, however, the scope of this chapter is mostly, although not entirely, limited to what comes within the scope of Art 5 of the ECHR.

For centuries the common law has sought to protect individuals from overenthusiastic actions by representatives of the state and in order to do so has developed procedures such as *habeas corpus* and judicial review. It has also recognised from early times the importance of lay involvement in legal process, and pays high regard to institutions such as the jury and lay magistrates. The man in the street is now, and always has been, right to treat government officials with some caution, and to extend that caution to others involved in administering the law including law practitioners, so it is important to recognise the value of these long-standing traditions and to think carefully before proposing and agreeing to the abolition of venerable protective legal institutions.

7.2 Human rights

The Second World War marked a turning point in many aspects of British life and in the following decades fundamental changes occurred, the importance and implications of which were

largely unrecognised at the time. The loss of empire and its replacement by the Commonwealth tended to delay recognition that the UK would eventually need to refocus on being a European state, and this still gives rise to scepticism even today.

Although the UK was largely instrumental in drafting the ECHR, most people were unaware of it or considered that the reason it was necessary was to force the realignment of the behaviour of other states, rather than it having much relevance to Britain. In the second half of the twentieth century, however, human rights were to become increasingly important and, although many of the ideas stemmed from common law principles, the emphasis and direction gradually altered – civil rights tended to develop into human rights.

7.2.1 Universal rights

The UN perspective of liberty and security shows a three-stage development:

1	Art 3 of the Universal Declaration of Human Rights (UDHR) states that 'Everyone has the right to life, liberty and security of person'.
2	Arts 9–13 of the International Covenant on Civil and Political Rights (1966) (ICCPR) expand the brief statement of principle in Art 3 of the UDHR and include other matters addressing fair and humane treatment whilst under arrest, juveniles, the right not to be subjected to imprisonment merely because of inability to fulfil contractual obligations, freedom of movement and similar provisions.
3	The First Optional Protocol to the ICCPR enables claims from individuals alleging they are victims of violations to be submitted to the Human Rights Committee established under Part IV of the Covenant.

7.2.2 The European Convention

By way of comparison, Art 5 of the ECHR is one of the longest and most complex in the Convention and expresses the provisions for liberty and security of person as follows:

'(1) Everyone has the right to liberty and security of the person. No one shall be deprived of his liberty save in the following cases and in accordance with a procedure prescribed by law, namely the:

(a) lawful detention of a person after conviction by a competent court;

(b) lawful arrest or detention of a person for non-compliance with the lawful order of a court or in order to secure the fulfilment of any obligation prescribed by law;

(c) lawful arrest or detention of a person effected for the purpose of bringing him before the competent legal authority on reasonable suspicion of having committed an offence or when it is reasonably considered necessary to prevent his committing an offence or fleeing after having done so;

(d) detention of a minor by lawful order for the purpose of educational supervision or his lawful detention for the purpose of bringing him before the competent legal authority;

(e) lawful detention of persons for the prevention of the spreading of infectious diseases, or persons of unsound mind, alcoholics or drug addicts or vagrants;

(f) lawful arrest or detention of a person to prevent his effecting an unauthorised entry into the country or of a person against whom action is being taken with a view to deportation or extradition.

(2) Everyone who is arrested shall be informed promptly, in a language which he understands, of the reasons for his arrest and of any charge against him.

(3) Everyone arrested or detained in accordance with the provisions of para (1)(c) of this article shall be brought promptly before a judge or other officer authorised by law to exercise judicial power and shall be entitled to trial within a reasonable time or to release pending trial. Release may be conditioned by guarantees to appear for trial.

(4) Everyone who is deprived of his liberty by arrest or detention shall be entitled to take proceedings by which the lawfulness of his detention shall be decided speedily by a court and his release ordered if the detention is not lawful.

(5) Everyone who has been the victim of arrest or detention in contravention of the provisions of this article shall have an enforceable right to compensation.'

It is perhaps ironical that the article which provides the fundamental rights to liberty and security should need to be expressed in such complex and conditional terms, but this just emphasises how difficult it is to establish and define freedom for one person whilst at the same time providing and maintaining a balance that would protect everyone else.

7.2.3 Circumstances permitting deprivation of liberty

The aim here is to provide a preliminary analysis of the article before moving on to a more detailed consideration of the case law, the emphasis of which has in some instances changed over the years. Liberty lies at the very root of European and American philosophy and, for example, was the driving force that propelled the UK into the Second World War, or the Falklands Conflict. It must also be said that perhaps mistaken ideas of liberty have steered states into other conflicts that maybe ought to have been avoided.

Art 5(1) defines six circumstances or cases in which a person can be deprived of his liberty, each of which is qualified by stating that it may only be done in accordance with a procedure prescribed by law. Arts 5(2)–5(5) stipulate some aspects of those procedures, three of which require promptness or speedy proceedings and the other an enforceable right.

The first exception in Art 5(1)(a) is confined to detention once a person has been convicted by a competent court, which precludes arrest as that will have occurred previously. Provided that due process has been observed, for example having regard to Arts 6 and 7 and provision of humane detention conditions, this accords entirely with traditional English civil liberties.

The distinction between 'arrest' and 'detention' in Art 5(1)(b) is not clear from the text of the sub-clause but in either case it deals with situations where someone has failed to comply with a lawful court order, or has not observed or fulfilled some other legal requirement.

Art 5(1)(c) also uses the alternatives of 'arrest' and 'detention' in three circumstances where the suspicion or justification is reasonable:

- to bring a suspect before a competent legal authority
- to prevent commission of an offence
- to prevent flight occurring following commission of an offence.

The second group of three exceptions justifying removal of liberty are based on other criteria, dealing with different situations each of which is distinct.

Art 5(1)(d) authorises lawful detention of a minor after an order has been made relating to his education or if it is needed to bring him before a competent legal authority. States have legal responsibilities to ensure that minimum educational provision is available for minors and it therefore follows that there should be some means of ensuring that those obligations can be fulfilled.

Art 5(1)(e) has a slightly old-fashioned ring to it, an echo of Victorian public health law, permitting as it does detention (but not arrest) in three types of medical case and dealing with one social problem:

- to prevent the spreading of infectious diseases
- to control people 'of unsound mind'
- to detain alcoholics or drug addicts
- to deal with the social problem of vagrants.

The sixth situation reverts to arrest or detention in circumstances involving restriction of freedom of movement. The ECHR does make some provision in this regard, for example Art 11 which governs freedom of assembly and association, but that is not what is being limited here. Some treaties provide for limited freedom of movement, for example Art 12 of the ICCPR, or give rights of asylum as in Art 26 of the Convention Relating to the Status of Refugees (1951), and the UDHR itself in Art 13 explicitly recognises the right to freedom of movement of persons, but these are not matters dealt with by the ECHR.

What Art 5(1)(f) of the ECHR provides for is lawful arrest or detention of a person either to prevent his unauthorised entry into a country, or with a view to deporting or extraditing him. The provisions are summarised in the following table.

Article	Criteria
5(1)	The right to liberty and security possessed by everyone is qualified by six provisions set out in paragraphs (a)–(f)
5(2)	The charge(s) and reason(s) must be given in a language the accused understands whenever a person is arrested
5(3)	This links with Art 5(1)(c) – everyone arrested or detained hereunder must promptly be brought before judicial authority for trial or release with guarantees to be provided if necessary
5(4)	Persons detained or arrested can test the lawfulness of their detention or arrest by speedy court proceedings and release if detention or arrest is unlawful
5(5)	Compensation should be awarded where arrest or detention was contrary to Art 5

 Figure 7.1 Prescribed criteria applicable to Art 5

CASE EXAMPLE

Guzzardi v Italy Series A, No 39 (1981) 3 EHRR 333

This case provides a useful introduction to the character of Art 5 and the nature of liberty under the ECHR. The applicant was a suspected Mafioso who was detained and had already been sentenced to 18 years' imprisonment for previous offences. In complaining to the Commission he relied on Arts 3 (inhuman or degrading living conditions), 8 (right to respect for family and private life), 9 (freedom to practise his religion) and there is also a rather unlikely reference to Protocol 1 Art 2 which would be his right to education.

Whilst all those arguments were rejected, the Commission of its own volition *ex officio* considered the applicability of Arts 6 (fair hearing) and 5. They unanimously found that there had been a breach of Art 5 but concluded that no other articles of the convention or of Protocol No 1 had been violated.

What is helpful in understanding the nature of Art 5 are the points made by the Commission about the scope and importance of liberty:

1. Art 5(1) is not concerned with 'mere restrictions on liberty of movement': in proclaiming the 'right to liberty' it contemplated the physical liberty of the persons and the need to ensure that no one was deprived of it in an arbitrary fashion

2. Art 5(1)(a) only allowed detention if it was established according to law that the claimant had committed an offence of either a criminal or disciplinary nature (here he was being detained pending further charges)

CONTINUED ▸

3. Art 5(1)(b)'s wording 'to secure the fulfilment of any obligation prescribed by law' only concerned cases where the law allowed detention in order to force him to fulfil a 'specific and concrete' obligation which he had failed to satisfy

4. Art 5(1)(c) did not justify the applicant's detention either because what this sub-paragraph allowed was detention of a person when it was 'reasonably considered necessary to prevent him from committing an offence' which was not adapted to support a policy of general prevention directed against an individual or groups of people such as Mafiosi

5. Art 5(1)(e) did not permit detention of Mafiosi, applying as it did to vagrants, persons of unsound mind, alcoholics and drug addicts. 'The reason why the Convention allowed the latter individuals all of whom were socially maladjusted, to be deprived of their liberty was not only that they were to be considered as occasionally dangerous but also that their own interests might necessitate their detention.'

It can be seen from the Commission's initiative in *Guzzardi* that great importance is placed on liberty, and this reflects the pride of place it takes in the French and American contributions to freedom.

7.3 Case law

7.3.1 Breach of the peace

To assess whether deprivation of liberty is 'lawful', it is necessary to be clear about the nature and extent of the particular domestic law in question. In *Steel and others v United Kingdom* (App 24838/94), Judgment of 23rd September 1998, (1998) 28 EHRR 603 there were five applicants all of whom had been convicted of breach of the peace but in three very different sets of circumstances. One had obstructed a grouse shoot by walking in front of one of the guns. The second had stood under a digger to impede motorway construction work.

The other three had been handing out leaflets and waving a banner protesting against the sale of fighter helicopters at an Arms Fair. They complained that the offence of 'breach of the peace' and the power to bind over were not sufficiently clearly defined for their detention to be 'prescribed by law', nor did they fall within any of the categories under Art 5(1). Because magistrates have immunity from civil process, they had all been denied the right to compensation under Art 5(5).

The European Court of Human Rights disagreed with these claims in respect of the first and second parties, although they found that there had not been justification for the arrest of the motorway protesters and, indeed, although they had been arrested and detained, no prosecution followed. Nevertheless, the outcome of the case vindicated the offence of breach of the peace and binding over procedures whilst leaving the circumstances in which they might occur as flexible as human nature and imagination can, and does, make it.

7.3.2 Detention without warrant and 'honest belief'

In *Fox, Campbell and Hartley v United Kingdom*, Judgment of 30th August 1990, Series A No 182; (1991) 13 EHRR 157 the applicants had been detained in Northern Ireland for periods ranging between 30 and 44 hours under s 1 of the Northern Ireland (Emergency Provisions) Act 1978 which allowed for arrest without warrant of 'any person suspected of being a terrorist'. The Commission found a violation of Art 5(1), (2) and (5) but not of Art 5(4).

Two of the complainants had been arrested and questioned on suspicion of intelligence gathering and courier work for the IRA and the third complainant was suspected of being involved in a kidnapping, although none of them were charged. The level of 'reasonable suspicion' needed in such terrorist circumstances might be rather less than for other types of case but, even so, there had to be an objective ground for the arrest.

The Court said that the reasonableness of the suspicion on which an arrest must be based forms an essential part of the safeguard against arbitrary arrest and detention. Having a reasonable suspicion presupposes the existence of facts or information which would satisfy an objective observer that the person concerned may have committed the offence. What may be regarded as reasonable depends upon all the circumstances.

The case is also authority for the proposition that honest belief in itself is insufficient to justify the claim to reasonableness, as there must also be an objective basis to justify the arrest and/or detention. This does not mean, however, that the authorities have to possess sufficient evidence to be able to charge a suspect before he or she can be arrested, and further enquiries can be made during the detention if additional investigation is needed (*Brogan and others v United Kingdom*, Judgment of 29th November 1988, Series A, No 258-B; (1998) 17 EHRR 117).

7.3.3 Courts martial

In *Hood v United Kingdom* (App No 27267/95), Judgment of 18th February 1999; (2000) 29 EHRR 365, the applicant was a soldier in the British Army who went absent from his unit without authority and was detained prior to his court martial. He claimed that this did not comply with his right to be given a prompt judicial hearing and speedy decision. The European Court found that there had been contraventions of his rights under Arts 5(3) and 5(5), but not of Art 5(4).

Both Commission and Court agreed that the commanding officer's dual responsibility for discipline and order provided good reason for Hood to doubt his impartiality when deciding on pre-trial detention. The Court recalled that courts martial proceedings were not satisfactory as decided in a previous judgment (*Findlay v United Kingdom* (App 22107/ 93); (1997) 24 EHRR 221) where there was a breach of the fair hearing requirements of Art 6.

7.3.4 Crime

The UK Government conceded in *Caballero v United Kingdom* (App 32819/96), Judgment of 8th February 2000; (2000) 30 EHRR 643 that there had been a violation of Arts 5(3) and (5) where the complainant was automatically refused bail pending his trial on a charge of attempted rape, the reason being that he had a previous conviction for manslaughter. The point at issue was that under UK law the judge had no power even to consider granting bail to Caballero whatever the actual suspicions necessitating his appearance in court, because of, yet regardless of, the circumstances of that previous conviction. This did not square with the Convention's requirement of prompt trial or release pending trial, with or without guarantees.

The offending statute was the Criminal Justice and Public Order Act 1994 s 25 which denied bail where the accused had a previous conviction for murder, attempted murder, manslaughter, rape or attempted rape. The government argued that the purpose of this section was to avoid the unacceptable risk of the court making an error of judgement and releasing a dangerous person pending trial, but did not identify any case where that had happened. In examining the relationship between the executive and the judiciary, however, it is essential that a judge has the power to order the release of someone who has been detained: otherwise, the safeguard afforded by an independent judiciary is removed.

7.3.5 Natural justice

A fundamental requirement where any question of deprivation of liberty arises is that the suspect must be given the opportunity to be heard, and failure to ensure this is likely to result in a breach of the rules of natural justice which would make an otherwise lawful procedure invalid (*Van der Leer v Netherlands* (1990) 12 EHRR 567). If there is no procedure under domestic law, or there is but it is not followed, that is also likely to be a breach of Art 5.

The lawfulness of the detention requires that it must be based on valid domestic law and conform to ECHR standards, but should not be applied in an arbitrary fashion. Therefore, there must be no abuse of power associated with the detention such as clandestine movement from one jurisdiction to another or turning a blind eye by the authorities should they have been aware of illegal activities on the part of a third party or state. Detention that is otherwise lawful may still be arbitrary if a discretionary power is fettered or proper regard is not had to relevant evidence (*Perks and others v UK* (1999) 30 EHRR 33).

It should be noted that Protocol No 4 prohibits imprisonment for debt, expulsion of nationals and collective expulsion of aliens and provides qualified guarantees of freedom of movement. Basically, what this amounts to is that the complainant must be deprived of his liberty and not merely have his movements restricted (this is covered by Art 2 of the Fourth Protocol) and to all intents and purposes there is little point in trying to establish semantic differences between liberty and security of person. Although the period of detention is important, it is not the sole determinant and a short period such as the time needed to take a blood sample may be sufficient to contravene the Convention (*X v Austria* (1979) 18 DR 154 ECmHR).

Rules of natural justice invoke notions of 'fairness' that are not always easy to pin down and which change through time and from place to place. This is an area where the margin of appreciation is important and where the balance between individual liberty and collective security needs to be carefully monitored.

7.4 Balancing liberty and security: detention without charge

The policy of the British Government is to extend as far as politically possible the time for which individuals can be held without charge whilst police investigations are undertaken. This is as much a political as a security agenda because, although it is the government's response to a number of terrorist outrages which demonstrate that these kinds of risks are ongoing, they have admitted that in no case were existing detention powers insufficient to allow the police enough investigation time. The objective was to extend detention without trial to 90 days in anticipation that one day such a period might be needed but eventually, in the face of concerted opposition, the period remained at 28 days.

There is conflict between this authoritarian approach and those who wish to uphold the long-established protection provided by common and human rights law. This is at the heart of the debate about the need for, and right to, liberty and security. It may well be the case, however, that an appreciable proportion of the general public would be prepared to accept detention without charge of those accused of terrorist activities for much longer periods of time, as they might support the reintroduction of capital punishment, were they to be asked.

Besides the obvious objection that everyone held in this way is innocent until convicted by a court, and the fact that some of the people so held may never be convicted and so actually are innocent throughout, there is the risk that such detention will alienate not only those arrested but important sectors of the general public.

In 1997, when the New Labour administration came to power, the maximum period that a person could be detained without charge was 48 hours, with the possibility that in exceptional cases that time could be extended to five days with the consent of the Home Secretary. Shortly afterwards the Criminal Justice (Terrorism and Conspiracy) Act 1998 was enacted which made it an offence to conspire to commit terrorist acts abroad, although subsequent events showed that terrorists within the jurisdiction perhaps constituted a greater danger.

Following the IRA Omagh bomb attack, the Terrorism Act 2000 extended the period of detention without charge to seven days and the Anti-Terrorism Crime and Security Act 2001 introduced indefinite detention without charge or trial for foreign terrorist suspects. The period for British citizens was extended to 14 days by the Criminal Justice Act 2003 and when the

House of Lords ruled that detention of foreign suspects without trial was illegal, the government's response in the Prevention of Terrorism Act 2005 was to introduce control orders. In 2007 these were held to be flawed too and, as indicated above, after a concerted government effort to increase the time that suspects could be held without charge to 90 days, almost three months, they were obliged to accept continuance of the 28-day time limit.

CASE EXAMPLE

A and others v Secretary of State for the Home Department [2004] UKHL 56; [2005] 2 AC 68

The government decided after the 9/11 attack on the twin towers in New York that there was a public emergency threatening the life of the nation within the meaning of Art 15 (derogation in times of emergency) of the European Convention. This was considered sufficient justification to derogate from the Art 5 liberty provisions of the Convention. Accordingly, the Human Rights Act (Designated Derogation) Order 2001 (SI 2001/3644) was made reinforced by the detention without trial provisions of non-nationals in s 23 of the Anti-terrorism, Crime and Security Act 2001.

The Home Secretary was empowered to authorise their detention based on his belief that their presence in the UK was a risk to national security in cases where he was unable to deport them because they would have been at risk from the regimes to which they were despatched (ie where he was prevented by international law from deporting them because they might have been tortured).

Seven law lords held that the courts were not precluded by any doctrine of deference from examining the proportionality of a measure taken to restrict such a right. The lords emphasised that personal liberty was among the most fundamental rights protected and the restrictions imposed by s 23 of the 2001 Act called for close scrutiny.

They found that the section was irrational as it discriminated against foreigners and did not provide for equivalent home-grown threats. It was a disproportionate response not strictly required by the exigencies of the situation within the meaning of Art 15, and did not comply with the UK's international human rights treaty obligations.

Although Lords Hoffmann and Walker dissented, the seven to two majority against the government was a humiliating defeat and provided confirmation of the illegality of both their executive actions and domestic law. It was because of this defeat that the control order provisions of the Prevention of Terrorism Act 2005 were enacted, which in turn were found to be less than satisfactory in *Secretary of State for the Home Department v JJ and others* [2007] UKHL 45.

CASE EXAMPLE

Secretary of State for the Home Department v JJ and others [2007] UKHL 45

The Prevention of Terrorism Act was enacted on 11th March 2005 and it repealed Part 4 of the Anti-terrorism, Crime and Security Act 2001, including s 23, which had been found by the House of Lords to be incompatible with Arts 5 and 14 of the Convention in *A and others v Secretary of State for the Home Department.* In the case of *JJ and others*, the government was also found to be seriously in breach of Art 5 requirements.

Six suspected terrorists, one of whom had absconded, were subject to non-derogating control orders under the Prevention of Terrorism Act 2005. The trial judge Sullivan J found that the provisions of Art 2 were breached and this was upheld by a strong Court of Appeal comprising the Chief Justice, Master of the Rolls and President of the Family Division. The Home Secretary's appeal to the House of Lords was dismissed. None of the suspects were charged with or prosecuted for any offence related to terrorism.

The court laid down that factors to be taken into consideration in making control orders included the nature, duration, effects and manner of execution or implementation of the penalty or measure in question. There had been no legal error in the reasoning of the trial judge or the Court of Appeal and the analogy drawn with detention in an open prison was apt except that the respondents were not allowed to associate with others, nor did they have access to entertainment facilities which a prisoner in an open prison would expect to enjoy.

The Home Secretary had no power to make an order that imposed any obligation incompatible with Art 5. An administrative order made without power to make it was, on well-known principles, a nullity. The defects in the orders could not be cured by amending specific obligations, since what the Secretary of State had made was a series of orders, applicable to the individuals named, which he had no power to make. Whilst it was true that, because public law remedies were generally discretionary, the court might in special circumstances decline to quash an order despite finding it to be a nullity, no such circumstances existed here, and it would be contrary to principle to decline to quash an order, made without power to make it, which had unlawfully deprived a person of his liberty. The administrative order was a nullity and the defects could not be rectified by amending specific obligations because the Home Secretary had no power to make them.

In his dissenting speech, Lord Hoffmann referred to the depth of revulsion in the UK against detention without trial and the right of liberty ordinarily to trump even national

CONTINUED ▶

> security. The reason it is so important is that it amounts to a complete deprivation of human autonomy and dignity.
>
> Lord Brown of Eaton-under-Heywood, expressing the majority view, said:
>
> > 'The borderline between deprivation of liberty and restriction of liberty of movement cannot vary according to the particular interests sought to be served by the restraints imposed. The siren voices urging that it be shifted to accommodate today's need to combat terrorism (or even that it be drawn with such need in mind) must be firmly resisted. Article 5 represents a fundamental value and is absolute in its terms. Liberty is too precious a right to be discarded except in times of genuine national emergency. None is suggested here.'

Because of this authoritarian agenda, the legality of the security legislation has been challenged in the courts on a number of occasions in recent years as the bases upon which individuals can be arrested, detained and held without trial have increased, but the House of Lords has been vigilant in seeking to protect the rights of individuals. The following two case examples provide more detail of this judicial diligence.

7.5 Anti-libertarian policies

Nevertheless, one important factor in electing a government is that people require protection from external and internal threats and few people would argue with the proposition that governments must take all reasonable steps available to protect their populations, especially in times of emergency, whilst at the same time infringing individual freedom as little as is practicable. The Civil Contingency Act 2004 defines 'emergency' and imposes duties of contingency planning, giving ministers powers to make regulations. The Third Schedule repeals much redundant previous legislation. Government planning for emergencies is co-ordinated by the Civil Contingencies Secretariat established in 2001 and situated within the Cabinet Office, which set up 'a UK-wide horizon-scanning capacity' and a 'national risk assessment process'. The requisite structural arrangements to anticipate and plan are therefore in place.

It is not surprising that given the UK's long and strong tradition of encouraging individual liberty there should be a considerable body of opinion concerned at the growing strength of the executive and the availability of new means of exerting control and protecting citizens. Their concerns could be expressed as follows.

The cumulative effect of this legislation since 1997 has been restrictive and anti-libertarian. The restrictions imposed on liberty and freedom of the individual are heavier than responses of other European states to the threats posed by terrorist gangs, and the decision of government to characterise criminal terrorist activities as a 'war' was a political rather than legally correct or logical response and followed the rhetoric of the USA. Wars can only be conducted against sovereign states, not criminal organisations, however extensive or subversive. In 2007 the International Development Secretary, Hilary Benn, announced that the government no longer used the phrase 'war on terror' because the way it had been portrayed by the Americans makes terrorists 'feel part of something bigger'. He also made the point that terrorists are not one organised enemy with a clear identity and a coherent set of objectives.

Other policies are being pursued, such as the introduction of ID cards when evidence indicates that the technology cannot cope, the data cannot be protected, the cost cannot be controlled, and government has a questionable record of losing information or allowing it to be transferred to third parties.

ACTIVITY

Self-assessment questions

1	English common law rules on liberty and security are wider than those that come within the scope of Art 5 of the ECHR.	True	False
2	Arts 9–13 of the International Covenant on Civil and Political Rights (1966) (ICCPR) cover the same ground as Art 5 ECHR.	True	False
3	Art 5(1) ECHR defines two circumstances or cases in which a person can be deprived of his liberty.	True	False
4	The ECHR does not contain provisions guaranteeing freedom of movement for individuals between countries.	True	False
5	Minors cannot be detained under Art 5 for purposes connected with their education.	True	False
6	The English common law offence of breach of the peace is incompatible with Art 5 of the ECHR.	True	False
7	The reasonableness of the suspicion justifying arrest is an essential part of the safeguard against arbitrary detention.	True	False
8	Detention without charge can never be justified, whatever the circumstances.	True	False
9	Art 3 of the UDHR states that 'Everyone has the right to life, liberty and security of property'.	True	False
10	Use of the phrase 'war on terror' is legally correct because terrorists cause death and destruction on a worldwide scale.	True	False

Only when people are convinced that the consequences of such policies and law might affect them directly do they tend to react to discourage government from restricting liberty further, as in the case of the abortive suggestion that vehicles should be monitored by satellite. The fact that there are more CCTV cameras in the UK than anywhere else in the world, and that most of the time they fail to identify clearly those who are being monitored and the pictures they produce cannot be used as evidence in court because of their poor quality, has not so far stopped the apparently inexorable increase in their use. Giving powers to local authorities that enable them to install surveillance devices in rubbish bins might also give pause for thought as to the value of the trend.

No doubt government pursues such policies from the best of motives and democratic process ensures that regular opportunities arise to question them. In recent years the judiciary and the House of Lords have played an important part in helping to maintain some sort of balance and the Government itself can take much credit from introducing new legislation such as the Human Rights Act and the Freedom of Information Act.

Internment in Ireland and the violations of human rights by the USA in Guantanamo Bay are in their different ways worrying precedents for suspension of civil liberties. The assumption that there is no risk in giving themselves these kinds of power because current governments regard themselves as benign and well-meaning not only begs the question as to whether it is true but assumes that future governments will behave well, and to human rights activists this attitude is somewhat short-sighted. Legitimately elected governments have been known to introduce illiberal policies.

7.6 Non-criminal detention under Article 5

It is important to note the other reasons why deprivation of liberty may be justified under the European Convention besides alleged commission of crime as set out in Arts 5(1)(b), (d), (e) and (f). Examples are summarised in the following table.

Purpose of detention	Example
To enforce a court order Art 5(1)(b)	To secure compliance with an order to deliver up property *Shobiye v UK* (1976)
To fulfil an obligation prescribed by law Art 5(1)(b)	Detention because of non-payment of the community charge might come within the ambit of this paragraph *Perks and others v UK* (1999) 30 EHRR 33
To detain minors to supervise education or to bring before a competent legal authority Art 5(1)(d)	The purpose is to ensure that the legal obligation to provide education can be fulfilled by ensuring school attendance of children *Re K (a child)* [2000] All ER (D) 1834
To detain vagrants, drug addicts, alcoholics and to prevent spread of infectious diseases Art 5(1)(e)	Such detention is only justified where the individual poses a threat to him or herself or others *Litwa v Poland* (App no 26629/95) [2000] ECHR 26629/95
To prevent unauthorised entry into the country or to facilitate deportation or extradition Art 5(1)(f)	All that is required here is that 'action is being taken with a view to deportation' whether or not that is justified under domestic or Convention law *Chahal v UK* (1996) 23 EHRR 413 para 112

Figure 7.2 Reasons for detention

7.6.1 Art 5(1)(a) Detention after conviction

Art 5(1)(a) says that 'no one shall be deprived of his liberty save in the following cases and in accordance with a procedure prescribed by law namely the lawful detention of a person after conviction by a competent court'.

There are some 8,000 prisoners in the UK who have indeterminate sentences, which means that they have been given a minimum tariff by the judge. This is the term they must serve before becoming eligible for parole. Only a small minority are given a whole-life tariff and there are strict guidelines to be followed by the judge whenever any indeterminate sentence is imposed. This aspect of sentencing, however, gives rise to questions of legitimate detention after conviction which may engage Art 5(1)(a) of the ECHR.

In *Secretary of State for Justice v Walker and others* [2008] EWCA Civ 30 the minister appealed against a decision that he had acted unlawfully by failing to ensure that where prisoners were serving indeterminate sentences, they were given the opportunity to demonstrate to the Parole Board that they were fit to be released. There was a policy (PSO 4700) showing the stages to be followed prior to release and prisoners had to attend offending-behaviour programmes in order to qualify. The prisoners in this case at HMP Doncaster had not been able to do so because facilities were not made available.

The Court of Appeal held that the Secretary of State had acted unlawfully by failing to provide suitable measures, although his contention was that he was not under any duty to do so. This argument 'lacked realism' as he had brought the provisions into force in April 2005 but not the resources to make them effective, which put him in breach of his public law duty in this regard. Two of the parties involved in this appeal were not in an acceptable situation as they had effectively been denied a review of the lawfulness of their detention.

If that state of affairs continued, it would be likely to result in a breach of Art 5(4) and their detention would cease to be justified under Art 5(4)(a). Although in Walker's case that stage had not yet been reached, it would occur when it was no longer necessary for the protection of the public or if such a long time elapsed without a meaningful review. In other words, at that point in time their detention would become disproportionate or arbitrary.

7.6.2 Art 5(1)(b) Non-compliance with lawful court order

Art 5(1)(b) says that 'no one shall be deprived of his liberty save in the following cases and in accordance with a procedure prescribed by law namely the lawful arrest or detention of a person for non-compliance with the lawful order of a court or in order to secure the fulfilment of any obligation prescribed by law.'

In *Perks v United Kingdom* (1999) 30 EHRR 33, Perks and other applicants were committed to prison by different benches of magistrates for failure to pay the community charge because of

wilful or culpable neglect. They had been unrepresented at their trials due to non-availability of legal aid but were later released on bail pending judicial review of the justices' decisions, all of which had been quashed. They complained that their rights, both to liberty under Art 5 and a fair trial under Art 6, had been breached.

The court held that in assessing whether there had been a breach of Art 5 it was necessary to determine whether the justices' actions had been *ultra vires*. The bench had not taken account of changes in Perks' circumstances, nor had they considered alternatives to imprisonment in the other cases, but neither of these amounted to a breach of Art 5 on grounds of arbitrariness because the sanction of imprisonment served the legitimate aim of securing payment of the charge and was therefore justifiable. There was, however, a breach of Art 6 in failure to provide legal aid in view of the threat to liberty arising from that omission.

This followed *Benham v United Kingdom* (19380/92) (1996) 22 EHRR 293 where Benham complained to the European Court that his Art 6 rights to a fair hearing and legal assistance, and Art 5 rights to liberty and security of the person, had been breached when he was committed to prison for three months. Additionally, he had not paid his community charge and had been refused access to legal representation. The Art 5 complaint was not upheld in that case but the Art 6 claim was, on the basis that although they were civil proceedings the nature and severity of the sentence meant that, in effect, it amounted to a quasi-criminal charge because his liberty was threatened. The legal issues to be determined were not straightforward because they involved determining whether Benham's default was due to culpable neglect.

Refusal to pay the community charge, which many people regarded as an unfair method of taxation, generated a number of legal cases in the 1990s and early 2000s. In *Beet v United Kingdom* (47676/99) (2005) 41 EHRR 23, Ms Beet applied for a declaration that her imprisonment because of her failure to pay the charge was unlawful and contrary to Art 5. Having found that this was due either to wilful refusal or culpable neglect, and having suspended her prison sentence so that she could make periodic payments, she failed to do so and spent two nights in prison before the High Court quashed the magistrates' order.

Specifically she argued that Art 5(1) was breached because the magistrates had failed to carry out an appropriate inquiry into her means as required by the Community Charges Regulations, and this contention was upheld by the President Judge Casadevall. Without such proper inquiry the magistrates were not in a position to decide whether it was culpable neglect or wilful refusal, so what had been decided was in excess of their jurisdiction and their order was unlawful.

Judge Casadevall also presided in the case of *Lloyd v United Kingdom* (29798/96) [2006] RA 329 in the following year when Lloyd was making similar complaints regarding imprisonment for non-payment of council tax. In that case the magistrates had failed to satisfy themselves that he had received proper notice of the hearing prior to his committal and again there was no legal aid or representation available. The complaints were upheld.

7.6.3 Art 5(1)(c) Prevention of commission of an offence

 Art 5(1)(c) says that 'no one shall be deprived of his liberty save in the following cases and in accordance with a procedure prescribed by law namely the lawful arrest or detention of a person effected for the purpose of bringing him before the competent legal authority on reasonable suspicion of having committed an offence or when it is reasonably considered necessary to prevent his committing an offence or fleeing after having done so'.

This provision deals with three possible situations, ie where the suspect:

1. is reasonably suspected of having committed an offence

2. needs to be prevented from fleeing after having committed an offence

3. needs to be detained where it is reasonably necessary to prevent the commission of an offence.

CASE EXAMPLE

R (on the application of Laporte) v Chief Constable of Gloucestershire [2006] UKHL 55

The Gloucestershire Constabulary were concerned that three coach loads of would-be demonstrators travelling from London to the RAF base at Fairford in Gloucestershire to take part in an anti-war demonstration were hard-core members of an anarchist group, although when searched they found that only eight out of 120 people in fact were. The Police Superintendent concluded that a breach of the peace was not immediately imminent but nevertheless forced the coaches and passengers to return to London with a police escort in order to prevent an anticipated later breach of the peace at Fairford.

The Divisional Court and Court of Appeal held that the police had acted lawfully in that a breach of the peace was likely to have occurred at Fairford, but that forcing the return of the coaches to London was unlawful. The case hinged on the interpretation of 'imminent' and Laporte was claiming that her Art 10 rights to freedom of expression and Art 11 rights of freedom of assembly and association had been infringed. Although her liberty had been curtailed, Art 5 was not argued. Under Art 11 no restrictions may be placed on the exercise of those rights other than as prescribed by law and are necessary in a democratic society. Both appeal and cross appeal were dismissed.

The House of Lords held that domestic law did not support the argument that action short of arrest could be taken when a breach of the peace was not so imminent as to justify arrest, the test here not being lawfulness but imminence. The action taken in such circumstances therefore had to be 'reasonable or proportionate' and here the police should have explored other options.

CASE EXAMPLE

Austin v Commissioner of Police of the Metropolis [2007] EWCA Civ 989

This case directly involved consideration of Art 5(1)(c). On May Day 2000, Oxford Circus in London was 'invaded' by a crowd of demonstrators. Although the police had an idea that something was afoot, the organisers of the demonstration had not given them notice of what was intended. Most people who entered the circus at 2 pm were not allowed to leave, and from 2.20 pm no one was allowed to leave except with police permission. By the end of the day some 3,000 people were trapped and some were held there for up to seven hours with physical conditions deteriorating to a state of unacceptability. Not all of the detainees were demonstrators.

The appellants in this case were an uninvolved bystander G, and L who had made political speeches at the demonstration, exercising her right to do so peacefully. Neither of them had been violent or threatened violence and each of them wished to leave. Having been refused permission by the police, neither attempted to do so. They had both been refused damages for false imprisonment [2005] EWHC 480 (QB) and under the Human Rights Act s 7.

Their appeal was dismissed. There had obviously been interference with their liberty which would have amounted to the tort of false imprisonment unless it was lawful. Although the police knew that not everybody within the cordon was a demonstrator, the trial judge's conclusion that the situation was wholly exceptional justified the containment, given the imminent threat of violence by others. The length of the containment could not reasonably have been foreseen and the situation was not static but 'dynamic, chaotic and confusing'.

The detention was not arbitrary within the meaning of Art 5(1). The distinction made by the court was that although it was an interference with the appellants' freedom of movement this did not amount to arbitrary deprivation of their liberty.

These provisions may lack some of the clarity attaching to the other Art 5 procedures provided by law, such as detention following conviction or failing to comply with a court order, and the case law shows that none of these situations is categorically clear cut.

7.6.4 Art 5(1)(d) Detention of minors

Art 5(1)(e) says that 'no one shall be deprived of his liberty save in the following cases and in accordance with a procedure prescribed by law namely the detention of a minor by lawful order for the purpose of educational supervision or his lawful detention for the purpose of bringing him before the competent legal authority'.

In *Re K (A Child) (Secure Accommodation Order: Right to Liberty)* [2001] 2 WLR 1141 (CA), K appealed against the latest in a number of secure accommodation orders made against him under the Children Act 1989 s 25, the argument being that s 25 was incompatible with his right to liberty under the Human Rights Act 1998 Sched 1 Pt 1 Art 5. His appeal was dismissed on the basis that although a secure accommodation order did amount to deprivation of his liberty 'by lawful order for the purpose of educational supervision', the local authority were obliged to fulfil their statutory obligation and 'educational supervision' was to be interpreted widely in order to encompass the many aspects of the authority's exercise of parental rights over the child, applying *Koniarska v United Kingdom* (App 33670/96) admissibility decision of 12th October 2000.

7.6.5 Art 5(1)(e) Detention on medical or social grounds

(A) Art 5(1)(e) says that 'no one shall be deprived of his liberty save in the following cases and in accordance with a procedure prescribed by law namely lawful detention of persons for the prevention of the spreading of infectious diseases, or persons of unsound mind, alcoholics or drug addicts or vagrants'.

Deciding whether a person is 'of unsound mind' is sometimes problematical as can be seen from *JE v DE (aka Re DE)* [2006] EWHC 3459.

The claimant wife alleged that a local authority had breached Art 5 requirements when it placed her husband in a residential care home, the court having to decide the preliminary issue of whether that action had deprived him of his liberty under the Convention. Her husband D was aged 76 and had been left with an impaired memory and blind after a major stroke, all of which tended to indicate that he lacked the capacity to agree to his confinement. Although he had known his wife J for many years, they had only been married for a few months when she had shut him out of the house saying that she could not care for him, which was the cause of him being taken to the care home. Obviously from the fact of her having commenced this litigation she really did wish to have him live at home, and his care notes and correspondence indicated that he was being held against his will. The local authority argued that his detention was in his best interests.

The preliminary issue was determined in the wife's favour because 'deprivation of liberty' under Art 5(1) has an autonomous meaning which meant that a person can be deprived of his liberty even though not technically 'imprisoned' for the purposes of the tort of false imprisonment. Applying *Guzzardi v Italy* (A/39) (1981) 3 EHRR 333 (discussed earlier in this chapter) the starting point had to be the actual physical situation that needed to take into consideration a wide range of criteria including the type, duration and effect of the restraint, and keeping in mind that deprivation of, and restriction upon, liberty differs only in degree but not in substance. The restraint did not need to be physical, the real question being: was D free to leave? The fact that he had a substantial amount of freedom within the care home could not mask the truth that he was not allowed to leave.

The question of how much justification is needed to interfere with or impede a person's liberty when not necessarily relying on specific statutory powers is one that arises in a number of contexts. There should be no problem if Mental Health Act 1983 powers are used to 'section' a patient, but less certainty when the patient voluntarily co-operates and ends up deprived of his freedom. In the case of *H v United Kingdom aka L v UK* (45508/99) (2004) 40 EHRR 761, the applicant suffered from autism and lacked the capacity to consent to medical treatment. He had been living in the community for about three years but one day became very agitated whilst attending a day centre and was assessed by two doctors as requiring medical treatment. He did not resist being taken to hospital but then wanted to leave and was prevented.

H commenced proceedings for *habeas corpus*, damages and judicial review and the House of Lords eventually held that the hospital could rely on the doctrine of necessity to treat patients against their will where they lacked capacity. However, the State had never shown that H was of unsound mind and he contended that his detention was unlawful under Art 5(1)(e) and Art 5(4).

His complaint was upheld and the fact that he had not resisted his detention was irrelevant on the ground that the right to liberty was too important to be forfeited solely for that reason. There was evidence to indicate that he was suffering from mental illness but, even so, his detention was unlawful because it had to be shown that it was not arbitrary, quite apart from the question of necessity. When this doctrine applied, there were no procedural rules that governed his treatment which meant that there was no provision for review of his case. Even judicial review and *habeas corpus* were insufficient to protect him in such circumstances because they could not provide the independent medical review of the hospital doctors' clinical assessment and diagnoses that was needed.

The juxtaposition of medical and social grounds in Art 5(1)(e) is perhaps indicative of attitudes at the time the ECHR was conceived. That would explain why vagrancy was regarded as a sufficient reason to deprive people of their liberty. Without further aggravating factors, it would be unlikely to be upheld today as a reason for deprivation of liberty. Alcoholism and drug addiction themselves might require temporary removal from society if they were causing immediate aberrant behaviour, but modern society would recognise that it is better to direct its efforts towards medical treatment rather than detention.

7.6.6 Art 5(1)(f) Unauthorised entrants

In the case of *R (on the application of Saddi and others) v Secretary of State for the Home Department* [2002] 1 WLR 3131 four asylum seekers appealed against the order of the Court of Appeal. This had allowed the Home Secretary's appeal against the High Court decision that their detention at Oakington Reception Centre was unlawful under the fast-track procedure which in Saadi's case took 10 days. It was argued that they presented no risk of absconding and the Art 5(1)(f) exception whereby a person could be detained to prevent his effecting an unauthorised entry into the country did not apply, either because he was making an authorised entry, having applied for asylum, or that the detention was a disproportionate response by the government.

The asylum seekers' appeal was dismissed. The short detention period in acceptable physical conditions was reasonably necessary and an asylum seeker's entry was obviously unauthorised, so the state had the power to detain without contravening Art 5. Detention in order to achieve speedy asylum decision making did fall within Art 5(1)(f) but this could be contrasted with Art 5(1)(c) which excluded from the prohibition a person's detention when it was reasonably necessary to prevent commission of an offence or flight.

Detention here was neither arbitrary nor disproportionate. A balancing exercise was required between deprivation of liberty and the need for speedy decision making, and the balance came down on the side of recognition of reasonable and proportionate detention under the Oakington procedures.

One of the features of Art 5(1)(f) cases involving unauthorised entrants is that the periods of deprivation of liberty are usually quite short. In *Saadi* it was 10 days, and in the case of *Amirthanathan* nine days (*R (on the application of Amirthanathan) v Secretary of State for the Home Department* [2003] EWHC 1107 (Admin)). The Secretary of State knew at the time he ordered the detention of A, a Sri Lankan national, that he intended to appeal but tried to justify the detention decision on the ground that removal from the UK was 'imminent'. The right of appeal arose under the Immigration and Asylum Act 1999 s 65 because of the refusal. The Secretary of State did not have a leg to stand on because the detention was contrary to his own policy, and so the application was granted. It could not be said that A's removal was 'imminent' if the appeal had to be heard first, especially given the known delays in immigration procedures. There was not only a breach of Art 5 but the Secretary of State had also breached the principle of proportionality enabling *Saadi* to be applied.

The Secretary of State appealed the Administrative Court's decision ([2003] EWCA Civ 1768) and lost. It was a conjoined appeal with another Sri Lankan, Nadarajah, who it was intended should be removed to a safe third country, Germany, whilst A was due to be returned to Sri Lanka where there had been armed insurrection for many years. On appeal, the Secretary of State argued that there were additional grounds to justify the detention, despite the findings at first instance. In N's case it was that he was being sent to a safe third country, and for A that it would assist in procuring the removal documentation. The Court of Appeal in rejecting the Home Secretary's argument pointed out that his policy was not generally well known and therefore was inaccessible, and in neither case was removal imminent, so the detention of both of them was unlawful.

7.7 Detention involving foreign states

Art 5 cases, such as the one just discussed, by their very nature involve unauthorised entrants from overseas who are attempting to gain access to the UK, but there are other circumstances involving UK nationals or residents that involve a foreign element where Art 5 needs to be considered.

7.7.1 Guantanamo

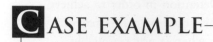CASE EXAMPLE

R (on the application of Abbassi) v Secretary of State for Foreign and Commonwealth Affairs [2002] EWCA Civ 1598

The inability of either the UK Government or courts to protect the liberty of British subjects held by the USA and categorised as 'enemy combatants' not subject to the Geneva Conventions was revealed in Abbassi's case. He was a British national detained at Guantanamo Bay in Cuba following capture by US forces in Afghanistan. His mother sought judicial review in an attempt to force the Foreign Office to make representations on his behalf to the US Government. Not only was his liberty removed, but he was unable to challenge the legitimacy of his arbitrary detention.

The Secretary of State did not see it as his responsibility to protect British subjects caught in this situation and was not prepared to challenge the US authorities, and argued that the English court could neither examine the legitimacy of action taken by a foreign sovereign state nor adjudicate on actions taken (or not taken) by the executive in its conduct of foreign relations with that foreign state.

The Court of Appeal refused the application for judicial review although accepting that the underlying fundamental principle of English law was that every imprisonment is *prima facie* unlawful and that no member of the executive could interfere with the liberty of a British subject unless the legality of the detention could be established before a court of justice, following *R v Secretary of State for the Home Department ex parte Khawaja* (1984).

Abbassi's status as an 'enemy combatant' might be justified but appeared to be objectionable in light of the apparently indefinite detention without trial. Even so, the Court of Appeal had to accept that there was no direct remedy in the English court and could not make an order affecting the US Government, which was not represented before the Court. Nor did international law recognise that a state had a duty to intervene diplomatically or otherwise to protect its citizens when threatened by a foreign state. The European Convention did not apply and neither did the Human Rights Act 1998 impose a duty on the government in such situations.

However, policy statements issued by the Foreign Office purported to preclude the possibility of judicial review. This is an example of the 'ouster approach' under which the executive tries (usually by statute) to prevent actions or omissions of public bodies

CONTINUED ▶

from being judicially reviewed by the Administrative Court. It would not succeed if the Secretary of State was simply refusing to apply the policy as such a blank refusal would be irrational and unreasonable. Ineffective efforts had been made here by the government in undertaking discussions and visits, and there was eventually to be some action taken by the US authorities in their appellate courts and by the Inter-American Commission on Human Rights. As to protecting the liberty of the British subject by the British Government or court, virtually nothing could be achieved.

Guantanamo Bay detentions are different from other situations as the USA has in effect politically removed the base and its inmates from conventional legal structures to a legally 'sterile' overseas location by inventing the status of 'enemy combatants' and denying the applicability of domestic and international law. This gives rise to serious human rights questions that are beyond the scope of this book other than to note that arbitrary political suspension of human rights law and principles is completely unacceptable. Removal of a human being from all protection of law, even for a short period, cannot be justified by any state that professes to observe the rule of law.

7.7.2 Iraq

A different issue arose in the case of UK policy in its conduct of affairs in Iraq after the invasion by British troops in support of the USA and other allies. Human rights questions here involved the question of whether, and if so how, the ECHR might apply to the conduct of British forces when outside the UK and Europe.

CASE EXAMPLE

R (on the application of Al-Jedda) v Secretary of State for Defence [2006] 3 WLR 954 CA

This was an appeal against the dismissal of an application for judicial review of the applicant's detention by British forces in Iraq. Born in Iraq, he had been granted British nationality and was arrested in Iraq in 2004 on suspicion of involvement in weapons smuggling and explosive attacks in Iraq. The trial court had decided that he was not entitled to Art 5 protection because those ECHR rights were qualified by UN Security Council Resolution 1546 which had to prevail.

The British forces were there as part of a multinational force acting under that resolution and other authority made by virtue of Art 42 of the UN Charter. The Security Council gave the multinational force 'authority to take all necessary measures to

CONTINUED ▸

contribute to the maintenance of security and stability in Iraq in accordance with the letters annexed to this resolution' and one of the letters annexed to the resolution indicated that the force could undertake internment where 'necessary for imperative reasons of security'.

The applicant's argument was that this could not be the case because UNSCR 1546 placed no obligation on the UK and because there were conflicts between the resolution and the UN Charter's human rights provisions. He further argued that the Human Rights Act 1998 created freestanding rights that could not be affected by international developments.

The appeal was dismissed. The Fourth Geneva Convention Art 78 established basic obligations on the state and UNSCR 1511 could be said to have extended the power of internment in favour of the multinational forces beyond Geneva Convention requirements. UNSCR 1546 gave the multinational force the power to intern people for imperative reasons of security and that power embraced people of every nationality whose internment was deemed necessary for imperative reasons of security. Art 103 did not give UNSCR 1546 precedence, in so far as there was a conflict.

There was nothing in the UN Charter creating a parallel obligation to give effect to the applicant's human rights, and therefore UNSCR 1546 qualified obligations under human rights conventions in so far as it was in conflict with them. Al-Jedda's reliance on the Human Rights Act 1998 s 6(1) and s 7(1) was nugatory because there was no breach of Convention rights in the circumstances.

Lord Bingham said that 'obligations' in Art 103 were not to be given a narrow and contract-based interpretation because the importance of maintaining world security and peace was overwhelming and that was the purpose of this UN mission, even though, as was well known, the majority of states chose not to contribute to the multinational force. Although the UK was not bound specifically to detain Al-Jedda, it did have to exercise the detention power and the action was therefore lawful.

The Court of Appeal's decision that the appellant could not claim damages for the tort of false imprisonment was also upheld by the House of Lords. If there was such a claim, it would lie under Iraqi law.

7.8 European Union

With regard to the EU, agreement has been reached by a Council Framework Decision 2002/584/JHA of 13th June 2002 on the European arrest warrant and the surrender procedures between Member States, as originally agreed at the Laeken Summit in December 2001. The effect was to simplify and speed up arrest procedures between states and to make the process subject to a judicial mechanism. The warrant applies in the case of offences punishable by imprisonment or detention order for a maximum period exceeding one year and where a final prison sentence or detention order has already been imposed for a period of at least four months.

It was used in July 2005 to allow Osman Hussain, one of the suspects in the London bombings of 21st July 2005, to be extradited from Italy back to the UK, but there have been concerns that it has been used in cases involving relatively trivial offences such as possession of minute amounts of cannabis or minor theft.

In *Dabas v Spain*, also known as *Dabas v High Court of Justice, Madrid* [2007] 2 AC 31 HL, Dabas appealed against a decision upholding an order for extradition to Spain under a European arrest warrant so that he could be tried on charges of collaborating with an Islamist terrorist organisation. He argued that although the proceedings were in the form provided for by the Council Framework Decision procedures, it nevertheless failed to comply with the Extradition Act 2003 s 64(2) because it lacked the necessary 'certificate' which could not be the warrant itself. The conduct in question had not constituted an offence under UK law at the time and did not show that it constituted an offence under Spanish law.

The appeal was dismissed using purposive interpretation, as a separate 'certificate' document was not necessarily required under the Act. It was not for the judiciary to remove from the Act provision that Parliament thought it right to include.

ACTIVITY

Self-assessment questions

1 Briefly explain your understanding of what is meant by 'liberty' and 'security'.

2 What was the purpose of the Human Rights Act (Designated Derogation) Order 2001 and did it achieve its objectives?

3 Which judicial decision identified the illegality in the Anti-terrorism, Crime and Security Act 2001 and what did the House of Lords decide in that case?

4 Which judicial decision identified further problems with the Prevention of Terrorism Act 2005 and what did the House of Lords decide in that case?

5 Explain the significance of *Abassi* and *Al-Jedda*.

6 What cases would you use to explain the way that the European Convention Arts 5(1)(a)–(f) operate?

ACTIVITY

Using the advice provided at the front of this book which suggests an approach to dealing with essay tasks, devise an answer plan for the following topic:

Critically discuss, by close reference to decided cases, the proposition that Art 5 of the European Convention of Human Rights too often fails to protect the liberty and security of the individual.

KEY FACTS

Principle	Authority
Everyone has the right to challenge the legality of their detention and to be released from custody if wrongfully deprived of their liberty	The ancient writ of *habeas corpus*
Everyone has the right to life, liberty and the security of person	Universal Declaration of Human Rights 1948 Art 3
Everyone has the right to liberty and security of person, prompt and fair trial, humane treatment, not to be imprisoned for inability to fulfil contractual obligation, freedom of movement and separate treatment of minors	International Covenant on Civil and Political Rights 1966 Arts 9–12
Everyone has the right to liberty and security of the person	European Convention on Human Rights 1950 Art 5
'Article 5 (ECHR) represents a fundamental value and is absolute in its terms. Liberty is too precious a right to be discarded except in times of genuine national emergency. None is suggested here.'	Lord Brown in *Re Secretary of State for the Home Department v JJ and others* (2007)

CONTINUED ▸

KEY FACTS

The Derogation Order would be quashed and s 23 would be declared incompatible with Arts 5 and 14, reversing the Court of Appeal	*A and others v Secretary of State for Home Department* (2004)
The ancient common law offence of breach of the peace, although very wide in scope and application, does not contravene the provisions of Art 5 of the European Convention	*Steel and others v UK* (1998)
When examining the relationship between the executive and the judiciary, the judge must have power to order the release of someone who has been detained, otherwise the safeguard afforded by an independent judiciary is removed	*Caballero v United Kingdom* (2000)
The law should be interpreted and applied strictly when any question arises regarding deprivation of an individual's liberty	Lord Atkin's dissenting speech in *Liversidge v Anderson* (1941)
It is a fundamental principle that any use of the procedures that existed for depriving a person of his liberty has to be carefully scrutinised	*Guisto v Governor of Brixton Prison* (2003)
We hold these truths to be self-evident, that all men are created equal, that they are endowed by their creator with certain unalienable rights that among these are Life, Liberty and the pursuit of Happiness	Preamble to the American Declaration of Independence made in Congress 4th July 1776

Useful resources

Labour Government policy on security and liberty: http://www.number10.gov.uk/Page15785.

Macovei, M, 'A guide to the implementation of Article 5 of the European Convention on Human Rights': http://www.coe.int/T/E/Human_rights/hrhb5.pdf.

Commentary on *Karl Anderson, Alexander Reid, and Brian Doherty v The Scottish Ministers and the Advocate General for Scotland* dealing with detention of untreatable psychopaths: http://medlaw.oxfordjournals.org/cgi/content/abstract/10/1/92.

Further reading

Feldman, D, *Civil Liberties and Human Rights in England and Wales* (2nd edn, Oxford University Press, Oxford, 2002).

Feldman, D, 'Deprivation of Liberty in Anti-terrorism Law', CLJ 2008, 67(1), 4–8.

Fenwick, H, *Civil Liberties and Human Rights* (4th edn, Cavendish Publishing Ltd, London, 2007).

Forsyth, C, 'Control Orders, Conditions Precedent and Compliance with Article 6(1)', CLJ 2008, 67(1), 1–4 (relevant to this chapter despite its title).

Sandell, A, 'Liberty, Fairness and the UK Control Order Cases: Two Steps Forward, Two Steps Back', EHRLR 2008, 1, 120–131.

Smith, A T H, 'May Day, May Day: Policing Protest', CLJ 2008, 67(1), 10–12; (Case comment on *Austin and Saxby v The Commissioner of Police of the Metropolis* [2007] EWCA Civ 989).

Walker, C, 'Terrorism: Prevention of Terrorism Act 2005 ss 2 and 3 – non-derogating control order – whether "deprivation of liberty" under European Convention on Human Rights Art 5', Crim LR 2008, 6, 486–503.

chapter
8 # RIGHT TO A FAIR TRIAL ■

AIMS AND OBJECTIVES

After studying this chapter you should be able to understand and explain the following:

- The role the common law plays in ensuring fair treatment in criminal trials and civil litigation

- The importance of fair process to people arrested on suspicion (although note that the chapter does not deal with the Police and Criminal Evidence Act (PACE) and codes)

- The full scope of Art 6 of the European Convention on Human Rights (ECHR) with its fundamental assumption of innocence until proved guilty

- The minimum rights available under Art 6(3) to everyone charged with a criminal offence

- Domestic and European case law under the common law and Art 6.

8.1 Trials and hearings

For clarity and convenience this book sticks fairly closely to the ECHR for most of its discussion so this chapter is entitled 'Right to a fair trial' to accord with the rubric of Art 6. However, as will be seen from the subsequent analysis, this is something of a misnomer because Art 6 deals with determination of civil rights and obligations as well as criminal charges, and in the civil context it is more appropriate to refer to 'hearings' rather than 'trials'. The 'right to a fair trial' is therefore part and parcel of the broader rights requirement of fair process, which includes Art 7 addressed in Chapter 9 which deals with no punishment without law and other aspects of process such as rules of natural justice.

8.2 Background

The ways in which English law has dealt with trials over the centuries would comprise a study in itself, but two brief examples can be shown to provide an indication of how some of these ancient provisions still have resonance in the twenty-first century.

KEY PHRASES

Key word	Meaning
Hearing Trial	From the context it is important to distinguish between the right to a fair *hearing* (civil proceedings in a court or tribunal) and the right to a fair *trial* (referring specifically to criminal cases).
Bias	There are different ways of classifying bias, for example judicial bias of the judge, or jury bias, with distinctions drawn between actual, apparent and presumed bias
Recusal	The act of excusing a judge or occasionally a prosecutor from proceeding with a case because he has some connection or relationship with a party
Sui generis	This Latin phrase means 'of its own kind' or having unique characteristics so that it cannot be incorporated into a wider context
Hearsay evidence	The Criminal Justice Act 2003 s 114 provides that a statement not made in oral evidence in proceedings is admissible in evidence of any matter stated only in circumstances provided for by the 2003 Act: the effect is to enable evidence to be admitted of 'implied assertions' reversing *R v Kearley* (1992) 2 AC 228
Desuetude	Obsolescence or disuse

8.2.1 Magna Carta (1215)

This seminal constitutional document was concerned with privileges conceded by the Crown, mostly to earls and barons and occasionally to freemen, but it is often assumed nowadays to be the origin of a variety of rights and privileges enjoyed by everyone subject to English law, even though the bases upon which the Charter's provisions were made are long gone. It may be argued from cl 28 that one of the fundamental requirements of fair process is that evidence should be provided by 'faithful witnesses', although the original purpose of producing witnesses was not directly to do with the alleged wrongful actions of an accused person.

'[28] No Bailiff from henceforth shall put any man to his open Law, nor to an Oath, upon his own bare saying, without faithful Witnesses brought in for the same.'

Clause 29 may be taken to comprise the foundation of crucial elements of fair trials, one example being the right to lawful judgment by one's equals (still evidenced by lay magistrates and the jury, although the jury's role has in recent years been much reduced). In the same clause there is the right for a person to be dealt with under the law, rather than in an arbitrary manner by the Crown or ministers, and the protection for everyone of not having verdicts bought and sold.

(A) '[29] No Freeman shall be taken, or imprisoned, or be disseised of his Freehold, or Liberties, or free Customs, or be outlawed, or exiled, or any otherwise destroyed; nor will we pass upon him, nor condemn him, but by lawful Judgment of his Peers, or by the Law of the Land. We will sell to no man, we will not deny or defer to any man either Justice or Right.'

Regardless of the exact relevance of these 800-year-old provisions to modern law, their psychological importance to the people of the UK in the absence of a clearly defined written constitution is significant.

8.2.2 English Bill of Rights 1689

When it became necessary to redefine the relationship between the Crown and Parliament in the late seventeenth century, the document by which this was done, the English Bill of Right, also contained provisions that had a direct bearing on how the law affected individuals. It did this by ensuring that the Crown could not arbitrarily suspend or dispense laws or impose unreasonable penalties or impositions unless due process of law-making had been observed.

In summary this removed the power of the Crown to make laws and recognised that Parliament duly (and nowadays more democratically) elected should legislate so that those subject to them would know what they are and what is required of them. It also reinforced and developed protections against excessive financial penalties and confirmed aspects of the jury system.

(A) 'That the pretended power of suspending the laws or the execution of laws by regal authority [and as it hath been assumed and exercised of late] without consent of Parliament is illegal … that excessive bail ought not to be required, nor excessive fines imposed, nor cruel and unusual punishments inflicted … that jurors ought to be duly impanelled and returned, and jurors which pass upon men in trials for high treason ought to be freeholders [and] that all grants and promises of fines and forfeitures of particular persons before conviction are illegal and void.'

However, it would be wrong to conclude that the right to be treated fairly under the law is restricted to public declarations occasionally promulgated at significant historical moments in contexts designed to protect the interests of influential minorities then in power. English law, enacted by Parliament and administered by the judiciary over the centuries, has long taken pride

in providing, clarifying and protecting the freedom of the individual and one of the most basic manifestations of this is the 'right to a fair trial' which everyone within the jurisdiction can claim.

8.3 Fair process

For criminal cases the common law developed the principle that a person is to be regarded as being innocent until properly proved to be guilty. Guilt has to be proved by the prosecution beyond reasonable doubt. In civil proceedings a different standard of proof is needed and decisions are reached on the balance of probabilities, ie which is the more likely version of events.

One reason for this is that criminal convictions carry social stigma and so are not to be reached lightly, whereas civil disputes have to be settled to maintain social justice between people and conclusions can be reached by accepting the more reasonable version of events based on the evidence. It would not be acceptable that civil litigation could not be brought to a conclusion because a sufficiently high level of proof was not achieved, leaving disputes unresolved. In both civil and criminal law the legitimacy and protective rigour of all aspects of how people are treated under the law is central to the quality of their human rights.

8.3.1 Kevin at the police station

How this operates can be seen by considering an example. Kevin is a 20-year-old music student who is not particularly interested in current affairs or legal matters although he has a good idea of what constitute his best interests. He has been arrested on suspicion of committing a serious criminal offence. In a refreshment break during his interrogation by the investigating police officers he makes a list of what he thinks might be some of the more important things necessary to ensure that if he is charged he will be given a fair trial, which he decides include the following in no particular order of importance:

- If he is charged he will not subsequently be subjected to indefinite ongoing questioning in conditions that might lead him to make untrue or forced admissions, whether from tiredness or fear.

- It should be clear what the charge means and then his case should be heard within a reasonable time.

- He might think about the pros and cons of having a public or secret trial:
  - public proceedings will give him a measure of protection from oppression by agents of the state or court, but,
  - secrecy might spare his blushes and embarrassment at his predicament, especially if he thinks he may well be guilty as charged.

- The judge should be independent and unbiased, and if there is a jury so must they be.

- He will be regarded and treated as innocent unless and until proved guilty.

- The evidence produced should be fairly and properly obtained, with witnesses available to be heard and cross examined at the trial and allowed to give only direct evidence of what they know rather than hearsay evidence of what someone else might have told them.

- He needs the opportunity to establish innocence or alibi, for example by requiring witnesses to pick him out at an identity parade, or to give evidence that he was somewhere else when the crime was committed.

- The resources he requires to defend himself should be made available such as legal advice, aid or translation services.

- If he is acquitted he will not want to be placed at risk of another prosecution at a later date (the principle of not being placed in double jeopardy), but he will have no assurance on that point as this protection has been removed.

- He has heard of the Englishman's right to be tried by a judge together with his peers as a jury, but is aware that there are relatively few serious cases where this is now the case, although initially his case may be dealt with by lay magistrates.

- His immediate concern may well be to call a solicitor, relative or friend to come to his aid.

He could produce a much longer list than this as he sits there, were he to be given sufficient time, and if Kevin is particularly thoughtful he might realise that just about anyone could end up in the predicament in which he now finds himself and conclude that the right to a fair trial is really pretty important. Perhaps his previous inclination to condemn others whose arrests are reported in the media as deserving what is coming to them might give him pause to reconsider.

His friend Gillian who is a law student would say that Arts 6 and 7, the latter providing that there should be no punishment without law, underpin some of the other ECHR rights and freedoms and form the first line of defence for an accused person. This being the case, the next consideration before examining the treaty is to look at the judges and juries upon whose decisions society depends for accurate interpretation of all aspects of law, protection against more powerful people, and dispensation of justice.

Kevin probably thinks that this is what the law is supposed to do, but Gillian knows that courts interpret and apply the law as it is in accordance with strict rules and are not in the business of simply deciding what is just or unjust.

ACTIVITY

Self-assessment questions

1 Think about Kevin's list of bullet points and consider whether you think there are any other important items you would wish to add to it.

2 Then put them into your preferred order of priority.

8.4 Judicial independence

8.4.1 Protection of judicial office

The Doctrine of Separation of Powers says that the executive (government), legislative (parliamentary) and judicial (court and tribunal) elements of the constitution should be kept separate, or as separate as practicable, in order to avoid any one branch becoming over-powerful and thus leading to corruption and dictatorship. The theory operates in a limited way in the UK, but applies more clearly to the judiciary than between the executive and legislature, where in the context of the political party system the executive is able to place pressure on and sometimes to control the legislature.

Steps have been taken in recent years to enhance the independence of the judiciary, one of the vital preconditions to ensuring that fair hearings are not only possible but actually take place. Ways in which judicial independence has been protected in the past or is being improved for the future include the following:

- Judicial immunity from suit; this means that judges cannot be sued for alleged negligence or defamation by disgruntled litigants or accused persons.

- Payment of judicial salaries is made from the Consolidated Fund in order to avoid the risk of financial pressure such as threats of pay cuts being brought to bear on them by the government or Parliament.

- Senior judges have security of tenure of office protected by statute until retirement age.

- The Lord Chancellor has lost his judicial functions as this office also encompasses an executive role as a member of the Cabinet responsible for a government department and formerly also a legislative function as the effective Speaker of the House of Lords.

- Removal of the direct power of the Lord Chancellor as a member of the executive to appoint members of the judiciary and replacement of that function by the Judicial Appointments Commission.

- A gradual widening of judges' background from white middle-aged public school Oxbridge males to include solicitors and in theory other candidates, more women, people of wider educational background, and members of ethnic minorities.

These are very different types of safeguard and factors but taken together they cohere into a regime which provides some measure of assurance to Kevin that the judge before whom he is likely to appear if he is charged will not be unduly influenced by the government, police or prosecuting authority.

8.4.2 Judicial bias in hearings

Independence in terms of judges' appointment is reinforced by the requirement of maintaining independence from the subject matter upon which they are adjudicating. This means that they should

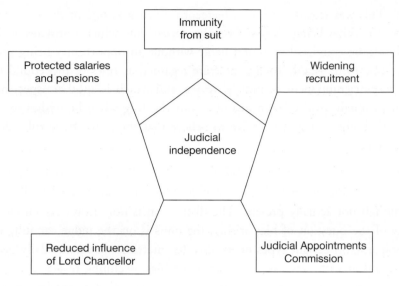

Figure 8.1 Judicial independence

have no interest of any kind in the case before them, nor must there be the remotest *appearance* of bias. There are different ways of classifying possible bias on the part of judges but a distinction sometimes drawn is that there seem to be two main forms. The first is where there is automatic disqualification whether or not there is an iota of suspicion attached to the judge or his state of mind, and the second is where the judge should be disqualified for presumed, apprehended or apparent bias.

Therefore, if a judge has a financial interest in the subject matter of the case, as did Lord Chelmsford in *Dimes v Grand Junction Canal* 10 ER 301, he would automatically be disqualified, but in other cases such as those discussed below, somewhat different factors are brought to bear. This is discussed by Lord Browne-Wilkinson in *Pinochet* below. These different ways of considering bias have been explained in slightly different terms by James Goudkamp in 'Facing up to actual bias' CJQ 2008, 27(1), 32–39:

> 'The common law of England recognises three species of bias: actual bias, apparent bias and presumed bias. Actual bias exists when a judge is in fact prejudiced against one of the parties. Apparent bias, which is also known as perceived and ostensible bias, occurs when the hypothetical fair-minded and informed observer believes that the judge may be biased. Finally, a judge is presumed to be biased if he has an interest, not necessarily pecuniary, in the outcome of the proceedings.'

Nemo iudex and *audi alteram*

Therefore, if a judge has an interest in the case he is trying he should be automatically disqualified on the basis of *nemo iudex in causa sua*, translated as 'no one should be a judge in

their own cause'. This was regarded in the nineteenth century as one of the two main principles of natural justice, the other being the *audi alteram partem* rule which translates as 'hear the other side'. No one should be convicted or found liable without an opportunity being provided for the other side of the case to be heard. Today, these are regarded as rules of procedural fairness which comprise an important component of judicial review and which is another aspect of the individual's right to obtain justice by means of a court hearing when he wishes to challenge a decision of a public body. It would be naive to believe that these two basic rules do not need further reinforcement.

If, on the other hand, it can be said that there is a real danger that the judge may come to a verdict that has been influenced by extraneous matters in some other way, the bias would be apparent even though not actually present. The distinction is not always crystal clear and if there is any possibility of the question of bias arising, the onus is on the judge carefully to consider his own position. Solicitors in certain types of practice (eg matrimonial) make daily decisions involving refusal to deal with new cases so as to avoid bias, declining to act in divorce proceedings for existing clients because they possess knowledge that might be prejudicial to one or other of the parties. Judges must make similar decisions, whether in magistrates' and county courts or the House of Lords.

(a) Actual bias

Goudkamp's article discusses how difficult and rare it is for litigants or their advisers to allege *actual* bias on the part of the judge, and although there may be a variety of reasons for this, the most apparent one is the fear of alienating the judge if he then declines to recuse himself. In a possession action in Luton County Court *Aldwyck Housing Association v Cunningham* [2000] CLY 52, a judge who had previously been in practice as a solicitor announced that he used to act for the claimant but had ceased to do so on his retirement from practice a year previously. The defendant was unrepresented and did not object at the time and the judge did not recuse himself. Subsequently Ms Cunningham lodged an appeal which was dismissed. The core question was whether there had been a real danger of actual bias and it was decided that previous instructions to act for a party did not constitute actual bias following *Locobail (UK) Ltd v Bayfield Properties Ltd* [2000] QB 451.

(b) Apparent bias

In *Howell v Lees Millais* [2007] EWCA Civ 720 where a firm of solicitors were involved, the Court of Appeal criticised Smith J who had been invited, prior to the original hearing, to recuse himself for not doing so. Previously, the judge had been negotiating with the firm to join that firm and those negotiations had broken down. In an exchange of e-mails the judge had told the firm that he was not very impressed with them. He was given a further invitation at the hearing to recuse himself but still refused to do so.

Sir Ivor Judge P said in the course of his judgment:

J 'There is no disguising the regrettable features of this case. The application to . . . Smith J to recuse himself was entirely justified . . . the [e-mail correspondence] demonstrates that the judge was extremely displeased that negotiations about his possible future with the firm of solicitors Addleshaw Goddard had broken down. His irritation is obvious.'

(c) Presumed bias

A classic example is *Dimes v Grand Junction Canal* 10 ER 301; (1852) 3 HL Cas 759 in which the Lord Chancellor was adjudicating upon a case involving the canal company in which he held a substantial number of shares. The House of Lords held that Lord Chelmsford should not have tried the case.

There have been some high-profile cases on the question of possible judicial bias, for example *Locobail (UK)* and *Pinochet*. In *Locobail v Bayfield Properties Ltd* [2000] QB 451, *Dimes* was discussed and it was said that in such cases the existence of bias is effectively presumed, so that disqualification is automatic because the judge has an interest in the outcome of the case. The rule in *R v Gough (Robert)* [1993] AC 646 HL (dealt with later in this chapter under jury bias) was followed, and subsequently *Pinochet* has shown that although non-financial interests as well as straightforward pecuniary interests could trigger automatic disqualification where they were related to the issue before the court, generally the fact of membership of professional, political or other organisations was insufficient to give rise to grounds for an allegation of bias.

Locabail also made it clear that other commonly cited triggers of accusations of bias such as ethnic or racial origin, class, sexual orientation, extra judicial activities or previous judicial references to parties or witnesses even if expressed in forthright terms would not suffice to found a successful challenge. What *would* be relevant was personal acquaintance with any individual involved in the case, particularly if antagonism was involved that would give rise to questions of credibility, as this would involve real danger of bias.

> 'In cases of real doubt recusal would be the obvious course, although judges should be as keen to guard against agreeing to do so if faced with a claim of little substance as they should be of ignoring meritorious claims. It was desirable for judges to disclose the existence of facts which were indicative of a danger of bias as soon as they became aware of their existence and failure to object on disclosure of such an interest would amount to waiver.'

CASE EXAMPLE

R v Bow Street Metropolitan Stipendiary Magistrate, ex parte Pinochet Ugarte (No 2) [2000] 1 AC 119 HL

The House of Lords had held that the former Chilean Head of State Senator Pinochet did not enjoy immunity from arrest and extradition from the UK in connection with allegations that he had been involved in a variety of crimes in Chile involving citizens from other states including Spain. It transpired that one of the judges, Lord Hoffmann, had been an unpaid director of Amnesty International Charity Ltd (AIC) since 1990. The relevance of this was that AIC was wholly controlled by Amnesty International (AI) which had been allowed to intervene in the case and so had become a party to the matter. Lord Hoffmann should have recused himself from the case but had not done so.

Senator Pinochet's application to have the previous decision set aside was granted, this being a direct application of the principle that a person cannot be judge in his own cause. Automatic disqualification did not apply but the circumstances did give rise to the question of whether a non-pecuniary interest in non-financial litigation (unlike the position of Lord Chelmsford in *Dimes v Grand Junction Canal*) was sufficient automatically to prevent Lord Hoffmann from sitting in this case. AIC had an interest in the outcome because one of its objects was 'to procure the abolition of torture, extra judicial execution and disappearance' and so they wished to ensure that Senator Pinochet would not be entitled to immunity.

> 'The fact that H was not a member of AI but a director of its wholly owned company, which carried on much of its work, was irrelevant if the absolute impartiality of the judiciary was to be maintained. The fundamental principle that justice should not only be done but be seen to be done had to be applied to a judge involved, either personally or as a company director, in promoting the same causes in the same organisation as a party to the action.'

In order to deal with Senator Pinochet's application, a differently constituted committee of the House of Lords had to rehear the Divisional Court's decision. Lord Browne-Wilkinson explained what he classified as two types of case and how the first one applied in *Pinochet*:

> 'The fundamental principle is that a man may not be a judge in his own cause. This principle, as developed by the courts, has two very similar but not identical implications. First it may be applied literally: if a judge is in fact a party to the litigation or has a financial or proprietary interest in its outcome then he is indeed sitting as a judge in his

CONTINUED ▸

own cause. In that case, the mere fact that he is a party to the action or has a financial or proprietary interest in its outcome is sufficient to cause his automatic disqualification.

The second application of the principle is where a judge is not a party to the suit and does not have a financial interest in its outcome, but in some other way his conduct or behaviour may give rise to a suspicion that he is not impartial, for example because of his friendship with a party. This second type of case is not strictly speaking an application of the principle that a man must not be judge in his own cause, since the judge will not normally be himself benefiting, but providing a benefit for another by failing to be impartial. In my judgment, this case falls within the first category of case, viz where the judge is disqualified because he is a judge in his own cause.'

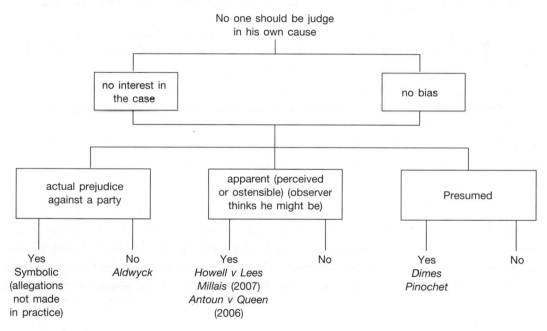

Figure 8.2 Types of bias

8.4.3 Jury bias

R v Gough (Robert) [1993] AC 646 established, applying *R v Spencer* [1987] AC 128 HL, that the correct test applicable where there was an allegation that a member of the jury was biased was whether there was a real risk of denial of a fair trial to the accused. A convicted robber appealed on the grounds that a jury member was his brother's next-door neighbour. The jury member swore an affidavit that she did not know of the connection until after the verdict had been delivered. The court dismissed the accused's claim of serious irregularity and said that the

test to be applied in all cases of apparent bias is whether there was a real danger that the appellant had not had a fair trial, and on that test the Court of Appeal had been entitled to decide as they did.

Gough was followed by *R v Conroy* and *R v Glover* [1997] 2 Cr App R 285 where Conroy and Glover appealed against convictions for kidnapping, false imprisonment and causing grievous bodily harm with intent. The evidence adduced during their trial about rival gangs in Newcastle was so unpleasant that one lady juror was discharged after a panic attack and another passed a note to the judge supported by her GP's medical report saying that she was unwell. It was not shown to counsel and although she did return to court after the weekend she was discharged at the end of that week. Conroy and Glover contended that their convictions were unsafe because the jury should have been discharged as it had ceased to be impartial. Their appeal was dismissed on the basis that they had been convicted on 'strong evidence and nebulous defences' so the convictions were not unsafe.

Changes in the composition of juries under the Criminal Justice Act 2003 mean that persons connected with the administration of criminal law may now be required to serve on juries whereas formerly they were exempt. The obligation to undertake jury service now includes police officers, practising lawyers and even judges. This soon gave rise to complaints of unsound convictions and the House of Lords dealt with the issue in a consolidated case in October 2007, *R v Abdroikov and others* [2007] UKHL 37. The cases involved charges of attempted murder, assault occasioning actual bodily harm, and attempted rape respectively. The jurymen to whom objection was made were police officers in the first two cases and a Crown Prosecution Service solicitor in the third.

The House of Lords were clear that the common law rule that justice should not only be done but should manifestly be seen to be done still applied and there was no difference between the common law test and the requirement under Art 6 of the ECHR that a person should be tried by an independent and impartial tribunal. Justice was not seen to be done if a fair-minded and informed observer on the facts of the case would believe there was a real possibility of conscious or unconscious jury bias.

The factors leading to two of the cases being overturned were: sharing the same local service background for one of the police officers; and, in the other case, the member of the jury to whom exception was taken was a full-time salaried employee of the prosecuting authority. They comprised two classic cases of justice not being seen to be done and it is interesting to see their lordships confirming that the Convention requirements of fairness are identical to the common law on this point.

ACTIVITY

Self-assessment questions

1 What is the difference between a fair trial and a fair hearing?

2 What is hearsay evidence?

3 What types of judicial bias are there and can you name a case that illustrates each?

4 What kind of bias applied in the case of Lord Hoffmann in *Pinochet*?

5 Briefly summarise in your own words the current law on jury bias.

8.5 ECHR Article 6 Right to a fair trial

The common law established a firm bedrock of principles regarding civil liberties and fair process, and provided a number of procedural safeguards such as *habeas corpus*, although the significance of the latter has been whittled away because it has been overruled by a variety of statutory provisions. Today, probably the first place most people would look would be the right to a fair trial provisions contained in Art 6 of the ECHR which are as follows:

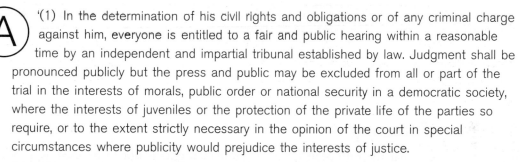

'(1) In the determination of his civil rights and obligations or of any criminal charge against him, everyone is entitled to a fair and public hearing within a reasonable time by an independent and impartial tribunal established by law. Judgment shall be pronounced publicly but the press and public may be excluded from all or part of the trial in the interests of morals, public order or national security in a democratic society, where the interests of juveniles or the protection of the private life of the parties so require, or to the extent strictly necessary in the opinion of the court in special circumstances where publicity would prejudice the interests of justice.

(2)   Everyone charged with a criminal offence shall be presumed innocent until proved guilty according to law.

(3)   Everyone charged with a criminal offence has the following minimum rights:

    (a)   to be informed promptly, in a language which he understands and in detail, of the nature and cause of the accusations against him;

    (b)   to have adequate time and facilities for the preparation of his defence;

    (c)   to defend himself in person or through legal assistance of his own choosing or, if he has not sufficient means to pay for legal assistance, to be given it free when the interests of justice so require;

    (d)   to examine or have examined witnesses against him and to obtain the attendance and examination of witnesses on his behalf under the same conditions as witnesses against him;

    (e)   to have the free assistance of an interpreter if he cannot understand or speak the language used in court.'

One reason why the ECHR is so important is that it has forced re-examination of English law in light of continental civil law legal systems, thus shining a spotlight into situations where English law may have become stultified or in need of modernisation or reconsideration. As indicated previously, although the detail in Arts 6(2) and 6(3) deals exclusively with criminal matters, Art 6(1) does make it clear that the article as a whole encompasses 'civil rights and obligations' which also come within the protection of the article's insistence on 'fair and public hearings . . . within a reasonable time by an independent and impartial tribunal established by law'.

• Example of the operation of the rule of law enshrining a number of important common law principles
• Covers civil rights and obligations and criminal charges
• Provides for fair and public hearings within a reasonable time
• Requires independent and impartial judicial tribunals
• Fundamental requirement is that there should be the presumption of innocence
• Limited restrictions are allowed to avoid publicity so as to protect morality, public order, national security, juveniles or private life
• There are defined minimum rights to clarity of charges, provision of time and resources to prepare a defence, fair use of witnesses and the right to understand proceedings

■ Figure 8.3 Summary of Art 6 principles

8.5.1 Types of hearing

It is important to note that the European Court of Human Rights is not to be used as a means simply of trying to obtain a rehearing of domestic case law when litigants or accused citizens are unhappy with the outcome. The role of the European Court is to examine whether the previous proceedings were fair and complied with the requirements of Art 6 when taken as a whole. This means that the Court will not formulate conclusions as to whether appropriate sentences have been reached, or even whether a conviction was safe.

The core of Art 6(1) is that 'everyone is entitled to a fair and public hearing within a reasonable time by an independent and impartial tribunal established by law'. In addition to court or mainstream tribunal hearings, other relevant types of hearing may be involved:

- fatal accident inquiries
- arbitration proceedings
- prison disciplinary hearings
- penalty schemes imposed on commercial firms to punish them for bringing illegal immigrants into the country on their vehicles (albeit inadvertently and unknowingly).

(a) Fatal accident inquiries

The Scots law case of *The Lord Advocate, Petitioner* 2007 SLT 849 decided that fatal accident inquiries were statutory proceedings *sui generis* and did not fall to be treated as ordinary actions, civil proceedings or administrative applications in relation to awards of expenses. This means that such actions do not engage the Art 6 rights of the European Convention, being neither a process for determination of civil rights and obligations nor of punishment in respect of a criminal charge. The decision demonstrates the necessity of having a hearing which has a bearing on the way that penalties or punishments may be imposed on individuals if the protection of Art 6 is to be secured.

(b) Arbitration proceedings

It is common in commercial transactions to agree that in arbitration proceedings the right of appeal is limited or excluded, but this is not onerous in the sense that it can still go to court in the absence of impartiality or where there is some other irregularity. Article 6 does not render a clause excluding right of appeal onerous or unusual (*Sumukan Ltd v Commonwealth Secretariat* [2007] EWCA Civ 243).

(c) Prison disciplinary hearings

Circumstances which clearly demonstrate failure on the part of a public body to understand or take notice of Art 6 requirements occurred in *Young v United Kingdom* (App No 60682/00); (2007) 45 EHRR 29. The applicant, who was virtually wheelchair bound, suffered from cerebral palsy and required medication to control urination, found herself imprisoned for breach of a probation order. This was despite the fact that her ability to process information was impaired and she generally required explanations in plain language and sufficient time for full comprehension.

She was required to provide a urine sample under the prison mandatory drug testing (MDT) policy and was unable to do so, leading to the prison authorities deciding that she had disobeyed a lawful order. Her punishment was an additional 14 days' incarceration imposed at a hearing where she was denied representation, although the punishment was later reduced to three days. The European Court of Human Rights held unanimously that this was a breach of Art 6. Her right to an independent and impartial tribunal had been denied, as had her right to be allowed to formulate an adequate defence.

(d) Illegal immigrants' regime

CASE EXAMPLE

International Roth GmbH v Secretary of State for the Home Department [2002] EWCA Civ 158; [2002] 3 WLR 344

The trial judge had held that the penalty scheme imposed on hauliers under the Immigration and Asylum Act 1999 Part II for innocently bringing clandestine entrants into the country was incompatible with the right to a fair hearing under Art 6, and interfered with their property rights. The scheme had been challenged by some 50 lorry drivers.

The Secretary of State appealed against the decision and although this was allowed in part on the basis that the trial judge had erred by finding that the scheme contravened EC treaty free movement requirements, the human rights elements were upheld by majority decision.

The unfairness of the scheme as a whole breached Art 6 according to Simon Brown LJ, and Jonathan Parker LJ held that the Secretary of State purported to be judge in his own cause. Laws LJ dissented, being of the view that although there were harsh aspects to the scheme, Parliament had struck a fair balance between the policy aim and the interests and fair treatment of carriers. However, features of the Secretary of State's scheme that fell particularly harshly on the hauliers, and which led to the injustice that invalidated it and did not provide a fair hearing for the defendants, were summarised by Simon Brown LJ:

'First, that the burden of establishing blamelessness lies on them (it being necessarily implicit in this that sometimes, if only rarely, the blameless will be penalised);

second, that the penalty imposed is fixed and cumulative, no flexibility whatever being allowed either for degrees of blameworthiness (or, in the case of owners or hirers, the fact that their liability may be purely vicarious) or mitigating circumstances such as a driver's co-operative conduct or financial means;

third, that even when a carrier is eventually determined not to be liable, whether by the Secretary of State under s 35(8) [of the Immigration and Asylum Act 1999] or by the court, his vehicle may well have been detained meanwhile and for this he will receive no compensation unless the Secretary of State acted unreasonably in issuing the penalty notice (which, given where the burden of proof lies, will be well-nigh impossible to establish).'

8.5.2 Fair hearings despite flaws

(a) Exceptional cases

It is possible for a conviction to be upheld even in a case where the Strasbourg Court has held that the appellant's Art 6 rights to a fair trial have been infringed (*R v Lewis* [2005] EWCA Crim 859). Circumstances where this can occur were identified by Rose LJ in *R v Dundon* [2004] EWCA Crim 621 where he said that quashing of convictions is not always necessary. In all cases factors that affect the outcome include 'the kind of breach and the nature and quality of the evidence in the case'. Thus it is that in some cases just and appropriate satisfaction could be provided by a reduction in sentence or a declaration of breach, rather than quashing the conviction. Occasionally there may have been some unfairness arising out of a legal misdirection but the evidence of guilt is still overwhelming.

(b) Need to give reasons

The obligation on the court to give reasons was addressed in *Tatishvili v Russia* (App No 1509/02); (2007) 45 EHRR 52. Art 6 obliges courts to give reasons for their judgments but does not require a detailed answer to every argument and the extent to which there is a duty to give reasons varies according to the nature of the decision. Courts are allowed a certain margin of appreciation when choosing arguments and admitting evidence but they have to justify their decisions and one function of a reasoned decision is to demonstrate to the parties that they have been heard as well as facilitating appeal and review. In this case that standard had not been achieved by the Georgian Court in failing to deal properly with her application for citizenship and it was found that there had been a contravention of Art 6.

(c) Failure to provide remedy

Even where domestic law fails entirely to provide a remedy, it does not follow that this will result in a breach of Art 6. In *Markovic v Italy* (App No 1398/03) (2007) 44 EHRR 52 the applicants were citizens of Serbia and Montenegro who had lost relatives in NATO military action in the former Yugoslavia in 1999. They issued proceedings in the Rome District Court against the Italian Prime Minister, the Italian Ministry of Defence and the Commander of NATO Allied Forces in Southern Europe.

Eventually the (Italian) Court of Cassation confirmed that Italian courts had no jurisdiction to hear claims arising out of the hostilities as domestic law did not recognise claims in such circumstances. There was no binding precedent in a case like this. There was plainly a serious and genuine dispute about the extent of the applicants' rights under domestic law and the case must have been considered to be arguable. The applicants were not deprived of any right to a determination of their claim. The claim was examined in the context of relevant domestic law and rejected in that context. The European Court held by ten votes to seven that there had been no violation of Art 6.

(d) Hearsay evidence

The problem of how to deal with hearsay evidence when it was the only or main factor in convicting the accused in criminal cases was addressed by the Court of Criminal Appeal in *R v Cole and R v Keet* [2007] EWCA Crim 1924. In the first case the prosecution sought to bring hearsay evidence from friends of the deceased to show the cause of injuries to the appellant's girlfriend who had committed suicide in circumstances where some of her injuries could not have been self-imposed.

The second case involved the appellant absconding which led to a five-year delay prior to the trial, by which time one of the victims from whom property had been obtained by deception was unfit to give evidence. The appellant objected to a five-year-old statement made to the Police being the sole or decisive evidence against him.

Both appeals were dismissed. Art 6 was based on the possibility of witnesses being called by the prosecution or defendant and did not address the situation where that was not possible. Admitting hearsay evidence at their respective trials was not precluded merely because it was the sole or decisive evidence against them, and on the facts of each case the evidence had been properly admitted.

8.6 Article 6(1)

Ⓐ 'In the determination of his civil rights and obligations or of any criminal charge against him, everyone is entitled to a fair and public hearing within a reasonable time by an independent and impartial tribunal established by law. Judgment shall be pronounced publicly but the press and public may be excluded from all or part of the trial in the interests of morals, public order or national security in a democratic society, where the interests of juveniles or the protection of the private life of the parties so require, or to the extent strictly necessary in the opinion of the court in special circumstances where publicity would prejudice the interests of justice.'

8.6.1 Access to the Court

There are various considerations that apply regarding access to the Court. It is a civil right although not absolute, nor is it expressly stated in Art 6(1), and there is room for implied limitations in certain circumstances. Nevertheless, the last recital of the preamble to the ECHR refers to the rule of law and this implicitly means that there must be access to legal advice and to the courts:

Ⓐ '*Being resolved*, as the governments of European countries which are likeminded and have a common heritage of political traditions, ideals, freedom and the rule of law to take the first steps for the collective enforcement of certain of the rights stated in the Universal Declaration, (*Have agreed* as follows) . . . '

ACTIVITY

Self-assessment questions

1 Name two types of non-court or tribunal hearings that still come within the remit of ECHR Art 6.

2 Identify one where the claimant succeeded and one which failed.

3 Identify two types of problem that may reduce the chances of a claimant being successful under Art 6.

KEY ISSUES

Key issue	Comment/explanation
The common law provided various types of protection for fair trials	There are constitutional provisions but also *habeas corpus*, trial by one's peers (lay magistrates and juries), rules of natural justice, independent judiciary and presumption of innocence
ECHR Art 6 reinforces common law with specific human rights protection	Clear written code of protection, recourse to external UK remedy, influence of civil law judges on English law, possibility of individual action against UK Government
ECHR Art 6(3)	Provides a short code of minimum rights
Judicial independence	Vital element in the constitutional context to provide protection against the executive and remedies for individuals achieved in a variety of ways
Protection against bias	Accused persons and litigants have recourse against possible judicial bias and in criminal cases against possible biased jurors
Shortfalls in protection	The right to a fair hearing is not absolute and some procedural or even substantive defects do not always give rise to protection or a remedy

The need to consider the substance and extent of the right of access to the court arises in a number of different contexts including:

- prisoners
- children
- protestors
- taking or defending defamation proceedings
- being subjected to inhuman or degrading treatment
- being deprived of the right to private and family life.

The right applies to people detained in custody, so where a prisoner was accused of assault and the accusation was subsequently withdrawn but he was prevented by the prison authorities from seeking legal advice about his treatment and from taking action against a prison officer, this amounted to a breach of Art 6(1) (*Golder v United Kingdom*, Judgment of 21st February 1975, Series A, No 18; (1979–80) 1 EHRR 524).

As an example of the right of access not being absolute or automatic, the existence of systemic failure to protect children over a period of years, whilst raising substantive and exceptionally serious issues of inhuman or degrading treatment, did not engage Art 6(1). Over a six-year period of time from 1987 to 1993 four children were subjected to what a consultant child psychiatrist described as 'horrific' treatment amounting to 'the worst case of neglect and emotional abuse that she had seen in her professional career'. During that time parental neglect and mistreatment was compounded by serious failures on the part of social services to take effective action to protect the children, despite a long string of warnings being given by a neighbour, the police, head teacher, general practitioner and health visitor.

The applicants complained that the House of Lords' decision that the local authority owed them no duty of care provided the authority with immunity from liability and thus violated Art 6. The Court held that there was no doubt as to the failure of the system to protect the applicants from serious, long-term neglect and abuse and consequently there was a violation of Art 3 of the ECHR.

However, with regard to Art 6 it was a Convention principle that the article did not guarantee any particular content for civil rights and obligations under national law. Thus, the non-existence of a domestic cause of action, even though it could be described as providing immunity by not enabling the applicant to sue for a particular category of harm, was nevertheless insufficient in itself. Competing public policy considerations had been addressed before the refusal to extend liability in negligence to a new area. The issues that did arise fell for consideration under Art 13 (right to an effective remedy) (*Z and others v United Kingdom* (App 29392/95), Judgment of 10th May 2001; (2001) 10 BHRC 384).

In another family case *TP v UK* [2001] ECHR 28945/95 involving violation of respect for private and family life, a similar conclusion regarding the non-engagement of Art 6 had been reached, although violations of Arts 8 and 13 were established in that case.

Legal aid is not available in the UK to assist people who need to defend defamation actions brought against them. This can present difficulty in what is called 'equality of arms', ie where one litigant is overwhelmingly more powerful in terms of resources than their opponent. If it is the powerful party who is taking action against the weaker, the absence of a right of access to the resources necessary to prepare a defence becomes an obvious disadvantage which is particularly unsatisfactory when the plaintiff has a global presence and the defendants are private persons with very few resources who are obliged to rely on *pro bono* assistance.

CASE EXAMPLE

Steel and Morris v United Kingdom (App 68416/01), Judgment of 15th February 2005; (2005) 41 EHRR 22

Steel and Morris were associated with London Greenpeace and during the course of a campaign were responsible for publishing a leaflet entitled 'What's wrong with McDonald's'? The company issued a writ claiming damages for alleged libel which the defendants contested. Not having substantial resources and not being entitled to legal aid to defend themselves, they relied on limited *pro bono* help from volunteer lawyers but for much of the proceedings were obliged to defend themselves during the 313-day trial against McDonald's experienced team of lawyers. There had been 23 interlocutory applications and the appeal took another 23 days.

They lost the case and substantial damages were awarded against them, and although these were reduced on appeal they were still substantial in comparison with the limited earnings and resources of the two defendants. The applicants' complaints under Arts 6 and 10 were both unanimously upheld by the European Court of Human Rights.

Equality of arms is central to the concept of a fair trial, and instituting and funding a legal aid scheme is one way of guaranteeing those rights. Whether it was essential depended on several things, including the facts and circumstances of the particular case, what was at stake for the defendants, and the complexity of the issues arising as this had an effect on the ability of lay individuals to represent themselves effectively.

The fact that the Art 6(1) right of access is not absolute means that any restrictions must pursue a legitimate aim and be proportionate and, whilst restricting use of public funds is legitimate, it must not place defendants at a substantial disadvantage *vis-a-vis* the adversary. The fact that they were resisting rather than instituting the proceedings was also a relevant factor, as were the particular facts which were so complicated that they turned out to be beyond the ability of a jury to understand.

All in all, 'the denial of legal aid to the applicants had deprived them of the opportunity to present their case effectively and contributed to an unacceptable inequality of arms with McDonald's. Accordingly, there had been a violation of Art 6(1).'

8.6.2 Fair and public hearing and judgment

(a) Accusatorial and inquisitorial proceedings

The role of an English judge in trial proceedings is to adjudicate. This may seem obvious, but it is not, because it is quite possible for judges to work in other ways. The role of the judge in a civil law legal system is to investigate. The English system of trial is a modern-day version of 'trial by battle' whereby two sides fight it out by presenting arguments to the court and he who presents the stronger case wins.

The combatants, ie opposing counsel, solicitors or parties in civil cases and the Crown or CPS and accused in criminal trials, often feel that they are required to fight this battle with one hand tied behind their backs because they are constrained by rules of evidence which prevent them from using each and every witness or piece of evidence in order to achieve procedural and substantive fairness.

In English law the opposing sides are involved in accusations and the facts that can be adduced must conform to strict rules of evidence, which means that often things that happened or circumstances that exist cannot be brought to the attention of the court, or can only be done so after a verdict has been reached. In civil law cases the broad thrust of the hearing is for the court, ie to inquire after the truth and, when necessary, direct that steps be taken to bring it out. For these reasons the common law approach is sometimes described as 'accusatorial' and the civil law system as 'inquisitorial'.

(b) Burden of proof

The burden of proof is much higher in criminal cases – 'beyond reasonable doubt' – and in serious cases there may also be a jury to convince as well as a judge. The reason for this higher standard is that conviction of a criminal offence results in punishment and social stigma. The burden of proof in civil cases is the 'balance of probabilities', ie which is the more likely version of events? The comparison might be 99 per cent certain for criminal cases and 55 per cent/45 per cent for civil cases.

The reason that there is a lower standard of proof is that disputes arise for many reasons, not all of which involve fault but all of which need to be settled, and whilst compensation is usually required, there is less or no stigma involved and it would not do to have the majority of these fail because there is not an overwhelming preponderance of evidence for one side or the other.

(c) Fair hearing

The right to a fair public hearing and judgment can be thwarted if the judge seems to interfere too much in the proceedings. In *CG v United Kingdom* (43373/98) Judgment 19th December 2001; (2002) 34 EHRR 31 the core of the applicant's case was that during her trial for theft the judge had interrupted and hectored her counsel repeatedly. Specifically, during cross-examination of the main prosecution witness the judge intervened so often that the defendant's counsel was

prevented effectively from challenging the accuracy of bank statement figures. Her examination in chief had been similarly disrupted so that her evidence was less coherent than she thought it should have been. Her barrister had felt so threatened that he had curtailed his examinations.

The Court of Appeal found that there was some substance in these complaints which were supported by the trial transcript. Furthermore, the judge's summing up on crucial points was described as 'very short' and 'somewhat laconic' and there were other criticisms of the judicial conduct of the trial. It was said that the trial judge was 'very experienced and highly regarded' but he had subsequently retired. Crucially, set against all this valid criticism, was the fact that the case against the accused was 'a strong one; indeed, the evidence was overwhelming'.

In addition to the general Art 6 provisions, the Court considered the Art 6(2) presumption of innocence and the specific allegations of violation of Art 6(3)(c)'s minimum right to defend oneself through legal assistance of one's own choosing, and examination of witnesses under Art 6(3)(d). However, taking all these factors into consideration the application was refused and it was held that, although the judge had intervened in an excessive and undesirable manner, it did not amount to breach of Art 6.

(d) Public hearing and delivery of judgment

The reasons behind the maxim 'justice must not only be done but be seen to be done' are apparent. Secret trials can lead to injustice, but no one other than the participants would be aware of the fact. Public confidence is necessary for any judicial system, but even more so when fundamental individual rights and freedoms are involved. This means in practice that court proceedings should be and usually are open both to public and press.

It does not mean, however, that all kinds of reporting are allowed in English courts, for example cameras are not allowed in court rooms, which is why television news reports of court proceedings are often accompanied by artists' impressions rather than photographs or film. In addition, there are some kinds of legal proceedings where there are much tighter restrictions on public and press attendance and reporting, two obvious examples being those involving official secrets and children although there are proposals to open up court hearings involving children.

In *B and P v United Kingdom* (Apps 36337/97 and 35974/97), Judgment of 24th April 2001; (2002) 34 EHRR 19, B's complaint was that he had been refused a public hearing and public delivery of the final judgment in previous county court proceedings. These had been to determine the residence of his son following divorce. The court had stipulated that if documents or information regarding the proceedings were to be disclosed it would be treated as contempt. Effectively the applicants were attempting to have the court reverse the effect of the provisions of the Children Act 1989 which provided privacy in order to protect children, based on the argument that it contravened ECHR Art 1.

The President Judge Costa gave judgment for the defendants, holding that exclusion of public and media is merited in residence proceedings for the protection of children. Presumption of

privacy in all children's cases enabled the judge to see the fullest possible picture and allowed parties and witnesses to express themselves freely without fear of public censure. The general presumption of privacy was not a breach of Art 6(1); in exceptional cases it could be reversed and transcripts are available for the court record.

8.6.3 Within a reasonable time

English law is highly reliant on the adjective 'reasonable' and frequently provides that things be done within a 'reasonable time' as well as requiring that people behave reasonably. Of course what is a reasonable time varies considerably according to the circumstances, but the courts have become adept at determining what it ought to be and, in the context of Art 6, it needs to be considered bearing in mind another perhaps partially contradictory maxim: 'justice delayed is justice denied'.

Civil law

In a civil law example, *H v UK*, the reasonable period of time for consideration in order to determine whether an applicant could have access to her child who had been taken into public care was two years and seven months and the court unanimously held that Art 6(1) was applicable and had been violated (*H v United Kingdom*, Judgment of 8th July 1987, Series A, No 120; (1988) 10 EHRR 95). The government argued that as the child had been removed into public care by valid judicial order no issue arose as to reasonable time, but that contention was rejected.

The relevant criteria applicable in assessing the length of proceedings depends on the circumstances but must have regard to the complexity of the case (here admitted to be considerable), the parties' conduct and what was at stake, which in this case was the future of the child, including adoption. The particular emphasis here was what was at stake for the applicant, which was the irreversible nature of the loss of her child by the 'statutory guillotine' of adoption.

'In cases of this kind the authorities are under a duty to exercise exceptional diligence since ... there is always the danger that any procedural delay will result in the *de facto* determination of the issue submitted to the court before it has held its hearing. And, indeed, this was what happened here.' That being the case and having weighed all the relevant factors, there had been a violation of Art 6(1).

Criminal law

In the following connected criminal law examples, the issue considered by the Privy Council was: what is a reasonable period within which to hold a trial? The appeals in question concerned the prosecution of a 13-year-old boy for alleged serious sexual offences, and the prosecution of two police officers on allegations of perjury. In the first case the delay between bringing the charges and the trial was 28 months and in the second 20 months (*Dyson v Watson; HM Advocate v JK*, [2002] UKPC D1, [2004] 1 AC 379). In both cases the Scots High Court of Justiciary had found that the respective delays breached Art 6(1) (2001 SLT 751 and 2001 SLT 1261).

The Privy Council held that the delay of 28 months in prosecuting the boy was a breach of Art 6(1) and in this case it was also necessary to have regard to the timing requirements of the UN Convention on the Rights of the Child 1989 and the Beijing Rules. Art 1 of that Convention defines a child as 'every human being below the age of eighteen years unless under the law applicable to the child, majority is attained earlier'. Art 37(d) entitles every child who is deprived of his liberty to prompt access to legal and other appropriate assistance and to a prompt decision. Art 40(2)(iii) goes on to provide that when a child is accused of having infringed the criminal law he is further entitled to have the matter determined without delay by a competent, independent and impartial authority or judicial body.

The 'Beijing Rules' are the UN Standard Minimum Rules for the Administration of Juvenile Justice adopted by General Assembly resolution 40/33 of 29th November 1985. Under r 13.1 detention pending trial should be a measure of last resort and kept to the shortest possible period of time. Rule 20.1 provides that each case must throughout be handled expeditiously, without any unnecessary delay. Taken together with the fair trial provisions of the ECHR Art 6(1), the procedure in the case of the child had taken too long, and the Privy Council concluded that no satisfactory explanation had been provided for the delay.

As far as the perjury trial of the police officers was concerned, although it was desirable that the period between charge and trial should not be as long as 20 months, that delay had not infringed the officers' rights. Apart from the exceptional case of *Mansur v Turkey* (A/321) (1995) 20 EHRR 535 ECHR, there did not seem to be any case where a 20-month delay had been found to infringe the reasonable-time requirement. Another factor mitigating towards justification of the delay was the need to investigate complaints against police officers very carefully as they are in any event susceptible to accusations of misconduct.

The provisions of Art 5(3) should also be considered when deciding what is a reasonable time:

'Everyone arrested or detained in accordance with the provisions of paragraph 1(c) of this Article shall be brought promptly before a judge or other officer authorised by law to exercise judicial power and shall be entitled to trial within a reasonable time or to release pending trial. Release may be conditioned by guarantees to appear for trial.'

8.6.4 Independent court and absence of bias

The issues to be discussed regarding the need for the court to be independent were addressed earlier in this chapter under bias and its various manifestations under s 8.4 judicial independence.

8.7 Article 6(2) presumption of innocence

The presumption of innocence is one of the cornerstones of English law and it is not surprising to find it at the heart of the ECHR in Art 6(2):

'Everyone charged with a criminal offence shall be presumed innocent until proved guilty according to law.'

The meaning of this under the ECHR was explained in *Barbera, Messegue and Jabardo v Spain* (1988) 11 EHRR 360 para 77 as requiring:

> '*inter alia*, that when carrying out their duties, the members of a court should not start with the preconceived idea that the accused has committed the offence charged; the burden of proof is on the prosecution, and any doubt should benefit the accused. It also follows that it is for the prosecution to inform the accused of the case that will be made against him, so that he may prepare and present his defence accordingly, and to adduce evidence sufficient to convict him.'

Addressing the presumption of innocence is not starkly black or white, however. There are several issues that may need to be considered. Internment during wartime, and detention without trial in peacetime in connection with threats of terrorism, may be justified by law and not fall outside human rights requirements, although in recent years the exact parameters of the latter have been the subject matter of anti-terrorism legislation and human rights test cases in the UK.

8.7.1 The reversed burden of proof

Another relevant factor is that, once the prosecution have proved the offence, the burden of avoiding or mitigating criminal liability might then transfer to the accused. It was argued in *R v Lambert (Steven) (and others)* [2001] 2 WLR 211 that the Homicide Act 1957 s 2(2) and the Misuse of Drugs Act 1971 s 5(4) and s 28 contravened Art 6(2). The sections provided defences to charges of murder and possession of drugs respectively, and placed a persuasive burden on a defendant to prove his case on the balance of probabilities. It was submitted to the Court of Appeal (Criminal Division) that the general burden of proof ought to remain with the prosecution.

In one of the conjoined cases the onus had shifted onto the defence to prove that the defendants were suffering from diminished responsibility under s 2 of the 1957 Act so that they would be convicted of the lesser offence of manslaughter, but the jury had rejected their defence. In the other case if the defendant could show that he was unaware of the contents of the container in his possession, this mitigated the offence. It was held in both cases that the provisions of the respective statutes did not contravene the requirements of Art 6(2).

The rationale for this was that although the principle that the burden of proof should lie with the prosecution was fundamental to the common law it could be displaced by Parliament where the statute was clearly worded, and the purpose of the ECHR was to strike a balance between the rights of individuals and those of society generally. Additionally, the relevant Acts did not require defendants to prove an essential element of the respective offences but, rather, gave them an opportunity to establish special defences which reduced the level of guilt and punishment.

The question of innocence and the burden of proof has been particularly problematical in recent years because of the steps needed to protect society against terrorist threats. In *R v DPP, ex parte Kebilene and others* the Divisional Court had made an order ([1999] 3 WLR 175) to grant declaratory relief to a number of people on the ground that the decision to continue prosecutions under the Prevention of Terrorism (Temporary Provisions) Act 1989 s 16A involved an error of law. This section, which dealt with possession of articles for terrorist purposes, reversed the legal burden of proof and so it was contended that it contravened Art 6(2).

The DPP's appeal was allowed (*R v DPP, ex parte Kebilene and others* [2000] 2 AC 326), the House of Lords deciding that, despite the uncertainty in the law, the prosecution was justified as being in the public interest. The Director's decision to agree to the prosecution was not susceptible to judicial review so long as there was absence of dishonesty, bad faith or other exceptional circumstances. Otherwise, it would have meant that the DPP was disapplying primary legislation, but the House of Lords left the issue of incompatibility of s 16A and Art 6(2) undecided.

The question of reversed burdens of proof regarding criminal evidence continued to be problematical after the House of Lords' decision in 2000 and similar questions arose in a consolidated case four years later, this time still involving terrorism but also driving whilst over the limit under the Road Traffic Act (RTA). The DPP was again involved in the RTA case, and the terrorist case was a reference by the Attorney-General (A-G) (*Sheldrake v DPP; Attorney-General's Reference No 4 of 2002*, [2004] UKHL 43, [2004] 3 WLR 976).

The DPP was appealing against a decision that the reverse burden of proof imposed by the RTA 1988 s 5(2) was incompatible with ECHR Art 6(2) ([2003] EWHC 273, [2004] QB 487). The A-G needed advice on the Terrorism Act 2000 s 11(2) regarding the decision of incompatibility in respect of the burden reversal reached at [2003] EWCA Crim 762, [2003] 3 WLR 1153. Sheldrake was the defendant in the RTA case and A the defendant in the anti-terrorism proceedings. In each case they contended that the respective statutory provisions infringed the presumption of innocence and so they should be read as imposing an evidential and not a legal burden.

The core of Sheldrake's arguments was that the likelihood of a person driving was the gravamen of the offence and s 5(1) of the 1988 Act was aimed at preventing a person from driving whilst unfit because of drink. This imposed a burden on the defendant to disprove an important ingredient of the offence. If he could not do so, his guilt would be presumed. An inexorable or at least a rational connection between the facts presumed and the facts proved was needed if the presumption was to be justified, which was not the case here.

Although Lord Rodger of Earlsferry and Lord Carswell dissented in part, the DPP's appeal was allowed and the A-G's question was answered. In each case the burden placed on the defendant

was not beyond reasonable limits or arbitrary and, in respect of the A-G's question, Parliament had clearly imposed a statutory legal burden on the defendant directed towards the legitimate objective of deterring people from becoming members of, and participating in, the activities of proscribed terrorist organisations, and in determining these questions of reversal of the burden of proof the crucial question was whether the provision was a proportionate and justifiable response to a legitimate problem.

8.8 Article 6(3) minimum rights

Some of the issues covered by the minimum rights provisions in ECHR Art 6(3) have been discussed previously in this chapter. The following table contains a reminder of what these are:

	Art 6(3) provides that everyone charged with a criminal offence has the following minimum rights:
(a)	To be informed promptly, in a language which he understands and in detail, of the nature and cause of the accusation against him
(b)	To have adequate time and facilities for the preparation of his defence
(c)	To defend himself in person or through legal assistance of his own choosing or, if he has not sufficient means to pay for legal assistance, to be given it free when the interests of justice so require
(d)	To examine or have examined witnesses against him and to obtain the attendance and examination of witnesses on his behalf under the same conditions as witnesses against him
(e)	To have the free assistance of an interpreter if he cannot understand or speak the language used in the court

■ Figure 8.4 Summary minimum rights

8.8.1 Article 6(3)(a) prompt information

The right to be informed promptly and in detail of the exact nature and cause of the accusation(s) against him in terms he can understand is central to the right to a fair trial. This rule applies to everyone, not just the accused, and occasionally lawyers finds themselves criticised in connection with how they choose to deal with their instructions. Thus, when a lawyer is instructed to defend someone charged with murder, he must be allowed to conduct that defence effectively and in a manner which includes cross-examining witnesses without interference by the court. If there is interference, the lawyer must be free to withdraw from the case without being accused of contempt of court.

In *Kyprianou v Cyprus* (Application No 73979/01, 15th December 2005, (2007) 44 EHRR 27, the defence lawyer objected to interruptions which he regarded as so damaging that he requested that he be allowed to withdraw from the case. When permission was refused the lawyer was reported as saying: 'You can try me.' He was sentenced to five days' imprisonment because of his alleged contempt of court and served an immediate term of imprisonment, although released early in accordance with Cypriot law. His appeal to the Supreme Court having been dismissed, he took his case to the European Court of Human Rights under the provisions of Art 6 of the ECHR.

Although it was not necessary to rule specifically on the provisions of Art 6(3)(a), the Grand Chamber held unanimously that there had been a violation of Art 6(1).

8.8.2 Article 6(3)(b) adequate time and facilities

The defendant and his legal representatives need sufficient time and resources – Art 6(3)(b) says 'facilities' – to prepare their defence, and if a prisoner is detained on remand, that right is particularly important. In a recent case the claimant, remand prisoner (E), applied for judicial review of decisions made by the Home Secretary to locate her at a particular prison and to treat her in a way that she claimed meant she did not have a fair trial in respect of terrorism charges *(R (on the application of E) v Secretary of State for the Home Department* [2007] EWHC 1731 (Admin); [2007] ACD 83).

The essence of her complaint was that she was held in a restricted status establishment some 20 miles away from the court. She alleged that this did not allow her sufficient time each day properly to instruct her lawyers, and the travel sickness her journey to court induced meant that because of the medical treatment provided, she was drowsy during the hearings and so was not fit to be cross-examined. She alleged that these circumstances constituted failure on the part of the Prison Service to ensure that she had the ability to benefit from her right to a fair trial.

The application was refused. Where appropriate, the Administrative Court could intervene in an ongoing criminal trial, but that was the primary responsibility of the trial judge and only in exceptional circumstances would such intervention take place. E had made no application to the trial judge to deal with her alleged difficulties, nor had she adduced any evidence to indicate that he was failing in his duty to ensure she had a fair trial or that he would not make allowances if requested; indeed, if anything, the evidence pointed the other way. Where she was being held was justified by the nature of the security risk she presented.

8.8.3 Article 6(3)(c) defending oneself and legal assistance

In order for justice to be seen to be done defendants must be allowed, if they judge it to be in their best interests, to defend themselves, although in most cases this may well not be the case, and such self-help is not likely to aid the smooth running of the trial process. Yet it would be wrong for a defendant to have dictated to him by the court what the law considers to be in his best interest. That is why the accused is allowed under Art 6(3)(c) either to defend himself, or to choose his own legal assistance. If he does not have the ability or wish to defend himself or the means to pay for legal advice and representation, the article says that it should be provided free 'when the interests of justice so require'. That can be achieved in a variety of ways.

Legal advice and assistance may be available and according to the Legal Services Commission's website they use their £2 billion annual budget to help around two million people access legal help each year (see link at the end of this chapter).

The 'cab rank rule' still applies to barristers, under which self-employed barristers must in defined circumstances under r 602 of their Code of Conduct accept any brief or instructions and represent a client whether privately or publicly funded. As long as he is appropriately experienced he cannot pick and choose if a client asks him to act, and this rule is meant to ensure that however heinous or unpleasant a client or his alleged conduct may be, he will find it possible to be legally represented. The rule is subject to a number of safeguards designed to protect the barrister as well as the potential client.

Other countries have different ways of ensuring that the substance of Art 6(3)(c) and, more generally, the rules of natural justice are upheld.

Under Belgian law, the Order of Advocates is obliged to make provision for helping people who require legal aid and in *Van der Mussele v Belgium* (1983) 6 EHRR 163 the applicant complained that as a pupil advocate he had been compelled by the Order's regulations to represent clients without payment. He alleged that this infringed a number of rights including his right under Art 4(2) not to be compelled to undertake forced labour.

Although Van der Mussele's claim against Belgium was not upheld, the European Court of Human Rights did find that Art 6(3)(c) was engaged because contracting parties cannot relieve themselves of their Convention responsibilities simply by imposing them by law on bodies such as the Order of Advocates. In that case, by not making provision for indemnifying pupil advocates, Belgian law implicitly acknowledged that the expense of compliance with the ECHR had to be borne by trainee lawyers. However, the result was that as these trainees knew what the provisions were yet still wished to join the legal profession, this was part of the price or cost they had to pay to do so, however inequitable it might seem that trainees should be penalised in such a manner.

8.8.4 Article 6(3)(d) witnesses

Circumstantial evidence must always be regarded with great caution, and the great majority of cases are decided on evidence provided by witnesses. It is therefore crucial to defendants in criminal cases and those defending their legal rights or attempting to prove facts in civil cases that the witnesses be produced in court in order to be subjected to vigorous scrutiny. Scientific evidence is often complicated and technical, and expert witnesses should be available to give and explain it to the court. Hearsay evidence, where a witness reports what someone else has told him, is dangerous because the direct truth of what is being said cannot be so tested. The best the law can do is to have the witness standing before the court, having sworn in whatever mode is culturally or religiously applicable to tell the truth, the whole truth and nothing but the truth, and then to be put to the test by close cross-examination of the evidence he has been led to give.

However, this is not always possible or desirable. One example of why not would be children who may be too young to stand in public in the witness box, and in such cases they may give evidence by video link, as may prisoners incarcerated in another part of the country if it is safe and more economic to do so. Another example is that of the witness who is or may be intimidated by the accused if his or her identity were to be made public. The police rely on information from many sources some of which are not and cannot be made public. They need to be able to give assurances to innocent witnesses that if they provide evidence necessary to help to convict dangerous criminals, they will not be subjected to reprisals and retribution. Such protection may vary from giving evidence from behind a screen, to having their voices electronically altered as is often done in the radio and television media, to provision of ongoing protection and new identities, in extreme cases.

These conflicting needs can mean that the accused person then finds himself at a disadvantage as his ability to challenge witnesses' evidence is severely curtailed if he does not know who the witness is, where he is coming from, whether he may have some ulterior motive for giving the evidence, and where the judge and jury are unable to see and assess the demeanour of the witness. It is impossible completely and fairly to balance these opposing criteria, and recent case law dealt a blow to the ability of the prosecution to use anonymous witnesses.

CASE EXAMPLE

R v Davis (Iain) and others **[2008] 3 WLR 125**

Davis appealed to the House of Lords from the Court of Appeal's dismissal of his appeal ([2006] 1 WLR 3130) against a murder conviction. Witnesses at his trial, without whose evidence he could not have been convicted, were allowed to give that evidence anonymously because they were in fear of their own lives. The Court of Appeal had rejected Davis's argument that the extensive measures taken in court to conceal witnesses' identities were contrary to Art 6(3)(d) of the ECHR. The House of Lords found in favour of the appellants, five in number altogether.

The common law had never responded to threats of intimidation to witnesses and the challenges they posed to the trial system. Even in 1972 at the height of the troubles in Northern Ireland the Diplock Commission had been unable to recommend legislation to change this principle. Strasbourg jurisprudence did not set its face absolutely against the admission of anonymous evidence in all circumstances, although it did say that a conviction should not be based wholly or to a decisive extent on anonymous statements, but the measures taken in this case would not conform to the requirements of the ECHR Art 6(3)(d) and an additional defect was the inability of the accused to cross-examine witnesses effectively. 'Ultimately, the protective measures imposed hampered the conduct of the defence in a manner and to an extent that was unlawful and rendered the trial unfair.'

Criminal Evidence (Witness Anonymity) Act 2008

The government introduced emergency legislation in the form of the Criminal Evidence (Witness Anonymity) Act 2008 on 4th July to overturn the judgment in *Davis*. The Bill received its third reading in the House of Commons on 8th July and a third reading in the House of Lords on 15th July. The following day the Commons approved the Lords' Amendments and the Bill obtained Royal Assent on 21st July 2008.

The Act abolishes the common law rules on witness anonymity and establishes a framework of witness anonymity orders which the Court may grant on application of either defendant or prosecution, but it does contain a 'sunset clause' which means that the Act will expire on 31st December 2009 unless Parliament extends it, which it may do for ongoing 12-month periods.

There are three conditions that need to be satisfied before an order can be made, ie that the:

1   order is necessary to protect the witness, prevent serious damage to property or real harm to the public interest

2   provisions of the order are consistent with the defendant receiving a fair trial

3   interests of justice require that it is important that the witness testifies, and that the witness would not testify if the order were not made.

It is likely that Parliament will need to return to this rushed piece of legislation which the noted human rights lawyer, Geoffrey Robinson QC, described in *The Guardian* on 8th July 2008 as a 'perjurer's charter'. He also questioned whether the Justice Secretary's statement that it conforms to ECHR criteria was correct.

8.8.5 Article 6(3)(e) interpreters

Adverse conditions in many parts of the world leading to refugees, asylum seekers and economic migration, increased mobility of workers within the much-expanded EU, and the existence of many communities throughout Europe whose members do not speak the language of their host states all provide reasons why the right to have the free assistance of an interpreter in court is important.

Courts intimidate those who can readily understand what is happening, but if the proceedings are conducted in a foreign language that the accused, litigants or witnesses cannot understand, that intimidation is magnified. It is especially important that persons at risk, such as asylum seekers, should be able to explain clearly why they fear being returned whence they came, but others in far less obvious predicaments may also need help.

For example, it may not be immediately apparent that a company director charged with tax evasion might be in need of an interpreter.

CASE EXAMPLE

Cuscani v United Kingdom (32771/96), (2003) 36 EHRR 2

Cuscani alleged that he had not had the benefit of an interpreter during the course of proceedings on tax-evasion charges, contrary to the provisions of Arts 6(1) and Art 6(3)(e). The trial judge had granted the request for an interpreter but in fact no arrangements had been made for this to be done and Cuscani's counsel had suggested that they would be able, in his words, to 'make do and mend' with the help of the accused's brother, although even that substitute repair kit had not been used.

The reason why these circumstances occurred may be because the accused pleaded guilty. He was sentenced to four years' imprisonment and disqualified from being a company director for 10 years. He subsequently argued that he could not fully understand the proceedings and without the help of a translator his conviction was unfair.

Judge Pellonpaa in the European Court of Human Rights held that, although the conduct of the defence was a matter for the defendant and his counsel, the ultimate responsibility for ensuring procedural fairness lay with the judge. The consequences of Cuscani's guilty plea were severe which placed a high onus on the judge not to leave the accused at risk and prejudiced by not fully being able to participate in the proceedings.

The court's duty in such circumstances was not discharged by acceding to the defence counsel's suggestions which failed to protect his client. Even had the brother been used, this would still have been less than satisfactory because his language skills were untested as far as the court was concerned.

Accordingly there had been violations of Arts 6(1) and 6(3)(e).

8.8.6 Misuse of Article 6(3)

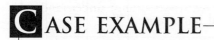

CASE EXAMPLE

R v Ulcay (Erdogan) and another [2007] EWCA Crim 2379

The minimum rights established by Art 6(3) are substantial when taken together, but they are not predicated on the proposition that an accused person should be able or allowed to manipulate them in order to sabotage what would otherwise be a fair trial.

CONTINUED ▸

The sequence of facts in *R v Ulcay (Erdogan) and another* is complex because of the devious behaviour of the accused but essentially, having been charged with conspiracy to facilitate the commission of breaches of immigration law, they set about giving contradictory instructions to counsel, repeatedly sought adjournments, and then changed their legal representatives three times before carrying on unrepresented.

Subsequently, they argued that these circumstances had prejudiced their respective trials, and an interesting contradiction became apparent with regard to the respective professional obligations imposed on barristers and solicitors:

> 'The Bar Council accepted that, in the circumstances faced by the new barristers, they should simply have "soldiered on" and done the best they could. However, the Law Society argued that that course was unavailable to a solicitor, who would be at risk of contravening r 2.01(b) of the Solicitors' Code of Conduct, which required a solicitor without sufficient resources or lacking the necessary competence to cease to act.'

In any event, the appeals were dismissed on the basis that the processes designed to ensure fairness in trials were not open to manipulation or abuse by defendants whose objective was to derail the trial. The judge had therefore been entitled to refuse the lengthy adjournments sought. The conviction was safe and the trial had been as fair as the accused had allowed it to be. The report of the case went on to provide a detailed discussion of legal representatives' responsibilities where the circumstances were diametrically opposed to those envisaged by the protective provisions of Art 6, namely where attempts are made by accused persons to manipulate the rules to defeat justice.

ACTIVITY

Self-assessment questions

1	The right to a fair hearing guaranteed by Art 6 only refers to criminal trials.	T	F
2	*Magna Carta* is now only of historical rather than legal importance.	T	F
3	The Bill of Rights 1689 redefined the relationship between the Crown and Parliament.	T	F
4	The importance of the role of the Lord Chancellor has been reduced in recent years.	T	F

CONTINUED ▸

ACTIVITY

5	Fatal accident inquiries are covered by the terms of Art 6.	T	F
6	Prison disciplinary hearings are not covered by the terms of Art 6.	T	F
7	The European Court of Human Rights will always intervene if a domestic tribunal fails to provide a remedy.	T	F
8	*R v Gough* and *R v Spencer* both found there had been no bias on the part of members of the respective juries.	T	F
9	The common law protection for accused persons against witnesses giving anonymous evidence was overturned by the Criminal Evidence (Witness Anonymity) Act 2008.	T	F
10	The Court can refuse to allow an accused person to defend himself.	T	F

KEY FACTS

The common law	Provided a number of important types of protection including independent judiciary, lay involvement in trials, *habeas corpus*, judicial review, protection from double jeopardy
ECHR Art 6(1) and (2)	Guarantee the right to a prompt and fair public hearing in criminal and civil matters and presumption of innocence until proved guilty
ECHR Art 6(3)	Establishes the minimum rights of those charged with a criminal offence including understanding the charge, having time and facilities to prepare a defence, availability of witnesses, legal assistance or representation and a translator if necessary
Judicial independence	Underpins the right to a fair trial and is achieved in the way that judges are appointed, their security of tenure recognised, and their immunity of suit from litigants and accused persons protected
Judicial bias	Litigants and accused persons are in turn protected from actual, apparent and assumed bias on the part of judges and juries
Types of hearing	A wide range of kinds of hearing are covered by Art 6 including fatal accident inquiries, arbitration proceedings, prison disciplinary hearings, and illegal immigrant penalties imposed by the executive

ACTIVITY

Practice essay title

Art 6 of the ECHR has expanded the scope of the long-standing protection of the right of the individual to a fair trial under English law.

Discuss.

Useful resources

English Bill of Rights 1689: http://www.yale.edu/lawweb/avalon/england.htm.

Legal Services Commission: (http://www.legalservices.gov.uk/public/what_legal_aid.asp).

Magna Carta: http://www.britainexpress.com/History/medieval/magnacarta-trans.htm.

Further reading

Goudkamp, J, 'Facing Up to Actual Bias', CJQ 2008, 27(1), 32–39.

Ovey, C and White, R, *Jacobs & White The European Convention on Human Rights* (4th edn, Oxford University Press, Oxford, 2006), Chapter 8, pp 158–215.

Foster, S, *Human Rights & Civil Liberties* (2nd edn, Pearson Education, Harlow, 2006) Chapter 7, pp 146–276.

NO PUNISHMENT
WITHOUT LAW ▪

AIMS AND OBJECTIVES ☐ ☐ ☐

- To consider issues relevant to the *nullum crimen, nulla poena sine lege* principle including due process and the theoretical unlimited power of the Westminster Parliament to legislate

- To review the UDHR and treaty provisions prohibiting retrospective criminal law and punishment

- To apply the 'Kevin test' (see Chapter 8) to the three main principles of Art 7 to show how it operates in practice

- To examine the case law on retroactive law and punishment.

9.1 Introduction

Nullum crimen, nulla poena sine lege

Law should be prospective, not retrospective, and the origins of this principle go back at least as far as Roman law. The Latin maxim *nullum crimen, nulla poena sine lege* means 'no crime, no punishment, without law'. It is the starting point for consideration of the presumption against retrospection in human rights. It expands the scope of the right to a fair trial provision, in effect, by requiring that a state must have in place a framework of validly made and administered law within which fair criminal trials can be held.

As will be seen from the subsequent discussion, the thrust of this chapter is that criminal law should be clear to everyone. It should not be altered retrospectively, and people should not be punished today for behaviour that was not criminal at the time it occurred. Implicit in this is a requirement, frequently not met, that law should be comprehensible.

Clause 29 of Magna Carta, discussed at the beginning of Chapter 8, is equally relevant and important in this context. It provides that 'no free man shall be seized, or imprisoned ... except by the lawful judgment of his peers or by the law of the land'.

9.2 Due process (of law)

In post-Roman times this proposition of 'no crime, no punishment, without law' came to be understood as 'due process (of law)'. The idea was taken up by the American colonists when they

achieved independence from the English Crown, driven by the belief that they were not being afforded respect equivalent to that given to English subjects of the Crown, limited though that was in the eighteenth century. The Americans were unrepresented in the English Parliament, yet were still taxed by the Crown.

In the emerging United States the idea was developed into *substantive* due process which concerned itself with matters such as privacy and free speech, as opposed to *procedural* due process which was to do with fairness of legal procedures including the right to be tried in person and to be legally represented.

The description 'due process' is not widely used these days in an English legal context but nevertheless it does incorporate vital principles such as: an accused being innocent until proved guilty; the right not to incriminate oneself; the right to silence; and the right not to be subjected to unjustified random searches or intrusions into one's private life. Perhaps one reason why the expression has fallen into apparent partial desuetude is that some of the protection that used to exist for the individual, mostly under the common law, has been eroded in recent years in response to modern threats and conditions. Also, the now prevalent European human rights regime has been heavily influenced by continental civil law jurisprudence, and so the law in this area now tends more commonly to be expressed in European human rights terms than by English common law, although that still exists as the bedrock of the English legal system.

Thus, an important part of the idea of due process of law is that governments should not be allowed to invent new criminal laws as they go along that can be applied retrospectively to their citizens.

9.3 Legislative power of Parliament

For centuries the power of the Crown was absolute so far as the ordinary subject was concerned, until the 'divine right of kings' was removed by Parliament with the Bill of Rights 1689. The theory developed during the Middle Ages that monarchs (mostly kings) were answerable only to God and it was therefore sinful, not to mention unwise, for their subjects to oppose or resist them. The Stuarts were rather keen on that idea but William and Mary were obliged to forego it as part of their bargain to be allowed to rule England.

The common law did develop a number of protective rules and procedures for the benefit of the Crown's subjects, but from the reign of William and Mary onwards it was Parliament that had effectively seized power, yet for several centuries thereafter Parliament was not representative of the majority of the population who remained mostly disenfranchised. By Victorian times it had become possible for Professor Dicey to state in his tripartite constitutional theory that the legislative power of Parliament was unlimited.

Although this theory was in the late nineteenth century basically tenable, in light of the passage of time it requires considerable qualification principally because, whilst it used to be *legally*

1	Parliament can enact laws about anything without restriction
2	No current Parliament is able to bind any future Parliament (which means it cannot pass any law that cannot itself be altered or repealed by any future Parliament)
3	As Parliament is the supreme law maker its legislation cannot be questioned or challenged by courts or elsewhere

Figure 9.1 Dicey's theory of parliamentary sovereignty

correct, it is certainly not *politically* correct (in the sense of being politically practicable). Members of the House of Commons usually pay considerable attention to safeguarding their seats, which in practical terms means they are not inclined deliberately to enact unpopular legislation that would be likely to lose them their seats in the following election.

The passage of time has also produced a variety of practical constraints on this theoretical unlimited power; for example, Parliament would be wasting its time trying to enact legislation to re-colonise the British Empire, and would encounter considerable difficulties if it attempted to repeal the European Communities Act 1972. To do this would almost certainly require a referendum in favour with a full public debate about the likely consequences, despite the absence of any constitutional requirement for referenda and politicians' flaky record for keeping electoral promises to hold referenda.

In other words, contemporary reality constrains traditional constitutional theory. Yet even so, Dicey's dicta may still hold true and Parliament may on occasion resort to retrospective legislation. For example:

- altering civil law as in *Burmah Oil*
- changing criminal law as with regard to genocide (further discussed at section 9.7.1)
- rectifying human rights law as in cases of the courts making declarations of incompatibility (see sections 3.5.3 and 3.5.4).

The House of Lords ruled in *Burmah Oil Company v Lord Advocate* [1965] AC 75 that although the act of deliberately destroying Burmah Oil installations during the Second World War on the orders of the British Government had been carried out lawfully by virtue of the royal prerogative, the Crown was not immune from paying compensation for the damage that resulted. The destruction of the oil installations did not result directly from battle damage, in which case such common law liability would not have arisen. Faced with having to make heavy reparation, Parliament enacted the War Damage Act 1965 which removed the government's liability to pay compensation and retrospectively changed the common law.

Other examples are the Genocide Act 1969 (since repealed but incorporated into the International Criminal Court Act 2001) which gave effect to Article II of the 1948 Genocide Convention and the War Crimes Act 1991. This treaty conferred retrospective jurisdiction for UK courts to try people for war crimes committed in Nazi Germany during the Second World War.

The War Damage Act 1965 deals with tortious liability whilst the Genocide Act and War Crimes Act both deal with criminal liability. In the latter cases there is a stricter onus on Parliament closely to limit the extent to which new law will be retroactive, because of the principles discussed in this chapter. In *Burmah Oil Company v Lord Advocate*, the House of Lords applied the common law rule, even though the economic effect of so doing was considered by the government to be unacceptable. The common law was clear and the House of Lords were applying common law principles rather than human rights provisions, and this was not the only occasion where their Lordships took this kind of stand.

CASE EXAMPLE

Waddington v Miah alias Ullah [1974] 1 WLR 683

Miah was charged on indictment on counts of being an illegal immigrant and possessing a false passport under the Immigration Act which was passed on 28th October 1971, although the relevant sections under which he was charged did not come into effect until 1st January 1973. Both charges related to offences allegedly committed on dates prior to the sections becoming law.

At the trial Miah moved to quash the indictment on the ground that the alleged offences were unknown at the relevant date but the submission was overruled and he was convicted on both counts. When he appealed, the Crown argued that although the provisions were penal they were retrospective and therefore valid, but the Court of Appeal rejected that argument and quashed the convictions.

The Crown's appeal to the House of Lords was dismissed. There was nothing in the statute to indicate that either section was retrospective, so therefore neither of them could apply to acts committed by the appellant prior to the Act and sections coming into force.

9.4 Development of the *nullum crimen* principle

The basic rule of not allowing punishment to be inflicted if there was no law in existence at the time the act was committed is, and was, by no means the sole preserve of Roman and English law, although some of the early English legal philosophers did write about it in the seventeenth century. The principle was developed in a number of continental legal systems and the German philosopher von Feuerbach incorporated the *nullum crimen* maxim into the Bavarian penal code in 1813 where it provided that judges interpreting criminal law had to adhere closely to the provisions of the code. In the meantime the idea had spread to the emerging American colonies and was applied in France following the Revolution. The reasoning is that the closer judges stick to a literal interpretation of statute, the less likely they are to stray from the true meaning.

The following brief summary gives an idea of some of the rule's main contexts over the last three-and-a-half centuries:

Item	Source	Year
1	Thomas Hobbes, *Leviathan*: 'No law, made after a fact done, can make it a crime . . . for before the law, there is no transgression of the law'	1651
2	American Constitution, Art 1 s 9(3)	1787
3	French Declaration of the Rights of Man, Art 8	1789
4	French Constitution (still part of the French Penal code)	1791
5	Bavarian Code	1815
6	German Penal Code	1871
7	Universal Declaration of Human Rights, Art 11	1948
8	European Convention on Human Rights, Art 7	1950
9	International Covenant on Civil and Political Rights, Art 15	1966
10	Rome Statute of the International Criminal Court, Arts 22 and 23	1998

■ Figure 9.2 Development of the '*nullum crimen*' maxim

After the Second World War, the first major statement of intent to apply the rule was contained in the Universal Declaration of Human Rights 1948, Art 11.

9.5 Modern international provisions

9.5.1 UDHR Art 11

1 'Everyone charged with a penal offence has the right to be presumed innocent until proved guilty according to law in a public trial at which he has had all the guarantees necessary for his defence.

2 No one shall be held guilty of any penal offence on account of any act or omission which did not constitute a penal offence, under national or international law, at the time when it was committed. Nor shall a heavier penalty be imposed than the one that was applicable at the time the penal offence was committed.'

9.5.2 The ICCPR Article 15

Art 11 of the UDHR presaged the International Covenant on Civil and Political Rights 1966 (ICCPR) which enlarged the Declaration's principle, expanded the scope of protection provided

from that contained in the ECHR Art 7 (see below), and enhanced the Declaration aspiration into a treaty obligation. Where adopted, it provided additional protection for an offender by allowing him to receive the lighter penalty if the punishment for his offence had been retrospectively increased.

'1. No one shall be held guilty of any criminal offence on account of any act or omission which did not constitute a criminal offence, under national or international law, at the time when it was committed. Nor shall a heavier penalty be imposed than the one that was applicable at the time when the criminal offence was committed. If, subsequent to the commission of the offence, provision is made by law for the imposition of the lighter penalty, the offender shall benefit thereby.

2. Nothing in this article shall prejudice the trial and punishment of any person for any act or omission which, at the time when it was committed, was criminal according to the general principles of law recognized by the community of nations.'

The UDHR provided the immediate background and justification for the English and European human rights law that prevents people from being punished in respect of actions and behaviour that were not criminal at the time they were committed, and the ICCPR reinforced it in 1966.

9.5.3 ECHR Art 7

Reference may be made from time to time by the English courts to the foregoing international treaty provision in the ICCPR but the law that is primarily applied is contained in Art 7 of the European Convention which says that there shall be no punishment without law:

'(1)   No one shall be held guilty of any criminal offence on account of any act or omission which did not constitute a criminal offence under national or international law at the time when it was committed. Nor shall a heavier penalty be imposed than the one that was applicable at the time the criminal offence was committed

(2) This Article shall not prejudice the trial and punishment of any person for any act or omission which, at the time when it was committed, was criminal according to the general principles of law recognised by civilised nations.'

9.6 The 'Kevin test'

At section 8.3.1 we encountered Kevin who was unfortunately languishing in a police station considering aspects of his need for protection, having come under suspicion of criminal activities. As Kevin goes about his daily business, trying to behave responsibly and in accordance with

ACTIVITY

Self-assessment questions

1 Explain in your own words the English meaning of the maxim *nullum crimen, nulla poena sine lege*.

2 Identify two documents prior to the twentieth century where the idea is mentioned or contained.

3 In Figure 9.2 items 7–10, which (if any) of the documents is not a legally binding international treaty?

4 Read carefully UDHR Art 11, ICCPR Art 15 and ECHR Art 7. Which of them do you think best expresses the rule against retroactive law and punishment?

5 Why?

existing law, he should be entitled to know that if the government decides that what he is doing today should be proscribed by law, or his behaviour classified as criminal, it must only be done after he and the public have been made aware of the changes in the law, which requires adherence to Art 7.

What Kevin did	Art 7 implications
Principle 1 Kevin stood on a soapbox in the Square and told passers-by that the government was run by dangerous characters who ignored the best interests of the people. Although this was not against the law when he did it Parliament later passed a retrospective law creating a criminal offence of 'dissing the government' and he was tried and sentenced to the maximum punishment, six months' imprisonment	This would clearly contravene the protective terms of the first sentence of Art 7(1) – 'dissing' was not an offence in any jurisdiction when Kevin spoke out and Art 7(1) is meant to prevent states enacting criminal laws applicable to these kinds of circumstance
Principle 2 When Kevin was released from prison he repeated his actions on the next market day. In an attempt to stop the spread of such dangerous behaviour Parliament passed a dissing amendment statute retrospectively increasing the maximum punishment to two years' imprisonment for which Kevin was also tried and convicted	This contravenes Art 7(1) second sentence by retrospectively increasing the punishment for what at the time had been made an offence (whether or not reasonable). Kevin was this time guilty of criminal behaviour, but should not later be subjected to more serious punishment for it, ie his maximum punishment should still be six months' imprisonment
Principle 3 When Kevin is next released from prison he mounts his soapbox for the last time. He speaks to his public and tells them that the end of the world is nigh and that the only answer is to sail away to a remote island. He tells them that it would be justifiable to attack and rob any other vessel encountered on the way in order to survive. For the sake of argument, 'incitement to piracy' is not a crime under English law	Piracy and analogous activities are crimes recognised by civilised nations whether or not particular states have specific national law addressing the suppression of piracy. Kevin can be tried and convicted and would not be entitled to the protection of Art 7(2) ECHR

■ Figure 9.3 The 'Kevin test'

This means that any such changes in the criminal law should only start to operate from now or from a future date. It enshrines three fundamental principles which we might call the 'Kevin test', as illustrated in Figure 9.3, to assess how they operate.

9.6.1 Example of Principle 1

The retrospective imposition of a confiscation order under the Drug Trafficking Offences Act 1986, in respect of a conviction for drug trafficking prior to 12th January 1987 when the Act came into effect, amounted to a penalty contrary to ECHR Art 7(1) (*Welch v UK* [1995] 20 EHRR 247) because conviction of drug trafficking was a pre-condition. In such cases the courts were entitled to make sweeping assumptions that the assets of the convicted person were drug-trafficking proceeds and so to take into account his degree of culpability.

The distinction being drawn was that in some circumstances the court can decide that confiscation is a species of reparation rather than punishment. The applicant's complaint that this confiscation order was a criminal penalty rather than civil reparation was upheld, so it was contrary to the provisions of Art 7(1) ECHR.

In its analysis of the essence of Art 7(1) the European Court said:

- If the order amounts to a penalty it is an autonomous Convention concept (analogous to 'civil rights and obligations' and 'criminal charge' in Art 6(1)).

- The Court must 'remain free to go behind appearances and assess for itself whether a particular measure amounts in substance to a penalty within the meaning of Art 7(1)'.

- Taking a purposive approach the Court examined the background to the 1986 Act, introduced to overcome the inadequacy of the previous powers of forfeiture, and to allow seizure by the Court even when the assets had been converted into other property.

- The severity of a measure is not the sole criterion on which to judge it as many non-penal measures nevertheless can have a substantial impact on the person convicted.

- All in all here, having looked behind appearances at reality, the conclusion of its being a penalty and thus in breach of Art 7(1) was justified.

9.6.2 Examples of Principle 2

In order to determine whether a measure taken against an individual is a penalty or not, ie to consider the criteria to assess possible penalties under Art 7(1) second sentence, *Welch v UK* (1995) discussed above said that the factors to be considered by the European Court of Human Rights are:

- Is it connected with a criminal conviction?

- What is its nature and purpose?

- What characterization is given to it by the relevant national law?

- What is its severity?

CASE EXAMPLE

R (Uttley) v Home Secretary [2004] UKHL 38; [2004] 1 WLR 2278

In the more recent case of *R (on the application of Uttley) v Secretary of State for the Home Department*, the Home Secretary appealed against the decision that a 12-year sentence of imprisonment imposed for a number of sexual offences, including rape, contravened the provisions of Art 7 ([2003] EWCA Civ 1130).

The reason for this decision was that the accused had committed the offence in 1983 and the punishment that was eventually administered was heavier than the one that could have been imposed at that time. Because of changes brought about by the Criminal Justice Act 1991, instead of only serving two-thirds of his sentence, he was released on licence, which he argued imposed an additional penalty.

Uttley's application for judicial review had been rejected but the Court of Appeal decided that there had been an infringement of Art 7 because he was liable to be recalled on breach, so the balance of his sentence was being held over his head that previously would not have been the case.

The House of Lords disagreed, interpreting the words 'the penalty . . . that was applicable at the time' under Art 7(1) to mean the maximum penalty the law could previously have imposed when the crime was committed. As the maximum throughout had been life imprisonment, there had been no breach of Art 7. The decision was subsequently followed by *R v McGuigan (William Joseph)* [2005] EWCA Crim 2861; (CA (Crim Div)).

Example of Principle 3

English law no longer regards wives as mere chattels and the property of their husbands. Many steps have been taken, particularly in the latter part of the twentieth and twenty-first centuries, to reduce inequality between the sexes and in other spheres (discussed in more detail in Chapter 16). Nevertheless, anomalies remain and sometimes rectifying what have long been unrecognised wrongs, or insufficiently recognised to have merited statutory rectification, is left to the courts. If it involves a principle, this is not the ideal way that law reform should be achieved because it is not judges but Members of Parliament who are democratically elected with a mandate who should bring about fundamental legal change, but it can and does happen under the common law. One such instance arose in the case of marital rape.

CASE EXAMPLE

SW and CR v UK [1996] 21 EHRR 363

Marital rape was a concept unknown to English law prior to 1989 but in that year for the first time English courts began to convict men who insisted on having sexual intercourse with their wives without their consent. SW and CR were convicted on charges of rape and attempted rape respectively and those convictions were subsequently upheld first by the Court of Appeal and then in 1991 by the House of Lords ([1991] 4 All ER 481).

Although not completely unrestricted, there was a general common law rule that a man could not be convicted of raping his wife, and the basis of the decisions reached in this case (which in effect was a change of policy by the courts) was that it is no longer appropriate in modern times. The courts took the view that they were not precluded from altering the common law rule by s 1 of the Sexual Offences (Amendment) Act 1976 which referred to 'unlawful' sexual intercourse. In 1995 the defendants appealed to the European Court of Human Rights.

The European Court held that the purpose and object of Art 7 was to ensure that nobody was subject to arbitrary prosecution. However, this does not mean that there can never be any retrospective application of the criminal law and it can be clarified by judicial interpretation. This is subject to the proviso that the development of such revised criminal liability was clearly defined and foreseeable. At the time the acts were committed by SW and CR the principle of marital immunity still applied, but both the Law Commission and Government had provisionally recommended its abolition, which led to the court concluding that adaptation and abolition of the then existing law could reasonably be foreseen.

In CR's case there had been an agreement to separate with the wife refusing consent to intercourse, so in any event that came within one of the pre-existing exceptions to immunity. The national courts' decisions did not violate Art 7 as they continued a perceptible evolution of case law which, at the dates of the applicants' actions, had reached the stage where they could be convicted of rape. In reaching this decision the European Court paid particular attention to the 'essentially debasing character of rape' which

> 'is so manifest that to convict the applicants in these circumstances cannot be said to be at variance with the object and purpose of Article 7, namely to ensure that no-one should be subjected to arbitrary prosecution, conviction or punishment. The abandonment of the unacceptable idea of a husband being immune against prosecution for rape of his wife was in conformity not only with a civilised concept of marriage but also with the fundamental objectives of the Convention, the very essence of which is respect for human dignity and freedom.'

9.7 Retrospective crime and punishment

9.7.1 Retrospective law

Sometimes law is *enacted* (rather than *interpreted* as in *SW and CR v UK*) at domestic or international level that makes an act criminal which was legal at the time it was committed. In such cases, whilst the act may or may not have been *morally* reprehensible at the time it occurred, it did not actually infringe the law. The question then to be asked is: should it be possible to insist later (ie retrospectively) that what was *then* done is *now* against the law and can *now* be punished? Art 7 clearly refers to criminal rather than civil matters, so apparently unfair law relating, for example, to retrospective imposition of higher taxation on selected types of vehicle would not come within its ambit.

This is a serious philosophical and human rights question, although not strictly a legal one, because as has been seen under the English constitutional doctrine of parliamentary sovereignty the legislature can and sometimes does enact retrospective legislation, for example windfall taxes. Some people would be quite prepared to see others punished by retroactive law if their behaviour infringes a perceived code of conduct, regardless of whether the action(s) in question were 'against the law'. The fact that many people might support this approach in certain instances cannot provide the basis of a just and fair judicial system or a properly functioning programme of protected human rights, but neither can the possibility of retrospective criminal law simply be dismissed as always being out of the question.

Genocide

A classic example under international law is what is now called 'genocide'. Mass murder coming within the modern definition of genocide has been committed throughout history. However, during the Second World War Nazi policies turned planned and calculated mass murder into a highly organised industrial process. Consequently, after the War, it was considered justifiable and right to designate that behaviour as an international crime and condemn a number of perpetrators to death on the strength of the retrospective introduction and classification of new international law. It was a step which required close consideration and moral justification, even given the scale and scope of the atrocities committed, because of those philosophical and human rights considerations. Otherwise, it would be liable to be dismissed as 'victors' justice', implying an absence of convincing justification and motivated by vengeance.

Generally, the Nuremberg Tribunals (1945–49) (the International Military Tribunal) which tried German war criminals has been accepted as legitimate, although there is rather more doubt attaching to the Tokyo Tribunal (the International Military Tribunal for the Far East 1946–48) conducted by General MacArthur in Japan. Less well known is the fact that China also convened as many as 13 tribunals of its own.

The problem can occur in domestic law as well, for example the removal of protection against double jeopardy which means that people who in the past have been acquitted under a regime that would not subject them to risk of further trial may today be tried again. The *ex post facto* creation of the crime of marital rape considered in sections 9.6.2 and 9.6.3 above (*R (on the application of Uttley) v Secretary of State for the Home Department* and *SW and CR v UK* are examples).

9.7.2 Retrospective punishment

Nor should it be possible to punish people in ways that were not available at the time of the alleged action, or to impose more onerous punishments. It is an important principle but of course can be used by smart criminals to protect themselves against retribution or justice when they knew that what they were doing was 'wrong'. This raises the question of what *is* 'wrong'? A further desirable characteristic is that the law should be clear and apparent so that no misapprehension would have arisen in the first place.

The 'defendant' is the innocent person who is accused of an offence or crime, until a properly constituted tribunal has determined otherwise. It is an important principle of the common law and of human rights that a person is innocent until properly proven to be otherwise. In Scots law a verdict of 'not proven' is possible but under English law the verdict will be 'guilty' or 'not guilty'. In either case the accused remains innocent until the verdict has been pronounced.

One problem facing human rights is that in an era tainted by terrorism the temptation may be for government to persuade Parliament to alter the law in favour of the executive in order to try to ensure that terrorists are neutered before they are able to attack, damage and paralyse society. Previous criminal law concentrated on identifying, locating, trying and punishing miscreants. With terrorism the risk for the government is that if they fail to take pre-emptive action and terrorists successfully commit outrages, the government will be criticised for lack of anticipation, inaction and incompetence.

Even taking this into consideration, during the last 10 years or so the government has created approximately 60 Acts of Parliament setting out some 3,000 new crimes, with other changes in procedure allowing previously excluded evidence to be introduced into court proceedings, for example disclosing previous convictions of the accused person. These all need to be measured against Arts 6 and 7 and, whatever the reasons, it is clear that the trend has been away from protecting individuals and towards what government believes is greater protection for society as a whole.

Traditionally, a person was tried on the indictment presented to the court but under some of this recent legislation he is apprehended on executive suspicion and may not be charged or sent for trial. Some people might think this is fair in the interests of protection of society and the greater good, but that does not address the human rights issues. Central to English common law and the Convention is the importance of the right to a fair hearing, whether criminal or civil, and this goes hand in hand with the right not to be punished unless there are already in existence treaty or domestic legal provisions clearly defining and setting out that the behaviour in question is contrary to law.

A useful rule-of-thumb test for the man in the street to apply is whether, if the pre-emptive or retrospective law were to be applied to him, his family and friends, he would still consider it to be fair and just for the greater good of society. The test works just as well if one is tempted to justify the use of torture, or to decide whether behaviour short of torture exceeds acceptable limits.

The following case example deals with two cases where the authorities were keen to show that a thoughtless action in one instance and maliciously founded behaviour in the other could be punished by law, and both hinged on whether the respective behaviour was unlawful at the time it occurred, or whether the legal parameters were being stretched too far.

CASE EXAMPLE

R v Goldstein; R v Rimmington [2006] 2 All ER 257 HL

Rimmington was charged with causing a public nuisance by sending 538 separate packages containing racially offensive material through the post and at the preparatory hearing the judge ruled that this was an offence known to law and the prosecution was not an abuse of process.

In a separate case, but one founded on the same alleged offence, Goldstein had posted an envelope containing salt to a friend, intending this to be a joke at a time when there was fear that terrorists were spreading anthrax in a similar manner, but some salt leaked onto the hands of a postal worker at a sorting office. This caused the building to be evacuated, following which he also was convicted of causing a public nuisance.

Their respective appeals against preliminary ruling and conviction having been dismissed by the Court of Appeal, they further appealed to the House of Lords on the basis that, as applied in their respective cases, the offence of causing a public nuisance was too imprecisely defined and the courts' interpretation of it too uncertain and unpredictable to satisfy the requirements either of the common law or of the ECHR. Additionally, public nuisance was now a statutory offence and therefore they should have been charged under the statute which provided for the question of *mens rea* to be taken into consideration.

Lord Bingham of Cornhill explained the problem of reconciling uncertain aspects of law with the Art 7 requirements by quoting Jeremy Bentham:

CONTINUED ▸

'The appellants submitted that the crime of causing a public nuisance, as currently interpreted and applied, lacks the precision and clarity of definition, the certainty and the predictability necessary to meet the requirements of either the common law itself or article 7 of the European Convention. This submission calls for some consideration of principle.

In his famous polemic *Truth versus Ashurst* , written in 1792 and published in 1823, Jeremy Bentham made a searing criticism of judge-made criminal law, which he called "dog-law".

> "It is the judges (as we have seen) that make the common law. Do you know how they make it? Just as a man makes laws for his dog. When your dog does anything you want to break him of, you wait till he does it, and then beat him for it. This is the way you make laws for your dog: and this is the way the judges make law for you and me. They won't tell a man beforehand what it is he *should not do* – they won't so much as allow of his being told: they lie by till he has done something which they say he should not *have done*, and then they hang him for it."

The domestic law of England and Wales has set its face firmly against "dog-law"… The effect of the Strasbourg jurisprudence on this topic has been clear and consistent. The starting point is the old rule *nullum crimen, nulla poena sine lege* (no crime, no punishment, without law).'

Lord Bingham of Cornhill

The House of Lords held in *R v Goldstein; R v Rimmington* that the courts could not abolish a common law offence but that it should be relatively rare for charges to continue to be brought under the common law when Parliament had made statutory provision. The definition of the offence of causing a public nuisance was clear enough but did not depend on harm to individuals, rather to the public in general, and the Court of Appeal's decisions were reversed.

Rimmington had not caused a common injury to a section of the public so his conduct lacked the essential ingredient of common nuisance, and in Goldstein's case it had not been proven that Goldstein knew, or should reasonably have known, that the salt would escape into the sorting office or in the course of the post.

Neither of them could be convicted of the offences.

9.8 Scope of Art 7 cases

9.8.1 What kinds of case?

The principle of no punishment without law can be applied to many areas of law. In *R v Goldstein* and *R v Rimmington* it was public nuisance and within the last few years it has also been considered in cases involving breach of the peace, immigration, manslaughter, and rape, marital and non-marital. In *Steel and others v United Kingdom* (1998) 28 EHRR 603 a number of people were charged with breaches of the peace in different contexts and the court held that the offence of breach of the peace was sufficiently well understood as to enable people to foresee the consequences of their actions.

R (on the application of Ullah) v Special Adjudicator; Do v Secretary of State for the Home Department [2004] 3 All ER 785; [2004] UKHL 26 decided amongst other issues that Art 7 was not likely to arise often in the context of immigration decisions to expel aliens, but it could do so and if it did the principles laid down by the European Court of Human Rights in respect of extradition and expulsion involving a real risk of a flagrant violation of fair trial rights would likewise apply. The article is among the first tier of core obligations under the European Convention and is absolute and non-derogable.

CASE EXAMPLE

R v Misra and another [2004] All ER (D) 107

In *Misra* a hospital patient died from a severe rare infection, and two doctors, Amit Misra and Rajeev Srivastava, were convicted of manslaughter based on gross negligence. The defendants contended that with hindsight they had made mistakes but genuinely had not realised the extent of the victim's illness and had acted in good faith and, in any event, the mistakes made were at most negligent, not grossly negligent. The trial judge certified a question for the Court of Appeal as to whether grossly negligent manslaughter complied with the requirement for legal certainty, pursuant to Art 7 of the ECHR.

The Court of Appeal dismissed the doctors' appeals on the basis that the law on grossly negligent manslaughter was sufficiently clear and did not offend the legal certainty requirements either of common law or human rights legislation. Doctors need to know that grossly negligent treatment of patients, exposing victims to risk of death and causing death, amounts to manslaughter.

In this case the jury was not deciding whether a particular defendant should be convicted of an offence of manslaughter by gross negligence on a legal basis but,

CONTINUED ▶

rather, on a factual basis. The question was not whether the defendants' negligence was gross and additionally a crime, but whether their behaviour was grossly negligent and consequently criminal, which indeed it was found to be.

The convictions were safe and would be upheld.

9.8.2 Strictly criminal in scope

As has been indicated, Art 7 is specifically couched in terms of the criminal law – 'guilty ... criminal offence ... penalty ... trial ... punishment'. In 2008 the Chancellor of the Exchequer proposed to impose increased taxation on certain motor vehicles with the implication that this was a 'green' tax to discourage people from driving 'gas guzzlers' and to persuade them to drive more ecofriendly vehicles. However, as the tax was to be imposed on vehicles purchased as long ago as 2001, it was argued by opponents that this could not be a green tax but was retrospective legislation, in effect imposing financial penalties by way of increased taxation on people who already possessed the types of vehicle to be covered. Could such retrospective legislation if enacted contravene Art 7?

An obvious weakness of the opponents' case is that this kind of taxation is often imposed by governments whose job it is to raise finance and who would find it impossible to do so effectively if there could never be an element of retrospection in their policies. Windfall taxes on what the government decides are excessive profits are another example. However, although the taxpayer may well be unhappy about these and similar schemes, there can be no question of them engaging Art 7. Only if the government went further and imposed retrospective penalties and punishment and designated the taxpayers' behaviour as criminal would that occur.

9.8.3 Presumption of innocence

In *R v Deyemi (Danny)* [2007] EWCA Crim 2060 Deyemi had been stopped and searched and found to be in possession of a stun gun which he said he thought was a torch. Although the judge accepted his evidence, he ruled that the offence was one of strict liability, after which Deyemi pleaded guilty. On appeal he claimed that the statutory provisions should not be read as imposing strict liability and that this was contrary to ECHR Arts 6 and 7.

The appeal was dismissed on the basis that mere possession was sufficient to obtain a conviction. Art 6 did not guarantee any particular content of civil rights and it had nothing to say about the content of the law creating an offence. Legislation that created an absolute offence was not in itself capable of infringing Art 6(1) or Art 6(2), but could be capable of affecting any evidential presumptions or statutory defences. Art 7 did not add anything to Art 6 in this case.

9.9 Conclusions

The importance of this prohibition is brought out by the fact that it was not buried as a sub-clause within Art 6 as it might well have been, but was given the status of a self-standing article in the ECHR. It relates not just to the rule that a person should not be punished for doing something that was not wrong or illegal, but neither should he be punished more severely than was provided for at the time the action was carried out. It does not arise anything like as frequently as some of the more obvious substantive rights or freedoms, but it is every bit as important in supporting the ground rules for protecting fundamental rights and freedoms.

ACTIVITY

Quick quiz

1 What is the problem human rights proponents have with retrospective legislation?

2 Why does Lord Bingham quote Jeremy Bentham and his dog in *R v Goldstein; R v Rimmington* (2006)?

3 Why is it preferable that for matters of principle and policy the law should be changed by Parliament rather than the judiciary?

4 Would there be any virtue in having a verdict in English courts of 'not proven'?

5 What bearing might such a verdict have on human rights?

KEY FACTS

Principle	Based on the Latin maxim *nullum crimen, nulla poena sine lege* which means 'no crime, no punishment, without law'
UN legal norm	Recognised in slightly different forms in UDHR, ICCPR and the Rome Statute of the ICC
ECHR Art 7(1)	Says that there must be no retrospective creation of new criminal liability nor imposition of a heavier penalty for existing offences
ECHR Art 7(2)	Emphasises that the article does not prejudice trial and punishment when what had been done was criminal at the time according to recognised principles of civilised nations
ECHR Art 6	The operation of the Art 7 prohibition is closely connected to the right to a fair trial provisions of Art 6

CONTINUED ▸

<table>
<tr><td colspan="2" align="center">KEY FACTS</td></tr>
</table>

Criminal matters only	Art 7 does not restrict government from enacting retrospective legislation on civil matters such as taxation
Retrospective law	Despite Art 7 and the unfairness of imposing retrospective law, it is used in English law and is hard to challenge under human rights law

Further reading

Atrill, S, 'Nulla Poena Sine Lege in Comparative Perspective: Retrospectivity Under the ECHR and US Constitution', PL 2005, Spr, 107–131.

Hannett, S, 'Focus on Article 7 of the European Convention on Human Rights', JR 2007, 12(2), 112–116.

Hoffman, D and Rowe, J, QC, *Human Rights in the UK: An Introduction to the Human Rights Act 1998* (2nd edition, Pearson Longman, 2006), Chapter 13.

Popple, J, 'The Right to Protection from Retroactive Criminal Law', Criminal Law Journal, August 1989, 13(4), 251–262, ISSN 0314–1160.

This can be accessed on the web at:

http://cs.anu.edu.au/~James.Popple/publications/articles/retroactive/0.html

Sullivan, C, 'The United Kingdom Identity Cards Act 2006: Civil or Criminal?', IJL and IT 2007, 15(3), 320–361.

chapter 10 PRIVACY AND RESPECT FOR PRIVATE AND FAMILY LIFE

AIMS AND OBJECTIVES

This is chapter addresses the following matters:

- Key concepts of privacy, breach of confidence, respect, private life, marriage and having a family

- Privacy under common law and development of domestic law following the HRA 'bringing rights home'

- Questions of how to categorise the nature and extent of the rights arising, and different approaches to doing this

- Discussion of a wide range of case law exemplifying the many facets of privacy, for example:
  - sexuality
  - family life, for example divorce
  - the home, for example eviction
  - correspondence, for example prisoners' communication rights

10.1 Introduction

It will be useful to keep in mind some basic explanations throughout this chapter.

KEY CONCEPTS

Concept	Commentary
Privacy	This is not recognised by English common law as a self-standing right worthy of legal protection (compare trespass or nuisance) but it does exist in limited form, for example by ongoing development of the common law breach of confidence, or application of Arts 8 and 12 of the ECHR

CONTINUED ▸

KEY CONCEPTS

Concept	Commentary
Breach of confidence	Occurs where information that complies with common law confidence requirements (for example because of contract or relationship) is communicated to someone who is bound by an obligation to keep the confidence but makes unauthorised use of that information to its owner's detriment
Respect	Respect is one of the fundamental qualities that underpins human rights. This problematical word was applied by Wall J in *Evans v Amicus Healthcare Ltd* [2003] 4 All ER 903 Fam D where two couples whose frozen embryos were being stored later separated. The women wanted to establish pregnancy and the men refused to agree and under the Human Fertilisation and Embryology Act 1990 Sch 3 para 6(3) the consent of each garnate donor was required. Respect for family life was not engaged as the four individuals all led separate lives, but respect for their private lives was. State interference requiring mutual consent was justified and proportionate to balance the four interests, but no weight or respect attached to embryos as potential human beings
Private life	'Private life' is a broad term not capable of exhaustive definition. Aspects such as gender identification, name, sexual orientation and sexual life are important elements of the personal sphere protected by Art 8 which also protects a right to identity and personal development, and the right to establish and develop relationships with other human beings and the outside world. It may include activities of a professional or business nature (*Perry v United Kingdom* (2004) 39 EHRR 3)

10.2 Privacy under the common law

Under the ECHR Arts 8 Right to Respect for Family and Private Life and 12 Right to Marry, together with Protocol 7 Art 5 Equality Between Spouses together provide protection for the home and correspondence which should not be interfered with by public authorities. They also cover the right to found a family, and relationships with children. What the ECHR does *not* provide is blanket recognition and protection of privacy for the individual as such and historically neither was English common law prepared to recognise privacy as an abstract free-standing right in itself worthy of protection.

For example, in *Bernstein v Skyviews Ltd* [1978] QB 479 the defendant company flew an aeroplane over Lord Bernstein's country house taking photographs which they then offered to sell to him. He regarded this as trespass but the court held that the owner's rights in airspace above his land is restricted 'to such height as was necessary for the ordinary use and enjoyment of the land and structures upon it, and above that height he had no greater rights than any other member of the public'. Accordingly Lord Bernstein was unable to succeed in what was essentially an attempt to protect his privacy, although he was obliged to categorise it as alleged trespass in order to frame his claim.

Looked at from the trespass standpoint the principle is sound because it would be impractical in the modern age to apply the law as originally formulated by the Romans and followed by the common law. This was that a person had property rights in a theoretical cone starting at the very centre of the earth and extending through the surface infinitely into space. The maxim was *cuius est solum ad coelum et ad inferos*, which means that he who owns the soil owns everything up to the sky and down to the depths of the earth.

Nowadays the ownership of a tunnel or of minerals such as coal or oil located under land is severed from ownership of the land surface and it would be impractical for a landowner to attempt to control over-flying aeroplanes, whether of the kind used by Skyviews or the jet planes flown by passenger and freight airlines. The landowner is 'seised' of the surface and sufficient subsoil to provide foundations and cellarage together with sufficient airspace to allow proper enjoyment of the property, but no more.

Had the common law been prepared to recognise a substantive right of privacy it would have addressed the question by looking at the purpose of (in this case) the intrusion into airspace rather than considering an ancient tort to provide a remedy for a problem that was inconceivable when the tort first emerged. The idea of privacy would not then have been particularly important because, with the remedy of trespass available, the landowner could simply keep people off his land, and there was then no way they could have the ability or temerity to fly over it.

Nevertheless, invasion of privacy can occur under many different guises, and on a much more personal and intrusive level, as the following case example illustrates.

CASE EXAMPLE

Kaye v Robertson [1991] FSR 62

Prior to the Human Rights Act 1998 the way in which the common law worked could be seen from a case involving the actor Gordon Kaye who was in hospital suffering from serious head injuries. A photographer and reporter from *The Sunday Sport* newspaper entered his ward and purported to obtain his permission to interview and photograph him, although because of his injuries he was in no fit condition to give willing and informed consent. The editor and publishers of *The Sunday Sport* appealed against an interlocutory injunction restraining them from publishing photographs and details of the interview.

The convolutions needed to protect Gordon Kaye's privacy are revealed by the actual decision. The court held that:

- it was arguably libellous to imply that the plaintiff had consented to publication and interlocutory injunctions should only be granted where any jury would inevitably have found that there was libel, but that was not the case here

- the use of the photographer's flashbulb could constitute battery where the subject was suffering from head injuries but there was no evidence here that damage had in fact occurred

- there had been no passing off because he was an actor and not a trader

- all the elements of a claim of malicious falsehood had been made out, however

There was no doubt that in non-legal terms a gross breach of privacy had occurred but the Court of Appeal held that there was no legal right to privacy. The judges made plain their dissatisfaction with this state of affairs but were unable to do anything about it and *inter alia* specifically held that 'there was no actionable right of privacy in English law'.

Glidewell LJ said in his judgment that:

> 'It is well-known that in English law there is no right to privacy, and accordingly there is no right of action for breach of a person's privacy. The facts of the present case are a graphic illustration of the desirability of Parliament considering whether and in what circumstances statutory provision can be made to protect the privacy of individuals.'
>
> Glidewell LJ

Bingham LJ, as he then was, indicated his concern and, quoting Professor Markesinis, compared it unfavourably with German law:

CONTINUED ▶

'This case nonetheless highlights, yet again, the failure of both the common law of England and statute to protect in an effective way the personal privacy of individual citizens. This has been the subject of much comment over the years, perhaps most recently by Professor Markesinis (*The German Law of Torts*, 2nd edn, 1990, page 316) where he writes:

"English law, on the whole, compares unfavourably with German law. True, many aspects of the human personality and privacy are protected by a multitude of existing torts but this means fitting the facts of each case in the pigeon-hole of an existing tort and this process may not only involve strained constructions; often it may also leave a deserving plaintiff without a remedy."

The defendants' conduct towards the plaintiff here (*Kaye*) was "a monstrous invasion of his privacy" (to adopt the language of Griffiths J in *Bernstein v Skyviews Ltd* [1978] QB 479 @ 489G). If ever a person has a right to be let alone by strangers with no public interest to pursue, it must surely be when he lies in hospital recovering from brain surgery and in no more than partial command of his faculties. It is this invasion of his privacy which underlies the plaintiff's complaint. Yet it alone, however gross, does not entitle him to relief in English law.'

Bingham LJ

The appeal was allowed in part. It was not possible to grant one on the grounds of libel as the case was arguable, nor for malicious falsehood as there was no evidence of either malice or falsehood. As Kaye's story was likely to be of value to him, however, and that value would be decreased if *The Sunday Sport* were allowed to publish their story and photographs, an amended interlocutory injunction would be granted.

Obiter it was observed that *Kaye v Robertson* demonstrated acutely the need for a law of privacy to protect individuals from press invasions. At the time, a number of learned journal articles were published discussing the subject but no immediate move to amend the law by statute. The then Conservative Government was experiencing economic difficulties, and was in decline at the end of an extended period of Tory rule, so were perhaps not inclined to become involved in law reform of this nature. On the other hand, the main opposition Labour Party were very much concerned with human rights and were determined to change English law radically in this area.

10.3 Rights brought home

What was the intention of the New Labour Government in this context when they 'brought rights home' by means of the Human Rights Act 1998? According to Lord Irvine LC, HL Debs, Vol 583, col 783, 24th November 1997:

'. . . the courts will be able to adapt and develop the common law by relying on existing domestic principles in the law of trespass, nuisance, copyright, confidence and the like, to fashion a common law right to privacy.'

Lord Irvine LC

What was not intended was creation of a brand new free-standing tort as he went on to explain at HL Debs, Vol 583, col 785, 24th November 1997:

'The scheme of the [Act] is that Parliament may act to remedy a failure where the judges cannot. In my opinion, the court is not obliged to remedy the failure by legislating *via* the common law either where a Convention right is infringed by incompatible legislation or where, because of the absence of legislation – say privacy legislation – a Convention right is left unprotected. In my view, the courts may not act as legislators and grant new remedies for infringement of Convention rights unless the common law itself enables them to develop new rights or remedies.'

Lord Irvine LC

10.3.1 Convention provisions

Convention jurisprudence having been 'brought home' by virtue of the Human Rights Act 1998 which came into effect on 2nd October 2000, the right to protection of private and family life contained in Art 8 of the ECHR was thenceforth available through domestic legal apparatus and made provision as follows:

'1.   Everyone has the right to respect for his private and family life, his home and his correspondence.

2.   There shall be no interference by a public authority with the exercise of this right except such as is in accordance with the law and is necessary in a democratic society in the interests of national security, public safety or the economic well-being of the country, for the prevention of disorder or crime, for the protection of health or morals, or for the protection of the rights and freedoms of others.'

Art 8 differs from other articles by requiring 'respect' which in turn implies a duty on states to ensure that a sufficiently robust regime is in place to protect people from potentially intrusive agencies that are not necessarily under direct government control.

10.3.2 Development of 'right to privacy'

The enactment of the Human Rights Act 1998 provided the opportunity for the English courts to develop some elements of a privacy law which they constructed on the improbable base of breach of confidence. What happened essentially was that the law of confidentiality was developed rather than a substantive human right to privacy. A number of cases contributed to this development:

- *Douglas v Hello! Ltd* [2001] 2 WLR 992 CA
- *Thompson and Venables v News Group Newspapers* [2001] 2 WLR 1038
- *A v B (a company)* [2002] EWCA Civ 337; [2002] 3 WLR 542
- *Wainwright v Home Secretary* [2003] UKHL 53; [2003] 3 WLR 1137
- *Campbell v MGN Ltd* [2004] UKHL 22; [2004] 2 AC 457.

Case	Court	Issue	Outcome
Douglas v Hello! (2001)	CA	*Hello!* appealed against an injunction preventing them publishing photos of the Douglas wedding because sole rights had been sold to a rival magazine who claimed breach of confidence	Appeal was allowed and the injunction was discharged – neither element is a trump card
Thompson and Venables v News Group (2001)	High Court Family Division	Child killers T and V sought injunctions limiting information about their identities to be made permanent on reaching age 18	Granted to protect their confidentiality because of threats to their safety
A v B (2002)	CA	Newspaper appealed against a decision refusing to set aside an injunction preventing publication of details of married footballer Garry Flitcroft's sexual relations with two women	Appeal allowed but as other cases were arising since enactment of HRA, guidelines were issued (see below)
Wainwright v Home Secretary (2003)	HL	Mrs W and son were strip searched prior to visiting another son in prison and appealed against setting aside of county court judgment in their favour of trespass to the person. She now claimed invasion of privacy	Claims dismissed: there is no tort of invasion of privacy, rather it is a value underlying the common law principle of breach of confidence
Campbell v MGN (2004)	HL	Naomi Campbell appealed against CA decision dismissing her claim against Mirror Group for damages for publishing details of her drug treatment, although she had lied about taking drugs	3:2 majority found in her favour. Basic publication of treatment was alright but not details and photographs which did breach confidentiality

■ Figure 10.1 Breach of confidence — privacy

The *Flitcroft* guidelines stated that it was 'appropriate to consider *inter alia* that:
• any interference with the freedom of the press has to be justified irrespective of whether publication of information is in the public interest
• the protection of any duty of confidence is dependent upon the relationship between the parties at the time of the actual or threatened breach
• the courts should not act as arbiters of taste in assessing the balance between the respective interests.'

■ Figure 10.2 The *Flitcroft* guidelines

Lord Hoffmann said in *Wainwright v Home Secretary* (2003):

> 'There seems to me a great difference between identifying privacy as a value which underlies the existence of a rule of law (and may point the direction in which the law should develop) and privacy as a principle of law in itself. The English common law is familiar with the notion of underlying values – principles only in the broadest sense – which direct its development.
>
> A famous example is *Derbyshire County Council v Times Newspapers Ltd* [1993] AC 534 in which freedom of speech was the underlying value which supported the decision to lay down the specific rule that a local authority could not sue for libel. But no one has suggested that freedom of speech is in itself a legal principle which is capable of sufficient definition to enable one to deduce specific rules to be applied in concrete cases. That is not the way the common law works.'

10.3.3 Framing the claim under Art 8

The practical result is that litigants and lawyers are to some extent left struggling to frame their claims to rights. A good example was the attempt by the Countryside Alliance to challenge the provisions of the Hunting Act 2004 which they considered to be a serious challenge to a long-established way of life for many country dwellers imposed by a government unsympathetic to the rural population and threatening many rural livelihoods.

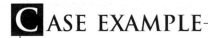

CASE EXAMPLE

***Countryside Alliance v Attorney-General* [2007] UKHL 52; [2007] 3 WLR 922**

The House of Lords considered Art 8 in detail in this case. The issue in the appeal before the House was the principle of whether the prohibition of hunting wild mammals with dogs and of hare coursing, imposed by the Hunting Act 2004, is incompatible with the ECHR or inconsistent with the Treaty establishing the European Community by reference to a number of articles including that of family life.

Lord Bingham of Cornhill said in his speech that the right has been described as 'elusive' and does not lend itself to exhaustive definition, which may be why the 'respect' mentioned above is required. The claimants had presented that part of their case based on Art 8 under a fourfold classification which provides a good summary of the case law for this subject. The introduction of the ban on fox-hunting had affected many people's way of life, but Lord Bingham was not convinced that under Art 8 any of the above categories was infringed and he dismissed them in the following terms:

CONTINUED ▸

Private life and autonomy

Fox-hunting is a colourful, noisy, public activity which attracts onlookers, so there is no analogy with very personal and private concerns which were the subject matter of such cases as *Bruggemann* and *Pretty*. It was also very different from interception of private telephone conversations in *PG and JH* and disclosure of closed circuit television pictures of the complainant in *Peck* who was preparing to commit suicide but changed his mind. These and similar cases referred to notions of privacy, personal autonomy, choice and the private sphere reserved to the individual. As such they were so different from fox-hunting as to provide no helpful guidance.

Cultural lifestyle

The comparisons that were attempted under this heading were Lapps in *G and E* and gypsies in *Buckley* and *Chapman.* In each case they had a traditional culture and lifestyle which were fundamental to their very identities, which could not be said to apply to the hunting fraternity who socially and occupationally were very diverse (and indeed they claimed that as one of their strengths).

Use of the home

The noun 'home' has an autonomous Convention meaning which can encompass premises other than where a person sleeps, as demonstrated in *Niemietz*. However, this does not mean that the word can cover land over which sporting activity is conducted and which no one in ordinary usage would refer to as 'home' (*Giacomelli v Italy* (2006) 45 EHRR 871, para 76). Some of the complainants feared that their actual homes would be threatened which did bring their claim much closer to Art 8 but the Hunting Act 2004 contained no intention to cause loss of any home and no one had in fact been evicted.

Loss of livelihood/home

The case of *Sidabras* was extreme on its facts involving as it did the employment of former KGB officers who were subsequently disbarred from many public and private employments and who complained of constant embarrassment. As they could not work, their ability to function as social beings was effectively blighted. None of that applied to the Hunting Act complainants and even on its own extreme facts there was no direct finding of a breach of Art 8.

Lord Rodger of Earlsferry developed the Art 8 discussion, pointing out that early decisions of the European Court on 'private life' tended to be about emotional and sexual responses in an intimate circle where people need privacy, but the Commission long ago rejected the Anglo-Saxon notion that respect for family life = privacy. What it does include are rights to establish and develop emotional relationships with other human beings in order to fulfil one's personality. Later cases advanced this further and it became a 'broad term'.

This Hunting Act case provides an interesting analysis of the history, impact and growth of the various rights contained within Art 8 that constitute a wide-ranging and powerful protection for the family. The essentials of Lord Bingham's analysis are summarised in the following table.

Description	Cases	Citation
Private life and autonomy	*Pretty v UK* *PG and JH v UK* *Peck v UK* *Brüggemann and Scheuten v Germany*	(2002) 35 EHRR 1 (App 44787/98), Judgment of 25th September 2001 (2003) 36 EHRR 41 (1977) 10 DR 100; (1981) 3 EHRR 244
Cultural lifestyle	*G and E v Norway* *Buckley v UK* *Chapman v UK*	(1983) 35 DR 30 (1996) 23 EHRR 101 (2001) 33 EHRR 399
Use of the home	*Niemietz v Germany* *Sheffield City Council v Smart* *Harrow LBC v Qazi* *Kay v Lambeth LBC*	(1992) 16 EHRR 97 [2002] EWCA Civ 4 [2003] UKHL 43 [2004] EWCA Civ 926
Loss of livelihood/home	*Sidabras and Dziautas v Lithuania*	(Apps 55480/00 and 59330/00), Judgment of 27th July 2004

Figure 10.3 Aspects of private and family life

ACTIVITY

Self-assessment true or false

1	Breach of confidence is a common law action that has been developed to enable claimants to obtain some protection of their privacy.	T	F
2	'Private life' is broad enough to include activities of a professional or business nature.	T	F
3	*Bernstein v Skyviews Ltd* (1978) demonstrated that English common law can find ingenious ways of protecting individuals' privacy from media intrusion.	T	F
4	*Kaye v Robertson* (1991) demonstrated that English common law can find ingenious ways of protecting individuals' privacy from media intrusion.	T	F
5	House of Lords debates on the Human Rights Bill confirm that English judges were to be given authority to create new types of privacy torts.	T	F

CONTINUED ▸

ACTIVITY

6	The *Flitcroft* guidelines' were formulated in the case of *Wainwright v Home Secretary* (2003) to explain the rules governing prison visits.	T	F
7	In *Countryside Alliance v Attorney-General* (2007) Lord Bingham defined Art 8 categories as private life and autonomy, cultural lifestyle, use of the home and loss of livelihood/home.	T	F
8	In *Thompson and Venables v News Group* (2001) an injunction was granted to protect the applicants' confidentiality because of threats to their safety.	T	F
9	'Autonomy' refers to the sport of fox-hunting described by Lord Bingham of Cornhill as 'colourful, noisy, public activity which attracts onlookers'.	T	F
10	Professor Markesinis compares English law unfavourably with German law in the way that it treats privacy.	T	F

10.3.4 Difficulty of categorisation

Lord Bingham is by no means alone in *Countryside Alliance v Attorney-General* expressing the view that the right is 'elusive' and does not easily lend itself to exhaustive definition. The problem was addressed by Dr N A Moreham in an article entitled 'The right to respect for private life in the European Convention on Human Rights: a re-examination' EHRLR, 2008, 1, 44–79. Five broad categories are identified:

1. freedom from interference with physical and psychological integrity

2. the collection and disclosure of information

3. protection of one's living environment

4. identity

5. personal autonomy.

The article points out that essential to understanding Art 8 are its basic positive and negative elements. The positive obligation is on states to protect the private lives of its individuals and the court must also address two negative considerations:

- Has there been interference with an Art 8(1) right?

- If so, was that interference justified under Art 8(2)?

Additionally, three requirements are essential if the interfering measure is to satisfy Art 8(2), ie it must:

- be made in accordance with national law and compatible with the rule of law

- serve the legitimate aims set out in Art 8(2)

- be necessary in a democratic society.

It will be useful to discuss Art 8 in light of these categories in order to avoid what otherwise tends to be a long list of disparate decisions.

1. Freedom from interference with physical and psychological integrity

Under this head Dr Moreham includes 'physical assault and exposure, unwanted observation, intrusion into home and the workplace, and the unwanted dissemination of images'. *Wainwright v Home Secretary* (2003) has previously been mentioned in connection with the development of protection of privacy, and is a good example of the way in which the absence of a distinct tort of privacy demonstrated how domestic law failed to provide a remedy leaving the Convention to rectify the position. The character of an individual's physical integrity is apparent from the circumstances.

 ASE EXAMPLE

Wainwright v Home Secretary [2003] UKHL 53; [2003] 3 WLR 1137

Wainwright v United Kingdom (2007) 44 EHRR 40

The first applicant, Mrs Wainwright, took her son, the second applicant (who had cerebral palsy, severely arrested social and intellectual development and was defined as a 'patient' under the Mental Health Act 1983), to see her other son and the first applicant's half-brother in HMP Armley (Leeds Prison) where he was detained on suspicion of murder. It was the first time either of them had been to a prison.

They were not aware prior to their arrival that the prison authorities were concerned about drug smuggling. On arrival they were separated and told that as they were suspected of carrying drugs they would be strip searched and if they refused to agree would not be allowed to continue their visit.

They were both obliged to remove all their clothing and to submit to intimate body searches, following which Mrs Wainwright was required to sign a consent form. Her son struggled to remove his clothing and when asked to sign his consent form told the prison officers that he could not read. His mother was not allowed to sign on his behalf. Both applicants were distressed by the procedures, had to shorten their visit, and suffered post-traumatic stress disorder. They succeeded in an action against the

CONTINUED ▸

Home Office for battery but that decision was overturned by the Court of Appeal whose decision was upheld by the House of Lords.

In the European Court the applicants did not succeed in proving inhuman or degrading treatment under Art 3 but were upheld unanimously in their claim under Arts 8 and 13 (right to an effective remedy) of the Convention. The specific findings regarding Arts 8 and 13 were:

'(a) There was no direct evidence linking the applicants with the smuggling of drugs into the prison. The application of strip-searches to persons who were not prisoners nor reasonably suspected of having committed a criminal offence was something which required rigorous adherence to prescribed procedures and the need to protect human dignity.

(b) It was clear that the prison officers had failed to comply with relevant regulations and procedures. It was for the authorities to ensure that such matters were complied with, not for individual citizens to request compliance.

(c) The behaviour complained of fell short of the minimum level of severity prohibited by Art 3. However, it was clearly a stressful and upsetting process and fell within the scope of Art 8.

(d) The actions of the prison authorities were both in accordance with the law and pursuant to a legitimate aim. They were not proportionate to that legitimate aim. The prison authorities failed to respect the dignity of the applicants and intruded more than was necessary.

(e) The searches were not necessary in a democratic society. Article 8 had been violated.'

In the House of Lords, their Lordships had encountered some difficulty with Art 8 and Lord Hoffmann said that there was nothing in the European Court jurisprudence which suggested that the adoption of some high-level privacy principle was needed to comply with Art 8. What did concern it was whether English law provided an adequate remedy in a given case if an unjustified invasion of privacy had occurred. With the enactment of the Human Rights Act 1998 and specifically ss 6 and 7, the argument in favour of the need for a general tort of invasion of privacy to plug the gaps was weakened. Lord Hoffmann rejected the invitation to declare that since, at the latest, 1950 there had been an unknown tort of invasion of privacy.

CASE EXAMPLE

Glass v United Kingdom (61827/00) [2004] 39 EHRR 15

Another example of intrusive physical bodily interference, this time in a medical context, occurred in the case of *Glass v United Kingdom*. The applicants were David Glass, a severely mentally and physically disabled child, and his mother. He had a history of severe respiratory problems and had been hospitalised on several occasions including an admission to the Portsmouth Hospitals NHS Trust in July 1998. Following an operation he suffered complications and was put on a ventilator. His mother was told that he was dying and that diamorphine should be administered but she objected on the ground that this would hamper his recovery even if relieving his immediate distress.

Over the course of his treatment the relationship between the family and hospital staff deteriorated because the family believed that David was being secretly euthenased and at one stage the stress became so serious that a fight broke out between family members and two doctors. Eventually David's condition improved and he was allowed to go home. His mother unsuccessfully applied for judicial review and was refused permission to appeal whilst the General Medical Council found that the doctors involved had not been guilty of serious professional misconduct. The Crown Prosecution Service took no action because of lack of evidence, at which juncture the Glass family had exhausted the available domestic remedies.

They complained that UK law and the practice followed by the hospital failed to guarantee David's physical and moral integrity, and the administration of diamorphine and placing of a Do Not Resuscitate (DNR) Notice with his medical notes, without his mother's knowledge, constituted a violation of Art 8.

This was upheld unanimously by the European Court. Although the actions of the hospital staff had been in accordance with UK domestic law, they had not been necessary and they could not explain why the consent of the High Court had not been sought for the proposed treatment.

2. The collection and disclosure of information

In this category there is some overlap with the developing tort of breach of confidence and it includes 'the right to be free from unwanted informational access – the right to be free from unwanted collection and storage of information, the reading of personal materials and the interception of correspondence'.

CASE EXAMPLE

Klass and others v Federal Republic of Germany (1979–80) 2 EHRR 214

Obvious examples of the kinds of situation applicable here are interference with mail and telephone traffic, covert filming and more recently the use of CCTV. In the 1970s West German law allowed state officials to open and inspect mail and monitor telephone conversations if 'imminent dangers' threatened the 'existence or security' of the state and the 'free democratic constitutional order', all of which were understandable provisions during the Cold War.

When such measures were taken they were subject to stringent requirements which meant they had to be:

- at the request of the head of one of the four security agencies
- authorised by the Supreme Land Authority or designated federal minister
- renewable but otherwise would lapse after three months if not renewed
- based on certain 'factual indications'
- supervised by an official qualified for judicial office and overseen by a statutory commission

After any such surveillance the subject had to be informed about it unless doing so would compromise the reason for the action, and regular reports had to be made by the minister to an all-party parliamentary committee.

The applicants were five German lawyers who claimed that these provisions infringed Arts 6, 8 and 13 ECHR. Although they accepted that the state had a right to undertake such activities, they challenged the legislation because it did not contain an absolute notification requirement to the subject and failed to provide a judicial remedy. The Government denied that it infringed the Convention and argued, in effect, that the applicants had no *locus standi* as they had not themselves been subject to surveillance, so were not 'victims of violation' within the terms of Art 25(1).

In 1974 the Commission declared the application admissible, deciding that the secret nature of the proceedings made it possible that they could have been victims, but that no breaches of the Convention had in fact taken place. The plenary court held unanimously that the lawyers were possible victims in the special circumstances of the case but that the safeguards indicated above were sufficient to comply with the Art 8(2) considerations as being 'necessary in a democratic society in the interests of national security'.

Klass was heavily relied on in the UK case of *Malone* in 1985.

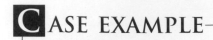

CASE EXAMPLE

Malone v United Kingdom (1985) 7 EHRR 14

James Malone was an antiques dealer who had been prosecuted for offences in connection with dishonestly handling stolen goods. During his trial it became clear that his telephone had been tapped by the police by virtue of a warrant issued by the Home Secretary. He was eventually acquitted and sought a declaration that the telephone tapping had been illegal, but this was refused by Sir Robert Megarry V-C although the judge did express serious concern about the state of the law in this regard.

The Commission found that there had been violations of Arts 8 and 13 and the Court also unanimously found that there had been a breach of Art 8 and, by 16 votes to 2, that it was not necessary to consider Art 13. The European Court held that the words 'in accordance with the law' referred not merely to domestic law but also to the quality of the law which had to conform to the rule of law. This meant, particularly, safeguarding citizens against arbitrary interference by public authorities and giving them adequate indication of circumstances in which 'secret and potentially dangerous interference' might occur which would damage respect for private life.

There had been a violation of Art 8 here because English law failed to indicate clearly the extent of the discretions available to public authorities and the ways in which they would exercise those discretions.

This problem of insufficient clarity arises in other contexts. For example, a verdict by the Crown Court was criticised by the European Court in the case of *Hashman and Harrup v United Kingdom* (2000) 30 EHRR 241 under Art 5 that the applicants' behaviour had been *contra bonos mores* (against good behaviour) because behaving badly (whatever that might mean) did not in fact amount to the commission of an offence known to law.

As a result of *Malone* the Interception of Communications Act 1985 was enacted, coming into operation on 10th April 1986. The Act made it an offence, punishable by fine or up to two years' imprisonment, unlawfully to intercept communications sent through the post or *via* a public telecommunications system. Section 2 provided that when the Secretary of State issued a warrant under the Act it had to be in the interests of national security or for the purpose of safeguarding the economic interests of the UK. There is also an Interception of Communications Commissioner appointed under the Regulation of Investigatory Powers Act 2000. The Commissioner prior to April 2006 was Sir Swinton Thomas, and Sir Paul Kennedy served the second term up to 2009. They are both retired Lords Justices of Appeal.

Unjustifiable dissemination

In 1997 in the United Kingdom a man called Perry had been arrested in connection with a number of armed robberies of minicab drivers in the Wolverhampton area of the West Midlands. He was released whilst identity parades were arranged but failed to attend them. To get round the problem this caused, the police sought and obtained permission to video him covertly. Subsequently he did attend a police station but continued to refuse to take part in a parade, so an engineer filmed him and the pictures were inserted in a montage of film which included other persons.

This was shown to witnesses, two of whom identified him as having been involved in armed robberies. Neither he nor his solicitor were aware or informed that this had been done and in March 1999 he was convicted of armed robbery and sentenced to five years' imprisonment against which he appealed unsuccessfully.

His complaint to the European Court on the ground of contravention of Art 8 was unanimously upheld (*Perry v United Kingdom* (2004) 39 EHRR 3). The Court made it clear that 'there is . . . a zone of interaction of a person with others, even in a public context, which may fall within the scope of "private life"'. What occurred in this case was not normal use of monitoring cameras in respect of the general public and this was sufficient to establish his claim.

In *Craxi v Italy* (2004) 38 EHRR 47 a former Italian Prime Minister was charged with corruption and related offences but did not appear at any of the trial hearings in 1993, and the following year he went to live in Tunisia. In 1995 the Public Prosecutor obtained permission to tap his telephone and transcripts of telephone conversations were produced at the trial and extracts were later published in a number of national newspapers. Craxi contended that the transcripts had provided no evidential value at the trials and that placing them in the public domain contravened his Art 8 rights.

His application was upheld. Press comment on criminal cases was important but should be limited to facts relevant to the charges and, as the transcripts were not relevant to the case against Craxi, there was no pressing social need for their publication. It was not necessary in a democratic society, and the state had not taken sufficient steps here to prevent the disclosure.

3. Protection of one's living environment

This fits perhaps a little uneasily into the categorisation but is important in the human rights context because of concerns that people have about their immediate environment, global warming and climate change. It should be noted that these are three entirely different things and the degree of interconnectedness between them, if any, is not widely agreed.

Nevertheless, many people would make connections and it is a useful and practical way of bringing together concerns that affect everyone in the present and future generations. Thus, in the wide context of human rights it needs to be considered and, although in the past such matters would not have been thought of in human rights terms, there are many older cases that in essence achieve at least some of the kinds of protection that today would be so expressed.

Examples of this are included in the following table:

- *Bliss v Hall* 132 ER 758; (1838) 4 Bing NC 183 Common Pleas
- *St Helens Smelting Co v Tipping* (1865) 11 HL Cas 642
- *Rylands v Fletcher* (1868) LR 3 HL 330
- *Sturges v Bridgman* (1878) 11 Ch D 852 CA
- *Halsey v Esso Petroleum Co Ltd* [1961] 1 WLR 683 QBD
- *Leakey v National Trust* [1980] QB 485 CA.

Case	Facts	Law
Bliss v Hall (1838)	Defendant candle maker's noxious vapours stank for three years before plaintiff arrived and complained	Plaintiff entitled to wholesome air and judgment against defendant unless the defendant could show that he had acquired a prescriptive right to cause smell
St Helens Smelting Co v Tipping (1865)	Plaintiff owned shrubs and trees which were damaged by fumes from copper smelting works	The smelting company was held to be liable in nuisance
Rylands v Fletcher (1868)	Defendants' engineers built a reservoir but failed to seal old mine shafts: water escaped and damaged neighbouring land	A person who collects and keeps anything on his land that may escape and do damage is answerable for all damage which is a natural consequence of the non-natural use of the land
Sturges v Bridgman (1878)	Confectioner used noisy pestle and mortar for 20 years with no complaints. Doctor built consulting room and alleged nuisance	Held on appeal that defendant had not acquired right to easement of making noise and vibration, and injunction granted to the doctor
Halsey v Esso Petroleum Co Ltd (1961)	Plaintiff's action alleged nuisance by atmospheric pollution of smuts and noise from boilers and vehicles	Applied *St Helens Smelting Co* so defendants were liable in nuisance and *Rylands v Fletcher* from damage done by acid smuts. Frequency and pungency of smell was nuisance, as was noise at night. Damages and injunction were awarded
Leakey v National Trust (1980)	Defendants aware that instability from natural causes threatened plaintiff's land but refused to deal with the problem.	Defendants were liable in nuisance and damages awarded. Appeal dismissed as occupier of land owes general duty of care regarding hazards on his land whether natural or manmade

Figure 10.4 Environmental torts

Thus, to be clear, the torts of nuisance and *Rylands v Fletcher* developed in the nineteenth and twentieth centuries enabling litigants to exert individual claims to protection of their environment, which is a narrow aspect of civil liberties but which today fits well into this human rights category of protection of one's environment.

(a) Noise pollution

In 1990 the European Court heard the case of *Powell and Raynor v United Kingdom* (1990) 12 EHRR 355 in which the applicants, who were owners of properties close to Heathrow Airport, complained of excessive aircraft noise around the airport. The allegation made was that there was absence of a right of access to the court under Art 6 and that there had been an unjustified interference with their right to respect for private and family lives under Art 8. The Commission had rejected both of these at the admissibility stage as being manifestly ill-founded and the Court found that there was no violation of Art 13.

The particular issues considered by the Court were that quite apart from the kinds of obligations placed on governments under Art 8 it was essential to strike a fair balance between individual and community interests. Operating a major international airport was a legitimate aim and a variety of steps had been taken to control, abate and compensate for aircraft noise.

It was held that the Government had not exceeded the margin of appreciation nor upset the requisite fair balance. Both applicants had suffered differing levels of disturbance but neither of them was able to make out an arguable claim of violation of Art 8 or entitlement to an Art 13 remedy. The aircraft were operating within the statutory domestic limits.

Airports give rise to a number of considerations both in human rights and environmental law terms, and the issues are more closely linked when the airport in question is situated in a heavily populated area. The problems of complainants in the neighbourhood of Heathrow were not going to go away and the matter came up again in 2003, this time because of the Airport Authority's policy on night flights. Ms Hatton also lived near Heathrow and again the claim was made under Arts 8 and 13 (*Hatton v United Kingdom* (2003) 37 EHHR 28).

Night-time noise levels were limited by allowing fewer flights under a noise quota scheme that allowed airlines to decide whether they wished to operate a larger number of quiet aircraft or a smaller number of noisier ones. It did not matter as long as the overall 'noise quota' was not exceeded. This may appear somewhat arbitrary from the point of view of the householder living underneath the runway flight path and indeed the scheme was successfully challenged twice, first at [1994] 1 WLR because it did not comply with the requirements of the Civil Aviation Act 1982 s 78 and later at [1996] 1 WLR 1460 because the consultation that had been carried out was unlawful. The policy alteration adopted as a result was based on stipulating an upper limit on the number of aircraft that could be operated, whilst at the same time retaining the noise quota scheme. Ms Hatton argued that this violated her Art 8 rights.

The claim was dismissed because the margin of appreciation granted to the UK was still too wide for her to overcome. The Court said that, in assessing whether the balance was appropriate, consideration was needed of what measures were being used to mitigate the effect of interference. There were complex issues involved but no substantive procedural flaws in the decision-making process contrary to the requirements of Art 8.

In the majority judgment it was pointed out that there is no specific right in the Convention to a clean and quiet environment and the role of the Convention is essentially 'subsidiary' in the sense that the national authorities had 'direct democratic legitimation and were in principle better placed to evaluate local needs and conditions'. What this meant was that 'in matters of general policy, on which opinions in a democratic society might reasonably differ widely, the role of the domestic policy-maker should be given special weight'.

However, there had been a violation of Art 13 and the main reason was that English law of judicial review was restricted by 'classic English public law concepts such as irrationality, unlawfulness and patent unreasonableness'. Prior to the enactment of the Human Rights Act, domestic law did not have to pay sufficient attention to the residents' rights.

Noise pollution is by no means confined to airports and can arise in other types of neighbourhood as demonstrated by *Moreno Gomez v Spain* (2005) 41 EHRR 40. Ms Gomez began living in a flat in a residential area in 1970 and four years later the local authority started allowing nightclubs, restaurants and bars to open and operate in the same area. She suffered from insomnia and her health deteriorated but in her domestic proceedings against the Spanish authorities she was unable to establish a causal link between the noise made and damage suffered. She complained specifically to the European Court that the issue of an unlimited number of licences had led to 'the acoustic saturation of the area'.

Her complaint was upheld on the basis that the national authorities had failed to discharge their positive obligations under Art 8. Breaches were not confined to those of a physical nature but could include noise and smells. The scope of the article extended to adopting measures that secured respect for private life in the private context involving relationships between individuals, and the authorities had failed to do that here.

(b) Eviction

Actual loss of one's home is a more proximate direct interference with a person's living environment, and the way in which local authorities went about the eviction process was tested against Art 8 in the House of Lords by *Harrow London Borough Council v Qazi* [2003] All ER (D) 569 (Jul) and in the European Court in *McCann v United Kingdom* [2008] All ER (D) 146 (May). Both cases involved secure joint tenancies under the Housing Act 1985 where the wife was no longer resident and the local authority landlord, were taking possession proceedings against the husband who was still living in the premises.

In *Qazi* the wife had moved out and served a valid notice to quit on the council, the legal effect of which was to terminate the tenancy. The Recorder made a possession order and decided that the premises did not constitute Mr Qazi's 'home' within the meaning of Art 8. The Court of Appeal agreed with Mr Qazi that the Recorder had adopted too restrictive an interpretation of what is meant by a 'home'. The authority appealed on the question of whether, in light of Art 8(1), 'it was unlawful for a public authority to recover possession from a former tenant by a procedure which led to possession being granted automatically, or whether the court had always to be given an opportunity to consider whether the making of a possession order would be proportionate'.

The House of Lords allowed the authority's appeal. Receiving a notice to quit, which had the legal effect of terminating the tenancy, enabled the council to exercise its unqualified right to obtain possession, thus making the premises available for another letting. Although the right to respect for the home was not irrelevant, earlier Strasbourg jurisprudence demonstrated that contractual and proprietary possession rights were not susceptible to defeat by a defence based on Art 8. This meant that the question of whether any interference was allowed by Art 8(2) did not need to be considered by the county court.

In property law, therefore, the service by the wife of the notice to quit on the local authority operated as a severance of the joint tenancy, and the action of one party doing this provided sufficient justification for the landlord to institute possession proceedings without concerning themselves with the human rights aspects of the 'severed' joint tenant.

The European Court adopted a more sympathetic approach in the case of *McCann v United Kingdom* in 2008. The applicant and his wife were joint tenants of a three-bedroomed local authority house and on the breakdown of their marriage the wife moved out of the premises with the two children. At that stage there was a contested hearing which resulted in Mr McCann being ordered to move out of the premises, which he did. Mrs McCann returned to the house with the children but it was alleged that subsequently the husband broke in using a crowbar and assaulted his wife who successfully asked the council to rehouse her.

As the house was then empty Mr McCann the applicant moved in and, when the council found out a few months later, an official visited the wife and obtained her signature to a notice to quit, although she was not advised that this would have the effect of terminating her husband's right to occupy the house or to exchange it for an alternative property.

The local authority landlord sought a possession order in the County Court and Mr McCann based his defence on Art 8 and won. The council successfully overturned this in the Court of Appeal [2003] All ER (D) 163 (Dec) whereupon the applicant sought judicial review of the authority's actions. At this hearing the judge decided that the authority had acted within its powers but that, in any event, the Court of Appeal had effectively adjudicated upon the relevant issues and, as the applicant was unable to take the matter further under domestic law, he complained to the European Court of Human Rights.

He contended that the way the authority obtained the notice to quit and restricted the resultant proceedings to bare property issues meant that respect for his Art 8 home rights had not been observed. Although the parties agreed that Art 8 was engaged on the facts, they disagreed about whether the impugned measure was 'necessary in a democratic society'. The government's case was that the council had simply been regularising the situation arising from the wife's departure and provision of alternative accommodation and, as *Qasi* showed, service of her notice to quit severed the joint tenancy. Mr McCann argued that the local authority's actions effectively

bypassed the statutory scheme which Parliament had established for the very purpose of protecting tenants such as himself.

The European Court held that the procedure used to dispossess one of the joint tenants of his home on service of notice to quit by the other joint tenant violated Art 8, and were forthright in declaring that:

> 'The loss of a person's home was a most extreme form of interference with the right to respect for the home. Any person at risk of an interference of that magnitude should in principle be able to have the proportionality of the measure determined by an independent tribunal in the light of the relevant principles under art 8 of the Convention, notwithstanding that, under domestic law, his right of occupation had come to an end. The joint tenant dispossessed had no possibility of having the proportionality of the measure determined by an independent tribunal and therefore there was a lack of adequate procedural safeguards.'

Had the local authority followed the correct statutory eviction procedure, Mr McCann would have been able to ask the court to examine the exact circumstances of his wife leaving the home, as domestic violence had been alleged but not put to proof. The judicial review proceedings were bound to fail because the local authority had not acted unlawfully in that they were entitled to seek possession. The net result was that the applicant had been deprived of his home without having the opportunity to obtain a ruling on the Art 8 issues and had suffered non-pecuniary damage by way of frustration and injustice which merited an award of €2,000.

4. Identity

The question of identity concerns 'the right to information about one's parents and early development, to recognition of one's sexual and cultural identity, and to change one's name'.

(a) Sexual identity and changing attitudes

It is important to bear in mind that all domestic remedies must have been exhausted before an individual attempts to exercise Convention rights in Strasbourg. The applicant in *Van Oosterwijck v Belgium* (1981) 3 EHRR 557 had been registered as female at birth but underwent a series of sex-change operations, following which he had attempted to alter his civil status under Belgian law. It was argued that the operations had resulted in 'civil death' and that Art 8 provisions were violated because the relevant documents did not reflect his real identity, which in turn prevented him from marrying and founding a family. The Commission had unanimously found a breach of Art 8 and, by majority, a breach of Art 12 but the Court subsequently held that because of his failure to exhaust domestic remedies the Court could not take cognisance of the merits of the case.

Some six years later UK law was challenged in the case of *Rees v UK* (1987) 9 EHRR 56. Mr Rees had been born with the physical and biological characteristics of a female; she had grown up with ambiguous appearance and exhibiting masculine behaviour as a result of which she underwent treatment for sexual conversion to the male gender. His claim was based on the UK authorities' refusal to change his original entry in the register of births nor to issue him with a revised birth certificate confirming his altered status, which prevented him from marrying a woman contrary to his Art 8 and 12 rights and effectively preventing him from entering into a recognised marriage.

The Court held that the refusal to accede to either of his requests did not violate the two articles because it was not arbitrary interference by public authorities in his private and family life and a wide margin of appreciation was allowed in this kind of case. Art 12 was not violated because of the 'traditional' understanding that marriage could only occur between people of the opposite biological sex.

Similar issues arose in *Cossey v United Kingdom* (1991) 13 EHRR 622 although in that case the applicant had been registered as a male and, having undergone treatment and gender reassignment surgery, purported to marry. The relationship broke down shortly thereafter and she applied to the European Court for a declaration that the UK had violated her Art 8 and 12 rights by not issuing a new birth certificate showing her to be a female.

Her application was also dismissed, with the court referring to the balance needed between the general interests of the community measured against that of the individual and stating that the UK was not under a positive obligation to modify its system of registration of births. However, what also had to be considered was the state of medical science and whether there had been any significant developments in science or in the social aspects connected with the traditional approach to marriage. In neither case had there been such a degree of change and it was not open to the Court to take a new approach to marriage. In other words, *Rees v UK* (1987) was applied.

In the late 1990s transsexuals were still encountering similar problems. In *Sheffield and Horsham v United Kingdom* (1999) 27 EHRR 163 Sheffield had been registered at birth as a male but from 1986 onwards started to live as a female. Despite gender reassignment she was unable to obtain an amended passport and driving licence, nor to change her recorded birth details and obtain a new birth certificate. Her contention was that this caused her considerable embarrassment and distress because of her need to disclose this to third parties and that, by still insisting on determining gender on the basis solely of biological factors, the UK was failing to take account of new research since the 1980s and more widespread understanding throughout Europe of the legal recognition of transsexuals' changed gender.

The European Court held by the slender majority of 11:9 that there had been no violation of Art 8. Previous case law had determined that Art 8 placed no positive obligation on the UK to alter its birth registration system which attempted to strike a fair balance between individual and public interests. Because Sheffield's complaints were similar to previous ones the question was whether there was still a fair balance between scientific and legal developments.

By this narrow margin the Court felt that the balance was still right and that Sheffield had failed to show that developments in medical science had laid to rest earlier doubts as to the causes of trans sexualism. 'The court was not satisfied that the detriment suffered by Sheffield in having to disclose her original gender in some situations was so serious that the UK was no longer entitled to rely on its margin of appreciation to continue to deny transsexuals legal recognition of their new gender.'

Gender Recognition Act 2004

By the turn of the century it was recognised in the UK that some change was needed and this occurred in 2004. The explanatory notes to the Gender Recognition Act 2004 state that its purpose is 'to provide transsexual people with legal recognition in their acquired gender'. Various provisions came into effect under the Gender Recognition Act 2004 (Commencement) Order 2005/54. The basic reform is clear from the first section of the Act:

'A person of either gender who is aged at least 18 may make an application for a gender recognition certificate on the basis of –

(a) living in the other gender, or

(b) having changed gender under the law of a country or territory outside the United Kingdom . . .'

Under Sched I, Gender Recognition Panels are established to provide the necessary machinery. A legal right now exists for a person to acquire a new birth certificate in their acquired gender after they have lived in the new gender for a two-year preceding period and having been diagnosed with gender dysphoria (deep discomfort, a condition difficult to bear). It also provides for an absolute right to privacy, thus dealing with one of the most serious practical problems of earlier complainants to the European Commission and Court, such as in *Sheffield and Horsham*.

(b) Traditional cultural identity

This category addresses cultural rather than sexual identity. Questions involving travellers sometimes involve a combination of property and identity rights. In *Burton v UK* (1996) 22 EHHR 135 the applicant was a gypsy who lived with her three children in caravans parked on land which she owned. She had been brought up since her birth in 1966 as a Romany but had abandoned that life in 1975 when her parents accepted an offer of council accommodation from the then Welsh local authority Ceredigion District Council. The family later moved to other council accommodation. From 1988 onwards the family suffered harassment because they were gypsies and applied for a further move.

However, the fundamental cultural nature of the applicant's claim arose from the fact that, despite removal of a cancerous tumour from her liver, it had returned and she was suffering from incurable pancreatic cancer. As the law report says, 'the applicant's knowledge that she is going to die in the near future . . . intensified her desire to live out her last days and die in a caravan, according to her Romany gypsy traditions'. The applicant's father had made a number of attempts to find a suitable location for their caravans, without success, and the local authority had determined that a mobile home was unsuitable for habitation. The specific cause of her suffering in human rights terms is also explained in the law report:

'The applicant complains that the Council is causing her anguish by preventing her from living out her last days in the traditional manner of a gypsy. She claims that this leads her to feel inferior and that the treatment is therefore debasing, humiliating and an interference with her dignity such as to constitute inhuman and degrading treatment within the meaning of Article 3 of the Convention.'

She applied in 1990 for retrospective planning permission which was refused by the local authority, following which they issued an enforcement notice requiring the caravans to be removed within a month. She alleged a violation of Art 8 of the Convention and it was held unanimously that it was applicable in the present case, although by six votes to three that there had been no violation of that article.

The Court considered various aspects of the need to balance the individual's right to a home with the wider interests of the community, and noted that many of the problems arising with regard to the travelling community are to do with conflict between them and 'permanent' residents. In assessing the community/individual balance and applying the proportionality principle, particular attention needs to be given to the procedural safeguards available to the individual. The regulatory framework must remain firmly within the margin of appreciation:

'Indeed it is settled case law that, whilst Article 8 contains no explicit procedural requirements, the decision-making process leading to measures of interference must be fair and such as to afford due respect to the interests safeguarded to the individual by Article 8. The Court's task is to determine, on the basis of the above principles, whether the reasons relied on to justify the interference in question are relevant and sufficient under Article 8(2).'

In light of the fact that the complainant had, in fact, been living in settled accommodation provided by the local authority since 1975 without interference with her altered lifestyle, the Commission found that there had been no violation of Art 8 and her further contentions under Arts 13 and 14 were also dismissed.

In *Connors v United Kingdom* (2005) 40 EHRR 9 a gypsy family had lived, with permission, on a local authority run site for 14 years with only one short absence, but was then evicted after a final written warning on the grounds of anti-social behaviour and nuisance caused, not by them, but by their relatives and visitors to the site. The notice to quit was not accompanied by a statement of reasons; a county court possession order was granted; and the Connors' application for judicial review was refused.

Complaints to the European Court were made under Arts 6, 8, 13, 14 and Protocol 1 Art 1. The complaint under Art 8 was upheld because the serious consequences of evicting the family required detailed reasons to be given. Gypsy sites enjoyed security of tenure and the requirement to give reasons for evicting long-term residents would not be affected by providing reasons. The local authority, in failing to do this, had acted in breach of the statutory procedural safeguards.

Another case which raised similar issues was *Chapman v United Kingdom* (2001) 33 EHRR 18 where the European Court held that Chapman's challenge of the local authority's refusal to allow her planning permission to station her caravan on green-belt land owned by her was not upheld. In addition she argued that the decision constituted discrimination against gypsies as an ethnic group, which also raises questions concerning autonomy.

There is a discussion on travellers and their needs in light of planning law in '"We'll go no more a' roving": seeking a new definition of gypsy and traveller' by Clorinda Goodman in JPL 2005, Sept, 1159–1163.

5. Personal autonomy

Closely connected to questions of identity are matters of personal autonomy which may concern development of relationships, sexual activity (as opposed to sexual identity), information about health and medical procedures, names and cultural identity, pregnancy and euthanasia.

Autonomy is the concept of intelligent, rational, informed beings voluntarily making decisions for themselves within (in these cases) a moral, bioethical and rights context. It derives from the Greek *nomos*, meaning law, so it means a person who gives himself his own law. It may otherwise be explained as personal self-government. The example of Diane Pretty discussed in section 4.5.1 under the heading of 'competency' demonstrates in a particularly poignant way one aspect of this issue, and more recent cases confirm that this is a serious gap in the law that urgently needs to be addressed by the legislature, although the attitude of the Government, as expressed by the Prime Minister at the end of 2008, is that they do not propose to alter the law.

In the previous absence of government or opposition proposals to provide terminally ill patients with autonomy, a cross-bench peer, Lord Joffe, introduced in 2005 the Assisted Dying for the Terminally Ill Bill into the House of Lords. The preamble said that it would 'enable an adult who has capacity and who is suffering unbearably as a result of a terminal illness to receive medical assistance to die at his own considered and persistent request; and for connected purposes'. It set out the duties of the assisting physician and provided protection for health-care professionals and other workers, whilst also making provision for conscientious objectors. There were requirements for medical records to be kept and for a monitoring commission. The Bill was strenuously opposed by the Anglican bishops and representatives of other religions and failed to become law.

In 2008 further high-profile cases were reported including the unsuccessful application to the Administrative Court by Debbie Purdy asking for immunity for her husband if he helped her, which decision she intended to appeal. Another case concerned Daniel James, a young sportsman who was paralysed in a rugby accident and after several attempts on his own life was taken by his parents to the Dignitas Clinic in Switzerland where he was helped to die.

This latter case shows particularly clearly the unsatisfactory state of the law. His parents and another person who helped with the travel arrangements were investigated by the police with a view to prosecution, and although assisting suicide is a crime under English law, after several months' investigation the decision was taken not to prosecute. Indeed there does not seem to have been any prosecution mounted for this offence in recent years. Thus, although the law is clear enough, it is not being enforced, yet distraught relatives and friends of terminally ill patients are being investigated and treated as criminals at what must be just about the lowest points in their lives.

The whole field of death (and birth) and respect for those unable or no longer capable of protecting themselves or making their own decisions is brought into question by autonomy considerations and may also bring into play other questions of cultural identity. A different aspect of this concerns the dignity of a person who is in fact capable of attempting to commit suicide as was the case in *Peck v United Kingdom* (2003) 36 EHRR 41.

Peck had been captured on local authority CCTV brandishing a kitchen knife in a public place shortly prior to attempting unsuccessfully to commit suicide by cutting his wrists on a high street. Photographs and images were subsequently broadcast at local and national level which Peck claimed was in breach of his Art 8 rights to privacy. No crime had been committed and the police took no action, but equally the local authority took no steps to prevent the consequential publicity nor to conceal Peck's identity. Indeed, the images had been incorporated into a campaign designed to promote the efficacy of CCTV in combating crime and, as neither to commit suicide nor to attempt to commit suicide are crimes, that in itself seems to have been an ill-informed and misguided project.

Peck subsequently appeared on a number of television programmes discussing the publications and he complained to the relevant media commissions and unsuccessfully sought judicial review. He subsequently lodged his complaint with the European Court where it was upheld. The Court found that there were not sufficient or relevant reasons to justify disclosure by the local authority which ought to have obtained his consent or alternatively hidden his identity. The disclosure was disproportionate and an unjustified interference with his right to privacy under Art 8 and there were inadequate remedies under domestic law. As with the case of Diane Pretty, the circumstances clearly go to the root of an individual's autonomy, although in this case the outcome was more satisfactory from the applicant's point of view.

Development of personal autonomy

As indicated above, autonomy is also concerned with other aspects of people's lives and not merely with their deaths, so questions involving development of relationships, pregnancy and cultural identity may from time to time also fall to be considered in this context. Included in

this list is the idea of sexual autonomy and the case of Max Mosley heard before Eady J in July 2008 appears to develop the law in this area (*Max Mosley v News Group Newspapers Limited* [2008] EWHC 1777 (QB)). The Human Rights Act has facilitated the development of the law on breach of confidence, which itself derived from equitable principles by affording protection to information where a person has a reasonable expectation of privacy. In the past this was usually understood to mean in a commercial context, but that has been extended to protection of a person's self-esteem and dignity: in other words, his autonomy. If there is a reasonable expectation of privacy, the fact that there is no pre-existing relationship does not preclude an individual seeking to protect his privacy even if, and perhaps especially if, he was involved in embarrassing activities.

The conflict here is between freedom of expression and the claim to protection of one's private life, and the balance to be achieved can only be reached by close and careful examination of the particular circumstances. This might well have the effect of reducing the sometimes apparently cavalier attitude of certain sections of the media which delight in revealing lurid information about public figures. The key to this is the proportionality of the issues raised, which means balancing the 'right to know' with the right to privacy and respect for one's private life.

In December 2008 another case was heard by the European Court in which two men, whose fingerprints and DNA were being held by South Yorkshire Police, were awarded damages because of the refusal of the police to remove the DNA from the database. Neither man had been convicted of any offence and the Court held that this violated their Art 8 rights. Details of some 4.5 million people are held by the UK, although some 20 per cent of these individuals do not have a current criminal record.

The Court was not impressed with the UK's attitude to this and was 'struck by the blanket and indiscriminate nature of the power of retention in England and Wales'. The government was failing to strike a fair balance between competing private and public interests and had strayed beyond any acceptable margin of appreciation. The judgment was remarkable for its strong wording and may influence policy on other surveillance programmes such as the ID card programme.

In Scotland, DNA samples taken from people during criminal investigations where they are not subsequently charged or convicted are destroyed. Whatever amended policy emerges as a result of this decision, it is obvious that there should be consistency within the UK if internal legal disputes and problems are not to arise. Recognition of autonomy and respect for the individual does here require that innocent people should not be stigmatised by being included on databases that are clearly compiled to keep tabs on criminals.

10.4 Exclusion of evidence

The Police and Criminal Evidence Act 1984 (PACE) s 78 enables the court to exclude prosecution evidence if it would be unfair to allow it to be admitted. State officials such as the police and revenue authorities use covert methods to obtain evidence and sometimes these methods go beyond what the law authorises and so the evidence obtained becomes inadmissible. In the first instance such actions might well breach the suspect's Art 8 right to respect for his private life but, if so, it is also likely to give rise to the question of whether the suspect's subsequent trial can be fair under Art 6 and whether if he were to be punished it would come within the parameters of the 'no punishment without law' provisions of Art 7.

CASE EXAMPLE

R v Khan (Sultan) [1997] AC 558 HL

The position is complicated by English privacy law as can be seen from Khan's case. He had been convicted of being knowingly concerned in the importation of a Class A drug, heroin, from Pakistan. He and his cousin had been searched at Manchester Airport and, although no drugs were found on Khan, his cousin was found to be in possession of heroin.

Several months later Khan visited the private house of a friend, who was under surveillance as a suspected drugs dealer, during the course of which visit the police obtained a covert tape recording in which Khan admitted to his friend that he had been involved in his cousin's importation of heroin. On arrest he did not admit to the offence, although at his trial he did concede that the taped voice was his. The Crown was forced to concede that they had obtained the evidence by committing a civil trespass, but nevertheless Khan was convicted.

On appeal the House of Lords held that there was no right of privacy in English law and relevant evidence remained admissible, despite being obtained improperly or unlawfully, subject to the court's discretion under PACE s 78 to exclude it following *R v Sang (Leonard Anthony)* [1980] AC 402 HL.

As explained by Lord Nolan in *Khan*, *Sang* is authority for the proposition that a judge has no discretion to refuse to admit relevant evidence on the ground that it was obtained by improper or unfair means, and the court is not concerned with how such evidence is obtained. The emphasis throughout Lord Nolan's speech, with which the other law lords concurred, was on Art 8 and the House of Lords concluded that, even if there had been a violation of that article, the evidence on which the prosecution was brought and conviction obtained was admissible and so the trial was not unfair.

Nevertheless the European Court subsequently found (*Khan v United Kingdom* Application No 35394/97; (2002) EHRR 45) unanimously that Art 8 had been breached but, by six votes to one, that Art 6 had not.

10.5 Importance of Art 8

The preceding analysis of Art 8 using Dr Moreham's categorisation demonstrates how wide are its parameters and how fundamentally important are its objectives. The right not to have one's private and family life laid bare before the world and one's home and correspondence opened up to scrutiny are amongst the most important kinds of protection available to the great majority of Her Majesty's subjects, despite the contemporary cult of celebrity.

Important though it is, it must be borne in mind that this right does not sit alongside the prohibitions on torture and slavery as being absolute and unconditional. Public authorities can, in accordance with the law and where necessary in a democratic society, justifiably interfere with the exercise of the right to respect for these things in six circumstances, in the interests of:

1. national security

2. public safety

3. economic well-being of the country

4. prevention of disorder or crime

5. protection of health or morals

6. protection of the rights and freedoms of others.

ACTIVITY

Self-assessment questions

1 What is meant by freedom from interference with physical and psychological integrity?

2 Give an example of a case falling within the above category.

3 What had to be done because of defects found in English law and procedure as a result of the case of *Malone v United Kingdom* (1985)?

4 How does English law of torts feed into modern environmental rights law?

5 Summarise a European Court case which addresses problems of noise pollution.

6 Compare the attitude of the European Court in the cases of *Qazi* and *McCann*.

7 How has English law adapted to medical and social developments in gender realignment?

8 Explain what human rights has to say about cultural identity.

9 What kinds of subject matter come within the purview of personal autonomy, and in what ways does current law not recognise personal autonomy?

10 How was the local authority at fault in the case of *Peck v United Kingdom* (2003)?

The case law provides a rich series of examples of this variety, although many of them demonstrate the need for states to be able to take advantage of the margin of appreciation.

10.6 Marriage and founding a family

The right to marry and found a family contained in Art 12, although expressed separately from the rights to respect encompassed in Art 8, goes hand in glove with the rules established for equality of private rights and responsibilities between spouses and towards children in the Seventh Protocol.

Art 12

'Men and women of marriageable age have the right to marry and found a family, according to the national laws governing the exercise of this right.'

Protocol 7 Art 5

'Spouses shall enjoy equality of rights and responsibilities of a private law character between them, and in their relations with their children, as to marriage, during marriage and in the event of dissolution. This Article shall not prevent States from taking such measures as are necessary in the interests of children.'

Article 12 has various cultural connotations as well as providing a specific human right to marry and found a family, which is why it is couched in terms that refer to the national laws governing its exercise. Clues as to other issues implicit in this right are indicated by the terms of Art 7 of the Protocol because it is not simply the participants' ages and qualifications needed to marry in the first place that are important.

Other factors for consideration are what happens after marriage in relation to responsibility for children, property rights, how and indeed whether marriages may be terminated by divorce, nullity, or legal separation and how far religious requirements or constraints have an effect on a state's civil laws, consanguinity, and much else beside.

There are two rights here, ie to marry and to found a family, but the qualification that applies is 'according to the national laws governing the exercise of *this right*' (author's emphasis) which seems to treat them as one. For most purposes they can be regarded as part and parcel of the same right but occasionally they may need to be separated. These topics are dealt with more fully in Chapter 14.

KEY FACTS

Art 8(1) provides for rights of respect for private life, family life, home and correspondence

Art 8(2) prevents interference by public authorities unless justified by law in a democratic society on one of the six specified grounds

The six specified grounds are:
- national security
- public safety
- economic well-being of the country
- prevention of disorder or crime
- protection of health or morals
- protection of rights and freedoms of others.

Lord Bingham designated Art 8 issues in *Countryside Alliance v A-G* (2007) as:
- private life and autonomy
- cultural lifestyle
- use of the home
- loss of livelihood/home.

Dr Moreham categorised the issues in a re-examination of Art 8 in EHRLR (2008) as:
- freedom from interference with physical and psychological integrity
- collection and disclosure of information
- protection of one's living environment
- identity
- personal autonomy.

Art 12 covers the right to marry and the right to found a family and the qualification is 'according to the national laws governing the exercise of this right'

Prot 7 Art 5 gives spouses equal rights and responsibilities regarding marriage, children and dissolution but allows states to take measures necessary in children's interests

Domestic and European case law is extensive and involves rapidly developing areas of private law

Useful resources

Kilkelly, U, 'The Right to Respect for Family Life': www.coe.int/T/E/Human_rights/hrhb1.pdf.

Personal autonomy (*Stanford Encyclopedia of Philosophy*): plato.stanford.edu/entries/personal-autonomy/.

Further reading

Amos, M, *Human Rights Law* (Hart Publishing, 2006), 343–409.

Foster, S, *Human Rights and Civil Liberties* (2nd edn, Pearson Longman, 2008), 558–629.

Goodman, C, '"We'll Go No More a'Roving": Seeking a New Definition of Gypsy and Traveller' JPL 2005, Sept, 1159–1163.

Marshall, J, 'A Right to Personal Autonomy at the European Court of Human Rights', EHRLR 2008, 3, 337–356.

Moreham, N A, 'The Right to Respect for Private Life in the European Convention on Human Rights: A Re-examination', EHRLR, 2008, 1, 44–79.

Ovey, C and White, R C A, *Jacobs & White The European Convention on Human Rights* (4th edn, Oxford University Press, 2006), 241–299.

FREEDOM OF THOUGHT, CONSCIENCE AND RELIGION ■

AIMS AND OBJECTIVES

These freedoms are very important, so important in fact that special provision is made in the Human Rights Act s 13 (see section 11.5 of this chapter), a privilege not accorded to the other Convention rights, freedoms and prohibitions. The aims of this chapter are to:

■ Provide a context for understanding that the freedom to think, exercise one's conscience and practise one's religion exists alongside responsibilities, especially when there is a wish to promulgate or impose views, beliefs and opinions on others who might take offence

■ Indicate a context for furthering understanding of the concept of 'freedoms'

■ Show that these freedoms exist in global and other continental regional instruments although not subject to equivalent enforcement procedures outside Europe

■ Demonstrate that the main vehicle for Art 9 is through religion and in particular *via* the manifestation or proselytising of religion, examining recent case law to support this

■ Explain why it is considered to be particularly important for domestic UK law

■ Show that in addition there is a wide range of secular beliefs that have been brought within the scope of Art 9

■ Examine in outline the EU context, and that of other European states.

11.1 Introduction

Previous chapters have considered rights to life, fair hearings, liberty and security, and to respect for private and family life. They have also discussed prohibitions on torture, slavery and forced labour, and on punishment not justified by law. This chapter deals with freedom of thought, conscience and religion, whilst the next two chapters address freedom of expression, followed by assembly and association. Rights, prohibitions and freedoms mean different things in plain non-legal English, and more so in the context of human rights jurisprudence.

Wesley Hohfeld, writing early in the last century, developed a complex analysis that encompassed rights and freedoms but which also recognised that there are other benefits to which human beings lay claim. The corollary of this is that where there are benefits to be claimed equal recognition should be given to corresponding responsibilities and obligations, whether considering human rights theory or the practical operation of rights claims in the real world.

Rights imply obligations, and the ECHR recognises this by stipulating that most rights are qualified. The words that people commonly use are 'human rights' although in some instances they will refer to 'freedoms'. In other cases more subtle distinctions might be made with reference to claims, powers, immunities and privileges, depending on the context.

Consider the following table:

Description	Dictionary definition	Qualification or comment
Human right	A right which is believed to belong to every person by virtue of being human	There is fundamental disagreement on this as many people believe that rights are culturally relative, ie dependent on one's society and background, not universal
Freedom	The power or ability to act, speak or think as one chooses	The implication here is that this reinforces different unspecified rights not to have the freedom in question interfered with or detracted from by others
Claim	An assertion that something is true, typically without finding or producing evidence that it is true	The presupposition here is that someone else has a duty to honour the claim. The qualification of 'typically' in the definition is open to challenge as claims may be true or false
Power	The capacity or ability to direct or influence the behaviour of others or the course of events	The implication here is that what one is able to do has consequential effects on other people
Immunity	Protection or exemption from something, especially an obligation or penalty	This implies the inability to challenge something
Privilege	A special right, advantage or immunity granted or available only to a particular person or group	Privileges would be considered by many people not to be part of human rights discourse but providing a special advantage to a selected or chosen group

■ Figure 11.1 Rights language table

The above table should make you start to think about 'rights discourse', the language of human rights. Many people do not differentiate between these different uses of language, using words interchangeably, but the distinctions are important and need to be balanced in the real world with corresponding obligations and responsibilities.

ACTIVITY

Self-assessment questions

Consider Figure 11.1 and then think about:

(a) how you might analyse the following concepts by reference to their dictionary definitions, and

(b) your further ideas about how they may need to be qualified:

  1. liberty

  2. duty

  3. liability

  4. disability.

There is perhaps an implication behind the word 'freedom' that it incorporates a raft of other rights, claims, powers, immunities and privileges. Freedom of thought is perhaps the least constrained of the freedoms, because apart from undergoing torture or brainwashing to force people to change their minds or beliefs, what goes on inside one's head is entirely private unless or until the thinker chooses to share his thoughts.

Freedom of conscience suggests an unlimited range of thoughts that one should be allowed to enjoy, without restriction apart from that which constrains the subject arising from his own moral attitudes and understanding. What it does not do is tell us very much about whether, and if so how far, those thoughts may become concrete or 'manifest' in the sense either of being expressed to others or more controversially promulgated in order to try to change other people's beliefs and opinions. This latter process then becomes an activity which causes practical difficulties under the ECHR when it comes within the description of 'proselytising'.

It will be seen that 'manifestation' and 'proselytising' are important ingredients of the freedoms, especially religious freedom. In other words, freedom of thought, conscience and religion is initially and primarily internalised and rights discourse is only engaged when it becomes externalised, echoing the Dembour analysis in section 1.5.5.

11.2 Freedoms interconnectivity

One way of conceptualising the relationship between these three Art 9 freedoms – those of association and assembly in Art 11, and of expression in Art 10 – is that they can be placed in a pyramidal structure, the base being thought, conscience and religion, with the right to belong and gather together growing out of that base, thus allowing participants to enjoy freedom of expression.

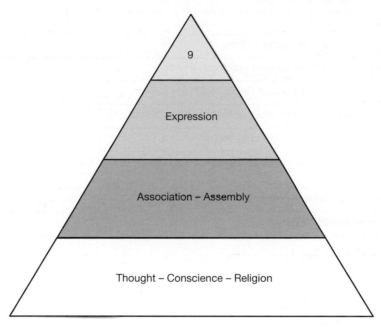

■ Figure 11.2 Art 9

What this is meant to show is that there is interconnectedness and growth between these six freedoms, although this chapter is only considering the 'ground floor'. Without them people could not develop ideas in society in order to associate with others of like mind, and join together to advance their views and opinions. This in turn enables and fuels one of the fundamental driving forces of human beings, the need to express themselves in ways that are as free as it is possible to achieve from the constraints and fetters that others (governments, political opponents, people with different beliefs, terrorists and many others) would impose on them.

It will be seen from the case law that the preponderance of litigation with regard to freedom of thought and conscience refers to religion, the freedom to practise it and, more controversially, the extent to which one may proselytise by trying to convert others to one's own beliefs. That is often where the trouble starts, and is bound to happen because it is the basic creed of some religions (not all) that believers should try to convert non-believers. Equally and from a fundamentally opposite stance, some people believe it is a mortal sin to convert from one's religion.

11.3 Analogous provisions

Recognition of equivalent provisions to these Art 9 freedoms is widespread in the global and regional rights context. There are similar articles in the International Bill of Human Rights and some regional conventions or charters, the relevant articles and documents being indicated in the following table which shows them in chronological order:

Convention/charter	Article	Year
UN Universal Declaration of Human Rights (UDHR)	18	1948
European Convention on Human Rights (and protocols) (ECHR)	9	1950
International Covenant on Civil and Political Rights (ICCPR)	18	1966
American Convention on Human Rights, Pact of San Jose Costa Rica	12	1969
African (Banjul) Charter on Human and Peoples' Rights	8	1981
Declaration on the Elimination of All Forms of Intolerance and Discrimination Based on Religion or Belief	All	1981
CIS (Minsk) Convention on Human Rights and Fundamental Freedoms	10–12	1995
Arab Charter on Human Rights	30	2004

■ Figure 11.3 Equivalent articles

As the above table indicates, human rights conventions do not operate in isolation but inspire and feed off each other. There are differences in wording and emphasis but, as this chapter will demonstrate, the advantage enjoyed by the European Convention is that its rights are directly enforceable, and this will now be examined in more detail.

11.4 Manifestation of religion

The principle of Art 9 is clearly and unambiguously stated in the first line and is expressed in absolute terms (author's emphasis below) but Art 9(1) immediately proceeds to provide examples which explain why most cases are based on *religious* freedoms rather than being grounded in the broader concepts of thought and conscience.

'1. *Everyone has the right to freedom of thought, conscience and religion;* this right includes freedom to change his religion or belief and freedom, either alone or in community with others, and, in public or private, to manifest his religion or belief, in worship, teaching practice and observance.'

'2. Freedom to manifest one's religion or beliefs shall be subject only to such limitations as are prescribed by law and are necessary in a democratic society in the interests of public safety, for the protection of public order, health or morals, or the protection of the rights and freedoms of others.'

Art 9(2) emphasises the right to *manifest* one's religion or belief, which is what lies at the root of many of the practical problems and case law that arise over freedom of thought, conscience and religion. Religious susceptibilities and the problems they can cause are the reasons for Art 9(2) containing such wide-ranging limitations.

Claimants frequently bundle together the bases of their claim, either in order to strengthen their case or because the issues are indeed confused or overlapping. Thus, they may argue that their right to freedom of conscience and religion under Art 9 is being stymied by restrictions imposed by a state on their ability to meet with fellow believers under Art 11, or to express themselves within the terms of Art 10.

CASE EXAMPLE

R (on the application of Playfoot (A Child) v Millais School Governing Body [2007] EWHC 1698 (Admin)

The claimant, Playfoot, applied for judicial review of a decision of the defendant governing body of the Millais School not to permit her to wear a 'purity ring' whilst a pupil at a maintained non-denominational girls' secondary school. The school's uniform policy imposed a general ban on wearing jewellery but had previously granted exemptions of some items for faith reasons.

The question was therefore whether Playfoot's belief as a committed Christian that she should be sexually abstinent before marriage could be signified by her purity ring which would thus entitle her to gain exemption from the school's policy. The school had found no evidence or explanation linking her belief in sexual abstinence to wearing a ring and concluded that this was not a legitimate manifestation of belief. Playfoot alleged that there was a contravention of Art 9 and Art 14 (discrimination) as girls of other religions were permitted to wear items that fell outside the policy.

The Administrative Court refused the application because, as she was under no obligation by reason of her belief to wear the ring, she could not be said to be manifesting her belief. Art 9 was not engaged so her Art 9 beliefs were not being transgressed. The Convention limitations took into account that the benefits of school uniform policy (including discipline, equality and cohesion), together with other factors, helped to provide a fair learning environment and so amounted to a legitimate and proportionate exception.

The rationale in *Playfoot* was that schools are justified in having school uniform and dress-requirement policies for good reasons prescribed by law that include fostering an atmosphere of allegiance, discipline, equality and cohesion which allowed children to study in an atmosphere and environment that minimised class, social and wealth differences. Banning jewellery clearly fitted into those objectives.

In March 2006 the House of Lords had considered a similar case in *R (on the application of Begum) v Denbigh High School Governors* [2006] UKHL 15 where the school governors appealed

against a decision [2005] EWCA Civ 199 that Begum had been unlawfully excluded from her school because she had not complied with the dress code. As a Muslim, Begum insisted on wearing a jilbab (a loose-fitting garment covering the entire body except for the hands, feet, face and head) to school rather than a shalwar kameeze (tunic and trousers) as provided for under the school's policy, although for two years previously she had not taken exception and had worn a shalwar kameeze.

The school's appeal was allowed, although Lord Nicholls and Baroness Hale dissented on the issue of whether there had been an interference with Begum's right to manifest her religion. It was held that what constituted interference depended on all the circumstances of the case and this included the extent to which an individual could reasonably expect to be at liberty to manifest her beliefs in practice. The focus of Strasbourg jurisprudence was on whether in any case under consideration a Convention right had been violated, not whether the challenged decision was the result of a defective decision-making process (which under English law would come within the remit of judicial review).

Following this House of Lords decision, but prior to *Playfoot*, the Administrative Court had heard a further case *R (on the application of X) v Headteachers and Governors of Y School* [2007] EWHC 298 (Admin). On the facts of that case the Muslim schoolgirl seemed to have a strong case in that her three elder sisters had attended the same school and had been allowed to wear to school the niqab veil which covered the entire face and head apart from the eyes. By the time X attended the school wearing the niqab, it did not conform to the uniform policy and dress code. The school made considerable efforts to assist X, however, by arranging and paying for tuition in some subjects and she was also offered a place at another school of similar standing where she could have worn the niqab, but she refused that offer.

Silber J in the Administrative Court decided in favour of the school because, although X's Art 9 rights had been engaged, the school's decision had not infringed them, especially where the individual had a choice which she had turned down. In particular, Art 9 does not stipulate that a person should be allowed to manifest her religion at any time and place of her choosing, and Strasbourg jurisprudence shows that there is no interference with an Art 9 right in situations where a claimant could manifest her religious beliefs in a different way. X's attendance some years after her sisters had left explained and justified changes in policy and attitude on the part of the school.

This line of cases, strengthened by the 2006 decision of the House of Lords, might have been thought to resolve the question and remove the likelihood of further litigation, but the 2008 application to the Administrative Court in the case of *R (on the application of Watkins-Singh) v Aberdare Girls' High School Governors* [2008] EWHC 1865 (Admin) was granted and the school severely criticised. The European Convention issues failed but in this case it was also Silber J who held that the school's decision not to grant Watkins-Singh a waiver to permit her to wear the Kara (a Sikh religious steel bangle) constituted indirect discrimination on grounds of race under the Race Relations Act 1976 and on grounds of religion under the Equality Act 2006, so on this occasion it was home-grown domestic legislation which provided the remedy.

Proselytising

Freedom to manifest one's religion implies the right to try to convince other people in the course of religious discussion, according to the decision in *Kokkinakis v Greece* (1993) 17 EHRR 397. In Greek law, proselytising is an offence under the constitution and legislation and in this case the conduct in question went beyond simple discussion so as to amount to 'taking advantage of [the listeners'] inexperience . . . low intellect and their naivety'. The Commission concluded unanimously that there had been a violation of Art 9 of the Convention.

In his Partly Dissenting Opinion, Judge Martens said that he concurred that there had been a breach of Art 9 but for different reasons, and some of his judgment helps to explain aspects of freedom to change religion and to try to persuade others to do so. He said that absolute freedoms explicitly include that of changing religion and beliefs, and whether or not someone does this is no concern of the State. In principle, therefore, neither should it be the State's concern if someone attempts to influence another person to change his religion.

Many religions count teaching one's faith to others as amongst the main duties of believers, and it is at the boundary of such teaching that the activity may shade off into proselytising which can create conflict. 'It sets the rights of those whose religious faith encourages or requires such activity against the rights of those targeted to maintain their beliefs (paragraph 15).' The reasons it is not within the State's responsibility to interfere in that 'conflict' are:

1 because respect for human dignity and freedom implies that the State must accept that in principle everyone is capable of determining his fate in the way that he deems best – there is no justification for the State to use its power to protect the proselytised unless a particular duty of care arises

2 even the public order argument cannot justify use of coercive State power in a context where tolerance demands that free argument and debate should be decisive

3 because under the ECHR all beliefs and religions should be equal so far as States are concerned.

The case reveals that European human rights law draws a distinction between bearing Christian witness or true evangelism as compared to improper proselytising. The latter comprises a corruption or deformation of the correct approach which leads to incompatibility with respect for the three freedoms contained in Art 9.

Thus, in a case where Greek air force officers tried to persuade soldiers under their command to become Jehovah's Witnesses that behaviour was improper because of the officer/other ranks relationship (*Larissis and others v Greece* (1998) 27 EHRR 329). Similarly, where a Turkish air force judge-advocate was forced to retire because the government took the view that his fundamentalist opinions were contrary to the requirements of loyalty to the secular state, this did not amount to interference with his freedom to practise his religion and there was no breach of Art 9 (*Kalac v Turkey* (App 20704/92), Judgment of 1st July 1997; (1999) 27 EHRR 552).

ACTIVITY

> **Self-assessment questions**
>
> **1** Why is religion such a fertile cause of contention under Art 9 ECHR?
>
> **2** What is the difference between manifesting one's beliefs and proselytising?

11.5 Human Rights Act s 13

Freedom of thought, conscience and religion, but as we have seen especially the latter, are regarded as being so important that the Human Rights Act 1998 specifically reinforces the Convention in this regard.

> **S** '13(1) If a court's determination of any question arising under this Act might affect the exercise by a religious organisation (itself or its members collectively) of the Convention right to freedom of thought, conscience and religion, it must have particular regard to the importance of that right.
>
> (2) In this section "court" includes a tribunal.'

The parliamentary debates on the Human Rights Bill drew assurances from the Home Secretary about the protection the clause was intended to provide for religious orders and adherents in the form of directions to the courts to pay close attention to freedom of religion. Concern had arisen because, as is usually the case, the susceptibilities of one group have to be weighed against the concerns of others. The effect of the incorporation of religious rights into domestic law, strengthened by s 13, was intended to remove some of the uncertainty that had previously existed about religious teaching in education law.

Religious organisations became worried when they realised that for some purposes they might be treated as public authorities. In such circumstances secular human rights might take precedence over religious ones. It was this that led to the insertion of the rather vague s 13 and the Home Secretary's extra-legal assurances, and it is significant that the section refers to 'a religious organisation' rather than to 'religion' or 'church'. In fact s 13 may well be superfluous as the Court is in any event bound to pay full regard to all the provisions of the Convention, subject only to derogations and reservations and the margin of appreciation.

ACTIVITY

> **Practice essay**
>
> With reference to what you have read so far in this chapter, consider whether, and if so the extent to which, it was necessary or desirable for Parliament to make special provision for religious organisations in s 13 of the Human Rights Act 1998.

11.6 Variety of religious beliefs

As far as religious, as opposed to secular, beliefs are concerned, considerable difference exists in the variety of religions for which recognition has been sought under the ECHR. Even mainstream religions provide a wide variation in their approaches to belief, whether and if so to what extent those beliefs are and should remain private or publicised, or be more forcefully taken out into the world and 'sold' to non-believers.

The rights claimed under the religious heading vary considerably also, from the Christian schoolgirl wanting to wear a purity ring (*Playfoot v Millais*), the Muslim schoolgirl wanting to wear a shalwar kameeze (*Shabina Begum*), and the Sikh girl wanting to wear her Kara to Hindus wanting to save the life of a condemned bull (*R (on the application of Swami Suryananda) v Welsh Ministers* [2007] EWCA Civ 893) and the Honoured Pendragon of the Glastonbury Order of Druids being prevented under the Public Order Act 1986 from holding druidic ceremonies at Stonehenge (*Pendragon v UK* [1999] EHRLR 223 (Commission)). Other cases can be cited to emphasise the variety of religious beliefs.

CASE EXAMPLE

R v Taylor (Paul Simon) [2001] EWCA Crim 2263

Paul Taylor was convicted of possessing cannabis, although the prosecution accepted that his Rastafarian religion used drugs as an act of worship, but the Court of Appeal held that there had been no violation of Art 9. The policy of the Misuse of Drugs Act 1971 and international law to which the UK subscribed was to combat public health dangers. A distinction had to be drawn between legislation of general application as opposed to laws relating solely to religious belief, and in this case the public policy of preserving public health in effect overrode recognition of the religious aspects.

A table of some of the beliefs that have given rise to Convention claims are summarised in chronological order in Figure 11.4:

Religion	Case	Year
Buddhism	*X v France*	1974
Divine light	*Zentrum Omkarananda and the Divine Light Zentrum v Switzerland*	1981
Sikhism	*X v United Kingdom*	1982

■ Figure 11.4 Variety of beliefs

CONTINUED ▸

Religion	Case	Year
Judaism	*D v France*	1983
Atheism	*Angelini v Sweden* (1986) 51 DR 41, ECmHR	1986
Druidism	*Chappell v United Kingdom* (1989) 12 EHRR 1	1987
Islam	*Karaduman v Turkey*	1993
Hinduism	*ISKONA and others v United Kingdom* (1994) 76A DR 41, ECmHR	1994
Jehovah's Witnesses	*Manoussakis v Greece* (1996) 23 EHRR 387	1996
Rastafarian	*R v Taylor (Paul Simon)* [2001] EWCA Crim 2263	2002
Scientology	*Church of Scientology Moscow v Russia* (18147/02) (2008) 46 EHRR 16	2008

■ Figure 11.4 Variety of beliefs (continued)

ACTIVITY

1 Research two of the cases in Figure 11.4 and compare and contrast the Art 9 issues that were considered.

2 Did they merit consideration under the ECHR? Why, or why not, and what are your reasons?

11.7 UK state recognition of religion

The importance of religion to the state and its citizens (or subjects in the UK) varies considerably in Europe and even more so throughout the rest of the world. In some states which regard themselves as secular, religion nevertheless plays an influential role in determining policy, for example Christian fundamentalism in the USA. In other states such as Saudi Arabia the legal system itself is religious in its substance and practice rather than secular, whilst in Turkey, which is overwhelmingly Muslim in religion, the state itself is strictly secular.

With regard to the UK, there is an established church and privileged legislative position for its senior clerics, yet the overwhelming majority of the population are not members of that church and there are sizeable minorities who are agnostic, atheist, humanist or members of non-Christian religions. History, rather than logic based on current considerations, maintains this anomaly.

How these disparities in approach stand up to rigorous examination in modern human rights terms is questionable. Although there has been some limited constitutional reform, the UK still retains privileges such as allocation of seats for 24 Church of England bishops and two archbishops in the House of Lords. Whether it is right to retain selective religious favouritism at all, let alone to prefer one Christian sect against others, or for that matter the Christian religion against other religions or creeds is part of a wider human rights discussion that is not pursued here, although the questions are pertinent to human rights discourse.

UK law discriminates against non-Church of England religions in other ways, for example by preventing a Roman Catholic from succeeding to the throne. The suggestion by the Prince of Wales that if he succeeds to the throne he might become the 'Defender of the Faiths' overlooks the archaic anachronism of religion still being constitutionally tied by an unwritten constitution to state governance. Were the first person in succession to the throne to be or become a Roman Catholic obvious questions would then arise under Art 9, and how an individual could have the status and responsibilities of heading the established church yet at the same time purport to defend other faiths, some of which are antipathetic to the aims and objectives of the Church of England, would give rise to a variety of constitutional problems.

Despite a number of reports published and statutes enacted since the New Labour administration took power in 1997, anomalies remain and there seems nowadays some reluctance to using traditional methods (such as Royal Commissions) of investigating and making proposals for important constitutional issues. Whether or not this view on how these important changes should be arrived at is sustainable, the reforms that have taken place have been piecemeal, incomplete and not entirely satisfactory. The Lord Chancellor and Secretary of State for Justice (as he then was) Lord Falconer of Thoroton said in the House of Lords in June 2007:

> 'My Lords, the Government are not at present proposing to establish a royal commission on the constitution . . . I wonder whether royal commissions are the appropriate way to deal with constitutional change now and whether there are ways of communicating with the public in a much larger way. I wonder whether bringing together the great and the good and saying this is the way that constitutional reform should take place is the appropriate way to deal with it. I suspect that the day of the royal commission determining what constitutional reform should take place may be in the past.'

Hansard 5th June 2007: Column 1015

On the other hand the secular viewpoint was trenchantly expressed by Peter Wishart MP on 6th March 2007 in the House of Commons:

> 'It is an absolute disgrace that in our multi-faith society we continue to favour one faith over all others. The fact that we are alone among western democracies in having religious representation in our legislature reinforces the view that the House of Lords is some sort of strange, eccentric, medieval throwback. We live in a multicultural, multi-faith society. Modern Britain is a society with great diversity of religions and non-religious beliefs, and continuing to privilege one denomination over others is preposterous and anti-democratic. If we are serious about modernising the House of Lords there can be no place for unelected bishops.'

Hansard 6th March 2007: Column 1462

Perhaps the universal rights answer would be to work towards instituting a secular state and to embrace disestablishmentarianism (removal of state recognition and privileges).

11.8 Secular beliefs

Although case law shows that it is religion that generates much of the controversy arising under Art 9, thought and conscience extends far beyond what can be classified as religion, so freedom of thought and conscience also needs to be examined in a secular context. Some examples of this are as follows:

1. Pacifism

Belief in pacifism can fall within the scope of Art 9 but does not necessarily cover all activities carried out in pursuit of that aim. This extends to conscientious objectors as in *Autio v Finland* (1991)72 DR 245, ECmHR and *Le Cour Grandmaison and Fritz v France* (1989) 11 EHRR 46, Ct).

CASE EXAMPLE

Arrowsmith v United Kingdom (1978) 19 DR 5, ECmHR

Arrowsmith was distributing leaflets at an army base, trying to persuade soldiers not to serve in Northern Ireland. She was charged under ss 1 and 2 of the Incitement to Disaffection Act 1934.

In the English court on appeal from her conviction Lawton LJ had described her behaviour as 'wicked' and, wicked or noble depending on one's views, with two dissenting members the European Commission upheld the UK Government's view that this came within the permitted restrictions under Art 9(2).

The case is discussed in more detail in connection with duties relating to national security, territorial integrity and public safety under Article 10(2) duties and responsibilities in section 12.7.

2. Anti-abortion

Throughout history people have refused to obey secular laws on grounds of conscience, and where such strong beliefs arise it makes little difference to the person in question whether this involves breaching criminal law or contravening other areas of law. A European example is *Knudsen v Norway* (1985) 42 DR 247, ECmHR for opposition to abortion, and similar cases have arisen in the UK.

CASE EXAMPLE

Connolly v DPP [2007] EWHC 237 (Admin)

Connolly appealed by way of case stated against the dismissal of her appeal against conviction for three offences under the Malicious Communications Act 1988. As a committed Christian opposed to abortion she had sent photographs of aborted foetuses to three pharmacies that sold morning-after contraceptive pills. The Crown successfully argued that the photographs were indecent or grossly offensive.

Her appeal was dismissed because her freedom of thought, conscience and religion were here subject to the Art 9(2) limitations protecting the rights and freedoms of others. The court said that the fact that a communication was political or educational in nature had no bearing on whether it was indecent or grossly offensive, and Connolly's conviction was necessary in a democratic society.

Her right to hold those beliefs about abortion under Art 9 and to express them under Art 10 did not justify the distress and anxiety that she intended to cause those receiving the images.

Although Connolly may have been devoutly religious and exercising her Art 9 right to freedom of thought, conscience and religion, the extent of her right to freedom of religious expression was no more important or worthy of protection than the freedom of secular expression enshrined in Art 10.

3. Sartorial self-expression

During the troubles in Northern Ireland, IRA detainees attempted to claim special status for themselves when imprisoned or interned, partly founded upon what they saw as their right to preferential political prisoner status. They argued that they should be entitled to wear their own clothes and be relieved of the requirement to undertake prison work, and generally to be distinguished from other prisoners convicted of criminal offences by the ordinary courts. They endeavoured to justify their refusal to wear prison clothing, partly based on their interpretation of Art 9 conscience and belief.

In *McFeeley and others v United Kingdom* (1981) 3 EHRR 161, in examining Art 9, the Commission said that they were of the opinion that the right to such preferential status for a certain category of prisoner was not amongst the rights guaranteed in general by the Convention or by Art 9 in particular. The Commission considered that the freedom to manifest religion or belief 'in practice' as contained in this provision could not be interpreted to include a right for the applicants to wear their own clothes in prison.

4. Animals

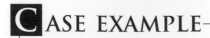

R (on the application of Swami Suryananda) v Welsh Ministers [2007] EWCA Civ 893

The Welsh Assembly Ministers appealed against a judicial review decision quashing their notice to slaughter a bullock under the Animal Health Act 1981 s 32, the animal having reacted positively to a bovine tuberculosis test. The respondent was a Hindu community which regarded the bullock as sacred and the preservation of life a fundamental tenet of their belief, imposing an obligation to prevent the slaughter to avoid a direct violation of their spiritual values.

It was held that the exception under Art 9(2) should prevail, so the slaughter was justified and necessary in light of the importance of eradicating bovine TB.

5. Veganism

H v United Kingdom (1993) 16 EHRR CD 44, ECmHR

H had been convicted of common assault and sentenced to three years' imprisonment but refused to work in the prison print shop because as a vegan he objected to working with the printing dyes which were products of animal origin. He was disciplined, punished, lost remission and eventually transferred to another prison, having been assessed as a risk to prison discipline, but in the meantime had himself declined to request a transfer to alternative work.

The Commission found that his vegan beliefs with regard to animal products fell within the scope of Art 9(1) but that the interference here was justified and prescribed by law because the Government's contention that it was necessary to impose a system of allocation of work that is fair and without favouritism was upheld. It was only one of H's reasons for refusing to work and a relatively minor one with insignificant penalties, so the principle of proportionality was not infringed.

6. Assisted suicide

The right to avoid a painful and lingering death or simply to die at a time of one's choosing – to commit suicide – used to be a crime at common law. More correctly, therefore, no such right existed under domestic law. However, suicide was relieved of criminal liability by the Suicide Act 1961 s 1.

S 'S1(1) The rule of law whereby it is a crime for a person to commit suicide is hereby abrogated.

s2(1) A person who aids, abets, counsels or procures the death of another, or an attempt by another to commit suicide, shall be liable on conviction on indictment to imprisonment to a term not exceeding fourteen years.

s2(2) If on the trial of an indictment for murder or manslaughter it is proved that the accused aided, abetted, counselled or procured the suicide of the person in question, the jury may find him guilty of that offence.'

Section 2 created the statutory offence of assisting suicide or attempted suicide with a heavy penalty and, whilst apparently providing a measure of protection in cases where undue pressure or downright wickedness might occur in unjustifiably persuading and helping a person to die, the law significantly fails to address circumstances where someone has the strongest of reasons to die at a time of her choosing but is physically unable to do so even though mentally entirely competent. This was the desperate position in the case of Dianne Pretty (whose case is also considered with others in section 4.5.1).

Lord Bingham of Cornhill, in the introduction to his speech in *The Queen on the Application of Mrs Diane Pretty (Appellant) v Director of Public Prosecutions (Respondent)* [2001] UKHL 61 *and Secretary of State for the Home Department (Interested Party)*, summarised her situation as follows:

1. 'No one of ordinary sensitivity could be unmoved by the frightening ordeal which faces Mrs Dianne Pretty, the appellant. She suffers from motor neurone disease, a progressive degenerative illness from which she has no hope of recovery. She has only a short time to live and faces the prospect of a humiliating and distressing death. She is mentally alert and would like to be able to take steps to bring her life to a peaceful end at a time of her choosing. But her physical incapacity is now such that she can no longer, without help, take her own life. With the support of her family, she wishes to enlist the help of her husband to that end.

He himself is willing to give such help, but only if he can be sure that he will not be prosecuted under s 2(1) of the Suicide Act 1961 for aiding and abetting her suicide. Asked to undertake that he would not under s 2(4) of the Act consent to the prosecution of Mr Pretty under s 2(1) if Mr Pretty were to assist his wife to commit suicide, the Director of Public Prosecutions has refused to give such an undertaking. On Mrs Pretty's application for judicial review of that refusal, the Queen's Bench Divisional Court upheld the Director's decision and refused relief.

> Mrs Pretty claims that she has a right to her husband's assistance in committing suicide and that s 2 of the 1961 Act, if it prohibits his helping and prevents the Director undertaking not to prosecute if he does, is incompatible with the European Convention on Human Rights. It is on the convention, brought into force in this country by the Human Rights Act 1998 that Mrs Pretty's claim to relief depends. It is accepted by her counsel on her behalf that under the common law of England she could not have hoped to succeed.'

Having lost the case at first instance and in the Court of Appeal, her penultimate hope was to ask the House of Lords to apply the European Convention in the domestic arena in a way that would overrule the effect of the Suicide Act, if their Lordships could find the Act incompatible with the Convention, but they declined to do so. Her appeal to the Lords was dismissed partly on the basis that the DPP had no power to give an undertaking not to prosecute Mr Pretty were he to help his wife, because any such undertaking would be a breach of the prohibition on the suspension or execution of laws without Parliament's consent contained in the Bill of Rights 1688. However, neither was there a substantive right to die under Art 2, and so the appellant's belief that she had the right to be helped to die was not supported by the Convention.

On 29th April 2002 seven judges in the European Court of Human Rights also ruled unanimously against her (*Pretty v United Kingdom* (2346/02) (2002) 35 EHRR 1), the court finding that her arguments were based on a misconception. Judge Pellonpa said that the law confers no *right* to commit suicide even though it had been decriminalised alongside attempted suicide for a number of reasons:

- Recognition of the common law offence did not seem to act as a deterrent.
- Categorising it as a crime cast an unwarranted stigma on innocent members of the suicide's family.
- It led to the distasteful result that patients recovering in hospital from a failed suicide attempt were prosecuted, in effect, because they had failed in their endeavour.

While the 1961 Act abrogated the rule of law making it a crime for someone to commit (or attempt to commit) suicide, it did not have the effect of giving a right to do so. Had that been its object there would have been no justification for penalising by a potentially very long term of imprisonment one who aided, abetted, counselled or procured the exercise or attempted exercise by another of that right. Thus, after its enactment the policy of the law remained firmly adverse to suicide.

Human rights law is therefore clearly unable as the Convention stands to deal with this serious and tragic problem, although it is quite feasible for domestic law to establish a legal regime that can do so, as is the case in the Netherlands. UK law makers have not been prepared to bite the bullet on this profound and tricky moral dilemma.

11.9 EU policy

All Member States of the EU are required individually to have signed and ratified the ECHR, whilst the EU's corporate policy contains analogous, but not identical, provisions. Under Art 52(3) of the EU Charter of Fundamental Rights the right guaranteed in para 1 of the European Convention corresponds to the EU's equivalent Art 9(1), and the EU must also take heed of the limitations in Art 9(2).

The difference between them is indicated below in italics and interpretation is in accordance with the EU's legal structure, so the outcome is that there may be a different route to enforcement but, at the end of the day, the EU as an entity as well as its Member States has to conform to the ECHR.

(A) EU Charter of Fundamental Rights Art 10:

'Everyone has the right to freedom of thought, conscience and religion. This right includes the freedom to change religion or belief and freedom, either alone or in community with others and in public or in private, to manifest religion or belief, in worship, teaching, practice and observance. *The right to conscientious objection is recognised, in accordance with the national laws governing the exercise of this right.'*

11.10 European examples

1. Greece

Manoussakis was a Jehovah's Witness who in 1983 rented a room in Crete for meetings, weddings and worship, but without obtaining official authorisation. Complaints were made on behalf of the local Greek Orthodox parish church. The use without authorisation resulted in conviction, fines and three months' imprisonment. It was held that these punishments constituted a violation of the Art 9 freedom, the requirement of obtaining prior authorisation having interfered with the freedom to practise religion which could not be justified as being prescribed by law (*Manoussakis and others v Greece* (1996) 23 EHRR 387).

A later case involved Serif, a Greek citizen and theology graduate who was elected Mufti of Rodopi by mosque congregations there in opposition to the government-appointed Mufti. He was subsequently convicted of usurping the functions of a religious minister and publicly wearing religious garments contrary to Greek law. It was held that his conviction was not justified and not compatible with the religious pluralism expected in a democratic society, precipitating a breach of Art 9(2) (*Serif v Greece* (App 38178/97, Judgment 4th December 1999 (2001) 31 EHRR 20).

2. Moldova

The Metropolitan Church of Bessarabia complained when the Moldovan authorities refused to recognise the church and this was upheld because it interfered with the church's right to freedom of religion. The thread of European cases demonstrating that the need to maintain true religious pluralism is inherent in a democratic society was continued, emphasising that refusal of recognition is not proportionate or necessary (*Metropolitan Church of Bessarabia v Moldova* (2002) 35 EHRR 13).

3. Turkey

Secularism is constitutionally particularly important in Turkey, where a number of religions coexist and it is important to avoid conflict between different groups of believers. A wide margin of appreciation was afforded when the question of wearing the Islamic headscarf in Turkish universities arose. There was no violation in the case of *Leyla Sahin v Turkey* (App 44774/98), initial judgment of 29th June 2004 confirmed by Grand Chamber judgment of 10th November 2005. The wearing of clothing and insignia has revealed a variety of problems throughout Europe as recent UK cases such as *Playfoot, Begum* and *Sarika Watkins-Singh* discussed above indicate, and similar issues have also arisen in France.

4. France

France adopted a law in 2004 which banned 'conspicuous religious signs' in public schools. Art 1 of the French Constitution states that:

 'France shall be an indivisible, secular democratic and social republic. It shall ensure the equality of all citizens before the law, without distinction of origin, race, or religion. It shall respect all beliefs.'

Nevertheless, following the black-listing of many religious groups, the About-Picard Bill provided the French Government with powers to dissolve religious denominations and spiritual movements if their leader, director, officer or members committed offences, regardless of whether or not the offence occurred in the name of the association. The law appears to be designed to ban the wearing of Muslim headscarves, Sikh turbans, Jewish skullcaps and large Christian crosses.

5 Denmark: Case Study

CASE EXAMPLE

It was reported on Danish television that in October 2004 a lecturer at the University of Copenhagen's Niebuhr Institute was attacked by five people who took exception to him reading extracts from the Qur'an to non-Muslims during a lecture. In 2005 a Danish writer, Kare Bluitgen, was writing a children's book about the Qur'an and life of the Prophet Muhammad but was having difficulty in finding an illustrator, and an article explaining this was published on 17th September 2005 in the *Politiken* newspaper. The Muslim religion forbids depiction of the Prophet's face.

On 30th September 2005 a Danish daily newspaper *Jyllands-Posten* (the *Jutland Post*) published an article comprising 12 cartoons entitled 'Muhammeds ansigt' or the 'Face of Muhammad', together with some text which criticised what it said was the special consideration for their religious feelings that Muslims demanded. Such sensitivity was incompatible with modern democracy and freedom of speech and it was argued that everyone had to be prepared to put up with ridicule, insults and mockery because otherwise censorship would take over.

The extent of the revulsion this caused to Muslims throughout the world, and the backlash it caused, had not been fully foreseen. Muslim organisations in Denmark pressed for prosecution under Danish blasphemy laws, without success. Imams presented petitions, and ambassadors from Muslim countries sought a meeting and action from the Danish Government, but were rebuffed by letter. Violence flared up around the world and in resulting riots and demonstrations it was reported that scores of people died.

In the following year there was a failed assassination attempt in Berlin on a newspaper editor who had reprinted the cartoons, and the would-be assassin later committed suicide in his cell, although many Muslims believed that he had been tortured to death. In Germany two suitcase bombs were found on a train but they failed to explode because of defective manufacture. In London a protest demonstration on 3rd February 2006 resulted in the conviction of six Muslim men for terms of between four and six years for inciting murder and terrorism.

Within the Muslim tradition, to depict the figure of Muhammad is regarded as a species of idolatry and insulting the Prophet is one of the gravest sins that can be committed. The case and its consequences provides a stark illustration of the kinds of problem that arise when the liberal human rights modernist movement, the bedrock of western democracies, comes up against the ancient, honourable and deeply respectful religious

CONTINUED ▸

299

tradition whose beliefs are more important to its adherents than life or liberty or the pursuit of happiness.

Although there are western laws against blasphemy, they were framed with the Christian religion in mind, and in any event many people believe they should be repealed. There are criminal laws designed to prevent disorder, and defamation laws to protect reputations, and the Convention which seeks to maintain a balance between the freedoms of thought, belief, religion and expression. None of these can always be effective when cultures clash, and only by acquiring understanding of others, and showing respect, will such disasters be avoided.

11.11 Scope of Art 9

The discussion in this chapter demonstrates the wide scope of Art 9 in both domestic UK and European contexts. Religion is more often than not at the heart of questions arising under this article, and on balance the Convention is working perhaps as well as might be expected in the modern world to address and deal with religious conflicts that arise across the continent, given the diversity of cultures and political systems that now exist in Europe, and their very different histories.

KEY IDEAS

Freedom	Quotation	Source
Thought	'Freedom of thought, conscience and religion is one of the foundations of a democratic society ... vital elements [of] the identity of believers ... but also a precious asset for atheists, agnostics, sceptics and the unconcerned'	*Kokkinakis v Greece* (1993)
Conscience	' ... emphasis on individual conscience and individual judgement lies at the heart of our democratic political tradition. The ability of each citizen to make free and informed decisions is the absolute prerequisite for the legitimacy, acceptability, and efficacy of our system of self-government.'	Dickson CJ Supreme Court of Canada *R v Big M Drug Mart Ltd* (1985)

CONTINUED ▶

<table>
<tr><td colspan="3" align="center">KEY IDEAS</td></tr>
<tr><td>Freedom</td><td>Quotation</td><td>Source</td></tr>
<tr><td>Religion</td><td>'Any examination of freedom of religion or belief today needs to address the massive religious revival which is characterising the end of the century. Should we anticipate in the wake of this revival an increase in tolerance, enlightenment and freedom or are we to be faced with greater intolerance and discrimination, condemned to a further period of extremism, darkness and inquisition?'</td><td>Prof Abdelfattah Amor, UN Special Rapporteur on Freedom of Religion and Belief, Preface to Freedom of Religion and Belief – A World Report (1999)</td></tr>
</table>

Useful resources

Bury, J B, The Critical Thinking Community, 'A History of Freedom of Thought':
www.criticalthinking.org/articles/history_freedom_of_thought.cfm.

Further reading

Foster, S, *Human Rights and Civil Liberties* (2nd edn, Pearson Longman, 2008), 631–660.

Gau, J and Arlow, R, 'Case Comment, Hindu temple – Slaughter of Sacred Bullock', Ecc LJ 2008, 10(1), 127–129.

Nathwani, N, 'Religious Cartoons and Human Rights – A Critical Legal Analysis of the Case Law of the European Court of Human Rights on the Protection of Religious Feelings and its Implications in the Danish Affair Concerning Cartoons of the Prophet Muhammad', EHRLR 2008, 4, 488–507.

Ovey, C and White, R, *Jacobs & White The European Convention on Human Rights* (4th edn, Oxford University Press, Oxford, 2006), 300–316.

Petchey, P, 'Legal Issues for Faith Schools in England and Wales', Ecc LJ 2008, 10(2), 174–190.

chapter 12 FREEDOM OF EXPRESSION

AIMS AND OBJECTIVES

At the end of this chapter, you should be able to:

- discuss the importance of freedom of expression

- provide an overview of the UDHR, EU and European Convention on Human Rights (ECHR) freedom of expression provisions

- consider in detail the extent of freedom of expression under Art 10 ECHR and its concomitant duties and obligations

- provide a selection of domestic and European case law examples.

12.1 The foundation freedom

'Freedom of expression and opinion is a foundation without which many other basic human rights cannot be enjoyed. Allowing people to publicly investigate and report on human rights abuses makes it much harder for those responsible for them to hide behind a veil of silence and ignorance. Similarly freedom of expression makes a valuable contribution to other key areas of concern – good governance, rule of law and democracy' (Statement on Foreign and Commonwealth Office website indicating international priorities).

12.2 Importance of freedom of expression

Freedom of expression is one of the most cherished rights enjoyed under English law. It is also known as freedom of speech and considered by many as perhaps *the* fundamental freedom or liberty of the Englishman. For example, Art 9 of the Bill of Rights 1689 guarantees freedom of speech and debate in Parliament so that debates there cannot be 'impeached or questioned in any court or place out of Parliament', which on a moment's reflection claims the right for Parliamentarians at the expense of everyone and everywhere else. Underneath the words the principle is sound: if Members are fairly and democratically elected as representatives of the people, their decisions must be respected against the rest of the world who are not so chosen.

However, freedom of expression is a wider term than freedom of speech as it incorporates and embraces other forms of imparting and receiving information regardless of the medium through which this is done. The general approach of the common law is that people are free and at liberty to do or say anything that is not actually forbidden by law. There is no requirement in English law that people should be *allowed* to think, say or do things only to the extent justified by law.

CASE EXAMPLE

Bushell's Case (1670) 124 ER 1006

Two Quakers, William Penn and William Mead, stood trial charged with unlawful assembly because they were challenging the Conventicle Act 1664 which prevented gatherings of more than five persons outside the Church of England. The judge had attempted to force the jury to convict by telling them that they would not be dismissed until they had reached a verdict that the court would accept. This posed what was essentially a starkly simple legal dilemma: was it the role of the judge or the jury to decide what facts had been proved? If it was the judge's task, the implication would have been that juries were at worst redundant or at best there to rubber-stamp judicial conclusions.

The jurors refused to take instruction and were fined but the chairman of the jury, Edward Bushell, refused to pay the fine. It was not uncommon for jurors to be treated in this manner: they were locked up without food or drink, fire or tobacco until they complied, and under such pressure juries usually would comply with the judge's wishes.

Edward Bushel was made of sterner stuff and he brought his own case in the Court of Common Pleas where it was established that the judge had been wrong in attempting to bully the jury. The case is significant in that it is regarded as decisive in establishing that juries must not be coerced by judges.

Important though this is, nevertheless the common law still imposed many constraints on freedom of speech and expression. Some of them have now been abolished as, for example, theatre censorship by the Lord Chamberlain, although only as recently as 1968 by the Theatres Act of that year. There is a considerable body of more recent legislation addressing the issue, in addition to obvious human rights statutes such as the Data Protection Act 1998, Public Interest Disclosure Act 1998, and Freedom of Information Act 2000.

Modern judges are well aware of the need and reasons for allowing and encouraging freedom of expression. In a consolidated case heard in July 1999 *R v Secretary of State for the Home Department ex parte Simms (and O'Brien)* [2000] 2 AC 115, Lord Steyn emphasised that in a democracy freedom of expression is the primary right and the rule of law could not operate without it. He said that it is *intrinsically* important, valued for its own sake, but it is also *instrumentally* important as it serves a number of broad objectives expressed in the following propositions:

- It promotes self-fulfilment of individuals in society.

- 'The best test of truth is the power of the thought to get itself accepted in the competition of the market' (quoting the American Justice Holmes and echoing John Stuart Mill).

- It is the 'lifeblood of democracy' as it:
  - provides free flow of information and ideas and informs political debate
  - operates as a 'safety valve'
  - acts as a brake on the abuse of power by public officials
  - facilitates the exposure of errors in the governance and administration of justice of the country.

The issue in *Simms and O'Brien* was that the criminal justice system had failed prisoners who had been wrongly convicted. Were they to be allowed to call in aid journalists who had available the resources that would enable further and thorough investigation to test whether there had been miscarriages of justice? Or was it legitimate for the authorities to limit free speech and not allow convicted prisoners to attempt to clear their names after conviction and appeal? The case reaffirmed the principle that free speech is not absolute but it was open to a prisoner to raise issues for debate with journalists if they wished.

The rules introduced by the Home Secretary that required journalists not to use information obtained from interviewing a convicted murderer were *ultra vires* in the blanket way they had been applied in Simm's case. Lord Millett said that the Home Secretary had claimed the right to impose an indiscriminate ban on all professional visits to prisoners by journalists or authors, no matter how strong a case might have been made to justify a particular visit, and he agreed with Lord Steyn that the Home Secretary had no such right.

In recent years the Government has had to be reminded of these important principles on more than one occasion as they strove to balance individual freedom with the rights of society as a whole and even the rights of those who see their mission in life to destroy those very freedoms. It is the fact that these freedoms continue to be available to people who reject them that proves their strength and worth. If these rights are diminished, albeit from the best of motives and undoubtedly sometimes for vitally necessary reasons, it means that traditional and hard-won rights are eroded and those who would plot to destroy them win their small but cumulative victories by diminishing civilised and humane society.

12.3 Treaty provisions

The Universal Declaration of Human Rights (UDHR) Art 19 establishes the basic modern human rights freedom of expression principle, the words 'through any media' indicating the extent of the right and 'regardless of frontiers' its universality. The EU Charter and ECHR define it in similar terms, although the Charter incorporates reference to the freedom and pluralism of the media and the Convention allows states to license broadcasting, television and cinema enterprises (in each case below identified by the author's italics).

The ECHR goes on to provide significant qualifications in para 2 that limit the exercise of the freedoms and accentuate the duties and responsibilities necessary in a democratic society on a number of grounds:

- national security, territorial integrity, or public safety
- preventing disorder or crime
- protecting health or morals
- protecting the reputation or rights of others
- preventing disclosure of information received in confidence
- maintaining the authority and impartiality of the judiciary.

UDHR Article 19

'Everyone has the right to freedom of opinion and expression; this right includes freedom to hold opinions without interference and to seek, receive and impart information and ideas through any media and regardless of frontiers.'

EU Charter Article 11

'Everyone has the right to freedom of expression. This right shall include freedom to hold opinions and to receive and impart information and ideas without interference by public authority and regardless of frontiers. *The freedom and pluralism of the media shall be respected.*'

There are two important things to note so far as the EU Charter is concerned:

1. Art 52(3) of the Charter ensures that the meaning and scope of the right are identical to those under the European Convention, and so the limitations that may be imposed also have to be the same whilst taking into consideration the EU's competition law requirements. The EU was primarily an economic community and remains so despite having developed from the European Economic Community into the European Union with a broader role that certainly wholeheartedly embraces human rights.

2. The freedom of the media is based on a number of things and it is important not to confuse European human rights cases with judgments of the European Court of Justice (ECJ):

   - ECJ case law regarding television, especially case C-288/89 (judgment of 25th July 1991, *Stichting Collectieve Antennevoorziening Gouda and others* [1991] ECR I-4007)

   - the Protocol on the system of public broadcasting in the Member States annexed to the EC Treaty

   - Council Directive 89/552/EC, particularly its 17th recital.

ECHR Article 10

'1. Everyone has the right to freedom of expression. This right shall include freedom to hold opinions and to receive and impart information and ideas without interference by public authority and regardless of frontiers.

This article shall not prevent States from requiring the licensing of broadcasting, television or cinema enterprises.

2. The exercise of these freedoms, since it carries with it duties and responsibilities, may be subject to such formalities, conditions, restrictions or penalties as are prescribed by law and are necessary in a democratic society, in the interests of national security, territorial integrity or public safety, for the prevention of disorder or crime, for the protection of health or morals, for the protection of the reputation or rights of others, for preventing the disclosure of information received in confidence, or for maintaining the authority and impartiality of the judiciary.'

Document	Article	Year
Universal Declaration of Human Rights (UDHR)	19	1948
Convention for the Protection of Human Rights and Fundamental Freedoms (ECHR, but note its full title)	10	1950
International Covenant on Civil and Political Rights (ICCPR)	19	1966
American Convention on Human Rights	13	1969
African Charter on Human and Peoples' Rights	9	1981
Commonwealth of Independent States Convention on Human Rights and Fundamental Freedoms (Minsk Convention)	11	1995

Figure 12.1 Freedom of speech and expression

12.4 Analysis of ECHR Article 10(1)

The basic components of Art 10(1) are:

1. the clear statement that everyone has the right to freedom of *expression* (wider than and not restricted to freedom of speech)

2. Although the declaration is unqualified, the second sentence elaborates by stating that 'freedom of expression' includes:

    (a) holding opinions, and

    (b) receiving and imparting ideas.

3. The basic freedom and the specific elaborations are strengthened by Art 10(1) making it clear that:
   (a) public authorities cannot interfere, and
   (b) frontiers are irrelevant.

4. Art 10(1) introduces the qualification that states shall have the power to license three types of activity:
   (a) broadcasting
   (b) television
   (c) cinema enterprises.

The combined effect of Art 10(1) without the third sentence is to provide a wide definition reinforced by reference to holding opinions, receiving and imparting ideas, absence of public authority interference and irrelevancy of frontiers.

The effect of the third sentence is to introduce three obvious ways in which freedom of expression can be controlled within the state, by the usual legal device of licensing for the three main types of activity that were apparent when the ECHR was drafted – broadcasting, cinema and television, although the latter was in its infancy in the early 1950s.

12.5 Analysis of Article 10(2)

Freedom of expression is not an absolute right, as is immediately apparent from Art 10(2), because it carries:

*   concomitant duties and responsibilities
*   the ability for states to subject it to:
    *   formalities
    *   conditions
    *   restrictions
    *   penalties.

These four types of limitation in turn have to conform to two criteria, ie they must be:

*   prescribed by law, and
*   necessary in a democratic society.

Art 10(2) then stipulates six types of situation that justify curtailment of an individual's freedom of expression, discussed in section 12.6.

12.6 Limitations on freedom of expression

12.6.1 Prescribed by law

In *The Sunday Times v United Kingdom* (1979) 2 EHRR 245 it was explained that a norm cannot be regarded as 'law', and therefore limited as 'prescribed by law', unless it is formulated

with sufficient precision to enable those bound by it to regulate their conduct in accordance with it. Thus, citizens must be able to foresee to a reasonable degree, depending on the circumstances, the consequences of a given set of circumstances and, given the complications of modern life, this might sometimes mean with the assistance of appropriate advice.

Conflict between the media's rights to publish information about famous people and their rights to maintain some confidentiality over their private lives, and especially their sex lives, frequently raises the question of how far limitations on freedom are prescribed by law. The case of *Tammer v Estonia* (2001) 37 EHRR 857 held that criminal penalties imposed when a sexual relationship was reported between the Prime Minister and a political aide could not be said to violate Art 10. Public figures are entitled to private and personal lives just like everyone else and should be free to enjoy personal relationships without interference or notoriety.

When that boundary is exceeded, the victim is entitled to be compensated by damages, but not by exemplary damages, as Eady J decided in *Max Mosley v News Group Newspapers Limited* [2008] EWHC 1777 (QB); 2008 WL 2872466. The judge's main reason for not extending what he described as an anomalous form of relief into a new area of law was that such a step would not be justified by reference to the matters prescribed by law or necessary in a democratic society under Art 10(2) of the ECHR. He was not satisfied that English law requires the additional weight of quasi-criminal financial punishment of the perpetrator, over and above ordinary compensatory damages and injunctive relief. There was no pressing need for it and the 'chilling effect' would be obvious. Mosley successfully sued the *News of the World* newspaper for defamation but using an action for breach of confidence and/or the unauthorised disclosure of personal information which infringed his rights to privacy under Art 8 of the ECHR.

12.6.2 Necessary in a democratic society

To be 'necessary in a democratic society' there should be a 'pressing need' and the limitation must be 'relevant and sufficient' according to *Handyside v United Kingdom* (1976) 1 EHRR 737. Handyside had been responsible for publication in the UK of *The Little Red School Book* which was a manual for children on how to challenge authority, but it also dealt with sex and drugs and the authorities thought it was obscene and he was prosecuted and fined £50. There were considerable and stark differences of opinion on the crucial question of whether the 'restrictions' and 'penalties' complained of by the applicant were really 'necessary in a democratic society' in this case 'for the protection of morals'. The Government and majority on the Commission were of the opinion that all the Court had to do was to ensure that the English court had acted in good faith and reasonably within the limits of the margin of appreciation given to Contracting States by Art 10(2). A minority of the Commission regarded the Court's task as not to review the Inner London Quarter Sessions' judgment, but to examine the offending *Little Red Schoolbook* directly and solely in light of the ECHR.

In 2007 the Scottish High Court of Justiciary had to deal with the case of a man who had been found guilty of contempt by insisting on appearing naked in court and elsewhere. His argument was that on the four occasions when this occurred he had not had the opportunity to be tried properly by an independent tribunal and the sheriff had decided on his guilt without due consideration. It was not an offence as such to attend court naked, and to be punished for it infringed the complainer's right to freedom of expression under Art 10. The matter should have been remitted to another sheriff to decide the question (*Robertson (Stewart) v HM Advocate; Gough (Stephen Peter) v HM Advocate;* also known as*: Robertson, Petitioner; Gough v McFadyen* [2007] SLT 1153).

The court held *inter alia* that the appearance of anyone naked in court is 'unquestionably a contempt' and not only was the complainer's conduct indecorous but it might have offended, upset or alarmed other people present and it added to the presiding judge's difficulties in such a way as to impair the administration of justice. There had been no violation of his Art 10 rights where the law of contempt simply restricted his right to express his views in his chosen manner. He could have expressed his belief in the right to attend court naked orally or in writing whilst remaining 'properly dressed' (although of course that would have meant that the complainer was obliged to deny his own beliefs by saying or writing one thing and being obliged to do another, and so effectively negating the freedom).

12.6.3 Legitimate aims

In *Handyside* the legitimate aims were the protection of morals, and perhaps they were underlying factors in Robertson's case also. Copies of *The Little Red School Book* were seized and destroyed, although publication had taken place and been allowed in other parts of Europe without interference from other state authorities.

The scope of legitimate aims is more fully dealt with in the following section. The plenary court held, by a majority of 13 votes to 1, that here the applicant's freedom of expression was both prescribed by law and necessary in a democratic society for the protection of morals under Art 10(2), so there had been no violation of his freedom nor, incidentally, of his property rights under Protocol 1 Art 1.

ACTIVITY

Quick Quiz

1 What is the significance of *Bushell's Case* (1670)?

2 What did Lord Steyn have to say in *Simms and O'Brien* about the instrumental importance of democracy, freedom of expression and the rule of law?

3 Under ECHR Art 10(1) what three kinds of licensing are allowed which will restrict freedom of expression?

4 What was decided about exemplary damages in *Max Mosley v News Group Newspapers Limited*?

5 To be 'necessary in a democratic society' what else is required according to *Handyside*?

12.7 Art 10(2) duties and responsibilities

Legitimate aims are wide and are construed allowing the state the benefit of the margin of appreciation, so the following are examples but by no means exhaustive of potential legitimate aims.

1. National security, territorial integrity, public safety

These three criteria are indisputably fundamental cornerstones to the overall integrity of the state. If it can be shown that by exercising freedom of speech a person or group of people is putting that integrity at risk, there is little doubt that the majority of those put at risk would agree that this is valid justification for curtailing the freedom. It thus becomes a real test for the three legs of Art 10, namely that the law in question be clearly defined, necessary in a democratic society and justified in pursuing legitimate aims.

CASE EXAMPLE

Arrowsmith v United Kingdom **Application No 7050/75 (1981) 3 EHRR 218**

Under the Incitement to Disaffection Act 1934 it is an offence maliciously and advisedly to endeavour to seduce a member of the armed forces from his duty or allegiance. Pat Arrowsmith was convicted under this statute for trying to persuade servicemen not to undertake military duties in Northern Ireland, by distributing leaflets to soldiers. She did this because of her belief in the philosophy of pacifism which, she argued, is allowed under Art 9(1) freedom of thought and conscience, and she relied on the concept of 'necessity' under Art 10(2) as a justification for restrictions and penalties. Freedom of expression here would have implied a pressing social need which may include the 'clear and present danger' test and which therefore required assessment in light of the particular circumstances of the case.

Her sentence of 18 months' imprisonment had been confirmed by the Court of Appeal, who granted leave to appeal against sentence and reduced the term so as to allow her to be released immediately, although by that time she had served nine months' incarceration. Her application was considered by the full European Commission in October 1978 and she submitted that s 1 of the 1934 Act was so vague that it threatened the right to liberty and security of person, prevented manifestation of her pacifist beliefs, and violated her right under Art 10(1) of the ECHR to freedom of expression.

Given the circumstances there was no doubt that her freedom of expression had been interfered with; the question was whether:

CONTINUED ▶

1. that interference had been 'prescribed by law'
2. it was made for one or more of the Art 10(2) purposes
3. the interference was necessary in a democratic society.

1 *Prescribed by law*: the Incitement to Disaffection Act 1934 certainly prescribed interference by law but despite the use of language such as 'maliciously and advisedly' and 'to seduce' in the Act, the Commission concluded that the Act was not so vague as to exclude any predictability as to what actions would come within its scope. Persuading soldiers to abandon their duty fulfilled the requirement.

2 *Pursuing Art 10(2) purpose*: the Commission accepted that deserting soldiers can threaten national security even in peacetime and maintenance of order within the armed forces needs strict measures to prevent desertion, so the aims pursued were in accord with Art 10(2). The leaflet went beyond simple political opinion and urged disaffection by refusal to serve, so the circumstances did engage an aim consistent with Art 10(2), namely the protection of national security and the prevention of disorder within the army.

3 *Necessary in a democratic society*: the applicant wanted to apply the US Supreme Court doctrine of 'clear and present danger' but Ms Arrowsmith's manifest intention to carry on her activities unless restrained from so doing made prosecution necessary and her sentence was not excessively severe. The Commission's overall conclusion by 11 votes to one was that the restriction imposed on the applicant's freedom of expression was justified under Art 10(2) of the Convention.

The content of the leaflet included quotations from soldiers who had deserted, contained information on Army regulations with regard to discharge, and advised how they could desert either to the Republic of Ireland or to Sweden.

2. Prevention of disorder or crime

In some ways this may be seen as analogous to security and public safety. An example of prevention of disorder or crime would be incitement to racial hatred. The Public Order Act 1986 s 18 makes it an offence for a person to use threatening, abusive or insulting words or behaviour or to display any material which is threatening, abusive or insulting if he or she does so with intent to stir up racial hatred or if in the circumstances racial hatred is likely to be stirred up. 'Racial hatred' is defined in s 17 as 'hatred against a group of persons defined by reference to colour, race, nationality (including citizenship) or ethnic or national origins'.

Again, it is unlikely that reasonable people would take exception to the objective of preventing disorder or crime but subject to the same qualifying criteria of prescription, democracy and legitimacy. These are valid aims of the law, and under the original Race Relations Act 1965 in order to uphold the human rights of accused persons it appears *per curiam* from Lord Parker CJ's speech that if there is a danger that a defendant has not had a fair trial the court would unhesitatingly set aside the conviction (*R v Malik* [1968] 1 WLR 353).

CASE EXAMPLE

R v Malik [1968] 1 WLR 353

Malik was a West Indian who was awaiting retrial on a charge of using words at a public meeting that were likely to stir up racial hatred, with intent to do so, contrary to the Race Relations Act 1965 s 6(1) when a newspaper had published derogatory references to his character in an article on race relations. Malik claimed that his understanding of the language used that came within s 6(1) differed from that which would be understood by English people, in that he sought to rely on his own personal interpretation of the meaning of the words used, rather than the plain English. He was convicted and the newspaper was fined for a serious contempt likely to prejudice a fair trial.

Malik's appeal against conviction and sentence was dismissed. No question of validity arose as he had admitted using language within the character of the section. The jury had decided on the true meaning of the words as understood by English people and so the appellant had used them with the necessary intent. The violence of the words used was one of the most important matters to take into account when considering sentence for an offence under the section. Limitations must be placed on the individual's freedom of expression when using that freedom in an unfettered way would cause real offence because of the racial nature of the views expressed.

3. Protection of health or morals

There is a considerable body of law designed to tackle indecency, pornography and other forms of behaviour that might prejudice the public's health or morals. Much of this by its very nature prohibits or inhibits freedom of expression which can give rise to tricky questions. For example, under s 160 of the Criminal Justice Act 1988 it is an offence for a person to have an indecent photograph of a child in his or her possession.

CASE EXAMPLE

R v Arthur Alan Murray [2004] EWCA Crim 2211; 2004 WL 1808966

In December 2003 Arthur Alan Murray was convicted in the Birmingham Crown Court of possessing an indecent photograph in the form of a video of a television broadcast showing scenes of a doctor examining the genitalia of a naked boy who suffered from a

CONTINUED ▸

genital defect. The original broadcast had then been altered by removing the commentary and slowing down the pictures leaving a slow motion version of manipulation of the penis, which was the reason for the charge.

The argument that what was merely a replication of the original programme, which the prosecution accepted was not indecent, could not itself be indecent was rejected by the trial judge and again on appeal. An abbreviated version of visual imagery, not otherwise altered, for example, by adding material, can become liable to censorship and thus limit an individual's freedom of expression because of the different emphasis and connotation that such manipulation can produce.

The judge found that part of the video could be so separated and that it was possible for it in that format to be indecent. He charged the jury that motive was irrelevant and the question to be decided was whether in its new form it was indecent or not. The Court of Appeal confirmed that this was the correct view of the law. What resulted was a second set of images, divorced from the first set.

4. Protection of the reputation or rights of others

The purpose of the law of defamation, ie libel and slander, is to protect the reputation of others and has long been accepted as a legitimate reason for restricting what one person can publish to the world about other people.

> 'The law of defamation seeks to resolve the conflict between the freedom of speech and publication and the right of the individual to maintain his or her reputation against improper attack.'
>
> A W Bradley and K D Ewing, *Constitutional and Administrative Law*, 14th edition, Pearson Education Ltd, Harlow, 2007

The rules of defamation are complex and not the concern of this book, but although it is broadly justifiable under human rights law to provide a remedy for persons who have been exposed to hatred, ridicule or contempt this does give rise to specific human rights issues and there are exceptions that apply where what would otherwise be classified as defamatory is protected if the defence of privilege, absolute or qualified, is available.

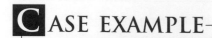

CASE EXAMPLE

Tolstoy Miloslavsky v United Kingdom (A/323) (1995) 20 **EHRR 442**

The European Court of Human Rights held in this case that a libel award of £1.5 million made in favour of Lord Aldington was a violation of the applicant's right to freedom of expression under Art 10 of the ECHR. This was because allowing the jury to set the amount of an award for non-financial damage but using 'fairly unrestricted discretion' was neither prescribed by law nor necessary in a democratic society. Insufficient safeguards were in place to prevent awards that were disproportionately high (in this case three times higher than any previous award).

An article had been published about Tolstoy Miloslavsky which alleged that he had committed war crimes after the Second World War by returning Yugoslav prisoners and refugees to the Soviet Union where they were liable to be persecuted. He appealed against the large award but was required to provide security for costs, which he could not do, and so his appeal was dismissed.

In the European Court he won his appeal against the UK and was awarded damages but not a declaratory judgment that the UK should indemnify him for an amount of his liability to Lord Aldington that exceeded what ought to have been adequate compensation, ie over and above what the jury should have awarded had they not made too high an award.

The original award and injunction violated the Art 10 principles because the UK's system that allowed juries to set the amount of awards for non-financial damage (ie not monetary compensation but for the purpose of addressing the defamation) allowed the jury too much discretion. The jury were not constrained by any scale of tariffs, nor were they subject to judicial guidance as to quantum.

The fact that in this case it was three times the size of any previous award rather spoke for itself on this point, however serious the libel perpetrated.

5. Preventing disclosure of information received in confidence

An action on the general ground of breach of confidence may be brought to prevent publication of matters that have been communicated on a confidential basis, and more particularly to protect government secrets. Again it means that freedom of expression is curtailed but for this head on the basis that it would be wrong to prejudice those who provided the information in circumstances where they believed that their confidence would be respected. A wide variety of other possibilities exists here encompassing the bases of trade and professional confidentiality. However, the courts will examine the particular arguments put forward in individual cases and only allow curtailment of freedom of expression where it is justified.

CASE EXAMPLE

Attorney General v Jonathan Cape Ltd; Attorney General v Times Newspapers Ltd [1976] QB 752; [1975] 3 WLR 606

The Attorney-General applied for injunctions to restrain the publishers Jonathan Cape and *The Sunday Times* from publishing the diary and extracts from it of the late Cabinet Minister Richard Crossman. His action was based on the proposition that expression of individual opinions by Cabinet Ministers in the course of Cabinet discussion is a matter of confidence which needs to be protected as such. This would mean that the Minister's freedom of expression regarding Cabinet discussions is reduced and, if permission to publish cannot be obtained, removed altogether. The Cabinet Secretary, having heard of the impending publication, wished to censor the diaries but, after protracted negotiations, agreement could not be reached as to what should be included or excluded.

Lord Widgery CJ, sitting in the High Court, held that this is indeed the law. However, although the doctrine of collective ministerial responsibility could be prejudiced by disclosure of information given to Cabinet in confidence and the court has the power to restrain such disclosure where it is clearly necessary in the public interest, here the public interest did not require such restraint because the events in question had taken place some 10 years previously.

Delayed publication in such circumstances was not likely to inhibit future free discussion in Cabinet. There was no power in the court to restrain disclosure of advice given by civil servants or of opinions expressed as to the ability of such civil servants. Lord Widgery applied *Rogers v Secretary of State for the Home Department* [1973] AC 388 HL.

6. Maintaining the authority and impartiality of the judiciary

The last of the six qualifications limiting the exercise of freedom of expression, and necessary in a democratic society, is where it is needed in order to maintain and protect the authority and impartiality of the judiciary. This is not the kind of case that is likely to arise much if at all within the English legal system, but it has occurred elsewhere in Europe.

CASE EXAMPLE

Worm v Austria (22714/93 (1998) 25 EHRR 454

Worm was an Austrian political journalist who investigated and reported on the former Austrian Vice Chancellor and Minister of Finance (A) who was involved in criminal proceedings arising out of alleged evasion of taxes. Worm's article stated as fact that A was guilty of tax evasion and although A was convicted, that was three months later. Despite the fact that his article had been factually albeit prematurely correct, Worm was then convicted under Austrian media law for having exercised prohibited influence on criminal proceedings. He was acquitted but on appeal by the prosecution was convicted.

He complained to the European Commission that this violated his right to freedom of expression under Art 10 but his complaint was dismissed because the conviction was prescribed by law and aimed at maintaining the authority and impartiality of the judiciary.

Applying the rules as the previous case law has demonstrated, the Court said that:

- the only issue was whether the interference was justified under Art 10(2)

- the impugned conviction was 'prescribed by law'

- Worm could reasonably have foreseen the result of this prescribed law

- the conviction aimed at 'maintaining the authority and impartiality of the judiciary' which is a legitimate aim under the Convention

- the reasons given by Austria in light of the case as a whole were 'relevant and sufficient'.

Worm's article had gone beyond the acceptable boundary because it intended to convey the impression that a criminal court could not possibly do anything other than convict, which in pre-judging the judge could have prejudiced the fair trial of the former politician.

12.8 Human Rights Act 1998

The paramount importance of freedom of expression is reinforced by specific provisions in the Human Rights Act 1998 ss 11, 12 and 13 (see section 3.8). The provisions of ss 11–13 of the HRA are intended to emphasise and reinforce the great importance that English law affords to freedom of expression. As Lord Steyn said in *Simms* (quoted above) 'it is the lifeblood of democracy'.

ACTIVITY

Self-assessment questions

1 How is freedom of expression defined in the ECHR?

2 What are the six types of activity named in Art 10(2) of the ECHR that may be used to limit freedom of expression.

3 Give an example of each of them.

4 Because exercising freedom of expression carries duties and responsibilities, to what three things, besides formalities, might it also be subject?

5 There are additional requirements to all of the above – what are they?

6 Give an example of each.

12.9 Anti-terrorism laws

Terrorist attacks in recent years have led to a considerable number of new or amended laws designed to create, define, counter and deal with an array of new offences, and inevitably these have an adverse effect on freedom of expression. The Terrorism Act 2000 s 1 provided a broad definition of terrorism and it applied where a person either acted or threatened to act in a way involving one or more of five criteria when it occurred for the purpose of advancing a political, religious or ideological cause.

The five actions to which this applies are those that:

1 involve serious violence against a person

2 involve serious damage to property

3 endanger a person's life, other than the life of the person committing the crime

4 create a serious risk to the health or safety of the public or a section of the public

5 are designed seriously to interfere with or seriously to disrupt an electronic system.

It is not immediately apparent that legislation of this nature and with such objectives will restrict freedom of expression, as they involve criminal activities that no right-minded person would be likely to consider as an illegitimate restriction on what people can think, say or do. This statute was enacted prior to the atrocities that started with the 9/11 attack on the American World Trade Center followed by terrorist attacks in the UK. In the climate that ensued there has been a considerable hardening of attitude in favour of authoritarian legislation and towards limiting or removing freedoms that were hard-won over the centuries. However, the point cannot be made too often that it is vital to maintain a balance between rights and freedoms and duties and responsibilities.

12.10 United Nations periodic review report

On 5th March 2008 the Ministry of Justice reported that the UK was submitting its universal periodic review report to the UN. The purpose of this report was to show how the UK is fulfilling its human rights obligations and it outlined the work being done in promoting and protecting human rights at home and abroad. This is a relatively new UN procedure and involved what the Government described as a constructive three-hour discussion of information provided by the UK, by stakeholders and by the Office of the UN High Commissioner for Human Rights.

The review took place in Geneva on 10th April 2008 and the report of the UK's performance is available on the Internet (referenced at the end of this chapter). A total of 28 suggestions were made to the UK representatives during the session from a variety of interested states including Algeria, Cuba, Ecuador, Egypt, Indonesia and the Russian Federation. Iran was particularly concerned about what they saw as a wide range of human rights abuses in the UK:

> '34. The Islamic Republic of Iran noted the concerns expressed by various human rights mechanisms about a series of human rights violations in the United Kingdom, including with regard to the increasing racial prejudice against ethnic minorities, asylum-seekers and immigrants, the increase in the incidence of domestic violence, including sexual violence against children within families, schools and detention centres. It also noted concerns expressed at the disproportionately high number of "stop and searches" carried out by police against members of ethnic or racial minorities, and the "profiling" in counter-terrorism efforts by the Government officials as well as the abuse of counter-terrorism laws which are perceived to target the Muslim population. It noted concerns at the grave situation of journalists and human rights defenders in Northern Ireland, including cases of death threats, arrests and detention, and cases of attacks on Muslim graves. The Islamic Republic of Iran asked about the concrete measures taken by the United Kingdom to address the said deteriorating human rights situation.'

Robert Burns' famous poem is a reminder of how important it is to be open to other people's perceptions:

> 'O wad some Power the giftie gie us
> To see oorsels as ithers see us!'

With particular regard to concerns about freedom of expression in the UK there were a number of points made:

- use of Official Secrets legislation to prevent matters of public interest from being aired, including gagging public servants, whether or not matters of national interest were involved

- reform of libel laws was called for to end 'libel tourism' where people from outside the UK 'forum shop' because they can obtain huge damages in English courts

- Official Secrets Act powers have been 'exercised to frustrate former employees of the Crown from bringing into the public domain issues of genuine public interest and can be exercised to prevent the media from publishing such matters

- the Terrorism Act 2006's 'broad and vague' definition of 'encouragement of terrorism' which can result in a jail sentence of up to seven years' imprisonment was criticised

- the intention to increase the period of detention without charge from 14 to 28 days caused concern, and more so when it was learned that the Government was intent on raising the time to 42 days

- the way the UK has treated the Chagos Islanders was also criticised.

On the positive side there were a couple of appreciative responses for action taken to abolish the common law offences of blasphemy and blasphemous libel, and for the enactment of civil partnership legislation recognising unions between lesbian and gay couples.

KEY FACTS

Freedom of expression is an ancient right found in the common law (for example *Bushell's Case* (1670)) and constitutionally embodied as Art 9 of the Bill of Rights 1689

It is *intrinsically* important being valued for its own sake and *instrumentally* important serving broad objectives essential to democracy and the rule of law

Its modern global expression is Art 19 of the UDHR and its European format is Art 10 of the ECHR

Art 10(1) freedom of expression is qualified by countenancing licensing of broadcasting, television and cinema enterprises

Art 10(2) says that because of the duties and responsibilities that go along with freedom of expression there must be a whole raft of circumstances where it can be restricted or removed in accordance with law necessary in a democratic society

Those circumstances are:
- national security, territorial integrity, or public safety
- preventing disorder or crime
- protecting health or morals
- protecting the reputation or rights of others
- preventing disclosure of information received in confidence
- maintaining the authority and impartiality of the judiciary

Useful resources

Article XIX Global Campaign for Free Expression: www.article19.org/.

The Chagos Islanders: http://www.chagos.org/home.htm.

UNIVERSAL PERIODIC REVIEW Report of the Working Group on the Universal Periodic Review United Kingdom of Great Britain and Northern Ireland, UN GA HUMAN RIGHTS COUNCIL Eighth session Agenda item 6 A/HRC/8/25 23rd May 2008: http://lib.ohchr.org/HRBodies/UPR/Documents/Session1/GB/A_HRC_8_25_United_Kingdom_E.pdf.

Further reading

Amos, M, *Human Rights Law* (Hart Publishing, 2006), 415–448.

Crumper, P, 'The Protection of Religious Rights under s 13 of the Human Rights Act 1998', PL 2000, Sum, 254–265.

Evans, C, *Freedom of Religion under the European Convention on Human Rights* (Oxford University Press, 2001).

Foster, S, *Human Rights and Civil Liberties* (2nd edn, Pearson Longman, 2008), 352–485.

McCormick, N and Riza, L, 'Case Comment: Privacy – The Bottom line', Ent LR 2008, 19(8), 178–179.

Ovey, C and White, R C A, *Jacobs & White The European Convention on Human Rights* (4th edn, Oxford University Press, 2006), 317–334.

Swepston, L, 'Human Rights Law and Freedom of Association: Development through ILO Supervision', (1998) *International Labour Review* 169.

FREEDOM OF ASSEMBLY AND ASSOCIATION ■

AIMS AND OBJECTIVES

By the end of this chapter, you should be able to:

■ explain the scope of each freedom and differentiate freedom of association from that of assembly

■ recognise the importance of association especially in connection with employment

■ identify the conflicting interests inherent in the right to assemble for purposes of legitimate protest and entitlement of others not to be unduly disturbed

■ identify international human rights law with regard to these freedoms

■ consider relevant domestic and European case law.

Freedom	Quotation	Source
Association	'The right to freedom of association also includes the right to independence from government and employer interference and the right for trade unions to elect officials and organise their own affairs.'	Freedom of Association and Protection of the Right to Organise Convention, 1948
Assembly	'In Northern Ireland there is no constitutional guarantee of freedom of assembly or to rights to public political expression. Rights exist only as common law in so far as that which is not prohibited or restricted is permitted. It has been suggested that any constitutional settlement in Northern Ireland should include a Bill of Rights.'	*Politics in Public: Freedom of Assembly and the Right to Protest – a Comparative Analysis*, by Neil Jarman, Dominic Bryan, Nathalie Caleyron and Ciro de Rosa

■ Figure 13.1 Association and assembly

13.1 Strength in numbers

People have long recognised that there is strength in numbers. Mutual solidarity and sometimes safety may be realised by standing together and presenting a united face, whether against oppressive rulers, potential invaders, powerful and self-interested employers or for that matter against anyone else who might pose a threat. Thus, although freedom to associate and to assemble are important rights for everyone, they are of especial importance to those who would otherwise be weak or ignored and who need to combine to further a common purpose.

13.2 Employment

Freedom to associate and assemble has special relevance to employment. The need for workers to protect themselves against powerful exploitative employers was recognised both domestically through the growth of trades unions and *via* the International Labour Organisation (ILO), the 'tripartite UN agency that brings together government, employers and workers of its member states in common action to promote decent work throughout the world' according to its website (referenced at the end of the chapter).

The ILO was the first specialised agency of the United Nations (UN) set up (or more correctly reconstituted) in 1946 and is the only surviving organ of the League of Nations originally established after the First World War. Its functions today are to promote social justice and ensure recognition internationally of human and labour rights. Its survival for almost a century is a tribute to recognition of the importance of protecting workers, which is manifested by international conventions laying down minimum employment standards. The purposes are to encourage and promote improved labour relations, working conditions, collective bargaining, recognition of workers' organisations and much else.

As societies developed, their ability to co-operate and organise grew and employers recognised the benefits of mass production. Therefore, understanding gradually emerged that collective capitalist and labour co-operation was desirable. Politically the ability to protest about matters of concern is an essential freedom in all societies democratic or otherwise and where it does not exist human rights are placed in jeopardy. Although this eventually grows into a wider freedom of expression it is a necessary prerequisite that people should have the right first of all to associate together and to reinforce this by joining together in organisations or assemblies to represent their views.

An early manifestation of what is now recognised by Art 11 of the ECHR was the growth of the trade union movement in the nineteenth and twentieth centuries in the UK and elsewhere. Although in the UK the influence of worker representation was heavily curtailed in the 1980s by the then Conservative administration in response to excessive workers' demands, strikes and disruption, it is important to recognise that only by collective resolve and organisation can individuals work together to resist the power of the employer, some of which are transnational corporations exerting influence way beyond that of many nation states.

Thus, although freedom of association and assembly exist as separate yet often interconnected rights, they are also frequently claimed and exerted in conjunction with other rights such as freedom of speech and expression, sometimes but not necessarily in an employment context.

13.3 Domestic law

Under domestic law some organisations such as the British National Party (BNP), whilst perhaps representing potentially divisive views, are usually allowed to go about their business provided that they do not overstep the mark, in which case statute has from time to time curbed undesirable activities. An example would be the Public Order Act 1936 s 1 which provides that:

 ' . . . any person who in any public place or at any public meeting wears uniform signifying his association with any political organisation or with the promotion of any political object shall be guilty of an offence:

Provided that, if the chief officer of police is satisfied that the wearing of any such uniform as aforesaid on any ceremonial, anniversary, or other special occasion will not be likely to involve risk of public disorder, he may, with the consent of a Secretary of State, by order permit the wearing of such uniform on that occasion either absolutely or subject to such conditions as may be specified in the order.'

The political background of the 1930s and the activities of Sir Oswald Mosley and his British Union of Fascists were factors in the enactment of the 1936 legislation, and the fact that perceived threats today come from elsewhere helps to explain what might otherwise appear to be an anomaly. Remembrance parades and similar occasions do not offend this statute but displays of defiance at funerals, by the IRA during the Northern Ireland troubles, did do so. It is understandable that such restrictions are still desirable so as to avoid raising levels of tension when society is under general threat from terrorist activities.

Over the centuries there have been occasions when the authorities have curtailed particular demonstrations. One instance was the 'Peterloo Massacre' at Manchester in 1819 when a demonstration, whose purpose was to call for parliamentary reform, was savagely put down by magistrates and militia at a cost of 18 civilian lives and some 500 injuries which included about 100 women. Some of the organisers were tried and imprisoned and Parliament enacted no fewer than six statutes to tighten up restrictions on public demonstrations.

Government has over the years used a combination of common law and statute to keep a balance between maintenance of law and order on the one hand and the limits of legitimate expression of views by the populace on the other, and what is acceptable to government has varied considerably from one era to another. The ideal position is that people should be able to do what they like so long as their behaviour is not threatening to others, and there should be a general unwillingness to ban individuals and groups of people purely because of their beliefs. If people's behaviour exceeds acceptable but clearly prescribed limits, however, the common law and more usually these days statute create and define offences which vary considerably in severity.

Thus, further to the Public Order Act 1936 there are today a number of UK statutes which impose more restrictions on individual freedom of association or assembly or both. The general context is that the ECHR allows restrictions that are 'prescribed by law' and 'necessary in a democratic society' to protect legitimate interests defined in Art 11.

Statute	Freedom of association
Public Order Act 1936	Creates offence of wearing a uniform in a public place, or at a public meeting, which signifies association with any political organisation or promotes a political objective
Terrorism Act 2000 and Anti-terrorism, Crime and Security Act 2001	Bans proscribed listed organisations if the Secretary of State believes they are concerned with terrorism
Terrorism Act 2006	Introduces new offences and extends the Home Secretary's powers

Figure 13.2 Examples of domestic provision

The right to freedom of association can be somewhat amorphous, whereas the right to freedom of assembly is more direct and obvious. The Public Order Act 1986 as amended by the Criminal Justice and Public Order Act 1994 statutorily defines a number of offences that may arise out of assemblies that are not discussed here but which include riot, violent disorder, affray, fear of provocation of violence, and causing alarm and distress. Some of these statutorily define ancient common law offences whilst others create new offences designed to address current threats to society.

A brief summary of some of the main provisions is contained in the following table:

Section	Provision
11	Imposes a duty (if it is reasonably practicable to do so) on organisers of processions to give six days' advance notice to the police
12	Gives the police power to impose conditions on processions
13	Provides limited power for police to ban a procession if the Chief Constable reasonably believes that the s 12 powers will not be adequate
14	Allows police to impose conditions on static public assemblies
14A	Authorises chief police officer to apply to local authority for an order prohibiting trespassory public assemblies
14B	Creates offences arising out of trespassory public assemblies for organisers and participants
14C	Gives police power to stop persons from proceeding to trespassory public assemblies

Figure 13.3 Public Order Act 1986 as amended

A trespassory assembly is one involving 20 or more people coming together on land to which the public have no rights of access, or only limited rights. The police still possess wide residual common law powers to take action against people where there has been a breach of the peace.

CASE EXAMPLE

Steel (and another) v United Kingdom (24838/94) (1998) 28 EHRR 603

Steel was arrested and detained for 44 hours whilst protesting against a grouse shoot by walking in front of the guns, and was charged with breach of the peace. She was convicted and sentenced to 28 days' imprisonment. N (the other person referred to above) was arrested at a conference centre where she was protesting against arms sales. She was held for seven hours but no proceedings were taken against her.

They both complained to the European Court of Human Rights contending *inter alia* that their arrests and detention were not 'prescribed by law' as breach of the peace is so widely based. Steel's treatment was held to be lawful and N had been innocent throughout. Although in the one case there had been violations of the ECHR, the offence of breach of the peace was not impugned despite the very different factual circumstances to which it could be applied.

13.4 International instruments

There are a number of conventions containing provisions designed to protect and promote freedom of association and assembly both in a general sense and for employment purposes. The number and variety of these indicate how important the principles are, and they may also relate to refugees and children. The following table sets out a summary of some of the more important ones.

Instrument	Subject matter	Article	Date
Universal Declaration of Human Rights	Freedom of assembly and association and right to join trade unions	Arts 20 and 23	1948
Convention Relating to Status of Refugees	Refugees' rights to participate in the same non-political, non-profit-making associations and trade unions as others enjoy	Art 15	1951
International Covenant on Economic, Social and Cultural Rights (ICESC)	Guarantees rights to form and join trade unions, establish national and international federations, and to strike	Art 8	1966
International Covenant on Civil and Political Rights (ICCP)	Elaborates in more detail the UDHR's principles of freedom of assembly (Art 21) and association (Art 22)	Arts 21 and 22	1966
Convention on the Rights of the Child	Specifically relates rights to associate and assemble to children with recourse in default to the UN Committee on the Rights of the Child	Art 15	1989
UN Basic Principles on the Use of Force and Firearms by Law Enforcement Officials	A UN 'standard setting' document emphasising that police forces should not refuse to allow peaceful and lawful demonstrations	Principles 12, 13 and 14	1990
ILO Conventions	Establish and build on principles asserting right of employers and workers to enjoy freedoms of association and assembly	1948	Various

■ Figure 13.4 International provisions

13.5 Assembly and association

'Assembly' has a number of meanings, but in connection with the ECHR it refers to people's freedom to gather or meet together or the place where they are able to do so, with the implication that this happens at a particular time and location and which also includes marches and processions.

'Association' is the act or process of organising in order to pursue particular interests and so is a longer term ongoing process.

These should not be construed as rigid or restrictive definitions. The two are often lumped together somewhat indiscriminately but it is important to keep in mind the differences between assembly and association. Art 11 is closely connected with Arts 9 and 10 and cases often involve all three. Freedom of assembly and association exists both generally and more specifically in relation to the right to be involved in trade union activities, but both are subject to limitations specifically in respect of:

- national security
- public safety
- prevention of disorder or crime
- protection of health or morals
- protection of other people's rights and freedoms.

For the avoidance of doubt the need to impose restrictions, over and above those applicable to other members of society, is acknowledged in relation to members of the armed forces, police and in connection with the administration of the state, and this is sufficiently vague to encompass a wide range of persons and so would, for example, include prisoners.

Art 11 refers to more than freedom to protest in a peaceful manner and to hold meetings and demonstrations. In some circumstances there may be a positive obligation on the part of the state to protect people with different views, so there is a balance to be achieved between demonstrators and counter-demonstrators.

13.5.1 UDHR Art 20

The Universal Declaration of Human Rights sets out these freedoms in the simplest form, establishing the principle that:

'1. Everyone has the right to freedom of peaceful assembly and association and protection from compulsion

2. No one may be compelled to belong to an association.'

13.5.2 EU Charter freedoms

Art 12 of the EU Charter covers similar ground but not in identical terms, making:

- specific reference to 'levels' at which the freedoms should be enjoyed, and
- identifying political, civic and trade union rights.

The scope is thus wider than that of the Council of Europe Convention and it operates at all levels from the EU down. The emphasis on civic and political rights is understandable in the context of expanding the EU.

'1. Everyone has the right to freedom of peaceful assembly and to freedom of association at all levels, in particular in political, trade union and civic matters, which implies the right of everyone to form and to join trade unions for the protection of his or her interests.

2. Political parties at Union level contribute to expressing the political will of the citizens of the Union.'

Freedom of assembly is here not limited to the state's duty to allow assemblies to take place, but places a positive duty (although not guarantee) on them to take appropriate positive measures such as providing adequate security. There is more of an economic dimension to Art 12 of the Charter.

13.5.3 ECHR Article 11

The European Convention says that:

'(1) Everyone has the right to freedom of assembly and to freedom of association with others, including the right to form and to join trade unions for the protection of his interests.

(2) No restrictions shall be placed on the exercise of these rights other than such as are prescribed by law and are necessary in a democratic society in the interests of national security or public safety, for the prevention of disorder or crime, for the protection of health or morals or for the protection of the rights and freedoms of others.

This article shall not prevent the imposition of lawful restrictions on the exercise of these rights by members of the armed forces, of the police or of the administration of the State.'

13.6 Analysis of 'association'

Freedom of association implies the right to convene with other like-minded persons and to organise actions and movements in order to pursue common interests. The main types of

organisation covered by the term 'association' are political parties and trade unions, but a variety of private bodies have been the subject of litigation as can be seen from the examples in the following table, in chronological order:

Type of association	Case	Citation
Professional bodies	*Le Compte and others v Belgium*	(1981) 4 EHRR 1
Doctors	*Platform Arzte fur das Leben v Austria*	(1991) 13 EHRR 204
Taxicab operators	*Sigurjonsson v Iceland*	(1993) 16 EHRR 462
NGOs	*'Negotiate Now' v United Kingdom*	(1995) 19 EHRR 93
Political parties	*Ahmed v United Kingdom*	(2000) 29 EHRR 1
Hunting clubs	*Chassagnou and others v France*	(2000) 29 EHRR 615
Trade unions	*Wilson and the NUJ and Others v United Kingdom*	(2002) *The Times*, 5.7.02
Freemasons	*Grande Oriente D'Italia Di Palazzo Giustiniani v Italy*	(2002) 34 EHRR 22
RSPCA	*RSPCA v Attorney-General*	[2002] 1 WLR 448
Hunting	*Friend v Lord Advocate*	[2007] UKHL 53
Racial hatred	*R v Umran Javed and Others*	[2007] EWCA Crim 2692
Political parties	*Galstyan v Armenia*	[2007] ECHR 26986/03

Figure 13.5 Associations

13.6.1 Case law on association

Article 11(1) specifically identifies the individual's right to form and join a trade union for the protection of his interests and is the only internal example of what the article is designed to address in protecting a person's right to associate. The need to protect people in connection with employment must therefore have been high on the agenda of the framers of this article. That makes the following case example particularly interesting because it concerns workers who were being forced by changes in the law to become members of a closed-shop trade union that they did not want to join, despite already being union members. Forcing association on employees in such circumstances was not what Art 11 was designed to do.

CASE EXAMPLE

Young, James and Webster v United Kingdom (1982) 4 **EHRR 38**

Three employees had each joined the staff of British Rail prior to 1975 when a closed-shop arrangement was agreed between three trade unions and the employer, which for the future required all employees to belong to one of the unions. The claimants regarded this as a breach of their right to freedom of association but could not claim exemption on grounds of religious belief, which would have been allowed both under the closed-shop agreement and by English law. The three employees were dismissed but prevented from claiming redundancy payments because their dismissal was not classified as legally unfair.

The Court held by a majority of 18 to 3 that there had been a breach of their Art 11 rights to freedom of association by reason of UK legislation. The UK was responsible for any violation because, although the immediate cause of the dispute was the 1975 agreement, it was really domestic UK law that made the agreement lawful and thus provided justification for their dismissal. The threat of dismissal involving loss of livelihood, especially where the employees in question had been engaged prior to this new legal regime coming into effect, constituted a most serious form of compulsion that struck at the very substance of the freedom of association guaranteed by Art 11.

One of the purposes of Art 11 was the protection of personal opinion, and the kind of pressure being exerted here to force them to join particular unions against those personal convictions also fundamentally contradicted the core purposes of Art 11, so much so that the mere fact that they were obliged to provide reasons for refusing in itself provided a further violation.

The restriction was not justifiable as being necessary in a democratic society as it had not been demonstrated to the Court that it was proportionate to the aims being pursued. No special reason had been advanced to require existing British Rail employees to join specific designated unions when the closed-shop agreement was concluded. The unions could have protected the interests of their members quite adequately without forcing employees who had objections to join a union to which they took exception.

Two years later there was a significant case that fell to be determined in the ongoing struggle between the Government and unions, the former being determined to reduce and where possible eliminate union power at GCHQ, the Government's communications headquarters. Closed shops are one thing, but when the executive cites national strategic and security interests to support its actions the courts are usually warned off and not inclined to challenge governmental decisions and action.

329

CASE EXAMPLE

Council of Civil Service Unions v Minister for the Civil Service [1985] AC 374

Council of Civil Service Unions and Others v United Kingdom App No 11603/85 (1988) 10 EHRR CD269

From 1947 onwards staff employed at GCHQ enjoyed trade union membership but in 1983 the Minister for the Civil Service (the Prime Minister) changed employees' conditions of service without prior consultation and refused to allow union membership.

Judicial review was successfully sought to challenge this before Glidewell J but the Court of Appeal allowed the Minister's appeal and the House of Lords held that although executive action based on common law or the use of prerogative power was not immune from review, the requirements of national security outweighed those of fairness, these being matters for the executive to assess and decide.

The European Commission of Human Rights had little hesitation in ruling that complaints made under Arts 11 and 13 were manifestly ill-founded. The restrictions were lawful under the second sentence of Art 11(2) even though they interfered with the applicants' rights under Art 11(1).

Art 11(2) provides the margin of appreciation for states to apply taking into consideration 'national security or public safety, for the prevention of disorder or crime, for the protection of health or morals or for the protection of the rights and freedoms of others', but there is specific additional provision to ensure that members of the armed forces, police and unspecified others involved in the administration of the state do not take advantage of the article. That, of course, does not prevent them from trying, as the next Case Example demonstrates.

CASE EXAMPLE

The Staff Side of the Police Negotiating Board, John Francis v The Secretary of State for the Home Department [2008] EWHC 1173 (Admin)

The police provide an interesting example to examine here because as Keene LJ said in this case they are probably unique amongst civilian workers because they are statutorily prohibited by ss 64 and 91 of the Police Act 1996 from engaging in strikes or other

CONTINUED ▸

industrial action and so cannot withdraw their labour in order to promote their working conditions and remuneration. Because they have thus indirectly been deprived of one important element of their freedom to associate in strike activity (although not prevented from assembling to protest) Parliament had provided them with independent negotiating and arbitration machinery to provide some measure of protection.

Although there are 43 separate police forces, pay is negotiated nationally. The Home Secretary is the government minister responsible and she deals with the Police Negotiating Board (PNB), a statutory body continued in being by the 1996 Police Act. In the event of failure to reach agreement the matter is referred to the Police Arbitration Tribunal (PAT) whose awards have the status of recommendations by the PNB as if it were an agreement by both sides. The final stage of the process is that this goes forward as a recommendation to the Secretary of State. This was done in December 2007 but the Home Secretary declined to implement it in full, the first time that had happened and causing widespread anger and dismay amongst police officers.

The police made an unsuccessful application for judicial review because since amendment of the regulations in 2000 the pay award no longer depends as previously on those regulations but the final determination is made by the Secretary of State. The police would seem to have had a strong case for judicial review based on legitimate expectation but Keen LJ said that he had first to deal with the Art 11 aspect, recognising the argument in favour:

> **J** 'What is contended on behalf of the claimants is that the Strasbourg jurisprudence establishes the "compensatory principle", that is to say, where there is no right to strike, the State must make available other means of securing the right to freedom of association. Reliance is placed for that proposition on *Schmidt and Dahlstrom v Sweden* [1976] 1 EHRR 632.'

However, there had been a clear contrary precedent in the case of *Council of Civil Service Unions v United Kingdom* where union representation had been summarily withdrawn from GCHQ by the then Minister for the Civil Service (and Prime Minister) Mrs Thatcher, who had been successful in that litigation citing national security.

CONTINUED ▸

> **J** 'I conclude, therefore, that well before the time of the decision now under challenge, it had become established that the legitimate expectation of police officers as to PNB recommendations/PAT awards on pay was that they would be carefully considered, would not be lightly set aside and would only be departed from for good reasons . . . I am quite satisfied that the claimants had no entitlement to an expectation that reasons of grave or serious national importance would be required for such a departure.'

Treacy J agreed without comment, and so although the boot would have been on the other foot had the government wished to accept an independent arbitration decision that was being resisted by employees, Art 11 was of insufficient weight here to protect the police from the Secretary of State.

There were similarities between the police case and that of the Prison Officers Association in *Ministry of Justice v Prison Officers Association* [2008] EWHC 239 (QB) where the Ministry sought to extend an injunction previously granted preventing strike action by prison officers because of another refusal by the government to implement the terms of a pay award in accordance with the recommendations.

An injunction being an equitable remedy, the POA argued that the government had behaved inequitably and it should therefore be lifted. The High Court found in favour of the government, holding that 'it was impossible to conclude that the claimant's conduct was so inequitable as to justify the withholding of the injunction' and bearing in mind that injunctions are equitable and therefore discretionary remedies.

It is clear, therefore, that the government is able within the law to exercise its executive discretion or powers to restrict the ability of its police and prison officers, and others in analogous positions, from enjoying the full scope or Art 11, constrained and qualified as it is by the provisions of Art 11(2).

13.7 Meaning of 'assembly'

The principles upon which the freedom of assembly have evolved were largely developed in the context of political demonstrations, according to Clayton and Tomlinson, *The Law of Human Rights*, para 16.57 which was quoted by Lord Hope of Craighead in his speech in *Whaley v Lord Advocate* [2007] UKHL 53; 2008 SC (HL) 107 at para 25.

The freedom to assemble peacefully sometimes overlaps with that of association and the example given by Lord Hope is where people assemble or move in procession in support of their right to belong to a trade union. When they are taken together they combine to provide protection in circumstances where people do not necessarily belong to any particular association, or where they have not previously formed any plan or intention, but do get together in an assembly to demonstrate about some issue of public interest.

He goes on to say that there is a threshold to cross before Art 11 becomes engaged. At the core of freedom of assembly is the guarantee that it is a fundamental right in a democracy and, as such, a foundation of such a society as expressed in *Rassemblement Jurassien Unitö Jurassienne v Switzerland* (1979) 17 DLR 93 @ 119. Lord Hope agreed with Lord Bingham that where the activity which brings people together is prohibited, the actual effect is to restrict their right to assemble.

The instant case was attempting to assert the right of assembly for sporting or recreational purpose and fell well short of the kind of assembly whose protection is essential and fundamental to the proper functioning of a modern democracy, and no decision of the European Court of Human Rights had gone anything like that far in defining and protecting the right of assembly.

13.7.1 Case law on assembly

ASE EXAMPLE

Ezelin v France (1992) 14 EHRR 362

This case involved an *avocat* who had been reprimanded by his professional body, the French Bar Council, for taking part in a demonstration against two court judgments that had been handed down. During the course of the demonstration graffiti were daubed on a building and judges were verbally abused by the crowd. It was not proved to the Commission that Ezelin had taken part in either of these activities but neither would he disassociate himself from them.

It was decided that, taking Arts 10 and 11 together, Art 10 dealing with freedom of expression was to be regarded in the circumstances of this case as *lex generalis* or general law whilst Art 11 which engaged freedom of assembly in this instance was to be treated as *lex specialis*, so it was not necessary to undertake separate consideration. Protection of personal opinions, secured by Art 10, was one of the objectives of freedom of peaceful assembly, so that Art 11 had to be considered in the light of Art 10.

A number of propositions were considered:

CONTINUED ▸

- The imposition of subsequent punitive measures may constitute a restriction on freedom of expression.
- The rules governing the profession of *avocat* are sufficiently clear to be prescribed by law and may apply even when carrying out non-professional activities.
- Prevention of disorder was a legitimate aim justifying interference with freedom of peaceful assembly and the punishment was because he had not disassociated himself from the unruly incidents during the demonstration.
- Proportionality when exercising rights of free expression and peaceful assembly means that restriction is not necessary in a democratic society unless the person in question has committed a reprehensible act whilst exercising his rights.
- The possibility that there might be counter-demonstrations does not remove a person's rights.

No charges had been brought after the criminal investigation into the events had been concluded and given that Ezelin's behaviour had been peaceful yet he was being punished, the Commission concluded by majority that there had been violation of his Art 11 rights.

 ASE EXAMPLE

R v Umran Javed and Others [2007] EWCA Crim 2692

An interesting comparison with this case is *R v Umran Javed and Others* involving the misuse of freedom of assembly. The appellants had been convicted and sentenced to six years' imprisonment for soliciting murder and four years for stirring up racial hatred contrary to Public Order Act 1986 s 18(1) at a demonstration purporting to object to the publication in Denmark of cartoons that were offensive to Muslims. The Lord Chief Justice, together with Davis and Simon JJ, upheld the convictions but reduced the sentences to four years and 30 months respectively.

The Lord Chief Justice quoted part of what the Common Serjeant had said at the outset of his sentencing remarks, which has a bearing on the freedoms under discussion here. Part of his judgment was that:

CONTINUED ▶

J

'. . . freedom of speech and assembly have long been jealously guarded by our laws but with freedom comes respect and responsibility, none of which was demonstrated by you and by the hard core of your fellow protestors on 3rd February last year ... but whatever your arguments with various European editors it is significant that no paper or magazine in this country followed suit ... What you were part of was the complete opposite of peaceful protest ... Everyone is entitled to freedom and protection under the law but no one is entitled to urge a perverted use of ideology to propagate distress and death'

The appellants did not appear to argue that their Convention rights were being contravened, but the case does provide insight into the other side of the coin, the misuse of available freedoms, and here the way in which the actual right of assembly was not curtailed or inhibited at the time of the demonstration. Rather, the police reacted as best they could to a dangerous situation, observed and recorded evidence, and subsequently brought effective prosecutions.

In some cases the behaviour of demonstrators seems to have been more of an irritant to others than to have comprised any choate offence and complaints made have resulted in the alleged miscreants being bound over to keep the peace. In *Hashman and Harrup v United Kingdom* (1999) 30 EHRR 241 saboteurs attempted to disrupt the Portman Hunt and on being so bound over they appealed to the Crown Court who depicted their behaviour as being *contra bonos mores* which seemed to translate as being 'wrong rather than right in the judgment of the majority of contemporary fellow citizens' and likely to be repeated 'unless it were checked by the sanction of a bind over'.

Although the Crown Court Judge agreed to state a case to the High Court, legal aid was refused and subsequent appeals having been lost; application was made to the European Commission, although the arguments were based mostly on freedom of expression rather than assembly. In any event the order did not comply with the requirement that the behaviour be prescribed by law, so the Convention had been breached.

KEY FACTS

1	Freedom of association means to be able to make common cause with others of similar interests in order to advance and develop mutual ideas and opinions
2	Freedom of assembly means being able to gather together in order to show solidarity and to march and protest in a peaceful manner, provided that this does not unduly interfere with other people's rights not be disturbed or threatened
3	In each case the ECHR Art 11 allows some constraints for everyone's benefit based on the following criteria: • a clear legal definition of any restrictions imposed • they must be necessary in a democratic society ie not arbitrary • for purposes of national security • public safety • prevention of disorder • prevention of crime • protection of health • protection of morals • protection of other people's rights and freedoms
4	The ECHR provisions reflect UDHR and EU Charter provisions fairly closely but with some variations
5	A wide variety of type of association is covered by Art 11
6	Rights connected with employment have played and continue to play an important role in Art 11
7	The continuing importance of the ILO also reflects the significance of labour relations in this rights area
8	Historically, government has always been concerned with maintaining law and order so there are fairly detailed rules backed by criminal sanctions for various types of unruly or provocative behaviour in public
9	Government is prepared to assert that national security overrules civil rights of association, ie to enforce executive authority over the judiciary which effectively precludes judicial review in some circumstances

CONTINUED ▸

KEY FACTS

10	The claim of priority because of national security has in recent years been extended from national security to cases involving the police and prison services to justify overruling pay and employment conditions awards

Useful resources

International Labour Organisation: http://www.ilo.org/global/lang-en/index.htm.

Further reading

Ewing, K, 'The Implications of the ASLEF Case, Case Comment', ILJ 2007, 36(4), 425–445.

Fenwick, H, *Civil Liberties and Human Rights* (4th edn, Routledge-Cavendish, 2007), 659–802.

Foster, S, *Human Rights and Civil Liberties* (2nd edn, Pearson Longman, 2008) 486–557.

Jarman, N, Bryan, D, Caleyron, N and de Rosa, C, 'Politics in Public: Freedom of Assembly and the Right to Protest – a Comparative Analysis': http://www.ccruni.gov.uk/research/csc/jarman98.htm.

Mead, D, 'The Right to Peaceful Process under the European Convention on Human Rights – A Content Study of Strasbourg Case Law', EHRR 2007, 4, 345–384.

Ovey, C and White, R C A, *Jacobs & White The European Convention on Human Rights* (4th edn, Oxford University Press, 2006), 335–344.

Walker, C, 'Case Comment: Police Powers/Public Order: Whether Commissioner of Police of the Metropolis may Delegate Functions Expressly Conferred on him by Statute', Crim LR 2008, 7, 562–567.

chapter 14 RIGHT TO MARRY

14.1 Global recognition

The right to marry and found a family is one that is recognised across the rights spectrum from the global provision in the Universal Declaration, reinforced by the International Covenant on Civil and Political Rights (ICCPR), to the European regime under the ECHR and in the EU's Charter of Fundamental Rights.

The UN Convention on Consent to Marriage, Minimum Age for Marriage, and Registration of Marriages is a treaty which stipulates standards that should be applied to marriage in respect of the matters referred to in its title. It came into force in 1964 but only has 16 signatories and 49 Parties. Whilst reiterating basic acceptable standards on the rights and obligations involved and the need for absence of discrimination, it nevertheless leaves it to individual States Parties to legislate on minimum age and does not even require the presence of the parties at the marriage ceremony.

A marriage ceremony where one or both parties are not present is called marriage by proxy and is legal in some parts of the world including the American states of California, Colorado, Texas and Montana. If neither party is present it is called 'double proxy'. Representation is achieved by using an attorney. Napoleon Bonaparte was married by proxy in 1810 to Archduchess Marie Louise and proxy marriages may occur during wartime when parties are not free to travel as they might wish. The concern with proxy marriages is that the absent party cannot be seen actively to consent to the arrangement.

In many parts of the world marriages are arranged for parties by their families; this sometimes gives rise to problems. The Forced Marriage (Civil Protection) Act 2007 was enacted to make provision for protecting individuals against being forced into marriage without their free and full consent, and connected purposes and whilst this does not have direct extra-territorial effect, it may help to influence courts in other legal jurisdictions to free people being held against their will.

The American Convention on Human Rights (1969) Art 17 recognises the institution of marriage as the natural and fundamental group unit of society to be entered into with the free consent of each party, recognising equal rights for children whether born within or outside wedlock.

The African Charter on Human and Peoples' Rights (the Banjul Charter) Art 20 requires States Parties to take appropriate legal measures to ensure that widows are not subjected to inhuman, humiliating or degrading treatment and to give them automatic guardianship and custody of their children, with the right to remarry the person of their choice.

The UN provisions do not acknowledge those cultures which provide for arranged marriages but the ECHR does, in that it says the right exists 'according to the national laws governing the exercise of this right'. On the other hand, the UDHR contains anti-discrimination provisions prior to, during and after marriage and the requirement of free and full consent of the intending spouses.

14.1.1 UDHR 1948 Article 16

'1 Men and women of full age, without any limitation due to race, nationality or religion, have the right to marry and to found a family. They are entitled to equal rights as to marriage, during marriage and at its dissolution

2 Marriage shall be entered into only with the free and full consent of the intending spouses

3 The family is the natural and fundamental group unit of society and is entitled to protection by society and the State.'

14.1.2 ICCPR 1966 Article 23

'1 The family is the natural and fundamental group unit of society and is entitled to protection by society and the State

2 The right of men and women of marriageable age to marry and to found a family shall be recognized

3 No marriage shall be entered into without the free and full consent of the intending spouses

4 States Parties to the present Covenant shall take appropriate steps to ensure equality of rights and responsibilities of spouses as to marriage, during marriage and at its dissolution. In the case of dissolution, provision shall be made for the necessary protection of any children.'

14.2 European recognition

14.2.1 ECHR 1950 Article 12

'Men and women of marriageable age have the right to marry and to found a family, according to the national laws governing the exercise of this right.'

14.2.2 EU Charter of Fundamental Rights 2000 Article 9

'The right to marry and the right to found a family shall be guaranteed in accordance with the national laws governing the exercise of those rights.'

14.3 Overview of ECHR case law

The right to marry in the UK involves a number of matters which encompass the right to found a family subject to the relevant national laws applicable. Courts may need to take into consideration the laws of consanguinity, issues of sexuality, migrants, prisoners, autonomy, nullity, separation and divorce. In some instances questions might also arise under the Art 8 right to respect for family and private life and possibly freedom of thought, conscience and religion under Art 9.

14.1 provides a summary for reference of some of these cases and indicates where each theme is discussed in this chapter.

Para	Context	Cases
14.4	Understanding the meaning of marriage	*Sheffield City Council v E* (also known as *Re E (Alleged Patient)*) (2005)
14.5	Relationship between Arts 8 and 12	*Marckx v Belgium* (1979) *R (Mellor) v Home Secretary* (2001) *Evans v United Kingdom* (2008)
14.6	Right of prisoners to marry and found a family	*K v Federal Republic of Germany* (1961) *Hamer v United Kingdom* (1979) *R (Mellor) v Home Secretary* (2001) *Dickson v United Kingdom* (2008)
14.7	Consanguinity and the right of in laws to marry	*B and L v United Kingdom* (2006)
14.8	Immigrants, illegal entrants, and asylum seekers	*R v Bhajan Singh* (1976) *F K (Kenya) v Home Secretary* (2008) *R (on the application Baiai and others) v Home Secretary* (2008)
14.9	Divorce/legal separation	*Airey v Ireland* (1980) *Johnston v Ireland* (1987)
14.10	Transsexuals	*Rees v United Kingdom* (1985) *Cossey v United Kingdom* (1991) *X, Y and Z v United Kingdom* (1997) *Bellinger v Bellinger* (2003) *L v Lithuania* (2008)
14.11	Tax	*Goodwin v United Kingdom* (2002) *Burden v United Kingdom* (2007)

■ Figure 14.1 Contexts

14.4 Understanding the meaning of marriage

Formulating a succinct definition of the legal meaning of marriage is difficult and the result would be oversimplistic because there are many rules to do with being male and female, same-sex partnerships, consanguinity, bigamy, domicile and residence, recognition of polygamy and so forth. Attitudes to marriage differ widely throughout Europe and elsewhere but the factors involved concern all legal systems in the modern world because of the widespread travel, work and migration patterns, and the very different standards and attitudes that are encountered. The picture is made more complex by the fact that religion is closely concerned with family status, so marriage may involve a combination of civil and religious contexts. Sometimes human rights law has to make difficult concrete decisions as to what lies at the root of marriage, which may require exercise of the inherent jurisdiction of the court.

CASE EXAMPLE

Sheffield City Council v E (also known as Re E (Alleged Patient))
[2005] 2 WLR 953

The preliminary issue to be decided was the extent to which one of the potential parties to a marriage had capacity to understand what was involved: in other words, what is the test for capacity to understand the meaning of marriage?

The local authority sought to prevent a female patient E, the first defendant, from marrying or associating with S, the second defendant. She was 21 years of age and suffered from spina bifida, and the local authority believed that she functioned at the level of a 13-year-old. S was 37 years old and had a history of sexually violent crimes and it was therefore a matter of concern to the authority that they proposed to marry.

The court was asked to determine first whether E was capable of understanding the general nature of the marriage contract and second the implications of the particular proposed marriage to S.

Munby J held that:

- it was insufficient simply for E to appreciate that she was taking part in a marriage ceremony and to understand the words used
- she had to understand the nature of the marriage contract
- it was necessary for her to be mentally capable of understanding the duties and responsibilities normally attached to marriage.

> **J** 'The test was capacity to understand the nature of the contract of marriage and not capacity to understand the implications of a particular marriage ... the analogy of consent to medical treatment was not appropriate because medical procedures varied whilst the contract of marriage was the same for everyone ... there was no true analogy between capacity to marry or the capacity to litigate.'

14.5 Relationship between Arts 8 and 12

The nexus between these two articles was tested when Paula Marckx and her infant daughter, Alexandra, complained that some aspects of Belgian law relating to inheritance and recognition of maternal affiliation infringed a number of articles of the ECHR, including Art 12. By majority the Commission had formed the view that Arts 8, 14 and Art 1 of Protocol 1 had been infringed but that Arts 3 and 12 had not and this was confirmed by the Court. The specific Art 12 aspect was consideration of whether parents of an illegitimate child were denied the rights of a married couple.

The Commission had previously expressed the opinion that Art 12 was not relevant but the applicants argued that the Belgian Civil Code failed to respect Paula Marckx's right *not* to marry and that this was, or should be, implicit in Art 12. The underlying reasoning was that if Alexandra was to be accorded the status of legitimacy, her mother would be forced to marry. The circumstances were that there was no legal obstacle affecting her choice either way. The Court could not accept the reasoning that because parents of illegitimate children did not have the same rights as married parents, this meant that Art 12 had been breached (*Marckx v Belgium* (1979) 2 EHRR 330)

CASE EXAMPLE

Evans v United Kingdom (Application No 6339/05) (2008) 46 EHRR 34

The umbrella effect of Art 8 over Art 12 can also be seen in *Evans v UK*. In July 2000 Ms Evans and her then partner J started fertility treatment but within a few months she was diagnosed with a pre-cancerous condition which meant that her ovaries needed to be removed. Before that was done she received IVF treatment and six embryos were conceived. Mutual consent was required under the Human Fertilisation and Embryology Act 1990, the effect of which was that either of them could withdraw consent prior to implantation of the embryo in her uterus once her ovaries had been surgically removed.

They were advised to wait for two years prior to implantation but by that time the relationship had ended and J withdrew his consent to further use of the embryos. Ms Evans sought an injunction to force him to restore his consent but the House of Lords eventually upheld the refusal to grant such injunction. In 2005 the President of the Chamber indicated that until final decision by a Grand Chamber the embryos should be preserved and on 10th April 2007 the case was finally heard by the Grand Chamber.

The basic point at issue here was whether Ms Evans had a right to be protected by the ECHR to found a family to whom she would be genetically related as there was no possibility of her conceiving her own child following the removal of her ovaries. The only links she had with that genetic possibility were the six stored embryos which under the 1990 Act were due to be destroyed. However, her complaint to the Grand Chamber relied entirely on Arts 2, 8 and 14 of the ECHR and no mention was made of the

CONTINUED ▸

specific Art 12 right to found a family. Under each of those headings the Court considered a number of matters as follows:

Art 2 Right to life	Art 8 Respect for private life	Art 14 Prohibition of discrimination
Beginning of life	Negative and positive obligations	Justification
Margin of appreciation	Margin of appreciation	
Embryo	Fair balance	
	Legal certainty	
	Decision to become genetic parent	
	IVF treatment	
	Embryo	

Figure 14.2 Interconnections

The Grand Chamber held that:

1   (Unanimously) there was no violation of Art 2 because in the absence of any European consensus on the scientific and legal definition of the beginning of life, the question came within the margin of appreciation and it could not be said that an embryo has a right to life (*Vo v France* (2005) 40 EHRR 12).

2   (By 13 votes to 4) there was no violation of Art 8 because although it was engaged, there were two irreconcilable interests here to be judged under a code established by primary legislation. The UK courts had treated this as an issue of the State interfering with private interests but it was more appropriate to decide whether competing public and private interests had been balanced and, as the requisite factor had throughout been 'joint treatment', it came within the margin of appreciation. A relevant consideration was the detailed and careful examination of the social, ethical and legal implications when the Act was passed. Greater weight could not be given to the one individual at the expense of the other.

3   The finding under Art 8 meant that no consideration of Art 14 was needed.

Besides demonstrating the thorough examination of issues and reaching a conclusion that at first sight may seem unfortunate and one-sided, this case shows how the specific right to found a family, apparently incidental but separate to the right to marry under Art 12, is in fact subsumed under the wider right to respect for family and private life provisions of Art 8 in which the scope of the qualification of Art 8(2) comes into play.

R (Mellor) v Secretary of State for the Home Department [2001] 3 WLR 533, and *Dickson v United Kingdom* (44362/04) (2008) 46 EHRR 41, discussed at section 14.6.2 below, are also relevant in this context.

14.6 Right of prisoners to marry and found a family

14.6.1 Marriage

In an early admissibility decision by the European Commission of Human Rights, *K v Federal Republic of Germany* (1961) 4 Yearbook 240; 6 Coll 17, it had been decided that a refusal to allow a prisoner to marry did not breach Art 12. Some 20 years later the Home Secretary sought to rely on that decision when a prisoner in England wished to marry and permission was refused (*Hamer v United Kingdom* Application No 7114/75 (1982) 4 EHRR 139). The Commission was not convinced by the comparison in light of the actual German law, to which reference had been made, and subsequent case law affecting prisoners and the conditions that prevailed at the time of the hearing.

It is legitimate for national law to regulate the exercise of the right to marry and it can take public interest into consideration on such matters as consent, capacity, consanguinity and the prevention of bigamy. The Commission recognised the twofold aspects of Art 12 and drew the distinction between the right to marry and to found a family. It was accepted that although the right to found a family is absolute, it does not follow that facilities to be able to procreate should always be made available: the fact that a person is in prison is, in effect, a handicap he has imposed on himself.

However, that is a different matter from preventing a prisoner from acquiring the change of status brought about by marrying. It involves no threat to the public, prison security or good order, and administratively it is only one of a number of practical arrangements that have to be made for prisoners, for example attending court, receiving visitors and so on. It might indeed be regarded as being the opposite of a threat to these things by helping to establish a stabilising and rehabilitating influence in the prisoner's life. The scope of national law to restrict the right to marry is not unlimited because if it was, Art 12 would be redundant. The Commission found unanimously that the Home Secretary's refusal amounted to a violation of Art 12.

14.6.2 Founding a family

National law can legitimately regulate the right to marry and prevent it occurring in some circumstances, for example by stipulating what consent or capacity is required, and preventing it on grounds of consanguinity or bigamy, but should not go further in depriving persons or categories of persons who otherwise have full legal capacity from marrying.

However, the distinction between marrying and founding a family *is* relevant in the custodial context. Early this century in *R (Mellor) v Secretary of State for the Home Department* [2001] 3

WLR 533 the refusal of the Home Secretary to give a convicted murderer serving a life sentence the opportunity to conceive a child with his wife by means of artificial insemination, and refusal of judicial review, were upheld by the Court of Appeal. The decision was made on the basis that there were no exceptional circumstances to justify the provision of facilities. Mellor argued that his Art 8 and 12 rights were infringed and the decision could not be justified on grounds of prison security.

The Court of Appeal held that the Home Secretary had not acted in breach of Mellor's Convention rights because part of his punishment was denial of the rights he sought. Interference with them did not amount to breach of his fundamental rights so long as it was proportionate to the punishment and deterrence aims of imprisonment. *Obiter* the court said that in some situations it might not be appropriate to deny prisoners the opportunity to conceive a child either naturally or by artificial insemination.

Whether it was the case that such circumstances did not breach the fundamental Art 8 and 12 Convention rights, and the separate question of what circumstances would justify allowing a prisoner to father a child in prison by artificial insemination, were tried recently in the case of *Dickson v United Kingdom* (44362/04) (2008) 46 EHRR 41. The first applicant was a convicted murderer who met the second applicant through a penal network and they subsequently married. They applied to be given the benefit of artificial insemination facilities as, given the age of the prisoner, it was unlikely that when he was eventually released it would be possible for them to conceive a child naturally, but permission was refused by the Home Secretary.

An application for judicial review was also refused and the European Court of Human Rights found that the refusal had not been arbitrary or unreasonable, nor did it fail to strike a fair balance between the competing interests involved. The principle was important and the matter was subsequently considered by a Grand Chamber, and primarily consideration was focused on Art 8 rather than Art 12, as is often the case where the right to marry and found a family is an aspect of broader issues arising from the right to respect for family and private life.

The UK Government relied on three grounds to maintain their so far successful policy of preventing prisoners fathering or conceiving children:

(i) Losing the opportunity to beget children was an inevitable and necessary consequence of imprisonment.

(ii) To allow prisoners guilty of certain serious offences to conceive children would undermine public confidence in the prison system by circumventing punitive and deterrent elements of the sentence.

(iii) Long-term absence of a parent would have a negative impact on any child conceived, and therefore on society as a whole.

In the Grand Chamber the previous decisions were reversed and the prisoner's complaint was upheld on four grounds:

(1) Applying *ELH v United Kingdom* (32094/96) (1998) 25 EHRR CD 158 Eur Com HR prisoners retained their Convention rights; restrictions on them had to be justified; and refusal of artificial insemination facilities engaged private and family life interests which incorporated the right to respect to become genetic parents.

(2) Applying *Evans v United Kingdom* (6339/05) [2007] 1 FLR 1990 (Grand Chamber) positive measures by the State were sometimes required even in the context of individuals with a fair balance to be struck between competing interests.

(3) With regard to prisoners, their inability to beget children was not an inevitable consequence of imprisonment, given the availability of artificial insemination facilities; forfeiture of rights should not automatically depend on not offending public opinion; rehabilitation was of increasing importance; and the State's positive obligations did not extend to preventing conception simply because two parents would not be available to care for the child until release.

(4) Government policy was not embodied in primary legislation here and failed to allow for genuine weighing of competing public and individual interests, which prevented the necessary assessment of whether the restriction was proportionate and placed too high a burden on the applicants to demonstrate that their circumstances were exceptional.

Given all these factors the case fell outside any acceptable margin of appreciation and it was held by the Grand Chamber by twelve votes to five that there had been a breach of Art 8, with no need therefore to consider Art 12.

ACTIVITY

Self-test questions

1 Which of the international instruments gives a widow the right to custody of her children and to marry the person of her choice?

2 Which one provides for protection of children?

3 Which one excludes discrimination?

4 What criteria does English law apply to ascertain whether a party understands sufficiently what marriage would involve were s/he to enter into a contract of marriage?

5 Do prisoners have the right to marry and/or found a family and in either case, if not why not?

14.7 Consanguinity

Close relatives are not allowed by law to marry and if such unions take place the crime of incest is committed. The reasons for this are social as well as the genetic undesirability of producing

children too closely connected by blood, although the two reasons may not always be connected. Consideration was given to prohibited degrees of relationship and how Art 12 impacts on English law in this regard in *B and L v United Kingdom* [2006] 42 EHRR 11. B had been cohabiting between 1995 and 2002 with his former daughter-in-law L, who was divorced from his son C, and in 2002 they enquired about getting married but were told that this was not allowed under English law which stipulates that whilst former spouses are alive the prohibited degrees of marriage prevent marriage by former father-in-law and daughter-in-law unless a private Act of Parliament was obtained to allow them to marry.

In this regard English law does pursue a legitimate aim in stipulating a bar on marriage between parents-in-law and children-in-law. It is aimed at protecting the integrity of the family and preventing harm to children who may be affected by changes in relationships between the adults in their family. It also aims to prevent sexual rivalry between parents and children, so for these three reasons the objective is legitimate.

The problem was that the bar was ineffective and could not prevent such relationships from forming; there was no illegality arising from the parties living together. In this case the child of the former marriage was living quite happily with his mother and his grandfather, was not suffering from any confusion or emotional insecurity as a result of his mother's relationship with her former father-in-law, and in any event there were no criminal sanctions to prevent such relationships. Indeed, it would be possible for them to marry if they petitioned for a personal Act of Parliament to authorise such marriage, and this had been done as recently as 1985 in the case of the Valerie Mary Hill and Alan Monk (Marriage Enabling) Act 1985. Although Parliament had been invited to consider the matter, no clear consensus had emerged and it seemed to be the case that domestic law here was based on tradition rather than on any modern justification and there was little incentive to change the law.

Inconsistency existed between the stated aims of this incapacity and the way that waivers had been obtained in the past which undermined the rationality and logic of English law. This was reinforced by the fact that where waivers had been obtained there was no evidence of any inquiries having been made into the possibility of harm occurring to children of the family. It seemed that there was little in the way of good reason for retaining an out-of-date law but no appetite on the part of the legislature for doing anything about it. For these reasons the Court held unanimously that this amounted to a violation of Art 12 of the ECHR.

14.8 Immigrants, illegal entrants, asylum seekers

Immigration law has been subjected to much change over the last 30 years or so and constant change over the last decade as it attempts to keep up with rapidly changing conditions in the modern world. The Court of Appeal held in the mid-1970s that an illegal immigrant who was detained in custody pending deportation could not insist on facilities being made available for him to marry someone who was a lawful UK resident (*R v Bhajan Singh* [1976] QB 198).

Singh entered the UK illegally in 1973 and, following his arrest and detention, he applied unsuccessfully to the Home Secretary to make facilities available so that he could marry at a local registry office. He argued that this was a marriage arranged by the respective families but that he had only found out about it after he had been arrested in April 1975.

His claim that the ECHR Art 12 gave him an inalienable right to marry, which could not be denied by the Home Secretary, was rejected by a strong Court of Appeal that included Lord Denning MR and Lord Widgery LCJ. The right to marry under Art 12 could be restricted and, in the circumstances of the appellant having been lawfully detained under ECHR Art 5(1)(f), the Secretary of State was entitled to refuse to facilitate his proposed marriage.

Because of the troubles in Kenya in 2007 many people fled from what had been one of the most stable of African states. One applicant for asylum in the UK (F) appealed against a decision by the Asylum and Immigration Tribunal that she could be safely returned with her daughter to Kenya if she relocated in a different area from that in which she had previously lived. She was a Kikuyu and her husband had refused to be recruited during the troubles by the Mungike, a violent militant traditionalist sect of which her father-in-law was a member. Because of her husband's refusal he had been murdered and she was threatened with forced marriage and female genital mutilation (FGM).

Her asylum claim was that she had a well-founded fear were she to be returned to Kenya that she would be subjected to FGM. The tribunal had accepted that that was the case but decided that it was not unreasonably harsh to expect her to relocate herself and daughter somewhere else in Kenya.

Her appeal was allowed (*FK (Kenya) v Secretary of State for the Home Department* [2008] EWCA Civ 119). The specificity of F's case, which related not to the existence of a well-founded fear of returning to her home village but to the reasonableness and safety of moving elsewhere in Kenya, had not been adequately addressed and F's case was remitted to the AIT so that the critical issue of the reasonableness of internal relocation could be properly determined.

In July 2008 the House of Lords heard a consolidated appeal involving Art 12 issues involving applications by a number of claimants: Baiai, Bigoku, Tilki and Trzcinska (*R on the application of Baiai and others v Secretary of State for the Home Department* [2008] UKHL 53. The Secretary of State was appealing against a decision ([2007] EWCA Civ 478) that the scheme established under the Asylum and Immigration (Treatment of Claimants, etc) Act 2004 s 19 involved a disproportionate interference with the respondents' right to marry under ECHR Art 12.

Under that scheme, anyone who was subject to immigration control had to have the Secretary of State's permission to marry and had to pay a fee of £295 unless they were settled or had been given entry clearance expressly so that they could marry. Permission would be granted if the applicant had a valid right to enter or remain for over six months and had at least three months' remaining time when the application was submitted.

The Secretary of State thought this scheme was reasonable on a number of grounds in that the right to marry is not absolute and the policy was proportionate. The House of Lords disagreed. It was lawful for a national authority to impose reasonable conditions to ensure that marriages of convenience were not being entered into, but the Strasbourg jurisprudence required the right to marry to be treated as a strong one and not subjected to conditions that would impair the essence of the right. Taken as a whole, the s 19 scheme did not come within the class of national regulatory laws which the article permitted.

> 'The vice of the scheme was that none of the conditions imposed by the Immigration Directorate's Instructions, although relevant to immigration status, had any relevance to the genuineness of the proposed marriage, which was the only relevant criterion for deciding whether permission should be given to an applicant who was qualified under national law to enter into a valid marriage.'

The blanket imposition of the rule had the effect of creating disproportionality. There had been a declaration of incompatibility but this was set aside subject to removal of discrimination between civil and Anglican ceremonies, and the House reinterpreted s 19 of the Act to conform with the ECHR and the Human Rights Act 1998.

Section 19(3)(b) should be read as meaning 'has the written permission of the Secretary of State to marry in the United Kingdom, such permission not to be withheld in the case of a qualified applicant seeking to enter into a marriage which is not one of convenience and the application for, and grant of, such permission not to be subject to conditions which unreasonably inhibit exercise of the applicant's right under article 12 of the European Convention'.

14.9 Divorce/legal separation

Although ECHR Art 12 deals with the right to marry and found a family, it does not address divorce or legal separation, and therefore any complaint made solely under Art 12 with regard to termination of marriage is unlikely to succeed. As Irish law used not to permit divorce, cases heard by the European Court have been concerned with judicial separation which was allowed. However, the fact that Art 12 deals with the commencement of marriage and establishment of the family does not mean that there has been no litigation, as can be seen from *Airey v Ireland* (1979–80) 2 EHRR 305 and *Johnston v Ireland* (1987) 9 EHRR 203.

Prior to 1995 Article 41.3.2 of the Irish Constitution provided that 'No law shall be enacted providing for the grant of a dissolution of marriage', which meant that it was not possible to obtain a decree of divorce in Ireland. By the mid-1990s this was thought to be discriminatory and a referendum was held to determine whether the constitution should be changed. By a slim margin of 50.3 per cent in favour and 49.7 per cent against change on a 62.2 per cent vote by the electorate, it approved amendment of the law relating to prohibition of divorce, which by virtue of the Fifteenth Amendment of the Constitution Act 1995 (amended Art 41.3.2) is now as follows:

'A Court designated by law may grant a dissolution of marriage where, but only where, it is satisfied that –

i. at the date of the institution of the proceedings, the spouses have lived apart from one another for a period of, or periods amounting to, at least four years during the previous five years

ii. there is no reasonable prospect of a reconciliation between the spouses

iii. such provision as the Court considers proper having regard to the circumstances exists or will be made for the spouses, any children of either or both of them and any other person prescribed by law, and

iv. any further conditions prescribed by law are complied with.'

One reason for the pressure for change can perhaps be gleaned from earlier case law. In *Airey* (1979) the applicant wished to petition for a judicial separation in the Irish High Court but no legal aid was available and she lacked the means to pay for the services of a lawyer. She was dependent on state benefits and maintenance from her husband but he had stopped paying her and would not agree to a separation agreement.

The European Commission held by majority that Art 6 had been violated, that consideration of Art 8 was unnecessary, and referred the matter to the European Court. The Court held by five votes to two that Art 6 taken alone had been breached and by four votes to three that there had been a breach of Art 8. Her right to the determination of her civil rights by way of a fair hearing had been effectively denied by inability to access the court, and this was compounded by the State having failed to provide an accessible legal procedure to determine the rights and obligations created by Irish family law. No decision was made under Art 12 for the reason given above.

In *Johnston v Ireland* (1987) 9 EHRR 203 a Grand Chamber of the European Court held by 16 votes to one that the absence of any provision for divorce in Ireland did not violate Arts 8, 9 or 12 nor was there any discrimination contrary to Art 14. Any questions arising with reference to divorce, nullity or legal separation are likely to be dealt with primarily under Art 8, together with any ancillary aspects that might arise with reference to Art 6 fair hearings, Art 13 right to an effective remedy, or prohibition of discrimination under Art 14.

Mr Johnston had married in Ireland in 1952 but since 1972 had lived with the second applicant who had borne him a daughter, the third applicant. They argued that Irish law violated the ECHR because of non-availability of divorce and that the consequential illegitimacy of the third applicant under Irish law violated Art 8.

The European Court held that neither Art 8 nor Art 12 was violated *vis-à-vis* the parents' relationship but that the illegitimate status of the daughter was a breach of Art 8 both in her own right and as it affected her parents.

> 'The natural family ties between the first and second applicants and their daughter required that she should be placed, legally and socially, in a position akin to a legitimate child. However, Irish law placed her in a legal situation which differed markedly from that of legitimate children. This resulted in a failure by Ireland to respect the applicant's family life.'

A recent House of Lords decision on the law in Northern Ireland, although based on Art 14 discrimination, has a close bearing on the effect of the status of marriage or not being married in connection with adoption, and endeavours to stay ahead of anticipated European Court jurisprudence were such an issue to be taken to Europe. In *P (A Child) (Adoption: Unmarried Couples), Re*, [2008] UKHL 38, the appellants were an unmarried couple, P and F, who were challenging a decision rejecting them as adoptive parents. P was the child's natural mother. F was not the biological father but had lived with P for 10 years and treated the child as a member of the family.

The rejection for adoption arose from the Adoption (Northern Ireland) Order 1987 which restricted eligibility as adoptive parents to married couples or single people. If marriage was a status, then so was not being married and the couple invoked ECHR Art 14 discrimination to support their appeal. The House of Lords, allowing the appeal, held that the state was entitled to take the view that marriage is an important institution and generally it is better for children to be raised by parents who are married to each other, but to apply such a rule in the present circumstances was quite irrational and defied everyday experience.

Getting to the nub of the matter, the present case was based on an obvious and straightforward fallacy that a reasonable generalisation could be turned into an irrebuttable presumption for individual cases, and although there was not as yet any European case on this particular brand of discrimination against marriage, the House anticipated that if one was heard it would find the existence of discrimination. The appellants were entitled to apply to adopt the child and the Northern Ireland's court decision was unlawful.

14.10 Transsexuals

There is some discussion of sexual identity in Chapter 10 in connection with the wider right of respect for private and family life. The issues arising in a number of cases involving transsexuals are similar in a number of respects, usually involving Arts 8 and 12 and sometimes Art 14. They indicate gradual changes in attitude and understanding over recent decades.

In *Rees v United Kingdom* (1985) 7 EHRR 429 the claimant was born with female characteristics but underwent medical conversion and lived as a male. The UK authorities refused to change his entry in the register of births or to issue him with a new certificate, which he claimed was contrary to Art 8, and he could not enter into a valid contract of marriage with a woman which he alleged was contrary to Art 12. The European Court held that the former was not arbitrary, given a wide margin of appreciation, nor was there any violation of Art 12, given that traditionally what marriage was recognised as doing was enshrining the relationship between persons of the opposite sex. This did not necessarily exactly deal with the question, however, as it left Rees as a female when he had been reassigned as male.

The opposite situation arose in *Cossey v United Kingdom* (1991) 13 EHRR 622 where the claimant was registered as male at birth but became female following treatment and gender reassignment surgery. She purported to marry, although the relationship broke down. Her claims were also based on Arts 8 and 12 in that her inability to obtain a replacement birth certificate invaded her right to privacy and neither could she contract a valid marriage. Her application was also dismissed because of the requirement to balance the general interest of the community with that of the individual. There had been no significant further scientific developments over the previous five years or so that would merit departing from *Rees* and there was no positive obligation on the UK to modify its birth registration system. Nor was there evidence to suggest any wholesale abandonment of the traditional concept of male–female marriage, and *Rees* was applied. No amended or new interpretation of Art 12 was required.

The case of *X, Y and Z v United Kingdom* (1997) 24 EHRR 143 differed from previous ones concerning transsexuals because it related to the granting of parental rights and the way the relationship between a child conceived by artificial insemination by donor and the person who fulfilled the paternal role should be treated in law. X was a female-to-male transsexual who had been living with Y since 1972. In 1992 Y gave birth to Z, who had been conceived through donor artificial insemination. Wishing to establish themselves in conventional family terms, X gave Z his surname and applied to be registered as Z's father, which was refused. The question was whether these circumstances breached Arts 8 and 14, and how this might differ from families created by marriage.

The Art 8 application was dismissed and the court did not consider Art 14. It said that 'family life' under Art 8 did not relate solely to families created by marriage and there were obvious *de facto* family ties between X, Y and Z. However, because there was little agreement between the Convention Contracting States on such issues and the law seemed to be in a transitional state on the subject, the UK would be allowed a wide margin of appreciation and was justified in taking a cautious approach. Amendments made in such times of transition might not turn out in the long term to be advantageous to children in Z's position. Generally, transsexuality raised difficult scientific, moral, legal and social issues which meant that the UK was not in breach of Art 8 by failing formally to recognise X as Z's father.

Following the enactment of the Human Rights Act 1998, domestic law became better able to address problems where earlier law had not been enacted fully taking into consideration the ECHR. For example, the Matrimonial Causes Act 1973 s 11(c) was found by the House of Lords to be incompatible with Arts 8 and 12 where a post-operative male-to-female transsexual appealed against a Court of Appeal decision that she was not validly married to her husband. She claimed that in light of the decision in *Goodwin* the previous year, her marriage should be recognised as valid from its inception and still subsisting (*Bellinger v Bellinger* [2003] UKHL 21; [2003] 2 AC 467).

Although her appeal was dismissed, a declaration of incompatibility was made. Were the House to make a declaration conferring validity on the marriage, this would represent a major change in the law on gender reassignment with far-reaching ramifications requiring consultation and it was not the function of the courts to undertake such responsibility in a piecemeal manner. The government had in fact announced the intention of introducing primary legislation on the subject and that was pre-eminently a matter for Parliament.

However, it was not possible for the House to construe the 1973 Act so as to give effect to the appellant's rights under Arts 8 and 12, and therefore a declaration of incompatibility under s 4 of the Human Rights Act 1998, following *Goodwin*, would have to be made.

A recent Lithuanian case illustrates some of the infelicities that continue to exist in this area of law and human rights. In *L v Lithuania* (2008) 46 EHRR 22 the complainant had experienced a number of administrative and medical problems including not being able to change his name on official documents and records or change his national identification number, which indicated he was still a female. He also wished to alter his university diploma so he could more easily apply for employment. He was concerned that he could not continue to secure hormone treatment and was being denied gender reassignment surgery because of Lithuania's failure to implement the necessary domestic law reform.

L's complaint was partially upheld because he was left in a distressing state of uncertainty in his private life and with regard to recognition of his true identity. Thus, in this regard the state had failed to strike the requisite fair balance between public and private interest. The judgment concluded that L's claim for pecuniary damages would be met provided that Lithuania enacted domestic legislation within three months but, failing that, he would be awarded €40,000 which would enable him to have the operation performed abroad.

ACTIVITY

Self-test questions

1 Why did English law on consanguinity violate the ECHR in *B and L v United Kingdom* (2006)?

CONTINUED ▸

ACTIVITY

Self-test questions

2 Do you consider it is reasonable for the Asylum and Immigration Tribunal (AIT) to rule that a woman should be sent back to her state of origin, where she was threatened with FGM, and told to live somewhere else than in her native village in (*FK (Kenya) v Secretary of State for the Home Department*) [2008])? Why did the AIT think it was a reasonable decision?

3 Consider the amended Art 41.3.2 of the Irish Constitution: giving reasons, do you think it now fully conforms to the ECHR?

4 Do you consider the House of Lords decision in *Bellinger* to be a good one or a compromise? What are your reasons?

14.11 Tax

Not all transsexual questions relate to the family or to relationships. *Goodwin v United Kingdom* (2002) 35 EHRR 447 involved a 65-year-old male-to-female transsexual who, because she was legally still a man, was obliged to continue paying national insurance contributions until the age of 65 whereas as a woman that obligation would have ceased at the age of 60. There was thus a financial element to her claim, but she was also concerned that her privacy had been breached because the retention of her former national insurance number meant that her employers had discovered her gender transfer: she having formerly been employed by them as a man.

The circumstances here were sufficient to allow the application to be granted. There were pension and retirement implications in her legal status remaining as that of a male, and this made her potentially subject to feelings of vulnerability, humiliation and anxiety. There did not appear to be any insuperable administrative problems such as would be involved by access to records, family law, affiliation, social security and insurance and no one else was likely to be prejudiced. What her situation did engage, however, was that the respect for her human dignity and freedom had been breached.

In particular with regard to Art 12, although it 'referred to the right of a man and woman to marry, such a right was not restricted to purely biological criteria. It was a fallacy to assert that post operative transsexuals had not been deprived of the right to marry since although free to marry an individual of the opposite sex to their former gender, they were precluded from marrying the opposite sex to their adopted gender. Accordingly, the fundamental essence of the right had been infringed'.

An unusual question arose in another recent case where complainant sisters alleged that their rights to peaceful enjoyment of their possessions were violated and they were discriminated against because they were cohabiting siblings and as such not able to take advantage of married status for other purposes (*Burden v United Kingdom* (2007) 44 EHRR 51). The violation of enjoyment of their possessions would occur because of the state's inheritance tax provisions.

The sisters were in their eighties and had lived together in their parental home for over three decades. Each had deliberately chosen neither to marry nor to take a partner. Because of house-price inflation the value of their house exceeded the inheritance tax exemption limit which meant that if one of the sisters died before the other she might be forced to sell the house to meet the tax liability. Despite having a stable and committed relationship they were denied the protection that married or civil partnership status would have provided to prevent that from happening. It was argued that this did not pursue a legitimate aim, but the complaint was ruled to be inadmissible as states enjoy a wide margin of appreciation in tax matters.

14.12 Protocol 7 Art 5

Although this says that spouses are to enjoy equality of private law rights and responsibilities between themselves and in relation to their children, this does not simplistically mean that in all situations such as on divorce there must be exact equality of division of assets, or that children must spend exactly half their time with each parent. UK discrimination law has tried and continues to try to prevent discrimination and foster equality, but individual circumstances still are (and it is to be hoped always will be) examined where appropriate by the court to determine what is fair and equitable. In other words, the rights and responsibilities are equal, not the disposal or allocation of assets.

KEY FACTS

1	The right to marry is recognised throughout the world but with very different regional emphases
2	UDHR 1948 Art 16 stresses mutual consent, equal rights during and after marriage with no race, nationality or religious limitations and the right to found a family
3	ICCPR 1966 Art 23 reinforces Art 16 by requiring States Parties to ensure equality of spousal rights and responsibilities during and after marriage with protection for children after dissolution
4	ECHR 1950 Art 12 guarantees that men and women of marriageable age may marry and found a family according to relevant national laws

CONTINUED ▸

KEY FACTS

5	EU Charter of Fundamental Rights 2000 Art 9 grants identical rights
6	The American Convention on Human Rights (1969) Art 17 recognises marriage as the natural and fundamental group unit of society to be freely entered into with equal rights for children born within or outside wedlock
7	The Banjul Charter 1981 Art 20 requires States Parties legally to ensure that widows are not subjected to inhuman, humiliating or degrading treatment, have automatic guardianship and custody of their children and the right to choose who to remarry
8	The UN Convention on Consent to Marriage, Minimum Age for Marriage, and Registration of Marriages 1964 merely provides for States Parties to legislate for minimum age requirements without stipulating protection for children
9	Issues arising regarding aspects of marriage have included: • prisoners • consanguinity • migration and asylum-seeking • separation and divorce • transsexuals • treatment of persons in situations analogous to marriage • taxation
10	Recognition of circumstances pertinent to marriage and founding a family are at the forefront of modern human rights because of rapidly changing social and medical developments, for example legislative recognition of civil partnerships and gender reassignment, and prevention of forced marriages

Further reading

Bainham, A, 'Arguments about Parentage', CLJ 2008, 67(2), 322–351.

Cretney, S M, 'Royal Marriages: Some Legal and Constitutional Issues', LQR 2008, 124 (Apr), 218–252.

Frimston, R, 'Marriage and Non-marital Registered Partnerships: Gold, Silver and Bronze in Private International Law', PCB 2006, 6, 352–362.

Hoffman, D and Rowe, J, QC, *Human Rights in the UK* (Pearson Longman, 2003), 243–248.

Thornton, R, 'Case Comment European Court of Human Rights: Consent to IVF Treatment', IJCL 2008, 6(2), 317–330.

AIMS AND OBJECTIVES

The intention of this chapter is as follows:

■ To identify typical contexts in which the need for remedies arise

■ To illustrate the principles that explain the origin and meaning of key ideas which in turn establish the reciprocal context of rights and remedies

■ To discuss those concepts so as to provide insight into their origin and meaning

■ To consider a number of cases illustrating circumstances where rights law needs to be developed further

■ To emphasise that a legal system providing adequate and appropriate remedies is not restricted to cases technically described as comprising 'human rights'.

15.1 Establishing the principle

Rights are only as good as the right-holder's ability to enforce them, whether they originate in custom, a written or unwritten constitution, convention or domestic law. This is true whether the claim is to an individual positive right, such as freedom of thought or expression, or a collective one which requires the state to ensure that the conditions are available and maintained to facilitate enjoyment, for example freedom of access to education or health care.

The fundamental need to ensure that appropriate remedies are available to enforce rights means that this chapter is more widely based and less concentrated on specific subject rights than the chapters dealing with Arts 2–12 and the relevant protocols. In this regard it is similar to Chapter 16 which deals with prohibition of discrimination and also has a wider scope.

The need for a symbiotic relationship between right and remedy has long been recognised and the Key Ideas chart provides wide-ranging examples illustrating this vital principle.

15.2 Rights must be enforceable

15.2.1 *Ubi jus, ibi remedium*

It is sometimes said that English law has been little influenced by Roman law, unlike Continental civil law legal systems, but until recently the use of Latin tags and Norman French

KEY IDEAS

	Right and remedy	Origin/meaning
1	*Ubi jus, ibi remedium*	Latin maxim meaning 'Where (there is) a right, there (is) a remedy'
2	'To no one will we sell, to no one will we refuse or delay, right or justice'	*Magna Carta* Clause 40
3	'Equity will not suffer a wrong to be without a remedy'	Equitable maxim developed in the Court of Chancery
4	'Be you never so high, the law is above you'	Thomas Fuller, quoted by Lord Denning in *Gouriet v Union of Post Office Workers* (1978) AC 435
5	'Law should be like death, which spares no one'	Baron de Montesquieu
6	'Where any person has a claim against the Crown after the commencement of this Act … the claim may be enforced as of right, and without the fiat of His Majesty, by proceedings taken against the Crown for that purpose in accordance with the provisions of this Act.'	Crown Proceedings Act 1947 s 1 authorises civil actions against the Crown in contract or tort
7	'Everyone has the right to an effective remedy by the competent national tribunals for acts violating the fundamental rights granted him by the constitution or by law.'	Universal Declaration of Human Rights Art 8
8	'Everyone whose rights and freedoms as set forth in this Convention are violated shall have an effective remedy before a national authority notwithstanding that the violation has been committed by persons acting in an official capacity.'	European Convention on Human Rights and Fundamental Freedoms Art 13

CONTINUED ▸

KEY IDEAS

9	'In this Act "the Convention rights" means the rights and fundamental freedoms set out in Articles 2 to 12 and 14 of the Convention … Articles 1 to 3 of the First Protocol, and Articles 1 and 6 of the Sixth Protocol, as read with Articles 16 to 18 of the Convention.'	Human Rights Act 1998 s 1(1), specifically omitting to implement Art 13 of the Convention which guarantees a remedy directly under the treaty

was widespread amongst common as well as civil lawyers. In the philosophical sense a right without a remedy can hardly be called a right and would be better expressed as a claim. There is little practical application of a 'right' if it cannot be enforced, although there are some circumstances where people have rights but are unable to obtain a (satisfactory) remedy.

Thus, if Debby is owed money by Owen who becomes bankrupt, then Debby's right to repayment of the debt is either devalued or lost, although there is no doubt that she has a 'right' to the money in the sense that she is entitled to it. If a constitution guarantees freedom but the Government enacts and enforces oppressive laws, the test of whether that right to freedom is real or illusory will depend on whether that right is enforceable or unenforceable by the citizens.

15.2.2 *Magna Carta* Clauses 39 and 40

MSN Encarta states that 'by most accounts only clauses 39 and 40 of the *Magna Carta* remain valid law in England' and it is the final 1297 rather than the 1215 version that survives as law.

Clause (or Art) 39 stated that:

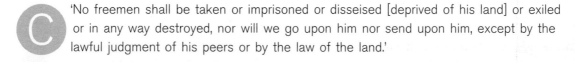

'No freemen shall be taken or imprisoned or disseised [deprived of his land] or exiled or in any way destroyed, nor will we go upon him nor send upon him, except by the lawful judgment of his peers or by the law of the land.'

In the absence of a written or codified constitution in the UK it is probably the case that even if this is all that remains on the Statute Book, people still believe that *Magna Carta* was the first rights document that protected them against overbearing authority, although in reality it was designed to protect the barons rather than common folk. What the clauses do provide for is due process under law. It is sometimes said that two other clauses may still be extant, guaranteeing the freedom of the English Church and the ancient liberties of the City of London.

Whatever the exact remaining provisions may be, Laws LJ, in identifying 'constitutional' statutes that could not be overridden by the doctrine of implied repeal in the 'metric martyrs' cases, singled out *Magna Carta* in *Thoburn v Sunderland City Council* [2003] QB 151; *Hunt v London Borough of Hackney etc* [2002] 3 WLR 247; [2002] 4 All ER 156, where it was being argued that the Weights and Measures Act 1985 had impliedly repealed s 2 of the European Communities Act 1972 (which gave precedence to EC Law over domestic law).

15.2.3 Equitable maxims

The Court of Chancery grew out of the King's Chancellor's responsibilities to overcome some of the deficiencies of the King's courts – King's Bench and Exchequer – by developing more appropriate and targeted remedies instead of simply awarding damages and insisting on settled rigid forms of writ and causes of action. The common law had become bogged down in excessive formality and there were gaps in the legal system that needed to be plugged. The ways in which this was done were many and ingenious, which lawyers explained by summarising as equitable 'maxims' or pithy explanations of remedial principles.

The word 'equity' is usually taken to mean 'fairness' but the technical meaning is the body of rules developed and applied by the Court of Chancery to mitigate the rigours of the common law, presided over by the Chancellor and developed under his authority.

This maxim 'equity will not suffer a wrong to be without a remedy' encapsulates the fundamental purpose of equity and so instead of, or in addition to, awarding compensation by way of damages when a litigant proved that someone had done him a wrong, imaginative and more appropriate remedies such as specific performance (making a party keep his bargain) and injunction (preventing the continuance or repetition of a wrong) were invented and developed, with direct action against the wrongdoing person (action *in personam*) if he remained recalcitrant and failed to obey the Court's order.

A good illustration of how equity will not suffer a wrong to be without a remedy is the equitable device of the trust. Originally placing property in trust occurred where the legal owner transferred the legal title to a second person or persons (trustees) who agreed to hold the property for the benefit of a third person or persons (beneficiaries). If the original owner (the settlor) died, the trustees could continue to carry out his wishes and there were incidental benefits such as avoidance of medieval taxes.

The many ways in which trusts can be used has developed enormously so that today, for example, if one person wrongfully attempts to take advantage of another a trust may arise without having been specifically created by a settlor which can be used to protect the person who becomes the beneficiary. One way in which this can occur is provided by the case of Mrs Bull senior, victim of a family dispute with her daughter-in-law.

CASE EXAMPLE

Bull v Bull [1955] 1 QB 234 CA

The claimant and his mother purchased a house in 1949, both contributing towards the cost although the property was conveyed into the son's sole name. Mother did not intend her contribution to be an outright gift as the objective was that it bought her the right to share the house with her son, which they did for four years. In 1953 the son married and it was then agreed that mother should continue to occupy two rooms and the son and his wife would occupy the remainder of the house. Differences arose between them and the son brought an action for possession of the rooms and thus to evict his mother from the property.

The Court of Appeal held that the son and his mother were beneficial tenants-in-common of the proceeds of sale and the house was held on a statutory trust for sale. Mother had an equitable interest that entitled her to remain in the house until it was sold.

In terms of remedies therefore she was protected in that she could not be turned out of her home arbitrarily because of the disruption brought about by her son's marriage, and if they could not settle their differences they were both protected because equity provided that in such a case the house would have to be sold and each would be entitled to a share of the net sale proceeds in proportion to what they had originally paid, as their respective contributions had not been equal.

Certainty v justice

An important aspect of understanding the nature of remedies is illustrated here. Law requires clarity and certainty so that everyone knows what it is and what is required of them by way of obedience and behaviour. Equity demands that notice should be taken of the individual circumstances of each case so that, where appropriate, any unfairness that might arise from excessive rigidity is mitigated. Achieving an acceptable balance between the two demands a high degree of knowledge, understanding and sensitivity on the part of the judge charged with the duty of hearing the case and awarding the remedy. However, when it comes to remedies, equity provided a fertile source of ingenious solutions to a variety of legal problems that arose over the centuries.

15.2.4 Rule of law

This is a complex and difficult concept, with a variety of shades of meaning attributed to it according to context, and it is often interpreted in widely different ways by states. Chinese lawyers would argue that the rule of law is relevant to and applies in China although, if so, it has a considerably different meaning than that understood in western democracies; but it is only fair to say that in the Western hemisphere there are also many shades of differing interpretation. In a basic form it is usually taken to incorporate the following major propositions:

- No punishment may be inflicted on anyone other than for a distinct breach of the law in ordinary manner before the ordinary courts.

- No man is above the law: irrespective of rank and status, all men are equal before the law.

- In the UK the rights and freedoms of Her Majesty's subjects are best protected under the common law: the uncodified constitution is pervaded by and is quintessentially part and parcel of the rule of law.

That was how it was identified by Dicey. If the law is above everybody one might expect it to follow that everyone is equal before the law, but in practice people are not always treated equally and it is clear that rich people can use the law to their own advantage and to the disadvantage of poorer persons. It is also the case that heads of state, diplomats, judges and Members of Parliament are all accorded privileges that do not apply to the rest of Her Majesty's subjects.

Equality was never a benefit guaranteed by *Magna Carta* or other enactments until much later in the twentieth century, so what is equality?

15.2.5 Equality before the law

Montesquieu's remark that 'law should be like death which spares no one' may contain the suggestion that the law is rigorously and unavoidably unpleasant but that at least it treats everyone in the same way, but does this imply equality before the law? At face value it perhaps means that every individual should be taken to have, and actually have, exactly the same rights as everyone else. There should be no distinctions drawn on grounds of birth, social status, religion, sex, political opinions and so on. In post-Second World War domestic UK law there have been considerable efforts to bring about such equality, examples including the:

- Race Relations Act 1965
- Equal Pay Act 1970
- Sex Discrimination Act 1975
- Civil Partnership Act 2004
- Equality Act 2006.

In addition to more obviously recognisable equality legislation, governments since 1945 have adopted policies intended to reduce or remove traditional barriers that have mitigated against equality in the past. Examples include: offering the opportunity to council-house tenants to acquire ownership after a qualifying period and at a discount on the market value (the 'right to

buy'); making legal aid and advice available so that poorer people could pursue legal claims and rights; and extending state educational and national health service facilities in an attempt to reduce some of the inequalities that formerly existed.

The point is that although equality by no means exists in the UK, attempts to reduce inequality are made on a wide front from specific laws designed to outlaw direct sexual or racial discrimination to more general policies that prevent or ameliorate the kinds of squalor which were widespread in Victorian England, and these policies and laws have been pursued by both major political parties when in government. The whole subject of discrimination is dealt with in detail in Chapter 16.

15.2.6 Petitions of right

Historically it was usually unwise to seek any kind of remedy against the Monarch, as for centuries they tended to hold a strong belief in the 'divine right of kings', whether expressed as such or not. Translated into modern terms this meant that they believed themselves to be chosen of God and thus neither prone to error nor answerable to mere mortals.

Crown Proceedings Act 1600

1600 c.23

THE negligence of the kingis officiaris may be supplyit be thair successouris

OURE Souerane Lord and Estaittis of parliament statutis and ordinis That the sleuth and negligence of ony of his hienes officiaris In the persewing or defending of ony of his actionis or causes in ony tyme bigane or to cum Sall nawayes be preiudiciall or hurtfull to his hienes bot that he and his officiaris successouris in that office May without ony ordour of reductioun and be way of exceptioun or reply vse and propone all and sindrie exceptionis replyis and defenses competent of the law quhilkis wer willinglie or negligentlie omittit be thair predecessouris And thairby supplie quhatsumeuir thing that hes bene neglectit or omittit be thair saidis predecessouris To the effect That his hienes and his crowne be nawayes hurte nor preiudgeit be negligent officiaris And that the benefitt of his lawes may be competent to him at all tymes quhair It sall pleis him and his officiaris to crave and vse the samyn (for the source see end of chapter)

Figure 15.1 Crown Proceedings Act 1600

In early times this did not need 'law' to justify it, as to challenge the King was tantamount to treason and likely to lead to rapid and unpleasant consequences. At the beginning of the seventeenth century a statute was enacted that showed how futile it was to challenge the Crown because 'his hienes and his crowne be nawayes hurte nor preiudgeit be negligent officiaris [and] nawayes be preiudiciall or hurtfull to his hienes [either]'.

The Royal motto beneath the lion and the unicorn says it all: 'Nemo me impune lacessit' means 'no one provokes/wounds/touches me with impunity'. It was the Scottish Crown's defiant challenge to anyone who dared call in question the authority of the Monarch.

After the Glorious Revolution (the series of events in 1688–89 which led to the final exile of King James II and the enthronement of the Protestant King William and Queen Mary), Parliament became sovereign in conjunction with the Crown, obliged as the new Monarchs were to accept the Bill of Rights as part of the price of their accession to the Throne of England.

ACTIVITY

Quick quiz – true or false

1	*Ubi jus, ibi remedium* means where there is a wrong the law should be changed.	T	F
2	'To no one will we sell, to no one will we refuse or delay, right or justice' is an example of an equitable remedy.	T	F
3	'Be you never so high, the law is above you' means that everyone should be treated as being equal before the law.	T	F
4	Actions in negligence and for breach of contract can be brought against the government since 1948.	T	F
5	The right to a remedy under ECHR Art 13 is explicitly included in the HRA 1998.	T	F
6	Complete equality under the law is guaranteed by the Human Rights Act.	T	F
7	The rule of law means that the courts are obliged to adjudicate on all complaints brought before them.	T	F
8	The Universal Declaration of Human Rights Art 8 says that an effective remedy should be provided by competent national tribunals.	T	F
9	In order to ensure that people enjoy their human rights, a balance needs to be struck between certainty of law and application of equitable principles.	T	F
10	A 'right' that cannot effectively be enforced is better called a 'claim'.	T	F

The description 'Glorious Revolution' expresses the idea that this part of the development of the English constitution (unlike, for example, the earlier civil war) and the ongoing rights that it represented were brought about peacefully and without further regicide or bloodshed.

Remedies in the modern world

However, it was almost 300 years later with the Crown Proceedings Act 1947 that Parliament eventually allowed civil actions in tort and for breach of contract to be brought against the Crown in the same way as against other parties. The Act retained the common law doctrine of Crown privilege but thereafter such actions were at least justiciable, although there remains to this day protection for the executive who may claim Public Interest Immunity.

The Second World War was profoundly damaging in so many ways, demonstrating for the second time in the twentieth century that modern man with his science and knowledge was little further forward in understanding how to treat his fellow men than his parents' generation had been in 1914. Radical reform was needed not only in the UK but throughout the war-ravaged world.

15.2.7 UDHR Article 8

Globally, the post Second World War rights regime proclaimed in the Universal Declaration of Human Rights established in clear terms that whatever rights are granted to individuals by their constitution or other law must be accompanied by effective remedies enforced by competent national tribunals if and whenever violations occurred. It should, however, be recognised that there was no general agreement to incorporate human rights into the charter and machinery of the UN itself, and so the declaration was just that rather than an enforceable treaty or embedded set of behavioural principles.

15.2.8 ECHR Article 13

In Europe the European Convention on Human Rights (ECHR) Art 13 reflected the UDHR Art 8 but with an important addition to make it clear that protection was intended even where the violation in question had been committed by persons acting in an official capacity: in other words, by state officials or operatives. This was influenced by the knowledge that Hitler had come to power legally and not by revolution, insurrection or *coup d'etat* so that the actions of his government and its functionaries were *prima facie* legal and legitimate.

15.2.9 HRA 1998 s 1(1)

Some 50 years later, when the Human Rights Act 1998 eventually 'brought rights home' to the UK, the Act made it plain that what was meant by 'Convention rights' were the rights and freedoms established by Arts 2–12 and 14 of the Convention, read together with various articles in Protocols 1 and 6, taken together with Arts 16–18 of the Convention. Art 13 itself is conspicuous by its absence from the legislation because the Act is supposed to ensure that adequate remedies are now available under domestic UK law.

15.3 Rights and remedies

15.3.1 Enforceability of remedies

It seems axiomatic that legal rights must be enforceable if they are to mean anything and it is usually taken for granted that this is done through legal process which is part and parcel of the rule of law. So far as human rights are concerned (as opposed to ordinary domestic legal rights such as pursuing a claim for a debt owed) in the UK there may be little difference, although there are some distinctions to be drawn. The omission in the Human Rights Act of direct implementation of Art 13 of the Convention restricts the horizontal effect between individuals affected by the Act.

The Latin maxim that where there is a right there is a remedy implies that if there is not a remedy the 'right' would not then exist. A remedy *does* exist where an authoritative body such as a court, tribunal, legislature or other effective agency is able consistently to ensure compliance with prescribed norms. If there are no effective enforcement procedures in a domestic forum, human rights mean little. This is especially the case if there is absence of, or weakness in, the rule of law or judicial procedures and in the international sphere where 'law' has a different reach and meaning.

15.3.2 Legal systems enforcing law

A 'legal system' enforcing 'law' implies a number of things. The 'system' has to exist in a recognised form. Effective enforcement machinery must facilitate pursuit of remedies, as being able to obtain a court order without the means to enforce the judgment to execution is merely an expensive and ineffective luxury. The 'law' in question must be clear but that in itself is insufficient without these additional criteria. If it is not, and cannot be enforced, the 'remedy' ends up as a 'no remedy' and the system has failed the claimant.

Customary international law, whether relating to human rights or not, is scant and tenuous in comparison with (say) English common law which is rich and in many areas comprehensive. Where English law legislates by statute, the rough international equivalent is treaties and conventions, and there is an abundance of those. The problem is that they only relate to and bind those states which choose to accept and adhere to them, and even the most widely acknowledged multi-lateral treaties, such as the Convention on the Rights of the Child (1989), is not universally recognised. There is a long list of States insisting on reservations and the USA and Somalia refuse or are unable to ratify it.

Even where a state has accepted some tenet of international law, the real test comes when it has committed a breach. In the case of the ECHR it is only since 2nd October 2000 that genuine access was made available to individuals within the UK; prior to 1966 the subject could exercise no rights at all under the Convention, and thereafter only with governmental consent. Nevertheless, compared to many international conventions the ECHR is pretty effective.

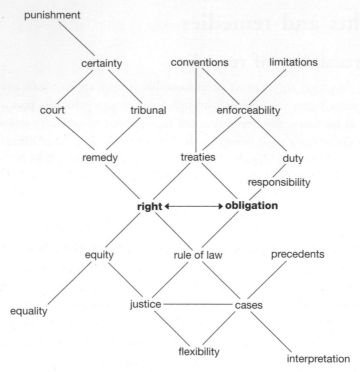

Figure 15.2 Mind map

15.3.3 UN global enforcement

It will be recalled that the League of Nations, founded in 1919, failed for a number of reasons, not least because it was not supported by the USA who then, as now, tended to take the view that their interests are best served by not tying themselves in to co-operative or collective international consensus. Of course, often that is the sensible attitude to take, given that co-operation is hard and consensus difficult to achieve, but as a starting point it is for human rights a rather negative attitude.

Nevertheless, the USA was instrumental in establishing the United Nations (UN) as the replacement for the League of Nations at the end of the Second World War. Despite the fact that the UN had been conceived during the War by the Western Allies and was not universally approved, there were much higher hopes that it would succeed where the League had failed.

To achieve any measure of success, compromises had to be made in the process and one of the more important of these was the need to provide some assurance that as an organisation there would be minimal direct interference in the sovereign affairs of Member States. This doctrine of respecting state sovereignty predicated a theoretical equality of status for every member regardless of size, wealth, population, military strength and influence in the real world. Art 2 of the UN Charter was born.

'The Organization and its Members, in pursuit of the Purposes stated in Article 1, shall act in accordance with the following Principles:

(4)   All Members shall refrain in their international relations from the threat or use of force against the territorial integrity or political independence of any state, or in any other manner inconsistent with the Purposes of the United Nations

(7)   Nothing contained in the present Charter shall authorize the United Nations to intervene in matters which are essentially within the domestic jurisdiction of any state or shall require the Members to submit such matters to settlement under the present Charter; but this principle shall not prejudice the application of enforcement measures under Chapter VII.'

The UN's main rules thereby indicate a strong intention on the part of the founding members that when remedies were needed, whatever transgression might appear to have occurred, direct action by individual members against other sovereign states would not be countenanced, subject only to exceptional circumstances where the Security Council were unanimous or their proposed actions were not vetoed by one of the permanent Members (the US, the former USSR and now the Russian Federation, China, UK and France). It is probable that the UN would never have got off the ground in the first place had its structure been otherwise.

Chapter VII

Chapter VII addresses the need to take action when there are threats to the peace, breaches of the peace and acts of aggression. It comprises Arts 39–51 of the UN Charter and enables the Security Council to determine the existence of any of the above and to make recommendations or decide what measures need to be taken to maintain or restore international peace and security. Initially, recommendations and non-military suggestions may be made but Art 42 says that should those prove to be inadequate, more drastic measures can be approved:

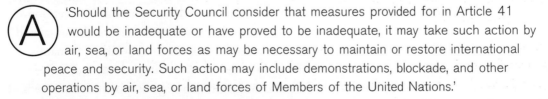 'Should the Security Council consider that measures provided for in Article 41 would be inadequate or have proved to be inadequate, it may take such action by air, sea, or land forces as may be necessary to maintain or restore international peace and security. Such action may include demonstrations, blockade, and other operations by air, sea, or land forces of Members of the United Nations.'

Art 51 provides a residuary but qualified safeguard for Member States concerned at this potential threat to their right of individual action:

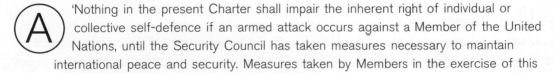 'Nothing in the present Charter shall impair the inherent right of individual or collective self-defence if an armed attack occurs against a Member of the United Nations, until the Security Council has taken measures necessary to maintain international peace and security. Measures taken by Members in the exercise of this

right of self-defence shall be immediately reported to the Security Council and shall not in any way affect the authority and responsibility of the Security Council under the present Charter to take at any time such action as it deems necessary in order to maintain or restore international peace and security.'

The reason it was possible to obtain agreement to this authority to act was that the Security Council was established as an elite body with extraordinary powers and the victorious allies ensured that their controlling members were not only on the Council but were permanent members each with a power of veto. They were thus assured that Chapter VII could never be used against their own particular interests, or against those of their friends.

Incidentally, the point is made today that although this is historically understandable, it does not adequately reflect *realpolitik* in the modern world, where economically powerful states such as Japan and Germany, and emergent states such as India, Brazil and others ought to be taken into consideration and have commensurate authority. No doubt, nuclear states such as Pakistan and Israel would also wish to stake a claim. Yet others such as Norway could argue that they should be accorded more influence because of their positive human rights record.

The overall effect is that the UN does have the power, ultimately, to impose remedies in cases where human rights are breached, but only where this occurs in the context of threats to the peace, breaches of the peace and acts of aggression, and only where there is unanimity on the part of the five permanent members. An example is the 1999 Security Council Resolution 1244 which authorised implementation of the Kosovo peace settlement that enabled the civil presence to protect and promote human rights including assuring the safe and unimpeded return of refugees and displaced persons, alongside other functions such as performing basic civilian administrative functions, maintaining civil law and order and establishing local police forces. Such unanimity is, however, rare as a number of African conflicts involving widespread rights abuses and large-scale carnage demonstrate.

The conflict between the Treaty of Westphalia 1648, which established the doctrine of non-interference in the internal affairs of sovereign states, and the somewhat theoretical interventionist Chapter VII provisions, has meant that in nearly all cases widespread human rights abuses caused by deliberate human action, or disasters arising out of natural events such as weather, tsunamis, cyclones or desertification, or a combination of both, in most cases remain without a direct interventionist remedy. Instead, it is left to NGOs and humanitarian organisations to promote and safeguard the rights of victims, and to pick up the pieces. It is a fact that the world often either turns a blind eye or declines to take effective action in response to human rights abuses such as those committed in the Democratic Republic of the Congo and Darfur.

Other UN remedies

There are other remedies available to the UN that should be mentioned. Direct military force was authorised in the First Gulf War in 1990–91, although it is significant that the human rights violated there were minimal in comparison with other situations and protection of strategic and economic interests much more the primary objective.

The UN General Assembly, as advised by the Security Council, has the power to suspend states under Art 5 of the UN Charter resulting in loss of membership privileges to the offending member, and in the event of arrears of contributions accruing, Art 19 of the Charter provides for exclusion. In these cases the available sanctions are unlikely to help in cases of human rights violations.

Another sanction is the use of embargo under Art 41, which interferes with an offending state's economic activities but almost inevitably this hits the wrong targets. One exceptional example of this was the slow but eventually successful use of sanctions that helped to abolish apartheid in South Africa. More often those imposing suffering on their citizens flout sanctions with impunity, as when the President of Zimbabwe travels abroad, despite the imposition of sanctions on him and his government.

15.4 Enforcement of ECHR remedies under HRA

15.4.1 Rights protected by the HRA

Enforcement of the ECHR in the UK is governed by the Human Rights Act 1998 s 1(1). Schedule 1 to the Act sets out the relevant rights in full and they comprise all the rights, freedoms and prohibitions covered by Arts 2–12 of the Convention, together with abolition of the death penalty under the Thirteenth Protocol and with First Protocol rights to:

* property
* education
* free elections.

From this it can be seen that the Act specifically and deliberately omits Art 1 of the Convention which is as follows:

'The High Contracting Parties shall secure to everyone within their jurisdiction the rights and freedoms defined in Section 1 of the Convention.'

The HRA 1998 is taken to achieve the ECHR objectives, and Art 13 provides that:

'Everyone whose rights and freedoms as set forth in this Convention are violated shall have an effective remedy before a national authority notwithstanding that the violation has been committed by persons acting in an official capacity.'

15.4.2 Summary of HRA remedies

The Act provides remedies in the following situations:

- Where a court determines that primary legislation fails to conform to Convention rights and makes a declaration of incompatibility under s 4
  - the practical result is that the government is obliged to amend the defective legislation, or in exceptional cases derogate from an unacceptable Convention requirement.
- Proceedings can be brought against a public authority under s 7(1) by a person who claims that it has acted or is proposing to act in a way which is made unlawful by s 6
  - this also enables the claimant to rely on Convention rights in any legal proceedings, in either case only if the claimant is or would be a 'victim' of the unlawful act.
- It includes a petition for judicial review under s 7(3) and (4).
- The court 'may grant such relief or remedy, or make such order, within its powers as it considers just and appropriate' by virtue of s 8(1).
- Damages is an option which must take into consideration any other relief or remedy granted and that it is necessary to afford just satisfaction to the person in whose favour it is made under s 8(3)
  - also taking into consideration European Court of Human Rights decisions under s 8(4).
- Power to take remedial action is governed by s 10.
- Special safeguards for freedom of expression, and of thought, conscience and religion are guaranteed in ss 11, 12 and 13.

15.4.3 Limitations on enforcement ability

As explained in Chapters 2 and 3 dealing with the Convention and Act, the scope of the ECHR has been increased several times since it was first opened for signature, whilst individual signatories including the UK have limited the extent to which they consider themselves bound by specific treaty provisions by reservation (eg education) or derogations in times of emergency (eg in respect of terrorist activities).

Additionally, most of the substantive articles are qualified anyway so what at first might appear to be an infringement may turn out on closer examination to be acceptable behaviour on the part of the State or one of its emanations. What often happens then is that an individual or group of individuals attempt to assert a right and the relevant state attempts to justify what occurred by reference to the appropriate qualification or limitation.

In particular, such limitations may relate to interference that might be justified by being:

- in accordance with law
- necessary in a democratic society
- proportionate in the circumstances of the case in question when otherwise it would amount to an infringement.

ACTIVITY

Self-test questions

1 In what important way does ECHR Art 13 differ from UDHR Art 8?

2 Why is the enforcement of human rights under international law usually much weaker than exerting rights within a state?

3 What steps can the UN take to enforce its will when human rights abuses have occurred?

4 Can you name the different kinds of remedy that are available under the Human Rights Act?

5 What is the significance of the Crown Proceedings Act 1947?

15.5 Case law

Art 13 is not in itself a free-standing right for obvious reasons. It is the means to rectify injustice where there has been a breach of other rights, freedoms or prohibitions. It operates in conjunction with Art 14 (see Chapter 16 proscribing discrimination) to ensure that a remedy or remedies are available to everyone and that no one is discriminated against in the process. The need for a remedy may arise in a wide variety of circumstances, as the following discussion of case law demonstrates.

15.5.1 Asylum seekers

The remedy sought must be against the actions of a public authority, and the HRA s 8(1) provides that the court may grant such relief or remedy or make such order within its powers as it considers just and appropriate. Whatever the court does, it should reflect the approach so far as is practicable with what the European Court would have done in the circumstances by virtue of Art 41 of the Convention.

CASE EXAMPLE

R (on the application of Anufrijeva) v Southwark LBC [2003] EWCA Civ 1406 (consolidated case)

A number of asylum seekers appealed against decisions dismissing claims for damages in respect of alleged breaches of their Art 8 human rights, and the Secretary of State appealed against a decision where damages had been awarded. The claims were

CONTINUED ▸

based on alleged maladministration by the local authorities because they had not provided benefits or advantages by means of welfare and national assistance payments.

The cases therefore needed to decide:

(1) when a positive duty arose on the part of the authority under Art 8
(2) under what circumstances maladministration would arise, and
(3) whether the remedy of damages arose and if so how they should be assessed.

The asylum seekers' appeals were dismissed and the Secretary of State's appeal was upheld on the basis that although Art 8 was capable of imposing a positive obligation on the state to provide support, it would only arise where family life was seriously inhibited or children's welfare threatened. Even culpable delay in the administrative process was not an infringement of Art 8 unless substantial prejudice resulted.

With regard to the remedy, damages were not recoverable as of right where Convention rights had been breached and courts had to look critically at such claims. The objective and concern was usually to bring the infringement to an end and compensation was of secondary importance. An equitable approach to the award of damages was therefore required and the need for damages should be ascertainable from an examination of the correspondence and witness statements.

15.5.2 Medical negligence and *stare decisis*

Sometimes when a trial judge is keen to provide a remedy he is not able to do so because he is bound by the doctrine of *stare decisis*. Decided case law, for example, established the principle that a claim in negligence for damages for lost years in respect of a young child was impermissible (*Croke (A Minor) v Wiseman* [1982] 1 WLR 71 CA (Civ Div)) but in a recent case where a child Khaled Iqbal had suffered from dystonic tetraplegic cerebral palsy because of a hospital's admitted negligence at the time of his birth the trial judge awarded him £42,402 calculated by a multiplier of 6.36 applied to a multiplicand of £6,667 which represented one-third of the agreed net earnings of £20,000.

There was no doubt that a remedy was called for but the hospital appealed on the basis that the judge was wrong in law because a claim for the lost years by a young claimant with no earnings record and no dependants was too remote to be capable of being compensated by an award of damages, and such a claim was not justified by the decision of the House of Lords in *Pickett v British Rail Engineering Ltd* [1980] AC 136 HL, and in any event the Court of Appeal were also bound by *Croke*.

In Khaled's case, *Iqbal v Whipps Cross University Hospital NHS Trust* [2007] EWCA Civ 1190, the Court of Appeal found that *Pickett* did not restrict a claim for lost years to adults with or without dependants and the decision in *Croke* was not consistent with the decisions of the

House of Lords in *Pickett* and *Gammell v Wilson* [1982] AC 27 HL. Nevertheless the principle of *stare decisis* bound the Court of Appeal here, applying *Young v Bristol Aeroplane Co Ltd* [1944] KB 718 CA, because Khaled's circumstances were not so rare and exceptional that the court could distinguish.

Thus, there is a significant constraint on both the High Court and Court of Appeal with regard to providing a satisfactory remedy because of the rules established by *Young v Bristol Aeroplane*. These are that the previous decision was:

- expressly or impliedly overruled by a subsequent decision of the House of Lords

- inconsistent with an even earlier decision of the Court of Appeal

- reached *per incuriam*, ie where the Court had not been referred to some other relevant authority.

For Khaled Iqbal none of these exceptions could be found to apply. There is some case comment on the decision in the suggested reading at the end of this chapter.

In another recent medical case, *K v United Kingdom* (38000/05), *The Times*, 13th October 2008, the European Court held that there had been no violation of Art 8 of the ECHR where an infant child was made the subject of an interim care order despite there having been a medical misdiagnosis. However, the parents' rights had been violated in contravention of Art 13 because there were no means available to enable them to challenge the way the local authority handled the procedure, nor was there any process by which they could claim compensation for the damage caused.

15.5.3 Higher education

Students will be particularly interested to know whether they have a remedy in cases where they have been excluded from their educational course. In an unreported case heard by Judge Pellis QC (*R (on the application of Daskaloulis) v University of West England*, Queen's Bench Division (Administrative Court), 22nd October 2008) a student, Daskaloulis (D), attending the Bar vocational course at the University of West England was required to withdraw as he had failed successfully to pass the requisite negotiating skills assessment.

In an effort to settle the matter the University offered to have a DVD of the failed assessment marked by two independent assessors applying the relevant criteria applicable at the time D failed, with further moderation by an independent examiner. Additionally, a resit was offered, again applying the criteria applicable to the academic year in which D entered the course. Although on the face of it these might seem to have been reasonable suggestions, D argued that more general remedies should have been made available together with the right to recover the fees paid to attend the course.

The application for judicial review was granted to the extent that the University's exclusion decision was quashed. The court said that D should be offered two alternative assessments comprising either the DVD offer previously made or a fresh one and in either case subject to the assessment criteria applicable in the year of entry. A cut-off point would be stipulated for the

choice to be made. D would not be awarded damages as that was not part of the permission given when seeking judicial review and if D considered there had been a breach of contract the proper forum for that to be tried would be the County Court or QBD.

In *Watson v Durham University* [2008] EWCA Civ 1266 an important point was emphasised by the Court in granting a professor's appeal against suspension by the University, where it was stated that the trial judge should not have been deterred from deciding it on the correct basis by the incompetent presentation of Professor Watson's case. The appellant had been suspended because of complaints about his behaviour and questions concerning his qualifications.

For anyone to be suspended from their employment pending allegations of misconduct was a serious matter. It meant that a shadow was cast over an individual and that was especially important where that person was employed in a public position or in higher education, and in this instance the suspension dragged on for too long a period. Regarding the balance of convenience it would be wrong to deprive Professor Watson of a remedy merely because the trial judge had failed to exercise his discretion to grant an injunction in an earlier hearing.

15.5.4 Deprivation of place of abode

Cyprus

In 1974 a Greek Cypriot woman, X-A, and her family were forced by Turkish soldiers to abandon their home and possessions in Northern Cyprus and had not since been able to return. The European Court found that this constituted an unwarranted interference with her right to respect for her home in violation of Art 8, and the continuing deprivation also violated her rights under Art 1 of Protocol 1 of the ECHR (*Xenides-Arestis v Turkey* [2006] ECHR 46347/99).

In considering this and other pending cases the Court also decided that Turkey had to produce a remedy pursuant to Art 46 ECHR. This led to Turkey adopting legislation for the compensation, exchange and restitution of immoveable (real) properties and appointing a commission for compensation for pecuniary losses.

With regard to X-A, the Court then found that although the new compensation and restitution mechanism had basically satisfied the requirements of the previous decision the applicant should not now be required to make a further application to the new commission so as to obtain her reparation. The European Court decided on an equitable basis to make an assessment in her favour and to award her €50,000 in respect of non-pecuniary damages.

Chagos Islands

Another case of long-standing deprivation of right of abode was considered in the following year by the English Court of Appeal. It upheld a successful application for judicial review which had found the UK Government guilty of abuse of power when two Orders in Council made in 1971 had the effect of compulsorily removing the inhabitants of the British Indian Ocean Territory the Chagos Islands so that the USA could use the main island as a military base.

The UK Government had accepted the court's ruling in 2007 but there was a later change of mind on the basis that the island was still needed for protection purposes and it would be uneconomic to resettle the islanders. The Secretary of State based the appeal to the House of Lords on two constitutional law grounds. The first was that the relevant 1971 Ordinance was primary legislation and therefore could not be challenged before a court, and the second was that review was precluded by the Colonial Laws Validity Act 1865.

The claimant's counter-argument was that the right of abode was so sacred and fundamental that the Crown could not remove it in any circumstances, relying on Lord Mansfield's statement in *Campbell v Hall* 98 ER 1045 KB that the King could not make changes in the law that were 'contrary to fundamental principles'. There was also the consideration that the government's assurance that it would accept the previous decisions gave rise to a legitimate expectation on the part of the Chagossians that they would be allowed to return to the islands (*R (on the application of Bancoult) v Secretary of State for Foreign and Commonwealth Affairs* [2008] UKHL 61).

In allowing the Secretary of State's appeal by a majority of 3:2 (Lords Bingham and Mance dissenting) and rejecting the right of the islanders to a remedy, the House of Lords reaffirmed the principle in *Council of Civil Service Unions v Minister for the Civil Service* [1985] AC 374 HL that there was no reason why prerogative legislation should not be subject to review on ordinary principles of legality, rationality and procedural impropriety in the same way as any other executive action. Here, however, too much was being read into Lord Mansfield's statement and the 1865 Act had in any event made the right of abode a 'creature of the law' rather than a constitutional matter. Crucially it was said in judgment that:

> **J** 'There [is] no support for any proposition that, in legislating for a colony, either Parliament or Her Majesty in Council must have regard only, or even predominantly, to the immediate interests of its inhabitants . . . taking fully into account the practical interest no legitimate expectation had been created (for) the Chagossians, the decision to reimpose immigration control on the islands could not be described as unreasonable or an abuse of power . . . no legitimate expectation had been created.'

15.5.5 Failures to provide remedy

Assisted suicide

A contemporary aspect of the failure of English law to provide a remedy (other than in the practice of turning a blind eye) is the question of assisted suicide, discussed in Chapter 4. There have been high-profile cases such as that of Diane Pretty in 2002 (*R (on the application of Pretty) v DPP* [2001] UKHL 61 and *Pretty v United Kingdom* 2346/02, (2002) 35 EHRR 1) but

attempts in Parliament to amend the law have been unsuccessful. Further challenges have been mounted, although it seems clear that the law can only be changed by Parliament. It might be argued that in practice the law is allowing the provision of a remedy *via* administrative non-enforcement by not instituting prosecutions under the Suicide Act. The arguments have been rehearsed previously so this point is not pursued further here.

Overriding interests

There are other completely different human rights situations where the law fails to provide a remedy. In *Aston Cantlow and Wilmcote with Billesley Parochial Church Council v Wallbank* [2004] 1 AC 546 the House of Lords affirmed that it was lawful to recover the costs of repairing the chancel of a church from a private landowner and that such a tax did not breach human rights obligations. This was despite the fact that the responsibility arose from historical circumstances when the Church had been entitled to tithes from land ownership. Their Lordships were not happy that this was the law but were obliged to uphold it. The liability had been foreseen by the Law Commission and its abolition recommended, but little has been done to protect individuals from this arcane financial penalty and the risk to what ought to be protected property rights remains for the unwary.

KEY FACTS

1	The key idea is *Ubi jus, ibi remedium* – where there is a right there is (or at least there should be) a remedy
2	A human right does not truly exist unless there is an enforceable remedy available – it would otherwise only be a claim to a right
3	Legal systems provide a wide variety of remedies, not all concerning themselves directly with human rights but which would diminish such rights were they not available
4	The growth of equity under the guidance of the Chancellor fostered the development of many remedies that are today taken for granted such as injunctions, specific performance, declarations and obtaining accounts
5	In addition to equity, legal systems must have at their core the right for litigants to seek appropriate remedies in their domestic courts
6	International declarations and treaties are important in identifying and defining the right to obtain remedies

CONTINUED ▸

KEY FACTS

	Examples of these include the UDHR Art 8 and the ECHR Art 13
7	Examples of specific domestic rights legislation affording remedies include the: • Race Relations Act 1965 • Equal Pay Act 1970 • Sex Discrimination Act 1975 • Human Rights Act 1998 • Civil Partnership Act 2004 • Equality Act 2006
8	Under the ECHR, Art 13 is not a substantive article but can be used to support such rights under Arts 2–12 and the protocols relating to education and property
9	Useful cases to explain why remedies are needed and how they operate include: • Asylum seekers: *R (on the application of Anufrijeva) v Southwark LBC* (2003) (consolidated case) • Medical negligence: *Iqbal v Whipps Cross University Hospital NHS Trust* (2007) • Education: *R (on the application of Daskaloulis) v University of West England*, Queen's Bench Division (Administrative Court), 22th October 2008) and *Watson v Durham University*, Court of Appeal (Civil Division), 24th October 2008 • Assisted suicide: *Pretty v United Kingdom* 2346/02 (2002) 35 EHRR 1

Useful resources

Ministry of Justice source for the Crown Proceedings Act 1600:
> www.statutelaw.gov.uk/content.aspx?ActiveTextDocId=1519242.

'What does the United Nations say about religious freedom?':
> www.interfaithstudies.org/freedom/unitednations.html.

Further reading

Amos, M, *Human Rights Law* (Hart Publishing, Portland, USA, 2006), 143–171.

Feldman, D, 'Remedies for Violations of Convention Rights under the Human Rights Act', EHRLR 1998, 6, 691–711.

Halstead, P, *Human Rights Key Facts* (2nd edn, Hodder Education, 2008), 148–160.

Hoffmann, D and Rowe, J, QC, *Human Rights in the UK: An Introduction to the Human Rights Act 1998* (2nd edn, Pearson Longman, Harlow, England, 2006), 67–78.

Lustgarten, L and Leigh, I, 'Making Rights Real: The Courts, Remedies, and the Human Rights Act', CLJ 1999, 58(3), 509–545.

McQuater, J, 'Case Comment Personal Injury: Clinical Negligence – Birth Trauma', JPI Law 2008, 1, C23–27.

Ovey, C and White, R C A, *Jacobs & White The European Convention on Human Rights* (4th edn, Oxford University Press, 2006), 459–506.

Shelton, D, 'Remedies in International Human Rights Law', reviewed by Chris Bleby, CLJ 2000, 59(3), 624–626.

Tortell, L, 'Monetary Remedies for Breach of Human Rights: A Comparative Study', reviewed by Merris Amos, PL 2007, Win, 855–857.

PROHIBITION OF
DISCRIMINATION ∎

AIMS AND OBJECTIVES

This chapter aims to do the following:

- Provide an overview of the development of anti-discrimination legislation in the UK since the 1960s

- Provide an outline of major UN declarations and treaties since the 1960s

- Consider the content and application of the European Convention on Human Rights (ECHR) Art 14

- Analyse the nature of Convention anti-discrimination provisions by reference to case law.

16.1 Background

16.1.1 Domestic legislation

There have been a number of statutes over the past four decades or so designed to address and eliminate various types of discrimination as indicated in the following table:

Act	Purpose	Method
Sex Discrimination Act 1975	Provided protection for men and women against unlawful discrimination in: • employment • vocational training • education • provision and sale of goods, facilities and services • management and letting of premises • exercise of public functions	Equal Opportunities Commission established by Part VI
Equal Pay Act 1970	Made it unlawful for employers to discriminate between men and women: • by virtue of their pay and working conditions • where they do identical or similar work • where work is of equal value or rated as equivalent	Enabled claims to be made to an Industrial Tribunal or the Industrial Court

CONTINUED ▶

Act	Purpose	Method
Race Relations Acts 1965, 1968, 1975 Race Relations (Amendment) Act 2000	Made it unlawful to discriminate against anyone on grounds of: • race • colour • nationality including citizenship • ethnic or national origin	Commission for Racial Equality
Disability Discrimination Act 1995	Made it unlawful to discriminate against disabled persons regarding: • employment • provision of goods, facilities and services • disposal or management of premises	Disability Rights Commission and National Disability Council
Civil Partnership Act 2004	Enabled same-sex couples to obtain legal recognition of their relationship provided that they are: • of the same sex • not lawfully married or in existing civil partnership • not within prohibited degrees of relationship • both aged 16+ or if under 18 appropriate consent has been obtained	By forming a civil partnership reciprocal rights and obligations are created
Equality Act 2006	Defined the CEHR's purpose and functions and renders unlawful various types of discrimination as explained in the following text It also creates a duty on public authorities to promote equality of opportunity between women and men ('gender duty') and prohibits sex discrimination and harassment in the exercise of public functions	Commission for Equality and Human Rights (CEHR) replaced and subsumed the: • Equal Opportunities Commission • Commission for Racial Equality • Disability Rights Commission

Figure 16.1 Anti-discrimination overview

16.1.2 Consolidation of domestic provisions

The dates of the various statutes enacted since 1965 provide some insight into the development of the general rights movement over the last 40 years or so, starting with race relations in the 1960s, equal pay and sex discrimination in the 1970s, and moving forward to disability discrimination in the 1990s. More recently, recognition has been given to civil partnerships and steps have now been taken in the Equality Act 2006 to implement some practical joined-up government and to bring some cohesion to the anti-discrimination legislation and practice. The Equality Act 2006 established the Equality and Human Rights Commission for England, Wales and Scotland which replaced the three previous separate commissions. Northern Ireland has its own arrangements.

In addition the Act also:

• makes it unlawful (with some exceptions) to discriminate on grounds of religion, belief or sexual orientation in providing goods, facilities and services, managing premises, education and exercising public functions

- creates a duty on public authorities to prohibit workplace sex discrimination and promote equal opportunities between men and women.

There are 17 commissioners and their objectives are to work towards eliminating discrimination, reducing inequality, protecting human rights and building good relations, thus ensuring that everyone has a fair chance to participate in society.

From 1st October 2006 regulations came into effect to provide legal protection against age discrimination. The intention is to:

- stop unjustified age discrimination in employment and work-related training
  - employers have to make sure that redundancy policies do not discriminate directly or indirectly against older workers, nor must there be any victimisation or harassment
- improve the rights of employees facing retirement
  - an employee can only be made to retire below the age of 65 if it is appropriate and necessary, six months' notice must be given, and consideration be given to any request to work beyond 65
- remove the upper age limit for unfair dismissal and redundancy rights.

What the provisions do *not* do is provide a right for a person over pensionable age to insist on continuing to work.

16.1.3 International declarations and treaties

Over a similar period of time international rights law was developing a series of conventions and declarations aimed at eliminating racial intolerance and discrimination, including apartheid, and addressing sexual, religious, national and ethnic prejudice.

Year	Declaration or Treaty	Comments
1963	Declaration on the Elimination of all Forms of Racial Discrimination	Article 1 declared discrimination between human beings on ground of race, colour or ethnic origin to be an offence to human dignity . . . (it) denies UN Charter principles . . . can disturb peace and security
1966	International Convention on the Elimination of All Forms of Racial Discrimination (CERD)	Entered into force 12th March 1969, 173 States Parties, monitored by the Committee on the Elimination of Racial Discrimination comprising 18 international independent experts
1973	International Convention on the Suppression and Punishment of the Crime of *Apartheid*	Crime of *apartheid* is defined in the Rome Statute of the International Criminal Court as inhuman acts 'committed in the context of an institutionalised regime of systematic oppression and domination by one racial group over any other racial group or groups and committed with the intention of maintaining that regime'

CONTINUED ▸

Year	Declaration or Treaty	Comments
1973	Convention on the Elimination of All Forms of Discrimination against Women New York (CEDAW)	Defines discrimination against women as 'any distinction, exclusion or restriction made on the basis of sex which has the effect or purpose of impairing or nullifying the recognition, enjoyment or exercise by women, irrespective of their marital status, on a basis of equality of men and women, of human rights and fundamental freedoms in the political, economic, social, cultural, civil or any other field.'
1999	Optional Protocol to CEDAW	Ratification of the 21 Article Optional Protocol means that a State recognises the jurisdiction of the Committee on the Elimination of Discrimination against Women, the compliance body, enabling individuals and groups to submit complaints
1981	Declaration on the Elimination of All Forms of Intolerance and of Discrimination Based on Religion or Belief	Proclaimed by General Assembly resolution 36/55 of 25th November 1981 and is regarded as an important international standard-setting instrument with respect to freedom of religion or belief
1992	Declaration on the Rights of Persons Belonging to National or Ethnic, Religious and Linguistic Minorities	Adopted by the General Assembly in its resolution 47/135 of 18th December 1992 it reaffirms a basic UN aim to promote and encourage respect for human rights and freedoms without distinction as to race, sex, language or religion

Figure 16.2 International provisions

16.2 ECHR Article 14

(A) 'The enjoyment of the rights and freedoms set forth in this Convention shall be secured without discrimination on any ground such as sex, race, colour, language, religion, political or other opinion, national or social origin, association with a national minority, property, birth or other status.'

16.3 Discrimination and equality

The positive promotion of equality of treatment of all human beings by virtue of their very humanity, or the polar opposite of aiming to protect people against every species of discrimination, is at the root of the universal understanding and interpretation of human rights, on a par with the absolute prohibition against torture and the fundamental and underlying precept that all people should be treated with respect and dignity.

This prohibition against discrimination is therefore central to the Universal Declaration of Human Rights and the two covenants, civil and political, and economic, social and cultural, which together comprise the International Bill of Human Rights. There should be no doubt about their core importance and the universality of their intended global application as well as at European and national level.

This means that:

(a) When Art 14 of the European Convention is applied it operates to supplement and support other rights and freedoms and in itself it does not enjoy an independent existence.

(b) The European Court has developed 'comparators' which it applies in considering cases to determine whether the complainant has been treated less favourably than others in a similar situation.

(c) The effect of this is that, applying comparators, there is not an absolute or even entirely objective standard that will determine that X has or has not been discriminated against in comparison with Y.

(d) Even though there might have been some discrimination in a given case the question still has to be considered of whether it was justified in the circumstances.

(e) What is *not* acceptable is arbitrary application of law so that some people end up being treated more badly than others where objectively the circumstances do not warrant such treatment.

Because of these constraints, consideration also must be given to positive and negative requirements on the part of the state. A considerable margin of appreciation is given to states because across Europe this allows for wide interpretation of the differences of history, culture and background that go to make up contemporary Europe and its rights regime.

16.4 Getting a case heard

Prior to 1998 a claimant applied to the European Commission of Human Rights which determined whether the Convention was engaged. When the Court was reconstituted as a full-time body in 1998 the Commission was abolished and application is now made directly to the Court.

CASE EXAMPLE

Nerva v United Kingdom (Application No 42295/98)

The case originated in an application (No 42295/98) against the UK that was lodged with the European Commission of Human Rights under the former Art 25 of the Convention. The application was transmitted to the Court on 1st November 1998, when Protocol No 11 to the Convention came into force (Art 5 para 2 of Protocol No 11).

The application was originally allocated to the Third Section of the Court (r 52 para 1 of the Rules of Court) which declared it admissible on 11th September 2001.

CONTINUED ▸

On 1st November 2001 the Court changed the composition of its sections (r 25 para 1). The application was allocated to the Second Section of the Court. Within that section, the Chamber that would consider the case (Art 27 para 1 of the Convention) was constituted as provided in r 26 para 1 of the Rules of Court.

The facts are briefly outlined in Figure 16.3 below.

Nowadays there is no need for such arcane Kafkaesque procedures, and application is made to a section of the Court which decides on the merits whether it is admissible or inadmissible. If admissible it will be heard by a Section of the Court, and if sufficiently important it will go to the Grand Chamber. Some examples of applications and the differing substantive bases on which they were made are set out in the following table:

Application	Basis of alleged discrimination
Corcoran v UK (App no 60525/00)	Men complained about their non-eligibility for equivalent to widows' social security benefits and tax allowances
Hepple v UK (App no 65731/01); *Kimber v UK Kingdom* (App no 65900/01)	Men complained about differences in the entitlement for men and women to certain industrial injuries social security benefits
Barrow v UK (App no 42735/02)	A woman complained that UK social security legislation discriminated against her on grounds of sex because she would lose entitlement to incapacity benefit when she reached 60, whereas a man in the same situation would benefit until 65: the applicant would receive a state pension from 60 but be entitled to receive less than she currently received in incapacity benefit
Hill and twelve others v United Kingdom (App no 28006/02)	Here there was different treatment under social security legislation between men and women whose spouses had died
Findlater v UK (App no 38881/97)	No compensation paid for reduction in value of business following changes in handgun legislation
Matthews v UK (App no 40302/98)	64-year-old male refused senior citizen's travel pass allowing free public transport travel because it was only available to men aged over 65 although available to women aged over 60
Eccleston v UK (App no 42841/02)	The applicant complained about the delay in obtaining access to personal files held by local authorities
Nerva v UK (App no 42295/98)	Waiters complained that tips included in cheque and credit card transactions were counted towards their earnings as part of the calculation of their minimum wage
Neill v UK (App no 56721/00)	Applicants claimed Armed Forces Pension Scheme was discriminatory and did not provide appropriate pensions for widows

■ Figure 16.3 Applications alleging discrimination

ACTIVITY

Self-test questions

1 What are the main objectives of the Equality Act 2006?

2 Name three of the international declarations or conventions which addressed discrimination from 1963 onwards.

3 How many kinds of discrimination are addressed in Art 14 of the ECHR and what are they?

4 What kinds of discrimination are addressed in the case law which engages Art 14 of the ECHR?

5 Name three cases and briefly outline their concerns.

16.5 What is discrimination?

16.5.1 Rational justifiability

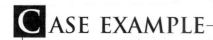

CASE EXAMPLE

R (on the application of Carson) v Secretary of State for Work and Pensions and Conjoined cases **[2005] UKHL 37**

What may comprise discrimination is sometimes not quite as obvious as one might suppose at first sight.

Annette Carson was a writer who worked for most of her life in the UK but in early middle age emigrated to South Africa. On her 60th birthday she became entitled to and obtained her UK retirement pension on which she had paid all necessary contributions including voluntary payments following her emigration.

However, when UK pensioners received subsequent annual increases Mrs Carson's pension continued to be paid at the original rate and she learned that it will not increase however long she lives. The reason advanced for this is that although there are arrangements between 'treaty countries', including the EU and USA to protect pensioners' increases these do not apply to other states, including South Africa, Australia and New Zealand, because the government has not concluded equivalent treaties with those states.

Her case appears to be typical of over 400,000 other UK pensioners living abroad and they contended that that amounts to discrimination contrary to Art 14. The House of

CONTINUED ▶

Lords did not agree and so such pensioners will have to live out the remainder of their lives on ever diminishing pensions despite having paid the same as everyone else in contributions. By a majority of 4:1 with Lord Carswell dissenting this was held not to amount to Art 14 discrimination.

To justify this, their Lordships made use of the word 'rational'. 'Severe scrutiny' is required when the question arises of discrimination against an individual, for example on grounds of sex or race, but 'merely . . . rational justification' suffices for grounds of residency or age because when collective considerations apply to the 'intricate and interlocking system of domestic social welfare' this is sufficient to 'preclude a claim for equality of treatment'.

Thus in such circumstances application of an economic policy takes precedence over recognition of pensioners' human rights and it would appear that to support it less severe scrutiny is required than would be the case were it based on sexual or racial discrimination.

16.5.2 The *Michalak* Catechism

One way of considering how to address Art 14 discrimination was adopted by Brooke LJ in *Wandsworth LBC v Michalak* [2003] 1 WLR 617 CA, sometimes referred to as the 'Michalak Catechism'. To understand this it is necessary to see what the court had to decide. Michalak was the brother in law of L's first cousin once removed and L was the secure tenant of a flat of which Wandsworth LBC was the landlord.

Michalak took up occupation of L's flat and paid L rent but after L died the council tried to evict him. He claimed he was entitled to be considered as the successor under the Housing Act 1985 s 113, although he was not in fact on the prescribed list of persons so entitled. He claimed that the list was not exhaustive but that in any event he was being discriminated against under the Human Rights Act 1998.

In order to determine whether this is the case the court asks four questions. If the answer to the first question is 'no' the case is likely to fail, but if 'yes' then the remaining questions need to be asked. At each step a negative answer probably precludes success.

The claim in *Michalak* was that he was being discriminated against contrary to Art 14 of the ECHR in that as a member of the tenant's family he was being treated less favourably than the members of a tenant's family listed in s 113 of the 1985 Housing Act. The Court of Appeal dismissed this claim on the basis that Parliament's intention in s 113 was to achieve certainty and avoid costly and time-consuming litigation as to who was or who was not a member of the tenant's family and that in itself could not amount to Art 14 discrimination.

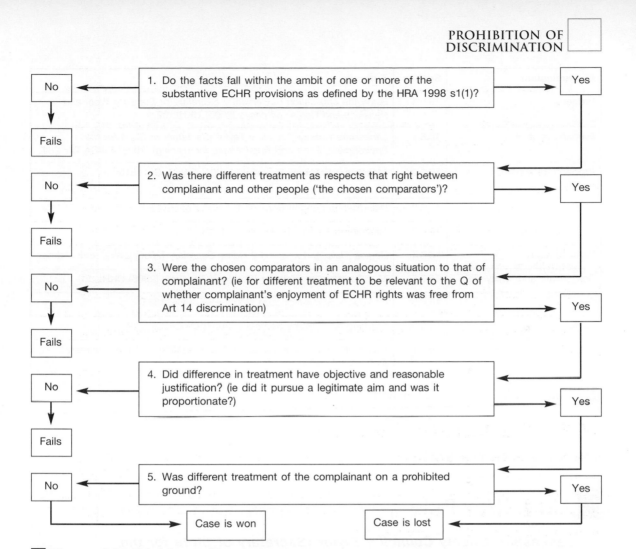

Figure 16.4 Michalak catechism

16.6 Other kinds of discrimination

The applications made to the former Commission or the present Court in Figure 16.3 related to a number of rights. The next table Figure 16.5 provides a summary of other examples of discrimination with relevant case law authority, which tend to be concentrated around property (status) rights, family relationships and status, asylum and crime.

Discrimination	Section	Authority
Property	16.6.1	*R (on the application of Carson) v Secretary of State for Work and Pensions and Conjoined cases* [2005] UKHL 37
Property (status)	16.6.1	*Lancashire County Council v Taylor (Secretary of State for the Environment, Food and Rural Affairs intervening)* [2005] EWCA Civ 284
Property (probationary tenancy)	16.6.2	*McLellan v Bracknell Forest BC* [2001] EWCA Civ 1510
Status	16.5.2	*Wandsworth London Borough Council v Michalak* [2003] 1 WLR 617 CA
Possessions on bankruptcy	16.6.3	*Malcolm In Re* [2004] EWCA Civ 1748
Right to marry	16.6.4	*Regina (Baiai and another) v Home Secretary* [2006] EWHC 823 (Admin)
Sex private and family life	16.6.5	*M v Secretary of State for Work and Pensions* [2006] UKHL 11
Sex 'spouse'	16.6.5	*Ghaidan v Godin-Mondoza* [2002] EWCA Civ 1533
Asylum	16.6.6	*F (Mongolia) v Home Secretary* [2007] EWCA Civ 769
Terrorism	16.6.7	*A and others v Home Secretary; X and another v Home Secretary* [2004] UKHL 56

■ Figure 16.5 Types of discrimination

16.6.1 Property status

CASE EXAMPLE

Lancashire County Council v Taylor (Secretary of State for the Environment, Food and Rural Affairs intervening) **[2005] EWCA Civ 284; [2005] 1 WLR 2668**

Taylor was in breach of agricultural covenants that required him to use tenanted land only for farming purposes rather than for food processing and distribution. He claimed that this contravened his right not to be discriminated against on grounds either of property or status, because there are different levels of protection available to agricultural tenants, depending on what kind of breach of covenant they are alleged to have committed.

The Court of Appeal held that the Agricultural Holdings Act 1986 did not contravene Art 14 of the Convention since the differential treatment applied to tenants alleged to be in breach of non-user covenants or covenants to improve their holdings, as compared to those alleged to be in breach of covenants to repair, depended solely on

CONTINUED ▸

the content of the covenant alleged to have been breached, or upon the nature of the breach alleged, rather than on the tenant's property or status.

Even if the 1986 Act did discriminate on a ground proscribed by Art 14 there was sufficient detail on the face of the legislation to demonstrate a rational and objective justification for the distinction between tenants who were at risk of inflated notices to repair, maintain or replace, for whom an early arbitration was desirable, and tenants facing other alleged breaches of covenant.

Taylor was not a 'victim' and not entitled to a declaration of incompatibility. Only a 'victim' could rely on Convention rights in legal proceedings and it had not been intended that members of the public should use the Act or the Convention to challenge legislation which they considered was incompatible with the Convention but by which they were not adversely affected.

16.6.2 Probationary tenancy

Introductory tenancy schemes enable local housing authorities to offer a 12-month probationary tenancy before upgrading to a secure tenancy, dependent on the new tenant complying with the tenancy conditions. There was concern that this might be discriminatory within Art 14 and this was tested in the Court of Appeal in *R (on the application of McLellan v Bracknell Forest BC)* [2001] EWCA Civ 1510.

Whether it is or not depends on the particular circumstances of each case. McLellan was a local authority tenant appealing against a possession order under the probationary scheme. He argued first that the review panel was not sufficiently independent and therefore he had been denied his right to a fair hearing under Art 6 and further that enforcement of the order would infringe his right to respect for private and family life under Art 8(1).

The appeal was dismissed. Even though the review panel 'did not exhibit the degree of independence required by Art 6, the court could find no reason why the review process could not be conducted fairly'. Judicial review provided an adequate method of challenge, and eviction was justified under Art 8(2) because it was necessary in a democratic society to protect other people's rights and freedoms. In any event county courts could adjourn hearings to facilitate judicial review.

The means employed by the introductory regime (which precludes security of tenure) were disproportionate and the regime was unnecessary for the control of anti-social behaviour as it could be invoked even where a tenant had not indulged in anti-social behaviour. Nevertheless, so far as Art 14 is concerned there was no discrimination on grounds of property status as once introduced, the regime applied to all tenants.

16.6.3 Bankrupt's possessions

CASE EXAMPLE

In re Malcolm [2004] EWCA Civ 1748; [2005] 1 WLR 1238

This case considered whether there was discrimination on bankruptcy in enjoyment of possessions for self-employed persons with retirement annuity contracts, compared with employees who had occupational pensions.

The applicant entered into a retirement annuity contract while he was self-employed but was made bankrupt in December 1996 with the result that, under the law then in force, the pension contract formed part of his estate, pursuant to ss 283(1) and 436 of the Insolvency Act 1986, and vested in his trustee in bankruptcy.

When he was automatically discharged from bankruptcy the assets remained vested in the trustee for the purpose of paying the outstanding bankruptcy debts, and in July 2002 the trustee sought to obtain the benefit of the pension contract for distribution among the remaining creditors.

The applicant applied in the bankruptcy proceedings for an injunction to restrain the trustee on the ground that the trustee's proposed use of his pension contract unlawfully discriminated against him in the peaceful enjoyment of his possessions, contrary to Art 14 read in conjunction with Art 1 of the First Protocol, because it disadvantaged the applicant on retirement as compared with an employee member of an occupational pension scheme with a forfeiture clause, who did not lose pension benefit on bankruptcy.

The judge dismissed the application and on the applicant's appeal it was held, dismissing the appeal, that to construe the Insolvency Act 1986 so as to include within the bankrupt's estate contractual pension rights vested in the bankrupt at the commencement of the bankruptcy was not inconsistent with the obligations, imposed on the UK by the Convention, to secure the applicant's enjoyment of his rights under the retirement annuity contract without discrimination.

The differential treatment in bankruptcy of the contractual pension rights of the self-employed and the pension rights of those employees who were members of an occupational pension scheme set up by way of a trust that provided for forfeiture of rights on bankruptcy was not a difference of treatment based on discrimination on the ground of status or any other ground. It arose because contractual pension rights fell within the description of property for the purposes of the 1986 Act. The rights of a beneficiary under an occupational pension scheme, after forfeiture on bankruptcy, did not fall within that description and in any event the words in ss 283(1) and 436 of the 1986 Act were not reasonably capable of being construed in such a way as to exclude contractual pension rights from the definition of 'property' in both provisions.

16.6.4 Right to marry

The application for judicial review made in *R (Baiai and others) v Home Secretary* [2006] EWHC 823 (Admin) following a change in the law requiring persons subject to immigration control who wished to enter into a civil marriage in the UK (ie a marriage other than according to the rites of the Church of England) to apply to the Home Secretary for permission. A certificate of approval had to be obtained; the application had to be in writing and to contain specified information; and a fee of £135 was payable.

Behind this was a raft of secondary requirements based on the Home Secretary's policy in considering such applications that required the applicant to have valid leave to enter or remain in the UK for more than six months, with more than three months remaining at the time of the application, or to have an initial application for immigration status, or an appeal remaining outstanding for 18 months, or to have compelling compassionate circumstances.

In the case of one application a male Algerian had been refused; in a second no response had been obtained for over three months; and in the third case there had also been untoward delay. Although the Home Secretary's policy was designed to prevent bogus marriages, it impinged on Art 14 requirements because it discriminated against those who did not subscribe to Church of England marriage rites and, whether the discrimination on grounds of religion or nationality was direct or indirect, weighty reasons were required to justify it.

On the evidence there was no reasonable and objective justification for the distinction in the treatment of marriages pursuant to Anglican rites and other religious marriages, with the consequence that the Art 14 claim must succeed.

16.6.5 Sex discrimination

M lived with her same-sex partner in their jointly owned house subject to a mortgage. She was the divorced mother of two children who spent most of each week with their father, M's former husband. Under the Child Support Act as the non-resident parent she contributed to the costs of maintaining the children incurred by their father as the parent with care.

Her partner's contribution to their joint housing costs was treated as reducing M's deductible housing costs whereas if she had been living with a man, whether married to him or not, his contribution to the mortgage would have been treated as part of hers so that her weekly child support payment would have been smaller.

M appealed against the assessment of her child support contributions on the ground that the assessment engaged her rights to respect for her private and family life and her home under Art 8 but also discriminated against her contrary to Art 14.

The House of Lords reversed the Court of Appeal and held (Baroness Hale of Richmond dissenting) that although the statutory scheme drew a distinction based on sexual orientation when assessing the amount of child support payable by a non-resident parent, that was not

sufficient in itself to bring M's complaint within the ambit of discrimination under Art 14 or the right to respect for family and private life under Art 8 (*M v Secretary of State for Work and Pensions* [2006] UKHL 11; [2006] 2 AC 91).

The case dealt more generally with discrimination aspects regarding same-sex relationships. In the present state of Strasbourg jurisprudence, homosexual relationships do not fall within the scope of the right to respect for Art 8 family life, and the respect afforded to those relationships was within the margin of appreciation allowed to contracting states. The UK reflected in domestic legislation such as the Civil Partnership Act 2004 the profound cultural changes which had occurred in most of Europe over the last two generations in attitudes towards homosexuality.

However, two generations was not a long time in which to change prejudices which had been deeply ingrained for many centuries, and both domestic law and Strasbourg case law were in a state of transition. The regulations of which M complained, and which had since been amended, represented the accepted values of society at the time, so the UK had acted with reasonable promptness and within its margin of appreciation in enacting them and they were not incompatible with M's Convention rights.

Inheriting a statutory tenancy provides more security than inheriting an assured tenancy. Thus, in another case where a person had for some 30 years lived in a permanent and stable relationship with a homosexual partner who was the protected tenant of a flat, he claimed that he was being subjected to Art 14 discrimination by interference with his Art 8 right to family and private life when the judge granted a declaration that he did not succeed to the tenancy as a surviving spouse but only became entitled to an assured tenancy as a member of the deceased's family (*Ghaidan v Godin-Mondoza* [2002] EWCA Civ 1533).

His appeal was allowed and it was held that his Art 14 rights had been infringed. The difference in wording under the Rent Act 1977 was that his succession 'as his or her wife or husband' should actually be 'as *if they were* his or her wife or husband' thus enabling him to enjoy statutory succession.

> 'Parliament having swallowed the camel of including unmarried partners within the protection given to married couples, it was not for the court to strain at the gnat of including such partners who were of the same sex as each other.'

To reach this decision involved the Court of Appeal in revisiting *Fitzpatrick v Sterling Housing Association* [2001] 1 AC 27 which was also concerned with the differences between paras 2 and 3 of the Schedule to the Rent Act 1977. That case arose prior to the enactment of the Human Rights Act and although it decided by a majority of 3:2 (Lord Hutton and Lord Hobhouse of Woodborough dissenting) that a same-sex partner of a tenant was now to be recognised as capable of being a member of the tenant's family for succession purposes, it did not find that the claimant was a 'spouse' or to be treated as such. The Court of Appeal in *Ghaidan v Godin-Mondoza* was thus able to apply the *Michalak* criteria, develop the Convention as a living instrument, and carry the law on tenancy succession by same-sex partners forward.

ACTIVITY

Quick quiz – true or false

1	The Equal Opportunities Commission was established by the Equal Pay Act 1970.	T	F
2	The Disability Rights Council and the National Disability Commission were established by the Disability Discrimination Act 1995.	T	F
3	The Equality Act 2006 established the Equality and Human Rights Commission for England, Wales and Scotland replacing three previous separate commissions.	T	F
4	The 2006 Regulations do not provide a right for persons over pensionable age to remain in employment.	T	F
5	The '*Michalak* Catechism' is a method employed by a judge to determine whether discrimination has occurred.	T	F
6	In *McLellan v Bracknell Forest BC* (2001) the introductory tenure regime was disproportionate and the regime was unnecessary but the court held there was no discrimination.	T	F
7	*In re Malcolm* (2004) there was no discrimination where a bankrupt's pension was used to pay his creditors.	T	F
8	*R (Baiai and others) v Home Secretary* (2006) is authority for saying that the Home Secretary can insist that foreign nationals marry according to the rites of the Church of England.	T	F
9	In *Ghaidan v Godin-Mondoza* (2002) the applicant's Art 14 right not to be discriminated against was upheld in the context of Art 12.	T	F
10	Same-sex partners do not have the status of 'spouse' under current law.	T	F

16.6.6 Asylum

F (Mongolia) v Home Secretary [2007] EWCA Civ 769 sets out the steps an asylum seeker had to take in order to reach a final Art 14 determination. The case eventually reached the Court of Appeal in seven main stages, but the applicant was still unsuccessful:

Stage	Action
1	F makes application for asylum to the Home Secretary, which is refused
2	F appeals to the single judge of the Asylum and Immigration Tribunal (AIT) who dismisses his appeal (in this case holding that to return him to Mongolia would not expose him to a real risk of persecution)
3	F applies for reconsideration of the single judge's decision by a Senior Immigration Judge (SIJ), in this case on the ground that it failed to demonstrate error on a ground of law by the single judge
4	F then applies for statutory reconsideration, also refused on the basis that there was no arguable error of law
5	The next step was to apply (unsuccessfully again in F's case) for judicial review of several steps in the previous procedure, ie the: (i) Home Secretary's refusal of asylum (ii) rejection of his appeal by the singe judge of the AIT (iii) refusal of the SIJ to order reconsideration
6	Permission was refused firstly on the papers and subsequently by consent
7	Finally there was a Court of Appeal hearing to ascertain whether a previous Court of Appeal decision was inconsistent with two earlier House of Lords decisions in order to address conclusively those of F's contentions based on legal grounds The Court held that there had to be shown the enunciation by the House of Lords of a clear principle that was plainly inconsistent with the approach to similar subject matter of the Court of Appeal authority under attack, which was not the case here F lost his battle to obtain asylum in the UK

Figure 16.6 Art 14 steps for asylum seekers

16.6.7 Terrorism

The legislation considered necessary by the government immediately following the attack on the twin towers in New York in 2001 was hastily enacted and consequently did not have the benefit of detailed parliamentary consideration. It was directed at a small group of foreign nationals who were thought to pose a risk to the national security of the UK. Under the Anti-terrorism, Crime and Security Act 2001 s 21 the Secretary of State was given power to certify people suspected of being international terrorists but who could not be deported because that would have meant sending them to a state where they might have been at risk of being subjected to torture or inhuman treatment contrary to Art 2 of the ECHR. The Human Rights Act 1998 would not allow this to be done.

The government's problem was that they were either not prepared or were unable to arrest, charge and try such suspects, perhaps because they had not committed any offences or that to do so could compromise national security by bringing information or investigative methodology into the public domain. The Act therefore provided that, once certified under s 21, they could be detained without charge or trial under s 23. In an attempt to render this procedure lawful the government had derogated from the Convention provision enacted as Art 5(1)(f) of Sched 1 Pt 1 of the 1998 HRA by virtue of the Human Rights Act 1998 (Designated Derogation) Order 2001.

The consequence of effectively branding a small group of foreign nationals as suspected Al-Qaeda terrorists by such targeted legislation gave rise to claims that the derogation was illegal and not done in accordance with Art 15 of the ECHR, that the right to liberty and security under Art 5 had been infringed, and that together these pointed to discrimination against the foreign nationals as defined by Art 14.

A small group of suspects were detained in this manner and eventually managed to have their case heard by the Special Immigration Appeal Commission (SIAC) which held that s 23 of the 2001 Act was incompatible with Arts 5 and 14 of the ECHR because they were being discriminated against by reason of their nationality. That decision was reversed by the Court of Appeal.

Bringing their appeal to the House of Lords, the alleged terrorists formulated three main arguments:

(1) The derogation from the provisions of the Convention under Art 15 was impermissible because there was no 'public emergency threatening the life of the nation' within the meaning of Art 15(1) so that the threshold test for reliance on Art 15 had not been satisfied.

(2) The derogation was not proportionate because the legislative objective could have been achieved by means which did not, or did not so severely, restrict the fundamental right to personal freedom.

(3) Section 23 was discriminatory in providing for the detention of suspected international terrorists who were not UK nationals but not for the detention of suspected international terrorists who were UK nationals.

The House of Lords allowed their appeal (*A and others v Home Secretary; X and another v Home Secretary* [2004] UKHL 56) (Lord Hoffmann dissenting on the public emergency issue and Lord Walker dissenting on the proportionality and discrimination issues). The relevant sections of the Act, ss 21 and 23, were disproportionate because they did not rationally address the threat to the UK's security in that they ignored threats from UK nationals and illogically permitted suspects such as these to go abroad to pursue their alleged activities unless prevented by rights abuses in the states to which they would have to be sent. The measures were not 'strictly required' by the exigencies of the perceived threat within the meaning of Art 15.

Detaining one group of suspected international terrorists, defined by nationality or immigration status, and not another could not be justified and violated Art 14. UK nationals suspected of the same things were dealt with differently, and certainly could not be detained indefinitely without charge or trial. The derogation failed because it had not been done on grounds of nationality or immigration status.

A further consideration was that the UK was in breach of other international obligations under Art 26 of the UN International Covenant on Civil and Political Rights and, because of these breaches, the government was unable to rely on the 'old rule' that a sovereign state could control

the entry and expulsion of aliens to its territory. The effect was that the 2001 Order had to be quashed and a declaration of incompatibility was made. The Order was disproportionate and allowed detention of suspected international terrorists in a manner that discriminated against them on the ground of their nationality or immigration status.

KEY FACTS

1	Since the 1960s a variety of anti-discrimination UK statutes have been enacted
2	Originally addressing discrimination in a piecemeal fashion, a 'joined-up' approach was eventually adopted by the Equality Act 2006
3	The subject matter of domestic law now covers equal opportunities, racial equality and disability rights
4	International declarations and conventions establish anti-discriminatory provisions to promote sexual, racial, religious, national and ethnic equality
5	The European regime standard and requirements are established in ECHR Art 14 which prohibits discrimination on a wide and unlimited range of grounds (because of the words 'such as' in the article)
6	The 'such as' grounds are sex, race, colour, language, religion, political or other opinion, national or social origin, association with a national minority, property, birth or other status
7	Art 14 does not stand by itself so if discrimination occurs it must do so in the context of one of the other substantive ECHR grounds
8	There is thus extensive case law covering a wide area and including various property rights, family, immigration and asylum seekers, sexual rights and terrorism
9	The courts may apply a 'rational policy' doctrine to justify what would otherwise be clear discrimination against a group of people, as in *Carson*
10	A wide margin of appreciation is permissible with regard to discrimination because of the different historical, cultural and developmental backgrounds of the 47 signatories to the ECHR

Useful resources

Equality and Human Rights Commission: www.equalityhumanrights.com.

UN Treaty Collection: http://untreaty.un.org/.

Further reading

Baker, P, 'Burden v Burden: the Grand Chamber of the ECtHR Adopts a Restrictive Approach on the Question of Discrimination', Case Comment, BTR 2008, 4, 329–334.

Fenwick, H, *Civil Liberties and Human Rights* (4th edn, Routledge-Cavendish, 2007) 1476–1603.

Foster, S, *Human Rights and Civil Liberties* (2nd edn, Pearson Longman, Harlow, 2008) 662–687.

Livingstone, S, 'Article 14 and the Prevention of Discrimination in the European Convention on Human Rights', EHRLR, 1997, 1, 25–34.

Ovey, C and White, R, C A, *Jacobs & White The European Convention on Human Rights* (4th edn, Oxford University Press, 2006) 412–431.

Shorts, E and de Than, C, *Human Rights Law in the UK* (Sweet & Maxwell, 2001), 637–697.

chapter
17 **REGIONAL RIGHTS REGIMES** ■

AIMS AND OBJECTIVES

This final chapter aims to provide a brief survey of the other non-European rights regimes that operate with differing degrees of effectiveness in areas adjacent to Europe and in other parts of the world in a variety of formats:

■ the Americas, north and south

■ Africa

■ Minsk (Russia and the Commonwealth of Independent States)

■ the Arab world.

17.1 The Americas

17.1.1 American Declaration of the Rights and Duties of Man 1948

This document pre-dated the Universal Declaration of Human Rights of the same year and has similar content that includes economic and social rights. A number of other articles set out the responsibilities and duties of citizens to ensure that children are educated, provision of civil and military service to their countries when needed, and the responsibility to vote for democratically elected governments.

17.1.2 Organisation of American States (OAS)

The origins of the OAS go back to the International Union of American Republics in 1890 but in its modern form it was established at the 1948 Bogota conference. The Charter entered into force in 1951 and has subsequently been amended by protocols on a number of occasions with its broad objectives including:

• promotion of democracy

• strengthening peace and security throughout the continent

• making provision for common action against aggression

• seeking solutions to political, economic and juridical problems.

The Inter-American Commission on Human Rights was created in 1959 and this led to a Convention of 1969 which came into force in 1978. There are 35 Member States, 25 of which have ratified the Convention and 20 of which recognise the jurisdiction of the Court. The concerns in the Americas have been different from those in Europe as Central and South America were slow to adopt democracy and until fairly recently most states were ruled by unelected military juntas, many of which had corrupt judiciary and indulged in torture and 'disappearances' of opponents. This resulted in different emphases from those that have interested the European states, and there is more diversity and less coherence in the Americas (stretching from Canada and Alaska in the north to Tierra del Fuego in the south) than is the case in Europe.

17.1.3 American Convention on Human Rights 1969

The Convention is a treaty based on the 1948 American Declaration and is sometimes called the pact of San Jose, Costa Rica. It followed the Third Special Inter-American Conference in Buenos Aires in 1967 and approved the incorporation into the organisation's Charter of broad standards of economic, social and educational rights with other more specific rights including the following:

- juridical personality   Art 3
- to have a name   Art 18
- rights of the child   Art 19
- to nationality   Art 20
- to property   Art 21
- freedom of movement and residence Art 22
- to participate in government   Art 23
- to equal protection of the law   Art 24
- to judicial protection by the law   Art 25.

It therefore includes objectives such as participation in government and nomenclature rights that go beyond the scope of the ECHR.

17.1.4 Forced disappearances

During the latter part of the twentieth century one of the worst kinds of abuse that seemed to be endemic in Central and South America was the incidence of forced disappearances. Unelected regimes tended to take care of their opponents simply by making them disappear, as occurred in Chile under the Pinochet regime. To address this particular transgression the Inter-American Convention on the Forced Disappearance of Persons (1994) was agreed. The preamble stated that the OAS members were:

- disturbed by the persistence of forced disappearances of persons, which was an affront to the whole hemisphere, and

- concerned at violations of many essential and non-derogable human rights which were supposed to be protected under the UN and American Declarations and the American Convention.

The 1994 Convention signatories therefore undertook not to tolerate or practise forced disappearances by reference to four essential elements:

1. depriving persons of their freedom in whatever manner
2. perpetrating any form of disappearance whether with or without state support
3. not providing information or refusing to acknowledge occurrences of the crime of 'disappearing' people (using the word 'disappear' as a verb)
4. impeding or negating legal or procedural remedies.

It was also provided that forced disappearances could not be treated as political crimes, nor could they be protected by limitation periods or by threats of political instability or other public emergency. Detained persons should be held in officially recognised establishments, be brought promptly before judicial authority and states should provide mutual assistance to search for and identify victims.

17.2 Africa

17.2.1 Organisation of African Unity

The Organisation of African Unity (OAU) was established in 1963 when 53 African states agreed a Charter, and in 1981 the Assembly of Heads of States and Government of the OAU adopted the African Charter on Human and Peoples' Rights which came into force in 1986. Implementation was by Commission but there were no enforcement provisions, so it was only able to operate as an advisory body, which partly explains why it has not been as effective as the American or European regimes.

The concern is with inviolability of borders and one African characteristic has been reluctance or inability to take effective action when violations have occurred, although sometimes this seems not to be the case as there are also many instances of incursions into, and attacks on, neighbouring territories. In 2002 the organisation was disbanded and a new African Union (AU) was launched in Durban. The OAU Charter did not specifically address human rights but they are now addressed in the AU Charter.

Art II sets out the purposes of the Organisation as follows:

a. 'To promote the unity and solidarity of the African States;
b. To coordinate and intensify their cooperation and efforts to achieve a better life for the peoples of Africa;
c. To defend their sovereignty, their territorial integrity and independence;

d. To eradicate all forms of colonialism from Africa; and

e. To promote international cooperation, having due regard to the Charter of the United Nations and the Universal Declaration of Human Rights.'

Art III establishes the principles upon which the purposes are to be based:

1. 'The sovereign equality of all Member States.

2. Non-interference in the internal affairs of States.

3. Respect for the sovereignty and territorial integrity of each State and for its inalienable right to independent existence.

4. Peaceful settlement of disputes by negotiation, mediation, conciliation or arbitration.

5. Unreserved condemnation, in all its forms, of political assassination as well as of subversive activities on the part of neighbouring States or any other States.

6. Absolute dedication to the total emancipation of the African territories which are still dependent.

7. Affirmation of a policy of non-alignment with regard to all blocs.'

17.2.2 African Union

Structure

The AU is broadly modelled on the EU and so is not primarily intended to be a human rights organisation, although it is now able to bring rights influence to bear should a sufficient number of Member States agree to devote priority to such purposes. The organisation is structured as follows:

- *Assembly*, comprising the members' heads of state and with functions including common policies, membership and (significantly, in this context) conflict resolution

- *Executive Council*, made up of the foreign ministers and dealing with trade, social security, food, agriculture and communications

- *Permanent Representative Committee*, consisting of the Ambassadors to the AU who are tasked with preparing the work of the Executive Council

- The remainder of the organisation comprises the Commission or Secretariat, a number of specialised technical committees, the Pan-African Parliament, the Economic, Social and Cultural Council, and three financial institutions.

AU human rights bodies

The reconstitution of the African arrangements provides an opportunity to establish more effective human rights procedures for the continent and to overcome the limitations of the

previous Commission. There is now an African Court on Human and Peoples' Rights which was established in 2005 and which integrated with the African Court of Justice, and a Peace and Security Council with 15 members who are responsible for monitoring and intervening in conflicts. They are to be advised by a Council of Elders and it is intended that there should be an effective African force to implement necessary action. The need for this is apparent in a number of parts of the continent and assistance is to be made available from the EU and elsewhere.

Year	Document	Content	Articles
1969	OAU Convention Governing Specific Aspects of Refugee Problems in Africa	Refugees, asylum, prohibition of subversion, non-discrimination	15
1981	African Charter	Rights and duties, measures of safeguard, general provisions	68
1990	African Charter on the Rights and Welfare of the Child	Freedoms, education, protection against abuse, responsibilities and organisational matters	48
1998	Protocol on the Establishment of an African Court on Human and Peoples' Rights	Governs relationship between Court and Commission, jurisdiction, access, administrative arrangements	35

■ Figure 17.1 African rights documents

17.3 Minsk Convention

The full title is the Commonwealth of Independent States Convention on Human Rights (1995) which was opened for signature in May 1995, originally signed by Armenia, Belarus, Georgia, Kyrgyzstan, Moldova, Russia and Tajikistan and subsequently ratified by Belarus, Kyrgyzstan, the Russian Federation and Tajikistan, entering into force in August 1998.

The CIS Commission on Human Rights is the control mechanism by which monitoring is meant to take place and recommendations issued. There has been concern in the Council of Europe that the CIS Convention does not offer as extensive protection as the ECHR and there is a possibility of conflict in states that are members of both: Armenia, Georgia, Moldova, the Russian Federation and Ukraine.

Problems could arise, for example, with regard to individual applications under the ECHR where the European Court's rulings are enforceable whilst recommendations under the Minsk Convention are not. However, other signatories are not eligible for membership of the Council of Europe so there is at least some alternative provision available for them although less satisfactory than the European arrangements in terms of effectiveness and enforceability.

17.4 Arab Declaration and Charter

17.4.1 Cairo Declaration

Following a conference in Cairo in 1990 the Arab world published its own Declaration to reinforce the UN global regime. It contained 25 articles and one of its objectives was to serve as general guidance on human rights for Member States following a report by legal experts. It differs from other approaches in that it is expressed in Islamic religious terms and so, for example, refers to the human family descended from Adam, subordinate to Allah, and with life being recognised as a God-given gift.

It addresses a variety of rights which along with family matters include:

- humanitarian concerns
- sexual equality
- prohibition of colonialism
- freedom of work and movement
- ownership of physical and intellectual property
- security, equality and freedom from hostage taking.

The Declaration goes on to say that authority is a trust, that abuse or malicious exploitation of authority should not be allowed, and that all the freedoms and rights set out in the Declaration must be subject to the Islamic Shar'ia which is the only source of reference for explanation or clarification of any of its articles.

17.4.2 Arab Charter on Human Rights

In 1994 further work was carried out on refining approaches to human rights, and the Council of the League of Arab States authorised the drafting of a document which referred to the Arab world as the birthplace of civilisation and cradle of religions. It rejected racism and Zionism, acknowledged the eternal principles of brotherhood established by the Islamic Shar'ia and other divinely revealed religions, expressed belief in the rule of law and reaffirmed the principles of the UN Charter and International Bill of Human Rights together with the Cairo Declaration.

However, there were an insufficient number of ratifications to enable the 1994 document to enter into force and in 2004 the project was carried forward and modernised in a new charter whose text was adopted by the Arab Standing Committee for Human Rights 5th–14th January. The approach was to start with the UN International Bill of Human Rights, place it in context with the Cairo Declaration, reject Zionism and racism and then incorporate specific categories of right. The result is a charter which provides a different emphasis to the UN and other regional materials, which came into force on 15th March 2008.

Concerns have been expressed about possible conflict between the Arab Charter and UN norms. For example, the death penalty might be applied to children in some circumstances. Article 7(1) says that:

'Sentence of death shall not be imposed on persons under 18 years of age, unless otherwise stipulated in the laws in force at the time of the commission of the crime.'

In December 2007 the General Assembly of the United Nations agreed to a global moratorium on all executions as a step in the universal agenda of abolishing capital punishment altogether. The Charter does not anticipate this happening at an early date, however, as Art 7(2) goes on to say that:

'The death penalty shall not be inflicted on a pregnant woman prior to her delivery or on a nursing mother within two years from the date of her delivery; in all cases, the best interests of the infant shall be the primary consideration.'

The governmental structure of most, if not all, Arab and many African states is bound to mean that the rights agenda enthusiastically adopted in Europe and less wholeheartedly in other parts of the world does not find itself at the top of the priority list of things that must be done and changes that must be made. Nevertheless, in a world of increasing movement and communication there are signs of a growing interest in fostering and protecting rights of more vulnerable people, and perhaps Arab and African states will soon become more focused and effective in their human rights aims and objectives.

17.5 Asia

Despite covering such an extensive part of the world, and for that very reason, Asia does not have any cohesive or comprehensive human rights organisations of the kind previously discussed in this chapter and in respect of Europe, although there is some machinery in force *via* the Asia-Pacific Forum (APF). The way it operates is explained as advancing human rights in the Asia Pacific through their member organisations, and facilitating the formation and growth of national human rights institutions by providing training, networking and resource sharing. The organisation was established in 1996 with the objective of providing a framework of human rights institutions that would work together and co-operate on a regional basis.

There are 14 full members under what are called the 'Paris Principles', which are rules made at a meeting in Paris under the auspices of the UN at which a comprehensive set of principles was drawn up to guide the establishment and operation of national human rights institutions. Accreditation under the rules means that the member institutions have a number of virtues:

• a clearly defined and broad-based mandate, based on universal human rights standards

• independence guaranteed by legislation or the constitution

- autonomy from government
- pluralism, including membership that broadly reflects the society
- adequate powers of investigation
- sufficient resources.

Nevertheless, a number of Asian and South Pacific states have a strong rights ethos and play their part in the development of global human rights.

KEY FACTS

The ECHR is the most advanced and effective regional human rights regime operating in the world today, since 1998 working through the full-time European Court of Human Rights and having its provisions and judgments complied with by 47 Member States of the Council of Europe

The Inter-American Human Rights System is sophisticated and elaborate and has played an influential part in encouraging and fostering the development of democratic governance in the Americas and reduction in widespread human rights violations such as forced disappearances

The African OAS was not primarily a rights organisation but the revitalised AU and the more recently constituted Court and Council may be able to develop a more proactive stance to the wide-ranging human rights abuses that blighted the continent in the twentieth century

The Minsk Convention of the Commonwealth of Independent States was borne out of the demise of the Soviet Union at the end of the Cold War and reflects some of the values of the ECHR, but without enforcement machinery giving rise also to some concern about possible conflict of purpose where membership is duplicated

The League of Arab States has 22 members and the 1990 Cairo Declaration and 1994 Charter have been updated and brought into force in 2008 expressing Islamic and Shar'ia human rights values, some of which may in future need to be reconciled with global provisions

Asia does not possess a formal regional rights structure because of its enormous size and diversity but the Asia Pacific Forum of National Human Rights Institutions provides a co-ordinating developmental and training role with other bodies, such as the UN, and is also poised to increase its range and influence

17.6 Conclusions

The first chapter of this book introduced a number of ideas and concepts that are important in understanding the nature and meaning of human rights. The second and third chapters explained the European Convention and Court of Human Rights and the introduction of the treaty law into domestic UK law.

Chapters 4–14 dealt separately with the substantive rights, freedoms provided by and prohibitions stipulated in the ECHR, the body of law developed throughout Europe which is meant to protect the interests of individuals across the continent. How to enforce those rights was the subject matter of Chapter 15 and the pervading principle of prohibiting discrimination was dealt with in Chapter 16. This final chapter provides a brief summary of other regional rights arrangements which if they are to be effective might learn much from the European example.

Human rights have come a long way since 1948 when they were proclaimed in the Universal Declaration of Human Rights. A cynical view might be that not much was learned from the catastrophic mistakes of the first part of the twentieth century as wars and crimes against humanity continue. What the ECHR shows, however, is that it is possible to institute a system that provides some justice for individuals who have been mistreated by their own people and perhaps this movement will continue to grow and spread its influence as time goes on.

Useful resources

International and regional human rights instruments:
http://www.diplomacy.edu/arabcharter/human_instruments.asp.
Inter-American Human Rights access (University of Minnesota Human Rights Library):
    http://www1.umn.edu/humanrts/inter-americansystem.htm.
Introduction to Arab Charter of Human Rights 2004:
    http://www.acihl.org/res/Arab_Charter_on_Human_Rights_2004.pdf.
Asia Pacific Forum of National Human Rights Institutions: http://www.asiapacificforum.net/.

Further reading

Bowring, B, 'Russia's Accession to the Council of Europe and Human Rights: Compliance or cross-purposes?' EHRLR 1997, 6, 628–643.

Chaskalson, A, 'The Widening Gyre: Counter-terrorism, Human Rights and the Rule of Law', CLJ 2008, 67(1), 69–91.

Otty, T, 'Honour Bound to Defend Freedom? The Guantanamo Bay Litigation and the Fight for Fundamental Values in the War on Terror', EHRLR 2008, 4, 433–453.

Rehman, J, *International Human Rights Law: a Practical Approach* (Pearson Education, 2003).

Scannella, P and Splinter, P, 'The United Nations Human Rights Council: A Promise to be Fulfilled', HRL Rev 2007, 7(1), 41–72.

Smith, R K M, *Textbook on International Human Rights* (3rd edn, Oxford University Press, 2007).

Steiner, H J, Alston, P and Goodman, R, *International Human Rights in Context: Law, Politics, Morals* (3rd edn, Oxford University Press, 2007).

Wallace, R M M, assisted by Dale-Risk, K, *International Human Rights Text and Materials* (7th edn, Sweet & Maxwell, 2007).

INDEX ▪

abode, deprivation of place of, 376–7
abolition
   corporal punishment, 131, 132
   death penalty, 38, 39, 40, 65, 85, 118, 371
   slavery, 6, 147–64
abortion, opposition to, 292–3
absolute unacceptability of torture, 124–5
access
   to court, 210–13
   to legal advice, 210–13, 221–2
accusatorial proceedings, 214
acronyms, commonly used, 22
actual bias, judge, 200, 203
adequate time and facilities, 221
adjudication role of judge, 214
admissibility criteria, European Court of Human Rights,
   46
adoption, 352
adults, (mis)treatment, 135–40
advisory opinions, 49–51
Africa, 402–4
African (Banjul) Charter on Human and Peoples' Rights,
   403–4
   widows, 339, 357
African Union, 403–4
age discrimination, 383
   see also retirement age
agreed rights, 19
Agricultural Holdings Act 1986, 390–1
aircraft noise, 265–6
Al-Qaeda, 41, 397
American Convention on Human Rights (1969), 401
   on marriage, 339
American Declaration of the Rights and Duties of Man
   1948, 400
Americas, 400–2
animals, 294
anonymity, witness, 223, 224
anti-abortion, 292–3
anti-libertarian policies, 176–8

Anti-Terrorism, Crime and Security Act 2001, 42, 75,
   174, 175, 324, 396
   see also terrorism
Apartheid, 383
apparent bias, judge, 200, 203
Arab Declaration and Charter, 405–6
arbitration proceedings, 207
armed services see military service
arrest
   detention and, distinction, 168
   fair process on, example (Kevin), 196–7, 234–6
   lawful (in ECHR), 166–7
Arrowsmith, Pat, 292, 310–11
Asia, 406–7
assembly, 321–37
   freedom of, 321–37
   meaning, 321, 326, 332–5
assisted suicide, 105, 106, 107, 108, 109, 272–3, 294–6,
   377–8
association, 321–37
   analysis and types of, 327–32
   case law, 328–32
   freedom of, 321–37
   meaning, 321, 326
asylum seekers, 137, 138, 139, 140, 373–4, 395–6
   claims for damages, 373–4
   detention, 184–5
   marriage, 341, 348–50
audi alteram partem, 200
Austria, media law, 316
authoritarian proposition and torture, 125
authority of judiciary, maintaining, 135–6
autism, 184
autonomy (personal), 272–4
   sexual, 274, 308

bail, refusal, 172
Banjul Charter, widows see African Charter
bankrupt's possessions, 392
barristers, 'cab rank' rule, 222

beating *see* corporal punishment; torture
Beijing Rules, juvenile prosecution, 217
Belgium
    forced compulsory labour/service
        habitual criminals, 155–6
        legal service, 158
    legal advice/assistance, 222
    marriage, 342–3
Bennett case, 113
bias, 194, 198–204
    judicial, in hearings, 198–203
    jury, 203–4
    protection against, 211
    types, 203
        see also specific types
Bill of Rights 1698 (English), 55, 60, 195–6, 230
    freedom of expression, 302
Bingham, Lord
    on assisted suicide, 295–6
    on hunting, 254–5
    on retrospective punishment, 240–1
    on security, 188
    on torture, 122
    on wartime deaths, 98
birching, 129, 130
Bland, Tony, 109–10
blasphemy, 299, 300, 319
breach
    of confidence, 248, 253, 308, 314–15
    of the peace, 170–1, 181
Bringing Rights Home, 59
Britain *see* United Kingdom
British National Party, 322–3
Bulger, James, Thomson and Venables killing of, 134–5,
        253
burden of proof, 214
    reversed, 218–20
Bush (George W) government, torture, 141–2
Bushell's case, 303

'cab rank' rule, 222
Cairo declaration, 405
Campbell, Naomi, 253
capacity *see* competency and capacity
capital punishment *see* death penalty
certainty v justice, 362
Chagos Islanders, 376–7
Chambers of European Court of Human Rights, 34
charge, detention without, 41, 173–6
chastisement of children, 129–31
children (minors)
    Arab Charter and death penalty for, 406
    begetting *see* family, founding a
    detention, 182–3
    Little Red School Book, 308, 309
    (mis)treatment, 129–35
    prosecution within a reasonable time, 216–17

protection, 212
    right to life, 83–4
    trafficking, 162, 163
    as witnesses, 223
Children Act 2004, 132–3·
China
    immigrants in UK from, trafficking, 161–2
    torture, 142–3
Christmas Island 1957–58 nuclear tests, 86–7
Civil Contingency Act 2004, 176
civil exceptions to forced labour in Art 4 of EHCR,
        157–60
civil law, justice delivered within a reasonable time,
        216–17
civil liberties, English, 165
Civil Partnership Act 2004, 382, 394
civil rights in Europe, historical perspectives, 6–8
civilians in war *see* non-combatants
claims
    for damages, asylum seekers, 373–4
    definition, 281
closed shops, 328, 329
cohabiting siblings and tax, 355–6
collection of information, 260–3
colonialism, end of, 10–11
combatants in trials, 214
Commissioner for Human Rights (Council of Europe), 33
Committee of Ministers (Council of Europe), 31–2
common law
    freedom of expression, 302–3
    no punishment without law, 230
    privacy, 248–51
    right to fair trial, 205, 211
    right to life, 117–18
    slavery, 148–9
Commonwealth of Independent States (CIS), Russia and
        see Russia
community charge, failure to pay, 179–80
competency and capacity (mental)
    in agreeing to confinement or treatment, 183
    in right to die, 105–7
        absence, 109–10
    in right to live, 111–12
        absence, 111
compliance
    with court order, failure, 179–80
    Milgram's torture experiment, 123–4
compulsory labour *see* forced or compulsory labour
concretisation, 18
confidence/confidentiality, breach of, 248, 253, 308,
        314–15
consanguinity, 341, 347–8
conscience, freedom of, 74, 280, 282, 283, 284, 285, 288,
        292, 293, 297, 300
conscientious objector, 151, 152, 156, 272, 292, 297
constitution, UK's, 60–1
control orders, 42

Convention(s), 23
    American, on Human Rights *see* American Convention
        on Human Rights
    Inter-American, on the Forced Disappearance of Persons
        (1994), 401
    Minsk, 404
    UN *see* United Nations
Convention against Trafficking in Humans, Council of
        Europe, 160–4
Convention for the Protection of Human Rights and
        Fundamental Freedoms *see* European Convention
        on Human Rights
Convention on the Elimination of All Forms of
        Discrimination against Women (CEDAW), 384
conviction, detention after, 179
corporal punishment, 127
    children, 129, 130, 131, 132, 133
Council of Europe, 10, 27
    Convention against Trafficking in Humans, 160–4
    institutions and personnel, 30–5
    prerequisite to membership, 85–6
council tax (community charge), failure to pay, 179–80
Countryside Alliance, 71, 254–5, 257, 278
court
    access to, 210–13
    independence *see* judiciary
Court of Chancery, 361
court martial, 171–2
court order, lawful, non-compliance with, 179–80
Craxi (former Italian Prime Minister) case, 263
crime
    no punishment without law *see* no punishment without
        law
    pretrial detention, 172
    prevention of commission of offence or, 181–2,
        311–12
    transnational organised, UN Convention against, 161
Criminal Evidence (Witness Anonymity) Act 2008, 224
Criminal Justice Act 1988, 144, 312
Criminal Justice Act 1991, 70, 237
Criminal Justice Act 2003, 151, 173, 194, 204
Criminal Justice and Public Order Act 1994 s 25, 172,
        324
criminals
    habitual (Belgium), forced labour, 155
    justice delivered Within a reasonable time, 216–17
    young, punishment, 134–5
Crossman diaries, 315
Crown, right to intervene, 71–2
Crown Proceedings Act 1600, 364
Crown Proceedings Act 1947, 366
Crown Proceedings Act 1948, 359
cultural identity, 270–2
cultural lifestyle, 256
    hunting and, 255
cultural relativism, 2, 14, 17
custody *see* detention

Cyprus, 45–6
    Greek Cypriots, in Northern Cyprus, 45, 376

de Menezes, Jean Charles, 91, 113
de Montesquieu, Baron, 3, 5, 359, 363
death(s)
    see also suicide
    in custody, 100–4
    right to die, 105–11
    wartime, 96–9
death penalty (capital punishment), 63, 84
    abolition, 38, 39, 40, 65, 85, 118, 371
    Arab Charter and, 406
    deportation and the, 137
declaration(s), 23
    Cairo, 405
    on discrimination, 383–4
    of incompatibility, 68–70
        remedial actions, 64, 65, 73
    on racial discrimination, international, 383
Declaration of the Rights and Duties of Man 1948,
        American, 400
Declaration of Tokyo 1975, 125
Declaration on the Protection of All Persons from Being
        Subjected to Torture and Other Cruel, Inhuman or
        Degrading Treatment or Punishment, 125
defamation, 313–14
defending oneself, 221–2
degrading treatment, James Bulger killers, 135
Dembour analysis, 19–20
democracy/democratic society, 4, 5
    limitations on freedom of expression necessary in a,
        308–9, 311
Denmark, freedom of religion, 299–300
deportation, 137–40
    see also extradition
    illegal immigrants, 138, 140, 232, 243
deprivation of place of abode, 376–7
derogations (art 15 of ECHR), 40–2, 397
    Human Rights Act and, 62, 74–7
desuetude, 194
detention/custody (deprivation of liberty)
    arrest and, distinction, 168
    in China, torture in, 142
    deaths in, 100–4
    foreign states, 185–8
    lawful or circumstances permitting, 167–70
    non-criminal, 178–85
    Northern Ireland troubles *see* Northern Ireland troubles
    without charge, 41, 173–6
    without warrant, 171
Dicey's theory of parliamentary sovereignty, 230, 231
die, right to, 105–11
dilemma, insoluble (on right to die), 107–8
diplomats, 11–12
disability, children with, 133–4
Disability Discrimination Act 1995, 382

disappearances, forced, 401–2
disclosure of information, 260–3
    see also confidence
    prevention, 314–15
discrimination, 381–409
    kinds/types, 389–90
    meaning, 387–9
    prohibition/no toleration, 15, 381–409
        domestic law, 381–3
        ECHR (Art 14), 36, 37–8, 384, 385, 388, 391, 393, 394, 395, 396, 397
        getting cases heard, 385–7
disorder, prevention, 311–12
dissemination (of information), unjustifiable, 263
divorce, 341, 350–2
DNA databases, removal from, 274
doctors
    medical negligence, 243–4, 374–5
    roles in interrogation, 127
doctrine of double effect, 108–9
domestic law/legislation, 136
    see also United Kingdom
    discrimination, 381–3
    equality, 363
    freedom to associate and assemble, 322–5
    transsexuals and marriage, 354
double effect, doctrine of, 108–9
Douglas wedding and Hello! magazine, 253
driving over limit, burden of proof, 219
drugs (illegal)
    importation, 275
    Rastafarians and, 289
due process (of law), 229–30
duties see obligations and duties

education (right to), 39, 63, 65
    higher, 375–6
égalité, 17
elections, free, right to, 65
embargo, UN, 371
embryo implantation, consent, 343–4
employment and labour
    see also pensions
    equal pay legislation, 381
    forced/compulsory see forced or compulsory labour
    freedom to associate and assemble, 322
        case law, 328–32
    retirement age see retirement age
enforceability of rights/remedies, 358–80
    limitations, 372–3
England (human rights and law in), 54–5
    Bill of Rights see Bill of Rights
    civil liberties, 165
    consanguinity and marriage, 348
    enforceability of rights, 358–60
    freedom of expression, 302–4
    slavery law, 4–6, 148–50

trial in
    fair, 193–4
    system, 214
environment, one's living, protection of, 263–8
Equal Pay Act 1970, 381
equality, 1, 17
    before the law, 363–4
    discrimination and, 384–5
Equality Act 2006, 286, 382, 382–3
equitable maxims, 359, 361–2
ethical issues, right to life, 84, 107, 109
Europe
    freedom of thought/conscience/religion, 297–300
    historical perspectives, 6–8
    right to life in, 115–17
    torture today in, 122
    UK's reluctant commitment to, 55–6
European Commission of Human Rights, 28, 30–1
European Convention on Human Rights (ECHR), 26–53
    categories of protection (Articles 2-14), 26
    derogations (under Art 15) see derogations
    discrimination and its prohibition (Art 14), 36, 37–8, 384, 388, 391, 393, 394, 395, 396, 397
    effective remedy (Art 13), 359, 366, 367, 371–3, 373
    fair trial (Art 6), 205–26
        Art 6(1), 210–17
        Art 6(2), 217–20
        Art 6(3), 220–6
    freedom of expression (Art 10), 304–5, 306, 306–7
        duties and responsibilities Art 10(2), 307, 310–16
    freedom of thought/conscience/religion (Art 9), 283, 284–5, 286, 287
        scope of Art 9, 300
    freedom to associate and assemble (Art 11), 327, 328, 329, 330, 331, 332, 333, 334, 336
    historical background, 26–30
    individual applications, 46–7
    inter-state applications, 44–6
    liberty and security (Art 5), 166–70
        circumstances permitting loss of liberty, 167–9
        non-criminal detention, 178–85
        UK nationals in foreign states, 185, 187
    marriage, 340–1, 342–5
        Art 8, 341, 342–5, 346, 353, 354
        Art 12, 340, 340–1, 342–5, 345, 346, 347, 348, 349, 350, 353, 354, 355
        divorce and separation, 351, 352
        Protocol 7 Art 5, 277, 356
    no punishment without law (Art 7), 234
        scope of Art 7, 243–4
    operating principles, 47–51
    principles, 35–44
    privacy (family/private life), 248
        Art 5 and 12, 277
        Art 8, 252, 254–6, 257, 258, 259, 260, 261, 262, 263, 265, 266, 267, 268, 269, 271, 272, 273, 274, 275, 276–7, 277, 278

European Convention on Human Rights (ECHR) –
  continued
  protocols, 38–9
  reservations *see* reservations
  right to life (Art 2), 84
    scope of Art 2, 86
  slavery/forced labour (Art 4), 150, 151, 152, 157–60
  torture (Art 3), 125
  UK's declarations of incompatibility, 68–70
  UK's Human Rights Act and, 63, 64–6
  UK's recognition, 55–6
  UK's reservations, 21
European Court of Human Rights, 30
  James Bulger killing, 134–5
  judiciary, 33–5, 78
European Court of Justice (ECJ), 30, 31
European Union, 29–30
  Charter of Fundamental Rights, 12–13
    freedom to associate and assemble, 327
    freedom of expression, 304, 305
    right to marry, 340
  liberty and security, 188–9
eviction, 266–8, 388, 391
evidence
  exclusion of, 174–5
  hearsay, 194, 210
exceptional cases of upholding of conviction despite trial
      flaws, 209
exclusion of evidence, 174–5
expression and speech, freedom of, 74, 302–20
  importance, 302–4
  limitations, 307–9
extradition, 137, 139, 145, 189
  see also deportation
  Pinochet to Spain, 11, 143–4, 202–3

facilities, adequate, 221
fair process, 196–7
fair trial or hearing, 193–228
  despite flaws/infringements, 209–10
  historical background, 193–6
fairness (notion of), 173
  equity and, 361
family, founding a, 277, 338, 339, 340, 343, 344
  see also relatives
  prisoners, 341, 345–7
family hearings, 212
family life *see* privacy
fatal accident inquiries, 207
Finucane case, 92, 95–6
fire service, compulsory, 158–9
first generation rights, 17
Flitcroft guidelines, 253
footballers, compulsory labour, 159
forced disappearances, 401–2
forced or compulsory labour, 147–50, 155
  definitions, 151, 151–2

difference between servitude and, 154–5
  in ECHR Art 4, 152
foreign language interpreters, 224–5
foreign states
  see also regional rights regimes
  detention, 185–8
  torture, 140–5
fought for rights, 19–20
foundation, freedom as a, 302
fox-hunting, 254, 255
France
  freedom of assembly, 333–4
  freedom of religion, 298
  slavery/servitude case, 152–4
fraternité, 17, 18
free elections, right to, 65
freedoms, 3–4, 17, 280–320
  see also liberty *and specific freedoms*
  definitions/meanings, 281, 282
  ECHR, 36
    Human Rights Act and, 63, 74
  interconnectivity, 282–3

gender identity *see* sexual identity
General Medical Council and right to live, 111
generational rights, 17–19
Geneva Convention, 4th, Art 78, 188
genocide, 10, 54, 231, 232, 239–40
Gentle, Rose, and *R (on the application of Gentle) v Prime
      Minister* [2008], 97
Germany
  collection and disclosure of information (former FRG),
      261
  compulsory fire service, 158–9
  right to life in (incl. former GDR), 116
given rights, 19
global dimensions *see entries under* international
Glorious Revolution, 365–6
golden rules, 67
goods, basic human, 16–17
Gough, Stephen (Naked Rambler), 308–9
Grand Chamber, 34
  marriage and, 343–4, 346–7
Greece
  freedom of religion, 297
  torture under 1967–1974 military dictatorship, 141
Greek Cypriots in Northern Cyprus, 45, 376
Guantanamo Bay, 178, 186–7
Gulf War
  first (1990–91), 370–1
  second *see* Iraq
gypsies, 270–2

habitual criminals, forced labour in Belgium, 155
Handyside case, 308, 309
hard law, 2, 23
heads of state, 11–12

health, protection of, 312–13
hearings, 206–10
    distinction from trial, 193, 194
    fair *see* fair trial and hearing
    judicial bias in, 198–203
    types, 206–8
hearsay evidence, 194, 210
Heathrow Airport aircraft noise, 265
Hello! magazine and Douglas wedding, 253
hierarchy of rights, 42
High Contracting Parties, reservations, 39–40
higher education, 375–6
historical perspectives, 4–12
    enforceability of rights, 358–66
    European Convention on Human Rights, 26–30
    fair trial, 193–6
    Human Rights Act, 54–62
    no punishment without law, 229–33
    slavery, 147–50
    torture, 121–2
        corporal punishment of children, 129–31
home
    see also living environment; place of abode; property
    enforceability of rights, 362
    eviction, 266–8, 388, 391
    rights brought, 251–2
    use or loss of, 256
        hunting and, 255
homosexual/same-sex relationships, 382, 393–5
Houses of Parliament, 78–9
Housing Act 1985, 268, 388
Housing Act 1996, 70
human goods, basic, 16–17
human right, definition, 281
Human Rights Act 1998, 54–82
    effective remedy, 64, 65, 73, 360, 366, 371–3
    freedom of thought/conscience/religion and s 13 of, 288
    historical background and genesis, 54–62
    implementation, 79
    privacy and, 251, 252
    proceedings under s 7 of, 72
    structure, 62–3
    terrorism and torture and, 396
human trafficking, 160–4
humiliation, James Bulger killers, 135
hunting, 71, 254–6, 257, 335
Hussain, Osman, 189

identity, 268–72
    sexual *see* sexual identity
illegal drugs *see* drugs
illegal (unauthorised) immigrants (in UK), 232
    detention, 184–5
    no punishment without law, 243
    penalty schemes on haulier firms bringing in, 206, 208
immigrants (in UK)
    deportation, 138, 140, 232, 243

marriage, 341, 348–50
    trafficking, 160–1, 162
    unauthorised/illegal *see* illegal immigrants
immunity, definition, 281
impartiality, judicial *see* judiciary
in extremis, torture, 124
inalienable rights, 15
incompatibility, declarations of *see* declarations
independence, judicial *see* judiciary
indeterminate sentences, 179
individual applications (to EHCR), 47–8
indivisibility of rights, 15
industrial action (incl. strikes), organisations prohibited
        from, 330–2
information
    collection, 260–3
    disclosure of *see* disclosure
inhuman treatment, James Bulger killers, 135
innocence, presumption, 217–20, 240, 244
inquisitorial proceedings, 214
insoluble dilemma (right to die), 107–8
Inter-American Commission on Human Rights 1959, 401
Inter-American Convention on the Forced Disappearance
        of Persons (1994), 401
Interception of Communications Act 1985, 262
interconnectivity of rights, 15
interdependence of rights, 15
interference
    bodily and psychological, freedom from, 258–60
    by UN in sovereign affairs of Member States, minimal,
        368–70, 372
International Convention on the Elimination of All Forms
        of Racial Discrimination 1966, 383
International Convention on the Suppression and
        Punishment of the Crime of Apartheid 1973, 383
International Covenant on Civil and Political Rights 1966
        (ICCPR)
    enforceability of remedies, 367
    liberty and security, 166, 168
    marriage, 339–40
    no punishment without law, 233
    right to life, 83
international dimensions (of human rights law)
    see also foreign states
    discrimination, 383–4
    enforceability of remedies, 368–71
    freedom to associate and assemble, 325
    marriage, 338–40
    no punishment without law, 233–4
    right to life, 83–4
    slavery, 150
    torture, 124
International Labour Organisation, 9–10, 322
    slavery and, 150, 151
international treaty, European Convention on Human
        Rights as, 28, 35
internment in Northern Ireland *see* Northern Ireland

interpreters, 224–5
interrelatedness of rights, 15
interrogation
   role of doctors in, 127
   terrorist, 135–6
      US government, 141–2
inter-state applications, 44–6
interventions by Crown, 71–2
intimidation, witness, 223
invasion of privacy, 249, 251, 253, 259
Iran on human rights abuses in UK, 318
Iraq (and Iraq war), 97–9
   civilian deaths, 100
   detention of British national in, 187–8
   torture by US forces, 142
Ireland
   case against UK, 44–5
   divorce and separation, 350–1
Islam (Muslim religion)
   Denmark, 299–300
   terrorism
      Al-Qaeda, 41, 397
      extradition of Islamist terrorist from UK to Spain,
         189
   wearing the jilbab, 286
Isle of Man, the birch, 129
Italy
   Craxi (former Prime Minister) case, 263
   deprivation of liberty, 169–70
   fair hearings, 209
   Mafia, 117, 169–70
   right to life in, 117

James, Daniel (paralysed young rugby player), 107–8, 273
Jehovah's Witnesses, 287, 297
jilbab, 286
Jordan case (Jordan's Application for Judicial Review 2004),
   92, 93–4
judgment, delivery, 215–16
judiciary (incl. judges)
   authority, maintaining, 135–6
   European Court of Human Rights, 33–5, 78
   independence and impartiality, 198–205, 211, 217
      maintaining, 135–6
   pensions, 63
jurisprudence constante, 159
jurisprudential nature, 14–21
jury bias, 203–4
jury service, 157–8
justice
   certainty v, 362
   delivery within a reasonable time, 216–17
   natural see natural justice
justification
   rational, 387–8
   torture, 124, 125
juvenile prosecution, 216–17

Kenya, asylum seekers from, 349
King (or Queen), remedy against the, 364–5

labour see employment
language (foreign) interpreters, 224–5
lawfulness of restrictions imposed on Convention rights,
   42–3
League of Nations, 9–10, 26–7, 368
legal advice, access to, 210–13, 221–2
legal service, compulsory, 158
legislation and its interpretation, Human Rights Act, 62,
   63, 66–71
legitimate aims, 309–16
libel, 250, 251, 254, 313, 314, 319
liberté, 17
liberty, 165–92
   balance between security and, 173–6
   case law, 170–3
   circumstances permitting deprivation, 167–8
   deprivation see detention
life, right to, 83–120
literal rules, 67
Lithuania, transsexualism, 354
Little Red School Book, 308, 309
livelihood, loss, 256
   hunting and, 255
living environment, one's, protection of, 263–8
   see also home
London, Treaty of (1949), 27
London Bombings (July 2005), 189

Mcbride case, 113–14, 115
McCann case, 87, 88, 91
McDonalds (McLibel Two) trial, 213
McKerr case, 92, 92–3
McShane case, 92, 94–5
Mafia (Italy), 117, 169–70
Magna Carta, 60, 61, 62, 194–5
   enforceability of rights, 359, 360–1
Malta, jury service, 157–8
manifestations, 282
   religion, 284–8
Mansfield, Lord (18th C), 377
   on slavery, 4, 6, 148–9
margin of appreciation, 23, 48–9
marriage, 277, 338–57, 393
   global recognition, 338–40
   rape, 238, 240
   understanding the meaning of, 341, 341–2
Matrimonial Causes Act 1973, 354
media, freedom of the, 305, 308
medical grounds, detention on, 183–4
medical negligence, 243–4, 374–5
mental capacity see competency and capacity
Michalak Catechism, 388–9
migrants, 12

Milgram experiment, 123–4
military service, 97–9, 113–15, 156–7
    see also court martial
    conscientious objector, 151, 152, 156, 272, 292, 297
minimum tariff, 179
minor see children
minorities, persecution and massacre, 10
    see also racial hatred
Minsk Convention, 404
mischief rule, 67, 68
mistakes (concerning right to life), investigation, 84, 90
Mohammed (Muhammad), depiction in cartoon, 299–300
Moldova, freedom of religion, 298
Monarch, remedy against the, 364–5
morals, protection of, 312–13
Moreham, Dr, on right to respect for private life, 257, 258, 276
Mosley, Max, 274, 308
Muhammad, depiction in cartoon, 299–300
Muslim religion see Islam

Naked Rambler (Stephen Gough), 308–9
national security see security
natural justice
    deprivation of liberty and, 172–3
    rules of, 5
natural law, 5
need to give reasons (fair hearings), 209
negligence, medical, 243–4, 374–5
nemo iudex in causa sua, 199–200
New York Twin Towers attack (of 9/11), 75, 174, 317, 396
9/11 Twin Towers attack, 75, 174, 317, 396
no punishment without law, 40, 229–33
    see also nullum crimen, nulla poena sine lege
    historical perspectives, 229–33
noise pollution, 265–6
non-combatants (incl. civilians), 12
    deaths, 12, 100
non-compliance with court order, 179–80
non-discrimination see discrimination
Northern Ireland, adoption, 352
Northern Ireland troubles, 41–2, 87, 89, 89–90, 92–5, 113–14, 292, 293, 310
    detention/internment, 178
        sartorial self-expression, 293
        without charge/trial, 41, 173
        without warrant, 171
    freedom to associate and assemble, 323
    interrogation of terrorists, 135–6
Norway, forced labour, 155
    military service, 156–7
not proven verdict (Scots law), 240
Nowak, Manfred, 126, 142
nuclear tests, Christmas Island 1957–58, 86–7
nullum crimen, nulla poena sine lege, 229, 232–5
Nuremberg trials, 54, 239

obedience, Milgram's torture experiment, 123–4
objection (to rights), torture, 125
obligations and duties, 15, 281, 310–16
    positive state, 99–100
offence, prevention of commission of crime or, 181–2, 311–12
Official Secrets legislation, 318, 319
Operation Pentameter, 162
Organisation of African Unity, 402–3
Organisation of American States (OAS), 400–1
Organised Crime, Transnational, UN Convention against, 161
overriding interests, 378

pacifism, 292, 310
Paris Principles, 406
Parker report, 136
Parliament (UK)
    legislative power, 230–2
        see also specific Acts
    procedure, 78–9
Parliamentary Assembly (Council of Europe), 32–3
parole, 70
Peck case, 273
penalty schemes on haulier firms bringing in illegal immigrants, 206, 208
pensions, 387–8
    judiciary, 63
personal autonomy see autonomy
pervasiveness, ECHR, 36
petitions of right, 364–6
philosophical influences in Europe, historical perspectives, 6–7
physical integrity, freedom from interference with, 258–60
physical punishment see chastisement; corporal punishment; torture
Pinochet, General, 11–12, 143–4, 202–3
place of abode, deprivation of, 376–7
Playfoot case, 285
Plenary Court, 33
police, restricted freedom of assembly and association, 332
Police and Criminal Evidence Act 1984, 274
political asylum, 137, 138, 139, 140
political factors
    Europe, historical perspectives, 6–7
    torture and its justification, 123
    UK's Human Rights Act, 58–9
political groupings, Parliamentary Assembly (Council of Europe), 32
positive law, 5
positive state obligation, 99–100
possessions, bankrupt's, 392
powers
    definition, 281
    separation of (doctrine of), 3–4, 5, 198
prescribed by law, limitations on freedom of expression, 307–8, 311

presumed bias, judge, 201, 203
Pretty, Diane, 105–7, 108, 134, 272, 273, 295–6, 377
prevention
    of disclosure of information, 134–5
    of disorder, 311–12
    of offence/crime, 181–2, 311–12
Prevention of Terrorism Act 2005, 42, 76, 174, 175
prison officers, restricted freedom of assembly and
        association, 332
prisoners
    see also detention
    deaths, 100–4
    disciplinary hearings, 207
    indeterminate sentences, 179
    marriage and founding a family, 341, 345–7
    parole, 70
privacy (and family/private life), 247–79
    aspects of, 256
    common law, 248–51
    invasion of, 249, 251, 253, 259
    meaning of concept, 247, 248
    respect for, 247–79
        categorisation and its difficulties, 257–74
privilege, definition, 281
probationary tenancy, 391
procedural v substantive due process, 230
process (of law)
    due, 229–30
    fair, 196–7
prohibitions
    see also abolition
    of assembly and association for police and prison
        officers, 330–2
    discrimination *see* discrimination
    in ECHR, 36
    torture, 124–9
proof, burden of *see* burden of proof
property
    see also home
    probationary tenancy, 391
    protection of, 65
    status, 390–1
proportionality principle, 47–8
proselytising, 282, 287
prostitution/sexual purposes, trafficking, 162, 163
protection
    from bias, 211
    of children, 212
    of health and morals, 312–13
    of judicial office, 198
    of one's living environment, 263–8
    of property, 65
    of reputation or rights of others, 313–14
psychological integrity, freedom from interference with,
        258–60
public authorities, Human Rights Act, 62, 63, 71–2
public hearing, fair, 215–16

Public Order Act 1936, 323, 324
Public Order Act 1986, 311, 324, 334
public safety, 310–11
punishment
    capital *see* death penalty
    no, without law *see* no punishment without law
    physical *see* chastisement; corporal punishment; torture
    retrospective, 240–2
    young criminals, 134–5
Purdy, Debbie, 107, 108, 272–3
purposive interpretation, 47, 47–8
    Human Rights Act and, 67–8
pursuing legitimate aims, 310, 311

Quakers in 1607, 303

racial discrimination
    international declarations and treaties, 383
    Race Relations Acts, 311, 312, 382
racial hatred/racism, 311–12, 334
    see also minorities
    Arab Charter on Human Rights, 405
rape, 172, 204, 237
    marital, 238, 240
rapporteur, UN, 126–7, 142
rational justifiability, 387–8
'reasonable time', justice delivered within, 216–17
recusal, 194
refugees, 12
regional rights regimes, 400–9
relatives and marriage and consanguinity, 341, 347–8
religion, 280–301
    discrimination, 384
    freedom of, 74, 280–301
    manifestation, 284–8
    Muslim *see* Muslim religion
    UK state recognition of, 290–2
    variety of beliefs, 289–90
religious law, 5
remedy/remedial actions, 358–80
    case law, 373–8
    enforceability *see* enforceability
    failure to provide, 209, 377–8
    Human Rights Act, 64, 65, 73, 360, 366, 371–3
reputation (of others), protection of, 313–14
reservations (ECHR), 23, 39–40
    Human Rights Act and, 62, 74–5, 77
respect
    for family/private life *see* privacy
    meaning of concept, 248
responsibilities, 281
retirement age, 383
    men v women, 154
retrospective crime and punishment, 240–2
reversed burden of proof, 218–20
right, human, definition, 281
road traffic offence, innocence and burden of proof, 219

Romany gypsies, 270–1
rule(s)
    of law, 3, 5, 362–3
    of natural justice, 5
    of statutory interpretation, 67
Russia (and the Commonwealth of Independent States),
        404
    fair hearings, 209
    torture, 141

same-sex relationships, 382, 393–5
sartorial self-expression, 293
Saudi Arabia, torture, 144–5
Schengen agreement, 30
school, manifestation of religion, 285–6
School Standards and Framework Act 1998 c 31, 131
Scots law
    Naked Rambler, 308–9
    not proven verdict, 240
    removal from DNA database, 274
second generation rights, 17
Second World War, 7
    aftermath, 10, 35–6, 54
    crime and punishment, 54, 231–2, 239
    effective remedy and the, 366
secularism
    Turkey, 298
    UK, 291–6
security, 165–92, 310–11
    see also Official Secrets legislation; United Nations,
        Security Council
    balance between liberty and, 173–6
    case law, 170–3
self-defence, 112–13
sentences, indeterminate, 179
separation
    divorce and, 341, 350–2
    of powers (doctrine of), 3–4, 5, 198
servitude, 147–50, 152–4, 154, 155
    definitions, 151
    difference between forced labour and, 154–5
sex discrimination, 381, 384, 386, 393–5
sexual identity (gender identity), 268–70
    marriage, 341, 352–4
sexual offences, 216
    see also rape
sexual purposes, trafficking, 162, 163
sexual relationships and sexual autonomy, 274, 308
    see also same-sex relationships
Siamese (conjoined) twins, separation, 111–12
siblings, cohabiting, and tax, 355–6
Siliadin case (France), 152–4
sisters, cohabiting, and tax, 355–6
slander, 313
slavery, 4–6, 147–64
    abolition, 6, 147–64
    definitions, 150–1

historical perspectives, 147–50
smacking a child, 130
social grounds, detention of, 183–4
soft law, 2, 23
solidarity, 17, 18
sovereign affairs of Member States, minimal interference
        by UN in, 368–70, 372
sovereignty, parliamentary, Dicey's theory of, 230, 231
Spain
    extradition from UK to
        General Pinochet, 11, 143–4, 202–3
        Islamist terrorist, 189
    fair trial, 218
Special Immigration Appeals Commission (SIAC), 138,
        139, 397
speech see expression and speech
sport, compulsory labour, 159
states, 23
    applications between, 44–6
    foreign see foreign states
    heads of, 11–12
    minimal interference by UN in sovereign affairs of
        Member States, 368–70, 372
statutory interpretation, rules of, 67
statutory reform, slavery, 149–50
strength in numbers, 321
strictly criminal in scope, 244
strikes, organisations prohibited from, 330–2
submissive compliance, Milgram's torture experiment,
        123–4
substantive v procedural due process, 230
sui generis, 194, 207
suicide, 105–7, 108, 109, 190
    assisted, 105, 106, 107, 108, 109, 272–3, 294–6,
        377–8
    common law and, 117

talked about rights, 19–20
tax and marital status, 341, 355–6
tenancy, probationary, 391
territorial integrity, 310–11
terrorism, 41–2, 75–7, 317, 319, 396–8
    detention without trial, 173–6
    detention without warrant, 171
    innocence and burden of proof, 219, 220
    interrogation of terrorists, 135–6
    no punishment without law, 240
    Northern Ireland see Northern Ireland
third generation rights, 17, 18
Thomson and Venables killing of James Bulger, 134–5,
        253
thought, freedom of, 74, 280, 282, 283, 284, 288, 292,
        293, 297, 300
time
    adequate, 221
    'reasonable', justice delivered within, 216–17
torts, environmental, 264

torture, 40, 121–45, 396
  changing perceptions, 127–8
  extra-territorial, 140–5
  historical background, 121–2
  meaning, 122–3
  prohibition, 124–9
trade unions, 322, 325, 327, 328, 329, 330, 333
trafficking, human, 160–4
Transnational Organised Crime, UN Convention against, 161
transsexuals, 268–70
  marriage, 341, 352–4
  tax, 355
Treaty
  of London (1949), 27
  of Westphalia (1648), 370
trespass, 249
  assembly and, 324
trial, 193–228
  detention prior to, 172
  detention without, 173–6
  distinction from hearing, 193, 194
  fair see fair trial
  Within a reasonable time, 216–17
Turkey
  Cyprus and, 45–6, 376
  right to life in, 115–16
  secularism and freedom of religion, 298
  torture, 140–1
Twin Towers attack (of 9/11), 75, 174, 317, 396
twins, conjoined, separation, 111–12

ubi jus, ibi remedium, 258–9
UK see United Kingdom
UN see United Nations
United Kingdom (UK/Britain)
  see also domestic law; England; Northern Ireland; Scot's law
  constitution, 60–1
  corporal punishment legislation, 131–2
  ECHR and the see European Convention on Human Rights
  extradition from see extradition
  freedom of expression, 318–19
  immigrants see immigrants
  Ireland bringing case against, 44–5
  liberty and security in, 170–8
    anti-libertarian policies, 176–8
    balance between, 173–6
    case law, 170–3
    non-criminal detention, 178–85
  liberty and security of UK nationals in foreign states, 185–8
  military service, 156
  periodic review report submitted to UN, 318–19
  religion recognised by state, 290–2
  retirement age see retirement age

rights today, 21, 79
United Nations (UN), 27
  Convention against Torture and other Cruel, Inhuman or Degrading Treatment or Punishment, 126
  Convention against Transnational Organised Crime, 161
  Convention on Consent to Marriage, Minimum Age for Marriage, and Registration of Marriages, 338
  Convention on the Rights of the Child, 84
    child prosecution, 217
  Convention Relating to the Status of Refugees 1951, 12
  Declaration on the Right to Development 1982, 18
  enforceability of remedies by, 368–71
  establishment, 10, 27
  General Assembly
    antidiscrimination declarations, 384
    power of embargo, 371
    power to suspend states, 371
    resolution 40/33, 217
    resolution 1386 (XIV), 83
    resolution 3452 (XXX), 125
  International Covenant on Civil and Political Rights see International Covenant on Civil and Political Rights
  Security Council, 369–70, 371
    chapter VII powers, 369–70
    Resolution 1244, 370
    Resolutions 1511 and 1546, 188
  special rapporteur, 126–7, 142
  Standard Minimum Rules for the Administration of Juvenile Justice, 217
  Stockholm Declaration 1972, 1
  Supplementary Convention Art 7(b) (1956), 151
  UK periodic review report submitted to, 318–19
  Universal Declaration of Human Rights see Universal Declaration of Human Rights
United States (USA)
  American Convention on Human Rights (1969) on marriage, 339
  liberty of UK nationals held in, 186–7
  torture, 141–2
Universal Declaration of Human Rights (UDHR; 1948)
  enforceability of rights (Art 8), 359, 366
  freedom of expression, 304, 305
  freedom to associate and assemble, 326
  liberty and security, 166
  marriage, 339
  no punishment without law, 233
  right to life, 83
  torture and, 125
universalism, 2, 14–16
university education, 375–6
'unsound mind', detention, 183
USA, torture see United States

Vasek's generational rights theory, 17–19
veganism, 294

Wainwright case, 253, 254, 258–9
war/wartime
    see also Gulf War, first; Iraq (and Iraq war); Second
        World War
    deaths, 96–9
    forced or compulsory labour, 152
    non-combatants *see* non-combatants
    retrospective crime and punishment, 54, 232, 239–40
    terrorist activities characterised as 'war', 177
War Crimes Act 1991, 231, 232
War Damage Act 1965, 231, 232
warrant, detention without, 171

Westphalia, Treaty of (1648), 370
widows, African Charter on Human and Peoples' Rights,
    339, 357
Withholding and Withdrawing Life prolonging Treatments:
    Good Practice in Decision making, 111
witnesses, 222–4
Woolf, Lord, 78–9
World Trade Centre (Twin Towers attack of 9/11), 75,
    174, 317, 396
World War II *see* Second World War

Zionism and Arab Charter on Human Rights, 405